# Understanding Homosexuality, Changing Schools

# Understanding Homosexuality, Changing Schools

Arthur Lipkin

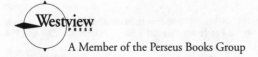

Westview
PRESS

A Member of the Perseus Books Group

Copyright © 1999 by Westview Press, A Member of the Perseus Books Group

Published in 1999 in the United States of America by Westview Press, 5500 Central Avenue, Boulder, Colorado 80301-2877, and in the United Kingdom by Westview Press, 12 Hid's Copse Road, Cumnor Hill, Oxford OX2 9JJ

Find us on the World Wide Web at www. westviewpress.com

Library of Congress Cataloging-in-Publication Data
Lipkin, Arthur.
  Understanding homosexuality, changing schools: a text for
teachers, counselors, and administrators / Arthur Lipkin.
    p.   cm.
  Includes bibliographical references and index.
  ISBN 0-8133-2534-X (hc.); ISBN 0-8133-2535-8 (pbk.)
  1. Homosexuality—Study and teaching (Elementary)—United States. 2. Homosexuality—Study and teaching (Secondary)—United States. 3. Homophobia—Study and teaching (Elementary)—United States. 4. Homophobia—Study and teaching (Secondary)—United States. I. Title.
  HQ76.3.U5L58   1999
  306.76'6'071—dc21

99-21973
CIP

The paper used in this publication meets the requirements of the American National Standard for Permanence of Paper for Printed Library Materials Z39.48-1984.

10    9    8    7    6    5    4    3    2    1

*I came to the mission of this book exhilarated by gay and lesbian students and teachers finding their dignity, their voices, and their allies in greater numbers than I once thought possible. Yet, for every one of them who attends a conference, wears a pink triangle, or speaks out in a class or assembly, there are many others who remain fearful and silent.*

*Some are intimidated by the vehemence of those who refuse to acknowledge the presence in schools of gay, lesbian, bisexual, and transgender people, never mind protecting and supporting them.*

*Others are frozen in their own internalized homophobia.*

*I understand their predicament. I taught in an urban public school for twenty years and for twelve of them was closeted, even to myself. Then, propelled by the energy of antiwar and antiracism struggles, I began to battle heterosexism too—first, by coming out. Although the response from some can be ugly, claiming one's authenticity and autonomy is a powerful step toward gaining dignity and freedom for everyone.*

*I dedicate this book to my parents*
*Philip Lipkin (1912–1988)*
*Rose Duchin Lipkin (1912–1994)*
*and*
*to my spouse*
*Robert Ellsworth*

# Contents

# Acknowledgments

I want to thank Henry Abelove for encouraging me to tackle this project. I am also grateful to my colleague Catherine Roberts and our students in T210A at the Harvard Graduate School of Education for their inspiration and support. My thanks go to Scott Heller, Irene Monroe, Brian Mooney, and Jeff Perrotti for reading the manuscript and responding with kindness and acuity—and to my former student Theresa Urist for helping me decipher my citations. I thank Carol Goodenow and Kim Westheimer of the Massachusetts Department of Education, both for the wonderful work they do and for taking the time to provide me details of it. I am indebted to Aleta Fenceroy, Jean Mayberry, Bill Stosine, and Jean Richter for keeping me abreast of developments around the country and the world. Their work is selfless. Thanks also go to Warren Blumenfeld, an information storehouse and beloved confidant. I also want to acknowledge Gordon Massman, Adina Popescu, Andrew Day, Tom Kulesa, and Jennifer B. Swearingen—all formerly or currently my editors at Westview Press—for putting up with a neophyte. A big embrace goes to the educators, students, parents, and community activists who have made the story that weaves through this book. And lastly, for their invaluable instruction, I bow to the hundreds of scholars who grace the footnotes of this volume.

*Arthur Lipkin*

# Introduction

Gay and lesbian visibility increased incrementally from the start of the gay liberation movement in 1969 through the early 1980s. Then, in the next fifteen years, the AIDS epidemic and civil rights battles pulled homosexuality dramatically into the public sphere. Commentators in the popular media regularly debate gay soldiers' sleeping arrangements, the "gay gene," "outing," "gay marriage," domestic partner benefits, "conversion therapy," and so on.

There are probably few over the age of toddlers who have not been exposed to public arguments about homosexuality and government policy toward gays and lesbians. Regrettably, many students have heard the sound bites and acrimony but have missed exploring these questions seriously in an academic setting—an omission with harmful, even violent, consequences.

Biological and philosophical theories about homosexuality are rife at some universities, along with discourses in gay-related law and politics, history, and culture, although original research is conducted by relatively few professors and graduate students, many of them gay or lesbian themselves. These topics are trickling down to undergraduate courses on some campuses, particularly in the context of women's studies. New histories and anthologies may stimulate wider interest.[1]

Gay/lesbian studies came to the academy too late, however, for most veteran elementary and secondary school practitioners. Without in-service training, they are generally unprepared for classroom engagement when the opportunity to discuss homosexuality arises, as it regularly does. Both the political risk and their lack of preparation lead them to avoid the subject. Even in those schools where faculty intervene to stop homophobic harassment, exploration of the topic is likely to be superficial—that is, a brief refutation of common "myths and stereotypes" or a guest speaker's thirty-minute show and tell.

Prospective teachers are lucky to encounter that much in college and graduate teacher preparation courses. Professors may be inattentive to current research and unaware of the subject's importance in education. They may be politically fearful or lack the pedagogy to deal with gay topics. In any event, teaching about school-related gay and lesbian issues is rare in both specialized and general courses.[2]

Inaccuracy and distortion often mar whatever brief mention of homosexuality may indeed appear in college texts, as in sociology, for example.[3] Evidence that some prospective teachers are both homophobic and uninformed renders these omissions and falsehoods inexcusable.[4]

Such shortcomings in teacher education and training will likely be rectified in the next decade, primarily because the plight of gay and lesbian adolescents is beginning to get the attention it deserves. The initial rush for quick fixes such as changing the harassment clause in the rule book or adding a panel to Diversity Day—necessary but insufficient steps—could lead to more thoughtful strategies. School personnel will eventually have to know more about gay/lesbian history and culture, identity development, families, and so forth.

I have tried to present these topics accessibly and with some thoroughness for both preservice and veteran educators "and for laypeople as well." The text covers a broad range of subjects because I want to make it easier for busy students and harried professionals to expose themselves to aspects of homosexuality unfamiliar to most educators, yet applicable to schools. I want to tempt my colleagues toward a wide exploration by having it all (albeit in abbreviated form) between two covers.

In a sense, there are two complementary books here: one to suggest means of making schools more affirming of gay and lesbian people and the other to provide a foundation of knowledge to support the arguments for such a transformation.

I hope this volume appeals to teachers, administrators, counselors, and other school staff, as well as parents, school committee members, and other policymakers. I believe that gay and lesbian teachers and their allies, who are the vanguard in campaigns for inclusion and equity, will find it useful. Lastly, I want this book both to affirm and to challenge gay and lesbian educators not widely read in gay/lesbian studies.

Some have asked whether it is fair to challenge teachers in conservative districts to action when there is a strong chance that they will end up muzzled and frustrated. My response is that all of us must have accurate information, if only to sharpen our awareness of the silences in schools. That consciousness is essential everywhere, including in those scary places where the steps toward inclusion must be discrete and tiny.

The goals of this text are

- to motivate teachers, administrators, counselors, and those who prepare and supervise them to understand the significance of gay and lesbian issues in education;

- to enable them to teach more comprehensively about the human experience through the integration of gay and lesbian topics into the core of learning in a range of disciplines;
- to promote the psychological and physical health and intellectual development of all students;
- to reduce bigotry, self-hatred, and violence by increasing tolerance for sexuality differences;
- to aid communication between gay/lesbian youth and their families and schools;
- to facilitate the integration of gay/lesbian families into the school community;
- to advance the professional development and well-being of all faculty, staff, and administrators;
- to encourage the schools' collaboration with the greater community in achieving these ends.

Educators need both extensive information on gay and lesbian topics and practical methods for dealing with them in schools. I offer this book to help make gay, lesbian, bisexual, and transgender experiences part of this nation's vision of democratic multiculturalism.[5]

# 1

# Overview of the Problem

### Diversity in Our Culture

There is a facile consensus in educational circles today, as well as in government and media, that diversity is a good thing. Although our commitment to immigration, affirmative action, affordable housing, representative curricula, and the like may not be deep, sociologist Nathan Glazer observes, "We are all multiculturalists now."[1] At the very least, xenophobia and racial supremacy are not to be directly expressed in polite discourse.

Ironically, the original metaphor for American heterogeneity was a melting pot. Newcomers were once expected to divest themselves of cultural differences except perhaps for colorful and harmless folkways. The American educational dream was that good public schooling would help an upwardly mobile second generation leave urban ghettos for suburban blending.

Sectarian and ethnic Americans still find comfort among their own and occasionally clash with others, but the old suspicions and rivalries, as between urban Irish and Italians for example, have greatly diminished. Prejudice has been countered with the blandishment, "We are all Judeo-Christian Americans, sharing the values of piety, work, and family—our differences are minor."

There are, of course, exceptions. Racism is abiding and pernicious. Although the question of whether one's forebears came on the Mayflower or in steerage has become increasingly the grist of good humor, the intractable legacy of the slave ships is not easily mitigated.[2] People of color who aspire to the middle class are not allowed to blend in to the degree that white ethnics have done.

Black people's liberation from illusory assimilation has helped transform the melting pot to a patchwork quilt, emblematic of the beauty and strength of our differences. The case for respecting diversity, however, still rests on the congruence of Americans' religious, moral, and eco-

1

nomic tenets—subsumed in the code words "family values." They are united in God, marriage, children, the comforts of home, and a disposable income. Thus, Bill Cosby's Huxtables became the most popular black family in American history.

Stitching homosexuals into the patchwork is still a great challenge. In 1996 alone, 228 instances of institutional antigay discrimination were documented.[3] (This pattern is consistent with abuses of homosexual human rights around the world.[4]) Even gays and lesbians with deep religious beliefs, conservative comportment, and manicured lawns face obstacles. Whatever else might qualify them for acceptance, homosexuals who merely live openly and without shame are seen by many as warring against God and the family. Those aspiring to marriage have been savaged.

The rhetoric of the homophobic opposition has a familiar ring: Some demagogues who have discovered the political utility of "the homosexual menace" in the '80s and '90s were likewise stridently racist in earlier decades.[5]

The denunciations regularly and unabashedly aimed at gays and lesbians prove the normativity of heterosexism in our culture. Although institutional racism and violent attacks on people of color have hardly disappeared, open expression of racial bigotry is tolerated far less than homophobic invective. So unfashionable is racism today that pollsters find white interview data unreliable for elections with African American candidates.[6] Most children are admonished not to use racial epithets; a similar standard does not apply to words like "fag."

Like white racists nostalgic for the Sambo days, some homophobes complain, "We always knew there were queers and bulldaggers around, but as long as they didn't flaunt it, nobody bothered them. Now they want rights and they're bringing trouble on themselves. They should just keep their sex lives private." The nostalgic bigot would have us believe that the two spinsters sharing an apartment or the artistic bachelor uncle had only intemperate gossip to fear. Left out of their recollection are the beatings, police entrapment, lost jobs and families, and suffocated souls.

In short, homosexuals are permitted to exist so long as they acquiesce to invisibility and inferiority. Even liberal editorial arguments, such as those favoring domestic partnership over gay marriage, betray an underlying injunction to second-class status. It is no wonder that many, if not most, gays and lesbians choose the closet.

## Attitudes Toward Homosexuality

The percentage of Americans who disapprove of homosexuality has ranged from 50–57 percent since 1982.[7] (Disapproval of homosexual relationships, 75 percent in 1987, stood at 56 percent in 1996.[8]) In American courts, gays and lesbians "are at least three times as likely to face a biased jury as a person who is white, African American, Hispanic, or Asian."[9] Among teenagers in one recent poll, 58 percent of boys and 47 percent of girls said homosexuality is always "wrong."[10] Oddly, 58 percent of teens in another poll felt that gays in this country get too little respect.[11]

*One Nation, After All,* an end–of–the–century study, concluded that middle-class Americans are morally pragmatic and tolerant of racial, gender, and religious differences.[12] The one exception to the nonjudgmental views of the "moderate majority" regards sexual orientation. "That is the one area where people use words like 'sinful, hateful, wrong, immoral'—the kind of words they never used on any other subject."[13] Still, although they rejected homosexuality, nearly three-quarters of the respondents said gays should be left alone in their personal lives.

That attitude does not prevent closely fought ballot initiatives to classify homosexuality as "abnormal, wrong, unnatural, and perverse."[14] Antigay referenda were proposed in 10 states in 1994, although they went to voters in only two and both were defeated.[15] In 1995, 39 antigay measures moved forward in 30 state legislatures.[16] In just the first three months of 1996, 72 antigay bills were introduced.[17] By 1998 only 10 states, 157 municipalities and counties, and the District of Columbia offered legal protections to gays and lesbians.[18]

At its root, homophobia is ignorance, yet the vast majority of schools are unwilling or unprepared to do anything about it. Other harmful prejudices are regularly challenged, in the interest at least of practical harmony if not of true multiculturalism. Yet a stubborn double standard prevails. It is easy to find schools, even some that are otherwise progressive, where "kids notice that when a racial slur is written on a wall, there is a fuss, but 'fag' on a locker remains for days, unremarked."[19] The consequences for students of the failure to address such issues are serious: a distorted view of human nature, bigotry, self-hatred, and violence.

Teaching about gays and lesbians and the diversity of their community would help reduce these problems. Yet school-based tolerance programs are almost always restricted to religious, racial, and ethnic understanding.[20] Although teachers might draw attention to the links among other prejudices, they often see homophobia as separate, unrelated, and beyond the scope of the K–12 syllabus.

Few school leaders recognize how homophobia is related to student promiscuity, substance abuse, academic problems, and suicide. Nor do they acknowledge its connection to violence among heterosexual youth: that is, boys often beat other boys and batter girls to distance themselves from gayness. The vast majority of juveniles arrested for violent crime are male.[21] They take foolish personal risks and shun academic success to prove they are not faggots.

## Homophobic Violence

When young men seek a violent outlet for their internal conflicts, disappointments, and rage, they commonly direct their attacks at the dehumanized, if not demonized, "other." They "displace their aggression more often onto a target whom they had earlier been led to dislike than onto a neutral target."[22] Not surprisingly, highly prejudiced people are likely to take out their anger on the targets of their prejudice.[23] Thus "social norms often dictate which group is to be the scapegoat":[24] "The most frequent victims of hate violence today are blacks, Hispanics, Southeast Asians, Jews, and gays and lesbians. Homosexuals are probably the most frequent victims."[25]

The incidence of hate crimes directed at those perceived to be gay or lesbian has been documented to some degree:

- In 1994 the overall number of bias-related crimes rose 25 percent nationwide, with gay and lesbian victims in 25 percent of assaults and nearly 66 percent of murders.[26]
- In 1995, the total number of hate crimes against gays and lesbians in 11 major cities had decreased by 8 percent, but the violence of the attacks escalated.[27]
- 2,399 incidents of antigay hate crimes were reported in just 14 locations across the country in 1996. These included 27 murders and 1,128 physical assaults.[28]
- 2,655 antigay hate crimes in 1997 (14 murders, 53 hospitalizations) were reported in 16 localities.[29]
- 2,552 antigay hate crimes were reported in 16 localities in 1998 (33 murders, 110 hospitalizations). There were stark increases in some weapon categories (guns, blunt objects, knives/sharp objects, and vehicles) and in verbal and physical abuse by police.[30]
- In New York City alone antigay bias crimes reported from January to October jumped from 46 in 1997 to 82 in 1998.[31]
- Antigay murders are often characterized by extreme viciousness.[32] Nearly 60 percent of 151 antigay slayings reported in 29 states from 1992 to 1994 involved "extraordinary and horrific violence," involving fewer guns than other killings, 26 percent versus 68 percent, and more knives, bats, clubs, and hammers.[33]

These statistics may reflect increased reporting, but many such hate crimes are in fact not reported because of victims' concerns about being revealed as homosexual or fear of hostile or indifferent police response.[34] Most jurisdictions lack discrete and sensitive community-based reporting mechanisms.[35]

The majority of hate crimes are committed for a thrill by white teenage males, sometimes substituting one minority person for another when a first target is unavailable.[36] In a nationwide 1994 study of lesbian and gay homicides, 98 percent of the killers were male.[37] As a rule, the victimizers are school-age.[38] Their crime, usually executed by more than one attacker and boasted of to others, is a ritual assertion of group membership and shared values.[39]

In a 1996 incident, eight 16 and 17-year-olds cruised the gay neighborhood of West Hollywood, California, where after taunting and beating a gay man, they loudly rejoiced.[40] In another case, a television newsmagazine reporter interviewed a like-minded group driving around a gay bar. One teen laughingly confessed they were looking for a "faggot" to beat up. Challenged by the reporter, the boy said he felt no compunction because faggots really were not human—the prank was like "smashing pumpkins on Halloween."

The ghastly 1998 murder of Wyoming college student Matthew Shepard could be the most notorious gay-bashing of the century.[41] The near crucifixion of the diminutive Shepard by two high school dropouts appalled the country, yet his fate was not much different from previous victims. For example, in a New York borough in the early nineties three young men went out looking for a "homo" to "tune up."[42] They used a knife, a wrench, and a hammer to kill a man they did not know and later bragged to friends of having done it. Only one had a violent reputation. Another attended college and the third went to art school. The one who did the stabbing said that his knife went in so easily it was "like sticking a watermelon."[43] He was the college student. It took police nine months to classify the case as a bias crime. Trial spectators spewed homophobic bile at reporters and others in the courtroom.

In Texas, eight homosexual men were stalked, terrorized, and killed by teenage boys between 1993 and 1995.[44] In Oregon, a man who executed two lesbians in 1995 admitted in a letter, "I have no compassion for . . . lesbians, or bisexual or . . . gay men. I can't deal with it."[45] In Baltimore, just a month after Matthew Shepard's killing, a cross-dressing man barely survived being pursued by a mob and shot six times.[46] Because he was black and a transvestite, the crime did not make the cover of the weekly newsmagazines. And in the same week a dozen teenage males invaded a gay pub in Palm Springs, California, and began hurling obscenities, ashtrays, and fire extinguishers.[47]

Greater gay visibility,[48] hysteria over HIV, and recurrent debates over gay rights probably play a part in the rising frequency of attacks. The more public and virulent expressions of homophobia become, the higher the incidence of gay-bashing. In 1995, 180 incidents of antigay actions by police, politicians, and public figures were reported, up from 134 in

1994.[49] One columnist has called the correspondence between defamation and violence "trickle-down homophobia."[50] The escalation of homophobic political rhetoric in 1998, such as the Senate majority leader's likening the "sin" of homosexuality to alcoholism, kleptomania, and sex addiction, is a classic example of reckless pandering to the Right.[51] Religious broadcaster Pat Robertson's 1998 warning that gay pride flags in Orlando can provoke tornadoes and "terrorist bombs" must have stoked the avengers in his flock.[52] The bomber of a gay Atlanta nightclub the year before appears to have been so motivated.

Gay-bashing is the extreme of what may begin as adolescent bullying. A 1984 survey of over 2,000 adults found that 45 percent of the males and 20 percent of the females reported verbal or physical assaults in high school because they were thought to be gay or lesbian.[53] Nine years later a major study of sexual harassment in schools reported the following:

- For school-age boys the most disturbing form of harassment was being called gay.
- 23 percent of boys and 10 percent of girls reported being called gay or lesbian when they did not want to be.
- 86 percent of high school students said they would be upset if classmates called them gay or lesbian.[54]

The power of the homophobic slur has driven heterosexual teens to suicide.[55] And at other times the rage is directed at the tormentors. In 1998, a Paducah, Kentucky, youth killed three classmates after years of teasing over middle school newspaper gossip that he had "feelings" for another boy.[56] Shortly after this Kentucky rampage, a Massachusetts student killed his harasser.[57]

Even the best students may be homophobic: 48 percent of top-achieving high school students in a major 1998 survey admitted to being "prejudiced against homosexuals," 19 percent more than the previous year. This startling increase among voluntary respondents who are mostly white females from two-parent nonurban homes is indicative of a worsening climate of hate. The number who admitted to being antiblack and anti-Hispanic also soared from 7 percent to 15 percent.[58]

Gay and lesbian students may be victimized in or outside of school or at home. In one study of gay minority youth, 61 percent of those who had been physically assaulted said their attacker was a family member.[59]

Many of those in charge claim that homophobic harassment is not an issue at their schools. The experience of a Massachusetts high school gives the lie to this kind of denial: Someone burned a swastika and the words "BOBO IS A FAGGOT" into the boys' lavatory ceiling. It was thought that the graffiti referred to a teacher who was a Jewish Austrian refugee. Treating the incident as an anti-Semitic hate crime, school authorities decisively summoned the police and the FBI. The homophobia was disregarded. Later, when one of the suspects stood drunk on a park table and wailed to his friends that he himself was gay, nothing was done for him. In the end, he dropped out of school and was hospitalized for depression.[60]

In another stark instance of denial, a caller to a 1996 radio program chided the Merrimack, New Hampshire, schools for their antigay policies and urged a school committeeman to consider that one of three recent student suicides in his community was committed by a homosexual teen. Instead of acknowledging the tragedy, the committeeman attacked the caller for defaming the grieving families by implying one of them had a gay child.[61]

### Barriers to Prevention and Treatment of Heterosexism

Although erotic imagery pervades advertising and sexual situations are the common currency of the popular media, many Americans are uncomfortable with sexuality as a serious topic for public discourse or school curricula. A 1996 study found that "three out of four shows in the 'family hour'—8 P.M. to 9 P.M.—now contain 'sexually related talk or behavior,' a fourfold increase since 1976."[62] Many parents allow their children to be exposed to this commercialized sexuality, while at the same time denying the appropriateness of sex education. This schizophrenia can be bizarre: Witness the banishment of a surgeon general who hinted that the topic of masturbation ought to be broached in school[63] and the months of joking about President Clinton's cigar.

The prospect of homosexual issues being introduced in schools provokes great anxiety and formidable resistance, responses that are exploited by those who allege a conspiracy of "radical feminists, the organized gay lobby, and the liberal news media."[64] Millions of dollars have been raised from people whose unease over modernity wants a scapegoat. They are told that gays need to recruit among the young. And the specter of cadres of not easily identifiable missionaries, like communists of the 1950s, evokes panic and resentment.

Opponents invariably target as exaggerated Kinsey's 10 percent figure, often used by gay rights advocates to approximate the number of homosexual Americans.[65] In fact, the arbitrary divisions of the Kinsey sexuality continuum are emblematic of the difficulties researchers have in determining the estimated percentage in each orientation category. Other estimates have ranged from 1 percent to 2.8 percent to 6.2 percent homosexual.[66] A 1989 meta-analysis puts the figure at between 3 percent and 6 percent of the male population.[67] In 1994, the acclaimed *Sex in America*, a study of over 3,000 subjects, found 2.8 percent of men to be self-defined as homosexual or bisexual and 1.4 percent of women to be so.[68]

These figures are all based on polls and interviews, both unreliable in assessing a stigmatized population. Moreover, the various definitions of homosexuality that are employed in such surveys, involving permutations of fantasy, behavior, and identity, have a decided impact on their results. In contrast to its 2.8 percent and 1.4 percent figures, cited above, *Sex in America*'s researchers found that 10.1 percent of their male and 8.6 percent of their female respondents exhibited some form of same-gender sexuality based on their desire, sexual activity, or self-definition.

Since 1992 two radical Right films, "The Gay Agenda" and "The Gay Agenda in Public Education," have been widely circulated, especially in communities considering antigay initiatives.[69] Over 100,000 copies of the first film were distributed and shown in churches and on community access television in just two years.[70] Using propaganda techniques reminiscent of the Nazi's "The Eternal Jew," they dehumanize gay people by sensationalizing questionable statistics. For example, their claim that 17 percent of gay men eat feces and 29 percent urinate on each other continues a long historical association of Jews and other despised groups with filth.[71] They also present discredited psychological theories[72] and repeatedly focus on gender-bending and bodily display, which are customary parts of gay pride celebrations.

The narration's cataloguing in lascivious detail of an imagined universe of kinky homosexual acts reaches the level of parody Shakespeare employed with puritanical Malvolio.[73] The films conflate gays and sex, using AIDS statistics to discredit antidiscrimination laws and tolerance curricula.

Nearly half of the antigay initiatives filed in 1995 dealt with school issues.[74] In 1996, 63 percent of Americans did not think schools should teach homosexual "lifestyles" and 58 percent disapproved of gay and lesbian school clubs.[75] Eight states actually require schools to teach that homosexual behavior is unacceptable and/or illegal.[76] The moribund Oregon Citizens Alliance, having failed with two antigay rights referenda in 1992 and 1994, sees its future in a narrower focus on keeping schools from condoning homosexuality.[77]

"The Gay Agenda in Public Education" begins with children frolicking on a swing set, like the girl in the 1964 campaign ad who picked daisies as the A-bomb loomed.[78] The narrator warns about perverts waiting for their victims. Scenes of families at gay pride celebrations with their fussing children are edited and scored to suggest that the youngsters' innocence is being ravaged. Alarming "expert" testimony on homosexual pathology is followed by an ingenuous high schooler's worries about the effects of tolerance lessons on his peers.

Such clever manipulation is meant to generate hysteria about fragile sexualities under assault from a homosexual menace. An experienced monitor of extremism observes that "the Right has mobilized a mass base by focusing on the legitimate anger of parents over inadequate resources for public schools on the scapegoat of gay and lesbian curriculum, sex education, and AIDS awareness programs."[79] Thus a parable from "Homosexuality, the Classroom, and your Children"[80] features Billy, a "small, shy" middle school boy whose parents' recent divorce has left him "torn up inside." When his husky classmate Chuckie gets him alone and invites him to "try" homosexual acts, Billy demurs. Chuckie reminds him that Mr. Carson, their gay health teacher with a Porsche (like Jews, gays are rich), said he experimented with it at their age. Then Chuckie mentions four other gay and lesbian faculty—and the police chief, other teachers, the newspaper, and the governor—who all "say it's OK," not to mention the gay pastor who told them in school that "God made him homosexual." Poor Billy, cajoled by the evidence, follows the skipping Chuckie to the secret "fort."

Anti-Semitism too was once fed by tales of child kidnapping and infant sacrifice, but some antigay rhetoric is more genteel than the unvarnished Billy and Chuckie broadsheet. A recent example of this type is "Straight Talk About Gays," by E. L. Pattullo, described as a former associate chairman of the department of psychology at Harvard University.[81] Pattullo's apparent acceptance of a Kinsey-type sexuality spectrum leads him to conclude, "There is a bit of the waverer in so many of us." Although he concedes most teens are firmly fixed in their orientations, he worries that "substantial numbers" of vulnerable ones are imperiled in today's tolerant environment. Society will send these youngsters the wrong way, he warns, if it does not clearly value heterosexuality over homosexuality. He holds schools responsible:

In a growing number of schools throughout the country, children are taught that the gay life is as desirable as the straight—if not indeed more desirable—and such instruction (which is often hard to distinguish from outright indoctrination) begins as early as the elementary grades. The same idea is increasingly propagated on television and in films. And it is strongly reinforced in colleges and universities.[82]

Pattullo condemns outright discrimination, yet his argument begs the question of how one convinces children of homosexuality's inferiority without promoting bigotry. His would-be moderate conclusions are not easily distinguishable from those of more feral adversaries:

1. Laws explicitly protecting gays from discrimination are bad because they betoken approval.
2. Regulations preventing gay adoption, gay scout leadership, or openly gay teachers are good because they protect youth from bad parenting and other nefarious influences.[83]

Pattullo feints with concessions. Perhaps we need do nothing to counter the gay movement. An awareness of the advantages of hetero-sexuality might already be inborn. Besides the causes of homosexuality are immune to societal influence. Maybe it's not so bad to have a few more homosexuals. And finally, it could be cruel to remind genuinely gay youngsters of their liberty's required limits. But his equivocation is pep-pered with telltale signs. Tolerance of gays has prevented the specter of AIDS from dissuading boys from homosexuality. Radical feminism is frightening proto-gay boys away from women. Ultimately, he concludes, "Society has an interest both in reproducing itself and in strengthening the institution of the family. . . . Parents have an interest in reducing the risk that their children will become homosexual."

For all his scholarly "straight talk," Pattullo engages in the arch decep-tion of the Right. He links the survival of the American family to the sup-pression of homosexuality. At a time when parents must work long hours to keep poverty at bay and when women are battered and children abused by heterosexual men, one must question his analysis.

But Pattullo's thesis is not just another forgotten opinion piece. A for-mer secretary of education and purported ethicist touts Pattullo's having gotten it right on the gay question,[84] and a syndicated columnist and tele-vision pundit uses Pattullo to attack New York City's Rainbow Curricu-lum.[85]

Some of Pattullo's readers might still wonder which schools teach the superiority of a homosexual life. In another article titled "On This Cam-pus, Straight Is Queer—Some 'Hets' Go Along to Get Along," a Santa Cruz professor likewise complained about a new conformist pressure: "You're not a real person unless you're gay or bisexual. The question is whether it is just a fad, or whether it is here to stay. I think it's seriously changing the way young people relate to each other in California."[86] His and Pattullo's carping is ludicrous in a country where most young peo-ple find it difficult to express a bit of homosexual desire.

Conservative screeds, political lobbying, and threats of parent orga-nizing can intimidate school authorities. Whether they agree with the protests or not, many educators have been reluctant to broach the topic of homosexuality, develop rules to punish homophobic behavior, or admit the presence of or provide services for their gay, lesbian, bisexual, and transgender youth.

Until the late 1990s, many in the homosexual community itself acted as if gay and lesbian young people did not exist. Gay organizations devoted few resources to youth programs and neglected schools entirely. Having to contend with civil rights infringements, hate crimes, antigay referenda, the military, and AIDS, gay leaders lacked the will and the resources to undertake school struggles. Leaving aside the fact that youth work is fraught with the hot-button issue of predation, adults might have shied away from a domain that reminded them of their own adolescent pain. Even when national attention was drawn to the Rainbow Curriculum controversy, no national gay or lesbian leader named schools as a priority.[87] The gay son of conservative figure Phyllis Schlafly observed, "The morality of homosexuality is controversial. The public schools should stay away from it."[88]

This adult avoidance has begun to change, mostly as a consequence of student and teacher activism. Two youth and education advocates were included in a 1997 meeting of gay and lesbian representatives with President Clinton, a gay rights ally.[89] The president later stated, "I don't believe that anyone should teach school children that they should hate or discriminate against or be afraid of people who are homosexuals."[90] In 1999 Clinton endorsed a middle school tolerance curriculum aimed at decreasing antigay and other hate crimes.[91] Yet the president had also said, "I don't think it should be advocated. I don't think [homosexuality] should be a part of the public school curriculum."[92]

Vice President Gore, on the other hand, has applauded television's antihomophobia teaching potential: "And when the character Ellen came out, millions of Americans were forced to look at sexual orientation in a more open light."[93]

Societal ignorance and fear still restrict appropriate responses to the urgent needs of homosexual youth and adults. Although 73 percent of Americans in 1996 were aware that gays and lesbians are the victims of some level of discrimination, only 27 percent thought that more needs to be done to protect gay rights.[94] Important connections between homophobia and youth violence, both self-directed and other-directed, are seldom explored. Government agencies have been unwilling or forbidden to sponsor research related to gay youth; pertinent results of some studies have been suppressed. Model government HIV prevention programs have not investigated the links between school environment, self-esteem, and risk behaviors.[95]

Some government actions have created a substantial barrier to school-based efforts. Despite conservatives' professed objection to federal interference in local education,[96] the House and Senate passed the Smith-Helms amendment to the 1994 Elementary and Secondary Education Act by votes of 301 to 120 and 63 to 36 respectively.[97] It contains the following language:

A. Prohibition—No local education agency that receives funds under this Act shall implement or carry out a program or activity that has either the purpose or effect of encouraging or supporting homosexuality as a positive lifestyle alternative.

B. Definition—A program or activity, for purposes of this section, includes the distribution of instructional materials, instruction, counseling, or other services on school grounds, or referral of a pupil to an organization that affirms a homosexual lifestyle.

Although the amendment was itself later altered to protect local control, the language appeared again in a joint amendment of a conference committee on the Education Act.[98] Through legislative legerdemain, another clause prohibiting the promotion of sexual activity of any kind replaced this amendment. Progressive forces succeeded in undoing the original intent, but only by appearing to concede that gay-positive instruction might have to be restrained.[99]

State and local authorities have taken their cue, and sometimes the exact wording, from Smith-Helms.[100] (See Chapter 13.) In the New Hampshire version of the debate, the father of an eighth-grader stated, "All we're trying to do is protect our kids from the 'homosexual agenda' that starts with sympathy and acceptance of gays and leads to 'special minority rights.'"[101] Allegedly spurred by the Traditional Values Coalition, a Michigan Republican convened a hearing under the banner "Parents, Schools, and Values." The gist of the session was that school-based AIDS education and tolerance for homosexuals are undermining parents' moral influence on their children.[102]

Hosts of Scopes-like trials are being plotted to punish liberal educators (see Chapters 13 and 14), and whatever the outcome of each case, the climate will be chilled for gay-related initiatives. Many schools are opting to do nothing that could upset conservative factions. Of course, inaction is not a neutral position when bigotry, harassment, and violence prevail. The equation "Silence=Death" applies as much in schools as anywhere else.

Without legal and policy mandates, some educators do not challenge even overt homophobic language because of their own moral beliefs or to avoid controversy or to escape being labeled gay themselves. They often try to elude responsibility with the disclaimer that they have no homosexual students. Of course, this blindness and insensitivity keeps young people from coming out to them. What gay or questioning youth would risk exposure in an ignorant and hostile school? If educators inform themselves and demonstrate their understanding and approachability, students will emerge seeking knowledge, support, and guidance.

Most schools still have a long way to go. The Gay Lesbian Straight Education Network (GLSEN) 1998 Report Card failed nearly one-half of the 42 largest school systems in the country for not having one policy or program in place to meet the needs of gay and lesbian students.[103] And despite the hand wringing after sensational hate crimes like the Shepard murder, the Congress's lopsided passage of the Defense of Marriage Act in 1996 does not augur much political support for school-based antihomophobia initiatives at the national level.

# 2

# The Theories of Homosexuality

"Queer theory," as it is now called, can illuminate how sexual orientation influences personal identity. Together with a good historical grasp, a theoretical perspective is essential to good teaching and counseling about homosexuality. This chapter probes the difference between experiencing gendered erotic attractions and developing an identity based on such feelings—a distinction that informs an important contemporary scholarly debate. The central questions are

- whether sexuality and sexual orientation have always been explicit dimensions of human identity;
- whether distinctions have always been made between homosexuality and heterosexuality;
- whether there have always been homosexual people.

But before delving into theory, a common vocabulary must be established. Sexual identity is comprised of five components:[1]

1. BIOLOGICAL SEX—a person's presented gender at birth. Today, when genital components of both genders are found, assignment surgery is often performed.[2]
2. GENDER IDENTITY—a person's internally perceived gender. It usually develops by age 3 and is probably a product of both biology and socialized learning.[3] Occasionally gender identity is not congruent with biological sex. Such incongruity, transgenderism, may eventually lead a person to seek gender reassignment, that is, transsexual surgery.
3. SOCIAL SEX-ROLE—the set of behavioral and other characteristics thought appropriate to each gender. Cultural norms dictate traits of male and female physical endowment, personality, comportment, speech, dress, and so on. Children seeking parental

and social approval and reward learn the prescribed repertoire between the ages of 3 and 7.[4] One may adopt sex-role elements of the opposite gender and still retain the gender identity of one's biological sex, as in transvestism, wearing clothes deemed inappropriate for one's own gender.

4. SEXUAL ORIENTATION—variously described as a person's
   - sexual experiences, attraction, and fantasy;[5]
   - behavior, fantasy, and affectional preference;[6]
   - all of the above plus social preference, self-identification, and lifestyle choice;[7]
   - sexual attraction, arousal, and gender(s) of love objects.[8]
5. AFFECTIONAL ORIENTATION—determined by the gender(s) of those with whom a person is inclined to share deep emotions and caring.

In this book I classify a person's sexual orientation by means of his or her erotic desire for another person or persons of the same, opposite, or both genders as expressed in behavior and/or fantasy.

### Historical Essentialism

It surprises many people to learn that although same-gender sexual activity has existed for as long as anyone can imagine, the concept of sexual orientation is relatively new. Clearly, for centuries various authorities have condemned sex between people of the same gender. There is ample documentation of punishment, usually by religious courts, of same-gender sex acts, yet other extramarital and nonprocreative behaviors also received harsh judgments, even the death penalty.[9] Scholars disagree whether there was something special about same-gender erotic activities that distinguished them from other proscribed behaviors and whether same-gender sexual sinners were viewed as people any differently from their opposite-gender counterparts.

John Boswell offered evidence that Christian churches have not always condemned same-gender sexual practices[10] and that one branch of Catholicism even blessed same-gender unions.[11] He further claimed that a special identity was indeed attached to same-gender lovers in ancient and medieval cultures. Boswell's work is viewed as "essentialist" because it seems to support the idea that a core (or essential) same-gender identity has existed through much of recorded history. Although essentialists admit that the names for same-gender activities and their practitioners have varied over time, they argue that such desire has always rendered a person significantly different from others. Same-gender lovers, they say, were socially labeled and internalized that distinction in their own minds. Boswell did not assert that this self-concept was the equivalent of a modern homosexual/gay identity,[12] but he did furnish examples of figures in history and literature whose sexual tastes, he claimed, set them apart categorically.[13] For example, he offered the following from an eighteenth-century Frenchman: "Because I have never liked women or [their sexual organs] does that mean I should not like passive men? Everyone has his tastes. . . . In nature everyone has an inclination."[14]

Boswell cited dozens of references to same-gender sexual behavior in classical, medieval, and premodern texts, making clear that there was no general expectation of bisexuality in the authors' cultures. On the contrary, he pointed to medieval poetry making fun of bisexuals as oversexed and quotes Plutarch on the exceptionality of bisexuality.[15]

Bernadette Brooten's investigations of love spells, astrology, dream interpretation, medicine, and other sources in the Roman Empire during the early Christian period provide an interesting lesbian counterpart to Boswell's scholarship.[16] She documents both open and hidden same-gender relationships, assertive ("masculine") lesbians who called their partners "wives," and both mental and surgical cures (i.e., clitoridectomy). For example, she presents evidence of Herais, Sophia, and Pantous, women who sought to get and keep the love of other women through magic charms, to prove the existence of "actual women in the Roman world who desired a female partner and went to some lengths to consummate the relationship."[17] Brooten also shows that lesbians were viewed with hostility as unnatural and repulsive—more so even than male homosexuals, since at least one of the female partners was thought to usurp the male sexual privilege. She presents evidence that the same-gender inclination was seen as an enduring character trait and that both male and female homosexuals were consigned to the identical spot in hell.

## Social Constructionism

Boswell and the essentialists have been widely challenged. Since Mary McIntosh wrote that the homosexual role is a modern invention,[18] most historians and theorists have concurred that no such identity existed before the late nineteenth century. These social constructionists believe that all identities are invented and shaped by social forces. One theorist insists there is no biological essence of sexuality that is immune to social influence, that even sexual fantasy is a socially learned script.[19]

It may seem that certain categories of identity are so salient they must have meaning in all eras for all cultures. Race, particularly, appears to be a universal criterion of identity, but anthropologists have found that members of one "race" may have less in common genetically than they do with members of a different "race."[20] These old denotations, based on visible differences, have perhaps never been biologically valid.

Neither is the social significance of "racial" difference essential. Just because there are differences such as skin color does not mean a particular culture will deem them important. Some folks like scrambled eggs and some like fried. Those tastes are not likely to construct identity. However, certain circumstances—like removing dark-skinned people from Africa by force and enslaving them in a predominantly white culture—create social conditions that promote pigment-based identities.[21] The culture dictates the criteria by which people are labeled and valued.

A society furnishes instructions and models for acting out the prescribed roles attached to these identities. The authorship of these sacrosanct scripts is often attributed to God or Nature, but in fact they are greatly influenced by those in power. In a patriarchal system, the maintenance of both gender and sexual roles serves the interests of men.

Although gender, racial, and sexual identities are arbitrary, often oppressive instruments, they still may become dear to minority people. An otherwise superfluous and limiting label may comfort and strengthen those it was meant to marginalize and weaken. Many women, blacks, and homosexuals find solidarity and resistance with others who resemble them in what might otherwise be a trivial aspect of their humanity. But others internalize the stigma. Racism has led some blacks to favor lighter skin, straighter hair, and so on,[22] and homophobia causes some homosexuals to shun effeminate men, butch women, and transvestites.

## Sexual Meanings in Ancient Greece and Rome

Social constructionists question whether any people would spontaneously focus on the gender of their erotic objects as a keystone of their identities. They assert that before the spread of Christianity same-gender sexual acts were not given particular notice[23] and that until the late 1800s when the label was invented , no one could have developed a homosexual identity. Although they agree that in classical Greece it was common for older men to have sex with younger men, they object to calling such relations homosexual because that implies the existence at that time of concepts for which there is no evidence. Social constructionists concur with Freud's position that the Greeks honored the (male) sexual instinct in all its forms with no regard for the sexual object.[24]

Ancient Greek society did, however, have standards, albeit different ones from our own. To them sexual activity was not homo- or heterosexual. An older male citizen, in the role of mentor to a younger man, could engage with him in sexual practices that current observers would call homosexual, yet the gender of the partners would not have been important to them. Sexual identity came rather from one's power status and literal position in erotic activity. An adult male was expected to penetrate a passive partner, who was inferior to him in some way, that is, younger male precitizen, male or female prostitute or slave, or wife (all women of the citizen class were confined to the legal status of minors).

Restraints on the older mentor (the *erastes*) and his young initiate (*eromenonos*) revolved around the *age* of the young man, the *type* of erotic activities permitted, and the *duration* of the relationship. Researchers disagree about whether the youth had to be physically beautiful or only of good character and whether the pairing was based on love, civic duty, or pre-Hellenic notions of passing power from older to younger men through transfer of semen.

To prove the distinction between the Greek practice and modern homosexual reciprocity, David Halperin employs a vase painting of a male coupling: a boy's apparently enthusiastic response to his older suitor is more cooperative than erotic, since the boy has no erection.[25] Halperin grants the pleasurable component of Greek pederasty without taking it as an indication of erotic fulfillment and certainly not as a sign of a homosexual identity. Enjoyment was not the issue. If same-gender penetration was thrilling to any of the parties involved, it proves only that a certain kind of virility was celebrated.[26]

Michel Foucault, the premier constructionist, goes even further, claiming that the privileged Greek male view of sexual morality was based on an exercise of power not only over the weaker other but also over the self.[27] The powerful Greek man proved his ethical caliber by restraining all his appetites, including the erotic. Amount, time, place, and position were regulated, but not the gender of the sexual object. His self-imposed elite regimen demanded an economy of sexual behavior: don't have too much, have it where and when appropriate, and don't be passive.

Contemptuous civil trial testimony and satirical poetry show that Greek men were mocked for ceding the prerogative of the phallus and yielding to penetration. In this pre-Christian system, condemnation hinged on the passive man's compromised status, not on the same-gender sexual contact.

For many years homophobic Greek scholars suppressed or bowdlerized the evidence of these activities in court records, literature, and art.[28] Others emphasized the civic and ritual nature of the relationships to underline the exceptionality of what they saw as homosexuality.[29] Like today's constructionists, but with censorious intent, they dismissed the notion that such liaisons could have had an erotic dimension. In 1978, however, K. J. Dover legitimized the study of Greek male same-gender erotics with the publication of his questionably titled book *Greek Homosexuality*.[30]

Boswell's observations about the criteria by which ancient Roman sexuality was regarded approach the constructionists' characterization of the Greeks:

- women were thought not to have sexual desires;
- attention was paid not to the gender of sexual partners but to their positions, that is, members of less powerful groups were expected to submit to higher status men;
- men's nonconjugal, nonprocreative erotic activity was generally accepted.

## The Emergence of Modern Sexualities

A different code evolved before and during the Christian era as erotic desire came to be seen as dangerous. Sexual fidelity in marriage became a virtue for early Christians.

Recent scholarship on the prevalence of male sodomy in Renaissance Florence has discovered general tolerance for a common male homoerotic culture, regardless of official disapproval.[31] Punishment of adolescents in the passive role was mild, whereas adult men who had sex together were penalized more severely. However, even in the presence of sexual networks, there is no evidence of a gay identity or conscious subculture.

Later, the agrarian economy of the preindustrial age greatly determined people's identities. The system was so dependent on furnishing child workers and conventional family production units there was little opportunity for developing any other sense of self beyond what the economy allowed. People took personal and group identities from family and religious life.

Those who had sex with people of the same gender had only religious terms by which to understand the significance of their desires. And, the constructionists remind us, those who lay with another man as with a woman, or with another woman, were not significantly differentiated from those who committed the sin of sodomy or adultery with opposite-gender partners or had sex with the cow. They would not have taken any identity beyond "sinner" from their transgression. They would not have been deemed a separate type of person. Everyone sinned.

The development of sexuality categories was made possible by economic changes. Industrialization, which allowed people to leave family farms and sell their labor in manufacturing centers, also permitted them to pay more attention to nonprocreative desires and to consider extrafamilial sexual arrangements. New social conditions led people to consider differently how they fit into the world and, thus, who they were.

Halperin sees the potential for a new awareness arising from the changing marriage and work patterns of northern and northwestern Europe after the Renaissance.[32] Mary McIntosh finds a homosexual subculture in late-seventeenth-century England, particularly London, where effeminate men were referred to as "Mollies" and "Nancy-boys."[33] Another scholar argues the emergence began in eighteenth-century London, when effeminate men were known to socialize and have sex in private clubs ("Molly houses") and the nighttime venues of parks and churchyards.[34] Jeffrey Weeks asserts the modern homosexual subculture began in the latter half of the nineteenth century.[35] In any case, by the 1800s, people who were sexually interested in members of their own gender could discover one another in the culture of growing cities.

*Scientific Classification.*   Having more opportunities than in rural isolation to fulfill one's same-gender desires could be a welcome development for anyone so inclined, but was it imperative that such an individual be seen as a different kind of person from everyone else? Coincidentally, science began at this time to compete with religion for preeminence. Priests had condemned sexual sin in its various forms. Now scientists began to study it, characterize it, and label in ways that had never been done before those who practiced it. Whatever their intent, scientists began to create a new entry for the church's demonic registry.

A few mid-nineteenth-century writers were interested in Greek practices and in male love as they were beginning to be understood. In 1836 a Swiss pastor published on the topic; and in 1837 a German scholar wrote for an encyclopedia. Karl Heinrich Ulrichs, who was to become a champion of tolerance, began his work in 1862. John Addington Symonds was the first to write about the subject in English in the 1870s, though he was not published until 1901.[36]

"Invert" was the first term used in the nineteenth century to denote a person exhibiting "deviant" gender behavior. The subjects, effeminate men and manly women, clearly mismatched in soul and body, seemed to have reversed their natural gender roles. Same-gender object preference was easily included in the inversion model but was not the only criterion and did not have to be present. Eventually, though, sex-object choice became paramount in the classification system. The actual term "homosexuality" had been coined by a pamphleteer in Leipzig in 1869, was repeated in a book in 1880, and was finally popularized by Krafft-Ebbing in the second edition of his *Psychopathia Sexualis* in 1887.[37]

The creation of our current sexuality categories occurred at the turn of the century. Although he stuck to some elements of the inversion concept as far as lesbians were concerned, sexologist Havelock Ellis transformed the notion of homosexuality. He made peripheral the varieties of same-gender sex practices others had studied (e.g., active and passive roles, gender role conformity) and distilled the whole taxonomy to the homo/hetero polarity, determined exclusively by the gender of the sex object.[38]

The case can be made that the idea of heterosexuality appeared at the same time. The actual term "heterosexual," although occasionally misapplied to bisexuality, had been used by the nineteenth-century Leipzig pamphleteer in a letter; however, he used "normalsexual" in his published work.[39] Ironically "heterosexual" was originally applied to males who enjoyed the "abnormal" gratification of nonprocreative sex.[40] It seems to have found its niche, however, as a convenient way to describe everyone who was not homosexual. In time it became a normative device to enforce compulsory sexual behaviors.[41]

Thus what one preferred to do sexually came to be considered secondary to the gender of the person with whom one wanted to do it. The science of psychology, which had begun to distinguish between healthy and unhealthy sexuality, made rabid use of this new system. A notion of categorical sexuality took root, becoming an accepted characteristic of the psyche and a major signifier of who one was. If the public had not previously sensed the significance of "inverted" erotic preferences, they would now.

Having their origin mostly in German medicine, culture and politics, the binary identity categories homosexual and heterosexual were adopted beyond Western Europe as instruments of social control.[42] Over the next hundred years these labels moved from scientific into popular application, reframing the parameters of identity. From a Marxist viewpoint, sexuality, like class, work, and public life, is a social imposition on the individual.[43] Only since the mid-1980s have some academics attempted to subvert it.

***Repression.*** The modern manufacturing society that lured homosexuals off the farm and gave them the economic freedom to pursue their sexual interests also made their lives difficult. Emerging sciences provided the means to identify and persecute them. One class of religious and civil authorities was replaced by another to equally repressive effect.[44] Individuals whose behavior alone had been condemned by articles of faith found themselves wholly typed and pathologized in published research and professional discourse. Inverts themselves, pitied or despised for their same-gender feelings, were being conditioned to accept the centrality of that desire in their own self-image.

Although the heterosexuality of the majority was valued for social maintenance, it was deemed almost incidental on the individual level. As the assumed status of all but a few, it was taken for granted, never imagined to embody their identities. Homosexuality, on the other hand, was thought to be the primary facet of the invert's life, a force that preoccupied, consumed, perverted, and criminalized them. It was a definitive illness.

Whose interests were served by this new social construction? In the late-nineteenth-century United States, the disruptions of industrialization, Darwinism, immigration, trade unionism, and feminism provoked reaction in both science and law. Nativist theoreticians propounded the inferiority of ethnic and racial minorities, while immigration and segregation laws distanced and contained the danger from those groups. Sexist psychological theories promoted diagnoses of neurasthenia and hysteria so that men might reassert their authority over women.[45] And a new psychopathological/criminal type was created—the homosexual pervert—so that any man who appeared to reject his sexual dominion over women could be punished.

*Female Inversion.*   And what of lesbianism? The political motive of nineteenth-century science was even clearer in its analysis of lesbians than in its interpretation of male homosexuality. The new scientific literature pathologized lesbians less for perverse erotic practices than for appearing to reject their feminine role in favor of a masculine one. In an 1872 decision upholding a state's right to prohibit women from practicing law, the Supreme Court made clear what a female's role was to be: "The constitution of family organization, which is founded in the divine ordinance, as well as in the nature of things, indicates the domestic sphere as that which properly belongs to the domains and functions of womanhood."[46] Likewise in the medical sphere, Krafft-Ebbing blatantly defended male privilege with a telling observation: the lesbian seemed interested more in the prerogatives of men than she was in the bodies of other women.[47]

Male physicians tried to put the "New Woman," the activist for social and economic justice, back in her place with a newly coined signifier, the "Mannish Lesbian."[48] Lesbians themselves might not have balked at the word "mannish." Like men and most other women, they had been brought up to believe normal females had no natural sexual appetite. Sex was thought to require male penetration and female passivity; therefore, how could two real women have sex together? A diagnosis of masculine dispositions helped explain their erotic desires.[49]

Sexologist Havelock Ellis's opposition to Victorian sexual repression made him in one sense liberal, but his opinions on lesbianism were not. He thought only a small number of women with masculine features and/or dress were congenital, unalterable lesbians with diseased sexual desires. The others inherited a weakness that might lead to lesbianism, if they were not protected from the influences of true lesbians. In brief, a cadre of intelligent predatory lesbians threatened the proper socialization of American womanhood.[50] Seen in the current light of sexual plasticity, bisexuality, and political lesbianism, Ellis's views, minus the pathology, were somewhat prescient. (See Chapter 6.)

## The Essentialist-Constructionist Debate

Extreme social constructionists argue that every aspect of sexuality is a cultural imposition.[51] They hold that sexual desire is an intrapsychic product of one's interaction with the environment—that people start out virtually blank and must be taught both how and what to want sexually.

Not surprisingly, many homosexual adults are uncomfortable with constructionism, as they are loathe to grant that what they experience as an integral, natural, if not inborn, part of themselves has been imposed by outside influences. Constructionists, for their part, concede that the discovery of an innate homosexual inclination would spoil their argument,[52] although a less radical analysis might turn instead on how the innate desire is given meaning and importance by the culture.

Boswell was accused of being the chief, if not the only, pure essentialist.[53] His work has been characterized as incorrect translation, misdirected emphasis, and transhistoricism, that is, giving modern meanings to old texts.[54] Halperin wonders what the term homosexual male can mean if it can be equally applied to:

- the Greek pederast who leads an apparently fulfilled life with his wife and occasionally penetrates a boy or male slave;
- the Native American berdache who lives his life as a married woman and religious figure;
- the New Guinea tribesman who leaves his youthful pursuit of younger male fellators in order to marry and become a father;
- and the American gay man who takes his sexual attraction as a important touchstone of his world.[55]

Other than performing certain sexual activities with other males, what do these men have in common?

Boswell replied that neither he nor anyone else would argue that the same meaning should be ascribed to all manifestations of homosexuality in diverse times and cultures.[56] Yet he faulted constructionists for challenging the validity of "homosexual," while permitting other changing terms like "family," "state," "religion," or "government" to be used transhistorically. Granting that all categories are subjective abstractions, he insisted that even without a distinct word for homosexuality in a past culture, some idea of the homosexual type might still have had currency. Same-gender taste might not have had all the implications of the modern "homosexual"—it may have had little or no social, ethical, or religious meaning or consequences—yet, Boswell maintained, it had some socially determined importance at the time in the broad culture and to the individual.

Boswell goes only that far toward constructionism. Although he agrees descriptors like "homosexual" are inexact, even today, he still sees value in a term that can be applied to a wide variety of people who appear to share only one experience:

> Because all of these people have erotic interactions primarily with their own gender, which is statistically less frequent in most human cultures, they have something interesting and important in common. It may not be a fundamental basis of identity in all cases (even on Castro Street), but it must play some role, as any noticeable and important divergence from the norm will.[57]

That is the moderate essentialists' most powerful argument: would not a persistent inclination among a relatively few people concerning the pressing matter of erotic interest be likely to serve as an identity reference point for them and those around them who do not share it?

Extreme constructionism will admit no means to prove which position has greater merit. Constructionism, or postmodernism, questions the very existence of objective scientific proofs, believing all observation to be colored by culturally learned biases.[58] Yet if any evidence exists to resolve the essentialist versus constructionist debate, it must be found in primary sources. Many statutes, court records, legal commentaries, sermons, and religious writings are extant concerning the sin-crime of sodomy and those who committed it, mostly men. Constructionists say that to all eyes such people were merely sinners; essentialists respond that their repeated and peculiar sin must have had a common effect on their identities.

What did it mean, for example, to Nicholas Sension, a New Englander tried in 1677 for sodomy with his unrelated male servant who called him "uncle"?[59] The younger man testified that Sension had not used "Loving Expressions" to induce him into sin. Did Uncle Sension not wonder why he was drawn to a male servant when other sodomites were attracted only to females? What, besides economic necessity, might have impelled the servant to continue to live with the allegedly bothersome Sension? Evidence of an emotional dimension to these relationships is so slim that the identity consequences of such attractions are unclear. Did the preindustrial world not allow for romance and its implications? (Even a pair of royal Egyptian manicurists from 2400 B.C. merited tomb images and inscriptions thought to be reserved to married couples.[60]) Strict constructionism may be faulted on exactly this point: "Constructionism has no theory of the intrapsychic; it is unable to specify the ways in which desire comes to be structured over the course of people's lives."[61] This psychological void is the central weakness of a schema concerned only with "the social articulation of sexual categories" and not with "what the sensation of being in love was like."[62] Orthodox constructionists would have to scratch their heads over the diary of Reverend Wigglesworth of seventeenth-century Harvard College. The entries include guilt-ridden confessions of the "filthy lust flowing from [his] fond affections for [his] [male] pupils."[63]

When constructionists do grant same-gender seekers a modicum of feeling, they minimize the social significance such emotions might have had. To the criticism leveled by Boswell, they respond:

> The argument has never said that people were not homosexual in the broader sense before the 19th or 18th century. It doesn't say that people didn't have a sense of being different. What it does say is that the idea that you can base your identity, your place in the world, on your sexuality, and specifically on your gay sexuality, is something very new to western civilization.[64]

### Toward a Synthesis

Halperin, though highly critical of Boswell, has wavered.[65] Citing certain little-noted Athenian vases, some depicting "reciprocal erotic contacts between adult males" and others showing "reversal of conventional erotic roles between man and boy," he confesses the artworks could necessitate some revisions of his prior analysis.[66]

Boswell too may have taken a step toward changing his position. He revised his definition of "gay people" from "those who are conscious of erotic inclination toward their own gender as a distinguishing characteristic"[67] to "anyone whose erotic interest is predominantly directed toward his or her own gender (i.e., regardless of consciousness of this as a distinguishing characteristic)."[68] That is, a person is gay even if he or she is oblivious to the distinction. Can this view be reconciled with his earlier claim that some form of cultural awareness of homosexuality has persisted throughout history? Perhaps the attachment of some cultural significance to same-gender sexuality makes the gay label valid, regardless of whether same-gender actors are aware of its application to them.

The three descriptors—homosexual, heterosexual, and bisexual—have widespread appeal. But why only three? What limits the construction of sexual categories? Several scholars observe that gender identity, gender role, sexual identity, sex role, and object choice can all be considered independently as masculine, feminine, or both/neither, leading to 243 potential labeling permutations, yet across history and culture there is no evidence of anywhere near this number of designations. One could venture that there is some "essential" number of meaningful designations.[69] In any event, the meanings of even universal distinctions like "male" and "female" are not uniform, intrinsic, or natural.[70]

Steven Epstein sensibly calls for a dialectic between the two critical camps, based on his view that "neither strict constructionism nor strict essentialism is capable of explaining what it means to be gay."[71] Although constructionism may seem to go too far, it provides a necessary balance to what has become politically expedient essentialism.

The earliest gay liberation rationale had a constructionist core: "We're all polysexual, so liberate your gay self to complement your straight self and soon these labels won't have any meaning."[72] Later, however, many activists turned essentialist to justify civil rights demands on the grounds that homosexuals were a distinct and enduring minority. This idea persists in the current assertion that homosexuality is neither new nor voluntary.

Identity politics depends on an identifiable, unambiguous gay community. Legislative lobbying particularly depends on fostering a minority group mentality. Essentialism supports the assertion of a "new ethnicity," used to obtain benefits in a multi-ethnic society.[73] Formerly ethnicity was employed to preserve ritual practices and prevent assimilation. As an affiliation based on symbolic and psychological factors, new ethnicity can be applied as easily to gays as to hyphenated-Americans.[74]

Those who choose, as well as inherit, their identity may seek rights; however, a group's claim appears to be enhanced by an ancestral record. That necessity helps explain the quest for homosexual antecedents, a gay and lesbian history. If a gay gene were to be discovered—the essentialists' dream—the inheritance would exceed the symbolic and psychological, giving homosexuals equal footing with other ethnicities.

To those who recall inchoate homosexual feelings from their earliest years, essentialism feels genuine. Besides its political usefulness, then, the homosexual identity is experienced as deeply rooted, "both strategy and reality."[75]

Others question both the theoretical underpinnings and the collateral effects of this strategy. Jim Sears blames essentialist activism for perpetuating male dominance: "Lacking a critical analysis of politics and human sexual behavior, homosexual activists help to drive the very engine of sexual oppression by reifying the sexual categories that serve a society based on male privilege."[76] This argument would fault all identity politics for reinforcing the legitimacy of inaccurate terms like homosexual, woman, or black. Echoing gay liberationist bisexual ideals, Sears asserts that no one is distinguishable by homosexual desire, since "*every* person has the capacity to form emotional, physical, and spiritual relationships with both males and females" [emphasis his].[77]

Essentialists are not the only ones targeted for their politics. Jacquelyn Zita, a constructionist, faults others in her camp for limiting their inquiries to sexuality while ignoring twenty years of feminists' dismantling of the binary categories of gender.[78] Further, she blasts the white male–dominated gay movement for slighting race, class, and gender issues. Zita observes that those gay male theorists who do pay attention to gender seem more attracted to its performance aspects (e.g., gender-bending) than to more serious matters of gender oppression. She calls for women's participation in "continuously reworking the intelligence and feelings of differences into a politic of effective consequence and conscience."[79]

All feminists would benefit from the demise of some essentialist assumptions about sexuality. This is the logic that underlies the lesbian feminist invitation to "choose" lesbianism in response to patriarchal oppression.[80] In similar fashion, all feminist men could be, but are not often, pressed to realize their homosexual capacity.

Like other groups, homosexual folks appreciate having a history, want to avoid blame for what is not a fault, and grow attached to a social mind-set that affords them rights. Essentialism meets those criteria. Yet dependence on essentialist positions can also imply that if homosexuality were a recent phenomenon or a choice, it would be less deserving of acceptance. The related essentialist argument that homosexuality is natural is not useful. Some have labored to discover homosexual counterparts among other species. Discovering so-called lesbian rodents should justify lesbianism as well as canine mating studies have justified rape.[81] The rationale lies not in nature but in a moral system.

A constructionist analysis would interrogate (i.e., deconstruct) the history, universality, and naturalness of identity signifiers and thus subvert the oppressive uses to which they have been put. Constructionism prompts gays and lesbians who have helped nurture an essentialist doctrine and politics for decades to cast off imposed categories and reject the essentialist claims of both their opponents and their friends.

And yet, the sure shot of constructionism, even as antidote to knee-jerk essentialism, is diminished by its insulting recoil. At its most strident, it charges that gays and lesbians are duped by false consciousness, trapped in a dictated script—that they are doubly victimized, first by internalizing a constricting sexuality and then in being reviled for it.

A more moderate constructionist argument should help gays and lesbians acknowledge the fluidity and intentionality of sexuality and the influence of culture on their understanding of desire:

> Constructionism may not turn out to be right in all of its preliminary claims, but in the meantime it encourages us to put some distance between ourselves and what we think we "know" about sex. And so, by bracketing in effect our "instinctive" and "natural" assumptions, it makes it easier for us to highlight different historical configurations of desire and to distinguish various means—both formal and informal—of institutionalizing them.[82]

Granted, even this qualified prescription can appear naive and impractical. Gays and lesbians facing palpable hatred cannot be expected to lead their lives as if homosexuality were a fiction, though they might be shown that both it and homophobia are socially produced. How can oppressed groups organize effectively against bigotry without giving credence to the identity that seems to bring them together? Would an anti-homophobia campaign adopt the line "Not only is homo-hatred wrong, but there's also no such thing as homosexuality?"

Some constructionists, in fact, condone the use of essentialist arguments in the tactical pursuit of civil rights.[83] Moreover an eloquent constructionist like Halperin still finds it counterintuitive to deny the meaning of same-gender desire in his personal life: "These categories aren't merely categories of thought, at least in my case; they're also categories of erotic response, and they therefore have a claim on my belief that's stronger than intellectual allegiance."[84]

Human beings seek their identities by trying on cultural labels and seeing what fits, what feels authentic, and what connects them with others in community. One's quest for identity is more interactive than passive, like the search for knowledge[85] or values.[86] In this vein, Epstein embraces a modified constructionism: Gay identity comes from an intrapsychic core of one's earliest memories and is given meaning from interaction with a "defining" society.[87] Gilbert Herdt and Andrew Boxer, an American anthropologist and a psychiatrist, add: "The earliest desires, we believe, are ontologically prior to and directive of all later cultural learning and teaching, especially after the entry of the child into school and diverse peer groups; subsequent socially learned desires build upon them."[88] Some suggest a parallel between language and sexuality acquisition, insofar as both depend upon a combination of "an inborn predisposition to learn . . . and key experiences at critical times in development."[89]

## Implications for the Present

Although it may seem burdened by jargon, this theoretical discourse is not merely an academic debate or a contest between scholars and activists. Its ideas can inform activism and public education by influencing how adults and adolescents view sexuality, identity, history, and politics.[90] It could have a profound impact on multiculturalism and democratic pluralism. Gay (or queer) theory clarifies the tension between the benefits and costs of identity politics among marginalized groups in what Audre Lourde called "the house of difference."[91] It is one tool for a larger analysis that might "create change and, ultimately, hope in the postmodern world."[92]

Revolutionary conclusions flow from these core constructionist ideas:

1. Society assigns significance to certain involuntary and intentional human differences.
2. Some differences are given their particular meaning to establish and/or maintain the social dominance of one group over another.

Teachers and students should be urged to examine this often oppressive heritage, whose categories can be deconstructed in the studies of history, culture, science, politics, art, and language.

Liberal educators traditionally try to counter prejudice by casting differences in a positive light. Occasionally they have actively helped minorities and women take pride in their identities and combat demeaning and false attributions. As a rule, however, they do not challenge essentialized categories or counsel resistance to inherited demarcations.

Given essentialism's appeal, they will have to broach delicately the suggestion that seemingly ennobling identity constructs could limit human potential. It is easier for the oppressed to condemn bigotry than to admit that they might be constrained by affirmations that have felt liberating. Many will be daunted by an invitation to join the deconstructionist enterprise

> To heighten our awareness of the various ways in which we are implicated in those regimes of power and knowledge within and against which we constitute ourselves . . . to glimpse contingency where before we had seen only necessity . . . to suspend, however briefly, the categories of thought and action within which we habitually conduct our lives.[93]

Although most minority people would be loath to abandon their identity communities, they need not stand alone at the end. As one comes to understand that *all* marginalized people share both the pride and tyranny of essentialized identities, one's capacity to form a greater community is enhanced. Sears, for one, advises that homosexual people will never recognize their authentic, nonhierarchical connection to other oppressed groups until they learn that "naming" is a form of oppression.[94]

The smooth biological continuum between male and female absolutes[95] is contradicted in many cultures by gender-role rigidity and cruelty toward those whose thoughts and behavior do not match their apparent physiology. Recognizing how much our social hierarchy depends on gender polarity and fixed gender role, Marilyn Quayle invoked an "essential" womanhood at the 1992 Republican convention and scolded those who would blur the imperatives of the distinct genders. In an increasingly controversial practice, babies born with indeterminate sex organs, some 1 percent to 4 percent of all babies born today,[96] are surgically assigned a gender as soon as possible.[97] Although Americans may toy with gender ambiguity as entertainment, we cannot bear really not knowing—thus the excruciating tease of "Pat" the late-night comedic television character of dubious gender.[98] Knowing the world appears vitally linked to telling male from female.

Even transsexuals can validate existing gender categories by aiming for a male or female gender, rather than blurring the distinctions between the two. Moreover, those who undergo surgery to align their anatomy with their psychology could give credence to the notion that particular feelings and ways of living are appropriate only in certain biologically gendered bodies. Biologically altered or not, however, most appear to want to undermine conventional readings and roles. They are "transgender warriors"[99] who violate gender proscriptions and oppositional labels to "challenge society's perceptions of gender."[100]

Upsetting the polarities of race, sexuality, and gender clearly demands sacrifice on the part of those who are advantaged in the constructed superiority of their identities. Some are not even aware of their privilege; others are, and cling tenaciously to it. Will they be convinced that the intellectual and emotional rewards of deconstruction are worth ceding some of their advantages?

Our social goal should not be to create a homogenized indistinguishable mass, to minimize our differences until they no longer register. Rather, aided by biology, social science, history, literature, and philosophy, we would try to understand and master our varied identities. With a nod to the arbitrary forces of nature and our struggle to comprehend and control the world by naming, we can recast the significance of our accidental and deliberate differences without dominion or rancor. Our subsequent readings of variance can still heed the inflections of cultural history, aesthetics, and spirituality, but our ultimate purpose must be to discover a humane preponderance of "agreement, commonality, and fellowship."[101]

This vision derives from the patchwork quilt theme of recent multicultural approaches, but it questions its essentialist assumptions. We now understand the quilt's pieces to represent not first principles but rather artifacts of social circumstance. Racial minorities have already reframed the boundaries through self-naming as "people of color." For most the label is a coalitional device for political organizing, not a repudiation of racial essentialism. Yet this opportune manipulation of given categories suggests their malleability.

Sexual minorities have acted similarly in taking the name "queer." Most homosexuals and bisexuals adopt it as expedient, inclusive, and conveniently concise. Others embrace it in opposition to categorical oppression and essentialist labels.[102] Taking a cue from political lesbianism, they invite those heterosexuals who renounce the baseless advantage of their signifier to validate the permeability of social constructs and be queer too.

Some people are offended by this old, still hurtful, pejorative. Others resist movement toward any more inclusive nomenclature. For example, JoAnn Loulan, a therapist and lesbian sexuality expert, insists she is culturally and politically a "lesbian," despite her continuing sexual relationship with one man she loves. Loulan adamantly rejects even the "bisexual" designation that would seem logically to apply.[103]

Gay (or queer) theory can be applied to the study of sexuality in contemporary world cultures. Although it has been shown that same-gender attraction is a cross-cultural phenomenon, there is also evidence that it is variously construed.[104] (See Chapter 7.) Halperin compares the modern Mediterranean pattern of youthful male homosexuality followed by heterosexual marriage to the practices of classical Athens.[105] Others similarly describe same-gender sexuality between boys and men in New Guinea and male bisexuality in Melanesia.[106] As in ancient Greece, these activities are not without erotic pursuit and fulfillment.[107] Sexuality norms in Mexico and some Arab countries likewise include erotic exchanges governed by power relationships between passive and active males.[108] Constructionism helps us resist applying twentieth-century Western taxonomies to these manifestations.[109]

When educators counsel ethnic and racial minorities and students from immigrant families about their developing sexualities, they must be aware that these students bring along sexual meanings that originate in their own cultural experience. Their adult sexual identities will emerge from a negotiation between these native meanings and American dictates. (See Chapter 8.)

Lastly, constructionist theory provides a paradigm for studying history. It becomes less important to name this or that figure as gay or lesbian than to examine what is known about their sexuality, to place it in their time, and to probe its possible impact on their lives and work.[110] If educators want to teach about sexualities in the past or the present or help students understand their own circumstances, they must bear in mind the following constructionist caution:

> It is really not possible to analyse sexuality without reference to the economic, political, and cultural matrix within which it is embedded. It would be more accurate to say, perhaps, that in modern society we have an *idea* of sexuality as a specific concept, but we cannot in actual fact understand it without contextualizing it. . . . What people want, and what they do, in any society, is to a large extent what they are made to want, and allowed to do.[111]

# 3

# Etiology

The first question most students and many adults ask when homosexuality comes up is, "What makes people gay?" Teachers should be familiar with some of the current etiologic speculation, but they should also be prepared to discuss the cultural and political issues that underlie both the question and its purported scientific answers.

Since the late nineteenth century, when homosexuality was first described as a condition and the homosexual as a type, medical doctors, psychologists, and biologists have probed for its cause. At times their hypotheses and alleged discoveries have attracted considerable attention. In the 1990s featured stories in popular journals on the latest genetic and other research signal the marketability of what might otherwise be obscure theorizing.[1] How do we explain this fascination?

Studies of the sexual relations between men and women are amply reported in the mass media, yet the causes of their orientation do not appear to interest most sexologists or editors. Normative heterosexuality is a relatively unexplored given. Any departure from that standard, however, invites scientific inquiry, if not voyeurism. Research grants have been forthcoming, and today the wizards of psychology and errant biology have a mass audience thanks to television and the press.

As long as heterosexuality is privileged, heterosexist biases may influence the research approach and/or its conclusions and reporting. Who frames the questions, who are the subjects, what is seen or ignored, and in what terms are the results made known? How, first of all, can sexual orientation be objectively studied when, for a century, many potential research subjects have been loathe to identify as homosexual, even to themselves? Secondly, but for sexist bias, how else do we account for the fact that the research on male homosexuality far outweighs studies of lesbianism?[2] As in heart and cancer research, many scientists and laypeople have incorrectly assumed that discoveries about men also apply to women.

This chapter is first a gloss on the putative causes of homosexuality, but it does not enter deeply into the arcana of biomolecular and other theories, especially since some experts, like the director of the Kinsey Institute, concede "we are very much in the dark" about the etiology of gender and sexual orientation.[3] The more important inquiry for this book is not what might predispose a person to same-gender desire, but rather whether it is important to know what does and what evolves from that knowledge.

Late-nineteenth-century European theorists centered on psychopathic perversion, twisted feelings, and female souls inside male bodies. Their American counterparts focused on gender confusion by way of a genetic flaw activated by contagion. Amused or disquieted, we can understand that these views were colored by social beliefs of the time. Most people, however, seem less inclined to see the cultural influences on contemporary science.

This chapter deals only with the origin of same-gender sexual desire. The development of homosexual identities is taken up in Chapter 6.

## Psychological Theories

Is the homosexual disposition an example of thwarted psychological maturation? Psychiatrists' responses to that question have changed over time. Freudians were influenced for some four decades by their mentor's view that homosexuality is not an illness, "no vice, no degradation," but rather an irreversible "variation of sexual function produced by a certain arrest of sexual development."[4] Unlike growing heterosexuals, who successfully redirected their polymorphous infantile bisexuality in the direction of opposite-gender relationships, homosexual men and lesbians got stuck at around the Oedipal stage.[5] Yet, Freud believed, unless they were beset by actual neuroses, adult homosexuals could be well adjusted. In fact some were "distinguished by specially high intellectual development and ethical culture."[6]

Freud rejected both the European idea that homosexuals constituted a separate sex and the American verdict that homosexuality was a moral failure. To him, homosexual desire, unconscious or conscious, was inherent in everyone, and all sexualities existed on a continuum. Although he may have seen exclusive homoeroticism as inferior to heterosexuality in some ways,[7] he thought it "nothing to be ashamed of"[8] and objected to the imprisonment of homosexuals and to their exclusion from the profession of psychiatry.

After his death in 1939, Freud's views on the universality of homosexuality were virtually ignored by his successors, especially by American psychologists.[9] They used some of his ideas to portray homosexuality as

a degenerate pathology requiring treatment. Typically ignoring lesbianism, they were fixated on male homosexuality as the result of overpro-
tective mothers and weak or emotionally absent fathers.[10] Feminized
boys were retarded at the Oedipal stage. Loving their mothers too much
to want sex with women, homosexual men developed a pathological fear
of women and craved male substitutes for missing fathers.[11]

Homosexuals were thought incapable of mature sexuality and stable
relationships.[12] The contemporary psychotherapist Charles Socarides
(the father of an apparently well-adjusted gay son[13]) represents the extreme of this position: He still claims that homosexuality is a severely debilitating illness originating in the pre-Oedipal stage, accompanied by
other symptoms, including schizophrenia and manic depression.[14]

If homosexuality were indeed caused by these factors and related to
these pathologies, how would their absence in the vast majority of gays
and lesbians be explained?[15] For instance, could not the budding effeminacy of sons precipitate the emotional withdrawal of fathers rather than
the reverse? Or might homosexual sons avoid recalling an attachment to
their fathers because of its erotic Oedipal component?[16] Could not individual repression and societal oppression result in the same adjustment
problems or illnesses that antigay therapists claim are caused by the orientation itself?

Some Freudian analysts, most notably Nancy Chodorow, have effectively challenged this pathologizing view. She cautions that diagnoses of
heterosexuality as healthier are offered "in the context of a normative cultural system," with biological assumptions, essentialist views of gender
and sexual differences, and gender inequalities.[17] She believes that judgments about the psychological merits of one sexuality over another, if they
ever can be made, will not divide on the homosexual-heterosexual axis.
The gender of one's sexual object choice does not determine one's psychological adjustment. In a chapter provocatively titled "Heterosexuality
as a Compromise Formation," Chodorow observes that the developmental and transferential histories of all sexualities involve "erotic feelings,
conflicts, defenses, accounts of relationships with parents, attempts to sort
out a self, accounting for what gives pleasure and why or for what is desired and what fantasized."[18] In other words, we must not take heterosexuality as an unexplored given or homosexuality as the departure or perversion. Indeed there are both normal and perverse versions of
heterosexuality, homosexuality, bisexuality, celibacy, and autoeroticism.[19]

## Genetic Theories

In a quest reminiscent of pre-Freudian times, clinical scientists today look
mostly for physical causes. Their findings have replaced, or more often

enhanced, psychological explanations. The reformulated research question is, To what degree is homosexuality biologically determined (i.e., genetic or hormonal) and to what degree is it learned or environmentally determined? Advances in biochemistry and genetics contribute to increasingly complex etiologic discourses.

The frequency of the homosexual orientation is much higher than any random genetic mutation would be.[20] Sociobiologists find that enduring human traits have been naturally selected through evolution. If homosexual desire is genetically influenced and persistent through the ages, they reason, there must be some justification for its failure to die out, especially since homosexuals appear to reproduce less than others do.[21] Indeed, this apparent genetic disadvantage leads some to speculate that homosexuality is caused by an infectious agent.[22] A number of explanations have been advanced to show how human gene pools could be advantaged by the presence of people with homosexual traits.[23] Homosexuality might figure in population control or perhaps some homosexuals' not having children of their own leaves them free to be caregivers, enhancing the survivability of other family members' progeny.[24]

Sociobiological reasoning is interesting but can only be taken seriously if genes for homosexuality are indeed found. A number of projects have begun to contribute to that goal.[25] Among the best known are two studies of pairs of twins in which one is homosexual.[26] These studies have demonstrated that the other twin is nearly three times more likely also to be homosexual when the twins are identical (i.e., they share identical genes) than when they are fraternal (i.e., they share as many genes as any other siblings would). This coincidence is used to prove that homosexuality is highly influenced by genes.[27] It must be noted that these twins were recruited through advertising and that homosexuals who knew their identical twin to be gay or lesbian might have had a higher rate of participation.

One of the researchers, Richard Pillard, also concedes that a greater incidence of bisexual self-identification among women makes female sexuality "a harder thing to study in the quantitative way that we've been doing."[28] The demonstrated likelihood is still impressive. Dean Hamer, a leading proponent of genetic origins, has targeted a sequence of five markers at the tip of the X chromosome (Xq28 region), found in pairs of gay brothers in 33 of 40 families.[29] No comparative analysis was done of this genetic region in gay-straight pairs of brothers, nor does Hamer offer any explanation for bisexuality.

If homosexuality were wholly genetic, every homosexual identical twin would have a homosexual counterpart. Since that is not so, we conclude that other factors are involved as well.[30] These influences may occur early, since the gender atypicality that signals homosexuality in some boys manifests itself in childhood. Extragenetic events may happen even in utero and affect one embryo only. A study is currently under way to count and compare finger print ridges of identical twins in which one is homosexual and the other is not; different finger prints, as well as sexual orientation, would be ascribed to the prenatal environment.[31]

## Hormones

If genes do cause homosexuality, how do they do it? Among other functions, genes dictate the production of hormones. Earlier in the century, it was thought that the so-called sex hormones had some connection to sexual orientation. These steroidal substances stimulate the development of primary (e.g., testicular growth, onset of menses) and secondary (e.g., facial hair, breast development) gender characteristics at puberty.

Rather crude therapies of injected testosterone or estrogen were once used to redress what was thought to be the imbalance in adult homosexuals of these male and female hormones. The cures all failed. Hormone supplementation was found to influence such variables as beard thickness, breast size, and the intensity of sexual desire but had no effect on sexual object choice. We now know that the great majority of homosexuals have normal levels of sex hormones.[32]

Current hormonal research is much more sophisticated, reaching to the cellular level. The target of one branch of study is the production and impact of prenatal hormones that control the differentiated development of male and female fetuses. The brain is of particular interest, with links proposed to male versus female behaviors (e.g., propensity toward violence).[33] Patterns of sexual attraction could well be programmed into the gendered brain.[34]

Substantial research has been devoted to the effects of sex hormones on the gender of the fetus and the subsequent gender role of the child.[35] All embryos have both male and female potential. Production of a masculinizing hormone in some fetuses prevents them from developing a uterus. Animal experiments have shown that prenatal hormones masculinize and defeminize the developing brain; conversely, their absence or insufficiency demasculinizes and feminizes.

In some individuals the gendering of the brain may be only partially completed. Parts of the brain may be able to respond in ways inconsistent with outward gender indicators. Injections of testosterone or other sex hormones into birds, rats, or sheep prenatally or at birth have proved that singing, mounting, posturing for urination, and other such gender-linked behaviors can be affected. A marine biologist has even discovered three kinds of fish that change both their brain structures and genitalia in response to their circumstances.[36]

Nonetheless, among sheep and particularly among higher primates, socialization more than hormone status has been shown to influence gender role. The behavior of hormonally masculinized female sheep and monkeys, for instance, appears not entirely dependent on chemistry.

Yet there are contradictory claims over whether nurture is paramount. In one case, when an eight-month-old's penis was accidentally severed during a routine operation, he was castrated, given a vagina and female hormone treatments, and raised as a female. At 14, however, the child renounced his ostensible gender, underwent further surgery to reconstruct his male genitalia and now lives as a married man.[37] In another case, a boy raised as a girl after a botched circumcision continued to live as a woman.[38]

Forms of hermaphroditism in humans suggest the possibility of a masculinized or feminized brain in our species. By natural happenstance or the mother's ingestion of drugs, hermaphrodites have been exposed in utero to atypical hormonal impact and are born with ambiguous, missing, and/or underdeveloped gonadal parts. John Money proposes that the sex-role behaviors of some hermaphrodites prove that the same hormones that control the development of internal and external sex organs influence the brain.[39] Some point to the masculine activities of certain females with high levels of androgen and masculinized genitalia to prove the influence of hormones on behavior, but these conclusions are disputed and no strong correlation has been shown with sexual orientation.[40]

A 1995 study of estrogen exposure to the female fetus claims to have found a higher tendency toward bisexuality and lesbianism than in non-exposed subjects.[41] Although the control sample may have been skewed away from those willing to admit homosexual tendencies,[42] the study supports the conclusion that the prenatal hormonal environment does play a role in determining the sexual orientation of adults. Other research observations from a 1995 study on androgen exposure suggest "a complex relationship among hormones, childhood sex-typed behavior, and sexual orientation."[43]

## The Homosexual Brain

Although some scientists argue over perceived differences between human male and female brains,[44] others profess to have discovered peculiarities in the homosexual brain. A Dutch researcher first found an anomaly in one part of the brain;[45] then American Simon LeVay spied a variation between gay and heterosexual men in the size of the hypothalamus, an area that had been connected with sexual behavior.[46] LeVay maintains gay men's larger hypothalamus resembles that of straight women, though he allows there is individual variation. (Lesbian brains are apparently less available for study than those from men who have died of AIDS.) LeVay's work brought him instant media stardom.

A year after his study, two researchers, whose work on gender had inspired LeVay, claimed to have found a gay/straight difference in the nerve fibers that link the two hemispheres of the brain, the anterior commissure of the corpus callosum.[47] This region of the brain is not involved in sexual behavior, but the same neurochemical agents that might affect sexual orientation could cause the perceived disparity. LeVay's findings on the hypothalamus had not yet been replicated when he too began new work on the corpus callosum.

Other studies have centered on left-handedness and spatial ability, both brain-related phenomena.[48] Gay men and lesbians are thought to be more disposed to left-handedness than heterosexuals are. Gay men and gender-nonconforming boys are alleged to be less spatially skilled than straight men. However, these not yet definitive findings sometimes appear to contradict themselves. Since left-handedness is said to be caused by high levels of fetal testosterone, one would not expect gay men to be more often left-handed then heterosexual men. Secondly, if higher spatial skills are associated with males, why then are straight women more spatially gifted than lesbians, who are said, after all, to be masculinized?

Although some of these theses show promise, we must be wary of research that

- uses cadavers that have been affected by AIDS;
- assumes AIDS cadavers to represent dead gay people without adequate corroboration;
- studies brains, such as those of postoperative transsexuals, that might have been affected by adult events, like surgery or hormone use;
- characterizes femaleness as the absence of masculinizing factor;
- jumps from one species to the next in making behavioral predictions.[49]

We should also note that some gay male hormonal research has been refuted[50] and that Money's gender work is based on the rare genetic variation in hermaphroditism and that he characterizes behavior by means of conventional heterosexual norms.[51]

In 1996, attention returned to previously studied phenomena: the effects of birth order and the gender of siblings. Homosexual men, and effeminate boys, appear to have later than average birth order and more brothers.[52] Psychologists had once opined on the effects of childhood fraternal sex play, but now they have turned to cellular science. Perhaps mothers, being female, produce increasing levels of antibodies to their successive male fetuses. An abundance of these substances might attack the developing male brain.[53] Of course this idea, like so many others in the field, lacks applicability to lesbian daughters.

It is tantalizing to link hormones or antibodies with embryos, brains, and sex-role behavior. One could then leap to insufficiently defeminized gay male brains, to slightly masculinized lesbian brains, to masculinized but not completely defeminized bisexual brains, to prepubertal sissified play habits, and to faulty brains telling men or women they are trapped in wrongly gendered bodies.[54]

But we should not be so facile. Allowing that prenatal variables like maternal stress, diet, and drug ingestion may have an effect on gendering the brain, perhaps predisposing it to certain sexual patterns, Money himself observes that sexual orientation does not inevitably follow. Erotic feeling and behavior in humans appears to be considerably influenced by socialization.

## Multiple Interactive Causes

Whatever inclinations certain regions in the brain might dictate, humans learn from their surroundings to behave, or even to desire, otherwise. Money nicely confounds nature-nurture oppositionality with the point that interaction with the environment actually changes the structure of the brain through "the biology of learning and remembering."[55] And even more tantalizingly, another seeker of the "cause" has demonstrated that having sex can actually alter the spinal chord nerves of rats.[56]

Expanding upon his predispositional yet interactive model, Money likens sexuality to language acquisition. He has coined the term "lovemap" for one's preferred sexuality menu. Both innate and fashioned by learning, it consists of an individual's sexual orientation, preferences, and acquired tastes. Money's paradigm applies to the origins and dynamics of all sexualities without sensationalizing or stigmatizing any.

What, then, makes some lovemaps homosexual? Despite recent claims that a single master gene controls the courtship activities of the male fruit fly,[57] neither one gene nor one environmental factor will likely be discovered to account for any complex human feeling or behavior. Even regular combinations of genes (i.e., alleles) do not always produce the same result in varying environments.[58] Although he purports to have found two genes that determine frequency of sexual activity and preferred number of partners,[59] Hamer imagines that sexual orientation depends on a number of biological causes: "There probably are other biological factors like hormones, for example, and other variables we simply don't know anything about yet."[60] He describes the research task as a search for *co-factors*, not *replacements*, for psychosocial causes.[61]

A multifactor model is consistent with the notion that sexuality exists along a continuum and is malleable. Sexual orientation, like musicality for example, is likely a product of both biological disposition and environmental influences. At any one time in their lives, different individuals may have reached the same point on the continuum by different routes, guided by different combinations of nature and nurture.[62] Both leave their marks on the patterns of the mind and the lovemaps of the heart in what is perhaps a lifelong process.

Lastly, although it has not yet been proven, it is possible that different arrays of both genetic and environmental factors account for lesbianism than for male homosexuality.[63] Hamer has indeed postulated that lesbianism is far more cultural than biological,[64] despite recent findings that lesbian hearing (and thus brain structure) veers toward male characteristics.[65]

## Why Ask—Why Now?

If scientists discovered the genetic factors that predispose some people to like codfish and others to prefer beans, would they receive such attention? Of course not—those preferences are inconsequential. Even research on the possible genetics of religiosity does not land its authors on the front pages.[66] Nonetheless, everyone appears interested in where homosexuality comes from.

Some want to know because they would like to change or prevent it. On the dark side of etiologic research, a faction of scientists, including some who worked for the Nazis, have tried to pinpoint a locus of homosexuality in the body so that it might be expunged. More recently, German doctors, following research on rats in the 1970s, claimed to have achieved a cure for homosexuality involving surgery in the area of the hypothalamus.[67] Similar operations were reviewed positively in 1974 in the *Journal of the American Medical Association*.[68] Some contemporary extremists are vociferous proponents of treatment.[69] We should be reminded that in the United States by 1940 some thirty states had enacted eugenics laws allowing forced sterilization of the feebleminded, the mentally ill, and the chronically poor.[70]

A cure would attract parents whose vigilance detected telltale signs in their youngsters; self-styled liberals might just want to protect such a child from a hard life. A test for causative factors could lead to preventive abortions by homophobic or stigmatized prospective parents, who would have the right to do so, according to one attorney who says he is "pro-freedom" as well as "pro-gay."[71]

James Watson, the co-discoverer of DNA, supports aborting gay fetuses.[72] Chandler Burr, a self-described Republican gay assimilationist admits the gay gene might yet prove to be a disease gene and is "not opposed to considering genetic surgery."[73] There is a market. Unhappy homosexuals have been paying therapists and praying for a cure for some time. Some would line up for DNA injections for the same reasons that other disfavored minority people have sought bleaching creams and cosmetic surgery.

Some researchers believe the discovery of a gene for homosexuality will protect gays and lesbians from bigotry by proving they are born that way. Pointing to surveys that show less hostility toward homosexuals among those who think the orientation is biologically determined,[74] LeVay hopes his findings are used to argue for civil rights. One might ask how well people of color have fared because melanin production is genetically caused or whether a biological predisposition toward obesity has protected fat people from ridicule. Biological theories single-mindedly advanced by early gay rights advocates like Magnus Hirschfeld may even have contributed to the Nazi persecution of homosexuals.[75]

Nor is it clear that the existence of lesbian seagulls[76] or gay silkmoths[77] and sheep[78] will dignify gay and lesbian people.[79] A long history of cultural stigma and religious proscription will not be easily reversed by scientific discoveries.[80] Many who already believe homosexuality is biological still demand that it not be expressed.[81] The most charitable response to homosexuality as an involuntary genetic condition may likely be toleration with pity.

LeVay's political strategy might indeed increase acceptance for the short term, but what of the future? Pinpointing a biological cause could also hasten the day when scientists learn "How Genetic Surgery Can Change Homosexuality to Heterosexuality."[82] The moment an effective treatment is found, pity could turn to anger at any who refuse the antidote. In the eyes of many, homosexuality will have been transformed wholly into an obstinate and perverse choice.

Current preoccupation with causation is essentially a reaction to the growing visibility of lesbians and gay men since the 1970s, and especially since the mid-1980s. This homosexual presence has created a new level of discomfort, if not of threat. There are precedents in the ways both race and gender have been examined in this country. For instance, the civil rights demands of people of color created a sudden mass interest in genetic theories of black intellectual inferiority.[83] The current appeal of *The Bell Curve* proves the continuing usefulness of such research in supplying a simplistic race-intelligence link to prove the futility of social education and welfare programs.[84]

Similarly, it is impossible to ignore the coincidence of research and popular articles on the female brain with women's struggle for equity. When feminists rise up in defiance of job discrimination and other gender-role limitations, conservatives almost cry out for studies that prove that women's genes render them unsuitable for "male tasks." The media hype these studies,[85] all but ignoring those that find gender differences minor and relatively insignificant.[86] "The idea that women are different has served to keep them out of the halls of power."[87] These race and gender tracts will some day probably share a library shelf with phrenological studies of Jewish skulls.

Of the connection between science and ideology, one female geneticist writes: "Scientists, and the data we produce, are not and cannot be free from the prejudices, ideologies, or interests of the larger society."[88] This dynamic was perhaps never so clear as it was in the early 1970s, during the American Psychiatric Association's debates about the classification of homosexuality as a disease. The vehemence with which reactionary forces dismissed the research findings of Kinsey, Hooker et al. (see Chapter 5) "provides an important indication of the extent to which 'facts' take on meaning only within the context of underlying conceptual schemes and do not in themselves have the capacity to compel fundamental changes in the way the world is viewed."[89]

In short, cultural and political orthodoxy infects the pursuit of scientific knowledge. Individual prejudices and neuroses play a role as well. One cannot overlook the possibility that an eminent thrice-married psychiatrist might cling to the idea of a cure for homosexuality because his son is an outspoken, politically active, self-accepting gay man.[90]

If a group observes something atypical and, for its own socially dictated reasons, labels it repulsive, an intense interest in its cause is likely to evolve. Because it is homophobic, our culture frets over the causes of homosexuality: "The search for a 'scientific' aetiology of sexual orientation is itself a homophobic project. . . . When the sexual racism underlying such inquiries is more plainly exposed, their rationale will suffer proportionately, or so one may hope."[91]

Perhaps as a product of internalized oppression, many gays and lesbians themselves puzzle over the genesis of their orientations. In a non-homophobic environment, they might be curious about why they are attracted to one individual or another, but they would probably have as much interest in what makes them seek a same-gender partner as heterosexuals now have in what makes them straight.

Whatever sparks homosexual desire today is probably related to what has caused it over centuries. It may be genetically predetermined like eye color, hormonally dictated like left-handedness, or environmentally influenced like sense of humor. The chief concern for educators, however, is not the source of this inclination, but rather what allows it to be expressed and what it means to people. Some folks' loving in a different way, whether by genetic disposition, nurture, or free choice, should pose no threat. Rather than rely on science for justification, gays, lesbians, and their allies would be better off with a long-term strategy of public education—one that honors equally all people's nonexploitative sexual desires and behaviors.

Why is sexual orientation or preference not treated with as much respect as religious preference? Experts should be investigating the etiology of the fear and repression of homosexuality. When those psychological and social factors are discovered, then perhaps a cure can be developed not for homosexuality but for the animosity that it evokes.

# 4

# Homophobia and Heterosexism

Two observations from a 1970s review of research on racism are central to this chapter:

1. Prejudice as an attitude held by individuals has not been adequately considered in terms of the societal context in which individuals exist.

2. Prejudice has been treated as an isolated variable . . . rather than as an interacting and interconnected aspect of an individual's complete self system (i.e., the organized, integrated set of personality, cognitive, ability, and self-perception factors that characterize the individual.[1]

Homophobia has only recently received media and scholarly attention. It too is a prejudice rooted in our culture, our politics, and our psyches. No fluke, homophobia is deliberately taught and persists because its social systemic manifestation in heterosexism serves a number of key functions. It will diminish as the social arrangement that it helps to maintain changes and its immoral and pernicious effects can no longer be borne.

Homophobia is the fear and/or hatred of homosexuality and homosexual persons. Its literal meaning, "fear of sameness," has no currency. In fact, the association of "homo" with homosexual is so common that references to *Homo sapiens* have provoked classroom snickers for decades. The word's second element, "phobia," however, is problematical. A phobia is technically an irrational fear that causes one to avoid contact with its triggering stimulus, and some people do indeed define homophobia as an irrational dread.[2] But homophobia is not always irrational; it is often a logical outcome of one's own predicament and perceptions about homosexuality.[3] Moreover, a dreadful number of homophobes, far from fleeing, actively pursue gays and lesbians for attack.

Contemporary conjunction with racism, sexism, and anti-Semitism confirm the gist of the "fear and hatred" meaning, although "heterosexism" is a more precise analogue to the others. Each of these racial, gender, and religious prejudices is elaborated into an oppression—an "ism"—in its social application and ramifications.

The 1960s gay liberationist view that everyone is inherently bisexual interpreted homophobia as a fear of what one could not accept in oneself. Now that gay liberation has virtually yielded to a minority identity position (see Chapter 2), homophobia is more readily seen to be directed toward an out-group.[4]

Hostility toward homosexuals may be linked to negativity toward women and ethnic/racial minorities,[5] suggesting to some that prejudice reaction is a function of the bigot more than the target.[6] Even assuming so, each group may be consciously despised for different reasons.

Yet if prejudice is indiscriminate ("hate one, hate all"), overt discrimination appears to be selective. Many seem less inclined to express racism and sexism than they used to be,[7] at least among strangers, yet seldom care what others think about their homophobia.[8] Among Americans 50 percent[9] to 66 percent[10] are willing to tell an interviewer they believe the homosexual "lifestyle" is unacceptable. Their unabashed prejudice is transmitted to the young with hateful consequences: A statewide survey of 2823 New York junior and senior high school students revealed greater hostility toward homosexuals than toward racial or ethnic minorities. Student responses often included threats of antigay violence.[11]

Before laying out a number of views on the nature and causes of homophobia, some problems in the supporting research must be highlighted:

- Some of the attitudinal studies do not exclude gay/lesbian respondents; therefore results could appear more positive than are justified.[12] Researchers who claim to have excluded gay/lesbian respondents[13] might be deceived, since student subjects in introductory psychology courses may be too unsure of or embarrassed by their sexualities to self-select out of the studies.
- Lab studies of interaction bear little relation to real-world interactions.[14]
- Considerably less attention is paid in the literature to lesbian targets of prejudice than to gay males.[15]
- Gender-related research studies are often influenced by factors in the experiment itself.[16]

Despite such limitations, existing studies provide valuable insights, which this chapter uses, together with moral development theory and observations about related biases, to sketch the challenge that homophobia and heterosexism present to schools. Chapters 11–14 investigate strategies and programs to mitigate homophobic fear and hatred.

### The Theories of Kite and Herek

Mary Kite lays out three reference points for analyzing stereotyping or prejudice:[17]

1. Sociocultural stereotypes
   - are provided by the culture and are stable across time and region;
   - are employed by individuals to demonstrate membership and loyalty to the culture;
   - can be based on the social role that particular out-groups play within the culture;
   - in the absence of personal contact, may depend on impressions from the mass media;
   - may vary among competing subcultures with differing values and interests.

2. Motivational prejudice
   - serves to bolster one's personal identity;
   - is related to one's willingness to subscribe to negative stereotypes;
   - is related to self-esteem or depression;
   - may serve different functions for different individuals.

3. Cognitive stereotyping
   - employed to categorize/interpret a complex world, is the compilation of lists of characteristics assumed to apply to all members of certain groups, for example, "all spheres roll";[18]
   - is protective, since one cannot know all individuals.

These three modes—social, psychological, or intellectual—may build upon each other. Prejudice begins as a blameless attempt to organize a puzzling world. Then, distorted by one's emotional needs and manipulated by social forces, it becomes a sinister bigotry.

Gregory Herek has studied the social/psychological function of homophobic prejudice.[19] In his analysis, clearly related to Kite's, attitudes toward gay/lesbian people can be characterized as follows:

1. Experiential/Schematic
   - categorizing social reality based on one's own interactions with homosexual persons;
   - can result in confirmation of negative stereotypes but more often reduces prejudice than exacerbates it.

2. Defensive
   - coping with inner conflicts/anxieties by projecting them onto homosexual persons;
   - actual contact often makes attitudes worse.

3. Self-Expressive/Symbolic
   - expressing abstract ideological concepts, closely linked to self-concept, social network, and reference groups;
   - needing high level of social approval;
   - more likely to be attending a religious service at least monthly, belonging to a conservative denomination, and endorsing an orthodox religious ideology;
   - pressured toward conformity by closely bonded social networks.

Herek stipulates that these functions may overlap and that no single frame can account for differences among heterosexual homophobes, yet his (and Kite's) categories appear to delineate three distinct kinds of homophobia: intellectual, emotional, or cultural.

There is no experiential domain that is not colored by intellectual and subjective factors. The experience of meeting a homosexual person is without meaning until it is both examined and symbolically recast. Regardless of the limits of one's interpretive capacities, the world is understood in the light of one's existing knowledge, feelings, and values, which have in turn been influenced by one's environment/culture. Therefore defensive homophobia cannot be separated from the symbolic. Feelings about sex and gender are not merely instinctive. One is uncomfortable with or frightened by homosexuality because it threatens one's understanding of self and society. To understand people's prejudice, we must examine their reactive thoughts and feelings and understand what exactly provokes them.[20]

Likewise, although heterosexism may serve a societal function, individuals will only subscribe to homophobic views that are personally meaningful to them. Following Kite, motivational prejudice makes sociocultural prejudice possible—and conversely, using a constructionist axiom, sociocultural prejudice helps dictate the terms of motivational prejudice. Three mutually reinforcing threads—analytical, emotional, and social—are woven into the fabric of an individual's prejudice.

Although bigotry may not be entirely rational and may indeed involve intuition and the intangible influences of context,[21] symbolic value is learned and therefore is an ingredient of prejudice upon which education may have some impact. Of course schools may also usefully provide for the expression *and examination* of feelings.

Kite claims that the cognitive perspective has not been adopted by most researchers into homophobia;[22] nevertheless one psychologist has said of prejudice in general, "Research shows a lot more cognitive influence than the public is aware of."[23] Antihomophobia educators must pay attention to cognition, particularly to why people construe difference as they do and how they respond to new knowledge that contradicts stereotype.

## Homophobia and Moral Development

Elisabeth Young-Bruehl writes that sexism and homophobia are related to "our rock bottom notion of who we are, who we ought to be, how we should be regarded by others and ourselves."[24] The pivotal question for antiprejudice educators is how people learn who they ought to be.

Children do not spring full-blown to mindful guardianship of heterosexism. Seventh graders, for example, do not consciously shout "faggot" in conspiracy to preserve male hegemony. Although they are being socialized into that repressive project, they have their own justifications for such harassment. And as they mature, their social awareness and reasons change. For teachers to intervene effectively, they must tailor their strategies to the students' level of rationalization.

This developmental view of prejudice reduction can be fleshed out with the help of moral development theory and feminist analysis. Although Lawrence Kohlberg does not emphasize bigotry (let alone mention homophobia) in his work, his findings can lead to a better grasp of bigotry as a product of moral judgment, Young-Bruehl's "who we ought to be."

Kohlberg studied how people determine right and wrong in a social context, how they find symbolic meaning in human interaction, and how they move from an instrumental to a more highly principled moral system.[25] His theory helps explain the relationships among the various functions of homophobia. It also exposes different layers within its symbolic and sociocultural meanings. From his moral development stages, one can extrapolate a methodology for addressing homophobia.

Despite substantial and rightful challenges to his ideas, based on the gender-skewing of his early research subjects,[26] Kohlberg's general schema should not be rashly caste aside, particularly since it can be so useful in reconciling the prejudice theories of Kite, Herek, and others. The success of bias reduction in a school program inspired by Kohlberg (see Chapter 11) also supports examining moral development more closely. Exploring how individuals at Kohlberg's developmental levels might think about difference is worth the effort.

## Cognitive Stages and Homophobia

**Stage 1.**  At Stage 1, the child views moral action as punishment avoidance: Whatever course prevents an authority figure's displeasure is good. Youngsters do pay attention to their elders' bigoted remarks and conversations.[27] If parents or older children speak apprehensively and derogatorily of a minority group, the child is likely to mimic their fear and hatred. There is good evidence that imitation of and identification with parents plays a role in socializing children to be prejudiced.[28]

There is no early need to persuade the child of the despised group's inferiority: "Majority-group children first learn affective, good-bad reactions to out-groups, and only later acquire specific beliefs about them."[29] The child learns that put-downs like "nigger" or "fag" are effective weapons approved by the powerful.[30] Children begin to see homophobic denigration as "expressions of cultural norms."[31] Of course, with a rather limited milieu at this age, his or her notion of culture is narrow.

Parents and others transmit their prejudice at varying levels of explicitness. They might discourage a child from associating with a gender atypical playmate or with the child of a gay parent. They may respond to questions about differences by changing the subject, looking pained or disgusted, or more directly, answering with stereotypes. They might even behave rudely toward or attack a minority person.

As elementary school teachers know, such learning begins well before children have any idea of what renders this group despicable. Challenged by his principal for using the word "faggot" and asked what it means, a second grader responded, "I don't know, but Francisco said it was the king of swears."[32]

**Stage 2.**  The individual at Stage 2 determines the morality of an action by calculating what its personal benefit will be. This stage subsumes the egocentric materialism of Stage 1 but adds the notions of instrumentalism and reciprocity. It is the "you scratch my back and I'll scratch yours" stage.

Because people want predictability in an exchange, they are probably suspicious of agents who appear different from themselves and their usual counterparts in the marketplace. One is comfortable with someone who clearly operates from one's own moral framework. That is, one cannot depend on reputed "outsiders" for a quid pro quo. The circumscribed world of a Stage 1 or 2 thinker would appear safer if there were no outsiders in it. This moral attitude builds on the child's earliest fears of the unfamiliar, wherein "young children react to superficial characteristics that are foreign to them."[33] Or, as history professor Robert Davidoff puts it, "Human beings have a real hard time with the fact that something that looks and feels totally different can be another form of love."[34]

*Stage 3.* The Stage 3 moral criterion is clan approval, to be acceptable to those with whom one directly associates in daily life. Intentions are important at this stage, and one behaves fairly toward another by virtue of common membership in the circle. Whatever list of aliens constitutes one's clan heritage becomes one's own phobic registry. One hates more for its value in making one fit with the clan than for any other reason. In some groups, prejudice toward an out-group (and the assumption that the in-group includes none of them) endears individuals to their cohort. Regardless of one's previous opinions, bigotry would become a virtue, as one moved from individuality and reciprocity toward such a group's norms.[35]

*Stage 4.* A Stage 4 moral universe enlarges from the immediate circle of the clan to a larger society of relative strangers. One's primary concern is the maintenance of the given familiar social order by means of rules and laws. At this stage, prejudice could emanate from a perception of social threat, rather than personal danger or a need to belong. As such the perceived danger and the response to it are abstract or symbolic. For example:

> Symbolic racism is a combination of the generalized feeling that the social, economic, and political status quo should be maintained with the belief that blacks are somehow responsible for threatening this status quo and, by implication, the whole American way of life. . . . [It] is centered around highly abstract or symbolic issues.[36]

Homosexuality also may seem wrong, if it is seen to challenge the existing social order.

Some researchers appear unsure what their interview subjects mean when they refer to the societal consequences of homosexuality.[37] For people at Stage 4, social preservation requires the enforcement of traditional patriarchy by various means, including controlling the gender and sexuality system. It is at this point that young people's homophobia becomes a systematic heterosexist practice. In fact, some may be so certain of a socially condoned and necessary homophobic license they are surprised when challenged. How else can we explain the reaction of a boy arrested for gay-bashing an undercover policeman? Led from the scene by other officers, he is taken aback and offers this justification: "I thought he was a damned fag!"[38]

The social symbolic danger of gender nonconformity and homosexuality is clear: "A 13-year-old tomboy and a 17-year-old drag queen do more than threaten persons with insecure gender identities; they threaten the social order."[39] This mentality leads to school rules forbidding boys to wear clothing associated with females.[40] Additionally, homosexuals become scapegoats for displacing the horrors of maintaining the patriarchal system: child abuse (2.9 million reported cases in 1993 and the primary cause of death for children under 4)[41] and woman battering.[42]

Under fascism, the extreme of Stage 4 thinking, homosexuals (and Jews) were singled out as antithetical to the cult of masculinity and were thought to sap the national strength.[43] In the United States today, less-homophobic people describe themselves as moderate or liberal, and more-hostile people rate themselves politically conservative.[44]

There might be a sociobiological aversion to the assumed childlessness of homosexuals, a societal extension of the hypothetical inborn prejudice toward anyone who appears to put one's family gene pool at risk.[45] But even gays and lesbians with children are often seen as enemies of social conservation.

*Stage 5.*   Moral reasoning at the postconventional stages casts aside rigid adherence to traditional law and order in favor of underlying principles, such as those articulated in the U.S. Declaration of Independence. A person at Stage 5 sees democratic lawmaking as a pursuit of justice and is occasionally conflicted over the failure of legislation to sustain values like liberty and equality. The area of individual and minority rights is rich with the potential for such conflict.

Difference does not upset the concept of social order at this stage. A number of competing interests are enjoined to resolve their competing claims under a system of amendable laws. One could support minority rights even if one felt personally uncomfortable about that minority. The following research observation illustrates such a possible Stage 5 mentality among college students:

> The willingness to accord civil liberties to homosexuals is not, however, to be confused with a generally favorable attitude toward homosexuality. Several studies report that for well-educated young respondents, favorable attitudes toward civil liberties often go hand in hand with repugnance toward homosexual activities.[46]

Some research shows that although most Americans think homosexuality is wrong on moral or religious grounds, they favor employment and free speech rights for homosexuals.[47] This may sound like a Stage 5 judgment, but it probably represents a Stage 3 or 4 parroting of glib American egalitarianism. The college students above might have a higher-stage reason than that for granting rights to people whose behavior disgusts them. The question they would have to answer is whether their disgust is prompted by morality or taste. If it is merely a discomfort with the unfamiliar (like the response of some to interracial dating), it is not a moral issue (and may abate with greater exposure).

Those who have not internalized higher principles of nondiscrimination can be swayed by low-stage arguments. The popularity of claims that gay rights are special rights, that military homophobia is caused by homosexuals, and that gays should not be allowed to marry proves that most Americans find such arguments appealing. Down deep, gays and lesbians are deemed second-class citizens toward whom it is acceptable to be bigoted.[48]

*Stage 6.* Stage 6 reasoning hinges on *a priori* principles. Its moral imperatives can lead to civil disobedience.[49] One Stage 6 criterion is universality: One weighs an obligation by asking if everyone ought to do the same thing. Should everyone tell the truth, for example, or keep a promise? Occasionally one principle must be sacrificed for a higher principle, ultimately the absolute value of human life.

Attacks on homosexuality often employ the test of universalization: "If everybody chose to be gay, the world would end because nobody would reproduce." Both the premise and conclusion are flawed: Most people do not choose their orientation; it is impossible that every human would lead an exclusively homosexual life; and gays and lesbians do have children. Should the human race be imperiled by underpopulation, many ethically driven homosexuals would have children, if they had not already had them.

What really motivates this argument is not alarm for the species but rather a Stage 4 concern that only heterosexual families can reproduce themselves as patriarchal institutions.[50] Here, an observation about homophobia among African Americans can be applied to the broader society: "'Homophobia' is not so much a fear of 'homosexuals' but a fear that homosexuality will become pervasive in the community."[51] Homosexuality is seen as dangerous because its acceptance could undo the community as it is currently constituted.

Stage 6 thinkers are not dismayed by difference. Human beings are seen not as means to preserve a system but as ends in themselves. Diversity is to be cultivated and celebrated as a reminder to value people individually.[52] This mind-set informs a commitment to pluralism that goes beyond mere tolerance.[53]

## Moral Development and Religion

Moral development stages may be reflected in one's religious views.[54] Those who hold that the rules are synonymous with the church are likely reasoning at stage 4 or lower. They believe that to alter traditional anti-gay doctrine would be to destroy the church itself. Homophobic people claim high religiosity and/or belong to conservative or fundamentalist denominations, whereas less-homophobic people see themselves as non-religious or belong to liberal denominations.[55] The extrinsically motivated, essentially at Stage 3, experience religion as group membership that brings social acceptance, status, security, support, and comfort. For the intrinsically motivated, religious principles determine everyday interactions with others,[56] a Stage 4 or higher faith standard.

Intrinsics are less likely to be racially biased than extrinsics,[57] but researchers have found largely negative views toward homosexuality in both groups, varying by denominational creed.[58] Stage 4 intrinsics would be governed by the dogmas of their churches, which tend in the United States to be nonracist but still homophobic. Stage 5 or 6 intrinsics would be more likely to depart from homophobic church teachings or belong to more tolerant denominations in the first place.

One should not confuse true believers with those who merely use the Good Book to justify views held on other grounds.[59] Sincere adherents to religious orthodoxy do not pick and choose which doctrines to follow. Hence, a thrice-divorced man who says gay marriage would destroy a God-given institution and an adulterous prosecutor of homosexual sodomy are likely to be homophobes even without their Bible.[60] For centuries those in power have used the Bible to justify oppression against out-groups, be they blacks, Jews, Catholics, or Protestants.[61]

## Formulating an Antibias Argument

Because most children and adolescents reason at preconventional and conventional stages, teachers might conclude that the homophobic attitudes of the majority of students are unalterable. That is not the case. Schools will, however, have to couch some of their appeal for tolerance in pre-Stage 5 values such as self-interest, peer group criteria, and rules. For example:

*Stage 1.*
• You will be punished if you discriminate.

*Stage 2.*
- You will not get what you want if you discriminate.
- How would you like it if they discriminated against you?

*Stage 3.*
- People you care about do not approve of discrimination.
- You must not discriminate against anyone in your group.

*Stage 4.*
- Discrimination is against the law.
- Discrimination is a threat to social order.

Literalist conservatism, the keystone of right-wing and fundamentalist bigotry, is ground zero for antihomophobia education with students, parents, and the community. Stage 4 thinkers must be prodded to step beyond a law and order mentality to postconventional reasoning, which is far less compatible with homophobia and heterosexism. New experience and persuasion can move them, but one must bear in mind that genuine social and religious Stage 4 conservatives are truly fearful that disorder, meaninglessness, and perdition lie on the other side of their certitude.

### Sexism and Homophobia/Heterosexism

Homophobic stigma is a powerful enforcer of conventional gender behavior.[62] Suzanne Pharr, noting how accusations of homosexuality are used to discredit those who challenge traditional gender norms, dubs homophobia "a weapon of sexism."[63] Conversely, sexism could be characterized as an indispensable ingredient of homophobia. Without gender role prescriptions, homophobia would lose much of its Stage 4 rationale.

Indeed, the hatred or avoidance of the feminine and of what is perceived as feminine in men is at the heart of male homophobia.[64] Men who are intolerant of homosexuality describe themselves as less feminine and more assertive and independent (i.e., masculine) than do more tolerant men.[65] Intolerant men also want others to know they are not sex-role deviant.[66] The worst insult a man can hear is to be called homosexual by another man:[67] "Whereas there is some grudging respect accorded women with masculine qualities, none is given to 'womanly' men. Even among children 'tomboys' are more acceptable than 'sissies.'"[68] Intimacy is permitted among females but raises alarms for boys and men.[69] Too tight or long a hug makes one suspect.

Jean Baker Miller describes in social constructionist terms how people come to have, and then might rethink, their ideas about gender:

It is true that the very ways we find to conceptualize experience are in large measure given to us by the culture in which we learn "how to think and feel." But people are also continually straining against the boundaries of their culture—against the limiting categories given by that culture—and seeking the means to understand and to express the many experiences for which it does not suffice.[70]

This engagement between past perceptions and new experience is a crucial developmental struggle. The cognitive dissonance Baker Miller describes can be resolved with postconventional thinking, but that difficult step demands that people reframe beliefs that have been critical to their identities. So much is invested in gender we should not be surprised when its reassessment is passionate.

Rethinking gender can shake conceptions of sexuality as well. That Baker Miller appeared to ignore lesbians in her call for a new psychology of women is puzzling.[71] There are, nevertheless, numerous correspondences between notions of gender and attitudes toward homosexuality. One recent study finds a high degree of correlation between attitudes toward women and homophobia.[72] College students, for instance, use gender-linked attributes in forming attitudes toward homosexual people:[73]

- women described as masculine are assumed to be lesbian more than women described as feminine;[74]
- when men are characterized by gender role traits commonly associated with women, those men are assumed to be homosexual;[75]
- the homosexual assumption is made for both men and women who show traits that are inconsistent with cultural gender norms;[76]
- nearly 70 percent of Americans think gay men behave like women.[77]

The idea that homosexuality is equivalent to gender inversion has persisted for over one hundred years. Those who revere traditional gender behaviors, therefore, are likely to disparage gays and lesbians generally for their perceived gender deviance.[78] They are more negative about homosexuality than other heterosexuals,[79] whereas less-homophobic people accept both nontraditional gender and family roles for men and women.[80]

### Gender as a Predictor

Some studies highlight differences between men and women themselves in attitudes toward homosexuality:

- heterosexual men harbor more negative attitudes than heterosexual women;[81]
- fear-based reactions are more common to heterosexual males than females;[82]
- heterosexual men are even more negative toward gay men than toward lesbians,[83] and AIDS may have increased this hostility.[84]

In a 1995 national poll, 54 percent of women said homosexuality should be accepted by society; 56 percent of men said it should be discouraged.[85]

Sexism might render lesbians less threatening to those men for whom women matter less. Moreover, lesbians may seem to undermine the patriarchal system less than gay males do. Heterosexual men sometimes believe they have the power ultimately to force lesbians "back" into their proper roles. They might even be titillated by images of lesbian eroticism.[86]

Gay men on the other hand may appear traitorous in seeming to yield their privilege of male domination over women. The supposedly weak homosexual man engaging in "female" behavior may feel like mockery to a heterosexual who fears losing his grip on masculinity: "Masculinity has to be constantly reasserted in the continuous denial of 'femininity' or 'feminine qualities.'"[87]

There are conflicting reports on whether heterosexual women view lesbians more negatively than they do gay men.[88] Theories of women's innate bisexuality suggest that lesbians could remind heterosexual women of what they have consciously given up or evoke what they have repressed. Proximity to a lesbian may precipitate discomfort in a heterosexual woman. Kite finds that intimate situations like sleeping in the same room with a known homosexual produce stronger negative reactions in both male and female heterosexuals than less personal interactions,[89] But a Kinsey researcher believes that men are more threatened by proximity than women because males are used to controlling their space.[90] Herek finds that both male and female heterosexuals are more negative toward homosexuals of their own gender but also reports that heterosexual males are more negative toward both gays and lesbians than heterosexual females.[91]

In the final analysis men appear to have more difficulty with homosexuality than women do, a finding reflected also in studies of racial prejudice and gender.[92]

## Internalized Homophobia

Internalized homophobia is the self-loathing that afflicts many gays and lesbians. Nearly all homosexual people are to some degree subject to this shame.[93] Examine, for example, the sentiments expressed by a national radio personality in an interview about his coming out as HIV-positive and gay: "I don't understand people who have to tell you what they do privately. . . . [Because of homophobes like a rival talk-show host] you become a one-dimensional man . . . but I'm not just gay. . . . Most of my friends happen to be straight, but my gay friends are good people. They're not just flibberty-gibbets."[94] In the course of a few lines, this noted libertarian intellectual equates sexual orientation with sexual activity, lets his enemies define him, and indirectly confirms a dismissive gay stereotype.

Internalized homophobia is the product of one's relational and learning environment. It flourishes or not, depending on the individual's psychological needs and capacity to resist,[95] which are also influenced by external factors. Race, class, ethnicity, religion, geography, family tolerance, and family psychologies can be determinants.

Internalized homophobia can cause depression[96] and low self-esteem[97] and has been associated with other problems in psychological and cognitive functioning.[98] Conversely, its diminution during the coming out process marks the progress of healthy adjustment.[99]

Although some homosexual people overtly despise, and sometimes wish to harm, themselves, not every case is conscious and direct. Ostensibly self-accepting gays and lesbians may harbor an unrecognized sense of inferiority that can generate self-sabotage and acquiescence to second-class status.[100] Some do not see that internalized homophobia contributes to their psychological ills.[101] Its consequences depend on which is stronger, the internal voice declaring, "You are bad, wrong, sinful and you must stop being gay," or the voice responding, "There is something burdensome, inconvenient, victimhood-inducing about being gay/lesbian and the solution is to stop homophobia."

A study among members of oppressed groups has shown that self-esteem suffers when the stigmatized blame themselves for their difficulties.[102] Such people have been known to act out self-fulfilling prophecies of inferiority.[103]

G. W. Allport found that internalized oppression can lead to denial of membership in the group, sometimes to the point of despising its members, including one's self.[104] People with fewer psychic resources might even wish they were not homosexual, not out of shame, but as a practical way to avoid the stigma imposed upon them by others.[105] One can be browbeaten to renounce something without agreeing that it is evil.

Reluctance to disclose is not necessarily a sign of internalized homophobia. Rational confident gays and lesbians often assess the consequences of coming out in a particular context and decide the potential costs are not worth the risk.[106] Those who refuse to tell anyone at any time, however, likely do have negative feelings about themselves.[107] In studies of gay males, lower levels of internalized homophobia are associated with:

- being open with more people;
- being more trusting;
- less frequent passing as heterosexual;
- sensing less negativity from significant others;
- being less lonely;
- having more support, at least as much gay as nongay support, and being more satisfied with support;
- socializing more with other gay men;
- having greater overlap between gay and nongay social networks;
- being less conservative about male and female gender roles;
- being more likely to adopt or have children by surrogacy after coming out;
- being more successful at coping with HIV seropositivity.[108]

Internalized homophobia is insidious and requires lifelong vigilance. Still, one must never assume that every discomfort gay or lesbian people have about their sexuality is related to a lack of self-esteem. The repeated blows of a homophobic society also induce mental distress.

How does one counter the glib assertion that every vocal homophobe is a repressed self-hating homosexual? The temptation to level that charge is particularly great when homosexuality-obsessed men seem to "protest too much." The accusation appears reactionary and facile on its face unless one takes seriously the proposition that everyone is to some degree bisexual. It is interesting to imagine the raging homophobe railing against the unacknowledgable in himself or herself. One fascinating study found over half the men in a homophobic group were aroused by gay sex videos, some perhaps as a result of anxiety rather than desire.[109]

Instead of drawing simplistic conclusions from such studies, let me offer that heterosexual men who are insecure about measuring up to the rigid demands of male gender and sexuality may cope with their anxiety by lashing out against the stigmatized other:

> As long as a sense of masculinity is built upon the systematic denial of "feminine" qualities, men are left in a continuous and endless struggle with themselves, in constant anxiety and fear of the revelations of their natures. They think they can control these fears within themselves, but they do so by projecting them . . . on to women, homosexuals, Jews, and Blacks.[110]

When authorities proposed the distribution of condoms in Jamaican all-male prisons, inmates rioted for three days, killing six of their fellows, assumed to be homosexual.[111]

## Homophobia and Behavior

Since behavior results from other motivations and inhibitions as well as moral reasoning, we cannot predict action solely on the basis of moral judgment.[112] Nor can social science forecast behavior toward others by analyzing a single interaction. Observation of a number of behaviors at a number of times in a variety of contexts is required.[113]

Context may actually outweigh attitude in influencing behavior.[114] Group pressure can overwhelm individual inclination in favor of group norms.[115] For example, even when a white student finds enough in common with a black person to sit next to or eat lunch with him or her, social pressure can prevent invitations home, consent to live in the same building, and comfort with a relative's marrying that black person.[116]

Moreover, habit may guide behavior as much as peer influence:

> Inasmuch as behavioral expectations have been clearly learned and a situation is well structured, people can be expected to do little thinking about their personal beliefs and attitudes, falling instead into the less taxing mode of responding with well-learned action rules. . . . Alternatively, in individuated situations in which attention is self-focused, people are likely to consider their attitudes and beliefs and are likely to behave in accordance with those ideals.[117]

One might, in short, be pressured and/or habituated to actions incongruent with one's principles, unless one is challenged to look within.

When it comes to how they treat gays and lesbians, otherwise well-meaning people may lack opportunity for or encouragement toward introspection. In one experiment, all respondents were found to be aware of discrepancies between how they should and how they would feel about, think about, and behave toward homosexuals in hypothetical situations. Those who were highly prejudiced felt global discomfort about the discrepancies but no compunction. Introspection evoked disgust and anger directed at homosexuals, rather than at themselves or at the interviewer. Lower-prejudiced people also felt global discomfort but theirs was accompanied by guilt and self-criticism.[118]

The unease experienced by both groups may be ascribed to moral reasoning dissonance or guilt over the gap between their moral judgment and their actions. It also could be the result of psychosexual factors triggered by the topic of homosexuality. Nevertheless, those with more developed senses of justice seem to turn more often conscientiously inward, and those who are less evolved and more self- and clan-centered look maliciously for scapegoats.

Controlled experimentation has yielded results on likely behavior toward homosexuals. Heterosexual subjects are:

- likely to decline, when given the opportunity to meet a person described as gay or lesbian;[119]
- unlikely to help a person wearing a pro-gay T-shirt;[120]
- less willing to interact with a homosexual person with AIDS (PWA) than with a heterosexual PWA.[121]

In direct interactions, heterosexual subjects:

- like a supposed gay person less than a supposed straight person;[122]
- remember less about a supposed gay person than a supposed straight person.[123]

Perhaps the only hopeful result of such studies is that heterosexuals may report more negative attitudes than they would actually display in meeting a gay or lesbian person.[124] Unfortunately there also must be some who report more positive attitudes than they would show in a direct encounter.

Studies of antigay/lesbian violence confirm many of these characteristics of homophobia:

- The bulk of these crimes are committed by male assailants, usually juveniles or young adults in groups.[125] Assaults by male assailants may be attempts to demonstrate loyalty, obtain peer acceptance, and solidify membership in the group.[126]
- Many males in this age group who manifest delinquent activities also reject culturally defined feminine characteristics and embrace masculine ones.[127] Antigay attacks could be a means, either conscious or unconscious, to assert masculinity and/or distance themselves from something in themselves—either the perception that they are not masculine enough or some homoerotic attraction.[128]

### Institutional Heterosexism

Homophobia, both blatant and subtle, can be used as an organizational tool. It is rampant in schools, where it is wielded regularly by adults and children to whip the mavericks who would stray from the socio-sexual conventions that schools are designed to transmit. The most common arena for adult expression is the gymnasium or athletic field, but classrooms, cafeterias, and hallways are not exempt. Too many educators resort to the easy homophobic barb, long proven to keep kids in line, whatever their transgression.

The particulars of the heterosexist school environment are detailed in subsequent chapters. We will take a closer look here at homophobia's uses in the military because they so mirror its manifestations in athletics and team sports—which have a long and profound impact on young people—particularly in annealing masculinity and controlling female autonomy. Indeed, one may accurately say many of homophobia's military guises are closely related to their schoolhouse incarnations. That should come as no surprise, since both institutions are charged with "building men" and (to a lesser degree in the military) "building women."

## Military Heterosexism

Military heterosexism plays a logical, if perverse, role in achieving the armed forces' goals. Military authorities argue that unit cohesion, preparedness, good order, and the integrity of the system of rank and command would be subverted by the open admission of homosexual servicepeople.[129] What they do not say is that homophobia is deliberately used to promote these ends.

Perhaps the most obvious example is the expression of homophobia to create solidarity, especially among recruitment-aged males. Organizers utilize common foes, stigma, and scapegoats to forge unity among strangers and to create an unquestioning nonindividuated mass of soldiers. Since antigay sentiments already prevail among adolescent males, homosexuality is a preferred target.

The armed forces also depend upon personal bonds between men and an ethic of self-sacrifice. Effusions about one's buddies and images of selfless heroism are a vital part of military lore—the soldier in a foxhole weeping over his friend's corpse or throwing himself on a grenade to save his platoon. As Senator John Glenn put it: "Marines do not fight and die for lofty ideological causes. They fight and die for the Marines to their immediate right and left."[130] The military situation provides a rare opportunity for men to express deep feelings to and about each other. Veterans often recall the trials of shared danger and appear to be drawn together by nostalgia for a deep and expressive male friendship.

Permission for such male bonding is contingent on the assumption of homosexual absence, especially among recruits. The ban on homosexuals in the military creates the fiction that any question of homosexuality in these attachments will have been ruled out beforehand. One may thus enter manly comradeship without scruple.

In a not-so-strange irony, induction rituals may require quasi-erotic performance: Incidents in the Coast Guard have included "a naked man sitting on the victim's face, and a practice where the victim would be restrained and a member of the deck force would use his genitals to strike the victim on the forehead."[131]

Besides the ban, two other features of military life contribute to the illusion that homosexuality has been purged: the constant mantra of homophobic invective and the creation of a hypermasculine environment. Soldiers are called to outdo each other in supposed proofs of gender and sexual qualification: courageous acts, feats of strength, the capacity for violence without remorse. Military planners must be loath to go without the homophobia that helps to spur these performances.

The need for heterosexism goes so far that anyone who enters the military with a tolerant view must be quickly disabused of it. In testimony before the U.S. Senate in 1993, an officer was asked whether some younger personnel come to the armed forces with an accepting attitude toward homosexuals. She replied that unlike trainees in the late 1970s, when she enlisted, some do appear unbiased. She insisted, however, "They go through a metamorphosis when they come into the military."[132] She attributed the change to the military's "unique community all-encompassing lifestyle" and the inability "to distance ourselves from the behavior" (as if homosexual soldiers engage in public fornication).[133] The military, it seems, is confident that homophobia can be instilled for the good of the service.

Although racial prejudice is no longer an appropriate or useful inducement to unit cohesion (unless the enemy is Asian or Arab perhaps), there is evidence that it still prevails, along with homophobia, among skinhead or neo-Nazi cults within the military. Some members sport tattoos signifying that they have killed an African American or a homosexual.[134]

Homophobia cannot be used to organize and prepare women recruits in the same manner as men. It is, however, routine practice to control the women's ranks with accusations of lesbianism. Periodic lesbian purges reduce the professional threat posed by competent female soldiers to their male counterparts.[135]

As women are integrated more into combat roles, some of the potency of military homophobia will probably be lost. Resistance to women in combat seems to derive less from concerns about their ability or safety than from the need to preserve hypermasculinity in combat units. Of late, the Army, with increasing female enlistments and a "don't ask—don't tell" policy regarding gays, seems to be losing gender-conservative Mexican-American recruits to the Marines.[136]

## Heterosexism in Other Institutional Settings

Sports teams value unity, morale, and aggressiveness. Athletes, like soldiers, luxuriate in an intimacy made possible by strident homophobia. Unacknowledged homoerotic elements may, as in the military, be a part of hazing ceremonies. Women's teams have contorted themselves trying to prove that they are lesbian-free. Female athletes have been pressured to leave their strength, independence, and practical clothing in the locker room before reentering the world.

Homophobia is salient in a number of other organizations. For instance, at their gatherings, leaders of Youth for Christ's "True Love Waits," a popular chastity movement, contrast virtuous abstinence with effete, and one assumes promiscuous, homosexuality.[137] In the Promise Keepers' emotional rituals, athletic stadium settings and homophobic harangues banish the gay taint from brotherhood in Jesus and commitment to male dominance.[138] The Boy Scouts[139] and various religious orders have gay/lesbian bans to permit bonding, while distancing themselves from discrediting allegations.

Sometimes organizational uses of homophobia are almost comic. Alabama state prison authorities could not find a way to stop male inmates from repeatedly exposing themselves to female guards. Even threatening to send pictures of their acts home to their mothers did not work. Finally they found a corrective: forcing the offenders to wear hot pink uniforms.[140] With similar intent, Fullerton, California, officials proposed changing the name of its gang-plagued Baker Street to Pansy Circle.[141]

Less colorfully, perhaps, but with devastating consequences, homophobic insult is employed in social service agencies, voluntary associations, churches, gangs, group homes, prisons, and families to shame young people into abiding by unyielding gender scripts and prescribed heterosexuality and, ultimately, into obeying authority.

# 5

## American History

To understand the position of homosexual people in the United States today, it helps to have a notion of their history. Most high school and college history texts have few lines, if any, on this subject—a mention perhaps of gay liberation and the gay rights movement of the late '60s and association of the AIDS pandemic with gay men.[1] Textbook publishers may slight the subject because of their own hostility, discomfort, ignorance, or anticipation of decreased sales.

For decades a pervasive homophobic impulse among scholars prevented the research that might have informed these texts. During that time, investigation of homosexuality appeared only in medical and criminal science literature. When notice was taken of homosexual communities in some cities, they were referred to with opprobrium.[2] The emphasis was on pathology, until psychologists like Evelyn Hooker began to attract attention in the 1950s.[3] Yet through the following decades, academics interested in gay history and culture were still commonly warned not to risk their reputations by investigating such a trivial topic; only a few independent scholars had the courage to ignore the stigma.[4]

These conditions changed in the 1970s, as women's and gay and lesbian studies were afforded increasing legitimacy and were actually encouraged at some universities. On the basis of publishing alone, one could conclude today that the field has burgeoned. A rich and colorful gay and lesbian American history has been documented. Informed of its details, educators could easily find opportunities to include the homosexual experience in their teaching. Like women and African Americans, gays and lesbians have a fascinating record as objects of oppression and subjects of self-discovery, perseverance, community, and creativity. They are also a compelling example of the changeability of human identity constructs over time.[5] (See Chapter 2.)

## Colonial America

White people living in North America in the seventeenth and eighteenth centuries had little opportunity to develop individual or group identities beyond those dictated by the requirements of their economy and their faith. At a time when labor was scarce and survival difficult, the agrarian life depended on the institutions of marriage and family to produce, train, discipline, and support workers. In a culture that spurned individualism, adult male dominance and the prerogatives of the propertied were part of a conservative hierarchical ideal that was reflected in the laws of church and state.

Biblically inspired regulations governing sexual morality were designed to create families and keep them together. Women had to submit their bodies to their husbands for procreation; husbands were enjoined to confine sex to child making with their wives. Numerous nonprocreative erotic activities were expressly forbidden and variously punished. The moral-legal classification of sexual acts required exquisite deliberation, since those offenses deemed to be sodomitical were capital crimes.

Although the Bible denounced both men having sex with men and women subverting the "natural use" of their bodies,[6] colonial statutes did not explicitly refer to female same-gender sex, except in an early New Haven proposal, later revised.[7] This omission illustrates that sexuality between females was not officially acknowledged. Court records of the period document trials of both men and a few women for same-gender sexual crimes. However, the light punishment meted out to the women for such infractions as "lewd behavior" rather than sodomy indicates the relative marginality of their offenses as perceived by the male-dominated religious and civil systems.

Because the sodomitical sinner appeared to offend the family and thus endanger the community, he was thought to deserve execution, especially in the early precarious days of the colonies. A case in point, one William Plaine of the New Haven Colony, a married man who had been convicted of sodomy in England, was executed in America for inciting youth to "masturbations," a wanton waste of seed.[8]

However, nothing in the statutes or other sources hints that sodomy was given such dire significance only when the partners were of the same gender.[9] Lust was lust, whatever its object. There is no convincing evidence in official documents, legal and religious commentaries or sermons, nor in any personal diary or letter that same-gender offenders were assigned to, or considered themselves to belong to, a special category of person. Use of the word "sodomite" was rare and did not imply membership in an identity class. "Buggery," the equivalent of sodomy in the more secularly founded southern colonies, was never imagined to be the product of the fundamental sexual disposition of a distinct and separate kind of men called "buggerers." On the contrary, they were sodomitical lapses to which, without vigilance and grace, everyone was subject. Such transgressions were thought to originate in idleness: Nonprocreative sex, like other lazy unproductiveness, was loathsome.

The majority of these men lived married lives with female spouses, even if they continued to sin in the same fashion from time to time. In the early colonies, the few male couples who maintained households together, presumably for economic reasons, were closely monitored for deportment. Later, single people were legally compelled to reside with approved married couples.[10]

## Industrialization

With changes in the economic system, men and women began to live different kinds of personal lives. By the last decades of the 1800s vast numbers of workers were no longer confined to family farms and small villages for their livelihoods. Individual wage earners, able to sell their labor to developing industries, became more independent and mobile. The birth rate dropped as numbers of single women left rural life behind for jobs in mill towns and other centers of manufacturing and commerce. Men too came to cities to work and associate with whomever they pleased.

In the wage-labor system people could concentrate more on individual fulfillment and self-definition. With increased anonymity, those who were inclined to do so had greater privacy for exploring unconventional and forbidden sexual interests. A larger urban population made for a greater chance of discovering others with similar desires for sexual liaisons and friendships.

Recent historiography describes the homosexual communities that developed in many American cities. They included people of different genders, classes, professions, and races. Women were, nonetheless, underrepresented in visible homosexual life because they had fewer opportunities for work outside the home, lower wages, and less freedom to move about and occupy public spaces.[11] Some people remained a part of this subculture for their entire adult lives and others for only a part.

Despite its importance in nurturing individual and group identity, this urban milieu was home to a relative few. Most homosexual Americans in this period did not know of its existence, and many experienced their desires in isolation and befuddlement or pain. If a few did encounter a mention of their orientation in a book or newspaper, it was unlikely to make them feel good about themselves.

*The Urban Scene*

Homosexual venues were not widely advertised or featured in the society columns of elite newspapers. On the contrary, the subculture was detailed in police files, court proceedings, and crime reports. Journalistic accounts of urban drag balls and other such events were published in marginal ethnic presses and working class tabloids.[12] The *New York Times* skipped the sordid details of the homosexual scandals it reported from 1880 to 1920, relying instead on euphemisms. Even the coverage in America of Oscar Wilde's 1895 sodomy trial was vague as to the exact nature of his crime.[13]

The sexual mind-set of the average early-twentieth-century person did not distinguish between homo- and heterosexual. Those rigid binary identity formulations were a recent invention of science and law, unfamiliar to most laypeople. Thus, it was possible for people to act on their same-gender erotic desires without realizing that such behaviors conferred a new identity on them. Working-class people, the most remote from scientific discourse, were the least affected by these new distinctions.

Those who did know of such labels used contemporary criteria in applying them to individuals. They would not have judged any man who behaved in a masculine manner to be homosexual. Rather, the homosexual "invert" was the effeminate "fairy." Gender-conformity in dress and behavior demonstrated that one was not inverted, even if one had sex with fairies.

George Chauncey's study of gay males in New York before World War II has shown that a rather open gay community thrived for about thirty years before a campaign of repression forced it completely underground.[14] Situated principally in ethnic neighborhoods and working-class sites like the waterfront, this gay culture developed its own signs and language, celebratory rites, and community network. They socialized within bars, function halls, street corners, parks, beaches, and other places that were also frequented by heterosexuals, as well as in gay speakeasies, bathhouses, and out-of-the-way cruising spots.[15]

Homosexual men had still to be careful about detection most of the time. They could be arrested, although the total number of arrests in the first part of the century was just a fraction of what it became after World War II. Hence they often communicated with covert phrases like "letting one's hair down," "being in the life," "coming out." Red ties and bleached hair were tokens of membership and availability. The relative openness of this gay community and its congeniality stand in great contrast to images of repression, misery, and hiding. Living a "double life," as it was called, was not stress-free, but it provided a thrill for some.[16]

Some of the words used by the public for homosexuals took on specialized meaning in homosexual argot. Although some used "queer" to distinguish themselves from their effeminate peers, the word eventually came to include both "fairies" (also called "nances," "sissies," "queens," "pansies," and other flowers) and "trade" (straight-acting men). "Fag" was used by straights, whereas "faggot" was used chiefly by black gays. "Flaming faggot" connoted flamboyance.

Once applied to prostitutes, the adjective "gay" came to mean "pleasant" or "lively," but with a certain inflection, a homosexual man could covertly indicate the exact nature of a nightspot's liveliness. "Gay" appears to have been popularized and even overused by "flamers." Over time, however, it was widely adopted to repair what some viewed as "queer's" implication of deviance.

Applying "gay" to all homosexuals signified that subgroupings based on gender role or affect were becoming less important than the gender of their erotic object. American gays were distinguishing themselves from heterosexuals more than from each other. Moreover, nongays who continued to consort with them began to jeopardize their own identities. Social forces induced both groups to map out their territories and validate the separation between them.

Jonathan Katz has assembled newspaper articles, letters, diary entries, and other material to document the urban American gay subculture at the turn of the century.[17] The homophobic bias of many of these collected observations by ostensible heterosexuals gives them a freak show tone. An antivice minister in 1892 New York described a scientist's reaction:

Each room [of The Golden Rule Pleasure Club] contained a table and a couple of chairs, for the use of customers of the vile den. In each room sat a youth whose face was painted, eyebrows blackened, and whose airs were those of a young girl. Each person talked in a high falsetto voice, and called the others by women's names. . . . The Doctor turned instantly on his heel and fled from the house at top speed. "Why I wouldn't stay in that house," he gasped, "for all the money in the world."[18]

In another, a Washington, D.C., doctor describes venereal disease "even in the mouth—the last abjection of vice," given to messenger boys by an older pederast. The diagnosis is followed by:

Only of late the chief of police tells me that his men have made, under the very shadow of the White House, eighteen arrests in Lafayette Square alone . . . in which the culprits were taken in flagrante delicto. Both white and black were represented among these moral hermaphrodites, but the majority of them were Negroes.[19]

The doctor studied lesbians as well. One was a "neurotic patient whose conversation showed an extreme erotic turn of mind" from whom he learned some details "as to the existence and spread of saphism." Another lesbian got her victims drunk before having orgies with them. Still others induced a "hystero-cataleptic attack" in a sexually curious prostitute.[20]

An 1893 medical journal article covered in outraged detail the dress and deportment of black Washington, D.C., "erotopaths" at a drag dance, featuring "a lecherous gang of sexual perverts and phallic fornicators," government workers among them.[21] The author, a St. Louis doctor, updated his work with a 1907 report of an arrest in his own city: "Male negroes masquerading in woman's garb and carousing and dancing with white men is the latest St. Louis record of neurotic and psychopathic sexual perversion."[22]

Although many homosexuals might have concurred with such characterizations, not all would have done so. Some refused to believe they were sick or to internalize the other homophobic notions of the time.[23] They may not have organized formal political resistance, but they found ways to live, even to celebrate their lives. An 1899–1900 New York State report reproduced testimony from law enforcement officials regarding the closing of some thirty gay clubs in New York City. One was described as a place where 25–50 degenerates gathered to talk and observe entertainment. At a second, where liquor where was served in the back, one could see and overhear "immoral actions and propositions by degenerates."[24] At another, men were solicited for immoral purposes and drinks were sold: "They have a piano there, and these fairies or male degenerates, as you call them, they sing some songs."[25]

Magnus Hirschfeld, the German sexologist and crusader for homosexual rights, studied homosexual life in Philadelphia, Boston, Chicago, and Denver through letters from Americans and an 1893 visit. One letter from a homosexual college professor lists cross-dressing, prostitution, Turkish baths, actors, dress and hat designers, military men, brilliant university students, men married to other men, and homosexual men married to women. It cites both a southern criminologist's view that the homosexual problem is caused by Italian immigrants and a supposedly popular notion that "yellow-skinned" people are prone to homosexuality.[26]

The British sexology pioneer Havelock Ellis declared in 1915 that 99 normal men out of 100 had been propositioned on the streets of America by inverts.[27] He represented the typical homosexual club as a dance hall connected to a saloon, usually operated by homosexual owners, waiters, and musicians. The drinking customers, almost all effeminate, were entertained by the singing and dancing of favorite performers. So well known were these clubs that one could be directed to them by policemen on the take. Ellis noted the significance of the red necktie. Newsboys, familiar with its meaning, made demeaning sexual gestures at men so attired. Homosexual prostitutes always wore one; savvy heterosexuals did not.

Since prostitutes were the only women allowed in most bars, many lesbians faced obstacles to community formation. Still, black lesbians and bisexual women were sufficiently tolerated in 1920s Harlem nightclubs to find refuge there. Indeed several major black entertainers were themselves lesbian or bisexual, including Gladys Bently, Ma Rainey, Alberta Hunter, and Ethel Waters. If a club got to be perceived as too gay, however, heterosexual patrons were known to find another venue.[28]

In smaller towns, lesbians often shared space with gay men, but in large cities one lesbian bar might be sustained. They were often in dangerous seedy neighborhoods and people risked life and limb to go unescorted, not to mention prosecution if they were discovered there.[29] Still, bars were an alternative to the streets, where women were denied cruising prerogatives that their brothers enjoyed.

### New Lesbian Possibilities

From the mid–nineteenth century, women's colleges were a propitious environment for privileged women to pursue their interests in same-gender relationships. "New Women" of the middle or upper classes entered college to break free of patriarchal restraints and pursue both economic and sexual independence. Although only 10 percent of women in the general population remained unmarried at the turn of the century, about 50 percent of college women stayed single.[30] Without equating gender role rebellion with lesbianism in the way Krafft-Ebbing, Freud, and others did,[31] one may still assume that numbers of women's college students, faculty, and administrators were lesbian. Indeed, these institutions were sometimes viewed with alarm as hotbeds of perversity.

The term "Boston marriage" was applied to cohabiting highly educated women living near Mt. Holyoke, Smith, Pembroke, and Radcliffe Colleges. Although there is often no proof of sexual activities between such couples, their "passionate friendships" could last a lifetime. Rather than wrangle over whether they were erotic, one historian suggests classifying these relationships as "gender nonconforming."[32]

M. Carey Thomas fought with her wealthy family just to go to college. She ultimately became president of Bryn Mawr and transformed it from a typical training school for wives and mothers to a liberal arts institution. After the departure of her first woman lover of 25 years, she lived with a female philanthropist for 11 more.[33] Mary Wooley, president of

Mount Holyoke College, lived with her professor companion Jeanette Marks for 55 years.[34]

A number of lesbian professionals also found employment in social work, education, and labor and peace organizations. Havelock Ellis fretted that women's colleges and settlement houses provided opportunities for feminist lesbians to prey on susceptible girls.[35] Jane Addams, founder of Chicago's Hull House Settlement, is probably the best known of these women who dedicated their lives to helping the poor. She booked hotel rooms with double beds during consecutive long-term relationships with two "devoted companions."[36] Miriam Waters, a prominent women's prison reformer, shared a home with a wealthy female partner, who maintained from afar her pro forma marriage to a man.[37]

Many of these romantic friendships would be called lesbian today. Yet there seems to have been considerable aversion to that term among the women themselves, even among those in demonstrably sexual relationships. Their objections may have been class-based. The first observations of female inversion were studies of working-class women, depicted as coarse, masculine, and hypersexual.[38] Higher-status women were not eager to take on a label with such connotations. They might have rationalized that their love was a more refined and spiritual thing, unrelated to the models of degeneracy and disease found in the medical writing on lesbianism.[39] Miriam Waters, for instance, clearly distinguished between the pathological condition of lesbianism and her own disposition. The Framingham, Massachusetts, reformatory she ran overlooked relationships between women not diagnosed as chronic lesbians. The psychic distance between upper-class, often educated, romantic friends and working-class, bar-culture lesbians endured for many years. It is ironic that its wellspring was an elite male medical discourse, motivated to a great degree by antifeminism.

*Medicine and Psychology*

Until the 1920s, it was the medical literature, not the popular press, that indulged in lurid accounts of homosexual practices. The superficial and sometimes bemused voyeurism of the tabloid and ethnic newspapers supports the idea of a relatively peaceful coexistence of gays with working-class ethnic cultures in New York City. And in the mainstream media, a facade of decorum was maintained for the respectable classes. The revulsion of the scientific and legal establishments, on the other hand, is well documented in treatises that were not widely read by citizens of any class.[40] The medicalization of homosexuality was the project of a specialized intellectual cadre.

Later, as psychiatric theory grew accessible through the mass media, more Americans came to see homosexuality as a sickness. The mass psychological screenings of draftees for World War II helped popularize this view. The armed forces, which had expelled men during World War I for committing homosexual acts, began to exclude male homosexuals from service because of an inherent diseased impulse. By 1944, after complaints of lesbianism in the Women's Army Corps, women were also screened.[41]

Despite Freud's views, homosexuality was universally pathologized in the West (see Chapter 3). Once threatened with hellfire and a jail cell, homosexuals were now confined to mental wards and subjected to behavioral and medical therapies. An elaborate and sinister hodgepodge of cures expanded over the decades: bicycling, rest, liaisons with prostitutes, marriage, sterilization, castration, testicular implant, clitoridectomy, orgasmic reconditioning, electric, chemical, and drug aversion therapies, electroshock and chemically induced convulsive therapy, hypnotherapy, cocaine, strychnine, testosterone, estrogen, Depro-Provera, x-rays, douches, hydrotherapy, cauterizations of the neck, back, and loins, lobotomy, analysis, acupuncture, and primal screaming.[42] It is hard to see how the compassion of the doctor was any better than the condemnation of the judge or the priest.[43]

### Early-Twentieth-Century Cultural Representations

After World War I the "sin that dare not speak its name"[44] was occasionally treated in a book or a play. In 1926, for example, *The Captive* opened on Broadway.[45] In the drama a husband wages a futile combat to rescue his wife from her female predator. This production and others aroused such opposition that by 1927, the New York State Legislature had passed legislation, which remained for forty years, forbidding "sexual perversion" as a dramatic theme.[46] In 1930 the Motion Picture Producers and Distributors Association adopted a code prohibiting the depiction of "sex perversion or any inference of it."[47] The ban persisted even through a revision of the code in 1956.[48]

*New York Times* reviews omitted the homosexual elements of some books, such as Sherwood Anderson's *Winesburg, Ohio* (1919). They utterly ignored major works like Radcliffe Hall's important British lesbian novel, *The Well of Loneliness*, though its censorship in England and unsuccessful suppression in the United States were covered in the news section. Mainstream arbiters pronounced the lives of homosexuals unfit for treatment even if they were depicted unflatteringly.

Writers and artists, nonetheless, continued to disagree. Through the 1930s, they produced an array of characters from scurrilous 1933 cartoons of "pansies"[49] to the lesbian schoolteacher in Lillian Hellman's *The Children's Hour* (1934). And more works dealing with homosexuality were produced in the 1940s: *This Finer Shadow* (1940), a novel with a neurotic homosexual main character, whose author committed suicide after completing the book; *Trio* (1944), a play that had difficulty finding a theater because it dealt with lesbianism; Isherwood's *The Berlin Stories* (1946); and Gore Vidal's *The City and the Pillar* (1947), a groundbreaking mainstream coming out novel. Many other works also dealt with these topics, not all of them great literature or contributors to the dignity of gay and lesbian people.

Until World War II the majority of homosexuals suppressed or hid their full identities and tried to live the lives that were expected of them in the communities where they had grown up. Many believed to some extent the hateful messages they heard and read about themselves. Organizing was scattered, feeble, and short-lived. The only clearly documented group of this period was the Chicago-based Society for Human Rights. Founded in 1924 by Henry Gerber, the society was inspired by Hirschfield's German movement, which Gerber had observed during the post–World War I occupation. Gerber was arrested along with his cohort, after police claimed to have found a powder puff during a raid of his home.[50] He was dismissed from his post office job for "conduct unbecoming" and the organization collapsed.[51]

### The Impact of World War II

The disruptions of World War II allowed large numbers of homosexual Americans to meet others like themselves. Many would not have previously called themselves homosexuals out of fear or lack of motivation toward self-identification. Then induction testing raised the identity question for millions, perhaps for the first time—and for some, just prior to entering a gender-segregated environment far from home. Those who remained civilians, particularly thousands of women who took jobs in wartime industries, had an unprecedented opportunity to explore their sexual desires, independent of family and marriage pressures.[52]

Whatever the official precautions, gay men entered the armed services, perhaps disproportionately, considering the military's preference for single men without children. Only the most obvious gender nonconforming men were likely to be rejected. Self-aware homosexuals would not have welcomed the consequences of admitting their orientation, even if it meant only being sent home to explain their dismissal to their families.

The chance of forming close friendships, particularly during warfare, was high. After induction, men lived in tight quarters. Intimate contact, including sleeping together, permitted sexual activity without detection.

Gay men found each other through eye contact and other subtleties. In American port cities, GIs cruised each other in crowded train stations, parks, and YMCAs. Networks of gay friends were established, and frequently groups of men in uniform spent their rest and recreation time in East and West Coast bars.

It is common knowledge that many GIs had affairs with women. Sex with prostitutes was so widespread, at home and abroad, that officers instructed soldiers on venereal diseases and use of condoms. It should come as no surprise then that the war gave homosexually inclined soldiers the chance to explore their sexualities, too. For the gay serviceman, however, the cost of getting caught was dire. Court martial, psychiatric examination, segregation and mistreatment in military prisons, and a record of undesirable discharge could have lasting repercussions.

Meanwhile military doctors took advantage of their captive subjects to develop new tests for identifying genuine deviates.[53] These criteria would be used after the war in the civilian sector.

The 150,000-member Women's Army Corps attracted a large percentage of lesbians.[54] The corps recruited young women who were, like GIs, mostly unmarried and childless and kept them separated from men as much as possible. Close female comradeship among such women was one incentive for lesbians to join the military. Moreover, the lesbian presence gave others whose sexuality was yet undefined a chance to discover themselves.

Military regulations requiring that lesbians be expelled were not strictly enforced, at least during the war itself. In fact, some officers were instructed to counsel rather than discipline offenders. A confidential 1943 lecture to WAC officer candidates urged the women to bond closely while serving together and went so far as to acknowledge the sexual potential of such relationships: "Sometimes [a relationship] can become an intimacy that may eventually take some form of sexual expression. It may appear that, almost spontaneously, such a relationship has sprung up between two women, neither of whom is a confirmed active homosexual."[55]

Women would be discharged only if their homosexual activities were habitual. Witch-hunting was discouraged. The army could not afford to lose people, nor could it stand the public outcry if large numbers of genuine lesbians were found in the WACs. An inquiry into charges of widespread addiction to mannish lesbianism at a Georgia basic training camp reached no conclusion and recommended no further investigation for the rest of the war.

Back on the home front, millions of women, some of them wives and mothers, joined the workforce for the first time. In the war industries, many of their workmates were also women. They often lived together in boarding houses or apartment buildings. Because they were expected to socialize among themselves, close female companionship did not necessarily arouse suspicion. Thus, the potential for lesbian relationships grew.[56] Working-class "butch" lesbians found some cover for their "masculine" appearance among the throng of "riveting Rosies." They forged strong ties with other lesbians in the bar culture.

### The Postwar Experience

When the war ended, the military's tolerance born of necessity also came to an end. Lesbians and gay men were purged on bases in Europe, Asia, and the United States. Five hundred women were dishonorably discharged from occupied Tokyo alone; and thousands of men were sent home on special "queer ships."[57] Some of the homosexuals who were thrown out of the military committed suicide rather than face further disgrace. Others lived in constant fear that the reasons for their discharge would become public when they applied for jobs.[58]

Many returning gay and lesbian soldiers stayed in the port cities where they disembarked, and many women remained where they had worked, determined to escape hometown scrutiny. New bars sprang up to accommodate them, even in the smaller cities.

Some books and a few underground magazines with gay themes were published after the war. Much of the literature reinforced the idea that homosexuals led sad lonely lives, doomed to tragedy, murder, and suicide. Gays and lesbians had not yet found a self-affirming voice.

A pivotal postwar event was the publication in 1948 and in 1953 of Alfred Kinsey's research on the sexual behavior of males and females. Based on face-to-face interviews with over 10,000 white men and women, the two books *Sexual Behavior in the Human Male* and *Sexual Behavior in the Human Female* became best-sellers, prompting widespread discussion of topics once forbidden.[59] Kinsey, an Indiana zoologist, reported in a scientific nonsensational manner a number of findings that surprised the American public, including the near universality of male masturbation, the sexual responsiveness of women, the frequency of extramarital sex, and the prevalence of homosexual practices.

Kinsey's findings about homosexuality, which even he had not expected, shook the nation.[60] He discovered that 37 percent of all males, and a slightly smaller percentage of women, had at least one postadolescent orgasm with a partner of the same gender. Adults, it appeared, were not always as fixed in their desires as had always been assumed. These statistics proved to Kinsey that homosexual feelings were rather normal; further, he theorized that social taboos prevented many people from acting on those impulses.[61]

Kinsey devised a sexuality scale based on people's behavior patterns. Zero represented absolute heterosexuality, six, exclusive homosexuality, and two to four, a continuum of mixed activity. He estimated that regardless of race, class, geography, and so forth, approximately 10 percent of men and 8 percent of women are more or less exclusively homosexual in behavior for at least three years between the ages of 16 and 55.

Kinsey's work was attacked as an affront to God, America, and the family. His assertions about women and homosexuals were especially reviled.[62] After all, it was thought that women could not be sexual on their own; and homosexuality was rare. Fairies had been assumed to be a pitiful few living in scattered urban cesspools. On the other hand, Kinsey's findings reassured most homosexuals that they were not as few as they had imagined and that their attractions were common to some degree, even to people who were primarily heterosexual.

## The Fifties

1950s reactionaries assailed independent women and demonized homosexuals and communists. Their postwar America would be put in order by herding women back into the home and imposing the heterosexual norm. It proved convenient to insert feminism and homosexuality into the greater anticommunist propaganda campaign. Lesbians, who allegedly rejected the family, and homosexual men, who were said to sap the nation's strength, were depicted as deliberately subversive.

Homosexuals were besieged, as military purges were succeeded by government and civilian crackdowns. Right-wing opponents claimed degenerate homosexuals could be blackmailed, making them easy prey for communist spy-masters. The government inexplicably judged both open and suspected homosexual employees to be security risks and began to dismiss them from public employment. The chief of the Washington, D.C., vice squad told the Senate that thousands of homosexuals held government jobs,[63] although the accuracy of his estimate was disproved in a newspaper report.[64]

Republicans tried to hurt President Truman by demanding an investigation. The Republican National Chairman warned that fear of offending the public kept the media from reporting a situation that would arouse the whole country.[65] In June 1950, the entire Senate approved a massive search for the "3,500 sex perverts" in government.[66] One year later, FBI head J. Edgar Hoover had identified 406 "sex deviates in government service."[67]

Ironically, Hoover himself may have been gay, as was his chief counsel, Roy Cohn. Later years brought allegations of Hoover's cross-dressing and sexual relationship with his aid, Clyde Tolson, and proof of Cohn's homosexuality and death from AIDS.[68] Moreover, the private diary of a prominent journalist noted that Senator Joseph McCarthy's rumored homosexual involvements were the subject of officials' gossip.[69] The level of internalized hatred and hypocrisy in these witch-hunts is stupefying.

Some politicians used Kinsey's assertion that homosexuality was common to every social stratum and was not outwardly identifiable to start a paranoid panic. In a 1950 interview, a Republican senator from Nebraska reported his conversation with another lawmaker:

> "In the light of these figures, Senator," I asked him, "are you aware of the task which the purge of all homosexuals from government jobs opens up?"
>
> "Take this straight," he answered, pounding his desk for emphasis. "I don't agree with the figures. I've read them all, but I don't agree with them. But regardless of the figures, I'll take the full responsibility for cleaning all of them out of government."[70]

Because homosexuals were thought to be morally weak and emotionally unstable, just one of them could corrupt an entire office, especially its younger staff. Besides the blackmail risk, homosexuals were so indiscreet they would blab government secrets to anyone who enticed them out on a clandestine date.[71]

Senators attacked government agencies for not firing known homosexuals or for permitting them to transfer to other jobs without alerting their new bosses. *Washington Confidential*, a 1951 book, declared a communist plot was spreading homosexuality in America and advised "with more than 6,000 fairies in government offices, you may be concerned about the security of the country."[72] In the chapter "Garden of Pansies," the authors cite a physician congressman's opinion that male homosexuals, though often able, suffer from menstrual-like periods of uncontrollable sexual appetite. Nor was lesbianism ignored—they estimated that because of a shortage of men, there were "twice as many Sapphic lovers as fairies."

In 1953, President Eisenhower issued Executive Order 10450, dismissing homosexuals from government. It resulted in the firing of forty people per month. Compassionate supervisors allowed others to resign quietly. Security clearance requirements established in 1947 had prevented many homosexuals from obtaining government employment in the first place.[73]

In the military, discharges for homosexuality rose from 1,000 per year in the late forties to 2,000 in the early fifties to 3,000 by the early sixties.[74] When there was insufficient evidence for court martial, they simply got rid of suspected homosexuals without letting them meet or question their accusers. One commander who advised her squadron of their rights during an investigation was relieved of her post.[75]

Many federal antigay policies were adopted by state and local governments and by companies doing business with the government. Suspicion was thrown on schoolteachers, who were accused of organized recruitment in the high schools,[76] and a few states passed laws so that school boards could use arrest and detention records alone to dismiss allegedly homosexual employees.[77]

The FBI compiled lists of suspected homosexuals and their associates. Postal inspectors lured men to write to them through "pen pal" clubs and if one of them was proved to be gay, the post office traced their mail to other men. A Florida state legislator began a hunt at the state university at Gainesville, which ended in the publication of unsubstantiated accusations and the firing of 16 staff and professors. That these people had also been active in the black civil rights movement led some to question the real motive behind the purge. The Florida Civil Liberties Union, however, did not support the homosexuals; they cared only that some heterosexuals might have been unjustly charged.[78]

Workplace discrimination was hardly the end of it. Police regularly raided both men's and women's bars. Between 1955 and 1958, hundreds were arrested in such places as San Francisco, New Orleans, and Salt Lake City. Just one raid netted 162 men in Baltimore, where parties in private homes were also broken up.

After a young boy was kidnapped and murdered in Sioux City, Iowa, 29 homosexuals were seized and committed to asylums without trial. In Boise, Idaho, in 1955, after arresting three men on charges of having sex with teenage boys, 1,400 residents were summoned to testify as to who was gay in Boise. Men fled the city to avoid exposure not as child molesters but just as homosexual citizens.[79]

Police set traps in public parks and movie theaters, often gesturing as though they wanted sex and then taking anyone who responded into custody. Arrests in Washington, D.C., numbered over 1,000 per year in the early 1950s.[80] Newspapers frequently printed the names of alleged homosexuals who had been apprehended in clubs and other places.

In their bars, neighborhoods, and homes gays were additionally victimized by robbery and violence. Extortionists, thieves, and thugs knew that these crimes would rarely be reported by homosexuals who dreaded both publicity and police mistreatment.

## The Homophile Movement

With all its horrors, the postwar era was still a time when handfuls of brave homosexual people came together to organize for systemic change and greater acceptance. The founders of this homophile movement were active in left-wing politics, some of them members of the Communist

Party. Harry Hay, the most prominent male homophile, helped start the Mattachine Society, first called "Bachelors Anonymous." The word Mattachine came from a secret medieval society of masked male performers. Hay originally conceived of the organization as a strategic defense against the scapegoating that he thought inevitable after the military purges.

Seeking basic human and political rights, Mattachine often relied on the opinions of heterosexual scientists to validate their claims. Hay hoped to garner endorsements from sympathetic ministers, sociologists, and psychologists by issuing a prospectus in 1950. It included the following:

> We, the androgynes of the world, have formed this responsible corporate body to demonstrate by our efforts that our physiological and psychological handicaps need be no deterrent in integrating 10% of the world's population towards the constructive social progress of mankind.[81]

This capitulation to homophobic diagnosis distinguishes the homophile movement from gay liberation, which followed in the 1960s. Only *ONE*, a small publication written by some members of Mattachine, flatly rejected the conventional psychiatric approach to homosexuality. It was not Mattachine's house magazine.

One of Hay's tactics was to tie homophile organizing to other progressive causes. For instance, he recruited members on a gay beach in Los Angeles while circulating petitions against the Korean War. As the movement grew in numbers and visibility, however, it moved to replace its left-leaning leaders with centrists. From 1953 on, Hay's vision of an alliance with groups demanding fundamental economic and social change was succeeded by a seemingly less threatening agenda: attaining civil rights for people who are just like other Americans except for what they do in bed.[82] The split between radical coalitionists and single-issue reformers has continued to this day.[83]

The Mattachine was ahead of its time in some respects. In 1952 they sent a questionnaire to candidates for the Los Angeles Board of Education asking whether they would support "a nonpartisan psycho-medical presentation of homosexuality" in required high school hygiene classes and a guidance program and counselors for young people beginning to show signs of variance.[84]

When Hay was called to appear before the House Un-American Activities Committee (HUAC) in 1955, he sought out a lawyer he had known for a long time, who represented heterosexuals summoned to the committee. The attorney's response was typical of a prevailing attitude among progressives: "We're not going to condone queers, you know."[85] It took Hay five weeks to find someone to represent him forthrightly. As it turned out, the committee was given such old information on Hay that he was not questioned about Mattachine.

Resistance to homosexual demands for justice was pervasive. Remarkably, both liberal groups and the organized Left turned their backs on gay and lesbian victims of government purges. Even the New York City *Village Voice* refused to run notices of homophile meetings in the early years.[86] Only a few individuals of conscience helped them.

### Lesbian Organizing

The lesbian couple Del Martin and Phyllis Lyon moved to San Francisco in 1953. Unhappy with the bar scene, they joined other friends in starting a social group, the Daughters of Bilitis (after an erotic poem, "Songs of Bilitis") and began thinking about how to educate the public. Since Martin and Lyon had already discovered the San Francisco chapter of Mattachine, it served as their model. Although some working-class women left the group to form another social club, the half dozen remaining DOB members affiliated with Mattachine to dispel myths about homosexuality through lectures and discussions.

In 1956 DOB began their own magazine, *The Ladder,* with a 200-copy first edition. Its only lesbian predecessor was the 1947 *Vice Versa,* a biweekly periodical with five carbons that had been passed hand to hand. *Vice Versa* had been written pseudonymously for nine months by "Lisa Ben" (i.e., les-bian), a Los Angeles film studio secretary, who secretly produced it at work.

Whereas the Mattachine's *ONE* was deliberately provocative and political, *The Ladder* was more personal in tone. It was aimed at the isolated, sometimes married, lesbian in the hinterlands. The importance of reaching out to women this way was underscored in the lives of Del Martin herself and of Barbara Gittings, her eventual collaborator. Martin, a divorced mother who had fallen in love with another woman, was unable to understand her own feelings until she read *The Well of Loneliness.*[87] Gittings's "hazy feelings" were diagnosed in her first months of college, and she was offered psychotherapy. Too poor for the treatment, she stopped going to classes and cloistered herself in the library, where she was only depressed by the medical papers on lesbianism. Ultimately, she found her way to novels that offered a fuller and happier understanding despite their consistently tragic endings.[88]

Gittings's interest in literature could not be satisfied in New York's lesbian bars. Only when she traveled to San Francisco in 1956 did she connect with like-minded women in the year-old Daughters of Bilitis. She helped establish an East Coast chapter (1958) and eventually edited *The*

*Ladder* in the 1960s. Like Lisa Ben, Gittings stayed overtime at the archi-
tectural firm where she worked, surreptitiously cutting stencils and stuff-
ing the magazine into purloined company envelopes.[89]

Gittings denied any strong political intent in DOB's formation as a separate group within Mattachine. She ascribed the move to women feeling
more comfortable with one another. Over the course of the 1950s, however, Martin and Lyon became frustrated with the neglect of lesbian issues in the homophile agenda. At a 1959 Mattachine convention Martin
defended the need for DOB, accusing Mattachine of relegating women to
"auxiliary" or "second-class" status.[90] Still, they remained with Mattachine, stressing their common purpose and voicing the woman's perspective. DOB's advice-giving function rendered it a temporary refuge
for women in need, but its middle-class leadership, denigration of
"butch" lesbians, and anti-bar crusading prevented it from attracting
masses of working-class women.[91]

Like Mattachine, DOB deferred to the opinions of "leading members of
the legal, psychiatric, religious, and other professions." They advocated
"a mode of behavior and dress acceptable to society" and refrained from
using the word lesbian, favoring "homosexual" and "variant." Grateful
to have anyone show an interest, DOB continued to invite pathologizing
experts to speak, even in the early 1960s.[92] Although proposing to eliminate prejudice through education and reform of penal codes, DOB's deference to mainstream authority proved its undoing.

For a decade, nevertheless, Daughters of Bilitis and Mattachine were
the only options. Even then, it appeared that organized homosexuals
were a small group indeed, clustering on both coasts. Ten to forty women
attended DOB–New York's two meetings a month. Some, of course, were
just looking for a date, a purpose that every gay and lesbian organization
had to deny or face prosecution.[93]

### Pre-Stonewall Militancy

In the early 1960s, the homosexual movement's plea for understanding
became an unapologetic demand for respect and civil rights. No longer
looking inward for the causes of their problems, gays and lesbians
began to fight the pathological diagnoses of the dominant heterosexist
culture.

To understand this change, one must consider the everyday pressures
and humiliations that even the most privileged homosexual people had
to endure. For instance, Doctor Howard Brown, chief of New York City's
health services, lived in constant fear of being found out. His liberal Republican boss, Mayor John Lindsay, was not tolerant of homosexuality
and bar raids were common during his administration. Brown moved his

lover of five years out of their home and avoided meeting socially with other gays in local government. Paranoia prevailed:

> We could not talk in our official cars because of the chauffeurs. We came to be wary of telephones—a secretary might pick up while we were talking, or our phones might even be tapped. One gay commissioner regularly sent a technician around to check out my office telephone. . . . At home I had two telephones, one of which was connected to an answering service. My commissioner friend warned me never to use the service phone to call a homosexual and never to speak of homosexuality. . . . My other phone was, like my office phones, regularly checked out by the commissioner's assistant.[94]

Is it any wonder that gay people did not want to live under such conditions in 1966?

Many, indeed, put up with worse. In one case a 24-year-old was forcibly committed to a psychiatric hospital in the South by his parents in 1964 because they suspected him of being gay. They had read his mail and disapproved of some of his "abnormal" friends. Doctors convinced his parents that his sexuality, as well as his argumentative and depressed behavior, should be treated with $6200 worth of electroconvulsive therapy. Although one new doctor thought he should never have been committed, he was given 17 shocks over 10 weeks and was sent home heavily tranquilized. The only result was the destruction of his memory: A New York lover wrote to him, but he had no recollection either of the man or of his five months in that city. When the therapeutic failure became apparent, some suggested that doctors had not gotten to him early enough. For 8 years he experienced memory lapses and panic attacks, sometimes not knowing who or where he was.[95]

Although the vast majority of Americans would never have considered homosexuals to be a minority group in need of legal protections from such violations, a small number of gays and lesbians did begin to make a case on their own behalf. An employee of the U.S. Army map service, Franklin Kameny, became one of the best-known activists. The brilliant young astronomer had worked in Washington, D.C., for only six months when he was fired in 1956 for being homosexual. After four years of appeals and a futile court case, he was reduced to eating at the Salvation Army. His health declined, but not his spirit:

> I am not a belligerent person, nor do I seek wars, but having been forced into a battle, I am determined that this thing will be fought thru to a successful conclusion, come what may. . . . I will not be deprived of my proper rights, freedoms, and liberties, as I see them, or of career, profession, and livelihood, or of my right to live my life as I choose.[96]

Because he could not get anywhere as an individual, he founded a Washington chapter of Mattachine with the son of an FBI agent and a small number of recruits.

A grassroots activist at heart, Kameny scorned private timid efforts. He had no use for lecture meetings with opposing views of homosexuality. Instead, encouraged by the black movement, he advocated taking direct action for homosexual rights and confronting opponents vigorously. He broke cleanly from the homophile past in a speech to the New York Mattachine:

> I take the stand that not only is homosexuality . . . not immoral, but that homosexual acts engaged in by consenting adults are moral in a positive and real sense, and are right, good, and desirable, both for the individual participants and for the society in which they live.[97]

Far from apologetic himself, he in fact demanded an apology.

Not all gay leaders were eager to adopt this new strategy. For example, Florence Conrad, research director for Daughters of Bilitis, continued to defer to medical authorities.[98] Edward Sagarin, a hero of the Mattachine years, also resisted Kameny. Sagarin had written *The Homosexual in America* under the pseudonym Donald Webster Cory. An insider's account of the gay subculture over 25 years, the book detailed the indignities homosexuals suffered, drew parallels to other minorities, and argued for understanding and justice.[99] But by the mid-1960s Sagarin had become a member of an old guard. For all his talk of rights, he would not give up the notion that homosexuals were as sick as alcoholics and equally in need of treatment. An opponent of militancy, the erstwhile great defender clung to the medical model and was passed by. Kameny vilified him as the "Senile Grandfather of the Homophile Movement."[100] Sagarin left the scene in 1964, pleading with Daughters of Bilitis to embrace their social purposes as much as their educational ones.[101] He eventually claimed to be a heterosexual sociologist of "deviance."[102]

The Washington Mattachine began a letter-writing campaign to Congress seeking a hearing on employment policy. Only two House members reacted positively. When Kameny and his allies descended on the offices of the Pentagon, the Selective Service, and the Civil Service Commission, they were insultingly rebuffed.

The Washington chapter of the American Civil Liberties Union, squeamish about taking a homosexual case, was finally persuaded to challenge the Civil Service Commission's exclusion policy. In June 1965 the federal court ordered the government to specify what conduct it forbade and to show why that behavior had anything to do with "occupational competence." Their decision merely opened the door to alleged proofs of homosexual incompatibility with government service.

With the support of the New York and Southern California branches, the Civil Liberties Union of Washington also tried to convince its parent organization to stop refusing cases involving homosexuality. The ACLU had insisted there was no constitutional right to practice homosexuality; it had also agreed with the government and military that gays and lesbians were unfit for employment.

Finally in 1964 the ACLU adopted the position that all sexual behavior between consenting adults should be decriminalized and urged local affiliates to accept gay rights litigation. Within four years they were involved in cases concerning lesbian bar and male bathhouse raids in Philadelphia and the arrest (for cross-dressing) of Houston lesbians wearing fly-front pants.[103] Kameny himself took on the District of Columbia, challenging raids in which bar patrons were beaten and jailed.

The success of the new Mattachine aroused the opposition of some conservative members of Congress. A bill to revoke the Mattachine's permit to raise money in Washington passed the House in 1964. The bill died in the Senate, but the publicity was enormous.

For all the accomplishments of the homophile groups, conditions in 1969 were still rather grim. The movement that had challenged the status quo on such issues as black rights, Viet Nam, and free love showed little concern for homosexuals. On the same day in May 1965 that Students for a Democratic Society turned out 20,000 for a Washington antiwar protest, only 10 people marched at the White House for homosexual rights.[104]

Moreover, the homophile force was weakened from within. In 1967 Del Martin took her energies to the women's movement, having come to believe, as many others would, that lesbians were better served by feminist activism than by second-class status in gay politics. Factionalism also divided civil rights–focused, mostly middle-class homophile leaders from New Left homosexuals, who urged a more radical stance.[105]

## The Stonewall Riots

In the early summer of 1969 a series of events occurred in New York City that would change American consciousness and the lives of millions of homosexuals. Although most people could not have realized how important these incidents would become (*Newsweek* and *Time* did not report them until October), some participants and observers sensed a historical turning point. Later that year a Philadelphia newsletter looked back:

When the New York City Plain Clothes officers entered the Stonewall Inn at 53 Christopher Street in Greenwich Village on Friday night, June 27, they had no reason to fear this raid would be different from all the others. The police claimed that the reason for the raid was that the bar, which operates as a private club, had been selling liquor without a license. The club was closed, the employees arrested, and the patrons ushered out. But, instead of dissolving into the night, grateful for having escaped the scene of someone else's crime anonymous and unscathed . . . [something else occurred].[106]

A crowd gathered on the street to watch. At first, some of those seized began waving to their friends and making wisecracks. Their audience responded by throwing coins at the police and shouting. As the arrested were loaded into a wagon, some spectators shouted to overturn it and one woman in custody fought back. When the wagon and several cruisers left, the remaining police retreated back into the building. Bottles and beer flew, while the police barricaded themselves in the bar. An eyewitness recounted:

> [Officer Pine] gathers himself, leaps out into the melee, and grabs someone around the waist, pulling him downward and back into the doorway. They fall. . . . Angry cops converge on the gay, releasing their anger. . . . The crowd erupted into cobblestone and bottle heaving. . . . The trashcan I was standing on was nearly yanked from under me as a kid tried to grab it for use in a window smashing melee. From nowhere came an uprooted parking meter—used as a battering ram on the Stonewall door. . . . More objects are thrown in. The detectives locate a fire hose, the idea being to ward off the madding crowd until reinforcements arrive. They can't see where to aim it, wedging the hose in a crack in the door. It sends out a weak stream. We all start to slip on water.[107]

Someone in the crowd responded to police threats to shoot by squirting lighter fluid toward the bar and setting it aflame. Just then sirens announced the arrival of more officers.

The riot lasted only 45 minutes that night, but the bar was trashed: "mirrors, jukeboxes, phones, toilets, and cigarette machines were smashed. Even the toilets were stuffed and running over." And the next day's chalked graffiti summed up the homosexual point of view: "Insp. Smyth looted our: jukebox, cig. mach., telephones, safe, cash register and the boys' tips"; "They invaded our rights"; "Support Gay Power"; "We are open."[108]

The weekend then became a series of protests against the Stonewall raid and the long history of similar harassment. One man claimed that five different bars in the Greenwich Village area had been raided in the three weeks prior to the Stonewall incursion. Another recalled that fifteen police wagons had appeared at a gay meeting place near the docks less than a month before and that people were beaten to the ground.

The night after the initial riot, the Stonewall bar was open again and crowds massed to cheer each other on:

Friday night's crowd had returned and was being led in "gay power" cheers by a group of gay cheerleaders. "We are the Stonewall girls/We wear our hair in curls.". . . Hand-holding, kissing, and posing accented each of the cheers with a homosexual liberation that had appeared only fleetingly on the street before.[109]

Older gays watched younger ones showing off in a way they might not have dared to. But as the crowd grew and did not disappear into the bar, the tactical police force arrived for the second night and chased people up and down the street. Some protestors blocked the way ("Christopher Street belongs to the queers!") and teased drivers. By 3:30 A.M. the police had dispersed the mob. Sunday crowds carried on for a third night, but were cleared without much fuss by 1 A.M.

More than a year later, a reporter for *Mademoiselle* looked back: "This time it was like the black woman who wouldn't give up her bus seat in Montgomery. This time, *our* time had come. We took to the streets . . . and we're not going back to the Closet, the back of the bus. . . . Ready or not, baby, here we come! We're freakin' on in!"[110]

The significance of the riots was not so clear to many others, however. Most considered it a one-time occurrence. Some sought the explanation in the full moon and the burial that Friday afternoon of Judy Garland, a gay favorite. One activist recalled, "To me the riot was just like a carnival. . . . I didn't see any massive energy. I just saw a riot. I wasn't able to interpret it any further than that."[111] A prominent gay writer later remembered the quasi-seriousness of Stonewall:

At the time we felt it was a big joke, very festive and funny. When we said things like "Gay is good," we were echoing "Black is beautiful." We felt presumptuous doing it, as if we were being slightly silly. We laughed at our own cheekiness. We didn't realize that what we were really doing was recasting homosexuality as a minority group rather than a disease. That was such a great leap of the imagination.[112]

Although a few days later Black Panthers, Yippies, and gang members from as far away as New Jersey came to add to the mayhem, the Stonewall eruption was essentially over. Its aftershocks, on the other hand, were just beginning.

*Why Stonewall?*

Located in a space where a straight bar had burned out, the Stonewall Inn was a ruin with black painted walls and no license. Hundreds of people crowded in on weekends, though there was only one exit and other hazards. It catered to those who could not afford other spots or would not have been wanted elsewhere: cross-dressing street queens, hippies, obvious drug users, underage runaways and kids who had been kicked out of their homes. All found a warm refuge for the night for a $3 cover charge.

Why would such a momentous event occur there and then? Although hardly noted after Stonewall, there had been prior resistance in California. Two years before, on New Year's Eve, plainclothes police who had infiltrated their parties raided several Los Angeles gay bars. When revelers kissed at midnight, the police tore the decorations down and began arresting people, dragging sixteen from one bar and forcing them to lie on the sidewalk, where they were badly beaten.

Contrary to the usual routine, the owners of that bar, Pandora's Box, objected. More characteristically, though, when gays began to organize a demonstration, one of Pandora's owners threatened to call it off if protesters used the word "homosexual." Several hundred people showed up to decry both the police abuse and the bar owners' refusal to acknowledge the victims' sexuality:

> We've been copping out to society for centuries, just as alot of other minorities were doing until very recently. Well, the Negroes aren't copping out anymore—and they're being listened to. . . . And God help the next one of us who lays down and takes it. . . . And what is our name? It has been Coward; Furtive; Hidden.[113]

The L.A. demonstrations were angry but well organized, politically oriented, and nonviolent. They resembled earlier San Francisco bar protests, which had been defused as soon as public officials agreed to cease the raids.

The Stonewall riots differed significantly from these California rallies. They were spontaneous, emotive, and bloody, not the product of cautious planning by established leaders. Sociologist Toby Marotta wrote of the first night:

> Partly because the extreme unconventionality of their lives gave them little status and security to lose, most of those dismissed from the Stonewall chose not to run to safety but to gather across the street to wait for their

friends. Laughing and joking, stoned on drugs and high in spirits, they applauded each time someone they recognized appeared in the doorway.[114]

Homophile figures like Kameny were indeed inspired by the example of the black civil rights struggle, but the spark at Stonewall was, despite the *Mademoiselle* reporter's analogy, quite different from Rosa Parks's deliberately plotted action:

> For most of the rioters, the impulse to protest came not from political perspectives but from feelings of resentment about official interference. Craig Rodwell, for instance, remembers stumbling upon the crowd in front of the Stonewall, seeing that there had been a raid, starting to chant "gay power," and being surprised that almost no one joined in. . . . A reporter writing for the *East Village Other* [a local underground newspaper] scolded the second night's demonstrators:. . . "Too many people showed up looking for a carnival rather than a sincere protest. Queens were posing for pictures, slogans were being spouted out, but nothing really sincere happened."[115]

To some critics the Stonewall demonstrators were not only unheroically apolitical, they were also an embarrassment. Many conventional gays and lesbians were horrified by drag queens, faggots, and hippies and wanted nothing to do with riots. Not unlike some older blacks who scorned their children's militancy in the 1960s,[116] they feared that such comportment only confirmed what many Americans thought about homosexual excess.

If some were put off, however, they were still resentful of the government attitudes and policies epitomized by the police action at Stonewall. More conventional and well-off homosexuals had also been dehumanized there and elsewhere. Martin Duberman, a distinguished professor of history at Princeton at the time, was a regular customer at the Stonewall Inn:

> Like other patrons, I had taken in stride the occasional raids. I can recall at least two evenings when the light signals suddenly went on (announcing the arrival of somebody suspect), dancing and touching of any kind instantly stopped, and the police stalked arrogantly through, glaring from side to side, demanding IDs, terrifying those not having them with threats of arrest. I remember hearing about another night, when a police raid bagged an illegal alien who, arrested and brought in to the station, threw himself in despair from a window, landing, impaled, on a spiked iron fence below. They worked for hours sawing the metal off the fence, lifting the young man's flesh off the metal. Somehow he survived.[117]

Whether the entire political spectrum of gays and lesbians was ready for confrontation and spontaneity or not, Stonewall roused great numbers of oppressed, justifiably angry homosexuals. Barbara Gittings thought it represented a popularizing of Kameny's assertiveness among masses who had hitherto remained, if not docile, at least relatively private.[118]

1968 had been a watershed year for protest and disruption in the United States: escalation in Viet Nam, turmoil on college campuses, and the assassinations of Robert Kennedy and Martin Luther King. In that environment, gay liberation was a cause waiting to explode. Stonewall was thereby mythologized into a kind of homosexual Boston Tea Party and was transformed from a rather amorphous outburst into a deliberate and unequivocal statement of political will.

The spirit and vocabulary of the gay movement had been significantly altered by the national mood. At a meeting in New York in July 1969, for example, an experienced organizer urged the crowd to contest police brutality with appeals to elected officials and a long-term educational campaign. A married woman suggested an amicable candlelight vigil. They were answered by a man who had burned money on the floor of the Stock Exchange as an antiwar protest:

> There's the stereotype homo again, man! . . . That's the role society has been forcing these queens to play, and they just sit and accept it. We have got to radicalize, man! Why? Because as long as we accept getting fired from jobs because we are gay, or not being hired at all, or being treated like second-class citizens, we're going to remain neurotic and screwed up. . . . Be proud of what you are, man! And if it takes riots or even guns to show them what we are, well, that's the only language that pigs understand![119]

There was no going back. Their future rhetoric might be mellow or radical, but the impatience for change that motivated this 1969 stridency was to become universal in the homosexual community. Gay and lesbian organizing and protests never before seen in the United States were on the way.

### Stonewall's Aftermath

The riots forever altered the terrain for the fifty associations that had met just before Stonewall at the fifth convention of the North American Conference of Homophile Organizations.[120] In the immediate aftermath, a number of activist groups sprang up. In New York, the Gay Liberation Front (GLF) was founded in the spirit of the New Left. GLF took its cue from Students for a Democratic Society (SDS), the Student Nonviolent Coordinating Committee (SNCC), and the Black Panthers in demanding complete systemic change. Spurning assimilation on behalf of poor, despised, and disenfranchised minorities, they trumpeted their difference and cultivated power through both separatism and strategic alliances.

The GLF positioned themselves within the antiwar, antinuclear, antiracism, and women's movements. The slogans "Black is beautiful" and "Black power" became "Gay is good" and "Gay power."[121] Tactics were also borrowed: Marches were followed by rioting, newspaper offices were occupied, police attacked, professional meetings disrupted, political candidates angrily confronted, and TV shows were invaded by guerrilla theater. Those who had marched peacefully in suits and dresses outside the White House would never have considered such options.

Open homosexuals in New Left groups inspired some closeted members to come out and take on a gay agenda; others, though, were frightened into a deeper silence. Surely, the majority of ordinary gay and lesbian citizens were not demonstrating in the streets. Many were afraid to take public stands, lived far from centers of organizing, or were uncomfortable with the Left's goals, rhetoric, or methods.

Splits developed even within the ranks of urban activists over linking gay concerns with the peace movement or the Black Panthers. Some critics formed splinter groups like the Gay Activists Alliance (GAA) in New York to narrow the focus. They may have resented the lack of reciprocity on the Left, which while welcoming homosexual support, rarely accommodated a gay and lesbian agenda. Like women, homosexuals were marginalized in a movement that often avoided sexual issues entirely. Indeed, some activists were hostile toward homosexuality in particular.[122] At their worst, the American New Left espoused the doctrinaire communist position that homosexuality, a bourgeois corruption, would be eradicated in a socialist state.[123] Most, however, tried to disguise their antipathy by declaring sexuality a personal matter that deserved no place in political discourse.

About that they were wrong. Like the Black Power struggle or any other revolt against injustice, gay liberation was both deeply personal *and* political. No political analysis becomes a movement without some degree of emotional identification on the part of its adherents. Steven Epstein suggests that the greatest successes in the gay and black movements are not legislative victories but changes in what it means subjectively to be homosexual or black in America.[124] Unlike more visible minorities, many homosexuals can remain hidden. To come out, then, is to defy personal shame and the patriarchal system. The step signals both a personal epiphany and an indelible political act, even for those with little political intent beyond asserting a libertarian prerogative.

Moderate or left-wing, many lesbians were discouraged by gay liberation's male-centeredness. With an emerging feminist awareness provoked by the women's movement, some lesbians became female separatists. Others doubted whether heterosexual women could ever be better allies than gay men.[125] Yet even those who continued to work closely with men began to insist that the collective word "gay" was indicative of their erasure. Gay women wanted explicitly to be named as "lesbians."

Meanwhile, heterosexually identified feminist women began to reevaluate their relationships with men. Some discovered feelings for other women that they had not previously recognized and some further acknowledged that they were lesbians. Homophobic feminists, on the other hand, opposed lesbian visibility in the movement. Some were alarmed by the antifeminists' charge that lesbians controlled women's liberation or that feminists were all man-hating lesbians at their core. Betty Friedan, founder of the National Organization for Women, considered lesbians a "lavender menace."[126] In 1973 she accused the CIA of infiltrating lesbians into the movement to discredit it.[127]

But for the most part, the alliance between the feminists and homosexuals grew stronger. Their agendas were compatible if not identical in critical respects: challenging rigid gender roles, insisting on the right to control one's own body, and asserting that pleasure is a valid justification for sex.

## The Seventies

In June 1970 thousands of people marched in a New York gay parade to commemorate the first anniversary of Stonewall. Over the next three years the number of homophile groups soared from 50 to 800, and pride events were held in cities across the country. Gay liberation reached the grass roots.

A National Institute of Mental Health study committee, chaired by Evelyn Hooker in 1969, had recommended civil rights protections and social tolerance for confirmed homosexuals but also supported "effective primary prevention" for those who might be saved from homosexuality.[128] Many pro-gay psychologists regretted that without scientific justification, medicine was being used to enforce moral, political, and religious views. After intense lobbying, the American Psychiatric Association's (APA) board of trustees removed homosexuality from its list of mental illnesses in 1973. They were helped to their conclusion by the work of Hooker herself, who in the mid-1950s had begun publishing her findings that gays are no less well adjusted than heterosexuals are. Many homosexuals who really were mentally troubled, Hooker discovered, became so in response to prejudice and stigma.[129]

Alan Bell,[130] Judd Marmor,[131] and others also offered supportive research. These psychotherapists rejected Freud's notion that everybody is in some degree bisexual and relied instead on the argument that gays and lesbians constitute a discrete minority group.[132] Marmor, an influential mainstream figure, originally considered all sexualities to be products of nurture and environment but felt that homosexuality, though not pathological, needed correction to become congruent with societal norms. His position did allow that norms might change to accommodate homosexuality, making treatment unnecessary. Later he came to believe that social prejudice was responsible for the classification of homosexuality as disease and that homosexuals could be as healthy as anyone else.[133]

Some homosexuals rejoiced in the APA's decision; others cautioned that whatever its opinion, gays and lesbians ought not to concede authority to the psychiatric profession.[134] That warning gained significance in the light of APA's record in the years after the vote. The Right decried the change as a capitulation to special interests. A vocal faction of conservative psychiatrists, led by Charles Socarides and Irving Bieber (see Chapter 3), attacked and undermined the board's decision until a general referendum was called in the spring of 1974. Although 58 percent of the voting members supported the removal of homosexuality from the Diagnostic and Statistical Manual of Psychiatric Disorders (DSM), a substantial 37 percent objected. Subsequently, in a 1977 poll of 10,000 psychiatrists, 69 percent thought that homosexuality was usually a "pathological adaptation."[135]

Prompted by the backlash, a draft of the 1977 DSM included a category for persons distressed by their own homosexuality—"dyshomophilia." Later revised to "ego-dystonic homosexuality," the term was approved for classifying subjects whose unwanted homoerotic feelings interfered with their preferred heterosexual functioning. The therapeutic goal was to get rid of the homosexual feelings imagined to cause the dysfunction, not to purge the internalized homophobia.

These debates over the nature of homosexuality reflected the sociopolitical shifts of the times, as both definitions and causation theories had done for nearly a century. Not until 1986 was ego-dystonic homosexuality deleted from the DSM. Replacing it was an unclassified disorder describing any person who is distressed by his or her sexual orientation.[136]

During the 1970s, the Civil Service Commission lifted its employment ban on homosexuals, politicians spoke out on gay rights, a handful of openly gay and lesbian candidates were elected to local offices, and sodomy laws were repealed in some states. Police no longer raided bars, although sweeps and entrapment in gay cruising areas (parks, restrooms, etc.) remained common. Some government agencies continued to pry into people's private lives, including their mail.

Also in the 1970s, gay and lesbian caucuses formed within professional associations (teachers, doctors, social workers, etc.). Gays and lesbians founded their own churches and synagogues and formed interest groups in many denominations. The gay community developed its own businesses, newspapers, clinics, choruses, theaters, sports leagues, and community centers.

Although coverage was often not serious or respectful, there was no denying the increasing visibility of gays and lesbians in American life. Most film and other portrayals continued the stereotypes and caricatures of the previous decades. One notable exception was the 1972 television movie, *That Certain Summer,* which featured prominent actors as sympathetic gay lovers. Print and television news, captive to the public appetite for the outrageous, persisted in sensationalism.

In 1973 Mayor Lindsay's health commissioner came out on the front page of the *New York Times* and became the chair of the new National Gay Task Force (NGTF). *Time Magazine* featured gay sergeant Leonard Matlovich on its cover in 1975, as he began a five-year semi-successful battle to stay in the Air Force. In the same year pro football player David Kopay became the first major league athlete to come out. Before him, only tennis star Bill Tilden, jailed in Los Angeles in the 1940s for having sex with minors, had been known as a homosexual athlete. In 1972 an openly gay man was elected as a delegate to the Democratic National Convention; and in 1976 an NGTF official was the first open lesbian in that role. Although the convention rejected a gay rights platform plank, she was invited to meet with a Carter White House minorities liaison in 1977.

On the darker side in 1977, former Miss America Anita Bryant began the infamous Save Our Children campaign to repeal employment protections for homosexuals in Dade County, Florida. Her referendum passed by a 2–1 margin. Within a year gay rights ordinances were repealed in three other localities (a fourth repeal failed), and two new protective ordinances were adopted. This spotty pattern would continue for at least twenty years.

Perhaps the hardest gay political battle of 1978 was fought over the Briggs Initiative in California. The referendum would have banned homosexual teachers and their open supporters from California public schools. It had just been defeated when a San Francisco city supervisor who had resigned assassinated both his gay colleague Harvey Milk and the mayor. When the killer was sentenced in 1979 to a 5–8 year imprisonment, the ensuing riot by 5,000 protesters received worldwide coverage. Later that year, when some 100,000 people marched on Washington for gay and lesbian rights, the demonstration was ignored in the major media.

## The Eighties

The new decade began with mixed signals as a gay rights plank was voted into the 1980 Democratic Party platform and a Senate bill was filed prohibiting the allocation of federal money to any gay-related project. The latter was only the first of many such bills offered at all levels of government over the ensuing years. Another discouraging turn was the birth of the Moral Majority, whose fundamentalist Christian opposition to homosexuality became the hallmark of their entry into politics.

In 1981, in response to the Matlovich case and others, the military adopted new regulations eliminating loopholes that had permitted some gays and lesbians to remain in the services. This action produced a new round of gay organizing and court battles, culminating twelve years later in the failure of the Clinton administration to reverse the ban. Also in 1981, attention was drawn to a mysterious illness spreading among gay men. First thought to be a gay pneumonia or cancer, the disease would eventually be recognized as a devastating immune deficiency—AIDS.

In 1982 Wisconsin became the first state to pass a gay civil rights law. It had been authored by an openly gay legislator. A similar Massachusetts bill, unsuccessful for seventeen years until its passage in 1989, was cosponsored by two state representatives, one an open lesbian and the other a closeted gay man. In 1983, following his censure for sexual misconduct with a page, Massachusetts Representative Gerry Studds was the first congressperson to come out. And Karen Thompson sued that year for custody of her injured lover, Sharon Kowalski. The couple became a cause celebre, while waiting nearly eight years for their legal victory. One hundred thousand gays and lesbians marched outside the 1984 Democratic National Convention in San Francisco. Meanwhile, the number of AIDS cases grew, and researchers announced the isolation of HIV, thought to cause the disease.

The Supreme Court handed down a stunning decision against homosexuals in the 1986 case of *Bowers v. Hardwick*. Found in his bedroom with another man, Michael Hardwick had been arrested by a policeman with a traffic summons. The court decided that the young Georgian had no constitutional right to engage in gay sex, thereby upholding the state's sodomy statute as it applied to homosexuals. Writing for the majority, Chief Justice Burger pronounced:

> Decisions of individuals relating to homosexual conduct have been subject to state intervention throughout the history of Western Civilization. Condemnation of those practices is firmly rooted in Judeo-Christian moral and ethical standards. . . . To hold that the act of homosexual sodomy is some-

how protected as a fundamental right would be to cast aside millennia of moral teaching.[137]

The court found no right of privacy had been violated. Three years after the decision, retired justice Lewis Powell, a swing vote against Hardwick, admitted that his opinion had been wrong.[138] Ten years after *Bowers*, Georgia's high court ruled in a new case that the homosexual sodomy law furthers "the moral welfare of the public."[139]

The second gay and lesbian march on Washington in 1987 drew from 200,000 (National Park Service estimate) to 650,000 (organizers' estimate). An AIDS quilt was spread over acres on the Mall and 600 Hardwick protesters were arrested outside the Supreme Court. ACT UP, the AIDS Coalition to Unleash Power, was founded in New York that year to pressure the government for research and treatment. The "in your face" activism of its worldwide chapters was reminiscent of the 1960s. ACT UP-New York's 1989 disruption of a mass at St. Patrick's Cathedral seemed to incite more controversy over tactics than it did opposition to the Church's positions on AIDS prevention. Some ACT UP members formed Queer Nation in 1990 to apply its provocative strategy more broadly in an antihomophobia campaign.

The third March on Washington in 1993, organized primarily to protest the military ban, had little political impact. Despite an enormous turnout, constituent lobbying of Congress was low. Although no one doubted the power of large demonstrations to galvanize grassroots organizing and public displays, hundreds of thousands were left wondering if the time for mass protests had ended. The gay community, long split over assimilation versus confrontation, was still torn between conventional politics and direct action. Many in the struggle conceded a need for both modes, but some bemoaned a change of focus. The original goal, they argued, was gay liberation, not legislation, and they criticized the elevation of civil rights over sexual freedom. Trying to pull the community back to its roots, they advised that subversive sex radicalism was more important than voting.

## AIDS

The epidemic itself and the organizing spurred by AIDS have given rise to extraordinary public discussion of homosexuality. Although most who have been afflicted with AIDS worldwide are not homosexual, it has had a grave impact on gay men in the West. It has also served homophobes as a convenient weapon. Misinformation and fear of AIDS have contributed to increasing antigay violence in the 1980s and 1990s.[140] (see Chapter 1). Failing to account for the small number of infected lesbians, religious extremists preach that AIDS is God's punishment for homosexuality.

Inconsolably jolted, the gay community has nursed and mourned thousands for more than fifteen years. Gay culture and relationships have also been altered by a necessary abridgment of sexual spontaneity. Yet AIDS has also united the community positively. In the face of social condemnation and early governmental and scientific indifference, gay people organized to save themselves. Lowering the incidence of risky behaviors, they have proved how effective preventive education can be. Through both militancy and cooperation they have brought drug companies and government agencies to change their research and drug testing protocols.

Perhaps never before have lesbians and gay men collaborated so closely with one another as service-providers, fund-raisers, and lobbyists. Previously apolitical people have also gotten involved. HIV/AIDS has drawn or forced some out of the closet. Many who have lived with the disease have shown great wisdom, courage, and will. No group would ever choose such suffering to demonstrate these qualities. But given the retroviral quirk that put gay men at the center of the epidemic in America, the community has proven itself, at least to itself. Whatever bigotry and ill-treatment has been precipitated by AIDS, only history will tell whether this hardship led to greater understanding and love for homosexual people.

### The Nineties

The last decade of the century witnessed an incremental infusion of the homosexual presence into the nation's consciousness. The repeated public articulation of the words "gay" and "lesbian" represents a remarkable change by itself. More representations of gays and lesbians appeared in the mass media than ever before. Some of them were silly or malicious, but perhaps fewer than before. The gay and lesbian publishing boom has grown apace. More public figures are coming out—not all of them reluctantly. Fewer straight and gay people appear to flinch at the proverbial "we're here" and "we're queer." They are even beginning to "get used to it," notwithstanding some stubborn symptoms to the contrary.

The Supreme Court's 1996 ruling in *Rohmer v. Evans* seemed to establish that states could not ban gay rights protections outright, although its inaction in a Cincinnati case two years later may have permitted localities to do so.[141]

Whatever the laws, many homosexual people are still unwelcome and unsafe on their streets and in their schools, workplaces, and families (see Chapter 1). Yet public education proceeds, particularly within conversations about HIV/AIDS, the military, youth and schools, employment protections, religious participation, marriage, and child rearing.

There are also signs that the sometimes-lonely campaign for antihomophobia education in the schools is picking up momentum. To judge by the ferocity of the opposition, one might think education proponents have gained more ground than they have. For all these right-wing alarms, a number of model educational and support programs have still been successful in promoting healthier gay and lesbian youth and more tolerant classmates.

Since for many gays and lesbians it continues to be more of a challenge to come out to their workmates and loved ones than to rally anonymously for their rights, the specter of shame has yet to be entirely vanquished. A focus on youth has therefore never been more crucial.

# 6

# Identity Formation

1–12–87

*Mr. Lipkin,*

*I would like to talk to you about a problem. I feel that you can help me make a strong decision. Considering we both ["do the" is crossed out] lead the same background. I really don't have anyone to talk to because no one knows about me. I need someone to talk to. I have my friends but that wouldn't help me much. Because words seem to go around. If possible please buzz me [phone number supplied]. Or write an appointment out. I would really appreciate it. If this is not possible, let me know.*

*Thanx.*

*p.s.    This letter will self-destruct in 2 min.—after reading—ha. ha. Please wrip letter in 1/2.*

*Thanx*
*[Signature]*[1]

How does a gay or lesbian young person come to his or her identity? What forms might it take in its development? How are stumbling blocks negotiated? Are role models helpful? Is there an end point? Psychologists once wrote as if homosexual adolescent development did not exist.[2] Now we know better.

The note that opens this chapter was jotted down during an English class by an African American high school senior and slipped to his white, openly gay, 41-year-old teacher. It is at once humorous, perhaps reflecting the class atmosphere, and a little desperate. The student almost writes that he and the teacher share a behavior, but he corrects himself—

it is a "background." He senses they have more in common than erotic practices—they possess a common identity.

This chapter takes homosexual desire and contemporary gay and lesbian identities as givens. Yet it comes to homosexual identity formation with a historical vision and with deference to the hazy border between genetic determinism and environmental influence. Although the gay/lesbian identity is in a theoretical dimension illusory (see Chapter 2), it is still real to most Americans. It may be an oppressive relic, but it also brings coherence to some people's desires, gives at least one dimension of meaning to their intimate relationships, and rallies them to community.

This chapter presents an overview of three models that trace developmental paths to gay and lesbian identification. They are paradigms of psychosexual growth and acculturation. Although they differ in some details, they have significant features in common: initial ambiguity, frequent questioning, disequilibrium, and information-seeking. In these regards they resemble other developmental patterns, like Piaget's cognitive model. Unlike those processes, however, the route to a homosexual identity is fraught with shame, guilt, and avoidance.

Furthermore, the supports commonly associated with the acquisition of other stigmatized minority identities—familial love, proximate community, adult models, and cultural history—are frequently unavailable to gay, lesbian, bisexual, and transgender youth.

"Coming out," a key element in their development, is not a single event. Some have called it an "acceptance and appreciation process"[3] that consists of affirming one's own homosexuality,[4] making contact with the gay/lesbian community,[5] and acknowledging oneself as gay/lesbian to others.[6] For many, it extends well into adulthood.

## Developmental Models

The most frequently cited scholars of gay/lesbian identity development are Eli Coleman,[7] V. C. Cass,[8] and Richard Troiden.[9] Taken together, they describe a progression from vague awareness of difference, through a gradual definition of sexual feeling, to identification with a social category, and sometimes beyond to a recontextualizing stage. These developmental models affirm the idea that the homosexual orientation is an inner potential, waiting to be discovered and expressed.

With the concession that much of the research that leads to these paradigms is based on adult recollections[10] and that Coleman and Troiden have been accused of male bias,[11] I begin with a short summary of each theory. I then offer a synthesis and discuss the limitations of such schemas.

*Coleman*

Coleman's is a 5-stage model: pre–coming out, coming out, exploration, first relationships, and integration:

1. Pre–Coming Out

    Rejection, denial, suppression, and repression. Being aware of stigma, one does not admit, perhaps even to oneself, that one might be or is homosexual. Stress may result in depression and suicidality.

2. Coming Out

    Initial acceptance of and reconciliation to one's homosexuality. First expression to others. Positive response, particularly from significant confidants, can lead to greater comfort and wider disclosure. Negative response can send one back to Stage 1, although hiding from oneself requires even greater levels of denial than before.

3. Exploration

    Trying out one's new identity socially and sexually. Contact with the gay/lesbian community. Often, a "homosexual adolescence" with promiscuity, infatuation, courtship, and rejection. For older people, possible shame at seemingly immature impulses. If one assumes this stage is representative of one's future gay life, one might try to flee.

4. First Relationships

    Sense of attractiveness and sexual competence can lead to the desire for deeper and more lasting relationships. Requires skills to maintain a same-gender connection in a hostile environment. Intense expectations, possessiveness, and mistrust can doom a first relationship. One partner may rebel by pursuing sex outside the relationship.

5. Integration

    Public and private selves become congruent. Growing self-acceptance leads to greater confidence and ability to sustain relationships. Possessiveness and mistrust lessen as openness and caring increase. Rejection is grieved, but not devastating.

*Cass*

The six stages of Cass's paradigm are confusion, comparison, tolerance, acceptance, pride, and synthesis.

1. Identity Confusion

   "Could I be homosexual?" Resistance—avoiding behaviors that seem indicative and shutting out information that confirm one's homosexual identity. One may also try to redefine the meaning of one's desires and behavior.

2. Identity Comparison

   "I may be homosexual." Alienated from heterosexual peers, family, and community, one does not yet have a sense of belonging to a gay community. One may react positively to being different but still hide from a homophobic world. Or one may react negatively to being different and seek to avoid gay behavior, gay identity, or both. May result in self-hatred.

3. Identity Tolerance

   "I am probably homosexual." Begins to tolerate homosexual identity and seek contact/acceptance from other gays/lesbians. Type of contact influences self-esteem and social skills. Purely sexual contact, without a gay identity or positive socialization, can retard development. More affirming interaction can lead to the next stage.

4. Identity Acceptance

   Tolerance replaced by self-acceptance. Self-concept refined in homosexual social spheres. Continued passing as straight in the outside world with possible disclosure to a few. Family contact is problematical.

5. Identity Pride

   Immersion in gay subculture brings preference for identity. Hiding is questioned as shame diminishes. Negative reactions to coming out can shake pride. Unexpected positive ones can lead to last stage.

6. Identity Synthesis

   Homosexuality viewed as one part of a multifaceted self. Reevaluation of separateness. Sexual orientation no longer chiefly determines identity and cohort.

*Troiden*

Troiden's four stages are sensitization, confusion, assumption, and commitment.

1. Sensitization
   Prepubertal feelings of marginality and difference, experienced as gendered more than sexual.

2. Identity Confusion
   Feelings of difference become sexualized. Younger adolescents experience turmoil over an ambiguous sexuality; older ones perceive homosexuality but avoid the label.

3. Identity Assumption
   Homosexual self-definition, toleration, and then acceptance. Regular association with and disclosure to other gays/lesbians. Selective disclosure elsewhere. Exploration of homosexual subculture and sexual experimentation.

4. Commitment
   The "why pretend" stage. Perception of homosexuality as natural and valid part of identity. Learning that sex and love may coincide. Happier, one discloses more generally.

*A Mega-Model*

Roughly congruent, these three models can be merged. Minton and McDonald have posited a three-stage combination: egocentric (genitality, emotions, and fantasies), followed by sociocentric (internalized conventional beliefs, guilt, and secrecy), and universalistic (social critique, self-acceptance, integration).[12] I propose a five-stage integration:

1. Pre-Sexuality (Troiden 1)
   Preadolescent nonsexual feelings of difference and marginality.

2. Identity Questioning (Coleman 1; Cass 1, 2; Troiden 2)
   Ambiguous, repressed, sexualized same-gender feelings and/or activities. Avoidance of stigmatized label.

3. Coming Out (Coleman 2, 3, 4; Cass 3, 4; Troiden 3)
   Toleration then acceptance of identity through contact with gay/lesbian individuals and culture. Exploration of sexual pos-

sibilities and first erotic relationships. Careful, selective self-disclosure outside gay/lesbian community.

4. Pride (Coleman 5; Cass 5; Troiden 4)
   Integration of sexuality into self. Capacity for love relationships. Wider self-disclosure and better stigma management.

5. Post-Sexuality (Cass 6)
   A diminishment of centrality of homosexuality in self-concept and social relations.

A number of embellishments can be added to this minimal framework: common pitfalls, developmental needs, stigma management, gender, class, ethnic, and racial differences. But before looking at these dimensions, we should consider the limitations of stage models in general.

## Limitations

Troiden himself cautioned readers not to take his identity formulations too literally.[13] They are gross generalizations, ideal types into which it is not advisable to try to force-fit individual cases. Still, however imperfectly, they do sketch the sequence and features of the identity passage.

Some question whether the stages are linear (i.e., invariably sequential) or if some may be skipped.[14] Gramick's research with ninety-seven lesbians found that such stages do not occur in universal order.[15] Preferring the term "gay trajectory,"[16] another researcher claimed that subjects entered her paradigm at any one of five developmental points.[17] Troiden carefully drew the geometry of his concept:

> Homosexuality is not conceptualized here as a linear, step-by-step process in which one stage precedes another and one necessarily builds on another, with fluctuations written off as developmental regressions. Instead, the process of homosexual identity formation is likened to a horizontal spiral, like a spring lying on its side.[18] Progress through the stages occurs in back-and-forth, up-and-down ways; the characteristics of stages overlap and recur in somewhat different ways for different people. In many cases stages are encountered in consecutive order, but in some instances they are merged, glossed over, bypassed, or realized simultaneously.[19]

In our culture, one would have to be superhuman to acquire a gay/lesbian identity without fits, starts, and slippage.[20]

Nevertheless, these stages are probably cognitively irreversible. That is, once one understands the concepts required for a later stage, one cannot "unlearn" them, although one might have trouble making feelings or actions correspond with knowledge. For example, the initial stages of gay identity assumption require that one first become aware of a homosexual category of people and then recognize one's connection to it. Individuals might repress but cannot absolutely forget these discoveries, although they might be uncomfortable adjusting to them. As for taking action to further one's identity acquisition, more factors than knowing one is homosexual motivate behavior.

The coming out process is a kind of moral development.[21] To embrace one's homosexuality demands engagement in a critique of conventional heterosexism. As in progression from sociocentrism to universalism (in Minton and McDonald's model), one moves beyond the received values of heterosexual superiority and "naturalness."[22] This enlightened view of sexuality may be occasionally strained, yet cannot be reversed.[23] Such moral perspective is crucial, yet cognition is only one part of development. The struggle to know disquiets more than the intellect, and when one finally gets it right in the mind, one may still be shaky in the heart. Coming out, therefore, requires ego strength and emotional support.

Some people try to get beyond the homosexual category altogether by adopting a less defined, more ample sexuality identity than is found in our "straight, gay, or bi" culture of oppositional labels. Some of them take the signifier "queer" (see Chapter 2), and others reject sexuality-determined identities entirely. The latter would be the Cass "post-gay" Stage 6-ers. Both groups balk at identities conferred on them by the majority culture but do not drop their sexual interests and self-knowledge or backslide into repression and denial. They want either to reframe sexuality labeling or to end it entirely.

### Pitfalls

Each of these models illustrates that the course of gay/lesbian identity formation is not smooth. Identity questioning, for instance, is rife with obstacles. Many try to evade the true nature of their feelings or acts with rationalizations based on ignorance and stereotype. "It was only a physical thing, I was just horny" is a typical male disavowal.[24] "It is too loving and beautiful to be homosexuality" is a common female disclaimer.[25] "It only happened this once," "It's just a phase," or "It isn't gay because neither male partner plays the woman" are also familiar. Sometimes drugs and alcohol enhance deniability ("It was the liquor that made me do it") or mask the guilt.

One may try to repair the "defect" by seeking a cure in religion or medicine. One might flee from people of the opposite gender or, conversely, have sex with them to avoid self-admission or detection. Heterosexual promiscuity and deliberate pregnancy are known covering strategies.[26] According to the 1997 Massachusetts Youth Risk Behavior Survey, 24.3 percent of homosexual/bisexual students who have had intercourse have either been pregnant themselves or gotten someone else pregnant (versus 12.2 percent of sexually active heterosexual respondents).[27]

Distancing can also take the form of shunning information about gays and lesbians. In the words of the main character in an early gay coming-of-age novel: "One ingenious defense was to remain as ignorant as possible on the subject of homosexuality. The less I knew, I reasoned, the less chance that I would start looking like one or acting like one."[28] At its extreme, distancing can be attempted through homophobic posturing, harassment, and bashing.

Some immerse themselves in hobbies or schoolwork, even to the point of perfectionism.[29] This is the "Best Little Boy [or Girl]" syndrome, common among gay and lesbian athletic and academic overachievers. These activities provide both distraction and refuge from heterosexual expectations: "Another important line of defense, the most important on a practical day-to-day basis, was my prodigious list of activities. 'Highly motivated; a self-starter,' the teachers would write on my character reports. Hell, yes, I was motivated."[30] Overachievement also serves as internal reassurance that in spite of one's monstrous secret, one is not worthless.

One can lose oneself in other people as well. In attention to the needs of others, the precocious caregiver can ignore his or her own needs.[31] The sexually troubled youth becomes the available friend and counselor. The son or daughter assumes a parental role in the family.

Another common refuge is acting out. "Cory" of *Growing Up Gay in the South* was one of a group of "little redneck hell-raisers."[32] Smoking, drinking, drug taking and dealing, he gave all his teachers problems and could not be bothered with schoolwork. At the age of twenty-one, still drinking, but with some perspective on his teen years, he confessed: "I built up walls in high school because I did not want to deal with other human beings. . . . If homosexuality would have been acceptable I wouldn't have built so many walls and been so angry."[33]

A young person in the identity questioning stage may acclimate to a gay or lesbian identity by first claiming a bisexual one to mitigate the stigma.[34] A feint toward normalcy, the bisexual label asserts that one is not completely twisted.[35] This mind-set is indicative of a transitional,[36] not mature, bisexuality.[37] One college counselor assesses the phenomenon this way:

It is unclear what proportion of adolescents will retain their bisexual identification after they explore more fully their homoerotic feelings. It is possible that for some of today's late adolescents, bisexual identity serves as a means of maintaining continuity with and acknowledgment of past heteroerotic experiences.[38]

A long-term bisexual identity is less likely to be established by age nineteen than a homosexual one.[39] Indeed, considerable heteroerotic feeling and experience appears necessary for the formation of a bisexual identity.[40] That might explain why bisexual males have reported not feeling different in childhood.[41]

Any bisexual identity is difficult to retain in the face of pressure to adhere to dichotomous standards. No less authority than sex guru Dr. Ruth Westheimer has opined about bisexuality, "There is just not that much hard evidence that such a state really exists."[42] According to the Kinsey continuum, nonetheless, the bisexual orientation spans erotic preferences and behaviors from point 2 to point 4 (on a 0 to 6 scale). Many at each extreme of this bisexual domain consider themselves either straight or homosexual, creating a barrier between themselves and those not far removed from them who identify as bisexual. One prominent sexologist sums up the arbitrary nature of the divisions with the observation, "I can't say a certain proportion of people are homosexual, heterosexual, or bisexual because I don't know where you draw the boundaries. Sexual orientation is more complex than that."[43]

Bisexuals can face hostility from two directions: from homophobes who fail to distinguish between bisexuality and homosexuality and from those gays and lesbians who view bisexuality as repression or false consciousness.[44]

Difficulties abound in the coming out stage, as well. Rejection can send one into retreat, followed by constant self-monitoring and trying to pass as heterosexual.[45] On the other hand, the emerging homosexual may capitulate to the negative expectations of an oppressive culture and adopt stereotypical appearance and behavior, even to the point of caricature. Both passing and minstrelizing are suppressions of the genuine self, the products of internalized homophobia.

## Developmental Needs for Successful Navigation

One does not usually vault effortlessly into the gay and lesbian community. Customarily the transition is difficult, as one yields one identity for another. Gilbert Herdt characterizes this coming into one's own as a rite of passage, attended by crisis rituals of loss and rebirth.[46] During an initial vulnerable period, one risks ostracism from the majority culture before one has found a new one. At the same time, often without consolation from family or friends, one mourns the loss of one's prior assumed heterosexuality, with its conventional roles and scripted future.

Getting through the identity questioning and coming out stages requires accurate information. Because media images of homosexuality are limited at best, those who are questioning or just coming out should have personal contact with other gay/lesbian people and access to their literature and subculture. Discovery of commonalities with other gays and lesbians and identification with role models should ease the passage into a new community.

In certain locales, the gay and lesbian world is now visible and available to its youth for unprecedented safe entrée. It offers language, humor, traditions, rituals, norms of conduct, a panoply of roles, and strategies for stigma management.[47] It also furnishes opportunities for friendship, sexual experimentation, and love relationships. Immersion in the culture helps one dismiss misrepresentations that are a part of everyone's conditioning.

Most gay and lesbian youth are victims of narcissistic injury, who need personal affirmation and group affiliation. From their first awareness of their sexualities they are subject to devaluation and rejection, both within themselves and from those who are closest to them.[48] Finding acceptance among self-affirming homosexual people plays a vital part in restoring their self-esteem.

## Stigma Management

As people come out they must learn to manage the social stigma that attaches to homosexuality. Carmen de Monteflores enumerates four coping strategies employed by lesbians:[49]

1. Assimilation—passing for straight while in the dominant culture. It may protect a woman from ridicule, harassment, and ostracism, but it can destroy her self-esteem by violating her own integrity as well as the values of the lesbian/gay subculture.
2. Confrontation—defiance through coming out and finding strength in her difference.
3. Ghettoization—finding shelter in psychological and even physical immersion in the subculture and living as much as possible in isolation from the majority.
4. Specialization—overcompensating by seeing herself as special, superior, or chosen by virtue of being homosexual.

There are significant drawbacks to all these mechanisms except confrontation, and even that presents risks.

Richard Troiden distinguishes among stigma management strategies at different stages. In the identity assumption stage, he proposes six:

1. Capitulation—one does not deny homosexual feelings or identity but, believing stigma is deserved, avoids activities that might lead to self-affirmation.
2. Passing—one leads a double life, hiding homosexual feelings and activities from others. (Both capitulation and passing are stressful and may be seriously self-destructive.)
3. Group alignment—one avoids the straight world.
4. Selection—one self-discloses to those assumed to be accepting.
5. Avoidance—one dodges situations that might result in disclosure, confrontation, or embarrassment.
6. Minstrelization—one expresses sexuality through stereotypical behavior, giving the dominant culture the embodiment of homosexuality it expects, often in defiant defensiveness, in the hope of escaping opprobrium.[50]

At the commitment stage, Troiden details three strategies:

1. Covering—one comes out to significant heterosexuals, while minimizing the import of the disclosure.
2. Blending—one is not shameful or trying to pass, yet asserts that sexuality is private and does not disclose.
3. Converting—one is direct if not defiant. Caution is replaced by a sense of entitlement, though not foolhardiness.

The same person may employ different stigma control modalities, depending on the situation and the relationships involved. This is a tactical decision rather than a developmental indicator.[51]

Many research studies point to individual and group differences in the developmental pattern. For example, Troiden found that those who are able to pass as heterosexual might come later to the process and proceed slowly. Opposite-gender sexual experience can also prolong confusion or aid denial.[52] On the other hand, the noticeably gender nonconforming with no heterosexual experience may begin earlier and move along quickly.[53]

## Gender Differences

The behavior of outsiders is clearly a factor. The straight appearing are not as likely to be pressed into declaring, whereas "obvious types," beset with harassment and probing questions might conclude, "Denials from me are unconvincing. Coming out may get these people off my back." Because gender unconventionality is tolerated less in males,[54] sissy boys may be sensitized to being different earlier than tomboyish girls.[55]

## Age of Coming Out

Herdt and Boxer found that although boys and girls experience same-gender desire and fantasy at about the same age, girls delay expression of their same-gender desire longer than boys do.[56] Girls may face greater pressure, especially from boys who want to be involved with them, to conform to heterosexual roles.[57] A common tactic for delaying lesbian identification is the "special case" excuse, in which a girl rationalizes that being in love with a particular female does not make her homosexual.[58]

Troiden found that gay males self-identified, typically between 19 and 21 years of age and that lesbians did so on average two years later.[59] These numbers are based on research that is rapidly becoming out of date (1971–1980). By 1989, another sample of young lesbians significantly lowered their age of identification to the midteens.[60] This narrowing gap is consistent with a third study that reports an identical mean age of 16 for boys and girls coming out to themselves.[61] In coming out to others, girls may be likely to disclose only to females, whereas boys might come out to either.[62]

## Gender Nonconformity

Extremely gender-nonconforming boys who were referred to mental health professionals have been studied over the long term.[63] They showed persistent interest in cross-dressing, playing with female dolls, and socializing with female peers. Some wanted to be female. The majority developed a gay identity; a few became transvestites or transsexuals. Richard Green dubs this pattern "the sissy-boy syndrome."[64] A recent meta-analysis of forty-one studies based on recollections of adult homosexuals found 51 percent of male sissies likely to become gay and 6 percent of female tomboys likely to become lesbian.[65] These numbers should be viewed cautiously, since adult homosexuals may be open to recalling gender-nonconformity and heterosexuals may repress such memories. In any event, there is a clear difference between the significance of gender nonconformity for girls and boys. A female's violation of oppressive gender norms is probably less indicative of sexuality than a male's opting for a lesser gender status.

## Relationships

Apparent differences have also been observed in how gay men and lesbians understand their relationships. Boys, regardless of orientation, are socialized to seek sexual contact before thinking about relationship.[66] As

a result, males tend to self-define as gay after sexual events[67] and generally equate gayness with being sexual.[68] Girls, though, are socialized to
put the relationship before the sex,[69] so it is common for a lesbian to self-
define after an intense affectional involvement with another woman.[70] In
one representative study, the establishment of a relationship was the
primary event that signaled lesbian identity formation, whereas phys-
ical/genital contact was secondary.[71] In fact, many lesbians have their
first same-gender sex with a known peer or established friend.[72] Unlike
gay males, who are thought to develop feelings of love only after sexual
liaisons,[73] lesbians experience sexual feelings in the context of love and
attachment.[74]

The primacy of relationality is said to lead some women from feminist
solidarity to political lesbianism, a nonerotic designation for women who
break from a world of patriarchal meanings.[75] This intense connection
with all women has the potential to become an emotional bond with individual women and perhaps evolve into erotic lesbianism. True or not
for women, one does not easily imagine men moving from brotherhood
to gay political identity to homosexuality.

There is yet no male analogue to Adrienne Rich's "lesbian continuum."[76] The typical boy, for whom carnality is primary, may experience
sex as physical pleasure relatively unaffected by relationality. In a study
by James Sears of gay and lesbian Southerners, boys might have sex
without affective connection, but none of the girls "engaged in homosexual behavior without first experiencing emotional and erotic attraction
for other women."[77]

Elements of the homosexual subculture may have served historically
to reinforce gender differences.[78] Urban gay males were often socialized
in the setting of the bar and bathhouse, where genital pleasure, pursuit,
and conquest were paramount. Lesbians, by contrast, were more often
socialized within small private friendship cohorts and in the women's
community, where relationships, mutual support, and solidarity were
emphasized.

Homosexual acts themselves may have different import for women
than for men. An apparently straight woman may engage in sex with
other women for a time without its affecting her identity; however, a heterosexual man's self-image is usually destabilized by homoerotic contacts.[79] It seems that such women would view a rare physical attachment
as a natural extension of a deep relationship, but men would be disposed
to consider a same-gender episode a symptom of repressed homosexuality.[80] Men would not find that such sexual acts were a natural extension
of emotional attachment. On the contrary, men in such circumstances distance themselves as much as possible from feeling and thus from the
taint of homosexuality:

I'm straight, but I need outlets when I'm away from home and times like that. And it's easier to get with men than women. . . . I would never stay the night with one of them, or get to know them. It's just a release. It's not like sex with my wife. It's just a way to get what you need without making it a big deal.[81]

At the commitment stage, gay men are likely to play the field longer than lesbians do, before settling into a relationship.[82] They also pay more attention to a potential partner's erotic compatibility and appearance.[83] In their sexual assertiveness, roaming, valuing physical attributes, and finding love after sex, gay men mirror their heterosexual counterparts.[84]

Although gender socialization could account for most of these differences, biology might drive them as well. Men may instinctively spread their seed as often and as widely as possible without relational encumbrances. And women may be genetically inclined toward nurture and mutuality. Even if valid, biology does not have to drive socialization. Men and women should not be constrained by nature or nurture to limit their repertoire to loveless sex or to sexless love. Instead of having feeling and relationality knocked out of them, boys could be encouraged to retain the affective qualities of their preadolescence. Girls, for their part, could be allowed a freer romp.

## The Lewis Model of Lesbian Development

L. A. Lewis proposes a 5-stage model for lesbian identity formation: being different, dissonance, relationships, stable lesbian identity, and integration.[85] In the dissonance stage women, particularly those who have been involved with men, may view their evolving lesbianism with anger, resentment, and sadness. They are upset by the prospect of losing heterosexual privilege and its predictable roles, relationships, and economic security. As observed earlier, both lesbians and gay males mourn the passing of their heterosexuality, but gay men, particularly those who appear masculine, still retain many gender privileges.

Lewis also asserts that women who have strongly identified as straight may, on the other hand, have more self-esteem as they begin to explore their lesbianism, since they have not suffered the long-term isolation of early lesbian identification. Their strength and genuineness could be challenged later, however, by "life-long" lesbians faulting their lack of adolescent lesbian experience.[86]

The self-esteem of both males and females who come later to homosexual identification probably hinges on the difference between having merely passed and having actually thought oneself heterosexual. Those who passed have undoubtedly suffered isolation and inner conflict.

Those who really believed themselves straight might be more likely to have developed greater self-esteem. Yet their habitual emotional fortitude is still tested in coming out. Young people who are "gender-typical, heterosexually active, and homosexually inexperienced encounter more confusion regarding their sexual identities because their characteristics are at variance with prevailing stereotypes."[87]

Lewis's relationships stage marks the onset of lesbian sexual experimentation. And just because they are female and might be veterans of profound friendship does not mean they are able to slide easily into erotic lesbian relationships. Like their gay brothers, they are probably inexperienced in homosexual courtship. Since women are conventionally sexual only in the context of a relationship, their exploration of same-gender sex may be halting.[88] The increasing popularity of unrestrained lesbian eroticism and pornography suggests sexual radicalism is already having an effect on lesbian norms, but many are still ashamed to articulate their erotic needs or to experiment sexually with their partners.[89]

Researchers have found that more lesbians than gay men are involved in committed faithful relationships, characterized as "quasi-marriages" and the "most viable option for most lesbians."[90] This coupling tendency might lessen with women's greater erotic and economic freedom.

There is a potentially enormous gender difference in Lewis's integration stage. After settling down with a partner in a committed relationship in the previous stable lesbian identity stage, a woman begins to integrate her sexuality into the rest of her life. Yet, remarkably, a relationship breakup or loss of community support can throw her back significantly "to earlier emotional stages."[91] Her reaction is described as emotional, not cognitive, regression, and she may still be lesbian-identified, if somewhat regretful for being so. Yet she may not feel like a lesbian for a while or forever. Of course men too can be hurt by a breakup, but men's relationship failures are not described as having sexual identity consequences, particularly in identity pride and other late stages.

The apparent changeability of women's orientation and identification may be connected to relationality. Their capacity to be drawn to both males and females upsets the polarities of homo- and heterosexuality. A woman may not, at any one time, have exclusive attractions. Moreover, during her lifetime, identity and behavior may fluctuate.[92] One scholar maintains stage models are inapplicable to lesbian identity formation, which she sees as more complex and fluid.[93] Rejecting the idea of an a priori orientation to which lesbians adjust and which they gradually make public, Laura Brown asks whether all women might not be capable of intense affection for other women:

It may be possible to better understand how lesbians hold on to and eroticize these attachments if we comprehend how such passions are lost or distorted for women who are not lesbian. In other words, we may be asking the wrong questions. We may need to ask not only why are some women lesbians and how do they come to that identity, but also why do some women lose their lesbianism as they develop?[94]

Adrienne Rich answered that question in advance with her notion that women are forced into "compulsory heterosexuality" by social conditioning, economic necessity, homophobia, and outright violence.[95]

### *Lesbianism as Choice*

Carla Golden builds on a theory that women are more interested in having emotional relationships with other women than with men,[96] offering that a mother's nurturance predisposes boys to heterosexuality and girls to lesbianism.[97] In her view, socialization reinforces the male predisposition, and only partially redirects females, leaving them with a bisexual potential. Recalling an earlier classification that made a distinction between primary and elective lesbians, Golden asserts that all women's sexuality is elective. Their devolution from a bisexual capacity into lesbianism or heterosexuality is a conscious choice.

Interviews with women who have come to lesbianism after lengthy heterosexual identification and activity can be interpreted to reflect Golden's views. C. Kitzinger and S. Wilkinson maintain that their subjects did not discover a preexisting and repressed condition but rather chose lesbianism as right for them in their circumstances.[98]

Once these choices are made, particularly as women get older and more attached to their cohort, their sexualities may be experienced as relatively fixed, though some remain open and flexible.[99] Most heterosexually identified women are startled by the idea that they might have chosen to be straight. A small number, however, acknowledge having made the choice, and some allow the possibility of lesbian involvement if the right woman came along or their man departed.

Attitudes may be changing quickly. A straight female Hollywood director is said to have remarked, "Every straight woman I know is trying desperately to arrange a lesbian affair. It's absolutely retro to be straight if you are female."[100] The Hollywood angle is not necessarily indicative, however.

### The Human Development Model

Such theories and observations undermine the seemingly inexorable progression within stage models. Furthermore, the stability of sexual orientation over the course of a lifetime has never been tested in large-sample longitudinal studies of males or females.[101] Sexual identity development may indeed be an ongoing, lifelong process with no maturation endpoint.[102]

Another schema, the "human development model," proposes that the acquisition of affectional interests and preferences is a multidimensional, dynamic, interactive process rather than a simple, fixed, biologically determined status.[103] This paradigm allows for more orientation and identity possibilities than are described or implied in customary stage models. It contends that culture, social norms and expectations, physical surroundings and interactions, and biology affect one's sexuality course. Its character may change over time as these determinants themselves change.

This paradigm does not imply that sexuality is like a reed bending compliantly with the currents of life. Rather it holds that affectional preferences and identity emerge at different points in life through a biologically and psychologically influenced combination of desire, yielding, resistance, and self-knowledge. People come to and go from homosexual feelings, behavior, and identity when outer circumstances and inner readiness concur. Many bisexuals, for example, emerge after years of considering themselves straight. Sometimes a bisexual identity leads to a homosexual one. For others, an established gay or lesbian identity is succeeded by a bisexual one.[104]

This dynamic model has been called antiessentialist because it contradicts the notion of a fixed sexuality.[105] But historical essentialism posits only a homosexual category that has persisted over the centuries; it implies nothing as to the permanence of an individual's identification with the label. The position this theory opposes would be called more accurately psychological essentialism, which asserts that an individual has a true and permanent sexual core.

The human development perspective eliminates the normative formulations that diagnose late coming out or bisexuality as repression, confusion, or immaturity. It recognizes that people come to their orientations via their singular constitutions and unique life experiences. It also respects the power of choice in recognizing and pursuing one's inclinations, affiliating with a gay/lesbian identity and community, and publicizing one's sexuality.

This view is supported by the results of the 1994 Sex in America survey.[106] Self-identified gay and bisexual men accounted for 2.8 percent of the 3,432 respondents; lesbians and bisexual women were only 1.4 percent. Yet, when desire and behavior over the previous year were assessed, the percentage of men exhibiting some dimension of same-gender sexuality rose to 10.1 percent and women to 8.6 percent. (Of that 10.1

percent of men, 44 percent experienced same-gender desire but did not act upon it and did not consider themselves gay; 22 percent engaged in same-gender behavior but reported both no desire for it and no homosexual identity; and 24 percent reported homosexual desire, behavior, and identity.)

Higher education proved to be a significant variable in the survey. Twice as many men and eight times as many women with a college education identified as gay/lesbian/bisexual than did those without one. Since there is no reason to believe that homosexuals are more likely to attend college or that colleges cause homosexuality, a sustainable conclusion is that higher education contributes to one's readiness to identify, through a number of factors such as distance from home, exposure to the homosexual community, and open discussion of sexual ideas and possibilities.

Like Golden's, the human development model highlights choice and points to the disincentives of stigma and prohibition for people in different phases of their lives. It is, of course, impossible to know the full range of anyone's sexuality potential as long as homophobia remains a factor in his or her affectional and sexual decisions. But the environment may change. More than three dozen movies issued or in production in 1997 alone featured youths having bisexual attractions.[107]

Although philosophically satisfying and emotionally reassuring, the human development model must be fleshed out and supported by longitudinal studies. Kinsey's interview research is widely accepted as referring to varieties of human sexual orientation and behavior but not necessarily to fluidity; he did, however, find that learning and conditioning could effect change in individuals. More recent studies have also noted such changes.[108] Complete sexuality histories across cultures will eventually yield details and reference points to illuminate how people travel their affectional/erotic paths and how they make sense of themselves as they do.

There is one caveat, nonetheless: theories of sexual fluidity and intentionality can be used for heterosexist oppression. Those who view homosexuality as a developmental aberration to be cured through inducements to normalcy would have gays, lesbians, and bisexuals swim the continuum stream in the direction of heterosexuality.[109] This one-sided prescription must be countered with the assertion that all sexualities are changeable and chosen—that the stream flows in two directions. Everyone should be freed from the restraints that impede their full sexual expression. The retort to the question "When did you decide to be gay?" used to be "When did you decide to be heterosexual?" Now it can take on an exquisite new twist: "When did you decide to be *permanently* heterosexual?"

# 7

# Multiple Identities

For centuries, disparate cultures have influenced whether and how same-gender desires should shape the identities of the individuals who experience them (see Chapter 2). What is new, though, is that mass communication and mobility have broken down ethnic, class, and national insularity to the extent that modern Western notions of homosexuality have broad impact, particularly in the multicultural United States.[1] American heterogeneity provokes public discourses and media representations of gender, sexuality, race, and religion, which have repercussions around the world. According to a Korean lesbian, for example, the Internet is helping people come out as never before in her country.[2]

Despite their differing moral positions, American subcultures are coming to have certain common, if not wholly accurate, notions about homosexuality, at the least that it is a real identity marker. Individuals with same-gender desires from various racial, ethnic, religious, and class groups may find it problematical to adopt a modern Western gay, lesbian, or bisexual identity. And if they do embrace it, they face the prospect of forging their multiple identities into a new coherent self.

Since racial, ethnic, class, and religious socializations are begun early, established identities may be threatened by budding homosexual self-consciousness. The visibility of the gay/lesbian community has generally facilitated young people's coming out, but some public images make it more difficult for immigrant, minority, working-class, and religious youth to accept the label. A pervasive white, Anglo, secular, middle-class stereotype can be off-putting. Adolescents might assume that in coming out they would have to sacrifice their neighborhoods, friends, cultures, faiths, and families. Their challenge is to find a way to be gay or lesbian that permits their multiple identities not just to coexist but to nurture one another and flourish.

The search for both intrapsychic freedom and social acceptance is daunting. Racial/ethnic/class prejudice and religious intolerance within the homosexual community and homophobia in the culture of origin are painfully alienating. If coming out means leaving their familiar minority community, they grieve the loss of a habitual refuge from bigotry and de-humanization, along with heterosexual privilege and predictability.[3]

This chapter is meant to provide possible reference points for under-standing individuals in the context of a multicultural society. Its analy-ses and prescriptions are not perfect for everyone. Despite the chapter's generalizations, these young people are not pure types; rather, like most Americans, each is a mixture of different heritages. Their families and native communities have to varying degrees played the roles of gate-keepers and value transmitters, but few youth are likely to be products of complete cultural isolation. If they have been long in the United States (particularly in urban centers) or in Western-influenced cultures, they have had considerable exposure to modern glosses on homosexu-ality.[4]

Without individual study, we cannot presume to know how any mi-nority youth navigates among a number of identity constructs. Still, we can be fairly certain that one of his or her life tasks is to integrate sexu-ality with gender, role, and the other variables that are the touchstones of this chapter. It is difficult to disengage sexuality, class, race, ethnicity, or religion from the matrix of features that define a human being. Their relative and mutual influences are a delicate tissue, which is not readily dissected, despite the fondness of social science for multivariate analy-sis.

One must not infer from this book that antigay/lesbian bias is worse in any single minority group than it is in another or in the majority culture. Each group has its own homophobic attitudes and behaviors.[5] Some va-rieties may be more subtle or discrete than others, but they are no less pernicious, particularly to the young. Attitudes vary from city to city and between rural and urban areas. The District of Columbia's large and vi-brant homosexual African American community must have a salutary impact on young people of color that is missing in Boston, for example, where black gays and lesbians historically have kept a much lower pro-file. So too, the cities of the West and Southwest attract Chicanos and Chi-canas from the smaller towns.

None of these minority groups is monolithic. There are subcultures within them that offer shelter and encouragement to gays and lesbians. The black feminist community is one such welcome ally.

Lastly, this chapter is somewhat limited by the uneven availability of research sources. There are fewer writings by and about Asian-American gay men, for example, than about their lesbian sisters and fewer of both than about African Americans. Within a few years, the disparity will probably change as more gay and lesbian scholars of all ethnicities produce their work.

## Class

More has been written about the relationship between homosexuality and race, ethnicity, and religion than has been written about homosexuality and class. Some historians, however, have observed significant details about working-class constructions of same-gender attraction and how they differ from those of the other classes.[6] Turn-of-the-century American homosexuals appear to have had greater freedom of association in poorer urban neighborhoods. At the same time, working-class ideas about homosexual behavior were highly influenced by conservative gender role mores. Although gender inversion was integrated into recreational milieus, it was still highly regulated. For example, stringent codes of lesbian dress and behavior known as "butch and femme" were more common to the working class than to middle-class and wealthy lesbians.[7]

Today as well, rigid gender role expectations influence working-class views of homosexuality. It is commonly thought that homosexuals want to *be* the opposite gender. In fact, working-class and minority gay/lesbian youth are more likely to engage in gender unconventional behavior than their more privileged peers.[8] These minstrelizers either accept that being homosexual requires gender inversion or believe that they will suffer less hostility if they conform to such expectations. The pattern is observed particularly among black and Hispanic cross-dressers.[9] A gay Latino testified to his predicament: "The only way I could survive as a young gay male was to act like a woman; to act differently would have meant physical violence."[10]

A 1993 study found that such conservative family values play a greater role in predicting coming out experiences than does race.[11] Since conservative views of gender and sexuality can be challenged by effective education (see Chapters 4 and 11), working-class gays and lesbians might suffer as a result of their families' lack of educational opportunity. Poverty also limits access to counseling services, particularly in times of government cutbacks, so poor youth who need professional coming out support are at a disadvantage.

There are of course many working-class families who show kindness and respect for human differences. Their homosexual children may have an easier adjustment than those in less tolerant households. Let it also be said, there is mean-spiritedness and bigotry among the middle-class and wealthy, including those with advanced degrees.

## Race and Ethnicity

*African Americans*

African American homosexual youth must contend with the racism of the larger gay/lesbian world and with the homophobia in communities of color. When racist prejudice bruises black children, black adults can heal them with dignity, love, and accurate information. Even sharing their rage can be soothing. However, the same institutions that promote racial pride and solidarity—family, community, and church—can be the sources of crippling homophobic messages that are heard well before adolescence.[12] Cornel West recalls, "I grew up in the Black community, in the Black church, on the Black block, and there's a lot of homophobia in all three sites."[13] Caught in the double bind of racist and homophobic deprecation, gay and lesbian African American youth must inevitably suffer.

*Scapegoating.* Ritual unification through scapegoating, common in many communities, is practiced here too. Consider, for example, male bonding through hypermasculine posing and antigay violence: "What I was or what I was becoming—in spite of myself—could be ridiculed, harassed, and even murdered with impunity. The male code of the streets where I grew up made this very clear: Sissies, punks, and faggots were not cool with the boys."[14] Homophobia enforces certain peer group norms. Any young black male who breaks the codes of the street by liking the wrong kind of music, doing well in school, or avoiding gangs, promiscuity, or violence can be gay-baited.

Part of African American heterosexism emanates from a passionate concern over the shortage of marriageable men within the community. Many are murdered, incarcerated, and debilitated by substance abuse, chronic unemployment, and other handicaps. A gay black man may represent an unforgivable dereliction of procreative responsibility for family and racial survival.[15] His supposed abdication may irritate those seeking providers and male role models for children. In the language of 1980s black nationalism, "Homosexuality is a genocidal practice."[16]

*Homosexuality as White.* Black homophobia also springs from the perception that homosexuality is a "white thing." The media reinforce the image of homosexuals as middle-class and Caucasian. The terms "acting white" and "acting gay" have become almost interchangeable among some young black males. The poet Essex Hemphill recalls searching in the library to understand his adolescent feelings and finding little connection with what he read: "If anything, I could have ignorantly concluded that homosexuality was peculiar to white people."[17]

Yet perceiving gayness as white is more than a simple reaction to media or literary stereotypes. The more homosexuality seems to threaten the black community, the more it is denounced as not indigenous to it. A black homosexual, it is assumed, *learns* to be gay by associating with whites.[18] It is an outside contagion:

Our folks, since the Black Power movement of the 1960s, have looked at us as doing the "white thing," as being totally immersed in the degeneracy of white America (in which homosexuality stood as an icon). . . . It represents a violent self-hate, one which is acted out by sleeping with white people to *become* them.[19]

He or she might be accused of switching affiliation and loyalty, a political betrayal. This charge was explicitly leveled at James Baldwin.[20] Moreover, because same-gender sex has traditionally had different social meanings in Africa than in the West, the gay identity is easily portrayed as a New World phenomenon to which black people, as involuntary immigrants, have been exposed.[21]

A sign protesting a gay book exhibit in Zimbabwe epitomizes the contemporary African version of this position: "Gays are from Europe. Leave Africa for the Africans."[22] Some African leaders have vowed to eradicate such "alien practices."[23] A lesbian in Cameroon was arrested, raped, and starved by police, then forced by her family to be cured of her attractions by a traditional healer.[24] A woman in Zimbabwe still bears the scars of "nips" all over her body, evidence of the scourge to which she was subjected after forced trips to psychiatrists and doctors yielded nothing. When she threatened to kill herself, her mother replied, "Carry on, then. It'll save me the embarrassment."[25] These attitudes threaten African Americans when Afro-centrism is invoked.

Significant in being overlooked is coastal Kenya, where Arabic influences persist. There one may find male couples in which the feminized "msenge" is trained to serve his "husband." Yet msenges are still pressured to marry women and father children and are routinely ridiculed.[26]

Black American views of homosexuality as genocidal and infectious can only have been amplified by the advent of AIDS. Although intravenous drug use and unprotected heterosexual sex are frequent routes of HIV transmission in communities of color, the image of AIDS as a gay disease remains strong in America.

*Homosexuality as Weak.* Another factor that makes African American homosexuality problematical is the historical issue of virility. Black men have suffered both *de facto* and *de jure* assaults on their traditional manhood. The ravages during and after slavery—not being able to provide and care for one's family, forced dispersal, castration, the routine rape of women, the epithet "boy," and the subsequent humiliations of the law enforcement, education, health and welfare systems—have left a legacy of sensitivity about emasculation. One critic actually claims prisons convert black men to homosexuality.[27]

And others in the community resent male homosexuality as feminizing and weakening. Speaking at a rally in support of Louis Farrakhan's leadership of the 1995 Million Man March, a prominent black minister asked, "What do you want, some Milquetoast sissy faggot to lead you into the promised land?"[28] And rapsters intone, "Real niggers ain't faggots."[29] Homosexuality renders one less than a man and less than fully black: "By the tenets of black macho, black gay man is a triple negation. . . . I am game for play, to be used, joked about, put down, beaten, slapped, and bashed, not just by illiterate homophobic thugs in the night, but by black American culture's best and brightest."[30]

Homosexuality, a resented white imposition, plays an internal scapegoating function as well. Black homophobia represents a psychic shifting of the burdens of racism:

> What lies at the heart, I believe, of black America's pervasive cultural homophobia is the desperate need for a convenient Other *within* the community, yet not truly *of* the community, . . . an essential Other against which black men and boys maturing, struggling with self-doubt, anxiety, feelings of political, economic, social, and sexual inadequacy—even impotence—can always measure themselves and by comparison seem strong, adept, empowered, superior.[31]

***Homosexuality as Sin.***   When religious proscriptions are added to these potent racial concerns, the authority of the African American minister seals the argument against homosexuality. Church members are exhorted to condemn it as sin and cast it out.[32] Repeated exposure to such views reinforces revulsion among many heterosexuals and causes black gays and lesbians great suffering: "The elders started coming down on me heavy. . . . I didn't want them to excommunicate me. I felt I wouldn't have anything to live for. See, I was told from day one that without the church you're nothing; you're as good as dead. So I ran from them."[33]

Although the church is a binding force for the community, it is a source of estrangement for its homosexual sons and daughters.[34] Nor are Christians alone in these views; proponents of Muslim and African tribal religions are not outdone in their fulminations. Farrakhan himself attacks homosexuality as "degenerate crap."[35]

*Class Aspirations.*   Attacks from the pulpit may be abetted by psychological inducements to sexual respectability. Some African Americans compensate for the myth of black hypersexuality by denouncing homosexuals as perverse and oversexed.[36] It has been suggested that poor and working-class "segregated" blacks are more accepting of sexual diversity than are the black middle class.[37] The aversion can be so strong that parents would rather have people think their sons contracted HIV through injection drug use than through homosexual activity.[38]

*Tolerance.*   Some charge that we do not hear enough from those who have lived contentedly in their communities.[39] Indeed homosexual African Americans, long a part of the black family and culture, have sometimes found a degree of acceptance. Yet it appears that their place is conditional. Toleration is contingent on their maintaining an old-style identity "in the life," that is, keeping quiet, not embarrassing the community, and perhaps having a family. They are "the invisible brothers, . . . the choirboys harboring secrets, the uncle living in an impeccable flat with a roommate who sleeps down the hall when family visits; men of power and humble peasantry, reduced to silence and invisibility for the safety they procure from these constructions."[40]

Claiming an open and proud gay identity is not permitted. Talking about it may itself be discouraged as a white practice.[41]

One of the saddest chapters in black gay history was the expulsion of Bayard Rustin, mastermind of the 1963 March on Washington, from the ranks of prominent civil rights pioneers. Black leaders and clergy, J. Edgar Hoover, and Senator Strom Thurmond coerced Martin Luther King Jr. to distance himself from Rustin in part because of his relatively unhidden homosexuality.[42] A popular black nationalist magazine dubbed Rustin "that little fairy."[43] Vilification of his sexuality continues today in the rhetoric of the Nation of Islam.[44] The homophobic denial that ignores Rustin's full story is also found in the criticism of a black gay writer for including minor homosexual characters in his novel about the Harlem Renaissance.[45]

*Lesbians.*   Religious and cultural imperatives for marriage and childbearing are as demanding on black women as on men. Failure to heed these obligations may be even less overlooked for women. Like other victims of the double standard, black women are not commonly allowed the sexual prerogatives available to males.[46] Some observe that, if he has position, power, and money, even a gay black man is given greater sexual leeway than his female or poorer counterparts. Black lesbians, lower in status than their heterosexual sisters,[47] are disparaged but are still expected to marry.[48] A triple restraint kept most black lesbians hidden some forty years ago: "It was hard enough to be Black, to be Black and female, to be Black, Female, and gay. To be Black, female, gay and out of the closet . . . was considered by many Black lesbians to be suicidal."[49]

In 1983, a black lesbian activist could still complain:

> A lot of Black Lesbians are still at a point where they don't want the Black community to know that they're lesbians. . . . Well how can you unquestion- ingly identify with the Black community when they are really not support- ive of who you are as a person or of your right to live in a society where you're not just tolerated, but accepted?[50]

A contemporary critique of the black liberation and women's movements decries the homophobia rampant in both and the erasure of black les- bians from black intellectual discourse.[51]

Public representations of African American gays and lesbians grew more frequent in the 1990s than previously. Yet, as popular as the novels of E. Lynn Harris have been among black women,[52] the majority of young people have not read his work or Audre Lord's essays or seen a Marlon Riggs film. They are more likely familiar with Eddy Murphy's fag-bashing humor, the limp-wristed caricatured black gay film critics on television's *In Living Color*,[53] the gratuitous gay rape scene in the popular black film *House Party*, the antigay lyrics of the Winans sisters' gospel single "It's Not Natural," or the public attacks of football star Reggie White.[54] One positive exception to the rule is the sympathetic gay man in Spike Lee's *Get On the Bus*.

Black lesbians are rarely depicted in mass media and then to mixed ef- fect. The lesbian in Lee's early film *She's Gotta Have It* is a troublesome rival to men. The sustaining lesbian relationship between the main char- acters in Alice Walker's novel *The Color Purple*[55] was removed in the suc- cessful film version, much to the annoyance of the book's author,[56] al- though heroic lesbian characters survived in the television rendering of *The Women of Brewster Place*.[57] Lesbian filmmakers have tried to balance the negative images with alternatives like *Go Fish* and *The Incredible Ad- ventures of Two Girls in Love*, but most young people's exposure to black lesbianism occurs via tabloid gossip on the sexuality of the stars.[58]

***Double Oppression.*** Many homosexual African Americans, unwill- ing to risk opprobrium, choose silence, but the cost of self-abnegation is high: "I cannot go home as who I am and that hurts me deeply."[59]

California Representative Maxine Waters has described a service at a black church whose minister was railing against homosexuals.[60] The con- gresswoman had been wondering why her gay friends would put up with such insults, when the organist-choirmaster rose from his seat and exclaimed, "There will be no more music today." He spun around and strode out, refusing any longer to settle for the old terms.

Some of the organist's pain may have ended with his departure, but the stresses of being black and gay do not necessarily diminish with coming out of the closet. Gay and lesbian people of color face additional conflicts. One of those is the matter of competing loyalties. The "black gay" versus "gay black" tug-of-war over the centrality of race or sexuality in one's life.[61] The question has been perennial in both the general and minority gay presses.[62]

Essex Hemphill once referred to a time when divided identity was thought to imperil the black civil rights struggle: "The defeat of racism was far too important to risk compromising such a struggle by raising issues of homosexuality."[63] For any multiple minority person, the relative significance of each of his or her identities seems to be proportional to the stigma attached to each. Homosexual people of color may have to decide which part of them attracts the greater penalty.

A putative hierarchy of prejudice often emerges in dialogues on heterosexism and other oppressions. Offended by white gay people comparing homophobia to racism, blacks accuse them of insensitivity and hyperbole. Heterosexism, sexism, and racism are of course not the same. Nevertheless, they do have some features in common. They are "linked yet different."[64] All three are driven by a systematic appropriation of power in which socially constructed stigma is used to demean and control.

Obviously racism and homophobia differ in the manner and form in which they are expressed. Second, members of some oppressed groups might have a better chance to escape attack by blending in with the powerful. Although race is usually more conspicuous, homosexuality, especially in the gender nonconforming, cannot always be hidden.

Rating oppressions either ignores the experience of those who are subject to more than one or offers to split them into fragments. Moreover, it is a futile exercise. Multiple minority people may relate differently, and with greater or lesser passion, to any of their identity components over a lifetime. Still it is unrealistic, even cruel, to require distancing from sexuality or race as a sign of allegiance to either one: "How do you choose one eye over the other, this half of the brain over that? . . . Which does he value most, his left nut or his right?"[65]

As a multifaceted whole person, Audre Lorde wrote, "There is no hierarchy of oppressions. . . . I simply do not believe that one aspect of myself can possibly profit from the oppression of any other part of my identity."[66] In founding a black women's writing collective, Barbara Smith observed:

> We are actively committed to struggling against racial, sexual, heterosexual, and class oppression and see as our particular task the development of inte-

grated analysis and practice based on the fact that the major systems of oppression are interlocking. The synthesis of these oppressions creates the conditions of our lives.[67]

Because of racism, black gays and lesbians often derive less support
from the larger gay/lesbian community than whites do and may thereby
experience psychologically damaging isolation.[68] "In this great gay
mecca,/I was an invisible man, still/I had no shadow, no substance./No
history, no place. No reflection."[69]

The antidote to this erasure is genuine inclusion, not tokenism, ideal-
ization, or sexual objectification. For example, gay photographer Robert
Mapplethorpe's use of the black male body, whatever its political or
satiric intent, has offended many people.[70] Although it might feel wonderful for a time to be intensely desired, it is dehumanizing to be turned
into a fetish. Of course, not everyone who finds beauty and allure in the
body of the "other" is exploitative, but the potential for objectification is
real: "Lionel was in love with black people but not in love with black individuals. He had an image that, because I was black, I was a stud, and if
I didn't continually portray that image, that would upset him."[71] Gay
and lesbian African Americans seeking inclusion must not be compelled
by gay racism either to lop off a part of their identity or to exoticise themselves.

It may be easier for some black people to protest their marginalization
in the gay community than to insist on a gay presence in the black community because they have long had articulate role models and ready allies for fighting racism. Still, gay and lesbian African Americans have
been summoned to come home aggressively, with pride, even in the face
of hostility:

> Confrontation means that we'll be called divisive. We can't let this accusa-
> tion determine our agenda. Too often the charge of divisiveness is just used
> to terrorize and repress. We will be about the business of nation building, for
> *true* nation building cannot be predicated on our exclusion from African
> American communities.[72]

The same political message can be expressed in personal terms:

> I ask you brother: Does your mama *really* know about you? Does she *really*
> know what I am? Does she know I want to love her son, care for him, nur-
> ture and celebrate him? Do you think she'll understand? I hope so, because
> I *am* coming home. There will be no place else to go that will be worth so
> much effort and love.[73]

Because he was gay, Marlon Riggs's manifesto to all black men had a powerful homosexual subtext: "In the context of so much violence, internalized anger, repressed emotions, and detachment, learning to love one another, to nurture one another would not just be *a* revolutionary act but *the* revolutionary act for black men in America."[74] His plea confirms the relevance of an antiheterosexist message in combating black male violence.

Riggs's language echoes that of an earlier figure. Huey Newton, a rarity among prominent black nationalists, condemned homophobia with the observation that "there is nothing to say that a homosexual can not also be a revolutionary. . . . Quite the contrary, maybe a homosexual could be the *most* revolutionary."[75]

The contemporary black community does not lack leadership on the issue of homosexual equality. Prominent elected officials have courageously taken positions ahead of many of their constituents. Thirty-eight of thirty-nine African American members of Congress in 1995 were unsurpassed in supporting gay rights.[76] During the 1996 debate on gay marriage, Georgia Representative John Lewis, a veteran civil rights activist, proclaimed: "I have fought too long and too hard against discrimination based on race and color not to stand up against discrimination based on sexual orientation."[77]

When debate reached the upper chamber, Senator Carol Mosely-Braun of Illinois likened gay marriage opponents to antimiscegenation campaigners of the past.[78] And on the thirtieth anniversary of her husband's assassination Coretta Scott King invoked his memory to demand gay and lesbian rights.[79]

Those who look abroad have inspiration from the new South Africa, where gay rights were explicitly protected in the 1996 constitution[80] (though less liberal provincial laws have been slower to change and incidents of cultural homophobia persist).[81] Outspoken Archbishop Desmond Tutu called rejection of gays by the church "nearly the ultimate blasphemy."[82]

In the United. States, groups like the National Black Lesbian and Gay Leadership Forum[83] and brilliant films like *All God's Children* increase the likelihood of healing old social and spiritual rifts.[84] The promise of full self-expression for gay and lesbian African Americans lies with such programs in their community of origin and with continuing antiracism projects in the greater homosexual subculture.

## Latinas and Latinos

The concerns of Latina lesbians and gay Latinos relating to gender, family, cultural survival, and church are similar to those of African Americans. Gender is especially vexing, as Latin American homosexual identity is constructed with particular reference to gender roles.

Latinas are frequently poor and devalued or ignored in Anglo culture both as people of color and as women. Yet they are often able to find visibility, economic support, and affirmation in the family as daughters, wives, and mothers. A lesbian identity threatens rigid gender role norms and puts the Latina's traditional rewards at risk.

*Latinas.* Latinas are said to have a special relationship with their mothers, who can be heroic models of resiliency against racism, poverty, and machismo. In the book *Chicana Lesbians: The Girls Our Mothers Warned Us About,* daughters write of straining this bond in revealing their unconventional sexuality.[85] In one case a mother who does not understand lesbianism and believes it to be a sin thinks her daughter's coming out is disrespectful.[86] The daughter in turn strives to preserve the relationship while still living out her sexuality.

Maintaining her racial consciousness in the predominantly white feminist/lesbian world is also crucial. Another Chicana lesbian, for instance, strives to keep lesbian solidarity from lulling her into racial betrayal. Trying to keep the memory of Mexican colonization alive, she deliberately lashes her white lesbian friend with the term "gringa," despite the latter's repeated objections.[87]

The demands of their native culture are another source of tension. Latinas generally are discouraged from discussing sex, acknowledging their bodies, and expecting or seeking sexual pleasure. They are expected simply to center on attaching to a man and catering to his needs. With that requirement come competition and suspicion among women in an anthropocentric order that favors women who are complicitous in their own victimization. A Latina's toleration of injustice is considered a virtue; her status as compliant wife and mother is deemed necessary to cultural survival.

The Latina lesbian's resistance undermines this gender system: She knows and loves her body; she seeks sexual pleasure; she needs no man to complete her identity; she does not compete with other women over men's attentions; and she objects to gender injustice. She is an affront to the women who accept the conventional arrangement and a traitor to the men who thrive on it. Open Latina lesbians are branded sell-outs to Anglo culture,[88] but if they keep their sexuality hidden, they may be allowed their places in the family and community.

Catholicism, another keystone of Latin American life, must also be grappled with. A perennial opponent of feminist positions on sexuality, the church's doctrinal condemnations help sustain cultural suspicions, ignorance, and animosity toward homosexuality. Latin lesbians and gays are therefore likely to become disaffected from their spiritual traditions.[89]

***Latinos and Dominance.*** Latino/Mexicano sexuality labeling has more to do with power than with gender. The evaluative criterion for men who have sex with other men is aggression versus submission. Because the female is considered inferior, a man who appears to take the female (i.e., passive) role in sex is devalued.[90] The "passivo," (also "cochón," "joto," or "puto") is therefore scorned: "The 'faggot' is the object of Chicano/Mexicano's contempt because he is consciously choosing a role his culture tells him to despise. That of a woman."[91] In the words of Octavio Paz, "The passive agent is an abject, degraded being."[92]

The "activo" (also "mayate" or "machisto"), however, is not derided—he is merely thought to be availing himself of the male privilege of insertion. An official of a Brazilian gay rights group observes, "Married bisexual Brazilians don't see themselves as gay. They'll harass gay guys, even guys they've had sex with, just so they aren't identified. A lot of the killers are people who have slept with their victims."[93]

Among Mexicano/Chicanos, an older activo often penetrates a younger effeminate passivo. The majority of these young men ("maricóns") begin such sexual activities before puberty, commonly with relatives, but they do not always remain passive throughout their adulthood. On the occasions when two activos have sexual relations, they are likely to assume active and passive roles, according to their relative virility, and never vary within that pairing, though each may take a different role with another partner.[94]

The conferring of respectability on the insertive partner resembles ancient Greek deference to the masculine ideal. But among Latin Americans, the practice may also spring from a need to identify with their conquistador forebears rather than with their vanquished Indian ancestors.[95] Sensitivity over "insertive" sexuality is a part of the African American sensibility as well, but it is hardly unique to either group. Patriarchal Arab and Mediterranean cultures attach greater significance to insertive and receptive roles than to the gender of partners.[96] Indeed, images of anal receptivity are common in American male insult and in metaphors for being defeated, cheated, or humiliated.

Among Latinos neither the active nor passive partner is usually considered gay in the European/North American sense. The identities of men having sex with other men are influenced by a number of factors including apparent masculinity, social class/mobility, contact with white gay culture, and capacity for survival as a cultural outcast.[97] Activos who adopt a modern gay identity put their male privilege at risk, although they are permitted to continue their domination of passivos, who, for their part, have less male status to lose.

Although effeminacy is seen as harmless entertainment and macho homosexual behavior can be overlooked as long as it remains relatively clandestine, a Latino's self-proclaimed gay identity, like open lesbianism, is seen as an assault on family and church, and hence on the lifeblood of the community.[98] Feigning and deliberate blindness flourish in this environment. "They may say they are horrified, that gayness is a taboo. But on the other hand, they can almost always overcome it by pretending."[99]

*Consequences.*   The burdens of conforming to community norms are intense. One young man in an East Los Angeles Latino men's group exasperatingly described his mother's denial, her encouragement that he have sex with a female friend, and her keeping his sexuality secret from his younger siblings. Another member explained, "Unless I bring home grandchildren, I'll never win mom's approval."[100]

In Central and South America, the consequences of exposure can be dire. A gay Venezuelan came out on a radio program in his country and was kidnapped, beaten, and repeatedly raped. Granted asylum in the United States, he later testified that his gay compatriots were routinely arrested, beaten, denied jobs, and expelled from school.[101] In Brazil, where 74 cities have gay rights protections, at least on paper, and thousands applaud flamboyant Carnival displays, one homosexual is killed every three days, often by stabbing.[102] A gay Brazilian, also an applicant for U.S. asylum, was raped at gunpoint by police, then taken to jail where the commanding officer invited other inmates to gang-rape and beat him.[103] Transvestite prostitutes are regularly attacked, degraded, and robbed, even by police and prison guards, in Mexico City.[104] And although Fidel Castro has reversed his position that homosexuality is deviant, social acceptance lags in Cuba.[105]

The Argentine military regime of the 1970s and 1980s denied gays full citizenship and sometimes arrested or murdered them. A new democratic government granted spousal benefits to same-gender couples in 1997 and discriminatory laws began to be repealed. Nonetheless, despite the apparent sexuality revolution in the urban centers, intolerance still festers in the provinces, as in North America.[106]

### Asian Americans

The Asian American community is composed of cultures as varied as Asia itself, and each generally identifies with its ancestral homeland. Moreover, recently arrived immigrants constituted some 60 percent of Asian Americans in 1989.[107] Despite differences of origin, however, homosexual Asian Americans have formed pan-Asian groups, such as Asian Lesbians of the East Coast, Asian Pacifica Sisters, Gay Asian and Pacific Islander Men of New York, Older Asian Sisters in Solidarity, Khush, and Trikone.[108]

Some participate more in lesbian and gay social and political affairs than in their ethnic communities.[109] This coming together might be made easier because of similarities in views toward homosexuality in various Asian cultures or even by common experiences of white racism.[110] Notwithstanding the exigencies of American identity politics, however, ancient and modern intercultural hostilities of constituent Asian groups are not always forgotten.[111]

Characterizations of gay and lesbian Asian Americans are based primarily on surveys and interviews with members of homosexual groups and on contributions to gay/lesbian anthologies rather than on more general samples. As in all the research on homosexuality, such sources are not necessarily representative.

Given then that the Asian and Pacific Islander gay and lesbian community is rather an ad hoc grouping, what are its common identity issues? Not surprisingly, they approximate African American and Hispanic concerns: community, family, gender, and multiple oppressions.

*Estrangement.* Like others, Asian American culture commonly regards homosexuality as a white, Western phenomenon.[112] Many gay and lesbian Asians end up feeling cut off from a community that will not recognize or honor their presence: "I wish I could tell my parents—they are the only ones who do not know about my gay identity, but I am sure that they would reject me. There is no frame of reference to understand homosexuality in Asian-American culture."[113]

Immigrant and American-born Asians are disturbed by having to find validation in "foreign" terms for their deep and seemingly unusual desires. This self-discovery process, "reframing the past with present knowledge,"[114] is not neat and linear but is a spiral of doubt and denial, beset with inherited taboos.

Self-exploration of any kind is incompatible with the Asian disdain for individualism. Self-concept is supposed to be subsumed in one's social, particularly one's familial, role. Chinese family members are rarely referred to by their given names, but rather by their family position—third sister, little brother, and so forth. The individual is constrained both in expression and action by reverence for lineage and Confucian emphasis on role and duty.[115]

Of homosexual Chinese Americans, 77 percent do come out to family members, yet only 26 percent of those come out to their parents.[116] A significant number also find it harder to disclose to other Asians than to non-Asians.[117] The prospect of dishonoring and being shunned by elders and families induces guilt[118] and frustration.[119] One gay Asian man wrote: "I'm an outsider, an outcast in my natural community, a hidden silenced nonperson. To participate in the life of my family, I bury my sexuality, my politics, my anger as deeply as possible; I suspect there's a secret dread in my family that I might ultimately shame them horribly."[120]

**Privacy and Shame.**   Sexuality of any kind is not a topic for Chinese public discourse, since one does not have a public sexuality. It is a private matter between partners that might be discussed with closest friends and family but often is not.[121] Private erotic expression itself can be so subtle as to appear nonsexual.[122]

In Japan, however, the open sale and popularity of pornography, even violent and misogynist comic books, are testaments to boisterous male-centered heterosexuality. But because homosexuality is discomforting, the Japanese pretend it is not there.[123] In one poll, 65 percent of Japanese said they did not "understand" homosexuality.[124] The nation's first march for gay and lesbian rights proceeded through Tokyo with 200 (lesbian-only) participants in the fall of 1997;[125] and a few months later, the family of deceased writer Yukio Mishima successfully petitioned a court to block the publication of his gay letters.[126]

Non-Christian, non-Islamic Asian proscriptions against homosexuality are not rooted in the concept of sin, but rather in the more practical soil of social maintenance—in gender role and family obligations. Although Satan does not lurk in its forbidden precincts, sex is for strengthening the family unit, not for individualistic fulfillment. Women are valued as deferential daughters, wives, and mothers; men are expected to carry on the family name, to provide, and decide. To refuse these roles brings shame to one's immediate family:

> If a daughter or son is lesbian or gay, the implication is that, not only is the child rejecting the traditional role of a wife-mother or son-father but also that the parents have failed in their role and that the child is rejecting the importance of family and Asian culture.[127]

> Shame, that's a big factor. Shame brought upon the family. You have to remember the Chinese, the name, the face of the family is everything.[128]

Because mothers are responsible for child-rearing, they are especially vulnerable to criticism.[129] An Asian American parent described her initial response to her daughter's disclosure: "I told her we would have to move away from this house. I felt strongly neighbors and friends in the community would not want to associate with us if they knew we had a child who had chosen to be homosexual."[130] Korean Americans are said to accept homosexuals "as long as they're not in their house, not in their life."[131]

***Cultural Differences.*** There are some variations on these themes in native homelands across Asia.[132] In Thailand, for example, men must not be publicly effeminate but are allowed homosexual relations as long as they are not all consuming. Even if they have no feeling for their wives, they should be married, procreate, and put their families first. In 1996 the Thai government ruled that gays would be banned from teacher-training colleges because they are not good role models.[133]

Similarly, a male Pakistani may enjoy private gay relationships because they are deemed unimportant, so long as they are quiet and do not interfere with his family role. Vietnamese homosexuality, on the other hand, more visible since the mid-1980s but hardly sanctioned, manifests itself mostly in male cross-dressing—the term for gay being "lai cai" (half man—half woman).[134]

The Communist Chinese government policy of persecution and arrest of homosexuals for hooliganism changed in the 1990s, becoming in some places more laissez-faire, apparently so long as there is no organizing or speaking out.[135] There are bars and discos in larger cities, but because of traditional pressures, many homosexual Chinese men lead double lives, meeting for sex in public parks and bathhouses. Ironically, unmarried men are often housed with their workmates in single-gender dormitories, where sleeping in the same bed is unremarkable.[136] A nascent gay rights movement, whose members call themselves "tongzhi," or "comrades," is led from outside the mainland.[137]

There is considerable power in Asian patriarchal norms.[138] For example, Indian women suffer from both male prerogative and religious prescriptions. For Indian lesbians, these are almost too much to bear:

> Stop it you men, you Indian men/ . . . Stop telling me to be quiet, to quit screaming/because you obviously know more/and good girls do not shout/Stop telling me I am not Indian, just queer/that I don't deserve my rich culture/ . . . And stop telling me to love you,/my God-Husband, my Pati-Parmeshwar/while you crush me to the ground with/your ton of good Hindu beliefs.[139]

Neither is it altogether comfortable to be Asian in the gay/lesbian community, where racism brings stereotyping and marginalization.[140] One lesbian chronicled her constant struggle: "I could not accept the blinding racism and assumptions about my mind, body, and culture that prevailed in the white lesbian community. . . . They were defensive and uncomfortable about confronting racism in their glorification of sister-hood."[141]

Particularly irksome to this woman was what she perceived as com-pulsory lesbian androgyny. Presenting her body with an eye to Indian standards of beauty, she resented the intrusion of politics and the sym-bolism of butch/femme representation. Her opposition to these imposi-tions originated in an earlier rebellion against universalized white aes-thetics. As a child and adolescent, she had internalized ideals of Caucasian beauty, thinking her own body and those of other Indian women unattractive.[142]

Historically some oppressed people have suffered from such colonized erotic preferences.[143] Although the attraction of "opposites" should not be unduly politicized or policed, self-revulsion is troubling: "To go out with another Asian was not a choice for me. . . . I'd been acculturated to see white people, white men in particular, as more attractive. Even though I was brought up in a city that was 90% Chinese, or Asian."[144]

Conversely, Caucasians might insult Asians with objectification as the mysteriously foreign erotic ideal of fragility and passivity: "Stop telling me I am beautiful/You see only my exoticism/WHO AM I?/I am not your little Indian doll."[145] As with other ethnicities, the personality and autonomy of the exotic object are erased by such an embrace.[146]

***Searching for Antecedents.***   Being ignored or disgraced in one's native community and racially oppressed in the white gay world make it hard for a gay or lesbian Asian American to develop an integrated sense of self. Some have sought to validate themselves by locating homosexuality in their cultural histories. This project has required straining modern Western categories to describe old Eastern realities. They have discov-ered gay love in the Chinese tradition of the "shared peach" (fourth cen-tury B.C.) and the "cut sleeve" (6–1 B.C.).[147] Others have found same-gen-der sexuality in Hindu erotic texts and sculpture; or women loving women in the Mahabharata; or a feminine world with lesbian practices being undone by Aryan invasion; or homosexual norms being undone by British colonialism; or repression originating with thirteenth-century Mogul rule.[148]

Perhaps the most commonly cited Indian gender/sexuality construct is the "hijra," a still-observed tradition of male-to-female transsexuality.[149] Some consider hijras hermaphrodites and a few are. Many hijras have undergone medically risky home-administered castration. Objects of fear, mockery, or respect, they are exaggeratedly feminine and refer to themselves with female pronouns. Hijras wander among villages, danc-ing at births and weddings and bringing blessings.

The ridicule and the dangers of their castration make this tradition dubious as a way to resolve the gender identity conflict of Indian men who think they are, or want to become, female. The custom also offers only one socially sanctioned path to those who simply have homosexual desires and no gender troubles. To be permitted to love other men, they must alter their gender through dress, comportment, and sometimes surgery. Their plight resembles that of adolescent gay minstrelizers in the West (see Chapter 6). Gay Indians should find little precedent or modern comfort in such a tradition.[150]

### Native Americans

Many gay and lesbian Native Americans, condemned by the colonial religions to which their peoples were converted,[151] have also looked to their histories for reassuring images of homosexual precursors.[152] They have found over 100 years of rich documentation, depicting the tradition of the "berdaches," or "two-spirits" in a number of tribes.[153] But were they homosexual?

Berdaches were males who, often from a very young age and occasionally with visions of a cross-gendered life, rejected the playthings and pursuits common to their gender. Tribal reaction varied from mild discouragement to active approval. In adulthood, these men took up the labors, the social status (including sometimes the marital position), and the clothing of females. Like the hijras, two-spirits were shamans, especially regarding venereal matters. In some tribes they had nursing and undertaking functions and carried supplies for war parties.

The pivotal factor in a male's assumption of the two-spirit identity was his preference for work commonly done by women. Although effeminate mannerisms and dress were expected to be consistent with those work preferences, his erotic desires were less central. Still, two-spirits did engage in same-gender sex, often with a spouse. Their work interests might have led to their gender identity, which could then generate *sexual activity* but not *sexuality identity*.[154] The fact that others who occasionally had same-gender sex were not called two-spirits could prove that sexual acts themselves were not the basis for identity formation. In any case, for the two-spirit the significance of erotic desire seems to have been obscured by, or at least trailed behind, other identity issues related to gender.

Some anthropologists, such as Evelyn Blackwood, undercut this cultural analysis by challenging the very notion of "cross-gender" occupation choice.[155] They believe that work roles often overlapped and that rigid gender role expectations did not exist. Objecting to the conventional characterization of the berdache as "less than a full man . . . but more than a mere woman,"[156] Blackwood preferred the term "third gender" for the two-spirit.

Those Native American women who behaved like men were rarely called two-spirit. When they were, the criteria were similar to those employed for males: their early visions of a cross-gender destiny, unconventional work preference, cross-dressing, and cross-marriage. It was also believed that they did not menstruate.

Girls were actively discouraged from gender crossing by parents and others.[157] Once they did, however, their gender role was male, and they might distinguish themselves in the male pursuits of hunting, battling, and so forth.[158] They also might marry traditional females, not others like themselves. And although their physiology could be overlooked in places like the male sweat bath, their marital sexual activities did not require them to pretend to be male.[159]

Some attention was paid to anatomical features of gender-crossers. Male two-spirits in the Southwest, for instance, claimed to menstruate or be pregnant. Nevertheless, there was not an anatomical focus such as the hijras endured.

It is important to note that unconventional erotic and gender behavior could produce stigma in Native American cultures. Without the justification of two-spiritedness, same-gender erotic practice was condemned as evil or foolish.[160] Even a male two-spirit could be regarded as the village whore.[161] There is evidence that the Mojave baited gender-crossers and that some other tribes were ambivalent.[162]

Will Roscoe has tried to find gay roots in the Zuni men-women, like the famous We'wha.[163] He proposes that rather than crossing from one gender to the other, the two-spirit bridged or combined the social roles of both. Instead of calling them homosexual, a term he limits to erotic practices, Roscoe offers the label "gay" for their distinct gender construct, involving unique religious, economic, kinship, and social, as well as sexual, roles.

On the other side, Ramón Gutiérrez argues against such upbeat essentialist readings of Native American history. He advises a broader view of pre-Columbian cultures to accommodate the fact that the two-spirit status evolved from the sexual domination and humiliation of conquered males.[164] In the Americas, as in East Asia and Islamic Africa, vanquished men were forced into female dress and occupations and had to submit to the sexual advances of the tribesmen who defeated them. They also provided a sexual outlet for young and unmarried males, who might otherwise have disrupted the sexual prerogatives of adult married men.

Although the two-spirit tradition might have begun as a ritual display of male power over the feminized enemy, it evolved into an intratribal practice. Certain men underwent initiation and lost status, wife, and children, if they had any. By the late nineteenth century, perhaps spurred by Christian influences, families were ashamed to have their men become two-spirits and scorned those who persisted.

Revered social role or ruthless punishment? Is the two-spirit just a benign example of one's destiny in Native American cosmology[165] or was the tradition a form of cultural tyranny?[166] Did Native Americans with persistent homosexual desires have to conform to cross-gender expectations in dress, occupation, and social role and perhaps endure sexual exploitation and opprobrium? If they had conventional occupational and gender role proclivities was there for them, like the hijras, still only one niche to occupy? If there was such a gendered reading of homosexual orientation, it was hardly unique to Native Americans or Asians. The theory of gender inversion as explanation for homosexuality appears to have been the dominant view in the United States and Europe before World War II.[167] (See Chapter 2.)

For many multiple minorities, having historical homosexual antecedents helps to counter the recurrent charge that homosexuality is a white Western contaminant. As one Mohawk woman said of the two-spirit, "It has everything to do with who we are now. As gay Indians, we feel that connection with our ancestors."[168] But an Asian lesbian proposes an alternate less essentialist strategy centered more on the present: "We can look to our own societies and cultures for examples of strong female friendships and of the heroic rebellion of all women dealing with aspects of patriarchy, including sexual and economic degradation."[169] Another woman concurs, "I think my sexuality came more through my politics than anything else."[170] Both demonstrate that dignity is derived as effectively from the present as from the past.

### Other Ethnicities

The variables of gender, family structure, culture, and religion are also important among ethnic gays and lesbians of European and Middle Eastern background, for whom rigidly prescribed male and female roles and behavior have led to gendered understandings of homosexual desire. Homosexual males are thought to want female identity; lesbians, insofar as they are acknowledged in patriarchal systems, are imagined to want male identity.

The treatment they are afforded in their native countries is appalling:

- A Russian lesbian was arrested, expelled from school, fired from jobs, and threatened with institutionalization to be cured.[171]
- The white South African Army routinely administered shock treatments to reprogram gay recruits during the Apartheid era.[172]

- Open homosexuals may be jailed for up to five years in Romania.[173]
- Adult homosexual acts are a capital offense in Iran and Saudi Arabia.
- Three Afghan men, convicted of sodomy, barely survived being buried alive for 30 minutes.
- A Kuwaiti professor was fired for stating that homosexuality ex ists in her country.[174]
- An Italian self-immolated in St. Peter's Square to protest his social abandonment and the routine killings of gay men in his country.[175]

Young gay and lesbian immigrants can be torn between marriage and procreation imperatives on the one hand and inverted gender expectations on the other. If they do come out, they may already have internalized the gender assumptions or conformed to them as a means of retention in their communities.[176]

Cohesive ethnic families may alternately require that gays and lesbians keep their sexualities to themselves, as a condition of remaining in the clan. Adolescents might be retained in the family as damaged and pitiable[177] or victims of American corruption. Girls may have particular difficulty getting out of the home for socializing.

Even if they find some level of acceptance within their families, they may still need to hide from intolerant communities. Sometimes they marry and have families for a cover, while engaging in same-gender relations on the side. This arrangement is common in Arab and Mediterranean cultures.[178] In the words of an Italo-Canadian male, "The big contradiction is not getting married and having kids. I think they would find it easier to accept a married bisexual guy, who fooled around and had a family."[179]

*Religious Identities*

Traditional ethnic values are often matched with conservative religious views. Jewish, Christian, Muslim, Mormon, and other orthodoxies are not accepting.[180] Moreover, churches governed by authorities in other countries may be allowed little discretion to accommodate gay and lesbian Americans and their families. A sad example of this control occurred when the American Conference of Catholic Bishops issued a pastoral letter in 1997, "Always Our Children," to assure parents that their homosexual sons and daughters were not damned and to urge them to accept them lovingly as they are.[181] Within months, the Vatican altered the document to classify homosexuality as a "disorder" and advised gays to repent and "convert their lives more fully to [God's] way."[182] Over precisely the same time period, the Pope repeatedly attacked officials around the world for endangering marriage and family life by offering civil sanctions and benefits for same-gender couples.[183]

One option for homosexual believers is to observe a gay/lesbian-inclusive liturgy in their own tradition. Many congregations offer one, especially in urban centers. For example, the gay-founded Protestant Metropolitan Community Church (MCC) is flourishing. Moreover, groups like Dignity (Catholic), Integrity (Protestant), and Am Tikva (Jewish)[184] support the integration of homosexuality and spirituality.

Although wrenching themselves out of familiar communities, families, and faiths can be traumatic, ethnic and religious homosexuals who remain may suffer more in being ignored, pathologized, or demonized.

### Definitional Pressures

Native constraints and racism in the gay community are not the only forces that make it difficult for these multiple minority people to forge genuine identities. They must also contend with the powerful social constructions of sexuality in the larger society.[185] America tries to impress them into a uniform homosexual category with a prescribed script: If you desire sexual intimacy with persons of your own gender, here is your name, your psychology, and the repertoire of your activities. The differences in sexuality labeling, the ranges of meaning and behavior, which are permitted elsewhere, are unsustainable here.

Multiple minorities become objects of a compulsory homosexuality,[186] whose norms are enforced by straights and gays alike, sometimes vehemently. Like some African Americans for whom it is never possible to be "black enough,"[187] some gays and lesbians are disturbed by others not sufficiently homosexual—bisexuals, for example. Multiple minorities may thank the Western gay and lesbian community for lifting their self-esteem and lessening their oppression, yet at the same time they may chafe at its controls on self-invention.

The American majority must respect that multiple minority people can form identities that depend less on Western parameters and more on their native culture's terms. Resisting public, or even private, subscription to gay and lesbian labels could allow a person greater latitude for living his or her sexuality across a fluid continuum.[188] Of course that freedom depends as well on the liberality of one's native identity constructs. There is little evidence that females in any culture are allowed as broad a spectrum of sexual expression as males.

At the same time, everyone should understand that minority people can have epiphanies of self-recognition that give authenticity to Western categories even within native subcultures. Same-gender orientation is validated by their experience as a key component of identity articulation. It seems just as vital to be recognized and named as any other constituent of the psyche's amalgam. Witness the example of a Cambodian, who, prior to discovering another like herself in the United States, had felt utterly isolated:

> It's really important for me to feel that I am not alone. That I'm not a freak. Yeah, there are Korean lesbians, there are Chinese lesbians, etc. But there aren't any Cambodian lesbians. I met you just a couple of months ago and I felt so good. I was in tears almost, because it was like looking at myself in the mirror. I'm not alone.[189]

Despite the power of such examples, gays and lesbians should be thoughtful when judging the rejection of American sexuality labels by non-Western people. Some would charge with "hypocrisy" those men who have sex only with other men but do not consider themselves gay. Indeed, they deserve the rebuke if their aversion to a homosexual identity is anchored in a need to degrade passive, feminized male partners, for whom they have a gay-equivalent label. Nevertheless condemnation based on culturally variable but morally irrelevant social customs is not valid.[190]

# 8

# Counseling Issues

*They all have this in common: the primary interest is the penis, not the person . . .*

*They have a compulsion to flaunt their sex in public . . .*

*One of the main features of homosexuality is promiscuity . . .*

*Live together? Yes. Happily? Hardly . . .*

*Female homosexual relationships . . . [are] no less stormy; the girls betray and deceive each other with monotonous regularity . . .*

*But basically all homosexuals are alike—looking for love where there can be no love and looking for sexual satisfaction where there can be no lasting satisfaction.*

—David R. Ruben, M.D.
**Everything You Always Wanted to Know About Sex—But Were Afraid to Ask, 1969**

Discovering one's sexual tastes and establishing one's sexual identity and values are just a few of the complex tasks of adolescence. This intimate work goes on at the same time a young person faces the challenges of friendship, family, faith, competence, and vocation. The disequilibrium, stress, and confusion inherent in this period are no small part of the school environment.

Most teachers want to promote their students' affective as well as intellectual development. Educators do have a responsibility to support adolescents and their families through their virtually certain crises. Few would argue today that a teacher's role is narrowly academic, and even those may be brought to see the link between students' psychosocial health and their ability to learn.

Lesbian, gay, and bisexual students have some adolescent tasks in common with their heterosexual peers but, like young people from other minority groups, must also confront the emotional consequences of stigma, even into adulthood.[1] In addition, they have their own developmental patterns (see Chapters 6 and 7), impediments, and sometimes, mental health problems.[2]

The following account of events in a Massachusetts town offers a clue as to their possible state of mind. To deal with complaints of boys sexually harassing girls, administrators banned students from having physical contact on school grounds. Of course, affection went underground and paranoia reigned: "Couples hold hands in dark corners, and friends hug only after checking to see that no teachers are close by."[3] If heterosexual teens can become unhinged by such constraints, what must be the effects on gay and lesbian students, who are routinely forced to hide not just affectionate displays, but the very nature of their attraction?

This chapter examines some of the obstacles that may impede homosexual young people's healthy growth and adjustment and suggests how school personnel can ease their way.

## Mental Health and Risk Assessment

Clinicians have called for more and broader studies of general gay/lesbian mental health and have urged more consistent definitions of the "nonheterosexual" in assessing this elusive research population.[4] These suggestions should surely apply to youth studies, many of which are based on subjects who have sought social services or come into contact with police and the courts. The results of gay youth research may have been skewed by the availability of teens with problems.[5] For example, a 1991 survey of 194 youth in community-based support groups paints a dire portrait of victimization and stress, with over half having seen professional counselors.[6] In a smaller study of 29 gay and bisexual male adolescents, ages 15–19, 72 percent had seen mental health professionals and 31 percent had been hospitalized for psychiatric reasons.[7]

Are such statistics representative of gay and lesbian youth as a whole? Or are conditions actually worse than reported: Might those youth who actively seek support be *more* stable than those who remain isolated?[8] Or does greater suffering drive them to counseling? There can be no definitive answers to these questions until the few studies that have been done on larger random youth samples are replicated. In the meantime one must be cautious about generalizing from those who self-select into support groups and from the runaway/street-youth population.

The federal government and most state agencies have sponsored little gay/lesbian youth research, and results of some official studies have been suppressed.[9] Some states utterly reject Centers for Disease Control youth research, and only two or three accept questions on same-gender behavior.[10] Overall, "sexual minority students have not been characterized as an 'at-risk' population."[11]

TABLE 8.1   Identity and Behavior (in %)

| | Identify as Gay, Lesbian, or Bisexual[a] | Have Had Same-Gender Sexual Contact[b] | Identify as Gay, Lesbian, or Bisexual and/or Have Had Same-Gender Sexual Contact[a] |
|---|---|---|---|
| 1993 | 2.5 | 6 | |
| 1995 | 2 | 6.4 | 4.4 |
| 1997 | 2 | 6.1 | 4.0 |

[a] Percentage of all students responding.
[b] Percentage among sexually experienced only.
Note: Approximately 50% of all students responding were sexually experienced.
SOURCE: Commonwealth of Massachusetts, Dept. of Education, *Youth Risk Behavior Survey Results,* 1993, 1995, 1997.

Ignoring homosexual students in such research is a flagrant dereliction by public and private research funders. If they make any gesture at all toward gay youth, it is usually in the context of AIDS risk. Then getting access to minors even for HIV studies is difficult.[12] For gay adolescent risk studies to rely on recollections of adults is doubly problematic: First retrospective data are inherently less reliable than direct observation, and second, older homosexuals' youthful lives may have been different from what young people experience today.

Despite such limitations, however, some government research has been done. The Massachusetts Department of Education Youth Risk Behavior Surveys (YRBS) are valuable statistical sources, for example.[13] Anonymous, random, and administered broadly to public high school students (grades 9–12), the last two surveys had approximately 4,000 respondents each. They have included questions about sexual behavior alone (1993) and both sexual behavior and identity (1995, 1997).[14] (See Table 8.1.)

In Vermont's YRBS 8.7 percent of 3,886 sexually active males reported one or more male partners.[15] Massachusetts students who are "unsure" of their identity are classified as "heterosexual," unless they indicate that they have had same-gender sexual contact. In a 1996 YRBS of 8,400 Seattle high school students, 5 percent reported being gay and 4 percent were not sure.[16] (In an earlier study conducted elsewhere, 4.5 percent of seventh- through twelfth-grade students admitted to homosexual attractions.[17])

Gay, lesbian, and bisexual YRBS respondents demonstrate high levels of problem behaviors. Moreover these surveys do not register the plight of those who have dropped out of school,[18] and they underrepresent those students who are chronically absent due to intimidation and other difficulties.

Based on the work to date, what is known about the causes of their dysfunction? Although there are some young people with underlying mental illnesses that can be exacerbated by their sexuality issues, emotional damage in most homosexual youth appears to be induced by heterosexism.[19] Indeed Gordon Allport emphasized how society can shape the personality characteristics of stereotyped individuals.[20] Yet Gregory Herek has tried to show that social stigma has no impact on people's psychological makeup and that their negative behavior is merely a coping strategy for certain situations.[21] Putting these two theories together, we might deduce that a stigmatized person's level of psychological immunity to his or her habitual coping strategies is a crucial factor in adjustment. (It has been suggested that many of those who do not adjust well suffer from previous psychological damage, affording them fewer resources to recover from ego-bruising homosexual self-discovery.[22]) No behavior appears to epitomize this conundrum better than minstrelizing, whereby a defensive surrender to stereotype can cross the line from coping with stigma to internalizing it.[23] (See Chapter 6.)

Although we should be aware of the possible ills to which these youth are subject, it would be wrong to assume such problems are unavoidable. To the contrary, many have survived and even thrived in unfavorable atmospheres.[24] In the words of one prominent researcher, "We need to know more about the personal resources that mediate or 'protect' gay and bisexual adolescents from such stressors."[25] Until recently there has been little reliable data, and it is still not clear who are susceptible and who are apt to be resilient.

Such an analysis of the Massachusetts YRBS began in 1998. Research Coordinator Carol Goodenow discovered a number of factors that seem to put some homosexual youth in greater peril. Those who had been threatened or injured with a weapon at school, for example, had 2 to 3 times greater risk on measures like substance abuse, gun possession, and suicidality.[26] Youth who had had sexual contact against their will showed similar profiles. Goodenow also found that those who had had same-gender sexual contact and also identified as gay, lesbian, or bisexual were at greater risk than those who had had the same-gender sex but did not self-identify. Much of this increased risk could be attributed to the harassment of those who are self-labeled or have little choice but to be identifiable. Further study is needed to confirm that abuse and intimidation are indeed the key variables. Whatever the final proportion of thrivers to casualties, there can be no doubt that gay and lesbian youth are in danger.

One comprehensive list of requirements for their and other adolescents' survival and healthy development includes the following: safety and structure; belonging and membership; self-worth and an ability to contribute; independence and control over one's life; closeness and several good relationships; competence and mastery; self-awareness.[27] Even a cursory look at these needs makes obvious the challenges to gay and lesbian youth for whom the risks outlined in this chapter are immediate and compelling.

Educators must remember that problems in these areas are commonly the consequence of stigmatization and rejection and not directly of the homosexual orientation itself.[28] Nevertheless, at the same time that schools focus on homophobia they should understand that it is probably not homosexual students' only counseling concern.[29] They are growing in more ways than one, after all. Furthermore, the problems that many do have as a result of their sexuality are not shared by all, nor are their responses to these difficulties necessarily identical.

## Counseling Areas

### Safety

Perhaps the most egregious obstacle to successful adjustment for gay/lesbian youth is the anticipation and presence of violence in their lives.[30] Statistics on antigay violence probably underrepresent the actual pattern of name-calling, harassment, and physical assault that is directed at homosexual adults and young people and those suspected of being so. A Washington State study found that for every homosexual youth who is harassed as gay, there are four heterosexuals who receive the same treatment.[31] One such was a Kentucky high school student. Repeatedly teased since the eighth grade because a school newspaper alleged he had feelings for another boy, he got revenge by shooting three classmates to death and wounding five.[32]

There is frequently no refuge from harassment and violence in the school, on the streets, and even in the home. One Colorado 14-year-old beat a gay schoolmate with a chain while shouting antigay epithets.[33] Four young assailants shouting homophobic epithets invaded the Maine home of two students thought to be gay and beat one so badly he was hospitalized.[34] A gutted raccoon was hung in the front yard and an evicerated cat was left at the front doorstep of the openly gay founder of the gay straight alliance at Sierra High School in Manteca, California.[35] And another student in the identical position at San Marin High School near San Francisco was severely beaten, once at a supermarket and then in the school parking lot, where his assailants etched "fag" into his arm with a pen.[36]

The 1995 and 1997 Massachusetts Youth Risk Behavior Surveys show startling disparities in violence-related experiences between homosexual

TABLE 8.2    Violence-Related Behaviors (in %)

|  |  | Homosexual[a] | Heterosexual |
|---|---|---|---|
| Property stolen or damaged in the past year | 1995 | 50.8 | 28.2 |
|  | 1997 | 42.9 | 26.8 |
| Being in a physical fight at school in past year | 1995 | 62.3 | 37.3 |
|  | 1997 | 24.1 | 12.4 |
| Being in any fight requiring medical treatment | 1995 | 12.3 | 3.8 |
|  | 1997 | 13.7 | 3.9 |
| Not going to school in the past month because of feeling unsafe at school or on the way to or from school | 1995 | 20.1 | 4.5 |
|  | 1997 | 18.0 | 4.0 |
| Being threatened or injured with a weapon at school in the past year | 1995 | 28.8 | 6.7 |
|  | 1997 | 28.1 | 6.6 |
| Carrying weapon at school in past month | 1995 | 27.7 | 8.1 |
|  | 1997 | 20.2 | 7.5 |

[a] Categorized by behavior or self-identification.
SOURCE: Commonwealth of Massachusetts, Dept. of Education, *Youth Risk Behavior Survey Results*, 1995, 1997.

(identified by gender of partner(s) or self-identification) and heterosexual high school students (see Table 8.2).

In one example of vandalism, a young lesbian's car tires were slashed several times in the school parking area;[37] and, in another, a gay boy's car headlights were broken three times in one school year. He had already attempted suicide at age 13.[38]

Both victims sensibly feared explaining the vandals' likely motivation to their parents, since half of gay/lesbian youths' parents in one study rejected them.[39] In a more recent national survey, 26 percent of parents *claimed* they would be supportive, and an additional 41 percent said they would be "OK," though unsure what they would do as a consequence.[40] It can result in worse than emotional estrangement. In a Philadelphia study, a family member had physically victimized 19 percent of male and 25 percent of female homosexual respondents.[41] Such family violence is even less likely to be reported to authorities than other forms because youth expect they will be trapped at home, having made matters worse.[42]

In an affluent Boston suburb in 1993, 97.5 percent of nearly 400 high school respondents had heard antigay comments in school. And in other Massachusetts high schools violent incidents have been the subject of personal testimony. For example: "We were picked on. We were called 'queer' and 'faggot' and a host of other homophobic slurs. We were also used as punching bags by our classmates, just for being different."[43] A student-led survey found the average Des Moines high-schooler hears about twenty-five antigay remarks each day.[44] Teachers may be complicit or even participate.[45] Although the number of teachers engaging in homophobic invective has to be small, the number who fail to challenge it is not.[46]

This violence includes rape. Anonymous reporting in Washington State over a 12-month period (1994–1995) documented the rapes of eight boys and girls for seeming to be homosexual:

> Overall, assailants [in each rape] outnumbered targeted persons by about three to one. Two severe beating incidents resulted in emergency room care for three people and in-patient mental health treatment for one. Fourteen incidents reported this year involved some form of sexual assault. . . . Six were gang rapes, with a total of eight people raped.[47]

Two male classmates raped a 16-year-old girl when they found out she was dating another girl. A 12-year-old boy was attacked and raped three nights in a row by four other sixth-graders and two older boys at a school-sponsored camp. Teachers had ignored much of the goading preceding these attacks, and in at least one case, joined the harassment.[48] Social workers note, "When adults tolerate abusive language, the next step is often physical violence."[49]

Fear of exposure and alienation from the community keeps young victims from seeking services and from reporting incidents to school personnel. Even adults who are attacked are known to remain silent to avoid being revealed or because they fear a hostile or indifferent police response.[50] Indeed, most jurisdictions lack privacy protocols and general awareness of victims' concerns.[51]

Schools seldom have explicit antiviolence protections for gay and lesbian youth, and those that do often lack discrete reporting and sensitive follow-up procedures. Parental notification, for example, a characteristic and advisable response in other circumstances, can be problematical. To escape calling attention to the underlying sexuality issue, some youth would prefer not to involve their parents. Combined with their assumption that squealing in general only makes things worse, this worry causes most young victims of homophobic intimidation and assault to suffer in silence.

Too often when they *are* called, authorities turn a blind eye to homophobic motive in order to avoid giving the impression that they support homosexuals. A second harm is done when both the attacker and victim pick up that underlying message.

*Belonging*

Can homosexual youth who are harassed or witness assaults on others develop a sense of belonging, particularly where few seem to care and where school leaders ignore even the membership of gays and lesbians in their community? Ultimately, they may drop out or run away from home, a dire loss of attachment.[52] The level of school threat is such that as many as 28 percent of gay and lesbian youth drop out of school because of harassment.[53]

Moreover, about 25 percent of these teens are forced out of their homes because of conflict over sexuality.[54] Boys are more likely to be thrown out; girls are often retained under physically and verbally abusive conditions.[55] In one national survey, 6 percent of all runaway youth were identified as gay or lesbian.[56] Reports in several large cities indicate that the real percentage may be higher.

Their isolation is threefold: social, emotional, and cognitive.[57] Narcissistically injured gay and lesbian youth rarely have a place to socialize, to share feelings, or to learn about gay/lesbian life: "I couldn't see or find a community of people like me and so I felt I had no home anywhere, no place to relax and be myself."[58]

The school and community youth groups that have sprung up across the country hardly meet the need. Sometimes, youth do not know about them: school-based support group signs are regularly defaced and torn down; administrators might not allow their meetings to be announced, possibly on the pretext of protecting their safety; community groups are regularly prevented from advertising their services in schools.[59] Furthermore, teens may be afraid to attend a group meeting in their school or immediate community and lack transportation to a more remote site.

Although some youth have opportunities to explore the increasingly visible adult gay world, roadblocks persist. Many live far from centers of gay and lesbian life, which tend to be urban. Studies have found that rural youth come out later than their urban peers do.[60] Potential adult role models in rural areas are more careful about revealing their sexuality, socialize more in private homes than in public spaces, and generally have less social involvement with other gays and lesbians than they do with heterosexuals.[61]

Community-based groups and some gay-straight high school alliances sponsor social events like movie nights, skating parties, and dances. San Francisco, Philadelphia, Boston, and other city youth have held alternative proms, supported by the larger gay/lesbian community.[62] A tiny number of openly homosexual couples have attended their school proms since 1980, when Rhode Islander Aaron Fricke shattered the heterosexual standard in federal court.[63] One Florida boy even won the right to attend his senior prom in a dress,[64] but persistent hostility makes such steps unthinkable for most others.[65]

As in the past, many youth first find affiliation through books and other printed material. The explosion of gay and lesbian publishing extends to works that adolescents find helpful for coming out knowledgeably.[66] They also discover antidotes to isolation through telephone information lines,[67] radio programming,[68] and in expanding cyberspace communities,[69] where those privileged to have links with the Internet can connect to news groups, chat forums, and bulletin boards. Some have been formed by and/or for gay and lesbian youth themselves.[70]

The confidentiality of the Internet holds the promise of increasing participation by geographically remote youth, those not ready for personal contact, and those worried about telephone billing records. If the information and advice they get is accurate and responsible, thousands of young people can be saved from loneliness, ignorance, and desperation.[71] Censorship of these on-line resource networks is therefore ominous.[72] Shadows have already been cast by the federal government's Communications Decency Act (found unconstitutional in 1997) and by retail filters like CyberSitter which block sites with any homosexual content.[73]

Regrettably for youth, the social epicenter of gay and lesbian communities continues to be the bars. Filled with smoke, alcohol, and conversation-inhibiting music, they are not ideal places for healthy acculturation. Although there is no great harm in underage youth sneaking in as a rite of passage, there is still risk in lack of supervision, alcohol, drug, and tobacco consumption, and impaired judgment.[74]

Adult mentoring in the community can also be scarce. Some homosexual adults avoid gay and lesbian youth outright to escape revisiting the struggles of their own adolescence or because they resent the prospect of young people coming out more easily and with more support than they ever got. But the most insidious factor limiting contact with the young is fear. Unsubstantiated cultural suspicions about recruitment and predation keep many from associating with minors. Unfortunately, the same misapprehensions lead youth to avoid adults or misconstrue outreach for attempted seduction. A deliberate intergenerational dialogue must begin to work through these misunderstandings. In the meantime, those teens who lack personal contact with gay and lesbian adults can find role models in books written expressly for them.[75]

In addition to being cut off from homosexual peers and adults, gay and lesbian youth are at risk of crippling estrangement from family, friends, school, community, church, and life itself:

- Family disapproval may alienate them from their natural support system.

- Unchallenged homophobia may convince them they cannot fit in with peers.
- Invisibility in school activities, in curricula, and in faculty role models may tell them they do not exist.
- Purported divine condemnation appears to deny them blessings.
- Dishonored status in civic and military life and caricature in popular culture may persuade them they have no future.

Unlike other low-status minority young people, whose families nearly always share their stigmatized status, homosexual adolescents are not regularly surrounded by loved ones to countervail societal prejudices. There is no family to say, "We're OK."[76]

Even in localities with vibrant gay/lesbian subcultures, homosexual teens can feel isolated. Their loneliness stems not from lack of exposure to a proud community but from factors related to their own families and friends. A clinical social worker who ran a rap group for gay teens in San Francisco found them shameful, guilty, and despairing over disappointing their parents. She wrote: "They've never heard anything positive about homosexuality. Without the background of peer and parental support, it seems there is no way out, no escape, and no prospect of things improving. The majority of kids I've spoken with have at least thought of suicide."[77]

Positive images and contact with healthy role models does not instantly cure this estrangement. Young people may think, "It's fine for those people to be gay, but not in my family, not with my friends, not in my church." And they may be right. Those they care about may not accept them.

Furthermore, it could take some time to build sustaining relationships in the homosexual community to compensate for the loss of those vital connections. Once gay and lesbian ties are established, however, they lead to better coping strategies and less stress,[78] a positive sense of well being,[79] better psychological adjustment,[80] and more intimacy in relationships.[81]

In the meantime, gay and lesbian youth are prevented by fear and self-monitoring from participating spontaneously in their school culture.[82] Sometimes their loneliness leads to depression and despair.[83] Indeed, depression often represents withdrawal from an unaccepting environment.[84] Ultimately, hopelessness and isolation from meaningful social relationships can lead to suicide.[85] The director of Gay and Lesbian Adolescent Social Services, a residential program in Los Angeles, observed: "When you go into hiding, you tend to feel more self-doubt, which very quickly turns to self-loathing and suicide attempts. All the messages these kids get from society say that they are no good."[86] Interpersonal conflict and rejection by family and peers trigger the vast majority of adolescent suicidal behaviors.[87]

## Self-Worth

**Suicide.** The American Psychological Association's *Let's Talk Facts about Teen Suicide* warns, "One of the most dangerous times of a teen's life is when he or she has suffered a loss or humiliation or some kind."[88] Thus, the suicide risk is high for homosexual teens, who often suffer the loss of a previous identity, abandonment by others, and repeated humiliations.

Statistics on gay/lesbian youth suicide are appalling. Paul Gibson's often-cited 1989 review of earlier reports makes the following points:

1. more than 50 percent of gay/lesbian youth have had suicidal feelings;
2. they are 2 to 3 times more likely to attempt suicide than their heterosexual peers;
3. completed suicide among this population may represent 20–30 percent of the annual total for all youth.[89]

However, Gibson's conclusions have been faulted for being based on little and unconvincing research.[90]

The study of youth suicide, difficult as a whole, becomes even more uncertain when sexuality is considered. First there is the general question, how are suicidal and other self-destructive behaviors to be defined?[91] Then, is sexual orientation to be categorized through self-definition, behavior, affiliation, or other indices?[92] Lastly, how does one find subjects? Convenience samples of runaways or service agency clients are nonrepresentative. Adult recollections are not reliable or necessarily relevant to today's young gays and lesbians. Youth who fail a suicide attempt aimed at escaping a homosexual identity are not likely to come out in counseling or even to receive it.[93] Nor do those who complete suicide over their homosexuality often want to leave definitive evidence of it behind.

Yet researchers other than Gibson have confirmed tragically high numbers in more current studies, some based on random samples. The 1995 and 1997 Massachusetts Youth Risk Behavior Surveys elicited shocking reports of suicidality.[94] (See Table 8.3.)

A similar Washington State report found more than 33 percent of gay and lesbian students had seriously considered killing themselves in the

TABLE 8.3    Suicide-Related Behaviors (in %)

|  |  | Homosexual[a] | Heterosexual |
|---|---|---|---|
| Attempted suicide in past year | 1995 | 36.5 | 8.9 |
|  | 1997 | 36.6 | 8.4 |
| Seriously considered suicide in past year | 1995 | 46.8 | 24.6 |
|  | 1997 | 53.9 | 22.3 |
| Planned suicide in past year | 1995 | 40.5 | 17.5 |
|  | 1997 | 41.3 | 18.3 |

[a] Categorized by behavior or self-identification.
SOURCE: Commonwealth of Massachusetts, Dept. of Education, *Youth Risk Behavior Survey Results*, 1995, 1997.

prior year and 20 percent had made attempts.[95] A study of gay and bi-sexual males revealed 29 percent had attempted suicide, and of those, half had made multiple attempts.[96] A fourth study found 59 percent of lesbian youth had contemplated suicide and 25 percent had attempted.[97] A fifth found 34 percent of gay male adolescents attempting;[98] and a sixth, by the same researcher with a larger sample, found 30 percent attempting near the age of 15.[99]

A 1994 study of 138 gay male youth found an attempt rate of 39 percent, contrasted with a 9 to 12 percent rate among adolescents in general.[100] Another in 1994, a random Canadian study, determined that 62.5 percent of male attempters were homosexual.[101] Lastly, 42 percent of a sample in community-based gay and lesbian youth groups acknowledged having made attempts.[102]

There is evidence that homophobic violence contributes to self-hatred:

> I just began hating myself more and more, as each year the hatred towards me grew and escalated from just simple name-calling in elementary school to having persons in high school threaten to beat me up, being pushed and dragged around on the ground, having hands slammed in lockers, and a number of other daily tortures.[103]

In one study suicide ideation was found in 44 percent of gay and lesbian youth who had experienced violent assault.[104] Washington State's study found 45 percent.[105] Researchers claim that the mental health consequences of low-level victimization may be mediated by family support,[106] but even students with accepting parents have reported suicide attempts brought on by persecution in school.[107] Robbie Kirkland, for example, was one for whom actively supportive parents and sisters, Internet links, and psychotherapy could not outweigh harassment, violence, a macho school culture, church rejection, and a failed crush. He committed suicide in an affluent Cleveland suburb in 1997.[108]

Although victimization can be damaging to all, those still struggling with the intrapsychic effects of stigma are more vulnerable than others with more established stigma management skills. Harassment might be more destabilizing for youth who are uncertain of their orientation than for those who have already taken on gay or lesbian identities.[109] However effeminate early- and middle-adolescent boys are particular exceptions. In a study of 137 gay and bisexual males, ages 14–21, suicidality was associated with greater gender nonconformity, lower age of self-definition and coming out, and earlier sexual activity.[110]

Gender nonconforming youth are less able to delay identification to themselves and others and are early candidates for self-reproach, isolation, and victimization(see Chapter 6). For these suicide attempters, the gender issue is a causative cofactor, along with a matrix of other problems such as sexual abuse, family dysfunction, substance abuse, and antisocial behavior. Sexual abuse was cited in another study as a primary constituent in a set of risk factors for gay men; John Gonsiorek suggests that the apparent vulnerability of some gay and lesbian youth makes them targets for abusers.[111] Gender nonconformity may increase likelihood of victimization.[112]

An important 1998 analysis of a 1987 Adolescent Health Survey of Minnesota seventh- through twelfth-graders found no connection between lesbians' suicidality and their sexuality. Gay male students, on the other hand, were highly suicidal, apparently because of a number of factors related to their homosexuality, such as female gender role and early self-identification.[113] Those boys who have sex only with other males but are able to disconnect their behavior from the gay or bi label appear to be at least risk in a number of categories, whereas boys with the same pattern of activities who accept that they are gay are at greatest risk.[114]

Many of these statistics may be challenged as inaccurate or exaggerated, but no one can deny that there are a significant number of homosexuality-related youth suicides each year. Two-thirds of a random sample of psychiatrists in 1987 thought the suicide attempts of homosexual adolescents were more serious and lethal than those of heterosexual youth,[115] yet few prevention programs acknowledge the urgency of the crisis or even address gay/lesbian youth as a population at risk.[116] The fact that former Secretary of Health and Human Services Louis Sullivan would not publicize or even comment on Gibson's paper typifies the resistance to this topic.

Meanwhile, over the cacophony of statistical and political arguments are heard the too common testimonies of despondency:

I was always an outcast at school. Books were my best friends. I ostracized myself from the rest of the world because I felt as if I could trust no one, not even my parents. The pressure of feeling so alone manifested itself in fits of manic depression, hysterical outbreaks, and eventually, suicidal tendencies.[117]

Some of the kids were putting notes into my knapsack with words like "faggot" or "fairy" written on them. My brothers, who always teased me about being gay anyway, really didn't talk to me or hang out with me. Nobody at school wanted to hang out with me because I guess they thought people would think they were gay, too. I just didn't see the point of, you know, being around, of living. So I decided I'd kill myself.[118]

I really felt alienated from the rest of the world. I didn't really have friends that I could relate to. I didn't want to die. What I wanted was attention. I wanted someone to look at me and give me that attention and realize that I was being overlooked.[119]

And from the diary of Bobby Griffiths, whose fundamentalist Christian parents rejected his sexuality as perverted and sinful: "I guess I'm no good to anyone . . . not even God. Life is so cruel and unfair. Sometimes I feel like disappearing from the face of this earth."[120] Bobby threw himself over a highway overpass into the path of a truck.[121]

*Other Self-Abuse.*    Mutilation and other self-abuse may also signal disrupted self-acceptance. Piercing, scarification, and anorexia might be attempts by gay and lesbian youth to punish themselves for their apparent shortcomings. Overeating too may derive from self-hatred or a lack of other fulfillments.[122] Moreover, obesity can shield one from dating expectations and questions about sexuality.[123] One researcher has linked body dissatisfaction and eating disorders with an obsession to impress men, hence with gay men and heterosexual women.[124] The Massachusetts YRBS has found gay males at greater risk than straight males for taking diet pills (18 percent versus 13 percent) and for using laxatives or vomiting for weight control (32 percent versus 3 percent). However, it finds little difference in these behaviors between lesbians and straight women: diet pills (10 percent versus 9 percent) and laxatives/vomiting (13 percent versus 8 percent).[125]

*Overcompensation.*    Self-worth depends on feeling that one can contribute. Many gay and lesbian youth give abundantly to their families and communities, often becoming caregivers as a distraction from their own needs. Some strive for perfection, perhaps to compensate for low self-esteem. They become overachievers, yet their accomplishments may ring hollow for them if their performance lacks authenticity. Stifling their deepest feelings and disguising their natures, they may feel like frauds. In fact, one study of gay male teens concludes that estranged from both the school and themselves, they suffer from a deep and abiding sense of personal shame.[126]

*Independence*

Adolescents strive for independence, both moral and practical. With the principles of their rearing as a baseline, they develop their own world-view and ethical sense. Reaching for self-sufficiency, many are confident they can fall back on family and other supports if they fail.

But gay and lesbian youth do not arrive easily at moral independence. They usually have difficulty affirming that gay is good in a culture that tells them it is wrong, if not evil, and that they must hide. Of those few that succeed it has been written:

> Their desire and struggle to come out is a new form of moral career. They are exercising a moral "choice," the liberty to come out and live as self-identified gays and lesbians, whose pursuit of happiness means that they no longer agree to live under the moral corruption and compromises of prior generations.[127]

How do they embark on such a moral quest? Opportunities for engaging in a balanced discourse about homosexuality are rare among their peers. Affirming literature in schools and public libraries is often scarce. Access to other information sources can be difficult. Positive adult role models may be few.[128]

Day-to-day independence, toward which most adolescents jostle on training wheels, is also more problematical for gay and lesbian youth. For them, the safety net of understanding parents, counselors, and friends is often missing. They undertake a private journey that can jeopardize that support. Homosexual minority youth especially, who always counted on homefolks for succor in an inhospitable world, risk emotional disinheritance in pursuit of their sexuality independence (see Chapter 7).

Sometimes support is removed literally. Being put out on the street is not safe means of gaining independence. Among other risks, homosexual teen homelessness can lead to survival prostitution and increased risk for HIV.[129]

In Minneapolis–St. Paul, 80 to 120 gay and lesbian youth are homeless on any given night.[130] One researcher found that 40 percent of street

TABLE 8.4   Substance Use (in %)

|  | | Homosexual[a] | Heterosexual |
|---|---|---|---|
| Alcohol use at school in past 30 days | 1995 | 19.9 | 6.1 |
|  | 1997 | 18.9 | 5.6 |
| Marijuana use in past 30 days | 1995 | 58.0 | 31.3 |
|  | 1997 | 48.5 | 31.2 |
| Marijuana use at school in past 30 days | 1995 | 34.8 | 10.4 |
|  | 1997 | 21.3 | 9.6 |
| Cocaine use in lifetime | 1995 | 31.0 | 6.8 |
|  | 1997 | 29.7 | 6.1 |
| Cigarette smoking in past 30 days | 1995 | 62.1 | 35.2 |
|  | 1997 | 54.1 | 33.6 |

[a] Categorized by behavior or self-identification.
SOURCE: Commonwealth of Massachusetts, Dept. of Education, *Youth Risk Behavior Survey Results*, 1995, 1997.

youth in Seattle identify as gay, lesbian, or bisexual and that up to half of the gay and bisexual males forced from their homes turn to prostitution.[131] The Streetwork Project in New York's Times Square reported 42 percent of 235 street youth over a three-year period acknowledged being homosexual; 73 percent of all the young people they surveyed admitted to being prostitutes.[132] Some 500 youth, many gay, have been known to gather at the piers in the West Village in the summer.[133] Offering gay sex for needed cash or shelter may also help some young men to rationalize their homosexual inclinations.[134]

Without genuine human connections, some youth become dependent on alcohol and drugs to salve the pain of emotional and interpersonal conflict and ease the intensity of constant self-monitoring.[135] Drug use may also provide an excuse for homosexual behavior[136] and cushion the blow of being discovered to be gay or lesbian.[137] The 1995 and 1997 Massachusetts Youth Risk Behavior Survey revealed dramatic differences in substance use between homosexual and heterosexual high school students. (See Table 8.4.)

Another study of gay male adolescents reported: 68 percent used alcohol, 26 percent once or more a week; 44 percent used drugs, 8 percent considering themselves dependent.[138] It also found 83 percent of adolescent lesbians used alcohol; 56 percent, drugs; and 11 percent, crack cocaine during a three-month period. The Seattle study found high risk or heavy drug use among one-third of gay youth.[139] The importance of bars in homosexual socialization and the use of drugs and alcohol to soften emotional stress are a double jeopardy.[140]

The onset of these abuses occurs before age 13 in a disproportionate number of gay, lesbian, and bisexual youth compared to straight youth: alcohol use (59.1 percent versus 30.4 percent); cigarette smoking (47.9 percent versus 23.4 percent); cocaine use (17.3 percent versus 1.2 percent); sexual intercourse (26.9 percent versus 7.4 percent).[141]

### Closeness and Good Relationships

According to Eric Erikson the twin tasks of adolescence are to find one's identity and to develop intimacy with another person.[142] Gay and lesbian youth are clearly disadvantaged if they are constrained to conceal an important part themselves from those with whom they seek relationships based in honesty and trust. Overheard homophobic remarks from unsuspecting family members justify their reticence. Neither is deceiving their peers prompted by paranoia: Only 12 percent of male youths ages 15–19 have felt they could have a gay person as a friend.[143] Some youth develop strategies such as immersion in academics or hobbies for avoiding closeness.

***Clandestine and Short-Term Relationships.*** Gays and lesbians who cannot be open may seek surreptitious impersonal intimacy. Boys in particular are known to sneak off to rest stops and other cruising areas,[144] but boys and girls both may go to bars for sex, not long-term relationships.

One-night and short-term relationships are not inherently harmful. They are common to many adolescents' entry into sexual relations and remain a feature of some adults' lives as well. When self-hatred and secrecy dictate these practices, however, there is less capacity to form sustaining loving connections. For some, physical but nonaffectionate liaisons keep a homosexual identity at bay—some going so far as to rule out kissing. (See Chapter 6.)

There are clear reported differences in sexual behaviors between heterosexual and homosexual students regarding incidence of intercourse, numbers of partners (in Vermont's YRBS over 3 percent of sexually active males reported six or more male partners[145]), pregnancy (see Chapter 6), and coercion. The statistics in Massachusetts have been relatively consistent over two surveys (see Table 8.5).

Both homosexual and heterosexual students who had had sex unwillingly were at significantly increased risk for alcohol and drug use, multiple partners, and suicide attempts. The three times higher rate of forced contact among the former merits full attention. This is a controversial finding that could be read as an indicator of widespread homosexual

TABLE 8.5   Sex-Related Behaviors (in %)

|  |  | Homosexual[a] | Heterosexual |
|---|---|---|---|
| Had sexual intercourse | 1995 | 87.7 | 46.1 |
|  | 1997 | 76.9 | 43.5 |
| Had four or more sexual partners in the previous 3 months[b] | 1995 | 20.9 | 4.3 |
|  | 1997 | 21.2 | 4.1 |
| Had four or more sexual partners in lifetime[b] | 1995 | 49.4 | 27.5 |
|  | 1997 | 44.4 | 23.8 |
| Been pregnant or gotten someone pregnant[b] | 1995 | 28.9 | 10.3 |
|  | 1997 | 24.3 | 12.2 |
| Had sexual contact against their will[b] | 1995 | 40.3 | 16.8 |
|  | 1997 | 40.2 | 17.5 |

[a] Categorized by behavior or self-identification.
[b] Among sexually experienced respondents only.
SOURCE: Commonwealth of Massachusettes, Department of Education, *Youth Risk Behavior Survey Results*, 1995, 1997.

rape. Yet, it is not clear if "against one's will" might be interpreted by homosexual youth to apply to undesired heterosexual contact, coerced or not.

One physician specializing in gay and lesbian adolescents believes that those who are sexually compulsive are so as a consequence of developmental deprivation.[146] A teenager so burdened is likely to compartmentalize his or her sexuality as a shameful, periodically quenchable desire, unrelated to the rest of life or to love.[147] As one young New Zealander expressed it, after frequenting public sex venues, "I thought toilets and what-not was what gay men did. I didn't realise there was anything outside that."[148]

*Health Risks.*   Furtive, alcohol-influenced sexual forays put one at greater risk for sexually transmitted diseases (STDs) and HIV. One-fourth of new STD infections each year are found in adolescents.[149] STDs infected gay and bisexual males (ages 15–19) at a rate approaching 50 percent in an early study.[150] Rates of HIV among younger gay men indicate significant numbers are engaging in high-risk behaviors.[151] Moreover, the extent of the HIV problem cannot be gauged wholly by the number of diagnosed cases. Because AIDS has a long latency period, one must look at the number developing the disease in their twenties to estimate how many contract the virus in their teens. A 1996 study puts the percentage of 15- to 17-year-old gay males with HIV at 2 percent in San Francisco.[152] The same study found seropositivity among young African American gay men at 12.5 percent, alarmingly higher than the 8.1 percent among whites.[153] A similar pattern of HIV infection was reported in preliminary findings of a multicity Centers for Disease Control "Young Men's Survey" among 15- to 22-year-olds: African American, 11 percent; Hispanic, 7 percent; white, 4 percent.[154]

On January 1, 1995, the total number of AIDS cases in the United States among males having sex with males (including those who also inject drugs) was already 51,422 (ages 20–29) and 477 (ages 13–19).[155] A study released in 1996 confirmed that AIDS was spreading fast among urban gay and bisexual men, ages 15–19 (5 percent infection rate) and ages 20–22 (9 percent), particularly among minorities (4 percent of whites, 7 percent of Hispanics, 11 percent of blacks).[156]

Some HIV incidence among young gay men is related to prostitution, substance abuse, and damaged self-image.[157] Research presented at the 1998 World AIDS Congress links high-risk behaviors to low self-esteem and prevalence of homophobia in the community.[158] A San Francisco study confirms that an individual's episodes of unsafe sex correspond to feelings of social isolation and low self-esteem.[159] A 1994 Boston study of gay men, ages 18–29, revealed that a significant number still engage in risky behaviors: 19 percent in unprotected receptive anal intercourse, 23 percent in unprotected insertive anal intercourse, 60 percent in unprotected oral sex.[160] The young men in this study who became intoxicated in bars and then had sex with new partners were in especially great danger. Indeed, a 1998 San Franciso survey disclosed that the biggest increase in unprotected sex among men with multiple partners was in the under-25 age group.[161]

HIV spread among young lesbians has been attributed to drug use, prostitution, and engaging in sex with multiple heterosexual male partners with the intention of getting pregnant.[162] It has also been related to sexual involvement with bisexual and gay male friends—50 percent of gay male adolescents have sexual intercourse with girls and are much less likely to use condoms with them than with male partners.[163] Older lesbians have been found to practice safer sex rarely with female partners and to be uncertain of what constitutes lesbian safer sex practices.[164]

Of course, HIV transmission is not solely the result of impersonal sex, prostitution, and drugs. Younger men, who are perhaps less experienced and assured, have a more difficult time negotiating safer sex under any circumstances.[165] Or they may equate risk-taking with erotic unconventionality and gay self-expression.[166] Some youth have illusions of invulnerability or assume that AIDS is an older man's disease;[167] others give up to the inevitability of infection or assume current treatments are the equivalent of a cure.[168]

Older gay men may engage in unprotected sex to affirm trust in their partners; in one recent study, the most likely predictor of unsafe gay male sex practice was being in a long-term relationship.[169] Among adolescents, any kind of monogamy may seem safe, even the short-term kind. New to falling in love, they might also feel that protection diminishes intimacy and that insistence on it would intrude in erotic communication or might offend their partner:[170] "If they have anonymous sex, they will use a condom, but if they're in love they think that will somehow magically protect them. There's also an assumed fidelity that's not always the case."[171] Or, "I call it a rite of passage. If they can get to the point where they can exchange bodily fluids, they see that as the greatest commitment they can have with another man."[172] One activist has even theorized that some uninfected gay men, identifying HIV with intimacy, intentionally convert to positive status to join a community that "live richer, more complex, more authentic lives."[173]

*Relationships.*    Establishing and maintaining good sexual partnerships demands some skill and practice. It is difficult, however, for gay and lesbian youth to learn what constitutes a good relationship and how to increase their chances of having one. Because of heterosexist assumptions, they have been prepared, from their earliest years, for straight relationships, courtship, and marriage. In their homes, their games, and their schooling, they have been provided only one pattern.

Standard health, sex education, and family life classes omit homosexuality and gay/lesbian families altogether, and only a few others include them freely and systematically.[174] It would be extraordinary, for example, for a class on dating violence and rape to consider the risks for same-gender couples.

Most homosexual youth do not have gay or lesbian parents to observe as they grow up, and only some have openly homosexual relatives or family friends. They have not been exposed to a range of literary, cinematic, or television depictions of homosexual partnerships. Although the media may have progressed from the freak show to the problem drama or light comedy, the details remain unexplored. Until the subtleties of homosexual relationships are treated with the same thoroughness afforded heterosexual ones, little can be learned from such sources.

Many of the pains in adolescent same-gender relationships are attributable to heterosexism and homophobia:

- Same-gender affectional or sexual play, alarming to many parents and teachers, is discouraged or punished. Gays and lesbians, therefore, have a late start at relations. If their sexual and emotional maturity lags behind their intellectual and physical development, relationship problems may arise.
- The need for hiding one's homosexuality can be a source of conflict in a relationship, particularly if the partners are at different

stages in coming out. Public exchanges of affection, normative among heterosexuals, can be dangerous for gays and lesbians. The need for constant vigilance diminishes spontaneity and may inhibit bonding.

- Bringing home a boyfriend or girlfriend to meet the folks is an affirming rite of passage often denied to gays and lesbians. Rejection of their homosexual partnering would deprive the relationship of an important support. Similarly, worries about losing friends can prohibit the introduction of a partner into one's circle. It is difficult to maintain a relationship that is a source of alienation from family, friends, and workmates. Mourning the loss of any of those bonds can affect the primary relationship.
- One's livelihood may depend on concealing one's sexuality at work, but having to hide one's social life and partner from one's employer is nerve-wracking. Gay/lesbian youth are even less inclined to come out to their bosses than to their parents.[175]
- There are few mainstream institutions that give social or religious sanction to homosexual relationships. The affirmations of state and church are important to some couples. The absence of material supports and privileges, such as health insurance, visitation rights, adoption rights, and survivorship, can make relationships unsustainable or demoralizing to the partners.
- The justifiable rage educed by heterosexism may diminish one's capacity to love and be lovable.
- Internalized stigma may cause one to think one's relationship is dirty and shameful.
- Beliefs about masculine and feminine roles can prevent flexibility and create discord. Expectations that one partner will assume a conventional gender role and that the other will take the opposite role are not limited to heterosexual couples. These patterns can manifest themselves in domestic, intimate, and breadwinning contexts. Questions about allocation of household tasks, passive and active erotic roles, or whose professional needs have priority might be troublesome.
- HIV and AIDS may affect relationships. Safe sex practices can be worrisome especially when only one partner is HIV positive. Grief over losses of lovers and friends to AIDS can inhibit bonding and intimacy.

Not all these issues are of immediate concern to younger gays and lesbians who are just starting to seek and form such connections, but they are nevertheless important in envisioning and preparing for their future.

*Friendship.*    Homosexual adolescents need friendships too, both with other gays and lesbians and with heterosexuals. A common stumbling block in relations among gay men derives from a lack of self-esteem. Having suffered years of denigration and internalized homophobia, they may be threatened by other gay men vying for partners, attention, or praise. Although lesbians can also succumb to these forces, the feminist ethos of caring and cooperation may be a mitigating factor.

Relations between lesbians and gay men also have not always been well cultivated. Gay men are not immune to sexism and have too often shown themselves ignorant or cavalier about women's issues. Some lesbians, on the other hand, have tended toward separatism, if not misanthropy. The AIDS crisis has mended the rift somewhat, due primarily to women's selfless work on behalf of their sick brothers. But many men do not get beyond token involvement in matters of importance to lesbians. There is promise, however, in the next generation, where cooperation and affection flourish between gay and lesbian high school and college students. The coed nature of their socialization into being homosexual is different from the single-gender passage that most of their predecessors experienced.

Genuine relationships with heterosexuals are sometimes hindered by the impact of coming out. Gays and lesbians often require a period of separation from prior friends and straight surroundings. Being among their own minimizes negative judgments and conflicts and provides a safe space for making new acquaintances and seeking intimacy. Some retreat more fully to live and work in gay ghettos, although most cannot or would not choose to do so.

One nettlesome feature of gay-straight relationships is that heterosexuals often seem oblivious to their privilege and assumptions. Inequities in acceptable discourse, for example, undermine good feeling. Habitually referring to their sexual partners and children, attractions, and tastes, heterosexuals appear to think everyone shares their orientation and the freedom to express it. Comparable statements by homosexuals about their love interests are often regarded as exhibitionism, hypersexuality, or callousness toward majority sensitivities. Gays and lesbians who find this double standard humiliating, or simply tiresome, cannot be faulted for wanting to withdraw from it.

## Competence

Confidence in one's own agency and abilities brings hope, goals, and resiliency to one's life. Gays and lesbians may have a hard time developing that sense of assurance: "I was under the impression that since I was gay, I wouldn't be able to do anything substantial with my life."[176] Regardless of whether one blames one's own homosexuality or faults others for being homophobic, this expectation of failure can be self-fulfilling.[177]

At their core, feelings of homosexual ineptitude relate to gender and sex-role stereotyping. Images abound of effete and frivolous gay men pursuing trivial "women's work."[178] A boy who is uninterested or unskilled in "masculine" endeavors, especially organized sports, is derided as "sissy," "fag," or "gay."[179] Gay has become synonymous with male incompetence and immaturity.

Girls, conversely, are expected to demur from aggression, competitiveness, and certain "male competencies." Powerful, assertive feminist women run the risk of being labeled "lesbian." Ironically, their skill in men's traditional pursuits casts doubt upon their competence, that is, their adequacy as women.

Most gays and lesbians are disconcerted, particularly when they are young, by challenges to their gender identity. Believing in gender differences, some may internalize the idea that their sexuality precludes them from claiming the stereotypical attributes and perfecting the conventional skills of their gender. They might be driven to achieve and appear satisfied by their apparent mastery, but underneath they think their incompetence awaits discovery. Combined with society's sexist/heterosexist expectations, such attitudes do not lead to expansive career ambitions, since "individuals develop interests for career-related activities for which they feel self-efficacious and expect positive outcomes."[180]

Some gay and lesbian youth doubt their own agency because they have struggled in vain against their sexual desires. Repeated denial of their attractions conditions them to deny all strong feeling and become numb.[181] Furthermore, psychological assault from family and others contributes to their giving up on themselves.[182] As adolescent girls, lesbians may feel doubly powerless and lose purposefulness. Schoolwork and attendance may suffer from their lack of confidence as well as fears of ridicule and attack.[183] Then academic failure just reaffirms their sense of incompetence. Some young men abandon safe sex practices, which call for a sense of proficiency and control over one's destiny.

### Self-Awareness

Homosexual youth are deterred from self-awareness by the twin ogres of denial and admonishment. Beset with fear and abetted by a culture that warns against and denies homosexuality, they sometimes are deluded into thinking that they can choose to be someone else.

Gay and lesbian adolescents have feelings that, once acknowledged, can explode their private and public identities. Inner conflict builds as they grapple with a new self and its certain social stigmatization.[184]

In search of an authentic self, some homosexual youth, and even adults, undergo a remarkable developmental recapitulation. After a first adolescence, in which sexuality is passed over or unresolved, they come out as gay or lesbian and then go back for another round of nascent adulthood. A previously heterosexual woman, for instance, might find herself in a same-gender relationship, trying to decide what it means for her identity and life course.[185] The new person can be at once exuberant and hesitant, giddy and abashed.

Heterosexism and internalized homophobia are not the only enemies of self-awareness. Young people have to contend as well with the limitations of sexuality categories to define them. They may struggle to integrate homosexual identity and customs into their lives while still maintaining their personal and spiritual authenticity. People coming out today are virtually instructed, "Your feelings make you a homosexual and here is the handbook for the rest of your life." It is important that developing gays and lesbians have role models and a vision of how their sexuality might be experienced from adolescence to old age. But homosexual (and heterosexual) scripts, even well intentioned affirming ones, can be smothering.

For the short run, finding one is gay or lesbian might clarify mysterious or troublesome feelings, but that new consciousness is just a part of self-discovery. What are the qualities of one's imagination, expressivity, spirituality, morality, lovingness, and lovability? Sexuality can inform these dimensions but does not define them. Accepting one's sexuality is a thrilling start, not an endpoint to mark the onset of complacency.

## Counseling Students

### Who Will Counsel?

Both institutional policy and their own personal hindrances might prevent homosexual youth from being counseled. Schools and communities may be reluctant to broach the topic, admit their presence, or provide services for them. Without the authority of explicit policy or law, individual school or social service personnel may fail to act because of moral or religious beliefs, fear of controversy, or being labeled gay themselves.[186] Closeted youth might shun services to avoid exposure or undermine their efficacy by not divulging their sexual orientation.

Assuming these hurdles can be overcome, who will counsel them? Responsibility may go to the schools by default. Despite a 1983 resolution of the American Academy of Pediatrics,[187] many physicians still do not discuss homosexuality with adolescent patients. Some feel the subject is outside their realm; others think it might upset patients or their parents.

Many are just uninformed, a serious indictment of their training.[188] A young lesbian has testified that in responding to her multiple suicide attempts "not one doctor ever broached the subject of sexuality. They later informed me that they were not equipped to deal with sexuality."[189]

But the neglect of homosexuality as a counseling issue may be caused by more than reticence or inexperience. Most medical, counseling, and school personnel simply operate under the assumption that everyone is heterosexual unless someone presents otherwise.[190] In short, they do not ask as a matter of medical protocol. A gay child psychiatrist in Boston has confirmed that his peers are often unaware of homosexuality as a relevant issue. As proof, he offers that he once gave some books on adolescent homosexuality to an inquisitive colleague, and the man began to carry them around and leave them on his desk during therapy sessions. Then, not so strangely, except to him,

> Over the course of the next few weeks, two adolescents who had been working with him for several years came out to him. It totally revamped the work they were doing in the psychotherapy and for the first time he had insight into the basis of the psychological conflicts. He would never have gotten to this information without giving a signal (in this case an inadvertent one) that he was someone they could talk to about being gay.[191]

Other therapists are indeed uncomfortable with the subject.[192] As late as 1990, surveys confirmed that negative biases and misinformation about homosexuality still prevail among many in their profession.[193] Several syndicated newspaper counselors are better informed than that.[194]

Some clinicians actually discourage clients from being gay or lesbian.[195] In the extreme, youth are sent against their will to psychiatric facilities where they are diagnosed inappropriately and forced into abusive therapies to change their sexual orientations.[196] Alarmed by the "latent homosexuality" of their sissy sons and tomboy daughters, parents may resort to such means.[197]

The barbarities inflicted on gender nonconforming children can begin with a diagnosis of gender identity disorder (GID).[198] In one recent case, a young lesbian was confined to a treatment center in Utah as a result of an individual educational plan (IEP) devised by her school and her mother.[199] Even a more humane-sounding therapeutic approach with young children is at some level coercive.[200] A youngster's distress over his or her gender (often reflective of family and community heterosexism) might just as well be alleviated through support and parental counseling as through behavior modification of the child.

Interviews with gay, lesbian, and bisexual teenagers from the early 1970s and the late 1980s indicate that many, if not the majority, consulted with counselors during adolescence through self-referral, professional referral, or compulsory treatment initiated by parents or courts.[201] Admired and trusted teachers are often counselors of first resort. Yet few teachers know much about gay or lesbian teens; even fewer receive formal training on the topic. Those who might refer a youngster for professional services sometimes balk, anticipating negative reaction from parents or supervisors. Out of ignorance, they might be concerned about entrenching a homosexual identity in an unformed young person.[202]

School counselors' perceptions of gay and lesbian students and of their responsibilities toward them are mixed. A 1991 study found that 54 percent of counselors strongly agreed that peers degrade students thought to be homosexual and 67 percent strongly agreed that they are thus more likely to feel isolated and rejected. Yet only 21 percent strongly agreed that helping them would be professionally gratifying and only 25 percent felt very competent to assist them.[203]

A large number reported they depend on professional journals, mass media, and professional conferences for information on homosexuality. Their lack of confidence and enthusiasm could arise from a paucity of in-service training, since only 16 percent cited such information sources. As if this survey were not discouraging enough, its 62 percent response rate leaves one to speculate about attitudes among some of the remaining 38 percent. The few studies that have been done of counselors-in-training show a consistent pattern of heterosexual bias and lack of knowledge and skills.[204]

James Sears confirms that counselors recognize the problems with which gay and lesbian youth contend.[205] However, in his study of 142 South Carolina guidance counselors he discovered that fewer than 33 percent thought their principal would approve of their counseling homosexual students about their concerns.[206] One must assume that many of the other two-thirds are inhibited by threat of sanction. Although most of his subjects favored civil rights for homosexuals, they also deemed homosexuality sinful and avoided contact with gays·and lesbians. This personal discomfort shows up again in their preference for workshops and readings over meeting with homosexual adults, including colleagues and parents.

Sears reports that counselors' attitudes and feelings about homosexuality were considerably more negative than those of their teaching peers, yet 80 percent said they would help students adjust to their sexual orientation. One has to wonder what their idea of suitable adjustment might be. Fewer than 20 percent of Sears's counselors had participated in programs to inform themselves about these issues, but those who had were far more inclined to provide services to concerned students.

When teachers and counselors are willing to support these young people, what exactly should they do? At present there is no research suggesting which school counseling strategies are the most effective in promoting healthy development and preventing self-destructive behaviors. What follows are commonsense suggestions, based on what is known about gay and lesbian adolescents.

### Alarmist Assumptions

For a start, educators must not assume that all homosexual students are in crisis. On the contrary, many show great resilience and good-humored adjustment to their socially problematic identities, although the public impression may be otherwise. Political expediency has required the use of grim statistics and horror stories to dramatize their needs. Indeed elected officials, policy planners, and benefactors have responded sympathetically to such alarms. Before the plight of these teens was spotlighted, a few modest programs with mostly volunteer staff limped along. Recent better-funded interventions have resulted from sympathy.

The dangers in this tactic are twofold. First, gay and lesbian young people repeatedly hear a shocking recitation of ills to which they may conclude they are greatly susceptible:

> I really felt like the students involved in this movement were really encouraged to act like victims. It's got more shock value and people are more likely to sit up and pay attention when somebody talks about getting beat up in high school than when someone talks about a positive coming out experience. . . . I mean I started thinking that I was going to commit suicide because of all these statistics I was quoting to people and I started thinking I'd start doing these things because I was talking about it so much and saying, "Look! Look! This is how it is!"[207]

Even if such suggestibility is rare, we should rethink a plan that regularly exposes these youngsters to such a ghastly picture of homosexual life. Second, we risk creating a self-defeating pathetic aura around them in the public mind. Trading hate for pity is not a wise course. We should take care to balance our representations of homosexual adolescents, affirming the joys and potential of their coming out, while noting their possible vulnerabilities.

Because of common hostility and rejection we can safely assume all such youth will benefit from ongoing support, but only those with psychological problems should be candidates for treatment. Then professional counselors and therapists should also know that where homosexuality is the issue, even the deeply troubled may recover quickly in a nurturing environment. The case of "Maggie," a young lesbian, illustrates the curative power of finding one's true voice, despite a significant history of psychological distress. Her therapist wrote:

> Specifically, I listened to Maggie speak about relationships and how they impacted her ability to resist and develop her own voice. I saw my job as helping her to acknowledge and learn about her own creativity, resiliency, and strength and then getting and staying out of her way as she listened closely to herself.[208]

### Broaching the Topic

Anticipating negative judgment, some young people are shy about broaching the topic of homosexuality with school personnel. Therefore, the counselor's projecting an accepting attitude best encourages disclosure.[209] He or she does not have to be homosexual to inspire students' confidence, but there is evidence that the more self-hating the clients, the less they open up to counselors who are straight or of unknown sexual orientation.[210] Counselors who are open to it should do what they can to invite disclosure:

- Put up gay-positive posters, "Safe Zone" stickers, or event announcements. Leave support service literature on information carrels, books and articles in the office or classroom.
- Take opportunities to show they do not assume everyone is heterosexual.
- Use inclusive language and refer specifically to gay/lesbian people in conversation with students and parents.
- Use nongendered pronouns when referring to student relationships and parents.
- Use the same terms that the student uses to denote his or her feelings and orientation.
- Assure confidentiality. (This assurance may not be possible in the context of suicidality or substance abuse, where reporting is mandated. Discretion is needed in deciding which underlying details of the problem should be divulged.)

Counselors may find they have made themselves available to homosexual students in unplanned and indirect ways. A lesbian student activist in Brookline, Massachusetts, chose to come out first not to her guidance counselor or her favorite teacher. Instead she sought out a teacher whom she did not know because another student had told her that the teacher once made a supportive comment about gays during a class.[211]

Students could give counselors reason to suspect homosexuality is on their minds. A student might

- dress or behave in a gender-defiant manner (though dress may be less an indicator in our gender-bending media-influenced culture);
- linger around in the nurse's office, even though they have no medical problems;
- refer to the homosexuality of a "friend";
- want to talk repeatedly about sex;
- relate a distant homosexual event in their own lives;
- show no heterosexual dating interest, while being otherwise gregarious.[212]

Counselors can bring up the subject of a student's sexuality obliquely by asking about relationships or initiating a dialogue on masculinity and femininity. Or they can ask more directly, "Are you wanting to talk to me about sexuality?" or "Are you concerned that you might be gay/lesbian/bisexual?"

*Labeling*

Students might seem to want an adult to decide for them what their sexuality is. Moreover, hearing their stories, sympathetic counselors might be inclined to clap them on the back and declare, in so many words, "You've just told me you're homosexual. How wonderful! I know what you must going through and here's what you can expect." That response could set a tentative student back.

Some have advised counselors to refrain from labeling or encouraging students to come out.[213] On the other hand, too restrained a response could send the message, "Let's not jump to conclusions. What you've told me doesn't *necessarily* mean that you're homosexual. You may still not be." This type of reaction is too negative, although it is less obviously so than "It's probably just a stage that you will outgrow," which is still sometimes heard.[214]

The conviction that adolescents cannot firmly establish gay or lesbian identities[215] is fading, but some counselors continue to dismiss or minimize students' same-gender desires, mistakenly fearing that discussing these feelings will encourage a student to become homosexual who would otherwise not.[216] A former U.S. education secretary has cited a school counselor's frustrated appeal, "What are we going to do with all these kids claiming they are bisexual or homosexual when we know they are not?"[217] When people did not come out until their mid-20s, it was perhaps easier to imagine that such identity definition was improbable in adolescence, but as the age of coming out drops, that position becomes less tenable.

A lesbian counselor confirms that clients can be reluctant to explore developing homosexual identities because of stereotype and stigma: They fret that they will be transformed into completely different beings, alien even to themselves.[218] She recommends respecting those fears and reassuring the client with the Kinsey continuum but also explaining the costs of repression.

A more complex alternative is to advise clients that socially constructed identity categories are illusory and that sexuality labels are less important than the quality of one's intimate relationships.[219] Counselors can explain the possibility for sexuality fluidity over time, yet also defer to the importance of understanding one's orientation at a particular point in one's life. They can suggest that the unsure advisee may or may not be homosexual and discuss what each of those possibilities would mean for him or her, stressing that either outcome can be part of a good life and would be fine with the counselor.

This counseling approach avoids sounding like, "It isn't real; it will pass; and don't, for heaven's sake, act on it." Rather its message is, "It may be real for you now; it could be right for you for a long time, perhaps all your life. Live the experience, but don't foreclose on any others." This kind of communication discards the assumption that coming out means finding one's true identity or that coming to homosexuality later in life is proof of long-term repression. The intent of this human development approach is to

- help struggling adolescents rid themselves of internalized homophobia;
- counsel them on coping with social stigma and family reactions;
- advise them to celebrate and cultivate their homosexual potential;
- caution them that sexual orientation is not static nor is identity fixed.

Adolescents may be dissatisfied with this kind of advice, even if they grasp its presumptions of social construction and sexual plasticity. Most do, after all, live in a nontheoretical heterosexist world that pressures them to develop a defined sexuality, and if it is the acceptable one, to make it obvious as soon as they can. Identity labels, even crude bipolar ones are important to them.

Young people police themselves and monitor others for signs of the sexuality script. How much attraction do they seem to feel and toward whom? How do they move? What clothing, music, hairstyle, and other preferences provide what clues? At exactly what point does one slip over the fateful demarcations from heterosexual to bisexual to homosexual or the reverse? Defining and displaying one's sexuality have real consequences, hence, the apparent relief in figuring out and assuming one's place.

It is one thing to help a confused, ambivalent, or rebellious adolescent understand sexual fluidity and the limited usefulness of arbitrary labels, but should counselors use the same model with young people who have begun to assume gay or lesbian identities and have come for affirmation? How would a student who is just beginning to find self-love, identity pride, and an exciting new community respond to this seemingly restrained and surely cerebral advice? Are these concepts not more appropriate to another time, when identity has solidified and relationships have matured?

Counselors may hope to free young people from the narrow identity constructs that society provides to control their behavior. Indeed, progressive educators should do everything they can to contradict the negative meanings and stifling dictates of these categories; but do they want to shield students from the positive affiliations and community that labeling brings? Would they warn adolescents that constructed meanings of race, ethnicity, and gender are harmful not only in their oppressive uses but also in their inducements to solidarity and pride?

Most adolescents are likely to concur with only the first part of Plummer's view:

> On the one hand, labels are useful devices—they give order to chaos, structure to openness, security to confusion. . . . On the other hand, labels are destructive devices—they restrict where other choices are possible, they control and limit possible variety, they narrow human experimentation. In the short run, labels are comforting; in the long run, they are destructive.[220]

However, some homosexual young people chafe against the label, sometimes subconsciously, and reject the socially imposed binaries.[221] As one high school student put it, "I also realized that although labels help us identify who we are, they are, in essence, degrading and often leave people feeling trapped."[222]

Homosexual counselors might be dismayed by their young counterparts' lack of identification with gay and lesbian history and identity. In their time they have seen harrowing discrimination and the milestones of gay liberation and civil rights gains. But their experience has shaped both an identity and a culture whose rigidity may not appeal to contemporary self-defining "queer" youth. Adults representing a community of support and celebration do not expect to be told by distressed youth that their proffered rescue is a mixed blessing.

If young people come to them rejecting sexuality labels, counselors should investigate. Do a student's objections spring from the inadequacy of sexuality categories or are they produced by internalized homophobia? It is terrifically intimidating to stand at the precipice of what they know is a momentous decision: to come out or not? Step over the edge and you fall into a transforming abyss from which you have been told there is no going back. One young woman, "Everetta," remembered her resistance: "I wouldn't admit to myself that I was gay, but I knew that I still had feelings. I didn't want any labels. At that time, I was still trying to be what I was supposed to be. And if you say you're a homosexual, then you are and you can't change it."[223]

Put off by the seeming irrevocability of a static identity, "Everetta" sounds like a candidate for a category-deconstructive "identities are fluid" kind of counseling. At the same time she dreads becoming someone she was not "supposed" to be. That is not a complaint about the narrowness or permanence of a label. It is a struggle with prejudice that has taken root in her moral system. Although proponents of one or another approach might want to claim her, "Everetta" is not likely to be helped by a single methodology.

A young male New Zealand rugby player is a purer case: "I just didn't know whether I was going to become some trizzie queen or something like that I'd been trying to cover up. . . . Suddenly I thought this monster was going to emerge."[224] Such students are clearly motivated by social stigma and internalized homophobia.[225] Like "Everetta's," their panic demands a comprehensive counseling strategy that combines the best features of both homosexual affirmation and a critique of categories.

These teens need to purge self-destructive thoughts and gird against societal prejudice. They must be consoled through their grief over the immediate loss of heterosexuality and helped to envision their capacity for homosexual relationships and family, as well as the possibility of orientational fluidity. They do not have to take on an identity and its community so exclusively that they cancel their individuality or truncate their developmental path. Whatever choices they make, whatever sexuality they assume, they need not abandon other aspects of themselves.

Young people in crisis are tuned to every nuance in those who might become their allies. In a society reeking of heterosexism, the main thrust of a counselor's response to adolescents who are just coming out should be congratulatory and enabling.[226] They should be directed toward positive information and role models (including career role models) and offered support for negotiating with family and peers. Cautions should be balanced by exhortations to make the most of their gay, lesbian, or bisexual potential, to enter the culture and tend to new relationships. For some, perhaps many, homosexuality will be the lifelong site of their erotic and spiritual lives.

## Students Who Want to Change

How should counselors respond to clients who want to be cured of their alleged perversity? The American Psychiatric Association, stopping just short of condemning conversion or reparative therapies[227] in 1993, stated that there is no evidence that they work.[228] Clearly, the record of successful therapy is not convincing,[229] and some research finds conversion impossible.[230] Still, therapists have offered cures and palliatives with varying degrees of optimism.[231] Moreover, church-affiliated groups, like the Exodus Ministries, have been adamant about their faith cures, though with little apparent justification.[232]

In 1997 the APA again failed to condemn the practice outright but did require therapists to make sure patients are not being coerced into treatment and to obtain their informed consent: They must be told that homosexuality is not an illness and that the risks and benefits of reparative therapy are not clear.[233] In 1998, the APA board voted unanimously to reject therapy that is aimed solely at a cure.[234] Its sister organization, the American Psychoanalytic Association, began to consider a similar resolution.

What constitutes a cure, upon whose veracity do reports of conversions depend, and how long do they last? Homosexual individuals have occasionally been conditioned to deny or ignore unwanted attractions and to engage in heterosexual behaviors, but the psychological consequences of such conditioning can be damaging;[235] furthermore their homosexual desire does not evaporate.[236]

The film *The Transformation*, for instance, documents the use of religion to convert Cuban émigrés who are transsexual prostitutes.[237] It is a heart-breaking example of the cruelty and futility of the practice. The very conditions said by reparative therapists to be requisite for a cure are not conducive to psychological health according to gay-positive counselors: conviction that homosexuality is disturbed, motivation to change, and avoidance of homosexual relationships and social contacts.[238]

Some therapists, while agreeing that homosexuality is not an illness or a sin, maintain that reorientation treatment must still be offered to patients who are unhappy with their sexuality, an echo of the old "ego-distonic" diagnosis (see Chapter 5). However, their ostensibly voluntary entry into such therapy is questionable. Client and therapist have merely colluded in pinpointing homosexuality rather than homophobia as the source of the misery. Reorientation programs, aimed tellingly at far more men than women, are not driven by objective science and pristine medical ethics; rather, they have been "shaped by pervasive and often unconscious social forces."[239]

Distressed homosexual teens could be helped to examine and cultivate their bisexual potential, if they have one.[240] But that course demands the exploration of the range of their orientation, not the amputation of one of its parts. Such counseling would not confirm or encourage a perhaps crippling gay or lesbian identity; rather it would affirm the homosexual component of a more capacious sexuality.

Some may grasp at bisexuality as a defense. Gay-positive counseling can help them cast off the shame that keeps them from complete self-acceptance. That does not mean they should be badgered. Dr. Ruth Westheimer's offhand-sounding advice to a conflicted 17-year-old, "I am sure that at some point you will fall in love with someone of one sex or the other and so be able to climb off of that roller coaster," is uncalled for.[241] One would have to work extensively with a counselee before concluding that his or her bisexuality was either transitional or maladaptive (see Chapter 6).

*General Responses*

More generally, when students come out to a teacher or counselor it is important to

- Express gratitude for the confidence.
- Assure confidentiality. (This may not be possible where reporting of suicidality or substance abuse is mandated.)
- Assess whether the student needs immediate extended counseling or if disclosure is enough for the time being.
- Make sure to see the student again, but do not assume that sexuality must be the focus of every subsequent interaction.
- Refer to the positive aspects of being gay/lesbian (solidarity, loving relationships, perseverance, diversity of the community, rich history and culture).
- Guide the student to sources of information and confirmation regarding these happy prospects.
- Discover the extent of disclosure to others and explore the consequences of coming out in various settings, including safety and shelter issues, reporting of harassment, stigma management, and possibilities for further support like referral to school or community-based groups.
- Ask about relations with family, teachers, and peers.
- Explore feelings about lost heterosexual identity and expectations.

- Discuss relationships, including courtship and breakup.
- Discuss alcohol and drug use.
- Discuss safe sex practices and the motivation to engage in them.

Discussing same-gender relationships helps students understand the special features they might encounter in their own partnerships. For instance, it is said that lesbians express a commitment to equality that is often not modeled in heterosexual relationships.[242] Some gay men, on the other hand, divide power according to income[243] or age discrepancies.[244] As a rule, however, gay and especially lesbian couples have been found to be more egalitarian than heterosexual ones.[245] Because many teens believe that coming out means abandoning hope of having children, they need to hear about creating families of choice.[246]

Young people must be given access to books and alternative film or theater, where homosexual relationships are presented in some depth. A stream of good fiction and a number of sociological studies and psychological self-help books have been published in the last fifteen years along with the production of a handful of creditable films.

Substance abuse advising should take into account the role of bars in the gay/lesbian community. AIDS counseling and education must be presented in consistent, detailed, and understandable terms within the context of realistic teen sexuality. Peer support and encouragement is essential.[247] The curriculum cannot be mechanistic, that is, restricted to anatomy, degrees of risk, and how to use a condom. Like effective pregnancy prevention programs, HIV education should be understood in relation to the determinants that influence sexual practices: self-esteem, love, communication, oppression, and cultural conditioning.[248] A democratic, pluralistic, respectful environment must be created for students to take account of their sexual lives and responsibilities.[249]

If any of these and related topics are beyond the counselor's knowledge or comfort level, she or he should refer students to someone better prepared to help, in either the school or the community. Lists of such resources should be available to all personnel. They may include health, counseling, and drop-in centers, advocacy groups, and shelters. Some communities provide residential options for homeless youth, including placements with gay and lesbian foster families.[250]

Even apparently well-adjusted gay and lesbian adolescents retain damaging bits of negativity about homosexuality, imprinted in their earliest years. A psychiatrist experienced in treating them observes that through each phase of life people strive to complete the unfinished developmental tasks of childhood, including for some the attainment of self-esteem.[251] Consequently, the counselor's chief role in working with gay and lesbian youth is to assist them in erasing the poisonous remnants of internalized heterosexism and homophobic stereotype such as those articulated by a young man from New Zealand: "I suppose I thought I was going to be very lonely and that everything I had planned for my life would be gone. . . . The hardest thing about coming out was having to change everything that I wanted out of life. . . . I had this nice middle-class family . . . with a nice little house which was what I always wanted."[252]

### Getting Perspective on Sexuality

School personnel, friends, and family may sometimes wonder at the apparent need of gay and lesbian youth to proclaim their orientation. When gay people merely correct someone's assumption that they are straight, they can be accused of flaunting their sexuality. Social conservatives and some liberals, squeamish about public displays of homosexuality, may offer such demurrers as "We don't care what you are, but why don't you just keep it to yourself." Of course these same censors see nothing wrong with "innocent" public expressions of youthful heterosexuality—puppy love!

Apart from representing a double standard, muffling homosexuality ignores young people's genuine needs. Even those who want to protect students from harassment may impede their growth by advising too much discretion. Disclosure is a necessary part of developing a positive gay/lesbian identity.[253] Coming out to others has been shown to increase personal integrity,[254] decrease feelings of isolation and help identity integration,[255] and increase intimacy in relationships.[256] Coming out and being accepted by other heterosexual adults than their parents can compensate somewhat for family disapproval. It is no fluke that the parents in P-FLAG (Parents, Friends, and Families of Lesbians and Gays) are the most warmly received contingent at gay pride events.

Occasionally, openly gay and lesbian youth tire of educating the rest of the world about homosexuality:

> Because I was out to everyone, people were always asking me questions. I felt like a permanent panel because I couldn't get away from the educator role. And I didn't want to blow people off because if you don't answer their questions sincerely then they are going to continue believing whatever it is that they are going to believe.[257]

Like some people of color dealing with racism, they throw up their hands, exclaiming, "I'm tired of this burden. Homophobia is *their* problem."

Unfortunately, they are only half right. Although adolescents do not bear sole responsibility, bigotry is everybody's problem. Adults should encourage their participation in the ongoing public campaign to dispel homophobic ignorance. Doing such work can be an essential part of a dynamic coming out process. At the same time, counselors should try to keep them centered on other important personal tasks as well. Students must not get so swept up in antihomophobia education that they neglect the rest of their lives.

The early stages of identity development can become a "bottleneck" that suspends schooling, career exploration, and other important life tasks.[258] Advising these young people how to manage coming out without slighting their intellectual growth and practical needs requires exquisite skill. It is like trying to counsel a student who has fallen in love for the first time: All else falls away for a while. In this case, the student has begun at last to love him or herself—and possibly someone else too.

## Exploring the Gay World

Some gay and lesbian adolescents are so relieved and excited to be able to express their sexualities that they throw themselves headlong into the subculture. It is natural for them to try out a number of possibilities in a community with many styles, affinity groups, and colorful people.

Like others, lesbians and gay men often identify by means of dress, comportment, and erotic interest. Lesbian identity may involve butch, femme, earth mother, jock, lipstick lesbian, baby dyke, bad girl, vanilla, and other signifiers.[259] Gay men might choose clone, jock, prep, disco queen, or any number of indicators of erotic taste. Likewise one finds club kids, athletic team members, AIDS activists, opera queens, two-steppers, gay rights activists, Gay Republicans, and so forth. Of course many are not wedded to any one appearance or affiliation, but adolescents often spend enormous energy trying to figure out where they fit in.[260] It can be a complex quest for costume, demeanor, community involvement, and erotic preferences.

For gay and lesbian youth, sexual activity is "normative, as a developmental marker of identity formation."[261] Furthermore they need relational and affectional, as well as erotic, fulfillment. Those who internalize the societal equation of homosexuality with sex may have some difficulty sorting their affectional longings from their sexual ones. Boys especially might find it hard to forge intimate nonsexual friendships with other gay males.

Their need for intimacy may not outweigh the risks of self-disclosure to peers whose orientation is unclear. Those without access to gay/lesbian youth groups therefore often lack opportunities for relational practice with their peers. Those who get into the bars will enter a sexualized venue with an increased likelihood for encountering older partners,[262] not by itself a worrisome entrée into the culture, but certainly worth discussing with a counselor.

Gay and lesbian youth need guidance and encouragement in these pursuits and consolation for their dead ends and failures. If they are inclined to feel foolish when they make a mistake, they should be reminded that most people are awkward when they enter a new environment. Unlike their heterosexual counterparts, who have had an often long head start with roles and relationships, they are just getting off the mark.

While urging them to loosen up and be patient, counselors should also advise moderation and circumspection, particularly noting threats to their safety. Are they acting out by flaunting their sexuality in places where they might be attacked? Are they being carelessly promiscuous? Are they being exploited? Are they dancing the night away and skipping school or letting activism interfere with their responsibilities? Many are justifiably angry, understandably love- or lust-possessed, and admirably dedicated to justice. They are also sometimes immature and filled with contradictions—in short, good prospects for affirmative but sober counseling.

Worried about his son's constant provocation at high school, one boy's father lamented, "He wears one sign on his front that says, 'Kick me, I'm gay' and another on the back that says, 'Feel bad for me, I'm gay and somebody kicked me.'"[263] The intent of this remark was wrong-headed. His son had been identifiably gay since the early grades and had suffered repeated harassment and suicidal thoughts. In wanting him to disguise his sexuality because it disturbed others, the father unfairly blamed the victim. Yet the boy did go out of his way to be confrontational, perhaps because he was "sick of running away." A good counselor would have talked with him about the personal costs of all direct action antiprejudice work and especially about finding allies for what appears to have been a crusade.

A good sense of humor helps in these counseling situations, as well as ability to reassure these adolescents that their experiences have been, and are still being, lived by others. When an advisor empathizes with a gay or lesbian youth on the basis of similar life experiences, an important bond can be formed, leading to more effective counseling on crucial topics like family dynamics, attraction and love, and safe sex practices. Some care is advised, however:

- Whether homosexual or heterosexual, counselors should not jump to conclusions about a gay or lesbian student's experience. Let the young person have the floor.

- Counselors should not provide details of their own intimate lives. Instead they can confirm that others have passed through similar territory and perhaps suggest readings and other materials.[264]
- Although gay and lesbian counselors can be role models, they should not let themselves be idealized. The greater the correspondence between the counselor's and the student's identities, the more caution should be exercised.[265]

Homosexual counselors occasionally find themselves targets of manipulation, including seduction and false accusation, from confused or angry adolescents.[266] This problem may be exacerbated when the counseling agenda is highly sexual. But gay or lesbian adults are potentially such important contacts for these youth, they should not flee. They must rather be clear about boundaries and be sure to alert a colleague or supervisor about what is going on. In some cases it might be advisable not to meet with a student unless another adult is within view.

Lastly, all teachers and counselors, whatever their own sexual orientation, should confront the homophobia within themselves. We all have vestiges of the prejudices with which we were infected early on. Admitting and discussing that painful fact with young people is a prerequisite for honest dealing on sexuality issues. When adults explain their own struggle with bias, they help defuse suspicion and give gay and lesbian counselees leeway to work on their self-hatred.

## Counseling Families

School personnel may be the first adults to whom gay or lesbian teens confide. As a result, teachers, counselors, nurses, or administrators may be called upon to counsel parents and other family members. Before meeting them, counselors should discuss with their counselees the extent to which they have come out to their families and how they have responded. Whole families or individual family members

- May not know yet.
- May know and pretend not to.
- May know and appear accepting but are not wholly so.
- May know and be accepting.
- May conceal from outsiders.
- May come out as a family.
- May know and not accept.

If the family are not yet aware, one must be cautious. Although the emotional consequences of hiding may be hurtful, the risks in "outing"

the student are also considerable: "When I did try to confide in a counselor at school, she did nothing but screw up my life. Basically, she went
back to my parents and told them all the things I had been saying."[267]
Being honest with a family may not always yield the best outcomes. One
study of male adolescents found that coming out to or being discovered
by family and friends was positive for half of the respondents and negative for the other half.[268]

### Rejection

Negative responses can range from shaming and verbal abuse to violence
and expulsion. The mother of the student quoted above came after him
with an iron and then called the police to eject him.[269] If support service
personnel are hostile or the level of services in the community is inadequate, the young person may be permanently harmed. When information about the family bodes ill, the better course is to collude with the
adolescent for confidential counseling and/or referral and leave relatives
out of the loop.

   Carol Gilligan observes that finding the silenced voice of an adolescent
girl is not a panacea for her patriarchal oppression. She warns in fact that
girls need to be careful about possibly harmful fallout from their authentic self-expression: "a voice whispers 'take cover.'".[270] Likewise coming
out to family is a course not always worth taking. Unlike independent
adults, adolescents who disclose to their families and schools may encounter emotional and practical consequences that are immediately endangering. They should do so with planning and care, if at all. Even
without the fear of drastic consequences, counselees might fret over
wounding their parents or letting them down.[271] These young people require periodic monitoring.

   Not notifying or receiving consent from parents or guardians about serious counseling concerns and referrals could be a violation of school
policy or of state law.[272] If that is the case, counselors should confer with
administration in advance of any real case on how to act in the best interest of the child when the risks of parental involvement are so severe.
Parental notification regulations regarding health status, harassment, assault, and sensitive curriculum could possibly be judged not to apply in
this circumstance. Even policies governing suicidality reporting could be
nuanced to the degree that notification need not include the reasons underlying the ideation. If the adolescent's confidentiality cannot be assured, at least with an administrator's wink and nod, the counselor is left
to conscience. One could still discreetly, perhaps indirectly, provide the
student with a list of community services (hotlines, mental health centers, and so forth).

All students should think through both their reasons for coming out to others and its timing. Using their sexuality in anger to spite their family will almost invariably provoke rejection. Moreover, if they are still wobbly, any ambivalence they show toward their own sexuality could influence the family's response. The counselor should probe: How are their overall relations with family members? Is the young person self-accepting and self-assured? What other sources of conflict or stress are evident in the family right now? With caring disclosure, accurate information, and support, a family's love can prevail.

Learning about the coming out experiences of other gays and lesbians with similar backgrounds might help the counselee anticipate some issues. Role-playing with the counselor as a family member might also be useful. Feeling a bit of pressure to come out is not always bad, since the nudging of an internal voice or a good friend may prompt risk-taking, growth, and improved communication. The process is delicate, and ultimately the decision should be left to the student. If counselees opt to go ahead and they fear ejection, they should have prearranged housing and support.

If students have already been thrown out or need to be removed from abusive homes, counselors should be meticulous in finding placements. The youth may be no more welcome in foster care or group homes than they were in their families. Verbal harassment and physical abuse, even rape, are too common in these settings. Foster parents and service providers may be homophobic themselves or lack knowledge and training to protect and counsel homosexual young people.[273]

Although politically and religiously conservative families tend to present a greater challenge[274] (see Chapter 4), counselors should know that even liberal parents might react poorly to a child's announcement. Their ostensibly progressive attitudes might stop short of gays and lesbians; or they may be more accepting of homosexuality in the abstract or in a friend than in their own children.

A son or daughter might fear to come out after another sibling has already done so. They may anticipate the reprise of a painful scene or detect lingering disappointment or disapproval that they dare not incur upon themselves.

A family may know or have strong suspicions about a child's homosexuality and still not acknowledge it. This silence, in which the youth is a coconspirator, is a symptom of group avoidance. The family members express interest in the child's life but are careful not to make inquiries that could bring an avalanche of truth telling. They may go so far as to treat lovers as "friends" to maintain the mutual deceit.

Families do not engage in this intentional delusion to be hurtful. On the contrary, they probably think they are doing what is best for all: sparing feelings and dodging conflict that would threaten family unity. This course is seductive but corrupting. Families that live with known yet un-broached secrets invite dishonesty at every level of interaction. Everyone must be on guard not to reveal what they know or suspect another knows. The self-esteem of homosexual adolescents is ultimately harmed, as they conclude they cannot be loved for who they really are, but only for the person they pretend to be.[275]

In a recent essay, a thirty-five-year-old man wrote that he saw no rea-son to try to "radicalize" his father with news that "would not be wel-come." After the father overheard one of his phone calls, the terms of the destructive game became clear:

> Detecting a certain tenderness in my voice during the call, he asked with sudden rage, "What is there between you and that friend? Tell me, is he straight?" He began to form another question, but he was unable to com-plete the sentence.
>
> In the trembling, awkward silence that followed, all had been asked and answered. My father's questions were, in fact, statements of his knowledge. We had played out our own peculiar battle and soon, while touring the sites we had mapped out that day, were back to reciting those of the Civil War.[276]

The casualties in this kind of familial conflict are both sad and pathetic. Adult gay men and lesbians often recall strained relationships, particu-larly with the parent of their own gender, prior to coming out.[277] They also report that concealment puts an alienating distance between them-selves and their families.[278]

Unlike those who may need to hide from families who really do not know, the adolescents in a pretending families waste energy in self-mon-itoring and self-protection. If their parents have not ejected or angrily confronted them with their suspicions, there is hope they will adjust to the truth after it has been spoken. Still there are families, as there are cul-tures, where the price of toleration is silence or second-class status. Com-ing out proudly and demanding respect equal to that afforded to other family members may be explosive. These possible outcomes should be explored as the student weighs his or her decision.

### Coming Out Selectively to Family

Research suggests that young people come out incrementally to family, starting with an emotionally sympathetic member, usually a sibling.[279] If a parent is told, mothers are more often confided in than fathers, and sons are less likely than daughters to inform their fathers.[280]

Adolescents should be warned that relatives will not always keep their secret. Developing circumstances might compel that confidante to tell others or it might slip out in the heat of a moment. If, on the other hand, the relative is a likely supporter with a record of probity, sharing the information could be advantageous. The adolescent would have a loved one to talk to and seek advice from, especially on family matters. Should the young person eventually decide to come out to others in the family, this relative could be a useful ally.

Nevertheless, when some family members are taken into confidence and others are left ignorant or pretending to be so, many of the harmful effects of silence, hiding, and hypocrisy remain. Those who are informed become codependent with the homosexual child in a system in which everyone's survival and happiness depend on maintaining an elaborate charade. Opportunities for guilt, emotional blackmail, and multifaceted deceit are proportional to the number of people who know. To prevent this result, the child, upon coming out to one family member, should plan with that person how to be open soon with the rest of the family.

## Family Adjustment

Of course, a family may appear to accept their child's homosexuality, but yet may not be happy with it. Discussion might reveal that they are trying to do right by embracing and loving their child as before; however, the news has made that difficult. Several studies confirm that time helps families cope.[281] If they are motivated to grow, experience and education should reconcile them to what may seem discomforting at the outset.

Family members should be treated gently through a period of adjustment that corresponds to the coming out process itself.[282] Parents often feel guilty that they must have raised their child incorrectly.[283] They may be aided in that conclusion by groundless psychological theories. They may also fear the stigma that could attach to them, if their circumstances become known.[284]

Family, especially parents, may experience a grieving period.[285] They mourn the loss of the child they thought they had and some of the expectations they had, just as the child grieved the loss of an old identity and its particular promises. When homosexual youth tell their parents that they are still the same children they were before the revelation, they really mean they still love them and want to be loved in return. Of course they are now different in a significant detail of their lives, and that takes getting used to. One parent recalled looking at his son and wanting to say, "I don't know who you are, but I wish you'd leave and send my son Ted back."[286] Another remembers, "As she was walking away from us, all of a sudden I felt like she was a stranger."[287] Family dynamics are disrupted with the appearance of a seeming stranger in the place of a child.[288]

It may be unfair or unreasonably optimistic to expect parents to rejoice. Even some of those who seem unruffled at the initial news experience aftershocks of grief, sometimes privately. Parents may take from six months to two years to process this information.[289] An Asian American mother's recollection distills this emotion poignantly: "The grieving process took a long time. . . . Not having her be a bride was a devastating change of plans for her life. . . . It made me feel when she said she was a lesbian that there was no place for me in her life. . . . I didn't know how to be the mother of a lesbian."[290]

Still, grief must have limits. As the family members learn more about gay and lesbian life, they would do well to revise their appreciation and expectations of the child and to renew their love. They must examine exactly whose plans have been altered. Getting stuck in denial, guilt, anger, or regret helps no one.

P-FLAG describes a six-stage process that families go through in coming to accept their gay/lesbian relatives: shock, denial, guilt, expression of feelings, return to rationality with varying degrees of acceptance, and true acceptance.[291] Another stage model cites subliminal awareness, impact, adjustment, resolution, and integration.[292]

Adolescents should be advised to be patient with their loved ones. They should consider the following:

- It took them time to adjust to the discovery of their own homosexuality.
- Family members need to express their feelings and be heard before they can move on to better understanding.
- Finding out a loved one is homosexual can shake one's confidence in an entire belief system.
- Family members may feel blameworthy when they hear how much a loved one has suffered, unbeknownst to them.[293]
- Each family member moves at a different pace.
- People sometimes regress in the progress they were making toward acceptance but usually recover.
- Most gay/lesbian people themselves spend years working out their internalized homophobia.

### Inclusion as the Goal

The goal in counseling family members must be complete and equal inclusion of the homosexual relative in the family unit. Conditional acceptance is not a lasting resolution. Restrictions on dress, dating, sexual activity should be consistent with those placed on heterosexual siblings. Nor should communication be rebuffed. "I accept what you are, but I don't want to hear about it" is not a satisfactory response. Conversely, families should not allow their natural curiosity to become voyeuristic. Gay and lesbian youth who come out to their families still have a right to privacy.

Overall, gays and lesbians want to feel that they are no less loved than others in the family and that their relationships are no less celebrated. The rest of the family must be sensitive to this need. They may take for granted the many social customs honoring heterosexual dating, courtship, and rites of passage and fail to provide the same for gays and lesbians. Valentine's Day, the prom, rings, breakups, and engagements are just a few examples. The wife of a rabbi and mother of a gay son came to this understanding after a while: "If we will it, mourning dissipates and love shines through. We discover that our gay and straight kids have much in common; they share attributes, friendship, creativity, love; they equally need security, support, acceptance, understanding."[294] It is not wise to counsel adolescents to be satisfied with long-term conditional love or second-class family status. Living under such terms is a source of constant pain and resentment.

## Needs of Accepting Families

Often families who accept their loved one's homosexuality also need education and guidance. They may want to learn more about gay and lesbian life than their relative is able to tell them. They may need help in examining their own attitudes or devising strategies for inclusion. They might seek support in telling others about their homosexual family member(s). Some fashion a closet for themselves and disclose to none or few. Others are more open, even activist. P-FLAG is a national organization with numerous local chapters working to foster acceptance and reconciliation within families and in communities.[295] Their meetings are more than group commiseration; they are also a forum for articulating pride and joy in all one's children.[296]

Some family members have a harder time adjusting or accepting than others do. Older people, perhaps influenced by generational attitudes, may be condemning or just believe that gays and lesbians live sad, shameful lives on the fringes of society. On the other hand, some older relatives might have reached a world-wise acceptance of difference.[297]

Siblings, conversely, may be too young to understand the meaning of the revelation or too immature to handle it seriously or well. At any age they can be angry and confused.[298] They might worry that they are or will become homosexual themselves. They may fear being taunted about their brother or sister's sexuality or having their own questioned. They should be counseled separately. Some of their concerns are reasonable, particularly if they are still in school themselves, and even more so if they are in the same school as their homosexual sibling.

The participation of extended family in any counseling depends on their closeness to immediate family members. Clearly, one does not want to invite bigots to the table. There is, however, the possibility that an uncle, aunt, or cousin might bring a better understanding to the conversation. When immediate or extended family members are openly gay or lesbian themselves, there is a history to build on.

Prior family experience can work to the advantage or disadvantage of the adolescent. One can imagine, for example, how much skill would be needed to deal with a gay or lesbian child coming out to a mother who was bitterly divorced from the gay father of this same child, or to counsel a gay adolescent about coming out to a closeted relative. These special cases remind us of the unexpected ramifications that can obtain in counseling adolescents and their families.

Parents and other family members should be

- given an opportunity to grieve;
- informed that homosexuality is nobody's fault;
- assured that the child's coming out is not an act of betrayal;
- cautioned not to blame homosexuality for any of the child's failings;
- educated about some basic facts of sexual orientation;
- assured that the child has not been recruited or forced into homosexuality by a lover or some other person;
- referred to gay-affirming religious teachings;
- encouraged to envision the child's productive and happy future.

If these steps have not set families on the route to acceptance, and especially if children are subjected to psychological or physical abuse, school workers have a responsibility to find healthier homes for them. That is not to suggest that homophobia must be virtually eliminated throughout the family tableau, but that extreme conditions dictate intervention.

## Counseling Multiple Minorities

All of the issues discussed so far in this chapter apply to gay and lesbian adolescents in general; however, as one might expect from observations of identity development, multiple minority youth raise additional concerns. (See Chapter 7.) Counselors who are themselves both minority and homosexual are likely to be most knowledgeable and sensitive to these issues, but they are also scarce commodities in schools. Even when referral to community-based counseling is feasible, all school counselors should be equipped with a basic understanding of these students' needs.

## Primary and Secondary Socializations

Minority adolescents resist adopting a homosexual identity for the same reasons as other teens do and then have reasons of their own that spring from their multiple minority status. Coming out for them demands a secondary socialization which may be inhibited by their primary socializations as members of racial, ethnic, class, or religious groups. The minority youth has likely already attained a level of pride in his or her minority status, perhaps after wrestling with bigotry and internalized stigma.

Racial, ethnic, and religious identity acquisition is commonly aided by family, church, and community, and possibly reinforced by the school. The nuclear and extended family is often "the emotional bond for the conscious self and personal psychology."[299] A minority youth's homosexual identity, however, is usually not fostered by the family or these other important formative institutions.[300] If the advent of a homosexual identity poses a threat to the adolescent's membership in the primary group, he or she may face a crisis. Coming out invites ostracism from the native community, while the prospect of refuge in a racist gay and lesbian culture is uncertain.[301] The stress endemic to this dilemma should not be underestimated. Several studies have found higher rates of attempted suicide among minority gay and lesbian adolescents than among their white peers.[302] The reasons for this discrepancy are not certain, although psychological isolation is strongly suggested.

It is probably useless to advise a minority youth that identity labels should not matter. Those who have invested considerably in a minority identity will not be comforted to hear that gender, race, and sexual identities are socially constructed. A better counseling strategy is to show that minority status and homosexual identity are not mutually exclusive. An African American gay man wrote: "Finally, we have to reach out to and foster leadership among gay and lesbian youth. We can only do this by working *within* (emphasis his) our communities. African American youth across the board need positive role models and we must be willing to fill those spaces."[303]

Counselors should facilitate acquaintance with such models. Gay and lesbian groups for people of color, Third World people, and people of faith usually welcome young folks to their meetings. Furthermore, in San Francisco, where multiple minority visibility is high, two youth groups,

"Brown BoyZ" and "Locas, Locas Y Que?" ("Crazy Girls, So What?") have spun off from adult support groups for Latin/Mexican gays and lesbians.[304] Students should also be introduced to the films and writings of Marlon Riggs, Gloria Andalzua, Essex Hemphill, Audre Lorde, John McNeil, Lev Raphael, and many others, and to periodicals like *BLK*, a magazine for gays and lesbians of African descent.[305]

Much needless anxiety has been produced by the conundrum "Which are you first, minority or gay?" Allegiance seems to be influenced by the proportionality of oppressions; hence, for example, the usual dominance of racism over homophobia may lead most gay and lesbian African Americans to identify more with race,[306] whereas a less virulent anti-Asian bigotry may lead gay Asians to feel more oppressed as homosexuals.[307]

The categories of race, ethnicity, and sexuality are given such importance in our culture that young people might have exaggerated expectations of the niche afforded by any one of them. Multiple minority adolescents may be frustrated and angry to find that they cannot feel entirely at home in any one community.[308] The answer to the "which are you first" question is ultimately that you should not have to choose: "I would be extremely unhappy if all my Latin culture were taken out of my lesbian life. . . . I identify myself as a lesbian more intensely than as a Cuban/Latin. But it is a very painful question because I feel that I am both, and I don't want to have to choose."[309]

It should be possible to integrate these identities. Although in practice, adolescents might have to deal with each issue separately, it helps for them to see not only the blending of identities within themselves but also the features common to all oppressions. In fact, it has been suggested that the skills employed in counseling racial and ethnic minorities are similar to those required for working with homosexual people.[310]

It is no disservice to advise multiple minority youth to risk coming out, so long as the counselor does so with an eye to all their needs for affirmation.[311] They cannot postpone the emergence of their sexual selves until racial, ethnic, class, and religious prejudices have been abolished. Sufficient conditions should obtain when the school commits itself to fighting all forms of bigotry.

*Immigrant Youth*

The impact of a Western homosexual identity for youth who have had, and perhaps acted on, same-gender attractions in a prior context may be different than it is for those who first become aware of their feelings in a new homeland. Even though Western identity paradigms are spreading throughout the world, young people, especially recent immigrants, might be shocked by sudden immersion into a culture that wants to impose a new identity on them. How do we counsel young people who confront sexual identity implications that have been previously unknown to them and perhaps remain unheard of in their families?

New gender and sexuality constructions are just two of many cultural immersions for immigrant youth. Adults who want to promote their autonomy and genuine self-expression must recognize how traumatic the process can be. Sensitive counselors, who would never force a sexuality label on them, still cannot ignore the potential of the majority to discomfort them. Nor can they overlook the possibility that the visible gay and lesbian community might evoke dissonance in the immigrant youth's established identity. The flexibility in sexual behavior that men especially are permitted in other cultures and the looseness or absence of labeling can be unsustainable here. Acceding to a narrowly defined and well-policed Western identity could constrict their sexual expression and cut them off from their families and other native cultural supports. One resister, a self-described "queer" Cuban-American who is editor of "Perra" ("bitch") magazine, defies what he sees as the rigid divisive labels of American liberalism: "Language betrays us. We need to accept sexuality as something fluid."[312]

If minority young people feel coerced to come out, they might turn their sorrow over alienation from family and native culture into anger toward their counselors. Family members might also blame advisors for the turmoil. Such resentments are similar to those one might face in counseling girls from patriarchal cultures. In fact, since sexism and heterosexism coincide in many cultures and religious traditions, young lesbians need more comprehensive support than their male counterparts.

## Common Concerns

Each ethnic, religious, and racial grouping encompasses a spectrum of constituent communities and family idiosyncrasies. As they should with any student, counselors ought to understand the student's family/cultural history, family power dynamics, level of assimilation into the dominant culture, and experience with oppression. They should explore what the youth and their families believe about such issues as procreation, religious observance, gender, and sexuality. Some parents who interpret sexuality differently might not have the language to discuss a North American "homosexual" identity to begin with.

Adolescents engaged in coming out might be accused of betrayal and threatened with excommunication.[313] As stunting as that community or family may be for their sexual identity development, it is also comfortably familiar, providing customs and roles from which they have derived pleasure and people of whom they have grown fond. They find sustenance as well as torment in these ties. No matter how expert a role model might be in arguing that a synthesis is possible between one's native identity and one's sexuality, the adolescent can still be petrified, reasoning, "It may have been possible for them, but it won't work for me!"

Coming out to their families may indeed bring estrangement and sadness. Counselors should point out that such outcomes may be reversed—that some remnant of connection can be retained and strengthened over time. Some will necessarily break from their past lives to establish their sexual identities and then find ways to be reunited with family members and reconnected with aspects of their abandoned cultural heritage. Even those who have felt expelled from their religious communities may find that churches are changing.[314] Others, having discovered love and fulfillment in new families, faiths, and communities, never go back to environments that promise only renewed conflict and misery.

Sometimes the terms and conditions under which reconciliation is offered are in fact unacceptable:

- coming back to a family that offers pity or second-class status;
- accusations that they have been corrupted by American or homosexual culture;
- proffering of cures, including heterosexual matchmaking or prayer;
- having to lead a double life (silence in the minority community, even in the face of blatant homophobia, and openness in the gay/lesbian community);
- conforming to norms of gender role and gender expression;[315]
- membership in a church that loves you but not who you are.

Why would anyone want to remain connected to such denigration? The question implies culpability for choosing to stay. Quitting the oppressive atmosphere might indeed be the eventual solution, but getting to that point calls for support and understanding, not blame.

## Counseling Minority Families

When counselors attempt family interventions, they can encounter barriers characteristic of particular minority populations. Chinese people, for example, tend to put away and not discuss painful or problematic issues, even within families.[316] Asian adolescents might be tempted to distract their parents by diverting their attention to achievement in other areas of their lives.[317] An Asian lesbian notes, "A friend of mine once said that Asian parents just didn't become P-FLAG parents. In my case, I thought he could be right."[318] Chicanas, for their part, are so loyal to their mothers, they shrink from causing them distress.[319] Coming out assertively may violate the face-saving custom of "personalismo" in Latin culture, that is, to be indirect in managing conflict.[320] On the other hand, quiet toleration is more a denial than an acceptance.[321]

For each culture, there are bound to be snares. Advisors who are not themselves members of a particular group might be hard-pressed to grasp the nuances of a family interaction, but they must try, since the number of minority counselors is limited. One solution to this shortage is to ask a sympathetic minority colleague or community-based minority psychologist or social worker to participate in the counseling for a while. It may be possible to get parents together with other parents of the same heritage who are also dealing with a homosexual child.[322] Such an approach might produce, for example, a Chinese couple who have come slowly to acceptance[323] or Indian parents whose affirmation brings them to Gay Pride Day.[324]

### Bias Within the Gay Community

Counselors should also be prepared to advise multiple minority youth on problems arising from stereotype and prejudice within the gay and lesbian community.[325] Incidents of racism and cultural arrogance persist in bars and clubs, for example. Patrons of color might be asked for identification at the door, whereas others are admitted without question. More subtle racism is manifested in political, social, cultural, and academic events in which representations of gay and lesbian life omit, marginalize, or minimize nonwhite, non-Western experience. Multiple minorities may be angered by lack of organizational outreach, noninclusion in community leadership, and having to take sole responsibility for their difficulties.

Gay and lesbian white people sometimes think homophobia should be the only item on their anti-oppression agenda. They can appear blind to other minorities' concerns and insensitive to the fact that gay and lesbian minority people always bring more than their sexualities to the table. It often falls unfairly on those minority members to instruct the rest on the interconnectedness of various oppressions and the critical importance of social class, gender, race, and religion to many gays and lesbians. These are the sources of persistent discouragement for multiple minorities. Adolescents in particular might need help channeling their responses into a forceful critique and effective participation.

*Intimacy and Relationships*

Intimate interpersonal matters may also be troubling. Sometimes the minority member of a mixed couple becomes the object of fetishization when the line is crossed between gratifying a particular erotic taste and becoming objectified. (See Chapter 7.) It is the political context that problemitizes these dynamics. A redhead is not likely to object to satisfying his or her partner's preference for a red-haired lover; a black person, on the other hand could find the eroticization of racial features dehumanizing.

Conversely, minorities can suffer from colonized erotic preferences, judging their own features unattractive in others. Minority people can be troubled by the possibility that their own tastes might be dictated by self-hatred.[326] In most instances, however, one ought not to be disturbed by the attraction of opposites, any more than we ought to ascribe narcissism to finding beauty in those who are similar.

Mixed race/ethnicity adult couples suggest that these issues are common in their relationships, but they might be unusual for teens. There is no need to raise them preemptively. Although counselors should anticipate certain areas of potential stress, including relationships, these erotic subjects could be far afield. When minority adolescents bring these matters up themselves, they should talk about their responses to objectification or about how relational preferences relate to their self-esteem. Counselors should help students see beauty in themselves and in all kinds of people and advise them to find relationships that are comfortable and nonexploitative.

It is clear that minorities encounter ignorance, callousness, and bias in the larger gay and lesbian culture into which they come out. Yet there are also instances in which minority people bring cultural baggage to their homosexual life that makes relationships more difficult. Habits of gender role are particularly portable. Although they are gay, men from cultures that promote machismo can scuttle their intimate connections through domination. Even women can internalize the cultural requirement that the sexual instigator be a "macho." One Latina lesbian complained of her inability to break from this tyranny, which she experienced as a compulsion to be "butch."[327]

*Reaching Congruence*

One model of identity formation for multiple minority gays and lesbians suggests a series of five states,[328] as opposed to sequential stages:

1. Denial of conflict—characterized by minimizing both race and sexuality as sources of stress.

2. Bisexual versus gay/lesbian—the use of the bisexual label to retain affiliation with the ethnic/racial group.
3. Conflicts in allegiances—anxiety over prioritizing memberships.
4. Establishing priorities in allegiance—during which ethnicity/race prevails and resentment arises from rejection by the homosexual community.
5. Integrating the various communities—commitment grows toward developing a wholly accommodating identity, even with continuing limitations.

Although this section has focused on obstacles in reaching the fifth state, multiminority youth should be reassured that congruence is possible. There is even a hopeful indication that those who have successfully navigated the acquisition of one stigmatized identity may have an advantage in negotiating another.[329] Gay and lesbian minority youth might be well advised to draw on those skills with which they confronted racism and other forms of bigotry to meet the challenges of homophobia and heterosexism. At the very least they must be supported in expressing their sexualities. The alternative is grim: "Silence is my cloak. It smothers."[330]

# 9

# Gay and Lesbian Teachers

*Dear Dr. Lipkin,*

*I am returning the Staff Development Manual. I had hoped that reducing homopho-*
*bia might be part of a new course here, but, ironically, I am inhibited by my friends*
*on the staff who are lesbians and who simply don't feel comfortable with the idea.*
*Thanks anyway,*

*[Signature]*

The above note from a public high school teacher represents one sad aspect to the subject of homosexual educators.[1] The following excerpt from a 1991 letter to a male public school teacher from a female former student illustrates a quite different one:

> You were a very singular figure in my life at [high school] and filled a need, a need for me that, for many reasons, few others had a chance at (they didn't want a chance at it either I'd guess). You were the first gay person I had ever known, and someone I had a great deal of respect for. It was because of these things that I was first able to entertain conscious thoughts of my own homosexuality, and more importantly, that I did not view them in a negative light. You have had a great and essential influence on the pride I take in being a lesbian.[2]

Their juxtaposition is not meant as an indictment of closeted teachers. As this chapter illustrates, the question of whether teachers should come out is complex and worrisome: Gay and lesbian teachers have been hurt, even fired, because of disclosure. On the other hand, a teacher's coming out can be both a personal and a community triumph.

This issue has been the subject of widespread public posturing in the last decade. With only 44 percent of Americans feeling comfortable having their children taught by openly gay teachers, according to one poll (the South at 36 percent and Midwest at 42 percent versus the Northeast at 55 percent and the West at 52 percent),[3] the specter of the gay teacher continues to be a convenient bogeyman in a volatile political environment:

- In 1998, the Oklahoma House of Representatives passed, for the second time since 1985 (when it was ruled unconstitutional), a law banning homosexuals from working in the public schools.[4]
- Film footage of Gay, Lesbian, and Straight Teachers Network members in the 1993 March on Washington for Gay and Lesbian Civil Rights was used in antigay propaganda to incite panic over recruitment and predation.[5]
- Paul Cameron, a talk-show favorite, presented a paper titled "Do Homosexual Teachers Pose a Risk to Pupils?" at the Eastern Psychological Association in 1995, basing his affirmative answer on bad research and illogical inferences.[6]
- An Idaho state senate candidate, outdoing Lillian Hellman's *The Children's Hour*, claimed in a fund-raising letter that a junior high school teacher told her class on the first day of school that she was a lesbian, although no support for the charge could be found.[7]

## History

Such sentiments and accusations are not new. Public opposition to homosexual teachers, provoked in part by fear that they will molest or unduly influence children, has fueled a number of campaigns since the 1970s. Among these was the notorious unsuccessful California Briggs Initiative in 1978. This referendum called for the dismissal of any school employee who "promoted" homosexuality in a manner that was aimed at, or might come to the attention of, schoolchildren or school employees.[8] Another milestone was the passage of an Oklahoma State law to the same effect in 1978. It remained in force for seven years.[9] Some have called for the explicit exclusion of teachers and child care workers from state and local civil rights and employment protections for gays and lesbians.[10]

These attacks followed a series of maneuvers, beginning in the 1950s, to deny due process to teachers involved in morals charges, regardless of guilt or innocence—all in the name of child protection. In fact, Anita Bryant's 1977 antigay rights crusade in Dade County, Florida, was cleverly dubbed "Save Our Children."[11]

Nor were such views restricted to benighted extremists. For instance, in his seminal *The Sociology of Teaching*, published in 1932 and twice reissued in the 1960s, Willard Waller wrote:

The homosexual teacher develops an indelicate soppiness in his relations with his favorites, and often displays not a little bitterness toward the others. He develops ridiculous crushes, and makes minor tragedies of little incidents when the recipient of his attentions shows himself indifferent. The favoritism which these crushes entail is of course fatal to school discipline. But that is by no means the worst danger that the homosexual teacher brings with him; the real risk is that he may, by presenting himself as a love object to certain members of his own sex at a time when their sex attitudes have not been deeply canalized, develop in them attitudes similar to his own. For nothing seems more certain than that homosexuality is contagious.[12]

In 1987, antiracism crusader, former cabinet member, and future vice presidential candidate Jack Kemp set the limit on his libertarianism with the remark, "I believe in civil liberties for homosexuals. I'd guess I have to say I'd draw the line at letting them teach in the schools."[13]

Some social workers and educators over the past 150 years, from Jane Addams to Paul Goodman, have been homosexual, but historians can only guess at how many there might have been. Single women at one time dominated the profession and then were discouraged from teaching.[14] From the mid-nineteenth century until after World War I, unmarried women were inexpensive to hire and thought to be good influences on developing children, inasmuch as they were pure, selfless, and innately maternal. Besides, those who intended not to be married found teaching to be one means of support that was open to them. At the same time, the low pay with which they had to be content may not have been enough for men with families. In 1900, 70 percent of all public school teachers were women; 95 percent of them were single, widowed, or divorced.[15]

During the early twentieth century, however, the invention of homosexuality as a deviant illness brought suspicion to some who chose spinsterhood. Single women were thought to be weakened by neuroses and other maladies that rendered them unfit for teaching. Fears about the declining white birth rate and the imagined feminization of boys led to crusades against unmarried women in the schools.

This reaction was a part of a broader male panic over women's economic, political, and marital independence (see Chapter 5). Unmarried, ostensibly independent female teachers and their bachelor brethren were deemed pathological role models for children. Waller expounded on this topic:

There remains a large and pitiful group of those whose sex life is thwarted or perverse. The members of this group, often consciously and usually with the best of intentions, carry sex problems into the schools, and transmit abnormal attitudes to their pupils because they have no other attitudes.[16]

Although for a time married women had been discouraged or even barred from employment in education because they were expected to live off their husbands' incomes and leave such employment for male breadwinners, these practices were gradually abandoned to bring healthy wifely women into the schools.

In 1940, 69 percent of female teachers had never been married, but twenty years later fewer than 30 percent of female teachers could be so classified.[17] The drop is likely attributable to gender role conservatism and heterosexism, as well as to families' need for two incomes. By 1994, only 12 percent of public school teachers had never been married, and 13 percent were widowed, divorced, or separated; 73 percent were female.[18]

A recent random anonymous survey of 289 urban, suburban, and rural high school teachers in Connecticut, for example, yielded 5 percent who said they were homosexual.[19] Other indicators of a gay, lesbian, bisexual presence in the ranks are reflected in the following:

- 90 chapters nationwide of GLSEN (Gay, Lesbian, and Straight Education Network);
- NEA-GLC (National Education Association Gay and Lesbian Caucus);
- AFT (American Federation of Teachers) Gay and Lesbian Caucus;
- the LTN (Lesbian Teachers Network);
- San Francisco BANGLE (Bay Area Network of Gay and Lesbian Educators, a part of GLSEN since 1997).

There are some regional and local groups as well. Moreover, because of the risks in being discovered, such membership rolls and survey responses are certain to underrepresent the true numbers.

### Concerns

Gay and lesbian educators' principal misgiving is that exposure of their sexuality will have negative professional and personal repercussions.[20] They fear harassment, if not violence, stymied advancement, demotion, or outright termination. In the words of one teacher in an affluent suburban school: "The old ones are in the closet because they fear the reactions of the student body . . . that their car will get keyed or something. The young ones are new to the system so they're not going to say anything."[21]

Another teacher at this same progressive Greater Boston school, where no adult is out, observed: "This is not thought by the gay faculty to be a safe school to come out in. This is a tough school in many ways. There are some kids who come from homophobic backgrounds."[22] Indeed, there is hardly a school in the nation that is not "tough." Even San Francisco, long an oasis of homosexual freedom, is no nirvana for gay and lesbian teachers despite the city's progressive politics.[23]

According to one study, teachers fear that their sexuality might become public in three ways: being accused of child molestation or improperly touching a student, being charged with influencing or recruiting students to homosexuality, or being observed in a homosexual milieu.[24] The insidious homophobic suspicions that began in the earliest years of the century and were stoked during the McCarthy period are still pervasive.[25] A gay New York public school teacher laments:

> Since childhood I have longed to teach, but every message I received reinforced the notion that respectable men did not become teachers. . . . So my real desire to teach grades four, five, and six was dwarfed by these capricious standards and my fear of parents accusing me of sexual abuse or statutory rape because I hugged some young boy.[26]

He is hardly alone in his worries, which are prompted by sexism, heterosexism, the equation of homosexuality with pedophilia,[27] and insufficient legal protections. Gays and lesbians seeking school employment, those without tenure, those who work with young children, and those who are likely to come into physical contact with students are particularly vulnerable to such anxieties.

## Legal Issues

Even teachers' consensual private conduct can be targeted. In 1998 the sodomy laws of nineteen states still criminalized homosexual erotic activities,[28] and in the last months of the twentieth century, men were still being arrested for making love in their homes.[29] Educators convicted of such "crimes against nature" could lose their eligibility to teach, although some states will restore credentials after "rehabilitation." In one noted case in Washington State, which had repealed its sodomy law, a court ruled that a twelve-year veteran teacher with an excellent record could be dismissed for immorality after being revealed by a student as a "practicing homosexual." His presence at the school was ruled inherently disruptive.[30]

One might fare better keeping sexuality private and observing community standards of decorum.[31] Otherwise one could end up like the school counselor who was fired when she told other school personnel she was a lesbian.[32]

Since 1974, when the National Education Association added "sexual preference" to its nondiscrimination language, its affiliate unions have had a basis for litigation on behalf of their gay and lesbian members.[33] Nonetheless, enforcement of the policies resides primarily with locals whose enthusiasm for gay and lesbian rights varies from place to place. Considerable courage, energy, and money are required to charge a local with failure to represent. Perhaps more to the point, many would not fight to keep a job in an inhospitable district with a homophobic union. Instead, they might prefer to negotiate a quiet leave-taking that conceals the reasons for their departure and then to seek a position elsewhere.[34] This sort of timid departure was probably common for a long time.

Some politicians insist homosexuals have the same rights as anyone else, yet no federal civil rights laws prohibit discrimination based on sexual orientation. Although the Supreme Court ruled in the 1996 *Romer v. Evans* decision that homosexuals as a group cannot be excluded by states from obtaining protections, it has not clearly outlawed local exclusions; nor has it banned discrimination based on actual or perceived homosexuality.[35]

A national Employment Non-Discrimination Act for gays and lesbians was defeated in the Senate in 1996, despite evidence that people are fired regularly because they are, or are thought to be, homosexual.[36] Several senators argued against the bill precisely because it would have protected teachers. One stated, "In hiring schoolteachers, or camp counselors, or those who deal with young people, you never just hire a teacher.... You are hiring a role model."[37] Another complained that a school would not be able to dismiss homosexual teachers who kissed or held hands in public with their partners.[38]

As of 1999 only 10 states, the District of Columbia, and 165 municipalities/counties had adopted civil and job rights provisions for gays and lesbians, and a mere handful of school boards had instituted inclusive nondiscrimination policies.[39] Many ordinances in fact omit or exclude public and independent schools. Local policy statements, application forms, and teacher contracts may not even reflect state protections. Moreover, since the late 1970s a number of jurisdictions have battled over legislation and referenda to restrict the rights of homosexual teachers.[40] In the 1990s several versions were introduced in a number of states and localities (for example, Oregon and Colorado).

Even preexisting protections have come under siege. A self-described Christian political action committee petitioned the Des Moines school board in 1996 to rescind antidiscrimination protections for gay teachers. A 5,850-signature counterpetition matched it, and after weeks of argument over definitions of "sexual orientation," the board declined to change the policy.[41] In the West, San Jose evangelicals turned out to oppose benefits granted to partners of homosexual employees.[42]

In the absence of explicit protections, judges will continue to weigh teachers' free expression and association rights against the prerogatives of school officials to limit the content of what is said in their districts and to restrict its employees' activities. For example, a 1998 federal court order, believed to be the first of its kind in the nation, required that an Ohio school district reinstate, with back pay and damages, a sixth-grade teacher whose contract had not been renewed because he was gay. This ruling was made despite Ohio's lack of protections for gay and lesbian workers.[43]

***The Gerry Crane Case.*** School authorities can be both mean-spirited and self-defeating. A notorious example is found in the treatment of Gerry Crane. An acclaimed music teacher in Byron Center, Michigan, Crane was called before school administrators who had heard that he was gay and planned to wed his partner. When he confirmed the story they told him they hoped the matter would blow over. Instead it exploded when a disgruntled former student distributed copies of Crane's out-of-town wedding program to school board members and ministers and phoned other students. Conservative citizens called for his dismissal. Someone mailed antigay videos to the parents of his 140 students. (A guidance counselor and one other employee were eventually disciplined for giving out addresses.)

Crane responded to his students' repeated questions with, "I know you've heard rumors about me. You have to ask yourself two things: Is it true? And should it matter? If not, then I have a job to do and you have a job to do. Let's get to it." He recorded his comments to prove that he never mentioned homosexuality or marriage. Still, the principal warned Crane to stop making an issue of his sexuality. He answered that he was not the one making the issue, but added that he would not lie either.

He was backed by the Michigan Education Association and a tenure law that requires just cause (for example, poor classroom performance or professional misconduct) for termination. The school board did not invite Crane to its first two hearings on the matter. When he did address the board at a separate meeting, they had no questions. They merely offered him a buyout in exchange for his resignation. He declined.

The board did not fire Crane. Instead, it published a statement declaring:

Homosexuality violates the dominant moral standards of the district's community. Individuals who espouse homosexuality do not constitute proper role models as teachers for students in this district. . . . The district continues to investigate and monitor the current circumstances and controversy and will take prompt and appropriate lawful action when justified.

Although he had had vocal student support, twenty-six students withdrew from his classes, including one girl whose church warned that her boyfriend would become gay if he remained in the school choir. Crane was formally reprimanded for speaking to the girl and reassuring her that her boyfriend would be fine. The board said he had ignored their order not to discuss homosexuality and violated a rule against religious harassment.

Within a year Crane resigned his position, blaming a poisonous environment and worn down by what one of his lawyers called "one baseless complaint after another." Six months later he was dead of a heart attack at the age of thirty-two.[44] In 1999 the district had to be forced by a court to pay Crane's estate the bulk of his severance pay.[45]

Ordinarily, teachers' extracurricular speech and advocacy are protected more than other kinds of conduct, unless the speech can be shown to interfere with or disrupt school activities.[46] Such disruption was the basis of a charge leveled at a veteran Utah teacher who came out at a state capitol press conference announcing the formation of a Gay Lesbian and Straight Teachers' Alliance in February 1996.[47]

Within the school, educators might be safer discussing homosexuality in general, rather than their own homosexuality, which can be deemed unfit even for adult peers to hear.[48]

*The Wendy Weaver Case.* The Wendy Weaver case has brought national attention to issues of speech and employment rights for gay teachers.[49] The Spanish Fork High School teacher-coach, who had taken her girls volleyball team to four Utah championships, became the object of a gag order. Weaver, a mother who was married for fifteen years and divorced, was asked point-blank by a student considering going out for the team whether she was gay. She told her she was, and in the resulting community firestorm, Weaver was dismissed from coaching and told not to speak of her sexuality to anyone connected with the school, even if asked. Her former husband, also a teacher, was issued a similar ban.

Although Weaver never intended to discuss her sexuality in the classroom, she found the order overly broad, even after the board stipulated that it was chiefly concerned with her speech as a professional, including extracurricular and parent-teacher duties. She sued with the help of the ACLU, claiming that many in her small town of fewer than 18,000 had school ties. She was then sued in turn by town residents who alleged that she had behaved inappropriately with her players by

- taking them on overnight trips to a cabin and to her home;
- presiding over all-night hot tub parties at the school;
- participating in a football game in which girls wore only bras and shorts;
- promoting a network of same-sex relationships;
- witnessing open displays of affection between the girls;
- discouraging them from having boyfriends and benching those who did;
- pulling their shirts up to inspect for "hickeys."

Two thousand seven hundred parents asked that their children not be assigned to Weaver's classroom. She was excommunicated from the Mormon Church for not renouncing her lesbianism.

One year after her ordeal began, a federal judge responded to Weaver's suit with an order that the school district reinstate her to her coaching position, lift the gag order, and give her $1,500 in damages.[50] She still faced trial in the state courts on the parents' charges, which were eventually reduced by the court to two: that she had criticized the Mormon Church in her class and that students' rights were violated by her mere presence in the locker room. Weaver declined the offer to continue her coaching.[51]

## Is Law Enough?

Legal recourse is of course important, but we must ask whether legislatures or courts can ever fully alleviate teachers' worries. This question is part of a larger one: Can a civil rights approach bring a just resolution to problems arising from heterosexist bigotry?[52] Some activists advise against pursuing equality through the political-legal process, which is by its nature both gradualist and compromising. There is also merit to their argument that liberation is not advanced by claims to privacy, as in *Bowers v. Hardwick*.

Even the patient and discrete may wonder whether granting employment or privacy protections will signal a change people's hearts and minds about homosexuality. Jubilation in the gay and lesbian community over the *Romer* decision was more than equaled by the outrage of those who savaged the Supreme Court for overturning a majority's wishes and forcing homosexuality down Colorado's craw. Justice Scalia's harsh dissent, representing a three-judge minority, characterized the state law that would have invalidated all gay rights ordinances as "a modest attempt by seemingly tolerant Coloradans to preserve traditional sexual mores against the efforts of a politically powerful minority."[53]

The courts might protect teachers' jobs, but they cannot be relied on to provide real security and comfort. Nor can one depend on politicians to assert unequivocally the full humanity of homosexual people. The rush to support the gay marriage ban in the Marriage Protection Act in 1996, even by the most progressive federal legislators, demonstrates the futility of expecting them to stand against popular homophobia.[54]

A teachers' employment rights case, *Acanfora v. Board of Education of Montgomery County* (1974), illustrates perfectly the limitations of court decisions and legislation. Although ruling against a homosexual teacher for lying about his gay activism on a job application, the judge's opinion included statements about homosexual rights that are still being hailed as precedent-setting and progressive.[55] Yet two premises in his remarks are troublesome. These two facets of Acanfora rank high in expediency but are deficient in dignity.

First, answering concerns that being around homosexual teachers might influence a student's sexual orientation, he found that such an effect was minimal since orientation is probably determined by age five or six. Implicit in the judge's reasoning, supported by expert testimony, was the notion that children must be shielded from inherently unhealthy homosexual role modeling. Heterosexual role modeling, one presumes, would be suitable and wholesome. Straight teachers would not be constrained to hide significant details of their identities like finding members of the opposite sex attractive or having a wife or husband.

Second, the judge relied to some extent on the assertion that homosexual people's rights hinge on their keeping their orientation private. Although every citizen deserves the right to be left alone, this imposed privacy—the mandated closet—is unacceptable.

Proponents of the privacy argument, otherwise moderate and reasonable, can be blind to this double standard. Arguing for the silence of gay and lesbian teachers, two of them write:

> Parents and school authorities have a right to demand that homosexual teachers refrain from using the classroom as a forum. This is not to single them out for special limitations. Heterosexual teachers are expected not to parade their political or sexual preference before the students.[56]

These censors do not understand that a simple personal declaration by a homosexual teacher creates a political forum only in a homophobic culture nor do they appear to notice the heterosexuality parade, marching daily through America's classrooms.

For some time and in most places the battle over teachers who are privately gay or lesbian has ceased. For all the past *causes célèbres*, such as the Briggs Initiative, the preponderance of case law does not support the assertion that reactionary forces are sniffing about for homosexual teachers to fire.[57] As they have found in their crusade to keeps gays and lesbians out of the military, it is harder nowadays to prove that *undisclosed* homosexuality is a danger to anyone. Rather they target the threat of homosexuality *revealed*. Students are expected not to ask; teachers, commanded not to tell. The bogeys of the Right are those whose words or actions teach schoolchildren that there is no inferiority, no disgrace, and no sin in being gay, lesbian, or bisexual.

As a result, even teachers who are bold enough to be identified as homosexual in the press might shrink from being open with students.[58] They rightly dread the repercussions of acknowledging their sexuality in school.[59] In one national study, more than 50 percent of junior and senior high school principals would seek to revoke the credentials of teachers who came out to students, whereas fewer than 10 percent said they would want to dismiss a teacher simply for being homosexual.[60] Some of these may fret over homosexual influence on students' development; others may know better. Yet they all share a common goal toward which closeted teachers perhaps unwittingly contribute: to communicate to students that there is substantial shame and no safety in having an unconventional sexuality.

There is no evidence that civil or employment rights guarantees are enough to bring homosexual teachers out. Other considerations hold them back, more subtle, and perhaps more immediately intimidating than the possibility of eventual job loss. The first is that supervisors can ruin teachers' working lives in ways that might be difficult to prove in an exhausting grievance process. Such factors as subject, class, student, and room assignments, numbers of preparations, schedule balance, extracurricular duties, evaluations, administrative, staff, and custodial support can mean satisfaction or misery. An attorney for the Lambda Legal Defense and Education Fund describes this tactic as "mak[ing] life so awful for the teacher that they can't bear to stay."[61]

Nor should one ignore the very real fear of direct homophobic responses, occasionally from antagonistic colleagues, but more often from students: harassment, vandalism, threats, and personal violence. In one instance a rural Michigan student with rumored ties to the Ku Klux Klan implied in his class writing and through the theft of shotgun shells that he intended to kill his lesbian teacher.[62] In another case, a California high school special education teacher was tormented on his campus with pornographic, antigay material, which "created a lack of safety in [his] world."[63] In a 1998 lawsuit, a Wisconsin teacher claimed to have suffered a disabling emotional breakdown because of vulgar phone calls, graffiti, name-calling at school and at home, and repeated harassment from students, parents, and school staff. Although a student had threatened in front of teacher and student witnesses to kill him, the boy was not disciplined. The administrator reasoned that middle school "boys will be boys."[64] Such threats and assaults often, but not always, come from students who are not assigned to these teachers and do not know them very well.

Sometimes homophobic reaction is camouflaged. One teacher who had successfully come out to his classes found his job in jeopardy on trumped up charges of "significant deficiency" having nothing to do with his sexuality.[65] Two others were fired for seven reasons, including misappropriation of school property and improper discipline of students as well as being poor role models and conducting a homosexual relationship. When one was vindicated by an adjudicator's ruling, the school board voted 5 to 1 to appeal.[66]

## Professional Losses

For some another apprehension is yet more weighty than fears over job retention, physical safety, and working conditions. It is that their school relationships would be unalterably harmed if their sexuality became known. Namely that they would forfeit the esteem of their peers and their effectiveness in the classroom. For them there is nothing more alarming than damaged collegiality and uncooperative students. Even those who would sacrifice cordiality with a few homophobic adults might balk at impeding communication with students, who will not learn from or be counseled by a teacher they do not respect.[67]

When relationships are wounded after disclosure the dagger can be delivered indirectly. It was not school officials' active opposition but their three-month silence that drove a San Leandro, California, science teacher to a stress-related medical leave and a voluntary job search. She might have survived the barrage of public criticism and even the death threat that followed her coming out during her school's diversity week: "I can withstand anti-gay comments from a handful of adults, but I cannot do my job with the school board and the superintendent not supporting me and sitting on their hands remaining silent in the face of threats and unfounded criticism."[68] The board's belated restatement of its nondiscrimination policy fell short of the affirmation she needed and deserved.

Educators have reason to believe that coming out would draw attention away from their teaching and toward their persons.[69] Each expects that parents and students will see him or her as the homosexual teacher, not the science teacher or the inspiring teacher. Even worse, some heterosexuals assume gays' and lesbians' values are so perverse as to render them incapable of the objectivity required of teachers and counselors.

*Administrative Opportunities.*   Although the rule is seldom explicitly stated, the closet seems to be the only option for those who want to become administrators. Systems may indeed welcome homosexual teachers, but the virtual absence of open gays and lesbians in their front offices is evidence of a lavender ceiling.[70] A random and anonymous Connecticut survey, for example, turned up not one homosexual principal, although one has been mentioned.[71] The public's dubiousness would likely be articulated in questions about commanding student and community respect. To some credibility, dignity, and "gravitas" may be synonymous with heterosexuality.

*Overcompensation.*   One small study found that gay and lesbian teachers strive for excellence to compensate for their homosexual status. They feel they have to be extraordinary professionals to defend against the effects of a possible disclosure.[72] Their perfectionism might also be a remnant of a similar stigma management strategy from their adolescence (see Chapter 6). Although teachers in general seem drawn to performing and being appreciated, gay and lesbian practitioners are perhaps even more intense in this regard than others:

> I see kids in the street and they always say "hi." Lately, I've been thinking, "I wonder what those kids would think if they knew." I was walking down the street the other day and a student I had last year gave me a hug and kissed me on the cheek. Would she have done that if she knew? I don't know.[73]

If as adolescents these teachers were estranged from or disparaged by their peers, their students' applause can represent a healing, if delayed, teen acceptance.[74]

The necessary relationships for good teaching and its rewards are endangered by disclosure. Argue as one might that honesty and integrity are at stake, the consequences can just as easily be disaster as relief. Even those who have previously come out to other classes approach each new occasion with trepidation.

*The Rodney Wilson Case.*   The cases of Rodney Wilson and Martin Bridge help clarify the risks. Wilson was a history teacher at Melville High School in Saint Louis.[75] As a young nontenured faculty member, he had thought about coming out to his students when they made antagonistic, even violent, statements about gays and lesbians during classroom civil rights debates. Although he remained closeted to students for almost four years, he was open with about a third of his colleagues.

Then, in March of 1994, after attending the National Education Association's conference "Affording Equal Opportunity to Lesbian and Gay Students Through Teaching and Counseling," Wilson came out to one of his classes during a presentation on the holocaust. Using a poster from the Holocaust Museum in Washington, D.C., he explained the significance of the various Nazi extermination camp insignia, including the pink triangle worn by homosexual prisoners. He stated that had he lived in Europe at that time, he would likely have been gassed as a gay man and then spoke of the history of gay and lesbian oppression. Greatly moved, Wilson's students urged him to have the same conversation with his other classes and he did with some. Their responses ranged from enlightened support to apparent uninterest.

But, as the word spread throughout the 2,000-student school, some negative and threatening words were uttered and written. Although they came to naught, the adult reactions came to matter. Initially the school administration seemed positive, but he was eventually sent a memo advising that discussion of "facts and beliefs of a personal nature" was "inappropriate conduct for a teacher." The superintendent admonished him to stick to the prescribed curriculum.[76]

Still untenured, Wilson began to fear for his job. Public testimony before the school board yielded both praise and condemnation. He did have support from some parents and colleagues, as well as from the NEA. After months of waiting, he was retained on his principal's recommendation.[77] Competence and popularity won out over a modicum of bigotry and suspicion. No parents took up Wilson's offer to confer with him about removing their children from his classroom, and all students remained.

*The Martin Bridge Case.*  Yet, for all the respected teachers whose ordeals are temporary, there are others who find legal protections an inadequate shield. One of them, Martin Bridge, was a popular high school educator in Los Angeles.[78] An English teacher, once named Teacher of the Month, Bridge was rated highly by students and administration. Everything fell apart, nonetheless, after a favorite student asked him if he was gay. He evaded the question, perhaps hinting embarrassment, and was subjected to a maelstrom of gay-baiting from his own classes and from others in the 2,300-student school.[79]

Despite the Los Angeles United School District's explicit policies against homophobic discrimination and programs for homosexual students in some locations, Bridge's school was decidedly homophobic. Its mixed-income, predominantly black and Hispanic students came mostly from religiously conservative homes. Although the principal offered to come to his classes to support him, Bridge refused, dreading further loss of control. Eventually, he left, declining to pursue his case with the Equal Opportunity Office.

Some might deem homophobia incidental to this story. They would claim Bridge's students just found a way to get to him, as young people often do with authority figures, but that theory ignores their established adoring relationship. Without preventative work or immediate strong intervention, this ugly set piece would have the same outcome in most schools. Rather than signal his vulnerability, Bridge might have thwarted his attackers with an out and proud demeanor or fought back with an official complaint. Wherever such actions might have led, this case demonstrates that laws and policies do not by themselves protect gay and lesbian teachers from the outcome that may dismay them most—losing rapport with their students.

## Identity Management

Homosexual teachers control their level of disclosure to prevent such employment and relationship losses. Pat Griffin describes a continuum of strategies they employ to manage their identities in the workplace.[80] Her reference points range from total hiding to public affirmation:

- Passing: lying, assuming no one knows, and wanting to be known as heterosexual.
- Covering: censoring oneself, assuming no one knows, and wanting not to be seen as gay/lesbian.
- Implicitly out: telling the truth without explicit gay/lesbian language, assuming some people probably know, not objecting to being seen as gay/lesbian.
- Explicitly out: affirming one's gay/lesbian identity, mutually acknowledging one's identity, and wanting to be seen as gay/lesbian.

"Passing" requires deliberate avoidance schemes like dressing in a supposedly heterosexual style, lying about the nature of one's relationships or the gender of one's lovers, and having decoy escorts.

"Covering" is lying by omission rather than deliberate falsifying. One lesbian teacher who was warned by a friend to concoct camouflage said, "Every nerve in my body tingled resistance. 'I don't want to live on lies,' I groaned. 'In silence for a year or two maybe, but not on lies.'"[81] Those who cover must shun situations that could lead to personal information sharing. When they do mention such matters they omit gendered pronouns instead of changing them, and if they appear with their lovers, they scrupulously avoid behavior that would indicate the depth of their relationship.

Covering appeals to those who are uncomfortable with lying but do not view selective truth telling as equally blameworthy. The lesbian teacher just cited did lie once, at the start of her job, and then took refuge in covering. She confided, "I never made a close friend on that faculty, though there were many people I liked and admired. I simply couldn't bear the moment when I would have to admit the lie, so instead I held my distance."[82] As Rita Kissen observes, "Closeted gay teachers miss the support of their colleagues in hard times as well as in good ones."[83]

"Implicitly coming out" drops passing and covering but does not name one's orientation. Choice of clothing and accessories may even intentionally imply one's identity. Assuming that many associates who remain silent about it already know one's orientation, one confirms that it is not to be discussed by not doing so oneself. One may refer to a significant other so as to acknowledge a relationship without using words like "lover" or "spouse." If someone else calls him or her one's "friend," it is allowed to pass.

This glass closet, maintained through unspoken agreement, affords a modicum of integrity to the teacher, who is not forced to lie. Since she or he has never been explicit, some latitude is maintained for denial should danger be signaled.

But even that deniability has subtle shadings. An eighteen-year veteran lesbian English teacher had great skill at partial truth telling. Asked by students about her living arrangements, "Ruth" replied that she lived with another woman and some pets and was not interested in marriage. When a persistent lesbian-baiter harassed her, she angrily demanded that her principal discipline the student. "Ruth" had one condition, however: The principal was not to tell him that "Ruth" was *not* a lesbian.[84] It is also excruciatingly clear that no one, particularly "Ruth" herself, could tell students she *was* a lesbian.

"Explicitly coming out" is irrevocable and therefore practiced selectively. In one study, 82 percent of ninety-seven gay and lesbian public school teachers were open with at least one person, but only 44 percent of these were out to another teacher. (Whether they were out to students was not even asked.) Of those who were out to someone, 70 percent reported a positive reaction.[85] That 80 percent of the respondents were recruited from gay and lesbian professional, social, political, or educational organizations implies a greater degree of openness in this sample than one would expect among other homosexual teachers without such affiliations. Only 8 percent of those studied were from the South, a socially conservative region.

Not all teachers employ the same strategy consistently at work. Some are more open with certain groups and individuals than with others. In one remarkable case, a teacher was out in his union activism but could not find a way to be direct at his school, even with his colleagues.[86] These patterns are consistent with identity disclosure strategies among homosexual people in other professions as well.

In an excruciating irony, several of Griffin's closeted subjects feared coming out to colleagues who were known or perceived to be closeted too. The former suspected the latter might betray the confidence in order to distance themselves from suspicion. Closeted teachers may even shun explicitly out colleagues in order to avoid being betrayed by them or characterized by association with them.

There appears to be a progression in disclosure to adults, punctuated by a forbidding boundary on the other side of which students dwell. Coming out to students is judged the riskiest action of all. Only one of Griffin's participants had told a student. Gay and lesbian teachers may suspect that certain students know their orientation but hesitate to confirm it to them, perhaps until they have graduated.

A teacher may be motivated extrinsically and intrinsically to scale the student barrier. They can be galvanized by gay pride events or other positive catharsis, or they may just grow weary of constant vigilance and avoidance. They can also be spurred by homophobia, especially when it is aimed at young people. A gay or lesbian student's injury, suicide, or attempted suicide can provoke an integrity crisis.[87] At schools with antihomophobia projects, they may participate in or observe the creation of a gradually more tolerant school environment and be inspired by open colleagues and students to take incrementally greater risks.[88] Conversely, demands for and inception of gay-positive school programs might startle teachers who are passing and covering. They could feel that unwarranted attention was being brought to a subject that would be better left unaddressed; or they might be torn between wanting to participate and fearing the suspicion that their involvement could bring. Like some minority teachers in the 1960s and 1970s, who preferred the apparent safe calm of the status quo to the tumult of a civil rights struggle, they might favor the relative comfort of their disguises over the disruptions of gay liberation. School-based activism might drive them deeper into hiding.

Thomas Juul's study of nine hundred members of gay/lesbian teachers groups in forty-one states and the District of Columbia found being open about sexual orientation to be positively correlated with youth, membership in a homosexual teachers group, and contact with AIDS-related death.[89] Even with their lack of experience and job security, younger teachers were more likely to come out than middle-aged and older colleagues. Second, peer support, and perhaps encouragement, could be incentives to openness, although actual group membership does not necessarily contribute to coming out. (In fact, teachers who are already out may be more likely to join such groups.) Lastly, those affected by AIDS mortality were tired of grieving alone. They needed the bolstering that could come only through sharing their losses. Survivors might also have reached a new life perspective that permits greater risk-taking.

As in the study cited earlier, Juul did not ask respondents whether they were out to students. Since his K–12 survey did not distinguish between responses from teachers of younger and older students, that question was deemed unlikely to yield meaningful results.

## The Personal Cost of the Closet

The balancing act for teachers who don't come out at school can steal their energy and attention. They often have to keep track of which identity strategy to use with whom, to monitor their confidences, language, gestures, and dress, to avoid physical contact, to demur from counseling homosexual students, and to look over their shoulders when they are away from work.[90] With less privacy and fewer opportunities to escape from their campuses, closeted boarding school teachers must find this regimen burdensome, especially those who endure the scrutiny given to unmarried teachers in single-gender institutions.

This dissembling is bound to diminish their self-respect. They can also be discomfited by having to be silent and unhelpful while gay and lesbian students or colleagues suffer—or resist and organize. A number of other researchers in addition to Griffin and Juul have noted these stresses[91] and their aftermath: drug and alcohol abuse, depression, detachment from students and colleagues, and other dysfunctional behaviors.[92] Even paranoia is possible.[93]

Juul found tenured teachers less stressed about their sexual identity but still not more predictably out.[94] Although tenure may bestow a greater sense of job security in the event of involuntary disclosure, it cannot eliminate all the apprehensions of the closet.

The agonies of Terri Gruenwald, for example, epitomize the fate of the closeted teacher and the cost to the school of her hiding.[95] Bitter over not being able to be a whole person at work, she sometimes took it out on the few colleagues who knew of her sexuality. She was sickened by the double standard that let her be a proud Jew in a predominantly Christian school, but not a lesbian. Unable to come out even to a lesbian student desperate for reassurance and knowing that many of her students detected her homosexuality anyway, she cringed when they asked about her alleged "husband." She wrote:

I love teaching with a passion. . . . But sometimes I wonder how long I'll be able to continue teaching. I live two lives: one in the classroom, and one at home. . . . It is a chasm so deep that I fear it will swallow me up. I worry that I may be forced to choose between being a teacher and living my life.[96]

Sadly, the teacher is not always the only casualty. There have been instances of closeted educators reinforcing their cover through tacit collusion in the bashing of homosexual students[97] and in the persecution of gay and lesbian colleagues.[98]

## The Benefits and Responsibilities of Coming Out

The chief rewards of disclosure are greater integrity, increased self-respect, and a more honest engagement with one's students and coworkers. Truth telling is appropriate to professionals who help students discover what the world is about, who they are, and who they might be. Each school day classroom teachers are judged. Are they genuine? Do they know valuable things? Do they care about us? Do they really want to find honest answers to our questions and theirs? Sensitive young people are eager to know whether their teachers and parents are honest about who they are and what they value.

When teachers are openly homosexual, they give students, colleagues, parents, and the community a chance to unlearn heterosexist stereotypes and present young gays and lesbians the rare gift of proximate role models.[99] Of course being a "model minority person" is never easy and not always joyful. One may bear an impossible obligation not to misstep, particularly with bigots ready to pounce on any shortcoming. Furthermore, the minority teacher must be a paragon so as not to let the minority students down. One out lesbian admitted that a gay colleague had her pegged when he observed, "You're being a superteacher, having to be extra good, extra dedicated to prove how wonderful lesbian teachers are."[100] Another teacher tallied the price of such a mania: "Like, you have to be the absolute best perfect model of a teacher all the time. You just end up driven."[101]

Additionally, openly gay or lesbian teachers often become native informants.[102] Everyone seems to turn to them with questions about homosexuality. Students with sexuality concerns are invariably referred to their door. When a teacher has been well regarded before coming out, he or she is often expected to lead the campaign against homophobia. That is exactly what happened to a respected teacher in a Boston suburb, who, after guilty silence during gay and lesbian student unrest, finally came out to the administration and instantly received their commitment to constructive action—and then she was left to initiate it![103]

Too often, gay and lesbian teachers alone are expected to furnish both the initiative and the execution for reform. Administrators assume that because teachers are homosexual, they are qualified and willing to assume the responsibility.

As if being experts and role models were not demanding enough, openly gay and lesbian teachers are subject to personal interrogation and occasionally to attempted seduction. Inevitably some students interpret a teacher's coming out as an invitation to inquiry at a level of intimate detail that is never assumed in a heterosexual context. When straight teachers confirm, indirectly or explicitly, the universal assumption of heterosexuality, young people often ask if they are married or have boyfriends, girlfriends, or children. When a homosexual teacher comes out, some students do not hesitate to extend their probe into the bedroom. However much it springs from legitimate curiosity about unfamiliar erotic practice, this questioning is intrusive.

Yet students do deserve a forum for questions about homosexual intimacy. If a gay or lesbian teacher is comfortable and competent to discuss homosexual practices generally, he or she should do so. Making sexuality the exclusive domain of sex education teachers renders it special, taboo, or sensational. To prevent that, most teachers should be relaxed and well informed to talk with students about both heterosexual and homosexual erotic expression. Of course homosexual topics should also be included in comprehensive sexuality classes (see Chapter 14).

Some gay and lesbian teachers recognize the importance of being out to their students but hesitate to spend class time discussing sexuality, particularly when they are expected to teach something totally unrelated to it like math or physics. Others do not feel as constrained by their syllabi.[104] Whatever the main subject matter, a few minutes spent on a serious sexuality question of interest to students is entirely proper.

### Effects on Students

Some heterosexual students are not ready to accept the fact of a teacher's homosexuality. They may insist others have misheard or claim the teacher was joking or testing their attitudes. Most however do not deny. They may have suspected, even speculated with others, or they might be surprised. Their reactions can be neutral, hostile, or accepting. Some straight students have even confided in their homosexual teachers as in no others, perhaps expecting greater understanding of their relationship quirks and family secrets.[105] Although research must determine what influences these varied responses, the following are likely factors:

- prior relationship with the teacher (level of mutual respect, affection, and honest exchange);
- student background—ethnic, racial, religious, class, and political;
- how and how often issues of difference have been addressed previously;
- level of commonality in values;
- extent of student leadership in modeling independent expression and tolerance;
- teacher's perceived attitude toward his/her sexuality;
- teacher's response to negative reactions.

Students' reactions mirror those in families. Some are disappointed in their assumptions and expectations, especially if they idealized the teacher. Given time, however, and a patient nondefensive teacher, even those most shaken can come back.

Students may be anxious about what their relationship with a homosexual teacher says about their own sexualities. At one extreme, having an openly gay or lesbian teacher can expose students to homophobic bashing. For instance, because their coach was an openly gay man, track team members at one California high school were regularly harassed and even assaulted by other students.[106] Students struggling with their own orientations may go so far as to disassociate from their out teacher.[107] Those having difficulties with the homosexuality of their parents or other family members may act out against the teacher, who is usually a safer target than any adult at home.

On the other hand, many students developing a homosexual identity welcome role models and allies against homophobia and invisibility. Some youth have testified that having out teachers is the most important part of their school experience as gays and lesbians.

### Student Crushes

A few homosexual students might even become infatuated with a teacher whose encouragement and nurturing can be mistaken for seduction. Teachers should understand what fosters this misperception. Educators of all sexualities have the capacity to turn students' heads. Many use this power to motivate their charges to scholarship and virtue. To love the person who stands in place of one's parent—to want to please and emulate him or her—lies at the heart of the learning dynamic. There is danger, of course, when the Platonic ideal is eroticized. All teachers must be clear in discouraging such a turn. Cornel West cautions, "And as teachers of students we know there's an erotic dimension, but it has got to be severed from any use of power for subordination, sexual pleasure, sexual manipulation, and so forth."[108]

Students will still have their crushes, willy-nilly.[109] They are the natural products of power relationships, role modeling, and the discovery that teachers are flesh and blood after all. But gay and lesbian teachers' support for homosexual students should not be perceived as a come-on by critical observers or the young people themselves. Homosexual teachers are no more responsible for inviting infatuation than are their heterosexual peers, albeit the eroticized understanding of homosexuality could lead to student fantasizing and even false accusations. This interchangeability in the public mind of homosexuality and sex might some day be corrected, when more people, including teachers, are out of the closet and their sexuality is normalized. Until then, teachers need not fret unduly, although they are wise, in a reactionary political environment, to be circumspect about student contact and sharing confidences.

### Sharing Personal Experiences

Gay and lesbian teachers who share their histories with their students should be careful not to pour out their pain indiscriminately, when just a few personal details could create a bond of common experience.[110] They are employed after all to teach and counsel students, not for their own therapy. They may have been marginalized and mistreated at the school and may yearn to rehearse their resentments for students, particularly those who are feeling that way too, but that is not advisable. Teachers can help students analyze and fight injustice without focusing on themselves. Instead, they need to find appropriate venues for their personal grievances, where inequities and injuries can be detailed and names can be named. The classroom is not usually the place for that.

Crises involving the teacher and the public are another matter, however. If a teacher faces firing, if curriculum is censored, or if books are banned, then students may be justifiably notified. It is proper for the teacher to inform students, parents, and other members of the community about the specifics of the charges or actions and to ask, without personal invective or unprofessional attack, for their support.

### When to Come Out

Timing is an important factor in successfully coming out. Although no one can say precisely when the most opportune moment arrives, teachers can be fairly certain that announcing their sexuality in the first sessions of a class is inadvisable. Even if a teacher ached to get it over with and wished that the homophobes would leave before they began to spew, it would be counterproductive. Some students could take an early declaration as an unwelcome, if not aggressive, challenge. On the other hand, when mutual respect, trust, and affection are allowed to develop, the odds favor student acceptance and growth.

If teachers' reputations or demeanors induce questions about their sexuality before they are comfortable answering directly, they have to make a judgment call. They could scold students into silence or to let them know they should desist or employ a host of evasions with which they are probably adept. Or, determining that intimidation and circumlocution will only make the situation worse, they could decide to answer truthfully and hope to work the matter through. If they do evade temporarily, they should resolve to come out as soon as they can, since the issue will arise again, at least in students' minds.

There is a downside to zigzag evasions.[111] Faced with an older closeted teacher, some young people assume that anyone over twenty-five must be too uncomfortable to come out. But the more harmful consequences of a transparent closet is students' concluding that a teacher is ashamed or that the school is really not as safe as some adults pretend.

Two examples illustrate the frequent self-delusion behind the dance. In the first, a lesbian teacher in Boston had thought her cover was so opaque to students, she was shocked to learn from colleagues in a workshop that several teens had asked them about her sexuality. Although none had betrayed her secret, the teachers admitted that changing the subject or double-talking had not laid the matter to rest. In the second instance, a lesbian alumna speaking before her alma mater's gay/straight alliance began her talk by asking if a favorite teacher she suspected of being gay had come out yet. Her embarrassed, but hardly surprised, audience merely giggled and shifted in their seats.

That is not to say that waiting cannot work. A teacher who came out to students in a letter to the school newspaper during a leave of absence, received the following reply:

> In your letter you spoke about how you wished you had told us the truth. I'm ashamed to say this, but I wasn't ready to hear that fall term of my freshman year. I probably would have rejected you like so many others have, simply out of ignorance. I can't speak for the whole class when I say this, but I think that by spring term you could definitely have told us, and that most of us would have accepted it. That just goes to show the wonderful influence you had on us (at least on me). It just goes to show that ignorance is the main thing to battle.[112]

## Preparing for Fallout

Finally, despite the many blessings of being open, there are still dangers for which one can never be wholly prepared. In one case an openly lesbian physical education teacher was sued for $300,000 by parents for playfully tugging at their daughter's basketball shorts after joking about how she wore them. The suit claimed the girl required counseling for emotional distress, affecting her sleep, grades, and social life.[113]

Despite such horror stories, gay and lesbian educators should be inspired by the courage of many of their peers. Among these must be mentioned three veteran teachers, one at Lake Forest High School in Illinois, another at Southwest High School in Minneapolis, and a third at Roosevelt Middle School in Blaine, Minnesota. The first two returned successfully to their workplaces after sex changes, and the third, newly hired, met with over three hundred parents to explain her transgenderism.[114] Sadly, even with school support, she felt forced to resign by the vocal opposition of some parents and clergy.[115]

All educators would do well to have such dignity and fortitude. And, regardless of the limited long-term efficacy of the legal system in bestowing those two assets, gay and lesbian teachers also must cultivate as many school and community allies as will fit in a courtroom.

# 10

## Gay and Lesbian Families

Two decades ago it was estimated that one in five lesbians and one in ten gay males had children.[1] Just before the "lesbian baby boom" of the 1990s,[2] researchers thought that between 400,000 and 5 million lesbian mothers cared for from 1.5 to 14 million children.[3] Current studies suggest that 4 to 14 million sons and daughters live with 2 to 8 million gay or lesbian parents.[4] Yet very few schools show evidence that they have changed to accommodate their needs.

Some teachers and counselors come to their duties with ill-founded assumptions and expectations concerning these families.[5] Those who are queasy or condemning may have prejudged the children's homes as dysfunctional; and even the more accepting may blame gay or lesbian parents' sexuality for problems the children might have.[6] Attitudes like these contribute to the hostility and ignorance that many homosexual parents encounter in health care, education, and work settings.[7]

### Legalities

The legal system has also been unaccommodating or hostile to gay and lesbian families. Historically, judges have allowed homophobic arguments to determine custody in divorce cases.[8] In one infamous 1995 decision, upheld on appeal, a Florida judge took an eleven-year-old girl from a lesbian mother and placed her with a father who had served an eight-year sentence for murdering his first wife.[9] (Months later the mother died of a heart attack.)[10] Women who have never been married have also lost their children on the basis of their lesbianism.

Gays and lesbians are commonly disfavored or banned from being adoptive and foster parents.[11] When one child's biological mother died, for example, a Florida court in 1985 snatched her from her lesbian coparent, who had helped nurture her from birth, and gave her to her grandparents.[12] In 1996, California's Department of Social Services began efforts to codify its exclusion of adoptions by unmarried couples; the regulations would also prevent partners from becoming legal coparents of a child of whom one is already the parent.[13] In Washington State, the validity of a lesbian adoption was challenged when the biological mother left her partner and moved with the child to North Carolina.[14] A similar case arose in Pennsylvania in 1996 after a lesbian separation.[15]

Courts have been known to impose conditions when awarding visitation to homosexual parents. If they have live-in partners, for instance, they might not be permitted to see a child in their home.[16] Virginia courts gave custody of Sharon Bottoms's son to his grandmother in 1993, first because Bottoms was a lesbian alleged to engage in criminal oral sex, and then because the boy would be ridiculed. Conditional visitation rights stipulated that Bottoms's partner not be present when the boy came to their apartment.[17] A ruling that the partner be barred from any contact with the child was later reversed,[18] then reinstated.[19]

Despite this dismal history, new legal precedents are being set. According to a family law expert, "There's clearly a door opening here."[20] A number of jurisdictions, including Massachusetts, Connecticut, Illinois, and Washington, D.C., have permitted both the adoption of one partner's biological child by the coparent and the coadoption of nonbiological children.[21] In late 1995 the Supreme Court let stand a ruling giving visitation rights to the female ex-partner of a lesbian mother.[22] In 1996 the Court of Appeals of Georgia ruled that the visits by a gay father ought not to be restricted solely because he lived with a male lover.[23] At the end of that banner year, an Illinois court upheld the custody rights of a bisexual mother living with a female lover[24] and a Washington State appellate court overruled an order that a gay father refrain from displays of affection with his partner during his children's visits.[25]

Still injustices persist, especially regionally. In 1997 the state supreme court of North Carolina revoked custody from a gay father because he lived with a male lover.[26] The next year the Alabama supreme court removed a daughter from a mother who lived "in an open lesbian relationship," which it found criminal, immoral, and detrimental to the child, despite no evidence of harm.[27]

### Societal Prejudice

Many Americans have been conditioned to believe that successful child rearing requires the presence of two opposite gender parents in the home. Inept conclusions from faulty research are often used in negative pronouncements against single and homosexual parenting. Thus the crux of the Hawaii attorney general's 1996 argument against same-sex marriage was that same-gender couples are inherently damaging to children.[28] (The judge ultimately ruled that the studies submitted by the attorney general failed to support his position.[29]) Moreover, many respectable studies confirm that the quality of family relationships and the availability of resources are far more important than the number of parents or their gender.[30]

Yet many stereotypes persist. Gay men are presumed to be pleasure hounds and sex machines, rarely monogamous, and not responsible or nurturing. Lesbians, on the other hand, are depicted as lacking the requisite grace and softness as well as the indispensable male child-rearing partner.

Lastly, of course, there is a pervasive unease over homosexual, particularly gay male, contact with young children. Informing this aversion are two fallacies: predation and undue influence—the beliefs that homosexuals are inclined to molestation and that children raised by gays and lesbians are more likely to become homosexual themselves. Judges, many of them male probably, show particular concern for the sexual development of the sons of gay fathers.[31] Even the Georgia court that gave a gay father the right to see his daughter couched its decision in the expectation that he would remain "actively" closeted from her.[32]

## The Research

A number of empirical and clinical studies have been conducted to investigate the mental health of homosexual parents, the quality of their home environments, and the effects on children of their parenting. Inquiry has been focused on lesbians, since more children live with mothers after divorce, nonmarital insemination, or adoption than live with gay fathers.[33] Moreover, a good deal of the research is prompted by custody questions involving lesbian mothers predominantly. Perhaps because of sampling difficulties, the subjects tend to be divorced, openly lesbian, white women who live without partners. The relatively scarce examinations of parenting lesbian couples have had small volunteer samples with children under nine years old.[34] There are very few studies of adolescent children, little longitudinal research, little direct observation, and few interviews with the children themselves.[35]

Little attention has been paid to mothers, and even less to fathers, who have become parents within homosexual relationships. Children living with lesbian or gay male couples have been underrepresented,[36] as have children of color, the nonaffluent, and those living with bisexual, still married, or closeted parents.[37]

Most gays and lesbians do not disclose their orientations to their children.[38] For children of divorced parents, the effects of the parent's sexual orientation may be difficult to cull from those related to separation and having a step-parent.[39]

Many interesting questions have yet to be considered. What, for example, are the effects of being raised in extended homosexual families, where the issues of biological relatedness and kinship may be different than in heterosexual ones?[40] How do children fare who are conceived by lesbians through gay donor insemination and maintain a relationship with their fathers? What happens when a child lives with a remarried heterosexual parent and has contact with the homosexual parent? If there are children from this second marriage, is the status of the child of a homosexual parent tainted within the blended family? The following sections highlight current research findings concerning lesbian and gay parents or caregivers and their children.

## Mental Health

1. Lesbians have no more mental health problems than heterosexual women do; some are more self-confident and independent, and enjoy support from alternative family constellations.[41]
2. Single lesbian mothers share concerns similar to single heterosexual mothers relative to providing for their children.[42]
3. Divorced lesbian mothers have added worries about disclosure of their identities and its ramifications regarding custody and family relations.[43]
4. Lesbian mothers with female partners have stresses about earnings, since female couples, particularly in the working class, earn less than heterosexual ones.[44]
5. Lesbian families in which one woman or both are stepparents to their divorced partner's children may face a more difficult adjustment than similar families with heterosexual remarried parents because of secrecy, legal status, and stigmatization.[45]
6. Noncustodial divorced gay fathers are subject to grief over losing quality contact with their children and stress over the integration of their parental self-concept/role and their often newly forming gay identity.[46]
7. Gay fathers who are open with their children about their homosexuality appear to have better relationships with them than closeted fathers.[47]

## Parenting Skills

1. Lesbians do not value their motherhood any less than heterosexual women nor do they perform differently in child rearing and problem solving.[48]

2. Lesbians and gay men are not less effective parents than heterosexuals.[49]
3. The nonbiological parent is likely to bond closely with the child and assume increasing responsibility for rearing after the child's infancy,[50] although biological mothers are more likely to be caregivers, and nonbiological mothers are more often in paid employment.[51]
4. The nonbiological lesbian parent is usually more involved in child rearing than fathers in heterosexual couples.[52]
5. Lesbians and gay men are not likely to molest their own children or anyone else's. (Heterosexual men have been found to be most involved in such abuse.[53])
6. The only evidence of parental dysfunction appears in cases of opposite-gender couples where the homosexual parent is closeted to the child[54] and in cases of closeted gay fathers, even those living apart from their families.[55]

## Mental Health of Children

1. Differences in mental and emotional health have not been observed between children of lesbians and those of heterosexual mothers.[56] Marital discord and divorce[57] are greater predictors than parental homosexuality of children's psychological problems.[58]
2. If there is any discomfort with a parent's sexual orientation, it comes when the child's situation is disclosed to others.[59]
3. Cognitive functioning and behavioral adjustment of the three- to ten-year-old children of lesbian couples are comparable to those of heterosexuals' children.[60]
4. Self-esteem of daughters whose lesbian mothers live with their partners may be higher than that of daughters whose mothers live singly.[61]
5. Children are better-adjusted and lesbian mothers happier when child-rearing responsibilities are more evenly divided.[62] (There is evidence that such an equitable division, and thus better parenting, is evidenced more in lesbian-headed families than in traditional ones.[63])

## Social Stigma

Children with homosexual parents are aware of societal disapproval and are often compelled to secrecy. However, children of lesbians are no more likely to lack self-esteem or feel less social acceptability than their peers.[64]

*Gender Role and Sexual Orientation of Children*

1. There are no significant differences in the gender identity, sex role behavior, or sexual orientation of children raised by lesbian versus heterosexual parents.[65]
2. Lesbian mothers are as likely as,[66] or more likely than,[67] single or divorced heterosexual mothers to ensure children's contact with adult men, including their fathers.
3. Lesbians and gay men may be more likely than the majority of heterosexual parents to influence children to challenge limitations of traditional sex roles.[68] Lesbian and gay male couples share household duties and occupational role to a greater degree than heterosexual couples.[69]
4. Daughters of lesbians are more likely to engage in rough play and to play with traditionally masculine toys than other girls are.[70] They also appear to cross-dress more frequently.[71] (These activities indicate a role modeling that speaks to freedom and comfort.)
5. Absence of a father has no correlation with sex-role behavior in homosexual or heterosexual families.[72]
6. Some parents and teachers see children of lesbian couples as more affectionate, responsive, and protective of younger children than are heterosexual couples' children, who appear more domineering and negativistic.[73]
7. Two out of twenty-five children (8 percent) raised by lesbian mothers became homosexual adults in one study;[74] in another study over 90 percent of adult sons of gay fathers were found to be heterosexual.[75] (These percentages are consistent with estimates of the number of homosexuals in the general population, who of course include children of both homosexual and heterosexual parentage.)

These findings underscore the basic unexceptionality of gay and lesbian families. Yet fears persist, especially regarding heritability. Recent scholarship on the etiology of sexuality suggests that genetics more than rearing influences the orientation of offspring. (See Chapter 3.) Although research already shows that the children of an individual homosexual are not more likely to be gay or lesbian themselves, can one be confident that two homosexual parents will not tip the odds? That is, if genes predispose one to homosexuality, would not the biological child of a gay man and a lesbian have an increased chance of being homosexual?

Perhaps that would be so. Nevertheless who is going to allow the presumption that having more gay and lesbian children is undesirable? Indeed there is dismay in the gay community over some homosexual parents' defensive insistence, "Why would we ever want our child to be gay, when it is such a disadvantage?"[76]

Still, some might argue against homosexuals' raising children of any sexuality. The kindly child protectionist could claim that these young people would encounter harassment and discrimination, yet such reasoning would apply as well to other stigmatized minorities. Not very long ago it was used against mixed race couples' having children. In the instance of children who are gay and lesbian, they may be helped by openly homosexual parents to embrace their sexualities, whereas closeted parents might exert an opposite influence.

## Problems and Concerns

Although no inherent shortcomings ought to be ascribed to gay and lesbian parents, we know that many of their children do have some unique concerns, particularly at school.[77] It must be emphasized, however, that their challenges stem from misunderstanding, bigotry, and concealment, not from their parents' sexuality itself.[78]

### The Home

Children of a gay or lesbian divorcing parent may have domestic disruption to contend with. As with heterosexual divorce, tension at home can result in academic or behavior problems at school.[79] Particular confusion may result when the parent is closeted. The home environment is usually better when a parent is open; yet children may be distressed over the prospect of public reaction.[80] Most fret, above all, over how their peers will respond.

The reactions of the children themselves to a parent's homosexuality may vary according to developmental and gender differences. The mean age of parental self-disclosure or discovery by the child ranges from eight to eleven years old.[81] Younger children and late adolescents appear to have an easier adjustment than early or mid-adolescents.[82] Anxieties may be triggered by heterosexist stigma, secrecy, a sense of being different, peer rejection, and fear of having their own sexuality questioned.[83] The last may help explain why young people seem to have a harder time when a parent of their own gender is gay.[84]

They may also begin to feel insecure about their own orientation. When mothers are lesbian, more daughters than sons are worried about becoming homosexual; when boys have gay fathers, the reverse occurs.[85] Gender differences may also influence the nature of their troublesome reactive behaviors: Research describes some girls competing with their mother's lover for attention and angry boys fighting with their peers.[86]

Most children eventually adjust to the disclosure, sometimes better than their parents anticipated.[87] Openness can even improve their relationship.[88]

## Children's Peers

Nevertheless negotiating with the outside world can be problematical. Children's concerns about peer relations are justified. They may face prank calls, derogatory jokes, harassment, loss of friends, and friends' parents' forbidding further contact.[89] As an extreme example, a twelve-year-old girl was verbally and physically assaulted over a period of two years at two different Fayetteville, Arkansas, schools because her mother was a lesbian.[90]

Many adolescents employ self-protective strategies:[91]

1.  Boundary control: regulating others' contact with parents, controlling parental behavior, and monitoring the home environment so as to hide evidence of homosexuality;
2.  Nondisclosure: not confiding, perhaps even denying, the parent's orientation and relationships;
3.  Discreet disclosure: selectivity in disclosure and careful monitoring of confidants.[92]

In policing boundaries, young people shield themselves and their parents from presumably homophobic friends. "Bill" confessed:

> I don't want anybody to know anyway. Because it would cause ridicule and lose me some friends. . . . It's hard feeling that there's something that you're not sharing with your friends. . . . Like when they ask if my father is dating right now, and I'm like, "No." . . . You feel like there's a little skeleton in your closet that you're not bringing out. . . . I used to do a sweep before I would bring a friend home, but now my dad keeps [gay magazines] in his room.[93]

"Bill," was so taxed he was occasionally envious of friends with straight parents. He clung to a painfully tense nondisclosure, even when he heard offensive remarks about gay people, "because you feel strongly, but you have to keep your mouth shut." In the end, perhaps because he could not continue to function otherwise, he found an outlet in a group for the children of gay and lesbian parents.

The skeleton in the child's "closet" resembles the universal stigma management metaphor of gays and lesbians themselves. Furthermore, just as homosexual identity development is influenced by such variables as race, ethnicity, and religion, so these children deal with their parents' sexualities in subcultural contexts. (See Chapter 7.) Teachers must recognize the potential for different responses among diverse students.[94] Young people could be torn between religious, ethnic, or racial disapproval on one side and their love for a parent on the other: "The pain you feel because your religion has shunned your mother, because your mother is hated by some people for just being in love. And the conflicts within yourself because your mother has made your life harder because of who she is, yet you wouldn't want her any other way."[95]

Imagine the distress of such a child, who is victimized by the public vilification of someone they love, and with whom they often live. Their anger is compounded when shame prevents them from defending their parent.

Just as proximity to sustaining homosexual peers and community can facilitate gay and lesbian identity assumption, these children's adjustment can be enhanced through contact with others in similar families. Those who live in geographical or cultural isolation find coping more difficult than do those who are connected to a visible and affirming gay/lesbian community.[96]

A likely determinant of children's adaptation is how their parents deal with their own homosexuality. One study asserts that children of lesbian mothers who accept their own sexuality were better able to respond to teasing, "just as Jewish mothers could help their children cope with anti-Semitism—because they did not feel guilty about being Jewish."[97] Children of less self-affirming homosexual parents may not be as well equipped.

Even if unintended, the legacy of secrecy may be the child's sense of shame. One gay dad who changed his strategy to be more open at his son's new elementary school observed, "So how can a child have a clear, positive concept and understanding about what this relationship is about if someone's telling him not to tell anybody?"[98]

## What Schools Can Do

Teachers, counselors, and administrators can make school life joyful for these families by fashioning a gay and lesbian-positive school culture. To that end, personnel must be trained to be sensitive to potentially worrisome issues. It is not imperative that gay and lesbian families are identified; rather schools should assume that both students and their parents represent sexual orientation diversity. Homophobic disrespect and harassment must be challenged. Moreover, gay and lesbian people must be acknowledged, honored, and celebrated.

Achieving those objectives will not only affect the school environment, it will also promote communication, and occasionally reconciliation, between students and their gay and lesbian loved ones. An accepting school lets children give up resentment toward their homosexual parents for the harassment they endured and the shame they were led to feel. It is a huge relief not to feel the need to monitor and control all the time. A study of gay fathers and their families found that social control strategies were employed more by those children, usually older and living with their father, who saw their parent's homosexuality as intrusive, and less by those who identified strongly with him.[99] Ultimately, school personnel should work toward the same end for the child of a homosexual as they do for a homosexual child: destigmatization through understanding.

Educators might be surprised to learn whom their gestures and lessons can touch: Just before Parent-Teacher Day, a first-grader approached his teacher and confided that he had not told her about something. He had always referred to a woman who lived with him and his mother as if she were a housekeeper or baby-sitter, but she was not. The two were partners and he was fearful that if they both came to the evening event, he would be thought a liar or the situation would seem strange. The teacher assured him that she looked forward to meeting them. Although the partner did not appear after all and the boy continued to refer to her in his habitual way in front of other children, he knew from then on that he had his teacher's support.[100]

The more ambitious objectives of inclusive counseling and diverse curricula must be part of a long-term training and implementation plan. In the meantime, however, schools should employ the following strategies:[101]

1. Eliminate the heterosexual assumption when working with parents:
   - School forms, intake interviews, and questionnaires should be modified so as to use inclusive terms.
   - School personnel who call or write to parents need to be sensitized.
   - PTAs should explicitly welcome gay/lesbian parents.
2. Encourage parents and children to be open with faculty and administration. It may be advisable to designate a school liaison (perhaps a gay or lesbian parent) with whom parents can make a comfortable first contact.
3. Be clear about who will or should be informed (for example, student teachers) and who is responsible for transmitting the information (principal, teachers, parents, and so on).

4. Understand that some gay/lesbian parents and their children may not want to disclose to students or to adults other than the child's teachers and administrators.
   - Be prepared to deflect questions on behalf of those children and help them deal with their impact.
   - Encourage and train teachers to break the silence discreetly with parents who have not disclosed.
5. Be prepared to respond sensitively when children reveal more than their parents wish them to.
6. Use the relationship names that children use for their gay/lesbian coparents.
   - Use acceptable terms in addressing both coparents directly (for example, "your daughter").
7. Recognize that a coparent may want as much as a biological one to be involved in the child's life.
8. Be prepared for reactions of educators, parents, and community people who disapprove of homosexual parenting.
9. Be aware that homosexual parents and families from conservative subcultural and religious traditions may have needs and coping behaviors different from the majority.
10. Be sensitive to the possible unease of closeted gay and lesbian teachers who have children of openly homosexual parents in their classes. The parents may feel awkward disclosing to and dealing with such teachers as well.

Although many adolescents are preoccupied with outside perceptions of their homosexual parents, for some gays and lesbians their identity as parents feels more central than their sexual orientation.[102] Surely, sexuality issues are crucial to student adjustment and performance and should be faced squarely, but school personnel must also be aware that not every difficulty that these families bring to school is related to sexual orientation. They are subject to the same exigencies that beset other families and share the same sustaining delights that others do.

This particular kind of inclusion and respectfulness has an impact beyond gay and lesbian families themselves. For all students, but especially for those who come from nontraditional and minority homes, these practices demonstrate the scope and sincerity of the school's commitment to diversity and multiculturalism. Homosexual parent visibility and pride within the school community also encourage gay and lesbian students who may want to be parents themselves some day.

Beyond these steps, schools should be able to assist gay and lesbian families with their unique difficulties through referrals to outside support. In some cities, groups have been formed to help with such matters as alternative insemination, adoption, foster parenting of gay/lesbian youth, gay men raising daughters, and lesbians with sons. National information sources are Gay and Lesbian Parents Coalition International (GLPCI) and Children of Lesbians and Gays Everywhere (COLAGE).[103]

Not surprisingly, defenders of gay and lesbian families often emphasize their similarity to heterosexual ones. Yet, in the end, teachers and counselors should be mindful of two things: First, all families, even outwardly conventional ones, are far from uniform in structure and dynamics; and second, differences are not always disadvantages.[104]

# 11

## School Change

The gay and lesbian liberation and civil rights movements have produced a level of national discussion that reaches adults and children.
From contentious religious, artistic, and political discourse to frivolous
pop cultural representations, homosexuality has gone public. And America's schools are not exempt from the din, even if many are officially
gagged on the subject. Mandated silence may prevent rational adult-led
conversation, but it does not stop all utterance at the schoolhouse door.[1]
Unfortunately, the most common forms for such expression are name-
calling, harassment, and the denigration of homosexuals generally. Indeed, some authorities would have the official silence broken only for
antigay lessons.

The prospect of ridding schools of homophobia has been unthinkable
until now. The gay and lesbian community has heretofore generally ignored the importance of what is going on in the schools or has shrunk
from tackling the problem. They may have been intimidated by anticipated accusations of molestation or recruitment that, despite statistics to
the contrary,[2] attach to gay and lesbian adult interest in young people. Or
they may have been loath to recall their own student days. Nevertheless,
a handful of courageous educators, parents, and students in a few states
have begun a school-based reform, and the response from the Right has
been so pronounced that gay and lesbian community leaders are at last
heeding the issue. Inspired by the example of racial minorities and
women bringing multiculturalism and gender equity to the schools, gays
and lesbians have begun to think it possible to transform schools into
places where

- gay/lesbian/bisexual/transgender identities are seen as a part
  of the school's diversity;
- homophobic harassment is challenged;

- students, parents, and school personnel of all orientations are affirmed;
- curriculum examines the nature of homosexuality, the character and experience of gay/lesbian individuals and communities, and the contributions of noted homosexual people to histories and cultures.

Most schools have a long way to go to accept, let alone reach these goals, yet a germ of momentum has begun to build.

Adult unanimity is not a prerequisite for beginning this transformation. Neither are legislative or central office directives. Although school board and administrative support can be crucial,[3] we cannot wait for progressive policy to develop. Nor do executive orders, by themselves, advance the cause very far. In fact, some top-down efforts are counterproductive, compared with collaborative campaigns.[4] Committed teachers and their community allies are better advised to put policy reform on a parallel track while activism begins in the schools themselves. There the focus should be on building a critical mass of teacher, student, and parent support for antihomophobia education. Carefully planned school-based interventions may even run ahead of policy, perhaps hastening it along.

Whatever its priorities, the overall campaign to sensitize, inform, and protect ought to be waged at a number of levels—the individual, the institutional, and the community. This chapter examines each of these points of engagement.[5]

## Changing Individuals

People's attitudes toward homosexuality are functional; they reinforce their view of the world. (See Chapter 4.) Heterosexuals' affective reactions and behavior toward gays and lesbians are influenced by a generalized belief system.[6] Homophobia, except in the most extreme cases, is not itself a psychopathology; in the main, it begs not therapy but persuasion.[7] For individuals' beliefs about gays and lesbians to change, they must be brought to see that homosexuality is not a threat to their moral system or be persuaded to change their values so as to accommodate it.[8]

One can try to persuade people who rely on the dictates of conventional morality and conservative religious dogma that homosexuality is misconstrued by the authorities on whom they depend. Or one can attempt to move them beyond the strictures of convention entirely. Neither is easy: "Where important issues are involved, information campaigns fail, because people are inclined not to sit still and take in information that is dissonant with their beliefs."[9] Therefore, those who are responsible for schooling must avoid one-way information giving in favor of transformative interactive education.

## Positive Propaganda

Some people believe that if gays and lesbians can be made to look like middle-class family people, they will be less unwelcome in the American patchwork.[10] A number of popular books recommend stressing the positive and eliminating the negative in the public image of gays and lesbians. Some, for example, condemn public sex, promiscuity, cavorting drag queens, and more than two alcoholic drinks a day.

One theorist has tried to bolster his argument in favor of the inclusion of "positive images" of homosexuality in school curricula in England with the following:

> To advocate, or even to condone, promiscuity and decadence under the alluring banner of liberality and emancipation would be not only a wicked and calculating imposture on the credulity of the young, but a policy pregnant with catastrophic social consequences. It would also bring into disrepute more temperate proposals which might be mistakenly associated with it. . . . However, it is possible to promote images of homosexuality which many can accept not—as some opponents fear—because they have been seduced into moral nihilism, but because their value system is flexible enough to accommodate homosexual relationships which are seen to share the morally significant features of comparable heterosexual relationships.[11]

There is reason in his focus on matters of moral significance, yet his tone invites the question, what does he think of cross-dressing or drinking more than two glasses of wine a day?

"Gays are just like every morally superior one else" is an ill-conceived and patently false inducement to tolerance. It does not allow gays and lesbians as a class the same universe of behaviors that everyone else enjoys. Homosexual people would be held to a higher standard for the sake of a propaganda campaign.

There seems to be a modicum of internalized self-hatred in prescriptions for cleaning up the gay act. Such exhortations will not admit that gays and lesbians ought to be accepted for their humanity, including their failings as some might see them. None of these authors would argue that only totally conventional or morally perfect heterosexual people are worthy of dignity or respect.

Some defend this double standard because they imagine heterosexism to be nonrational:

Trying to argue people out of their homohatred is, however, founded on a completely false assumption—namely, that prejudice is a belief. But prejudice is not a belief; it's a feeling. Argument *can* change beliefs, but not feelings. . . . Even where argument seems effective, one rarely, if ever, persuades intellectually: rather the appeal succeeds for emotional reasons.[12]

Hence, to these crusaders an image campaign is far more effective than any discussion could be.

It might indeed help to manipulate people's emotions so that they *feel* that homosexuals are not different from them, but any effort that depends on the pretense that gays and lesbians are totally conventional or morally perfect is bound to fail. The truth is that they *are different* in a way that stands sexual convention on its head and that they *are like* everyone else in many respects, including being fallible. Nongay people must come to understand that and not hate or fear it.

An antihomophobia strategy that depends on reforming the fallen and the misguided or tries to repackage the gay image is either utopian or cynical. Gays and lesbians do pay mortgages and repair people's plumbing—some are indeed Catholics and Republicans—but those facts can never erase the fact that they are also sexual outlaws, whose desires and behaviors fly in the face of sexism and Puritanism, of the Right and Left.[13] Only when a society is nonpatriarchal and sex affirming can homosexuality be uncontroversial.

### Appealing to Reason

A realistic plan for fighting homophobia in the schools must recognize the centrality of the intellectual-moral domain in forming beliefs about difference. It will acknowledge the importance of both beliefs and feelings in motivating behavior. Teachers, after all, are not propagandists. They should value the proposition that challenging heterosexist notions and homophobic feelings can change how students think, feel, and act.

Moral development theory suggests a strategy for combating homophobia.[14] (See Chapter 4.) Lawrence Kohlberg, like Piaget before him, tried to show that the stimulus for an individual's moving from one ethical stage to the next is the disequilibrium prompted by the inadequacy of his or her reasoning to resolve a moral conflict. With similar logic, Milton Rokeach has attempted to prove that creating dissonance among one's important, or "higher order," beliefs can lead to prejudice change. For example, showing people how race prejudice is inconsistent with their own core values challenges their self-perception and forces them to reexamine their racism.[15]

The ultimate cognitive aim in antihomophobia education is to raise a person's moral judgment to include respect for the dignity and rights of all. Moral education practitioners recognize both the intellectual steps that lead students to such a vision and the importance of affective factors in supporting that growth.

Although moral development is a cognitive process, it does not occur in an affect-free vacuum, especially among teenagers learning about sexuality in a classroom or discussing equity in school governance and decisionmaking. Teachers must provide them with emotional support for the rigors of cognitive dissonance and assist the ego development of students. If they do not attain a positive sense of themselves, moral behavior might well slip, although their principles have soared.[16]

The topic of homosexuality and contact with gays and lesbians might disconcert even the well meaning. For some, the subject evokes images of predation, unfamiliar relationality, and alien erotic practices. Those who squirm need reassurance that their response is understandable. It may just take a while for affect to catch up with intellect.

## Encouraging Contact

The cognitive component in antiprejudice work is sometimes given short shrift. Some integrationists appear to think that contact by itself eliminates intolerance. It is certainly easier to assemble a diverse student body or faculty, mouth a few multicultural platitudes, and hope for the best than it is to tackle the roots of bigotry and misunderstanding in the minds of teachers, students, and families.[17] Although daunting, promoting cognitive development is a surer path to lasting change.[18]

That does not mean that integration has no value. Although proximity is not a panacea, it can still assist students' comprehension of human equality. Getting through the earlier stages of moral development particularly requires a sense of familiarity with others. Speaking of education for multicultural understanding, Alvin Poussaint recommends "an integrated environment, where the students are actually living with, talking to, and meeting people from different backgrounds."[19]

Common membership in a larger, even temporary, entity "may permit positive bonds to develop . . . and thus change the basis for future interaction."[20] Yet teachers should not conclude that contact is enough for the long haul. It may indeed alter behavior, but often only during the contact period itself. The change may not be maintained outside the work or school setting.[21] If the school does not help students grasp the principle of human equality, its victory over bigotry may be fleeting.

Schools often bring disparate people to cooperate only within a concrete universe, a circle of familiar faces. How often has one heard, "Oh I like her. She isn't like the rest of them"? Schools may encourage majority and minority students to get along for a time, yet is their prejudice really shaken and are attitudes changed? Even if daily contact with the unfamiliar teaches students to tolerate a kind of difference that becomes routine, what hope is there that they will deal fairly with other kinds of human variance with which they have had no direct experience?

Research reveals that less homophobic people have had positive personal contact with gays and lesbians, whereas more hostile people have had less contact.[22] Of course that may be because homosexuals make themselves known in the first place to those they think will be accepting. It appears that highly educated, politically liberal, young, and female people are more likely to have such contact. They are also clearly the kinds of people to whom one is likely to come out. Undereducated, conservative, older men do not often invite such confidences.

Contact might still help somewhat in changing attitudes.[23] Even in homophobic groups, persons who know someone gay or lesbian tend to have fewer negative attitudes toward homosexuals than other members of the group.[24] Furthermore, the number of Americans reporting they have a gay friend has jumped from 22 percent in 1985 to 56 percent in 1996.[25] This increase could account for the rising percentage of Americans who think homosexuality should be considered acceptable, from 34 percent in 1982 to 44 percent in 1996.[26] That is why universal coming out has been heralded as the eradicator of homophobia.[27] Gays' and lesbians' most productive disclosures are not to strangers but to those who have already been their admirers, friends, and loved ones.

*Effective Contact*

Casual connection, however, is not likely effective for long. It might change behavior while the contact lasts but probably does not change fundamental attitudes.[28] What can be accomplished during contact that will lead to less ephemeral results? On integration in the armed forces, a university psychologist writes: "Under the proper circumstances, prejudice is reduced by bringing the prejudiced and the prejudiced-against groups together and putting them in a situation where each group can learn more about the other and the two can develop lasting relationships."[29]

The key to changing fundamental attitudes and values lies in the nature of the contact and what is learned about the "other." Poussaint himself admits the limits of school integration: "I think the attitudes of a lot of these kids have changed to some extent because now they know blacks personally, but it hasn't changed the attitudes of some of the more insecure and threatened people."[30]

In the absence of deliberate examination of those insecurities and the nature of the perceived threat, contact would accomplish nothing for some people. Just putting groups together may even worsen attitudes.[31] Successful prejudice reduction demands planned interaction. Regarding racial integration, one psychologist has asked: "In what types of contact situations, with what kinds of representatives of the disliked group, will interaction and attitude change of specified types occur—and how will this vary for subjects of differing characteristics?"[32]

The complexities of planned interventions can be daunting. G. W. Allport offered some thirty variables for such interactive situations,[33] but four major determinants stand out: status of the interacting groups, cooperative and competitive factors, intimate versus casual contact, and the degree of institutional support.[34] The following detailed conditions are deemed conducive to ethnic/racial prejudice reduction:

- equal status contact;
- positive perceptions of other group as result of contact, even under unequal status conditions;
- contact between members of majority and high-status members of minority;
- contact requiring cooperation;
- contact involving interdependence, common goal, or separate goals requiring cooperation;
- intimate rather than casual contact;
- promotion of contact by authority or social climate;
- contact that is pleasant or rewarding.[35]

The following unfavorable conditions are thought to inhibit ethnic/race prejudice reduction:

- competition;
- unpleasant, involuntary, tension-laden contact;
- lowering of prestige or status of one group because of contact;
- groups or members being in state of frustration;
- groups having moral or ethnic standards that are objectionable to each other;
- having their status in the contact replicate their unequal status in the real world.

It is advantageous for the institution to sanction the contact and to set an expectation for its success and continuance,[36] yet this position may also provoke resistance. When contact is seen as involuntary or an invasion, resentment is greatest among those who think they will lose most in status, opportunity, or values.[37] Equal status contact with gays and lesbians might threaten heterosexuals who have always rested securely in their presumed superiority. They may fear that a proud homosexual presence endangers heterosexual privileges and patriarchal values. Those fears are well founded whatever else may disturb them.

Nevertheless, in his studies of racial contact, Elliot Aronson found that the more forceful the integration, the less the resistance.[38] Faced with certain contact with blacks, whites tended to cope with their repugnance by finding reasons not to dislike black people.

Gays and lesbians do not have to be bussed into a school; they are already there. It is their coming out that may be considered invasive. When school authorities, support their presence and refuse to pressure them back into the closet or into alternative placements they are in effect saying to resisters, "They've been here, they're queer, get used to it."

"Belief dissimilarity theory" postulates that the right kind of contact leads to the conclusion that "they" are more like "us" than we thought.[39] Problems arise when coming face to face does not get at the similarities, or worse, when it exacerbates the differences. Strongly resistant people may become more stubbornly prejudiced through contact, whereas willing participants who are predisposed to give up prejudice may do so after contact.[40]

When membership in one's own group requires belief in the negatives about another group, then contact does not improve attitudes.[41] That finding is troublesome in light of the compulsory heterosexism of hypermasculine culture. Moreover, proximity may aggravate homophobia in those whose prejudice is based on inner anxieties, such as feelings of sexual inadequacy.

Subcultural histories and belief systems often influence attitudes toward homosexuality. (See Chapter 7.) Hence, contesting homophobia and heterosexism within various ethnic, class, racial, or religious groups requires an understanding of its varied underlying determinants.

## Analogizing to Other Oppressions

Although heterosexism is fundamentally linked to sexism and has some features in common with racism and religious intolerance, the oppressions are not the same. People may be enlightened to find elements of shared experience among stigmatized groups. However oppressed groups can also be angered either by the equation of all bigotry on the one hand or by the suggestion of a hierarchy of oppression on the other.[42]

It is pedagogically risky, for example, for a white teacher to compare being homosexual with being a racial minority or even to point out similarities in the social dynamics of heterosexism and racism. Teachers may be tempted to use analogies to race because racism is a familiar concept to all Americans and widely condemned. Nonetheless, they must appreciate that people of color may resent a privileged person's using blacks' experience to curry sympathy for the homosexual position—"pimping on my pain," as one African American graduate student phrased it in a class on homophobia.[43] Teachers of color may have greater license to draw parallels among biases, but even they must tread carefully.[44] Multiple minority gays and lesbians can at least speak to the convergence of oppressions in their experiences.

Ultimately, teachers want students to relate other people's lives to their own. Such comparisons occur spontaneously and are the first empathetic step toward understanding another person. The educator's role is to make it possible for young people to see their similarities where they exist and not to misconstrue or fear their differences. In the ideal multicultural classroom students would speak about themselves, elucidate what they have in common, and negotiate their differences. When they come to school unconscious of their privilege or claiming a monopoly on oppression, the process is arduous but worth the effort.

*What Can Schooling Do?*

How much can schooling actually contribute to lessening heterosexism? Surveys of students entering college in 1997 show negative attitudes toward homosexual relationships at a record low of 30.6 percent[45] (down from 53 percent in 1987[46]), indicating a trend among the college-bound. Nearly 50 percent went so far as to support gay marriage. Positive views were strongest among women, those with better high school grades, and those attending four-year colleges. Research often shows that highly educated individuals express less negative attitudes toward gays and lesbians[47] and that the less-educated express hostility.[48] Moreover, a 1998 Harris poll found education (along with gender and political philosophy) to be a better predictor of support for gay rights laws than having a gay friend or relative.[49]

These observations are consistent with findings about race prejudice[50] and may mean that educated people know better what responses the researcher expects. These results might not represent real attitudes or predict behavior.[51] The raw prejudice of an honest unschooled bigot might not be much different from and could be  less dangerous than that of a subtle genteel homophobe with a college degree and a hand on the tiller of power.

Racial views of whites improve after having a black teacher, perhaps confirming the theory that contact with a high status minority member encourages tolerance.[52] In the same fashion, homophobic students could be prompted to change when they learn of an admired teacher's homosexuality. Those who are entrenched in their thinking might excuse the teacher as an exception while their bigotry continues to simmer. Others might begin to ask themselves whether gays and lesbians are so bad after all.[53]

However the moment of their cognitive dissonance may evaporate under group pressure. Such may have been the case in Los Angeles, where high school students drove out a once popular teacher when his homosexuality was revealed (see Chapter 9). He and his colleagues were unprepared or disinclined to engage the young people in dialogue or to advise a group for homosexual students at the school. An important opportunity was lost.[54]

No teacher would deny that "it is difficult to change attitudes through education,"[55] yet it is still possible. To reduce homophobia an intervention must overcome human tendency to act habitually and reduce adolescents' susceptibility to peer pressure. The key is to create an environment in which conventional peer, family, community, and cultural norms can be examined critically. Students must have exposure to new information, intellectual prodding by the teacher, emotional support, and most important, peer debate. When some of the participants in such a project are gay and lesbian or have friends or family who are, the discourse can be most compelling and effective.

### Changing the School

In a homophobic school or community, how can the individual be brought to heed his or her highest principles and to argue for tolerance? It takes courage to interrupt a group's habitual thoughts and actions, to begin articulating one's perhaps newly forming ideals, and to plead with one's peers and others to change their attitudes and behaviors. "To develop an open, accepting attitude toward minorities when all of your friends and associates are still prejudiced is no easy task."[56] It can be as intimidating for heterosexuals to dissent as it is for gays and lesbians to stand up for themselves. One heterosexual male ally has said that challenging heterosexism makes him "vulnerable to shunning and possibly violence. Traitors to this system are given a special hell by those who maintain it."[57] A much younger ally recalled what happened when she objected to her eighth-grade classmates' degrading remarks about gays: "Because of my standing up for what I believed, people said I was gay. I was harassed verbally, emotionally, and physically for a full year. . . . But I am not sorry for the stand I took."[58] It is just her sort of peer challenge that is needed, with appropriate safeguards, to jostle the typical teen mind-set.[59]

*Cooperative and Democratic Learning*

Some reformers call for sensitivity training, a group process of values clarification. This approach allows for the expression of hostilities but attempts to control them. It has had mixed, though generally positive, results in lessening racism.[60] However, the best tolerance education goes beyond promoting sensitivity and good feelings to seek deep understanding and long-term cooperation.

Antiprejudice interventions have the greatest chance of success in classrooms with an ethos of justice, caring, and mutual endeavor. Cooperative learning has been cited as a positive factor.[61] Such an environment was the goal of the teachers, students, and parents of the Cluster School, which, among their other achievements, effectively tackled issues of race.[62] With consultation from Lawrence Kohlberg and the staff of the Center for Moral Education at Harvard, this program forged itself into a small community within a large bureaucratic city high school. Through democratic town meeting governance and a curriculum centered on moral issues in history and literature, students and faculty sharpened their sense of justice and struggled to deal fairly with one another.[63]

For example, when teachers, African American students, and some white peers voiced antiracist beliefs, the majority of white students voted for affirmative action in recruitment and admissions. Some students gave their support for lower-stage reasons, such as not wanting to face retribution; others genuinely wanted to make their black schoolmates more comfortable, and a few articulated more general principles of social equity.

Moreover, the very process of democratic debate and decisionmaking helped to bridge differences. New studies of prejudice have shown that "when kids work together to achieve something they value, they begin to look better to each other."[64] A democratic school or classroom requires that students labor to form and govern their small community. Likewise, cooperative classrooms foster the growth of interdependence and empathy.[65] In the domain of race relations, the prospects for change are good in such settings: "Optimistically, shared group identity and the development of a sense of partnership can eliminate manifestations of even . . . subtle, indirect, and rationalizable forms of racism."[66]

*Appeals to Caring and Fairness*

Using exhortations that are accessible to relatively low moral reasoning, schools can enlarge their circle of caring to include gay, lesbian, bisexual, and transgender people. To create the spirit for this growth the school or the class must articulate regularly the following declaration: We have gays and lesbians in our town and our school, and they must feel comfortable here because these places are as much theirs as anyone else's.

When such a direct appeal cannot be truthfully or safely made, something can still be done to bring the issue home to the school. The argument for caring can be indirect and simple. Heterosexual teachers or students can plead that homophobia hurts them personally. They could say, for example, "Every time you say those cruel things or use that language, I think about a relative (or a friend) whom I like alot and who doesn't deserve those insults. It makes me feel really bad." It may not be as dramatic as having a student or teacher come out, yet it does make the point that you do not have to be homosexual to be hurt by homophobia and to stand up for gays and lesbians.

Even those who would have to say they are unaware of having any homosexual relatives or friends can offer a valuable perspective on the issue. When they urge tolerance, they can truthfully claim the high ground of disinterested communitarianism. They have no personal ax to grind or favorite person to defend. Their advocacy can summon students at the stages of egocentric reciprocity to think of unspecified others, particularly members of the group who might not feel safe enough to reveal either their own or their loved ones' homosexuality.

Whether by means of personal testimony or indirect report, adults who are professionally committed to care for young people should be particularly moved in hearing the plight of gay and lesbian students in their school. And classmates who want to "be nice" should be amenable to empathy for how their peers *feel* having to listen to cruel comments day after day. The majority would probably not yet relate to other homosexuals outside their immediate sphere, but they might be on their way. In a caring school, at least the harassment and violence would abate.

However, one ought to be wary of portraying homosexual youth as a class of pathetic passive victims; that characterization does not help them muster the self-esteem to resist stigmatization and could also contribute to further victimization.

Schools must be made safe as well for gender nonconforming people.[67] Whatever the degree of their gender role violation and whatever their sexual orientation, sissies, tomboys, and other transgender people alarm conventional thinkers and might even distress homosexuals who have internalized heterosexist gender stereotypes. Effeminate males and butch females are a Rorschach test for an individual's gender confidence and a litmus test of a school's acceptance of diversity. Gender education is an indispensable part of any antiheterosexism campaign.

***Being Nice to Our Own.*** School and classroom members themselves, preferably students, are the most credible advocates for fairness. The optimal adult contributions are periodic appeals to caring and restatement of arguments. The more homosexual people are seen as "one of our own," the more cogent the argument. Openly gay and lesbian students and their family members have great leverage in the discussion, as do gay and lesbian teachers and staff. If none will undertake the plea, another good choice would be a recent graduate. Or, less immediate, but still useful is a member of the outside community.

Solicitations for compassion and fairness made by homosexual youth are exceptionally effective with adults. When they are not available personally, or by mail, film portraits of other youth may suffice. Most faculty and administrators want to do right by their charges. Many are disturbed to learn of current or former students, of whose suffering they were ignorant and for whom they were not available. Some are snapped out of denial that they ever had homosexual students and are spurred to help the ones who may sit before them now. Massachusetts high school students have even addressed their former middle school teachers to good effect.[68]

Such is the strategy behind Gay Lesbian Straight Education Network's (GLSEN) "Back-to-School Campaign," which organizes gay and lesbian graduates to write their former teachers and principals. Over 5,000 letters were sent in 1996. The following is an excerpt from a 1992 letter:

> I graduated from Affton High School in 1982 as valedictorian of my class. . . . I earned a 4.33 grade point average, sang in the choir, performed in every play and musical, competed on the speech team, and wrote a musical my senior year which got me and Affton High School on the TV news magazine "PM Magazine." . . . My high school years were wonderful except in one important area. I'm gay, and though I fell in love for the first time my sophomore year, like many other kids, I could not tell anyone because the object of my affection was another boy. . . . Everywhere I turned it was made clear to me that I was a freak. . . . The most popular insults among kids were implications of homosexuality, and teachers never said a word to stop it. It was a terrible, empty, lonely feeling. . . . School is supposed to be a place to explore ideas, cultures, and people different from us, a place to try to understand the wonderful, varied, diverse world we live in, . . . where kids can feel safe, respected, encouraged, nurtured. . . . I owe many of my accomplishments to the teachers and administrators of Affton High School, but they are also directly responsible for some of the most difficult and painful times of my young life.[69]

When this letter appeared in the Affton Senior High School newspaper, it "stirred discussion among teachers, students, and administrators."[70] An accompanying article made clear with testimony from another gay alumnus that ten years after the writer's graduation nothing had changed.

***Adult Pleas.*** If parents of homosexual youth from the school or from elsewhere are able to participate, they can describe their families' experiences. Faculty and students alike are often touched by parents' travails and impressed by the love that prevents or heals their estrangement from their children.

Gay and lesbian faculty voices are important too. There is overlap in the measures that schools need to take to make adults and students feel honored and supported. Still, because schools are constituted to serve students and because peer argumentation is most persuasive, students should take their major cues from other students. Homosexual faculty concerns can be detailed among other adults.

Discussion will probably center around "kindness to people we know" but it should include higher moral persuasion as well. Students who are capable of making more abstract arguments about minority and human rights should be encouraged to speak up. If there are none who can do that, adults might weave such themes into their pleas for mutual respect and caring; however, it is crucial that the group process not devolve into oratorical grandstanding by adults ranged against reluctant uncomprehending students.

## Imposing Rules

School leaders seem to rely primarily on rules changes from above to prevent homophobic acts. Though useful, these prohibitions are not an effective stimulus to moral development. Most school codes, initiated and enforced by adults, are perceived by youth as arbitrary means to regulate their behavior. Additions to discipline handbooks about which students have not had a substantial say have limited effect. They may help set a tone, but if students think they should obey the rules only to please adults or not be punished, then they are not disposed to examine their own heterosexism.

That may be exactly the intent in some instances. In Maryland, for example, a school board member contorted herself to describe an antiharassment rule that had just been broadened to include antigay/lesbian behavior: "This new policy will not require sensitivity training or anything like that. It merely gives students and staff some expectations that if they are the victims of harassment or discrimination, we will take steps to make sure it stops."[71]

Prevention through empathetic understanding seems unthinkable to her. In this district, the victims are merely offered a shred of protection, which they must take the initiative to obtain. Perpetrators are to be deterred from further offense by threat of punishment, never to be made aware of the nature of their offense to human rights. And for the basher who asks "Why?" one supposes the response, "You broke a rule." Never mind whom it protects or why we have it.

In the absence of democratic rule making, ethical thinking, and peer pressure, although harassment might be curtailed within the school, it will probably be resumed on the street, like drug use and other forbidden behaviors. If, on the other hand, the rules result from school discussions in which gays and lesbians are imbued with humanity and misperceptions are challenged, tolerance may be internalized and practiced even when the teachers are not looking. Educators must come to see the futility of punishment and reward for the promotion of moral development beyond early childhood.[72]

### Dealing with Dissent

Transforming beliefs is not a short-term project. Nor is it achieved without sparking antagonisms, but schools must not retreat when the process becomes difficult. Such is the discouraging course being taken in some corporations with regard to diversity training. For instance, because animosities were stirred up in multicultural workshops, AT&T changed its course:

> At the crux of a lot of bad situations with diversity training is often the misunderstanding that the training is going to be aimed at changing the way you think, changing your beliefs—which kind of gets at the heart and soul of someone. Diversity programs here now are more aimed at behavior modification and workplace respect, so we are not really interested in our employees' hearts and souls, but in their actions at work.[73]

Of course, the corporate goal is to maximize cooperation for productivity—"profitability correctness, not political correctness."[74] For schools, though, democracy, not profit, is at stake. Their practical aim in reducing bias is not just to change behavior for seven hours but to advance good citizenship and, beyond that, to foster respect and cooperation for humanity's sake.

The liberal argument is that homosexuality is as natural and good as any other orientation for the individual and for society. It advocates the same tolerance of sexuality differences as many seek for gender, race, ethnicity, and faith diversity. If a majority of parents, staff, and students can agree to include sexual orientation in their respect for diversity, what is the school's responsibility toward those who dissent on cultural, moral, or religious grounds? How should they be heard? Open discussion and debate are essential to persuasion and growth. And students want to know what their peers, parents, and teachers really think. Yet adult arguments over homosexuality can be dangerously divisive and hurtful to young people. How can the school respect an antigay point of view and still maintain a tolerant, even affirming, environment?

At one school, it was suggested that objections to positive characterizations of homosexuality be answered as follows: Homosexuality just *is*, and so schools must deal with it.[75] Hardly an adequate justification! Homosexuality does indeed exist, as do racism, sexism, cheating, stealing, and violence. How is the school to engage with each issue and to what end? Not many teachers would propose a value-neutral approach to any of these human phenomena except homosexuality. It provokes little controversy to take a stand against the last five. Only homosexuality gets a pass.

Notably, the principal of this same school took a strong stand against homophobic name-calling. Where gays and lesbians are concerned, it is easier for a school to justify an antiharassment policy than an affirming one. In 1992, when presidential candidate Bill Clinton was asked if he supported teaching about homosexuality as "normal and natural" to children in public schools, he answered: "Affirmative teaching is very different. . . . I'm not talking about embracing a lifestyle that you may think is wrong or even immoral; I'm talking about the absence of discrimination."[76]

Each side in this debate thinks the other poisons the school atmosphere in a way that harms young people. Liberals have argued for the welfare of homosexual students, teachers, and families and for enriching the diversity of the school community. But opponents to positive gay messages fear the consequences of hiding from students what they perceive as the dangers of homosexual immorality.[77] They profess to be as caring as the proponents are, albeit their approach might oppress some youngsters.[78] Thereupon, gay allies countercharge: "The premise that society somehow helps gay teens by rejecting them defies logic."[79]

The antigay stance is commonly cloaked in the professed concern of the "I'm beating you for your own good" variety. One objector to a Maryland antiharassment school policy preferred that harassment continue as a preventative: "You can never come up with a practical, political compromise with a moral imperative. . . . Their behavior is killing them, so therefore it is not okay to be gay."[80] If they concede that some youth are irredeemably homosexual, they still insist that others be protected from their influence or from a message of acceptance.[81]

*The Limits on Adult Free Speech*

Competing claims over whose prescription is more ethical are not just background noise; they can be a tangible part of the school culture. The

case of the Boston Latin School provides an object lesson. A school newspaper article lauded the Safe Schools for Gay and Lesbian Youth Program
in Massachusetts. The reporter himself was the first openly gay student
at the school and a founder of its new gay/straight alliance (GSA). A
teacher's rebuttal was then published, berating the state initiative and asserting that homosexuals are evil. In the ensuing controversy, a group of
teachers wrote a letter on behalf of gay students, and several administrators, including the headmaster, made it clear that the gay/straight alliance had their approval. Some students also expressed their solidarity.
No one was disciplined.

This controversy could be offered as proof that open debate can move
a school to express greater tolerance than had ever been articulated before. On the other hand, it raises a number of disturbing questions.
Would further voicing of bilious homophobia be permitted in ongoing
discussions? What were the views of the faculty majority who did not
sign the support letter? Could openly homosexual students or parents
expect fair treatment in every classroom? Would homophobic students
be drawn to the teachers they perceived to be on their side?

Two years later another teacher in the school mocked a group of students for planting bulbs in an AIDS memorial garden, asking them in a
mincing voice, "Did you all plant tulips, today?" A few homeroom teachers continued to refuse to read the GSA postings along with the other
club announcements that are read aloud from the daily bulletin.[82]

The Boston Latin School debate did not occur among students thrash-
ing out diversity issues in a habitually democratic and cooperative educational milieu. It was not guided by teachers who had crafted a faculty
position after privately working the issue out among themselves. The
result was spontaneous, genuine, and messy—not unexpected or bad
qualities in student discourse—but it was also dangerous because it involved adults, who were by virtue of their positions, not equal participants. Students are probably drawn more effectively into moral disequi
librium by the arguments of their peers, whereas teachers might be
merely intimidating.[83]

*Power Inequities.* The power difference in the school between adults
and students puts an extra burden on teachers to be careful how they express their opinions about ethnicity, religion, class, race, physical ability,
gender, and sexuality, and of course, politics. Most Americans today
would be irate if a teacher suggested that any ethnic, racial, gender, or
religious status is lower than another, and many are coming to feel the
same about physical ability. No one would condone a teacher's saying
that Spanish-speaking students, or students of color, or those in wheel-
chairs are inferior human beings. Even bigoted teachers have learned

not to imply so, especially when members of stigmatized groups are present.

A conscientious educator would never participate carelessly in classroom debates about intelligence bell curves, bilingual education, or signing for the deaf. Open applause for a principal who tells a mixed race student that she is a "mistake"[84] is rare. Homosexuality, however, appears to be a trait about which teachers may say anything negative they please without compunction or broad disapproval.

Young people and their families are worldly enough to know that teachers have shortcomings, including harboring biases. However, when students are attacked or detect signs of abiding prejudice, they may legitimately challenge the teacher's capacity to treat them fairly.

It is one thing to encourage students to express their own opinions in order to promote dialogue and understanding, but is it too much to ask that teachers openly subscribe to a principle of human equality? Some might answer that teachers should be free to condemn certain behavior. The Catholic Church now takes such a position on homosexuality: Love the sinner—hate the sin. But many people, particularly the young, do not make the distinction, as many instances of gay bashing prove. Even the U.S. military acts as if the homosexual orientation by itself is the equivalent of a disallowable behavior.

***Public Expression of Personal Convictions.*** Where, then, does the free speech argument lead us? Most understand why public school teachers should not proselytize or use sectarian argument to sway young people's opinions. But should they also be forbidden from expressing their convictions? There can be only one answer. When a teacher's religious views or personal morality conflict with the school's expressed ethos, the teacher must leave those values at the schoolhouse door. If they cannot in conscience take an egalitarian stance, they should be respectfully silent. At a minimum, they cannot be permitted to deride, attack, or advocate hostility toward gays and lesbians. The Catholic Church itself has called for "respect, dignity, and delicacy" in dealing with homosexual teenagers.[85] Sadly, some teachers flout such advice.

***Must Both Sides Be Presented?*** To avoid accusations of one-sidedness, administrators in one western Massachusetts district allowed a parent to mount a high school book display in response to a GSA-organized "coming out day." Her exhibit featured titles such as *Healing Homosexuality* and the jacket of a video on Christian "conversion" counseling for gays.[86] When students use sectarian arguments in the classroom, teachers have to be sensitive in trying to limit religion's role in the discussion. However, admitting a parent into a public school for what amounts to an attack on some students strains the meaning of accommodation.

A bold example of the enforced separation of religion and public school teaching has been set in Canada. The British Columbia College of Teachers, which certifies teachers in that province, has refused to permit graduates of a fundamentalist-Christian university to teach in its public schools on the grounds that, in banning homosexual behavior, the religious school "follows discriminatory practices which are contrary to public interest and public policy."

If teacher and parent heterosexism is muzzled to protect certain students, then some might wish on the same grounds to forbid advocating for homosexuals. Two evangelical parents, for example, brought a complaint to the Brookfield Connecticut school board in the interest of their high-school-aged daughter. They opposed her teacher's putting pink triangle "Safe Zone" stickers in her classroom and urging acceptance of all kinds of people. "This is a homosexual agenda. This is homosexual recruiting. This is disgusting. This is illegal," they wrote.[87] When the teacher filed a lawsuit against the parents for libel, they countered that their free speech rights were being abridged.

In Brookline, Massachusetts, a lesbian social studies teacher came out to a freshman class in 1993.[88] The parents of one student claimed their daughter was traumatized by the event and by the alleged derogation of her fundamentalist beliefs by her peers. They sued the school system for damages and the cost of sending their child to a private Christian school. The parents, both public school teachers in another town, had rejected an offer to transfer their daughter to another teacher's section of the same course because the two classes occasionally had joint field trips.

In a similar case in California, five male students were transferred out of their science class at parents' request because their sixty-one-year-old "Teacher of the Year" openly criticized a public official for saying homosexuals are sick. The principal reluctantly deferred to parents who felt their moral beliefs were being violated. The teacher, James Merrick, was gay but was not out to students and had not made his remarks in the school.[89] Merrick lodged a discrimination complaint with the state's Division of Labor Standards Enforcement, the California Teachers Association, and the local school board. The school board dismissed his charge unanimously,[90] but the state ruled against the district, instructing them to stop removing students from the class and ordering them not to discriminate any longer on the basis of an employee's sexual orientation.[91]

Because he was just a few months from a planned retirement, Merrick decided not to return to the classroom, which was then too hostile an environment.[92] Instead he agreed to undertake administrative duties in exchange for an apology from the district and their agreement to allow him to consult with a committee set up to "improve staff understanding of the new policy."[93] At least one parent hoped to file a suit to preserve parents' rights "to decide who can educate their children and who they don't want them to be around."[94]

To answer these parents' concerns for their children's well-being, teachers must guarantee all students respectful treatment in the school. That stipulation does not include that teachers be gagged or forced into the closet. In the public schools, religious conviction must surrender to democratic values. To allow otherwise would condone such travesties as letting a Jewish student transfer out of a self-declared Muslim teacher's class or other variations on that ugly theme.

It does, however, seem fair to ask whether honest peer debate among students is prevented when teachers are openly gay, lesbian, or gay-supportive. Would students dare object to homosexuality without fear of reprisal? Everyone has weighed the risks of not telling teachers what we think they want to hear in their classes and on their exams. Telling powerful adults that you think them sick or immoral goes beyond reason. It is not like dissenting to their interpretation of a sonnet.

Teachers' exhortations must, above all, be consistent with the espoused values of the school. Teachers, parents, and school leaders are obliged to work through their opinions on diversity in their adult cohort before broaching the subject with students. One hopes professionalism and collegiality will prevail in reaching a consensus that values all students and families equally. Then faculty can develop a pedagogy to promote tolerance.

## Staff Development

When they undertake staff development as an initial step toward making schools safer, workshop leaders must be selective about the training modalities they employ. Techniques that might work with students are not always transferable to adults. Ice-breaking and values clarification exercises can sometimes seem frivolous. Likewise patronizing facilitators may incite resentment.[95] Furthermore, sessions can bog down in vocabulary lessons. Terminology is important, but accurate and polite language is initially less crucial than genuine feelings.[96] Workshop leaders can assume that some have already thought about such matters and are capable of engaging with each other and with less conversant colleagues.

Warm introductions, acknowledgment of unease, and clarity about goals are a good start. The best clarion is an institutional summons to understanding, safety, equity, and action. With an obeisance to reasonable confidentiality, the sessions should permit the frank expression of feelings, encourage dialogue, provide basic information, arouse compassion, promote personal growth, and prompt school reform.

When time is short, the factual segment is best limited to the healthy development of gay and lesbian youth. As for compassion, teachers always respond well to students' and parents' stories. At the end, participants should be encouraged to agree on a framework for making the school safer.

Any compromise short of complete acceptance and equal treatment is not justifiable. Silence or second-class status as the price of membership in any public institution is as unsatisfactory as it is in the family. Witness, for instance, the inner contradiction in the "inclusionary formula" of the Republican Party chairman: "We're very strongly against it being taught in schools as an acceptable alternative lifestyle. But there are, I am sure, scads of homosexual and lesbian Republicans, and certainly they're welcome in our party."[97] A gay or lesbian schoolchild would see through those open arms.

### Student Debate

The requisite student debate about homosexuality must occur with teachers and tolerant peers acting as buffers against threatening speech and other hostile behavior. This refereeing calls for good judgment: If true feelings are stifled, resentment increases. Yet if students are personally denigrated, they may get so defensive they cannot hear the other side.

Older students should be trained to make diversity presentations and moderate debate among those younger than they are. They can act as role models of acceptance and can communicate information colorfully. Members of gay/straight high school alliances in several Massachusetts towns have visited middle school and junior high classes to good effect.[98]

Educators are regularly encouraged by the capacity of younger high school students to discuss such matters. For example, two dozen Massachusetts ninth-graders were brought together by the National Conversation on American Pluralism, Identity, and Law. They exchanged views about the case of the Brookline student who objected to having a lesbian teacher:[99]

- "I think by letting her avoid all contact with people who are different from her, the school isn't fulfilling their purpose." (Bharat)
- "It seems sort of absurd that she should be forced to deal with the teacher that makes her physically sick; she'll never be able to learn anything with that teacher." (Nick)

- "Lots of people have problems with teachers. . . . She should have probably made more of an effort to work it out." (Suparna)
- "A teacher coming out in class . . . is not trying to convert anyone into becoming a lesbian. . . . They are not expressing who should be like this, or that you're evil because you are not. . . . As opposed if you come out in class and say that all Jews are evil, gay people are evil." (Matt)
- "I find that more acceptable than if she came in and said, 'Anyone who doesn't accept me is wrong.'" (Josh)

These students are exceptionally articulate, yet most students are able to have heartfelt and reasoned conversations about fairness and differences.

While championing these debates, schools cannot ignore the safety of gays and lesbians. Such was his probable concern when the principal in Pennsylvania forbade the posting of organizing leaflets for an "Anti-Gay Coalition," saying he could not condone any group whose purpose was to make an uncomfortable environment for any other members of the student body.[100] In another instance, a Wisconsin high school newspaper's April Fool's Day edition was pulled by a principal for an item expressing nostalgia for the days when "flag-burning pansies" could be shot.[101] These administrators acted prudently, but it is important, nevertheless, to give homophobic students a forum in which to argue their position.

School authorities should act to keep ruptures from becoming permanent when, inevitably, emotions run high and feelings get hurt. They should consider how any minority students might feel during a classroom "debate" over their worth. Gay and lesbian students could misconstrue the promotion of free expression as the encouragement of hate speech. They also might read their teachers' restraint in the debate as lack of support for them. Sympathetic teachers and counselors should touch base individually with homosexual students and those from gay and lesbian families, if they are known, to reassure them and give them a chance to process the feelings that come from hearing their own or their relatives' humanity questioned. A gay/straight student alliance is a good place for students to get teacher and peer support and to organize for school reform. The Gay Lesbian Straight Education Network has instituted a Student Pride Program to provide resources to and foster communications among student activists.

All students need to hear that they are cared for despite heated words that might be exchanged. Homophobic students also need assurance that they are personally valued, even if their views are contested. Calls for mutual respect should permeate the school's discussions of difference, and caring should be cultivated as a developmental necessity.

## Invoking Public Values

These school change strategies depend upon the principles of equality and respect that schools universally proclaim. However, prejudice in many forms continues to flourish despite admirable pronouncements. When the lived reality of students and faculty stands in stark contrast to the platitudes of multicultural deference, an opportunity still exists to call upon the school to live up to its own credo. It is the frame within which progressive antibias reformers can fashion their appeals.

Although gays and lesbians may have had no place in people's minds when the school's diversity principles were first enunciated, it is imperative to dare the community to make the leap to include them. People do not always say no to a personal appeal. For example, when a fourteen-year-old Massachusetts boy was followed home by gay-baiters, his mother expressed her fears to other parents who had previously fought against antihomophobia programs and won them over.[102] In Miami-Dade, Florida parents obtained the nation's first charter for a gay-oriented PTA to offer support to gay teens and their families.[103]

## Impasse and Evasions

When a significant majority are against extending tolerance to homosexuals and even advocate abandoning them, progress may seem impossible. The ensuing despair bolts the closet doors in many schools, and some, usually those who are too conspicuous to hide, are driven to refuge in alternative placements. A small percentage of gay and lesbian students must indeed be given such options. They deserve a new safe and sympathetic environment for learning, supervision, and counseling, particularly after they have been victimized. Alternatives like the EAGLES Center in Los Angeles, the Harvey Milk School in New York City, and the private Walt Whitman Community School in Dallas are necessary for gay, lesbian, bisexual, and transgender youth because so many schools disregard or are unable to protect and sustain them (see Chapter 13).[104] But it is unfair to send students elsewhere who would prefer to stay in their own schools under better conditions.

Siphoning them away also takes the pressure off the mainstream schools. Pretending to resolve the issue by purging these "problem students," administrators allow themselves to ignore other gays and lesbians who remain and suffer silently. An alternative program should serve only as a temporary refuge until the rest of the schools are transformed. Furthermore, the students who are assigned to them should not be written off as maladaptive. In most cases, it is the schools that have failed, and students have been driven from their rightful places.[105]

Not every school will be reformed with all deliberate speed. Nor is it always advisable for a few to risk their safety in a seemingly doomed campaign, just for the sake of some future breakthrough. At the same time, the successes of some courageous individuals should inspire them not to underestimate their own ability or resiliency. Even in Cambridge, Massachusetts, renowned for its liberalism and the site of the first public high school gay/lesbian/bisexual support group in the East, the road was not direct or easy. For several years a handful of teachers had lobbied the administration but gained nothing: no staff training, no help for homosexual youth. It took a harassment complaint by a gay teacher against a colleague to produce a legal settlement requiring staff sensitivity workshops. That little-supported action was the start of a comprehensive antihomophobia plan for all Cambridge schools.[106]

### Radical Versus Gradual Reform

Some university-based reformers want school leaders to align themselves with "social reconstructionist schooling,"[107] by developing a critique of inequalities based on race, class, sexuality, and other factors:

> Administrators and faculty can change this status quo via critical self-examination . . . [and] can gather data to become more critically aware of power differentials in all aspects of the curriculum, instruction, and culture of educational organizations . . . to guide actions that nurture empowerment in the culture and instructional organization, reaching out to make a difference in our communities and, ultimately, in society.[108]

Social reconstructionists disfavor "human relations" approaches to multicultural education, deeming them assimilationist and noncritical of majority values. They also fault "single-group" studies for not examining the common experience of all out-groups and not encouraging coalitions. Lastly, they criticize a cultural democracy model that stresses diverse views and a community of learning but that does not offer explicit lessons in social transformation. Rather than expect them to remake the world on their own after contrasting their school lives with the outside, they would provide students with direct "social action skills."[109]

Progressive antihomophobia educators would likely approve most of the social reconstructionist vision. Some would agree that assimilationism is an enemy of homosexual authenticity and liberty. Some would also see the importance of linking their cause with that of other oppressed groups. Homosexuals have suffered a number of the failures of liberalism. Consequently, a radical analysis can be appealing.

But the rhetoric of social reconstructionists is hardly geared to the sensibilities of most teachers, let alone school administrators. "Tear it down" can never be as appealing to the stewards of convention as "do it better." One must come back to meeting people where they are and call them to the highest principles they have already articulated. With the right language, there can be a convergence of social reconstructionist aims and hallowed democratic virtues: "The multicultural literature pays too little attention to the fact that the multicultural education movement emerged out of Western democratic ideals."[110] Activist teachers should nurture school democracy as a means to cultural transformation. The encouragement of a diversity of voices in a community of caring can lead to both individual and group growth and to social change.

This strategy is indeed indirect and gradual, but the charge that it does not contribute to revolutionary aims is unfair.[111] A developmentalist stance summons administrators, and others, to critical inquiry as a path to both leadership and reform.[112] Developmentalism harbors no illusion of utopian consensus. Rather it embraces rationality and caring democratic practice as both a means and an end of education.[113]

A reasonable teacher would concede that "persistence does not resolve all conflicts, that some problems are not solvable but only manageable, and that a level of mystery and perplexity accompanies all attempts at human understanding."[114] Nevertheless, those who remain in the profession must never give in to the paralyzing suggestion that power inequities in our culture make dialogue across differences and community building impossible.[115]

## Changing Administrators

Jim Sears calls for societal reform based on two components of "sexual praxis": "Critical-reflective thought about (homo)sexuality . . . and immediate administrative action to address the long-neglected needs of lesbian-, gay-, and bisexual-identified students and faculty are the twin vectors of sexual praxis."[116] We cannot ignore the role played by administrators in this or even in less grandiose visions of school change. Making the tone of the institution less homophobic requires backing from principals and superintendents and their associates.

Although this chapter has argued that unilateral directives are not advisable, it does not discount the value of the not-too-bullying pulpit, particularly in rallying the faculty. Heterosexual leaders can signal that the battle against homophobia is everyone's responsibility. Genuine ones are as supportive in public as they are behind their office doors. The best are pro-active and positive; they do not wait for a crisis.

In trying to enlist administrators, one begins with several disadvantages. First, an underlying discomfort with sexuality as a school matter causes many to be obstructionist. Second, the current male majorities at every level of administration are subject to all the sexist and heterosexist tendencies that afflict men generally. Research on administrators reveals a pattern of sexual harassment, abuse, and disrespect for women and gays, as well as a tendency to condone or overlook such behavior in others.[117]

Even well-meaning administrators cannot be blind to the disincentives to pursuing an antihomophobia agenda. Political pressures are ubiquitous. The patriarchy favors school leaders who are loyal to the interests of the powerful, interests regularly framed as "traditional values." Administrators have good reason to anticipate opposition to programs that upset convention.

School administrators are good candidates for denial. Many are safer believing there are no homosexuals in their school and that gay and lesbian issues have no relevance to the education of heterosexual students. They are usually wrong on the first count and always wrong on the second. To begin with, there are probably some homosexual people in the school population and there are certainly some with family who are gay or lesbian. Second, there is often a notable discrepancy between administrators' and students' willingness to acknowledge that heterosexism is a palpable problem in the school.[118] The invisibility persists because a denying and hostile school culture keeps homosexual students and parents from coming forward and silences their allies. A gesture of acceptance would elicit a swarm of revelations. Lastly, administrators are simply misinformed if they think straight students have nothing to gain from studying all forms of sexuality. Not only might their prejudice abate, but they could also make discoveries about themselves along the way.

## The Power of Persuasion

There are a number of practical routes to convincing administrators that something should be done. Recommendations from higher officials can help as well as pressure from parents, faculty, and students. One Massachusetts principal was swayed by the spirit of a gay student who insisted his closet was more excruciating than blatant homophobia could ever be.[119]

Mandates from state or central offices, on the other hand, are of mixed consequence. Although they may move school leaders to act, too often the response is half-hearted and pro forma. On such matters as sexuality and multiculturalism they might well hold their breath through some token event and then move quickly away from controversy. Some appear convinced that the best course is the one that brings the fewest opponents and the least disruption.

If we want to deepen administrators' commitment, we must convince them of the value of antihomophobia interventions and involve them in the planning and execution of events and activities. When possible, they should have direct contact with gays and lesbians who speak the language of schools. Finally, as pressed as they are by a multitude of problems, they should be dissuaded from delegating these tasks entirely to others. As easy as it might be for them to they send a representative to a workshop—often the health specialist or the gay/straight alliance advisor—it is crucial for principals and superintendents to go too.

Their most credible motivators are other administrators who have taken risks and emerged as the beneficiaries. Their inspiring stories may even rewrite history a bit in the afterglow of a successful school experience. One principal, having admonished a teacher that coming out would be a disaster, later effused to a roomful of administrators about the transformations at his high school that resulted from having an openly gay faculty member.[120]


## The Power of Law

There is also the power of the law to galvanize action. Only five states and a handful of localities have protections for homosexual students. Without explicit regulations in most jurisdictions, case law is still uncertain as to the liability of principals and others. Some elucidation is available through publications, such as the Gay and Lesbian Advocates and Defenders'(GLAD) volume on the legal rights of homosexual students and teachers in public schools.[121]

**The Nabozny Case.**   Groundbreaking cases like that of Jamie Nabozny have also begun to clarify the schools' legal responsibilities in these matters. With the aid of Lambda Legal Defense and Education Fund and his parents, the twenty-year-old Jamie sued his former school district and several school officials in Ashland, Wisconsin. Nabozny claimed they failed to protect him against the attacks that eventually drove him first from the eighth grade, then from high school.[122] Beginning in middle school he was subject to repeated abuse, such as being kicked unconscious, mock raped, and urinated upon. He accused the district of condoning these activities for five years. Providing him with a private bathroom or separate seat on the school bus was not enough, he said, since none of the perpetrators was ever punished. In fact, his middle school principal warned he had to expect such treatment, if he was openly gay.[123]

The school system denied culpability, insisting that the harassers' upbringing caused their behavior. A district court ruled that the schools were not liable, unless it was their policy or custom to endorse or ignore the harassment, and that they "did not have an affirmative duty to protect [the] plaintiff from private violence." However, that decision was overruled on appeal and the case was sent back for trial.[124] This resubmission was the first time that federal law was held to apply to antigay discrimination in schools.

In November 1996, a federal jury found three administrators, though not the district, guilty of violating Nabozny's rights by ignoring his plight. Having antiharassment language on the books protected the system but not those who failed to enforce it—the middle school principal, the high school principal, and his assistant. One day after the verdict, and before jury consideration of damages, Nabozny won $900,000 in an out of court settlement with the school system.[125]

***Other Cases.*** Perhaps in light of the Wisconsin judgment, Maine's attorney general filed a civil rights complaint against a high school student for a violent attack and repeated harassment of a fifteen-year-old that school authorities and even the police were unable to stop for at least four months.[126] A similar suit was subsequently brought on behalf of a former high school student in the Kent (Washington) School District, where two teachers stood by as he was assaulted and another remarked, "I already have twenty girls in my class. I don't need another."[127] Also beaten by eight others in front of a crowd across from the school security office, he eventually received a settlement of $40,000.[128]

Suits have also been filed against Morgan Hill (California) Unified School District[129] and in Sussex County, New Jersey,[130] with charges ranging from name-calling and spitting to death threats and a beating that resulted in severe hearing loss. A harassment case on behalf of a twelve-year-old in Pacifica, California, was settled out of court when the boy was awarded $125,000 and the system agreed to teacher training and better enforcement.[131] The mother of a Denver high school bisexual cheerleader has brought a complaint against some of the other cheerleaders for tormenting her daughter and against their coach for doing nothing to stop it.[132]

In a 1995 Illinois case, a "Mario Doe" sued his high school for taking little or no action against harassment directed at him.[133] Riverside-Brookfield District answered they were sorry but not legally responsible. Although he felt obliged to dismiss the federal complaint, the judge chastised the school for not doing "the right thing," that is, protecting the boy. Further, he sent the case back to state court, where a second student joined the suit. One of the youths said his counselor had merely advised him to learn karate.[134]

In 1998, the "deliberate indifference" of school officials led to a jury award of $220,000 to a girl, taunted from age eleven for four years in a rural county near Louisville.[135] An important point was made by a former student who sued his Duluth, Minnesota, high school in 1999 for ignoring his humiliation and terror: The case was based not on his sexuality but on the treatment he received because of his "perceived sexuality."[136]

*Title IX.*    Another 1998 case has encouraged legal advocates even more as it has broken new ground. The federal Office for Civil Rights (OCR) ruled that by permitting antigay harassment, Fayetteville, Arkansas public schools were in violation of Title IX regulations that bar discrimination based on "sex."[137] The interpretation hinged on the sexual content of the taunts. Though admitting no culpability, Fayetteville officials agreed to prohibition, monitoring, and punishment of antigay acts, teacher training, and other preventative actions.

Whether sexual harassment regulations cover sexual orientation is subject to interpretation.[138] It appears that for the federal Title IX to be applied to sexual orientation, the harassment itself must be sexual in nature, as in threatened sexual assault.[139] One deputy assistant secretary in the Department of Education's Office for Civil Rights admitted they are "still struggling" over this matter but also hinted that anyone who is harassed over gender behavior might be covered.[140] Further court decisions are awaited. In the meantime, then, to be useful in preventing heterosexist harassment, policies should expressly cite sexual orientation. In 1999 the Office for Civil Rights issued *Protecting Students from Harassment and Hate Crimes, A Guide for Schools,* which does address antigay acts.[141]

Examples like the Nabozny and the Kentucky and Arkansas cases could have a profound impact. Nevertheless, one must question whether legal threats, though useful as a last resort, are the most effective means of getting administrators to cooperate. Fear may give them pause, while they search for means to evade the true intent of the law. Legally acceptable remedies may not be consistent with reform. For example, a town might offer to pay tuition at another school for a harassed gay student who claimed denial of educational access. That response might satisfy the court or even the student but would do nothing to meet the larger equity goal.

## Changing the Community

In the larger community outside the school, democratic dialogue is more difficult. Too often public forums on safe schools for gay and lesbian youth degenerate into political posturing and demagoguery. Since it is the nature of conservatism to defer to convention, progressives can only hope to prevail by invoking civic principles to which even their opponents claim allegiance.

## A Place for Religion

As for religious principles, let them be heard as well. Antihomophobia proponents would find it difficult to call for their exclusion from public discourse, when, in 1996, 54 percent of Americans believed churches should be involved in politics (up from 40 percent in 1968).[142] Rather than ban religion from the debate, school reformers would do well to cite the most humane tenets of the major religions. Better still to let the clergy cite them. Letting the public know that there are religious leaders who stand up for gay and lesbian youth[143] corrects the misimpression that all churches are opposed to them.[144] In some Contra Costa County (California) public schools, for instance, Catholic Charities has cosponsored antihomophobia trainings.[145]

But fair-minded people of faith who engage in civic discourse should not be tempted toward protracted Biblical elucidation to dispute the notion that God hates homosexuality. As the Right have so often proved, scriptural exegesis quickly becomes a quagmire. The dean of the Harvard Divinity School argues that religious viewpoints cannot practically be banned from democratic debate, nor should they be, so long as those who hold them abandon their claims to absolute truth. However, he concludes that we ought to be governed by the core values that underlie our secular and religious traditions: liberty, equality, and tolerance.[146]

## Heterosexual Allies Among the Laity

Besides enlisting the churches, one should locate heterosexual allies among the laity. Parents and Friends of Lesbian and Gays have a record of testimony that only the most callous can disregard. Parent accounts of their often difficult path to acceptance are dependably effective. Resistant people might first identify with their shock and dismay, yet might eventually understand how loving parents ultimately want their children to live genuine lives. P-FLAG's message is, "I know how you feel, because I have felt the same way. I did not welcome homosexuality right away just because my child is gay. I had to work at it. I had to rethink all we have been told." Theirs is the perfect inducement to moral development.

Nonhomophobic adults of all backgrounds have the ability to inspire tolerance and re-form community. Heterosexual allies without gay or lesbian loved ones are particularly convincing because they avoid the charge that their relationship with a particular homosexual person has led them to rationalize.

## Family Values

Nor should activists wither under the assault of family values arguments. First, they must counter with the contributions that gays and lesbians make to their families of origin. Second, they must hold up the example of those homosexual people who bring remarkable values to their intentional families. Third, they must point out the historic failure of conventional values to foster growth and well-being for every family member.

And finally, they may argue that family cohesion and indoctrination can lead to insularity and prejudice. Sometimes democratic institutions have to counter the effects of family values. Allport's vision united school, church, and state against the transmission of prejudice from parent to child. Speaking of the conflict that arises in children when they begin to question their parents' values and their social attitudes, he writes:

> The primacy of the family does not mean, of course that school, church, and state should cease practicing or teaching the principles of democratic living. Together, their influence may establish at least a secondary model for the child to follow. If they succeed in making him question his system of values, the chances for a maturer resolution of the conflict are greater than if such questioning never takes place.[147]

If an antihomophobia campaign finds the church and family arrayed against the state and school, constitutional ideals of freedom, equity, and justice become even more crucial.

The best hope for changing community views lies in engaging people in small groups with some of the same modalities that are employed in teacher workshops: clear goals, personal stories, facts, and invitations to reform rooted in the espoused best values of the community itself. A proactive strategy would begin such a dialogue immediately in the PTAs and parent councils.

### What One Teacher Can Do: A Checklist

1. Inform yourself about gay/lesbian/bisexual people and about homophobia.

### Low Risk

- Learn about gay/lesbian history, culture, and current concerns by reading books, journals, and periodicals.

### Some Risk

- Attend gay/lesbian film series or lectures.
- Attend a meeting of a gay/lesbian organization.
- Attend an "allies" meeting (for example, P-FLAG).
- Have conversations with openly gay/lesbian people.

### Greater Risk

- Engage heterosexual people, including your family and friends, in discussions of homosexuality/homophobia.

2. Create a safe and equitable classroom.

### Low Risk

- Change your assumption that everyone is heterosexual unless they tell you otherwise.
- Use inclusive language that implicitly allows for gay/lesbian possibilities (for example, "parent" rather than "mother" or "father"; "spouse" rather than "wife" or "husband"; "date" rather than "boyfriend" or "girlfriend").

### Some Risk

- Challenge homophobic language and name-calling.
- Put up gay/lesbian-friendly posters, pictures, or signs.
- If you are heterosexual, don't be quick to inform others of your heterosexuality. Ask what they might think if you told them you were gay or lesbian.

### Greater Risk

- Be clear about your willingness to support gay/lesbian students.
- Use language that explicitly allows for gay/lesbian possibilities (for example, "Emily Dickinson and her boy- or girlfriend").
- Invite gay/lesbian speakers to your classroom.
- Use gay/lesbian curriculum.
- If you are gay/lesbian/bisexual, come out to your students.

3. Create a safe and equitable school.

## Low Risk

- Be a role model of acceptance.

## Some Risk

- Challenge name-calling and harassment.
- Work to establish policies protecting gay/lesbian students from harassment, violence, and discrimination.
- Call for the inclusion of gays, lesbians, and bisexuals in diversity presentations.
- Work to form a gay/straight alliance and/or support group for gay/lesbian students.
- Call for faculty and staff training in gay/lesbian youth issues (including crisis intervention and violence prevention).
- Call for counseling services for gay/lesbian/bisexual youth and their parents.

## Greater Risk

- Invite gay/lesbian/bisexual and transgender speakers to your school.
- Join a gay/straight alliance.
- Call for and develop a gay/lesbian/bisexual awareness day.
- Work with the PTA and other community-based support groups regarding the educational and health needs of gay/lesbian students.
- Solicit the cooperation of gay/lesbian/bisexual alumni/ae in motivating the school to meet the needs of students who succeed them.
- Call for faculty training in gay/lesbian studies.
- Encourage colleagues to develop and use gay/lesbian curriculum.
- If you are gay/lesbian/bisexual, come out to the school community.

# 12

## The Massachusetts Model

Setting a standard for policies that have been advocated since the early 1980s,[1] the Massachusetts model is unprecedented in scope and cogency. Its recommendations, programs, laws, and regulations are a major advancement for the welfare of gay and lesbian youth.

In 1992, William Weld, the recently elected governor of Massachusetts, issued an executive order creating the Commission on Gay and Lesbian Youth to study the status of homosexual young people in the state and issue recommendations. It was ordered to meet quarterly with the Secretaries of Education, Health and Human Services, and Communities and Development, and with the Public Health Commissioner, as well as to advise the Executive Office of Health and Human Services on an ongoing basis. The commission held five public hearings across the state, soliciting testimony from students, parents, teachers, principals, government figures, and others. One year later, in its first report to the governor,[2] the commission recommended the following:

1. School policies protecting gay and lesbian students from harassment, violence, and discrimination.
2. Training teachers, counselors, and school staff in crisis intervention and violence prevention.
3. School-based support groups for gay and straight students.
4. Information in school libraries for gay and lesbian adolescents.
5. Curriculum that includes gay and lesbian issues.
6. School-based counseling for family members of gay and lesbian youth and community-based assistance in the P-FLAG model.
7. Education of families through information in public libraries.
8. Parent speakers bureaus to advocate for fair treatment of gay and lesbian youth in schools.

Shying away from the library and curriculum recommendations, the governor advised the state Board of Education that schools be encouraged to

1. develop policies protecting gay and lesbian students from harassment, violence, and discrimination;
2. offer training to school personnel in violence prevention and suicide prevention;
3. offer school-based support groups for gay, lesbian, and heterosexual students;
4. provide school-based counseling for family members of gay and lesbian students.

When the board approved these objectives unanimously in May 1993, the state Department of Education (DOE) established the Safe Schools Program for Gay and Lesbian Students to implement them.

### The Safe Schools Program

Over five years the Safe Schools Program grew from a half million to a 1.5 million dollar enterprise.[3] It has two full-time staff, a fractional-time supervisor, and secretarial support at the Department of Education and a full-time project manager at the Department of Public Health. A significant amount of its work is contracted out to other organizations. By 1998, Safe Schools and the Governor's Commission had achieved the following:

- provided technical assistance to over 350 schools;
- held over 700 regional and local presentations and faculty trainings;
- trained over 60 workshop facilitators (with GLSEN, the Gay Lesbian Straight Education Network);
- trained over 75 parent speakers (with P-FLAG, Parents, Friends, and Families of Lesbians and Gays);
- coordinated over 500 P-FLAG speaking/outreach engagements;
- trained over 150 student speakers;
- distributed almost $800,000 in grants of up to $2,500 to over 140 school districts for program assistance;
- spurred the establishment of 140 Gay Straight Alliances (GSAs);
- published a manual for starting GSAs;
- allocated $120,000 in grants over three years for established GSAs to mentor fledgling GSAs in their region;
- given grants to college gay and lesbian student organizations to mentor high school GSAs;

- developed a resource manual for teachers and counselors;
- initiated a youth pride retreat for GSA members and their advisors (subsequently administered by other agencies);
- sponsored the attendance of several GSAs at Outward Bound–Boston island retreats, designed to help teachers and students reach Safe Schools goals;
- allocated $60,000 for the purchase and distribution of books requested by schools;
- begun a Young Leaders Conference for 100 students and GSA advisors;
- conducted workshops with the Massachusetts Secondary Schools Administrators Association and other educational leadership organizations;
- and held workshops with Interscholastic Athletics Associations and others, focusing on coaches and athletes.

The DOE embellished its offerings by cosponsoring activities with the Massachusetts Department of Public Health (DPH). The 1996 two-day youth retreat, Standing Out Together, featured such workshops as When Your House Doesn't Feel Like Home; Transgender History/Culture; Conflict De-Escalation; Dating and Relationships; Talking About Sex and HIV; On Being a Straight Ally; Internalized Homophobia; and a Roundtable on Alcohol, Tobacco, and Other Drug Use. A similar 1997 retreat drew over one hundred adolescent participants for three days.

Beginning in 1996, the Governor's Commission and the DPH launched a complementary initiative, the Gay and Lesbian Youth Support Project (GLYS). Modeled on Safe Schools, it trains community-based social service providers through regional and on-site workshops, ongoing consultation services, information sharing, and support networking.[4] Within two years they had coordinated two-day intensive trainings for seventy community agencies and have been particularly effective in reaching beyond the metropolitan Boston area. By involving school personnel in their sessions, GLYS has spurred the welcoming of providers into the schools for cooperative work, often without charge.

### New Laws and Standards

The Board of Education's Safe Schools recommendations were purely advisory. However, the elected Student Advisory Council to the Board of Education, several GSAs, and a number of community youth groups lobbied the state legislature to add sexual orientation to an existing student antidiscrimination statute. They were successful at the end of 1993. The amended Student Rights Law now reads:

No person shall be excluded from or discriminated against in admission to
a public school of any town, or in obtaining the advantages, privileges, and
courses of study of such public school on account of race color, sex, religion,
national origin, or sexual orientation.[5]

The law applies to school and course admission, guidance, curricula, and
extracurricular activities, including athletics. Under it, students must
seek remedy first from principals and then from designated school-based
compliance coordinators; thereafter, they may file complaints with superintendents and school committees, and ultimately with the DOE.
They can also bring suit in court at any time.

This law would likely support a claim that gay and lesbian students
are not being served when the Board of Education's Safe Schools recommendations are ignored. Indeed, it may go even further than those parameters, since it has been held previously to require curricular representation of other protected classes, such as women and minorities.

In 1994, the Board of Education similarly reformed their certification
standards. Equity competencies now require that a teacher master "effective strategies within the classroom and other school settings to address
discrimination based on each student's race, sex, sexual orientation, religion, socioeconomic class, or disability."[6] They stipulate that a qualified
administrator "accepts and respects individual and group differences
with regard to gender, language, race, sexual orientation, religion, socioeconomic background, and values."

Because of these explicit mentions, sexual orientation may also be in-
terpolated into related certification provisions regarding current equity
issues for students and their equal treatment, freedom of expression, self-
esteem, unique developmental and cultural needs, and family backgrounds. Since 1996, the DOE has contracted 39 three-hour workshops in
colleges and graduate schools to help teacher education faculty prepare
their students to meet these standards.

## Responses from the Schools

A number of Massachusetts school systems have responded with enthusiasm and intelligence. For example, the town of Arlington, a middle-
class community (75 percent of graduates go on to four-year colleges; 15
percent to two-year schools; 10 percent to work or military) has made
great progress:

1.  formation of a systemwide Safe Schools Task Force (faculty, ad-
    ministrators, students, school committee member, clergy, and DOE
    consultant);

2. revision of the school committee's K–12 antiharassment and discrimination policies and the student handbook;

3. cooperative development (students, deans, and principal) of a comfortable reporting procedure for harassment;

4. training for counselors, K–12;

5. mandatory middle and high school faculty workshop;

6. middle school assemblies with student skits on gender and sexuality harassment and open question and answer sessions;

7. mandatory elementary school faculty workshop;

8. training for eleventh- and twelfth-grade peer counselors working with younger students;

9. book, video, and film purchases for the high school guidance library;

10. high school field trips to film and drama presentations (for example, "Philadelphia," "The Sum of Us," "Beautiful Thing," and "Ma Vie en Rose"), followed by discussion groups led by trained personnel;

11. establishment of a high school GSA (membership, ca. 50), advised by the Director of Health and Physical Education (activities include improvisational theater, trip to a gay-themed play, dances, meetings with town officials and civic committees, State House testimony, and yearbook pictures);

12. high school human rights days about gender and homosexuality;

13. Days of Dialogue, in which GSA members invite nonmembers to panels and discussions;

14. voluntary faculty trainings on transgender issues;

15. detailed coverage of all Safe Schools activities in the high school parent newsletter.

Arlington's great success has been bolstered by the participation of nearly every administrator. At the first faculty training the new superintendent wept as she compared her own mother's immigrant girlhood isolation to the experiences of gay and lesbian students today. The principal later said the event, unlike most "boring, banal, force-fed professional development," was the best in-service in twenty-nine years.[7]

Long and careful planning has brought this system many successes, including a plan for curricular integration of gay and lesbian issues in grades K–12. Scattered opposition from some town conservatives has not caused backsliding.[8] Yet, as in any other school, the Arlington faculty's good will is not unmitigated. For example, in a roomful of ninth-graders, a teacher can still ask a student who says his father does all the cooking, "What is he, a fag?"[9]

A twenty-eight-page screed titled *An Intelligent Discussion About Homosexuality* was mailed to every household in the community of Sherborn by a man trying to stop Safe Schools activities in the state.[10] Filled with tired antigay boilerplate (for example, gay men's life spans are thirty years shorter than married men's are), the mailing raised a great outcry.[11] The high school GSA hosted a well-attended educational "coffeehouse" for the town and a crowd of gay-supportive citizens came to a public meeting and wrote letters to the editor, excoriating the pamphlet and its author.

Other school districts have also distinguished themselves. In western Massachusetts, with Pat Griffin of the University of Massachusetts as consultant, Amherst High School formed a Lesbian Gay Bisexual Study Group to assess school attitudes, policies, and resources and to propose action objectives.[12]

Closer to Boston, the veteran Newton South principal, a student of gay and lesbian youth issues, has promoted staff training, encouraged his only openly gay teacher, and helped the GSA and Committee on Human Differences with a number of Gay and Lesbian Awareness Days. Standing up to a conservative *Boston Herald* columnist in point-counterpoint school newspaper editorials, the principal has championed openly homosexual teachers.

Spectrum, the GSA at Concord-Carlyle High School has

- conducted and published a school homophobia survey;
- sponsored lectures and films on gay/lesbian history;
- donated books to the school library;
- held a parents' night;
- instituted "Bring a Homophobic Friend to Spectrum Day";
- sent members to conferences;
- invited community-based groups to their meetings;
- petitioned to make the curriculum of the "Junior Lifeskills" course more inclusive;
- helped students come out and attend school dances in same-gender couples.

The Collins Middle School in Salem distributed a booklet to accompany its "Safe LGB Zone" sticker project. The publication includes such topics as "What Might It Be Like to Be Lesbian, Gay, or Bisexual at Collins?" "Making the Decision to Become an Ally: A Checklist for Readiness."

The principal of the Mount Greylock Regional High School appealed for Safe Schools initiatives in a 1995 letter mailed to every principal in the state.

In 1994, GSAs came from as far as sixty miles away to attend a dance sponsored by the Brookline High School GSA. The evening began when the heterosexual Brookline headmaster took another man onto the dance floor. What began in Cambridge in 1987 as antiharassment policies, faculty workshops, and a student support group (see Chapter 11) had been replicated and embellished ten years later throughout Massachusetts. The shift in perspective that has come with these changes is perhaps best illustrated by the remark of one high school principal in 1999: "There's something wrong here—we're the only school in the area without a GSA!"[13]

## School Policies

As suggested by the Governor's Commission, a school's first priority in protecting students who are, or are perceived to be, homosexual should be to have explicit policies. Two random examples illustrate why these are imperative:[14]

- A high school girl was the target of bathroom graffiti. The male janitor would not enter the girls' lavatory during school hours. The girl herself was left to monitor and clean the walls. She became suicidal.
- An eighth-grade boy was being tormented. His teacher feared twenty angry parents if she intervened. The boy's appeal that "even gays have rights" caused the principal to ask him if he were gay. Since he did not identify, the school took no action.

If they are written and accessible in school board regulations and faculty and student handbooks, rules represent the school's intentions unmistakably.[15] To be most clear and forceful, moreover, they must outline non-intimidating procedures for complaint, judgment, and appeal.

Legal experts stress that complainants should compile written documentation of the abuse and of their dealings with school personnel, particularly when school officials might be legally liable.[16] Notarized witness statements and signatures of document receipt may be advisable. Beyond reporting to superiors, counselors and teachers may not be legally obligated to intervene. Principals and central office officials, on the other hand, may be required to take remedial action. When the response is too slow or the discipline is insufficient, they should be appealed, even to state officials and the courts.

A major problem in relying on written policies and legal remedies is that students might be loath to use them. They could be fearful about reporting incidents to an unsympathetic authority figure or about the repercussions of their telling, such as intensified harassment or public scrutiny. The latter possible result could make a closeted, uncertain, or heterosexual youth worry that complaining is tantamount to coming out.

Moreover, parental notification is mandated when children are attacked or put at risk. Students might feel that flagging their sexuality to their families is worse than putting up with peer abuse.[17]

For all these reasons, the complaint mechanism should incorporate a sympathetic student advocate, reasonable confidentiality, protection from retribution, and discretion in reporting to parents. If these parameters can be respected, peer mediation would be a sensible approach to resolving complaints at the outset. Incidents of physical violence, however, must be handled decisively and punitively, with mediation as a possible follow-up to set standards for future behavior.

Many schools already have harassment policies to which they may add sexual orientation protections and sensible enforcement procedures. A school should echo the language of municipal and state laws, where they exist, while couching its regulations in a school ethic of caring and multicultural respect.

As with its older law against sexual harassment in schools, Massachusetts requires that certain conditions be met for a charge of sexual orientation harassment to be upheld. The behavior in question must

1. be unwelcome;
2. pervade the educational environment;
3. focus on sexual orientation;
4. affect the student's ability to learn.

Because the aim is to terminate the behavior, the following questions are likely:

1. Does the school have a published policy and procedure?
2. Has the behavior been documented and reported to the administration?
3. Has the administration investigated as confidentially as possible?
4. Has the administration taken prompt remedial action, including various levels of discipline, on a case by case basis?

If a Massachusetts school system has not responded conscientiously and expeditiously to the charges, it leaves itself open to censure from the DOE's Division of Program Quality Assurance and to lawsuit. Particularly after the Nabozny verdict, the threat of court action may spur superintendents and school boards to act. (See Chapter 11.)

In 1996, the DOE began the Student Hate Crimes project to improve reporting and documentation of harassment and violence. It includes high school presentations, as well as wallet cards, posters, and a web site. This initiative has brought to the schools an approach that has worked on the streets. During the 1996–1997 school year, one hundred incidents were reported to the project staff, mostly at on-site presentations in school and community workshops. The use of an 800 number telephone system has been less effective.

## Staff Training

Well-executed trainings can have a profound effect. My own study assessed the impact of a 12-hour workshop series on the attitudes and professional practice of sixteen heterosexually identified staff participants at Cambridge Rindge and Latin School, the city's public high school. (Six gay male participants were not studied.)[18] The voluntary workshop, "Gay and Straight at CRLS: Creating a Caring Community," took place in 1989. Through the remarks and behavior of colleagues who did not enroll, all the participants became aware of significant skepticism or hostility toward the workshop among the faculty.

At its conclusion, fifteen members rated the workshop positively and said the most memorable activities were a role-play, in which a young woman came out to her family, and the stories told by parents and gay/lesbian staff and alumni/ae. They characterized the sessions as moving and found the experiences of homosexual staff and students troubling, yet most did not recall feeling uncomfortable. Many enjoyed the collegiality among gay and straight workshop members.

Most felt that their participation strengthened their initial view that homosexuality was indeed an issue at the school. Almost everyone believed that homophobic name-calling should be interrupted and negative comments discussed. A few described the workshop as a personal breakthrough in understanding the dehumanizing of homosexuals. Finally, 75 percent thought the workshop itself was the catalyst for the group's near unanimous support for the formation of a gay/lesbian student group at the school. Two participants, one gay man and a heterosexual woman, subsequently helped start Project 10 East.

In the following years Project 10 East evolved into a flourishing GSA. It has a full-time faculty advisor. Student members distribute information at freshmen orientation day and speak in high school and elementary classes. Their gay history and photography exhibits are showcased outside the principal's office. Gay, lesbian, and bisexual speakers from all walks of life have addressed National Coming Out Day assemblies, while students, staff, and faculty of all sexualities have worn pink triangles as symbols of solidarity. At the high school's annual Awards Day, the Cambridge Lavender Alliance, a local political group, presents a prize to the senior who has done the most to advance the well-being of gay and lesbian students.[19] And with remarkable daring, transsexual speakers have begun to challenge the social meanings and conventions of gender.

Some negative reactions have been heard, mostly from conservative faculty. Early on, an anonymous flyer, "SODOM HAS RETURNED . . . !" caused a flurry. Then, a few years later the superintendent approved the display of *Love Makes a Family* in a grammar school lobby,[20] causing a few parents and politicians to protest. Although the theme of the pictures of lesbian and gay families was not apparent until one stopped to read the matching texts, the school committee agreed that children could be kept at home, with lessons to be sent for the duration. Nonetheless, the exhibit stayed up. The six-year dialogue within the school system prior to this crisis helped prevent a retreat. Doubtless, three openly gay and lesbian elected city officials and progressive city council and school committee majorities contributed to this resolve as well.

Capping its unique record in 1997, the Cambridge School Department hired a half-time parent liaison/advocate for gay and lesbian families.[21] In her first year the parent liaison achieved the following:

- formed an advisory committee, including other Cambridge parent liaisons (Hispanic, African American), teachers, and community people;
- published a monthly newsletter;
- met with nearly every elementary school principal;
- sent informational mailings to all teachers and staff;
- established a gay, lesbian, bisexual, and transgender (GLBT) family liaison in every K–8 school;
- held a six-session discussion and support group for middle school students from GLBT families;
- began a gender identity support group for fourth- through eighth-graders and a gender discussion group for parents;
- conducted a five-session workshop for K–5 teachers;
- organized a pre-K, K, 1, and 2 GLBT parent group;
- won a grant for book and film purchases for classroom use and training;
- began an annotated bibliography;
- developed and distributed a packet of materials for student advisory groups in grades 6–8;
- met with eight school teams regarding GLBT issues and name-calling;
- worked cooperatively with a community organization of GLBT parents;
- held monthly potluck suppers, featuring films and discussion.

## Gay/Straight Alliances

GSAs have come to represent the flagships of the Safe Schools Program.[22] Faculty and students often leave workshops, resolving to start such a group. They might run into opposition from a frightened administrator or irate politician, and their posters are almost always mysteriously torn down for a while; yet GSAs have still been launched in 140 out of Massachusetts's 368 public secondary schools.

Safety and confidentiality are their initial concerns. In one town students fretted through their first session that the football team was lying in wait; in another, a teacher stood outside the room taking down names and then followed one boy enjoining him to quit the group.[23] Although some have considered meeting off campus, most have chosen to stay at school as a commitment to visibility. Adult advisors are alert to potential harassment but cannot monitor students all day.

It was a strategic decision to form alliances with straight allies rather than constitute as gay/lesbian support groups. Since many homosexual adolescents fear to identify openly and some are uncertain of their orientations, the GSA offers a place for a range of students to feel welcome. A group aimed at homosexual students alone would attract only the out, the brave, and perhaps the desperate. Project 10 East had difficulty getting more than a few members in its first years until they became an alliance. Most GSAs make a point of not pressuring students either to decide or announce their orientation, allowing those who are questioning or frightened to proceed at their own pace in a secure affirming environment. It has even been suggested that having refreshments at meetings not only improves attendance by appealing to adolescent's appetites but also offers a cover for those who are reluctant to be seen with a GSA.[24]

One consequence of this policy is that the groups are less likely to function as gay and lesbian peer counseling forums. Rather they gravitate toward a gay rights agenda with educational, activist, and social components. One Project 10 East student confided: "I'm here because it's important for me to belong to a political group . . . so I can open up the newspaper every day and feel good that I'm doing something."[25]

That leaves those who have already assumed a homosexual, bisexual, or transgender identity wanting access to counseling and a space to socialize with their cohort.[26] Some form a GSA subgroup or find another setting outside the school for gay and lesbian peer and adult counseling and bonding. Community-based groups, lacking the constraints of a school, also allow for more relaxed and explicit discussion of relationships and more sexually expressive behavior. There were some twelve community alliances of gay and lesbian youth (AGLYs) in Massachusetts as of 1998.

GSA advisors in Massachusetts have grappled with a number of challenges in starting groups and keeping them afloat. Although some are unique, others are common to any youth organization:

- fighting GSA invisibility vis-à-vis other school clubs;
- leadership development;
- working effectively with overcommitted students;
- reaching out to new members;
- preventing cliques;
- making the group comfortable both for new, perhaps intimidated students, and for veterans;
- dealing with multiple levels of openness—students who come out to the advisor and a few peers but are not ready to come out in the group, or come out in the group but not in the school;
- focusing the group;
- resolving the tension between activist and social agendas;
- motivating students to follow through on projects;
- networking with other GSAs;
- working out relationships with community-based youth and adult groups;
- dealing with community resistance and hostility.

A GSA is a haven for some of the school's neediest youth. A small survey in one school supports the notion that homosexual students who have attended GSAs or community-based groups might be more inclined than their peers toward worry, suicide, and other negative health outcomes.[27] There is no reason to think that the organizations themselves cause these outcomes. More probably, such groups are a lifeline for those who are already at risk.

The prominence of such students has given some GSAs a "freaks and misfits" image that puts off better-adjusted youth who would otherwise come to meetings. A group in Washington State has begun to document the impact of such groups in making schools safer, keeping GLBT students from dropping out, and reducing suicidality.[28] Still more research is needed on the membership, role, and the effects of GSAs on individuals and institutions. (In 1997, the Massachusetts DOE provided modest funding to begin a multiyear study on the impact of Safe Schools interventions on students, and researchers at the University of Massachusetts have also begun a separate study.[29])

GSA advisors have a difficult job. They can be caught in a political maelstrom if they advocate strongly for their students and blamed if one of them becomes destructive. Some youth come out with such abandon that schoolwork suffers; some are drawn to activism, a few into prominence in the workshop and media circuit. The adults who encourage and use these students' talents are occasionally insensitive to the perils of their overcommitment. Although their enthusiasm is wonderful, they should be counseled toward moderation and reminded of their mundane responsibilities. (See Chapter 8.) When GSA advisors are themselves homosexual, they may take on the extra burden of role-modeling.

Furthermore, students' anger is sometimes misdirected at those who labor for them. As many parents know, adults who are close by, willing to listen, and imperfect make ready targets. Once, for example, Arlington High School GSA students lashed out at administrators and teachers at both a town meeting and a State House hearing. Injured for years at home and in school, they blamed their allies for not setting everything right instantly. One casualty of this outburst was the GSA advisor, a soft-spoken heterosexual man, who had wanted to be a counselor, not a political referee.

Still, for all the pitfalls, the GSAs have been important school and community change agents. Even when they are just comfortable after-school hangouts, their mere existence broadcasts an inclusionary message. They also become institutional monitors, whose watchful presence makes it harder for schools to regress. Some GSA members also speak aloud and eloquently to the powerful:

> Nobody tells Latino kids in the high school that nobody cares if they're Hispanic so long as they keep it to themselves. Jewish kids aren't told that they're sinners, and they could change into Christians if they wanted to. People don't tell black kids they should put up with racism because they've come so far from when they were slaves. They don't have to defend why there is a black history month, or why people want black studies included in the curriculum. People don't say, "That's so Korean!" when they mean something is stupid or weird. People don't tell disabled kids that the community isn't ready to defend their equal rights and inclusion yet. You never hear anyone argue that breast cancer is God's way of killing off the women, and it's a good thing. If a teacher hears anyone use a slang insult for a Chinese kid, they jump on it. When foreign exchange students ask teachers about dating in the school, they aren't sent to see a guidance counselor.[30]

In the spring of 1995 nearly one thousand GSA youth, friends, and families participated in the first Gay/Straight Youth Pride March in Boston. Buoyed by a governor's proclamation of Gay and Straight Youth Pride Month, the event was sponsored by the Governor's Commission and assisted by the DOE. Almost one hundred Massachusetts high schools were represented as the students rallied to demand GSAs in every school, penalties for harassment, gay-inclusive curriculum, out gay teachers, and open communication with parents.[31] A yearly May march and rally, with increasing representation, has been held ever since. In 1998, 7,500 participants joined in the event.[32]

## Limitations of the Massachusetts Model

What has been accomplished in Massachusetts is unprecedented and nearly incredible, even to those who have been a part of it. The Safe Schools success may be attributed to be a combination of liberal and libertarian politics, gay and lesbian activism, heterosexuals who "get it," a critical mass of progressive schools, and hard work by students, parents, and teachers. Nonetheless, mistakes have been made and flaws must still be addressed.

### Emphasizing the Negative

Although it provides political leverage, spotlighting suicide and other woes in hearings, reports, and policies is a problematic tactic. The intent is to play on people's hearts, but the litany risks further pathologizing homosexuality in the public perception. That result could exacerbate the stigma of gay youth and may even convince them of an inevitably bleak future. Moreover, it relies on the efficacy of victimhood to win rights and respect. There is already evidence in the politics of the late twentieth century that the majority of Americans are tiring of that strategy.

Furthermore, when the government gives the impression that programs like Safe Schools are merely expedient responses to whining rather than justifiable initiatives in their own right, it gives those who prefer to do nothing a cynical excuse for ignoring official recommendations.

### Political Fears

A second problem with the Massachusetts model is that the governor walked away from his commission's library and curriculum recommendations. In the wake of the defeat of New York's Rainbow Curriculum,[33] he distanced himself from the sin of "teaching homosexuality" in what became a headline: "'There'll Be No Gay School Lessons': Weld Vows He Won't Change Curriculums."[34] Weld may have trumped his right-wing critics,[35] but he also dealt a blow to the Safe Schools' potential.

On the other hand, by dropping these recommendations from his list, the governor allowed a constituency for curricular and library changes to emerge over time at the local level. And it is locally, after all, where school committees have complete curricular authority. A school's antiviolence and counseling initiatives can thus create a constituency for a more honest and complete approach. Indeed, by 1997, DOE contractors had compiled bibliographies, sample lessons, and book collections to give to those schools who are ready for them.

Weld's deference to local sentiment was evident also in two of his subsequent positions on legislation. The first was his opposition to a bill setting state standards in comprehensive health education, which failed in the legislature.[36] The second was his backing of a parental notification bill, which gives the general public and parents the right to preview curricula and remove their children from courses, course units, assemblies, and other instructional activities that focus on human sexuality or sex education.[37] Advanced by the religious Right, this bill became law and is doubtless having a chilling effect on curriculum designers and classroom teachers.

That is regrettable, as the Weld administration's leadership on gay and lesbian teen suicide and safety testifies to its recognition that communities sometimes need persuasion and encouragement to act. An articulate justification from the governor of more inclusive health, history, literature, art, and science education might have stood up as well as his antiviolence and counseling messages.

In 1996 the DOE stopped offering Safe Schools grants to elementary and middle schools just as the Governor's Commission asked for extension of antiharassment teacher training to the lower grades.[38] When requested by an elementary, middle, or junior high school, the state still provides staff development trainers. It will not, however, fund local initiatives for students below high school age. Even in Massachusetts, politicians are cautious.

The DOE's final advisory curriculum frameworks may help. However, as of 1999 the frameworks address homosexuality explicitly only in the context of health, counseling, and violence. It remains to be seen how much they will lead to contextual, comprehensive lessons about gay and lesbian issues for all students. Even less promising, several 1996 gubernatorial appointees to the Board of Education weakened the multicultural provisions of the 1995 proposed frameworks. The social studies frameworks had recommended that students analyze the "individual and cultural components of identity," including sexual orientation. That was eliminated in the final version.

### Uneven Responses

The advisory nature of the original Board of Education's recommendations has also weakened reform. Among the 330 school districts in Massachusetts, response has been uneven, with greater receptivity in suburban than in rural or urban settings.[39] Parents in the working-class community of Orange, for instance, contested a revised health curriculum and the flying of a gay-rights rainbow flag, despite student council and administrative approval of the gesture. "Either they're going to have to climb back in the closet or be a little bit more low-key," one father pronounced.[40]

Northampton is regarded as a liberal community and boasts a significant lesbian population. Yet, because it is set in the rural western part of the state, its district vocational school has a reputation for intolerance, especially about gender issues. Although he never said he was gay, a fifteen-year-old male student there responded to homophobic teasing over his dress by stabbing to death one of his tormentors in 1998. Only then did the school seriously consider forming a gay/straight alliance.[41] A former staff person at the state-run Gender Equity Center declared, "I was probably in almost every high school in western Massachusetts, and I found homophobia to be rampant."[42]

Although in June 1994 the Boston School Committee adopted all the Safe School's recommendations as policy, the city's schools have barely responded. Only a handful of faculty have attended trainings, and only one or two high schools have GSAs. At one middle school a panel was arranged and then canceled by school officials, with no explanation to the on-site planning team.[43] At a meeting of the School Committee's subcommittee on Health and Human Services in 1994, the superintendent said she was disinclined to "promote" homosexuality by holding parent information meetings. When she offered that she had more pressing problems to deal with, like violence, she was urged to consider the relationship of gender roles and sexuality to aggression and assault.[44] Although her successor is friendlier on these matters, heterosexism is not yet high on his action agenda.

Other urban districts are more encouraging. Greater Lawrence Vocational Tech has a GSA (though some Latino parents organized the evacuation of some four hundred children out of Lawrence on the day of its first Gay Pride Parade).[45] Lowell High and Lowell Vocational have alliances. Brockton and Lowell hosted regional workshops with good racial and ethnic representation. At Brockton High, what once had to be called a "diversity" group made the transition to a GSA. Springfield's DOE grant was aimed at starting Safe Schools task forces and GSAs in every high school. Waltham High's GSA held a groundbreaking Day of Dialogue in 1999. Worcester has held community meetings.

*Minority Access.*   One serious consequence of Boston's and other cities' underparticipation is that minority students miss out. The chair of the Governor's Commission has lamented the relative absence of minority youth at most regional workshops.[46] So long as GSAs, are seen as a "white thing," it will be difficult to convince youth of color to try them out and risk both ostracism from their cultural networks and misunderstanding from nonminority gay peers. Cambridge's Project 10 East fails to attract more than a few youth of color, although a majority of the school's students are racial minorities and for four years a charismatic African American gay mayor chaired the school committee.

Suburban school models seem not to be working in city schools. The primary reason is that heterosexism is not likely to galvanize teachers and principals when they are preoccupied with other crucial problems. Homosexual minority youth might actually be more comfortable attending groups away from their own school. At the same time, however, it is unrealistic to expect urban youth to travel to unfamiliar surroundings in other parts of town or in other communities, where they could expect little awareness of multiple minority concerns. Many already enjoy socializing at particular urban hangouts, and some have found their way to community-based groups and racially diverse gay nightclubs that are accessible to underage youth.

One way to bring more minorities into school GSAs is to seek members among

1. those who attend community-based gay/lesbian support groups;
2. peer leaders and student activists from urban youth groups who are assisted by health grants for work that is not primarily about gays and lesbians.

The DOE has given two grants to increase minority participation in Safe Schools. One, the Youth of Color Outreach Project, is administered by the community agency Boston Children's Services as part of its Every Person Counts program. It is having some success in training young people up to age twenty-three for peer education on sexual orientation. Sessions with significant black and Latino representation have been held with the Massachusetts Prevention Centers' Protect Teen Health and Teen Empowerment programs. In its first two years, they conducted fourteen and then thirty-eight workshops. In its second year Every Person Counts peer leaders received thirty hours of general training with peer leaders from other programs and then by themselves received an additional ten hours on diversity issues within the GLBT community.

This project still has very little contact with youth of color within the public school system, with the possible exception of East Boston High School. Ironically, in 1997–1998 it reached more youth of color in the suburban high schools of Brookline and Newton, both of which participate in a Boston-to-suburb busing program.

The other DOE outreach project, Family Outreach: Focus on Diversity, seeks to involve parents of color in Safe Schools work. The contract was given to P-FLAG to recruit minority parents of gay and lesbian students through community agencies. They were to be invited to workshops and peer support activities and recruited for the Parent Speakers Bureau. After faltering in its first year, the program may have gathered momentum in its second.

One program with a significant percentage of gay/lesbian youth of color is a Boston area theater workshop, involving some forty teens. Funded by the Massachusetts Cultural Council, it has received additional money for parent outreach from the DOE.

*Outright Resistance.* Some principals and superintendents have actually defied the homosexual student protections in the Student Rights Law. In Quincy, just south of Boston, the superintendent refused to permit a high school GSA to form. He sent a memo to principals stating that sexual orientation "is a social issue which is not within the province of our mission as a school system," adding: "I have strong feelings from my own professional experience as an educator that it would be a serious mistake to have young people define themselves as to their sexual orientation at such an early age."[47] Asking respect for all, he attached a magazine article by stridently homophobic Joseph Nicolosi, a regular television advocate of reparative therapies for homosexuality. (See Chapter 8.) The article rued the day the American Psychiatric Association removed homosexuality from its list of disorders and ended by urging schools to "teach tolerance while not actually teaching students to value sexual diversity."[48]

Safe Schools is reaching out to resistant administrators by developing a relationship with the Massachusetts Secondary Schools Administrators Association. The first Safe Schools workshop sponsored by MSSAA, at the urging of several principals who had successes to report, was a partial breakthrough in 1996. A modest number of schools were represented, but the majority of attendees were principals' designees. Apparently, most are discomfited by the topic or think it unimportant. Nevertheless, the MSSAA has not given up and continues to invite Safe Schools to be a part of its events.

In the semi-rural community of Westhampton, the Hampshire Regional School Committee blocked the volunteer Safe Schools Task Force from receiving state funds. It criticized the Governor's Commission Report for contradicting the values of many families and tried to add members to the Task Force to make it more representative of parents who "will not tolerate schools advocating gay and lesbian lifestyles."[49] And in the suburbs, over fifty parents flocked to a Hamilton-Wenham Regional

School Committee meeting to protest an impromptu gay role-play that was used as an ice-breaker at the high school's Human Rights Day. It "downgraded religious convictions," according to one parent, who also claimed that his daughter "was made to feel that she was wrong for believing in her own convictions."[50]

Even liberal suburban schools set limits on inclusion. When the Newton North GSA brought "The Shared Heart" to the high school, the faculty generally ignored the teaching opportunity inherent in the photo-text exhibit by and about gay and lesbian youth.[51] In Wellesley too the absence of blatant opposition masks homosexual erasure and rigid conformity to heterosexual norms: One hundred library books on gay issues are not much used because teachers do not assign research on such topics and no students in the 1996 GSA dared be out of the closet.[52]

Hearings were held at the close of 1994 to assess the progress since the emendation of the Student Rights Law one year before.[53] Testimony from earnest, sometimes frantic, students and teachers confirmed widespread resistance to Safe Schools. Witnesses detailed obstructionist school practices and desperation:

- "Our administrators are extremely hesitant to do anything about harassment; therefore nothing is done to combat it. The majority of teachers are not aware of what the law implies."[54]
- "Last school year we had three suicides where it is known within the faculty that one . . . young man did commit suicide while trying to determine his own sexual identity. . . . They set up a community-wide suicide task force. Unfortunately . . . not one mention was made about sexual identities or problems."[55]
- "I should feel optimistic about all the things that have happened, but at the same time I think that there are a lot of problems. Last year two people in my high school attempted suicide and I was one of them and that was largely because of gay issues—because people were uninformed, because I had to live through a health curriculum that didn't teach anything about being gay, didn't mention it even once."[56]
- "Today we started a bulletin board at our school when we put up information and it didn't last more than six periods before it was ripped down and destroyed completely."[57]
- "I am forced to be in a private gym class for mentally handicapped seniors now so that I am not physically or emotionally abused. That I guess is their way of . . . handling my being gay. . . . I leave every class 10 minutes early and get there 10 minutes late so I'm not hurt or beaten up."[58]

The state's own evaluators reported that schools where harassment is more frequent are more likely to be following some Safe Schools recommendations.[59] That finding could mean, as the report suggests, that schools with the worst problems are acting to solve them. However, it could indicate just as well that only the schools that take Safe Schools recommendations seriously are recognizing and documenting their homophobia. In either case, self-reporting on levels of homophobic harassment should not be given too much credence. Moreover, how accurate is an assessment of school environment made through a voluntary survey with a 39 percent response rate and a 2 percent rate of student representation?

This critique of the Massachusetts initiative is not intended to imply that decades of neglect can be corrected in a few years by state fiat. It will take more time for grassroots community and school-based constituencies to organize in some localities. Toward that end, educators who are succeeding in their schools must be given the opportunity to inspire, coax, and reassure their well-intentioned, perhaps overly cautious, colleagues in other places. State authorities, for their part, must back up both established programs that want to improve or expand their offerings and others just getting started. Moreover, government agencies cannot permit local districts to flout the Student Rights Law with impunity or stand by while some ignore Safe Schools recommendations.

### Reaching Parents

Of all its recommendations, the state board's proposal that schools counsel the parents of gay and lesbian youth has been least observed.[60] Of course, the record of the high schools' contact with parents on all matters is spotty. Their level of inertia regarding sexual orientation is understandable, especially when a student does not appear to be at risk.

Then there is the matter of finding the parent constituency. Even in schools with large GSAs, the number of young people actually identifying as homosexual is small.[61] Coming out in school is still a major step, particularly for those who can pass for heterosexual. The number who have come out to their parents might be even smaller. (See Chapter 8.) The school is left with little incentive to involve the families. Most parents who become aware of their children's homosexuality are left to get help from P-FLAG, clergy, physicians, social workers, and other community resources. Schools might reach more families of gay and lesbian students by making presentations to all parents through PTAs and parent councils, a good idea in its own right. (See Chapter 11.)

## Long-Term Monitoring

The DOE has not provided the means to check on the progress of the schools after its trainers depart. Participants are encouraged to devise action plans, but unless they call for further assistance, they may drop out of sight and grow moribund.

At one time, 70 percent of those schools that participated in Safe Schools offerings were solely involved through regional workshops; nearly 50 percent held personnel trainings at their own sites; about 30 percent asked for and received further technical assistance.[62] This pattern reveals that it is relatively easy for an administrator to send a few faculty to a workshop, perhaps as insurance against the complaint that the school has done nothing. But some degree of dedication is needed to have a workshop at one's school and involve the DOE in the development of an action plan.

A further commitment is required to continue the reforms after the DOE team departs. One-time events starring imported talent may not yield lasting improvements.[63] Implementation is better advanced by means of an ongoing Safe Schools Task Force or the like. Yet, even so, school teams need follow-up collaboration and guidance in their program and curriculum planning. Once they have gone back to the real world of their classrooms, they benefit from periodic consultation.[64]

Experts can help, for instance, in the thoughtful selection of classroom materials. A horrifying example of what can happen without such consultation was the distribution of a "heterosexuality questionnaire" to Framingham sophomore health classes. The handout contained such items as, "If you never slept with someone of the same sex, how do you know you wouldn't prefer that?"[65] Some students and parents failed to understand or approve of the irony of that pedagogical device. Nor did they appreciate the "list of famous homosexuals," naming three popes, two cardinals, and others of ambiguous sexuality. Conceding that such items obtained at a teacher workshop might have been intended for adults, school administrators fortunately upheld the intent of the lessons, while promising to prepare better materials for the future.[66]

**Keeping Track of GSAs.** The rapid proliferation of GSAs could also be cause for concern. Safe Schools should know how each is doing. Some apparently exist only on paper. Others have difficulty maintaining their membership numbers and staying effective from year to year. Adult advisors need support with a job that is always exhausting and sensitive and sometimes controversial. Some have been able to confer with other advisors for mutual advice and cooperation at DOE-sponsored sessions, but they are infrequent. Internet communication could be a boon. For now, the state has given contracts for GLSEN/Boston to publish a thrice-yearly GSA newsletter and for more experienced GSAs to mentor newer groups.

At one suburban school, an attempted lesbian suicide and a fracas over a lesbian couple going to a dance indicated the advisability of a GSA. It was finally initiated through the persistence of a gay student, but the attitude of a counselor whom the principal ordered to attend caused students to become disaffected. The group floundered when its leader, a senior with outside affirmation, grew tired of the hassle. After he graduated, some students felt they were better served in a community-based group in another town and in involvement with the Governor's Commission. They had even written a play but could not get the school to hold an awareness day during which it could be performed. They correctly perceived that faculty and administrative backing for their objectives was weak.[67]

"Gay/Straight Alliances: A Student Guide," by the DOE is good reading for adult mentors as well, but more is required. The whole Safe Schools Program could be discredited by a serious failure in a GSA. One suburban advisor has publicly warned that most GSAs lack a mechanism for dealing with kids in crisis.[68] Principals ought to solicit their best teachers and counselors to serve as faculty advisors and afford them professional development opportunities beyond the average two- or three-hour general Safe Schools workshop session.

It should not be assumed either that advisors who are gay and lesbian themselves have already been prepared for the role by virtue of their sexuality. They might in fact require special consultation to deal with the unexpected feelings that often arise from working with homosexual youth whose experiences are different from their own. They might also need help keeping their past grievances with a heterosexist system separate from the GSA's struggle.

Ongoing DOE regional workshops for new and veteran GSAs should help. With sessions like "Building Relationships Across Differences," "Making What's Great Even Greater," and "Coalition Building in Schools," and with separate roundtables for students and GSA advisors, they have begun to address the ongoing needs of those in the trenches. Still, these sessions are for the already committed. They do not attract the general faculty and administrators who are the critical mass for broadening the impact of Safe Schools institutionally.

Moreover, GSAs should not be asked to take over the entire reform of the school. Groups must be free to set their own agenda for activism or counseling or both. The formation of a GSA is not a finale but an invitation to the rest of the school to become active. At the outset of its campaign, Arlington had the foresight to create a Safe Schools Task Force with broad representation.[69] Although a few members have taken leadership roles, it has not been left to one person such as the GSA advisor to assume responsibility for everything. If she leaves or is ill, the project will not be thrown into disarray, as has happened in other communities.[70]

*Supporting Teachers.*   More attention must also be given to the consequences for teachers of their involvement with Safe Schools programs. An official of the Massachusetts Teachers Association has charged that some have suffered various forms of harassment.[71] Although what has been done to them might be sufficiently subtle as to be nongrievable, they have to get support from both the system and the union. Openly gay and lesbian teachers often have this kind of experience. (See Chapter 9.) It is not surprising that their allies are getting the same treatment.

### Student Privacy

No clear provisions have been made to ensure student privacy. Referral to school or community-based counseling about sexual orientation asks a higher level of confidentiality than may be available under current regulations. Students have legitimate fears about their personal concerns getting bruited about the school or reaching their families. Some districts actually require that parents be consulted when a student sees a counselor more than a few times about an issue or before a referral. And the state's 1996 parental notification law's provisions for sex and sexuality instruction can only make this predicament worse.

### Certification Follow-Through

The outcome of the new certification/recertification requirements is still vague. It remains to be seen how prepracticum and veteran teachers will be provided the information and skills to confront discrimination and affirm homosexual youth. Nor is it certain how rigorous the Department of Education will be in monitoring compliance.

Considerable curricular revisions are needed to give education and counseling students more than superficial exposure to the topic of gays and lesbians. Yet, the optional DOE-sponsored college faculty workshops were unevenly attended. Many professors, though eager to invite guest presenters into their classes, seem less motivated to master the subject themselves; and some college and graduate programs have declined to participate at all.

The State Board of Higher Education has unfortunately never been involved, and the Governor's Commission seems loath to solicit their help. The DOE's Certification Division is the only leverage available for en-

couraging compliance. Since a state crisis has arisen over teacher education and credentialing in general, there is little hope that much attention
will go toward enforcing one, perhaps thorny, piece of the Equity Standard.

### Political Support

**The Board of Education.**  Governor Weld's and his successor's ap-
pointments to the State Board of Education may undermine the state's
accomplishments.[72] Unlike his predecessor, whose compassion for homosexual youth was demonstrated in proactive leadership, the board's chair
from 1996 to 1999 has a record as a college president of outright hostility
toward gays and lesbians.[73] Furthermore, his stated intention to eliminate certification altogether imperiled staff development, as did Governor Weld's periodic threats to abolish the Department of Education.

**The Legislature, the Departments, and the Commission.**  Although
the legislature passed the Student Rights Law, they did not fund Safe
Schools explicitly for its first three years. Money was committed behind
the scenes by the governor and included in other DOE accounts. Although it was no secret to most lawmakers, some preferred not to go on
record in favor of such spending. The absence of a specific line item successfully protected the program from political attack; however, it also ne-
cessitated repeated lobbying of the executive branch and DOE to spend
the money as promised. This arrangement might have been politically
palatable, but it invited intrigue in the governor's office and state agencies.

This practice ended in 1997, when both House and Senate passed ap-
propriations explicitly dedicated to protecting gay and lesbian youth.
Yet, despite clear support from both the executive and legislative
branches, there have been periodic clashes between the Governor's Commission and the DOE over budget and program decisions. Some com-
missioners have charged the DOE with foot-dragging, and some in the
DOE have accused the Governor's Commission of micromanagement.
Moreover, a number of education and public health subcontractors have
felt caught between two masters.

In five years, the volunteer Governor's Commission has indisputably
accomplished more for gay and lesbian youth than has been done in any
other state. They have gotten public bureaucracies to provide unprecedented direct support to students. But because they have sometimes confused political ends with educational ones, they have also irritated a
number of experienced gay and lesbian service providers. Ideally, the

commission would help formulate policy and then leave it to state agencies and their professional contractors to carry it out. They would of course retain the right of periodic review and would continue to advise the governor and his or her department heads about the quality of the work being done. They would not, however, be involved in day-to-day decisionmaking.

Perhaps with some of these problems in mind, the Governor's Commission hired a director of programs in 1998 to oversee all contracts. As an employee of both the Department of Public Health and the Governor's Commission he might improve communication with the people in the field. But it is difficult to see how hiring him makes any clearer the advisory Commission's authority to supervise Safe Schools work.

Because politics and education so often intersect, the task of making schools safe for gay and lesbian students is inherently complex. It may therefore always require precarious and uncomfortable cooperation between effective state house lobbyists and master teachers.

# 13

## Reform and Opposition

Massachusetts may be something of a paragon, but it is not the only place in the country where law, policy, activism, and caring have led to safer schools for gay and lesbian students. In fact Lambda Legal Defense and Education Fund (LLDEF) has published an impressive list of model state laws and school policies.[1] Wherever it has occurred, however, progress has not been achieved without marked, sometimes ugly, resistance from conservative religious and secular groups and from alarmed individuals. The poignant vignettes in Dan Woog's *School's Out* provided a national perspective on this transformation in the mid-1990s.[2] During the 1990s newspapers across the country supplied an almost daily record of schools being challenged by students, teachers, and parents to change their attitudes and policies regarding homosexuality. Of course vehement opponents have received at least equal media coverage. This chapter examines some of these advancements and recent battles over heterosexism in education.

### State and Municipal Reforms

As of 1997 Connecticut, Massachusetts, Minnesota, Pennsylvania, Vermont, and Wisconsin prohibited discrimination based on sexual orientation in their education law.[3] The Florida Department of Education's Code of Ethics required schools to "make a reasonable effort" to protect students from such harassment. The Rhode Island regents issued a 1997 policy statement regarding harassment, discrimination, and exclusion,[4] but almost a year later it was not being followed by many teachers.[5] Reformers in other states still struggled for legislation. For example, despite a comprehensive 1992 report on the needs of gay youth in Hawaii, officials had not responded through 1998.[6] Also in 1998 more than one hundred students rallied in Austin in support of a bill banning school discrimination in Texas.[7] In 1999 a "posthumous hearing" was given a similar bill, already dead in Washington State.[8]

## California

California's AB 101 made it to the floor in 1997 and 1998 but was narrowly defeated.[9] Youth Lobby Day in 1999 brought seven hundred teens to the capitol to promote the bill, which was given a strong chance of passage after making it through the Education Committee in the State Assembly.[10] It would add sexual orientation to the law protecting public school students from kindergarten through the state university system. Activists have also sought to amend the state's curriculum frameworks.

*San Francisco.* San Francisco has had a number of heartening successes. Among them:

- electing an openly gay person to the united school district board of education in 1990 (later elected chair);[11]
- hiring a director of support services for gay youth in 1990;
- designating a sympathetic staff person in every middle and high school;
- distributing curriculum supplements to all teachers;
- developing an antislur policy;
- halting ROTC recruitment (a result of the military ban on homosexuals);
- banning Boy Scout activities in schools (due to their discriminatory practices);
- developing comprehensive AIDS education and making condoms available in schools;
- holding the first public hearings by the city's human rights and youth commissions on the issues and needs of GLBT youth in 1996.[12]

Gay and lesbian organizations, including political, parent, and teacher groups have helped bring about these achievements. The citywide Lesbian and Gay Parents Association pushed to make school workers more sensitive, forms more inclusive, and family portrayal more diverse. The Bay Area Network of Gay and Lesbian Educators' (BANGLE) five chapters lobbied for the student support services position, assist with workshops, and donate books. The Contra Costa chapter sponsored a groundbreaking video, *Gay Youth,* which has been shown in workshops nationwide.[13]

The half-time ombudsman and referral agent for the schools' Health Programs Department is a psychotherapist from the lesbian/gay parents group who

- is liaison to the designated adult(s) in each school;
- counsels youth, families, and faculty;
- runs workshops for middle and high school staff;
- develops curriculum on name-calling, diversity, and homophobia and enforces the antislur policy;
- develops counseling guidelines and trains teachers and guidance staff.

The designated adults are available in a safe space to youth and their families for information and referral. They also promote HIV/STD/drug education and enforcement of the antislur policy. Counselors have approximately 300 contacts with students regarding sexual orientation in a year.[14]

The Support Services program recommends and/or offers the following:

- school and classroom visuals reflecting family diversity;
- books for display in school libraries;
- Support Services signs and posters;
- promotion and enforcement of antislur policies;
- curriculum review with Gay/Lesbian Sensitive Adult and health liaisons;
- implementation of "Name-Calling" and "Family Diversity" curricula (grades 6–8);
- use of inclusive language when discussing teen sexuality, dating, and families;
- inclusion of gay/lesbians in "diversity days";
- publicizing Designated Gay/Lesbian Sensitive Adults.

Gay/lesbian groups have been formed in at least seven San Francisco high schools. One at George Washington began meeting openly with more than one or two members in 1995.[15] They told a receptive faculty meeting that it is easier to be open at more academic middle-class schools.[16] At Richards High School, where a middle- to low-income student population is made up of over two-thirds youth of color, progress was hampered in part by the community's religious sentiments.[17] Even with two out teachers, signs for the "underground" support group were torn down, announcements were not read aloud by faculty, and students were harassed. Hayward High's Gay Straight Alliance (GSA) led a faculty in-service and perceived a positive change in its first year

(1996–1997), whereas at Hayward's Mount Eden High, a tiny GSA with mostly straight-identified female members got a weak reception.[18] Despite intervention, one harassed San Francisco eighth-grader dropped out in 1996,[19] proving it is still hard to come out in middle school, no matter how proactive the system.

The only apparent shortcomings in San Francisco's impressive record are those that it shares with Massachusetts: the failure to move every school to undertake reforms and the lack of emphasis on comprehensive curriculum. A district resolution of the school board in 1996 finally led to a two-day training of 1,500 employees of twenty-one city schools early in 1998.[20]

*Los Angeles.* In Los Angeles's Fairfax High School, two blocks from West Hollywood, science teacher Virginia Uribe founded Project 10 in 1984 to prevent gay and lesbian youth from dropping out. Begun as an informal lunchtime discussion, this school-based group was the first of its kind in the country. Project 10 is regularly pilloried by opponents, yet they have always been defended by the principal and school board, whose president in 1984 was a lesbian. The National Education Association and others have recognized Uribe for her vision and courage.

Like other schools in cities noted for their gay and lesbian enclaves (for example, Provincetown and Northampton High Schools in Massachusetts), Fairfax is not bias-free.[21] Perhaps to compensate for teasing they have received from homophobic peers in other schools, straight students have been known to lash out against homosexual classmates.

In 1996, Jeff Horton was elected as the first openly gay president of the Los Angeles Unified School District. Horton, who came out shortly after he was first elected to the board in 1991, has been hailed for initiating policies and programs for gay and lesbian and other underserved students.[22]

Project 10 has tried to replicate itself in other Los Angeles high schools but has not been universally well received. Particular effort is still needed to enlist schools in Latino and African American neighborhoods.[23] Eight years after the establishment of Project 10, the school district opened the EAGLES Center, a high school alternative for a small number of gay/lesbian dropouts.

The Board of Education asks schools to commemorate June as Gay and Lesbian Pride Month. It has also published "Educating for Diversity," which calls for instruction on "the contributions of gay and lesbian people in history and culture and the current status of homosexuals as it relates to social policy, family diversity, and human relations."[24]

This document followed the establishment in 1991 of a Gay and Lesbian Education Commission with a paid director. They offered curricula on famous historical and contemporary homosexuals and on gays in the

Holocaust, but their use was unenforced among Los Angeles's 35,000 teachers. Progress was measured instead by the number of staff workshops being conducted by the teachers' union and other groups; the performance of gay/lesbian student support mechanisms; and the enforcement of antiharassment policy by the Safety Committee of the Assistant Superintendent for Intergroup Relations.

Los Angeles's resolutions and goals are referred to as mandates, which schools are encouraged to observe. Nevertheless, half the district's fifty high schools do not have counseling provisions, and curriculum revision is largely ignored. In 1998, Proposition 209's ban on affirmative action terminated the Gay and Lesbian Education Commission along with others on gender and ethnicity.[25]

*Other Districts.*   Despite the strides in some urban centers, many nearby communities are still struggling. Fearing accusations of endorsing homosexuality, the Fremont school board refused to rewrite their antiharassment policies to bar homophobic acts, all the while assuring advocates that gay/lesbian youth were protected.[26] Later, religious groups forced them both to water down a faculty antiharassment training and to take responsibility for conducting it away from the gay educators, who had run a previous administrators' training.[27]

Current and former students at Morgan Hill High School filed a federal lawsuit in 1998, accusing school officials of ignoring their victimization by repeated harassment. Livermore High School students, and others from nearby Granada High, conducted a sit-in to protest homophobic incidents at their schools.[28]

A heterosexual African American teacher who cofounded a high school GSA in San Leandro was reprimanded for pro-gay "proselytizing" in his class. He was responding to students' concerns about antigay initiatives in the community.[29] He later sued the district for its ban on discussion of "controversial issues."[30]

A Project 10 in Alhambra had ten years without controversy,[31] but at Hoover High School in Glendale, students lobbied against a parent notification requirement for participation in all clubs, seen as an attack on the GSA. An approved compromise required that parents receive a list of all clubs at the beginning of the year.[32] Objections to another GSA in Orange County were answered by officials changing its name from a "club" to an "equal access organization." The GSA at Los Alamitos High School endured heckling, torn posters, teachers' ignoring or mocking announcements, and angry calls from parents; the president of Huntington Beach High's GSA received death threats.[33]

When a young man at Argus High School in Ceres was attacked and beaten by fellow students, the principal implied that he had brought it on himself: "The kids chose to react. Wearing a T-shirt that advertises your sexual preference—to me that is no different than a gang member who wears a shirt. . . . It's inflammatory."[34] An administrator at an Oakland high school declined to classify a student beating as gay-bashing because, he maintained, "We don't have any gay students at our school."[35]

Because there are no school-based services in Modesto, gay students are referred to an off-campus group.[36] Similarly, a student at Oakland's Skyline High School had to find refuge outside. When he approached school personnel about support for him and three others who were closeted, one counselor said there was no need and another worried that he would be suspected of being gay if he offered assistance.[37] The local newspaper in San Marino editorialized that its school district's plan for Project 10-style lunchtime counseling would "mess with kids' heads."[38]

Las Lomas, the Contra Costa County high school from which Bobby Griffith graduated before his suicide (see Chapter 8), continued to wrestle with the issue. When a straight student reporter wrote sympathetically about his gay peers in 1995, some gay and lesbian students were able to be open and others remained hidden. Homophobic schoolmates protested the very idea of such an article.[39]

## New York

The New York State Department of Education's policy prohibits discrimination on the basis of sexual orientation in its own offices. Its Director of Civil Rights and Intercultural Relations believed that homosexual students are covered more generally under federal Title IX provisions against sexual harassment. (See Chapter 11.) Heterosexism is ignored in the State Department of Education's guidebook on sexual harassment.[40] Indeed, few districts in the state have taken a position on the issue. The prevailing attitude was reflected in the comments of an assistant superintendent: "We never had any agreement among the community as to how to address it. The position that the school takes is that it's a topic for home."[41] The Coalition for Safer Schools of New York State (CSS-NYS), a gay advocacy group, has been trying to change such attitudes. For instance, it recently appealed to the state's education commissioner to include same sex questions on the New York Youth Risk Behavior Survey.[42]

*New York City.* New York City school officials have consistently refused to acknowledge antigay bias as a school problem.[43] Nevertheless, since 1985 the city has offered one haven for gay and lesbian youth at risk. The Harvey Milk School enrolls twenty to thirty young people, some of whom have been homeless. It is funded by the city, the Hettrick-Martin Institute (a community-based gay youth agency), and private contributions. Fewer than 10 percent of the youth seen at the Hettrick-Martin Institute are referred to the Harvey Milk School. The staff of two teachers, paraprofessionals, and volunteers caters primarily to students whose unconventional appearance or behavior makes them targets of oppression in mainstream schools. Many are minority and most are poor. Many have had family and truancy problems. Of the one hundred enrolled in the first six years, only fifteen graduated.[44] Since then graduation rates have improved. Some finish their schooling at Harvey Milk; others go back to their original schools after a time.

For a short time in the 1990s the debate about the city's "Children of the Rainbow Curriculum" became a rallying point for public discourse about the nature of sexuality and families. That battle over the inclusion of gay-positive instruction in a multicultural curriculum evinced a homophobic barrage from a multi-ethnic chorus. Adopted by Chancellor Fernandez's office in 1991, Children of the Rainbow had been conceived as a teachers' resource guide rather than a formal curriculum. It was intended to help foster awareness of diversity in first-grade students, while teaching them academic and social skills.[45]

Children of the Rainbow's recommendations were being largely ignored when members of the all-white community school board in Queens, where 70 percent of students are children of color, began an offensive. They decried the curriculum's homosexual content and turned out busloads of religious Latinos, blacks, and working-class whites.[46] Teachers also complained, although their union president discovered only five of six hundred disgruntled members had actually read the document.[47]

The curriculum was characterized, with some justification, as having been foisted upon the community by middle-class gays and a remote central office.[48] Attempts by Rainbow proponents to compare gays to blacks in the old South provoked outrage rather than empathy. It was particularly irritating for parents of color, who had long sought greater curricular representation of their own experience, to think that gay outsiders, not "real minorities," were being catered to.[49] Local communities had had little involvement in the curriculum's development.

Long-festering school inadequacies had also created hostility toward the central administration in many districts. And at about the same time conservatives organized against the chancellor's support for K–12 non-"abstinence only" HIV/AIDS education and condom distribution.[50] Resentment peaked when the chancellor fired the Queens school board. The central board then reinstated them and ultimately it was the chancellor who was fired.

Unfortunately, the inclusion of two books in the resource list provided effective ammunition to the opponents. *Heather Has Two Mommies* and

*Gloria Goes to Gay Pride*[51] were too advanced for first-graders to read and raised issues perhaps more appropriate for older students. The former, which had actually been written for lesbians to use with their children, explains alternative insemination. The compilers of the list may have erred in their haste to complete their task. On the other hand, the readings were targeted to teachers, not students.

Some Rainbow supporters faulted liberal parent groups for not taking their side.[52] In any event, the curriculum was revised, and many local boards opted to delay teaching about homosexuality until fifth or sixth grade.

In 1995, the Board of Education narrowed its multicultural policy to include only ethnic, racial, and linguistic groups. This move was a last retreat from the Rainbow concept, albeit board members professed to support a separate antidiscrimination curriculum that would cover sexual orientation, religion, gender, and disability.[53] The decision left in limbo a seventh- and eighth-grade social studies unit, *Struggle for Equality: Lesbian and Gay Community*, prepared in 1989 as part of the Multicultural Education Curriculum by the Mayor's Office for the Gay and Lesbian Community.[54]

The inclusion of gays and lesbians in the Rainbow Curriculum was hobbled primarily by a disregard for community sensibilities, an overreliance on administrative authority, and too few good materials. Nonetheless, it is doubtful that community outreach, democratic decisionmaking, and finely drafted curricula would have won the day. Such strategies may only have avoided a total disaster and have better begun the dialogue. Gay and lesbian activists might have had greater success had they united with other minorities in their long-term effort to improve education across the board.[55]

At least one homosexual group, People About Changing Education, was organized precisely for that purpose.[56] And after the imbroglio, three openly gay or lesbian candidates were elected to local school boards. These are both more promising steps toward solid, if gradual, reform.

## Pennsylvania

In 1993, the Pennsylvania Board of Education adopted a prohibition against discrimination on the basis of sexual orientation in educational programs.[57] It also passed an "Appreciating and Understanding Others" goal, which left unspecified the breadth of diversity it envisioned. This section, however vague, was attacked as pro-gay and removed from the ten-item package by the governor, leaving only the Educational Equity Principles of the State Board of Education, which cite race, gender, and other categories, but not sexuality.

The following year the Philadelphia Board of Education passed a Multiracial-Multicultural-Gender Policy (Policy 102), referring to sexuality. It offered new equity possibilities in schools, even though it lacked enforcement provisions. The District's Policy 102 Collaborative, which represented more than seventy professional and community-based organizations, including gays and lesbians of color, urged a new superintendent to commit to Policy 102. He refused, confessing a fear of homophobic backlash.[58]

A decade's research and lobbying by the Philadelphia Lesbian and Gay Task Force has, however, led to some policy improvement and an inclusive "Equity in Diversity" teacher training. Small-scale local changes have become the rule. For example, through the persistence of one senior, a support group was launched at Lower Merion High School in Ardmore.

## Minnesota

In 1991, the Governor's Task Force on Lesbian and Gay Minnesotans asked schools to "take the lead in developing a climate where diversity is respected and protected."[59] In 1993 Statute 363.12 was passed, prohibiting discrimination on the basis of sexual orientation and other categories.

Two years later, after visiting thirteen cities, the task force again called for school and community affirmation and counseling for gay and lesbian teens and for public employee training. They referred to _Alone No More: Developing a School Support System for Gay, Lesbian, and Bisexual Youth_, a 1994 booklet prepared by the Minnesota Department of Education's Prevention and Risk Reduction Team (HIV/STD). This well-crafted manual employs AIDS in the same way that the Massachusetts Governor's Commission uses suicide and violence as an inducement to a comprehensive approach to teen homosexuality. Schools are encouraged to perform the following:

- examine and change school and classroom climate and access to student services;
- have at least one person, preferably a team, to advocate for homosexual youth;
- develop classroom presentations on sexual diversity;
- institute clear policies to protect homosexual students and staff;
- develop school-based peer discussion and support groups.

_Alone No More_ offers pointers for devising policy, hiring for diversity, creating an inclusive environment, developing curriculum, and improving instructional effectiveness and counseling techniques. It also provides specific guidelines for school-based peer groups.

The state was aided by earlier initiatives in Minneapolis–St. Paul. Wingspan, a Lutheran outreach ministry, sponsored a coalition to fight homophobia in schools. The St. Paul schools' 1990 prohibition against antigay behavior prompted the establishment of a support group of nurses, health educators, and students at Central High School. Since then Out for Equity has aided students and trained teachers throughout the St. Paul district. Originally funded with state, federal, and foundation money, Out for Equity's $40,000 budget was assumed by the city in 1997, despite some carping that the state Human Rights Act prohibits the "promotion" of homosexuality in the schools.[60] By then, ninety-two students had joined eight groups in St. Paul's high schools.[61] "Out 4 Good" became their Minneapolis counterpart. In the same year, the "Love Makes a Family" project began bringing parents into first through fourth-grade classrooms to read stories about family diversity. Sponsored by a $10,000 grant, the program is optional for students, parents, and teachers.[62]

The Youth and AIDS Project at the University of Minnesota has been an important ally, bringing together doctors (including pediatricians), public health professionals, social workers, educators, and even a Master of Divinity. Project Director Gary Remafedi's research has drawn national attention (see Chapter 8).

Minnesota has yet to muster greater commitment across the state. The Governor's Task Force reported in 1995 that away from the Twin Cities and college communities, many gay/lesbian youth live isolated despairing lives. When a religious conservative assailed *Alone No More* at a U.S. congressional hearing, a spokesperson for the state's Children, Families, and Learning Department answered emblematically that the booklet was sent to schools only upon request, adding, "It's an old dead issue. It's a one-time project that is no more."[63] The fourth annual survey of the state attorney general's office in 1997 revealed that gay and lesbian students are still prime targets of violence in the schools.[64]

## Other States

Responding to a 1995 survey by its Committee on Hate and Violence, the Montgomery County, Maryland, school board prohibited antigay discrimination but barred homosexual speakers from classes, to avoid advocacy or endorsement.[65] In Fairfax County, Virginia, there is one high school "human sexuality discussion group."[66] Washington-area youth are perhaps best served by the community-based Sexual Minority Youth Assistance League (SMYAL).

Official Kansas inertia did not deter P-FLAG parents and others from holding a daylong public session in a church to document the struggles of homosexual youth. Although high school students were afraid to appear, recent graduates testified before a handful of progressives—politicians and others, including the chairperson of the state board of education, who was moved to tears.[67] A non-government-sponsored forum was also held in Rhode Island. The superintendent from Woonsocket attended, the only community with a high school GSA.[68] Maine, which repealed its gay rights law by referendum in 1998, has only one GSA—on Mount Desert Island.

The Detroit chapter of GLSEN issued a report and recommendations, "Bruised Bodies, Bruised Spirits," based on comprehensive surveys in the metropolitan area, revealing that half of the schools had no services for homosexual students.[69]

Despite Connecticut's legal protections, gay and lesbian youth are given scant attention in most schools. There are a few GSAs scattered throughout the state, one of them founded by a Manchester High School student after repeated snubs from her principal. Officials finally relented when she agreed to change the group's name from "Gay and Straight Pride" to "Gay Straight Alliance for Tolerance." Like many schools, New London has a diversity group but no GSA. And the principal of East Hartford High School equated its word-of-mouth support group to the student Alcoholics Anonymous meeting.[70] The greatest impetus for school change comes once a year from Children from the Shadows, a non-school-sponsored conference for students, teachers, and social workers. The sixth conference, held in 1999, featured two days of panel discussions, workshops, plenaries, and other affirming activites for students, school and mental health workers, parents, and others.[71]

Most Illinois communities find the topic too controversial. A dozen schools in the Chicago area have GSAs and both Skokie and Lincolnshire offer confidential support groups,[72] while a "Spectrum" club in Zion-Benton Township meets behind locked doors with security on alert.[73]

Jefferson County, Colorado's largest system (nearly 90,000 students), amended its Student Conduct and Discipline code in 1996 to protect gay and lesbian teachers and students.[74] The Denver Public Schools considered a discrimination ban on the basis of sexual orientation and gender identity in both hiring and educational practices.[75] In the end the ban was passed without the gender provision.[76] Jefferson, El Paso, Pueblo, and Boulder counties have also begun gay and lesbian student groups.[77]

Many large urban high schools in Washington State have gay-positive counseling and GSAs for their students. For example, the Seattle School District's Creating Safe Schools for Sexual Minorities program conducts groups at eight of the city's high schools. Yet smaller and more rural districts are likely to offer nothing.[78]

In Florida, Dade and Broward County school regulations protect homosexual youth, but more advocacy has been called for. A retired University of Miami professor, who also assists Project Y.E.S., a community gay and lesbian youth group, has trained forty high school guidance chairs and eighteen counselors in Dade.[79] Project Y.E.S. also offers a G.E.D. program.[80] Pinellas County has also approved student and employee protections.[81] But Palm Beach opted not to adopt such a policy for fear that explicit prohibitions would make it more vulnerable to lawsuits,[82] perhaps a perverse consequence of Wisconsin's Nabozny decision (see Chapter 11).

Exceptional people have fostered incremental change in Portland, Oregon,[83] Seattle,[84] Birmingham, Michigan,[85] and Denver.[86] In Portland, for example, parents and teachers set up Love Makes a Family, Inc. to start a dialogue in school, community, and church groups. Student-initiated groups met at two Tucson high schools, under the two-year shadow of legislation proposing to ban such meetings from kindergarten through public university.[87] When another Arizona school support group was formed, the student council tried unsuccessfully to abolish it.[88] In Chicago, an openly gay student was elected a nonvoting member of the Board of Education.[89] The St. Louis School Board added sexual orientation to its antidiscrimination code[90], as did the Ames, Iowa School Board.[91] A Detroit student, inspired by an Ann Arbor GSA, waged an extraordinary campaign at Novi High School and was honored for his leadership.[92]

As in Massachusetts, reform most often happens in suburban, affluent, and liberal cities and towns and in progressive neighborhoods. A recent survey by the National Association of Secondary School Administrators (NASSP) found only 16 percent of urban middle and high schools have gay teen support groups or alliances and only 11 percent have groups led by a faculty member.[93] Chapel Hill (N.C.) High School's Gay/Straight Alliance, and school groups in Decatur and Cobb County, Georgia, are rare phenomena in a rather solidly antipathetic South.[94] Indeed, the father of a gay former student received threatening phone calls at work after writing to two school principals about the plight of gay and lesbian students.[95] Pro-active culture- and class-sensitive strategies to reach working-class youth and conservative school districts have yet to be widely applied.

Governors, in addition to Weld of Massachusetts, have begun to take progressive stands. Washington's governor, on his last day in office in 1997, wrote a request to every superintendent to "adopt and aggressively enforce school policies that explicitly forbid discrimination and harassment based upon the perceived or actual sexual orientation of students, family members or school staff."[96] His insistence on the language reflects Washington activists' concerns that without explicit protections, antigay harassment is not reported.[97] Vermont's governor used a high school speech to the same effect in 1998.[98] He subsequently authorized funding for a Safe Schools effort, modeled on the Massachusetts program.

### National Organizations

Some prominent national organizations have weighed in on behalf of homosexual students. Resolutions to sustain gay and lesbian youth have been passed by the American Psychological Association (1981, 1988, 1993), the National Association of Social Workers (1987), the American Association for Counseling and Development (1987), the American Federation of Teachers (1988, 1990), the Association for Supervision and Curriculum Development (1990), the American School Health Association (1990), the Council for Exceptional Children (1997), the National Education Association (1990, 1994, 1995), the Child Welfare League of America (1991), the National School Boards Association (1991, 1993), the National Association of School Psychologists (1993), the National Middle School Association (1993), and the National Association of State Boards of Education (1994).

The American Friends Service Committee's Bridges of Respect Project has labored for increased understanding of homosexual young people with written materials and collaborations on such events as the Lesbian Gay Bisexual Youth Empowerment Speakout, a two-day conference in 1993 for two thousand youth and their allies.

In 1996, the American Civil Liberties Union of California's First Amendment Project held summer trainings on gay rights in schools for the first time. Research results and training curricula have also come from the Center for Population Options (1992), the Sex Education and Information Council of the U.S., and the Phi Delta Kappa Educational Foundation (1993).

The prominent inclusion of gay and lesbian concerns by Teaching Tolerance, a curriculum project of the Southern Poverty Law Center, is atypical. Erasure is more common in mainstream diversity forums and mass-produced curricula. The article coincidentally titled "Teaching Tolerance" in *The Executive Educator*, for example, is an appeal to schools to "tackle head-on the tough issues of violence, prejudice, civil rights, and bigotry."[99] It contains not a word about homophobia.

The Anti-Defamation League of B'nai Brith's World of Difference program promotes tolerance and understanding through the schools. With bases in thirty-two cities in the United States, it has had over 300,000 teacher participants. After being lobbied,[100] the ADL now includes sexual orientation in its official antibias pledge. Its New England chapter stood by this decision, even when attacked[101] and prominently features homophobia in its teacher trainings.[102] In 1997, moreover, one of the ten students they honored was an open lesbian working against heterosexism in her school and community.[103] The California chapter also incorporated materials from the Gay and Lesbian Alliance Against Defamation.

Facing History and Ourselves, an acclaimed curriculum project designed to counter prejudice through study of the Holocaust, the Armenian genocide, and other instances of inhumanity, has made exemplary progress in addressing homophobia. Its 1989 sourcebook of "Holocaust testimonies" contained only two unelaborated references to the Nazi persecution of homosexuals and no personal account to match the testimonials and memoirs of Jewish and other victims.[104] (Its 1990 American history resource book, alas, missed gay oppression entirely.[105]) But its 1994 resource book on the Holocaust is a model of integration.[106] (In 1999 Georgia's Commission on the Holocaust deleted two paragraphs about treatment of homosexuals from its proposed teacher's guide, which is distributed around the state.[107])

Attention to homosexual youth by federal departments is rare, for example, the documentation in *A Guide to Enhancing the Cultural Competence of Runaway and Homeless Youth Programs.*[108] Omission or token mention is almost certain in many government programs, even those dealing with high-risk youth and suicide. This invisibility results from ignorance, cowardice, or a lack of government and foundation funding for research on homosexual youth. Mention of "sexual orientation" in the federal government's 1997 "Healing the Hate" curriculum (for middle school bias crime prevention) may signal a more vigorous approach in at least some departments.[109]

Gay and lesbian youth services are frequently left to the homosexual community, although their record on educational matters is spotty as well. P-FLAG's Respect All Youth Campaign oddly does not aim at schools. The platform of the 1993 Gay and Lesbian March on Washington included a demand for "full and equal inclusion" in the educational system, yet the education sessions of the yearly National Gay and Lesbian Task Force Creating Change conferences draw the smallest audiences, compared to other civil rights and political organizing panels. Homosexual parents, teachers, and students are too often the sole proponents of education activism.

This historic neglect by the gay movement is being reversed by such relatively new organizations as the Gay Lesbian and Straight Education Network (GLSEN) and the Hettrick-Martin Institute's National Advocacy Coalition on Youth and Sexual Orientation.[110]

Since its founding in 1991 as a committee of the Independent School Association of Massachusetts, GLSEN has grown into a respected national institution of ninety chapters. GLSEN and its constituent groups host national and regional conferences and sponsor many programs aimed at K–12 school reform through teacher and student advocacy, staff and curriculum development, and political and legal activism. GLSEN has begun issuing a yearly "Report Card" to rate school districts on their efforts.[111] Some of its other successes, like the Back to School Campaign and the film "Out of the Past," are cited elsewhere in this volume.[112]

## The National Education Association

*First Resolution—1990.* The actions of the National Education Association (NEA), a 2.2 million member union with a history of progressive policies, are a somewhat tortured case study of mainstream national organizing against homophobia and heterosexism in schools. In 1990, the NEA Representative Assembly (that is, convention of elected delegates) resolved as follows:

> The National Education Association believes that all persons, regardless of sexual orientation, should be afforded equal opportunity within the public education system. The Association further believes that every school district should provide counseling by trained personnel for students who are struggling with their sexual/gender orientation.[113]

This resolution was a praiseworthy stand for equal rights and services for gay and lesbian school-age youth. It was limited only by its failure to consider the education and counseling needs of homophobic students. Formulating the issue as a compensatory one, the NEA did not acknowledge the full scope of the problem. (See Chapter 11.)

Despite recognizing that homophobia "operates to prevent peer group interaction," the guidelines accompanying the resolution were similarly focused only on the hated and not on the bigots: "The NEA believes that the public schools can help reduce homophobia and discrimination against gay and lesbian students and improve their success rates in school through student services and staff development."[114]

Possible approaches for "consideration" by public schools were to be framed by "the right [of all students] to positive role models, both in person and the curriculum." There was no indication that these positive homosexual role models would have a salutary impact on heterosexual students as well their homosexual schoolmates.

This ambivalence is further illustrated in the language of the "What Can Be Done" section of the Action Sheet:

The NEA supports effective educational and counseling efforts to encourage responsible behavior by all students. Appropriate educational and counseling strategies, policies, and procedures must be put into place to permit all of our young people to fulfill their own promise, regardless of sexual orientation or other condition.[115]

The second sentence appears to limit the "responsible" behaviors to those that are related to the students living out their own sexualities and not to interacting with those who are different. It may be a fine distinction, but it does reflect what must be a fear within the NEA that it not seem to propose teaching heterosexual students what homosexuality is or that it is acceptable. That educational content is reserved for teacher training.

*Second Resolution—1994.* In July 1994, the NEA Representative Assembly passed a better resolution on Sexual Orientation Education:

The National Education Association recognizes the importance of raising the awareness and increasing the sensitivity of staff, students, parents, and the community to sexual orientation in our society. The Association therefore supports the development of positive plans that lead to effective ongoing training programs for education employees for the purpose of identifying and eliminating sexual orientation stereotyping in the educational setting. Such programs should attend to but not be limited to:

1. Accurate portrayal of the roles and contributions of gay, lesbian, and bisexual people throughout history, with acknowledgment of their sexual orientation.
2. The acceptance of diverse sexual orientation and the awareness of sexual stereotyping whenever sexuality and/or tolerance of diversity is taught.
3. Elimination of sexual orientation name-calling and jokes in the classroom.[116]

This new resolution for training faculty and informing students is better because, although it again emphasizes the protection of homosexual youth, it does so with an eye toward teacher training and combating heterosexism in the classroom. At least that is what it appears to do. Subsequent events might have rendered that interpretation moot.

*History Month Resolution—1995.* On July 6, 1995, the NEA adopted amendment "d" to the above section: "Support for the celebration of a Lesbian and Gay History Month as a means of acknowledging the contributions of lesbians, gays, and bisexuals throughout history."

The History Month project, patterned after observances for African Americans and women, was the idea of St. Louis teacher Rodney Wilson (see Chapter 9) and was organized with GLSEN to acknowledge the history and contributions of homosexual people in America.[117] October was selected because National Coming Out Day, when gays and lesbians are encouraged to be open about their sexuality, is observed on October 11.

Passage of the History Month resolution, which had been defeated the year before, gave a substantial boost to the year-old project. The governors of Connecticut and Massachusetts issued proclamations on its behalf for the second time and were joined by the governor of Oregon and the mayors of St. Louis, Boston, and Santa Fe.

*Retreat and Compromise.*   On the other side, the Concerned Women for America (CWA) had an organizing field day. Dedicated to putting religiosity into schools, among other goals, they took out half-page newspaper ads attacking both homosexuals and another favorite target—the NEA.[118] Portraying Gay History Month as a "threat to morality and decency," and claiming that "49 percent [of homosexuals] admitted to having sex with a minor,"[119] the CWA offered free "action information" packets and a toll-free number. Over 20,000 protest letters and phone calls to the NEA were generated in two weeks.[120]

Throughout the country bilious citizens demanded that their school boards reject the History Month project.[121] The superintendent in Rodney Wilson's own district told critics, "At no time have we as a district even considered celebrating Gay History Month."[122] And Wilson himself had to reassure the school board that his curriculum advocacy was part of his private activity and did not affect his professional duties.[123]

The Alabama State Board of Education unanimously commended a local board for its proclamation that the History Month celebration does not represent the values of its citizens nor its employees. This same board, whose president is the governor of Alabama, had voted previously to promote creationism.[124] And at the end of 1995, Indiana's East Allen County School Board embellished its condemnation of the NEA's gay initiatives by denouncing "drug use, premarital sex, violence or gay and lesbian behavior or the support of such activities."[125]

Because of this exponential reaction, the positive momentum of years of NEA declarations was interrupted by a sidestepping fiasco. Some figures in the usually staunch organization backed away from the resolution. "There are no plans in Tennessee to do anything on this issue, none whatsoever," said one local union president.[126] The president of the Montana Education Association stressed that the measure was not binding and was really aimed at students who are struggling with their sexuality. Out of ignorance or guile, he characterized accusations that the NEA vote represented a move to advocate curriculum as a "really rather fantastic stretch."[127]

The leader of the Rapid City, South Dakota, union dismissed the resolution as merely "an idea," claiming it had been tacked on to past language at an emotional and divided convention. Her defense that "no money goes toward any action about the resolution" was doubtless meant to reassure her audience that intentions don't mean anything without a price tag.[128] The same defense from the Mehlville (Mo.) Community Teachers Association and the Utah Education Association, all of whose 110 delegates voted against B-9,[129] hinted at a conspiracy of denial.

One national NEA spokesperson announced that the resolution dealt only with gay and lesbian teens and that the union was not preparing curriculum materials.[130] Another claimed the language was directed only at teachers, observing inanely, "The resolution deals principally with tolerance—and has nothing to do with anything going on in the classrooms or hallways."[131] Union leaders in Oklahoma, Louisiana, and Nebraska also demurred.[132]

At the top, the president of the NEA tried to inject coherence in a position paper stating:

- the NEA is a democratic organization;
- B-9, like other resolutions, was an expression of opinion or belief;
- B-9 was aimed at increasing understanding for the special needs of gay and lesbian students and decreasing intolerance;
- B-9 does not advocate any lifestyle nor direct anyone to observe Gay and Lesbian History Month;
- and that NEA would not be distributing curriculum materials.[133]

His seeming retreat was unnecessary and disingenuous. Surely, no other such celebration was barred from classrooms and hallways and aimed only at teachers or a certain group of students. Black History Month was not observed in a closet nor Women's History Month in a boiler room. They were intended to be commemorated within the academic and social life of the school. Furthermore, despite their detractors, the value of these special months was not restricted to African American and female students, although they were perhaps their first beneficiaries.

Jessea Greenman of Project 21 eloquently observed that according to the NEA's own handbook, its resolutions "are formal expressions of opinions, intents, beliefs or positions of the Association" that "shall be consistent with the goals of the Association."[134] The NEA must have known that evasion and defensiveness are unworthy of their profession. Caught in an ugly fight, cynically stoked by perennial foes who would capitalize on public homophobia, they did not shine. Once the resolutions were passed, clear-minded progressive leadership should have countered the spate of disassociation on the part of reactionary or frightened state and local affiliates and used the occasion to educate its membership.

The NEA were not alone in seeming unprepared. The National Gay and Lesbian Task Force fell into a similar trap by reiterating the claim that the History Month was devised for isolated homosexual youth. They appeared to ignore its wider educational importance.

For the 1996 Representative Assembly, the Resolutions Committee devised a solution to the controversy in consultation with various minority caucuses. New language eliminated previous sections on racism, sexism, and sexual orientation education and also deleted explicit references to six History Month recommendations devoted to separate minority cultures. A revised B–6 on Diversity called for tolerance and celebration of specifically named minority statuses, including sexual orientation, and stated the importance of "programs and observances which accurately portray and recognize the roles, contributions, cultures, and history of these diverse groups and individuals."

A new B-7 Resolution on Racism, Sexism, and Sexual Orientation Discrimination sought the elimination of discrimination and stereotyping on the basis of various characteristics, including sexual orientation. It stated the association's support of "plans, activities, and programs for staff, students, parents, and the community" to

- increase tolerance and sensitivity;
- eliminate discrimination and stereotyping in the curriculum, textbooks, [and so forth];
- foster the use of nondiscriminatory, nonsexist and nonstereotypical language, resources, practices, and activities;
- eliminate institutional discrimination;
- integrate an accurate portrayal of the roles and contributions of all groups throughout history and across the curriculum;
- identify how prejudice, stereotyping, and discrimination have limited the roles and contributions of individuals and groups;
- eliminate subtle practices that favor the education of one student on the basis of race, ethnicity, gender, and sexual orientation over another.

Further, the proposed language encouraged NEA affiliates to develop and implement trainings on these matters. Both sections, B-6 and B-7, passed by a substantial margin on a voice vote. The majority of the NEA Gay and Lesbian Caucus, however, were opposed.[135]

There is no denying that these revisions came in reaction to the right-wing onslaught. However, their cooperative fashioning signified progress. Uniting to craft an inclusive, and explicit, multicultural document seems to have made all minority groups stronger. They appear to have given up, without resentment, their separate, hard-fought, positions in favor of a common stand.

In the end, these important questions must still be answered. Will multicultural constituencies remain allies? Will they all labor for every group's advancement in every school, no matter what its cultural profile? Will the NEA leadership stand unapologetically behind each section of B-7 and commit its resources to its recommended trainings? And most importantly, will the proponents of multiculturalism challenge the assumption that they advance the interests only of minority groups? B-7 should be more than an amalgam of sops to the underrepresented. If it is honored, it will indeed benefit the invisible and self-doubting, but it will also help those who have been hobbled by a narrow vision and a superior attitude.

In the final analysis, the history month flap illustrates the limited effectiveness of policymaking from above and afar. Such resolutions are perhaps useful only as a backup for efforts that are begun at the grass roots. Without local support they are window dressing, or worse, divisive and half-hearted. Once passed, however, the NEA should use the mandate of such votes to offer direct assistance to educators campaigning at the district level against homophobic attacks and for gay-positive curricula.

Perhaps there is reason to hope for such an outcome. In the fall of 1998 NEA President Bob Chase spoke out clearly to his board of directors on the need both to protect gay students from harassment and to "teach tolerance."[136]

## Opposition

The following is a representative tableau of oppositional responses to antiheterosexist school reform and community programs for gay and lesbian youth:

1. Colorado-based Focus on the Family attacks a proposal to display posters in ten high schools informing students of a gay/lesbian community counseling center. "The poster's intent is clear: it is meant to promote same-sex romance among teens," says the Focus president.[137]

2. A group tries to block publication of phone numbers for two gay support groups in the "Yellow Pages for Frederick County (Md.) Teens," a booklet distributed by high school guidance counselors.[138]

3. Indiana parents backed by a Virginia-based conservative law center and local supporters demand that a heterosexual teacher remove a tolerance poster, which had hung for six years in her classroom, because the depiction of ten famous gay people offended their son.[139]

4. A Brookfield (Conn.) high school teacher sues parents for libel after they accuse her of "homosexual recruiting" because she brought a Pink Triangles sensitivity and "safe zone" sticker program to her classroom. Insisting that the father's sister became a lesbian after bad relationships with a series of men,[140] the parents are supported by the American Center for Law and Justice, founded by right-wing Reverend Pat Robertson.[141] The Board of Education votes to discontinue the safe zone program.[142]

5. An Indianapolis-area high school principal does not allow the student newspaper to publish a nonexplicit article about two anonymous gay underclassmen who asked the reporter to write about their lives and show that they were not "weird."[143]

6. Sparked by pro-gay articles in a student newspaper, Colorado for Family Values barrages the Colorado Springs school board with nearly 7,000 postcards demanding a policy that "discourages promiscuity and affirms traditional marriage."[144]

7. Fearing negative community reaction, a Corrollton, Texas, high school principal cancels her school paper's story about efforts to start a gay support group.[145]

8. The Merrimack, N.H., School Board votes to ban "any program or activity that has either the purpose or effect of encouraging or supporting homosexuality as a positive lifestyle alternative," though no program has been contemplated by the system. They forbid materials, instruction, and student referral to gay-positive counseling. Teachers are afraid to explain AIDS statistics from a newspaper, assign *Twelfth Night,* or use a video about Walt Whitman. A subsequent school board substitutes language prohibiting the promotion of any sexual orientation or activity.[146]

9. A Vatican document asserts that sex education is the fundamental right of parents and that teachers "need to respect the right of the child and young person to take themselves out of any form of sex education" that goes against their home teachings.[147]

10. The Catholic Defense League goes to court in St. Paul (Minn.) to obtain details about the high school support group "Out for Equity," claiming that the approach taken by the year-old program violates

Church teachings and the wishes and rights of parents and students.[148]

11. The Internal Revenue Service withholds tax-exempt status from a North Carolina youth support group until it can be assured that minors will not be encouraged to develop "homosexual attitudes and propensities."[149]

12. Calling the Kinsey studies fraudulent and criminal, a Texas congressman files a bill to deny federal funds to any program based on Alfred Kinsey's research. Meanwhile, the Traditional Values Coalition claims Kinsey's finding that 10 percent of the population is homosexual is the basis for hundreds of millions of dollars in federal grants.[150]

13. Jonathan C. Wilson is defeated for reelection to the Des Moines School Board after disclosing his homosexuality during a debate with antigay protesters.[151]

14. After its lesbian president is defeated in a homophobic election campaign, Michigan's Wayne-Westland school board rescinds sexual orientation harassment protections for students and faculty.[152]

15. After hearing evidence of violence against a fourteen-year-old gay student, the school board of Allen Park, Michigan, rejects the pleas of the boy's mother and others to add sexual orientation to its antiharassment policy.[153]

16. Just months after adding "sexual orientation" to their antidiscrimination policy, a Metro Detroit, Michigan, school board drops the change under pressure.[154]

17. Incensed by the Modesto city schools' purchase of the GLSEN video "Teaching Respect for All," a California assemblyman proposes to prohibit the use of state funds for "materials and instruction that promotes or advocates homosexuality as a viable alternative lifestyle."[155]

18. The West Covina (Calif.) Unified District School Board refuses to allow middle school teachers to attend a conference, one of whose thirty-six sessions is on homosexuality. The board chairman says that "issues of sexual preference are better left up to the parents."[156]

19. After adverse public reaction, a conference for and about gay youth at Washington State University is canceled out of concern for the safety of the participants.[157]

20. Two hundred fifty middle and high school students march out of classes in Pennsylvania to protest the Elizabethtown School Board's "pro-family" policy forbidding "pro-homosexual concepts" in the schools.[158]

Each of these vignettes represents hundreds of hours of bitter contention. Sometimes opponents prevail, but some discredit themselves

with extreme language and a radical agenda that goes beyond the repression of homosexuality to the abolition of bilingual and multicultural
education and the promotion of creationism and classroom religiosity.[159]
A majority of state senators in Tennessee, site of the Scopes Trial, threatened to fire any teacher who presents evolution as fact.[160]

## The Utah Struggle

A 1990 U.S. Supreme Court ruling that schools cannot discriminate between other extracurricular activities and a Bible club has been a boon to
more than the Christian Right.[161] This opinion and the 1984 federal Equal
Access Act, favoring religious study clubs, have been used to protect
gay/straight alliances in Salt Lake City and elsewhere. Utah Senator
Orrin Hatch bemoaned this defense as "an unintended consequence" of
federal law.[162]

When the Utah attorney general was thus compelled to sanction the
first GSA, the state Board of Education scrambled to permit localities to
stop such groups.[163] And as other schools began to plan alliances, the
pressure on conservative lawmakers increased.[164] Rather than permit the
GSA to meet, the Salt Lake School Board ended up abolishing all clubs.[165]
Spurred by that edict, resentful students petitioned to start Anti-Homosexual Leagues in two high schools.[166] Others rallied to uphold the
GSAs.[167] At one such event, a public school teacher came out, the first in
Utah to do so.[168]

Utah lawmakers tried to close down GSAs by passing a bill to prohibit
teachers or volunteers from "encouraging, condoning, or supporting engagement in illegal conduct."[169] GSAs were also said to disrupt school
order and harm students.[170] Utah senators claimed they had to act decisively after viewing an antigay video in an illegal closed session.[171] The
governor vetoed the legislation on free speech grounds; yet in the end a
law was passed and signed banning student clubs that "promote bigotry,
encourage criminal behavior, or involve human sexuality."[172]

During the process many opinions were aired, but threats, agitation,
and political posturing distorted what could have been a healthy exchange. One state representative asserted that his brother, dead of AIDS,
had been dragooned into a gay "lifestyle" by members of his Boy Scout
troop.[173] A senator introduced a letter by the notorious reparative therapy proponent Charles Socarides (see Chapter 8), inveighing against the
clubs for bringing "individual tragedies to our young people both now
and in the future."[174]

Months after the Utah ban passed, a debased discourse continued with
one legislator proposing an amendment to permit counseling for students with gender-identification problems and a senator answering that

the existing language encourages students to be cured of homosexuality.[175] Although some thought gay students might be allowed to rent school space as a chaperoned nonschool group,[176] others conceded the law would end up in the courts.[177]

Rules adopted by the Utah Board of Education in early 1997 permit GSAs to meet but reserve the right of local boards to

- alter group names that might be disruptive;
- prevent clubs from harassing others;
- forbid the advocacy of illegal sexual activities;
- bar presentations that violate sex education and privacy statutes.

These rules did not resolve the issue, however. For instance, the Granite school board's policy on noncurricular clubs effectively ruled out GSAs as antithetical to state policy.[178] However, several other high schools in the area petitioned to start GSAs.[179] And in 1997, as the original GSA met amid increasing harassment in their rented East High School space, two members sued, claiming the ban is arbitrarily enforced and unconstitutional. Attempts at mediation before trial were not promising,[180] and a federal judge refused to issue a summary judgment or an injunction in the GSA's favor.[181] After ruling that the GSA's attorneys could not question the motives of the school board, the judge set a pretrial conference for April 1999.[182]

### Fallout in Other States

Meanwhile, inspired by Utah, school authorities in Idaho considered an identical ban.[183] And officials in other states became embroiled in their own GSA battles, with tactics that ranged from patently absurd to subtly evasive. In Alaska, one school board member claimed that a high school alliance was a violation of Alaska's child sexual abuse statute because it was likely to induce minors to engage in sexual penetration. In a mollifying gesture, the Anchorage board voted 4–3 for a compromise regulation requiring parental permission for membership in all school clubs.[184] The GSA in Niskayuna, New York, was allowed the same meeting privileges as other clubs, but the board would not officially sanction it, because officials judged antidiscrimination to be "inherently political."[185]

The first GSA in Colorado sued the Cherry Creek School District near Denver to achieve full recognition as a school club, then had to agree to have a civil rights focus without being a support group. (A second GSA began in Denver's East High in 1998,[186] but the next year a principal in School District Eleven refused to sanction a GSA on the grounds that doing so would open the door to devil worshipers and Nazi sympathizers.[187]) The Minnesota Civil Liberties Union failed to gain club status for the Orono High School GSA, settling instead for a "limited open forum," that is, no public address or general postings and exclusion from student handbooks and yearbooks.[188]

Students in Fort Lauderdale's Wellington High School were hard-pressed to begin a group they called "Working Against Sexual Prejudice" (WASP). An enthusiastic junior first encountered a hard rule against petitions, then met with a tepid principal who said she would only permit such a club because other clubs were allowed, and finally faced the sad reality that no teacher would chaperone the group. The seventeen-year-old sighed, "Teachers seem to support the idea of my group. But when it comes down to being directly involved with it, they back off."[189]

Fear certainly influenced the principal at Whitney Young High School in Chicago to advise the nearly thirty gay and straight students in the Pride Club to keep quiet about the group's existence, prompting one recent graduate to observe, "It did bother us. It felt like the school was ashamed of us. They were saying, 'We can have you, but we don't want anyone to know about you.'"[190]

## Censorship

A number of so-called "traditional values" and "pro-family" organizations have sectarian affiliation and censorious intent. With hundreds of local chapters, Citizens for Excellence in Education (CEE), for example, is a part of the National Association of Christian Educators. CEE's leader has warned:

> Every day Christian children all across America are quietly sitting in their public school chairs while, unbeknownst to either the church, their parents, or the children themselves, they are being subjected to a subtle but systematic mind-altering and faith-destroying curriculum . . . full-blown indoctrination in moral relativity and secular humanism.[191]

CEE offers to assist parents to "change a curriculum" to make "the Christian impact . . . felt in the classroom" and advises ministers to get involved in public education.[192] Civil libertarians have called the group "the most active censorship organization in the schools today."[193]

Filed on behalf of the Interfaith Coalition, the original Massachusetts parent notification bill would have banned instruction about sexuality, sexual or physical abuse, alcohol or drug use, marriage, divorce, family life, death, grief, self-esteem, and emotional health.[194] The legislation was a clone of the Parental Rights Amendment, proposed by "Of the People," a national organization. People for the American Way says of this amendment:

> By adopting language that is intended to give parents absolute authority over what their children are taught, PRA-backers would greatly strengthen the hands of those who would censor schoolbooks, or seek to control curricula on ideological or sectarian grounds. . . . The Christian Coalition has adopted the "parental rights" cause. . . . Federal legislation was introduced in the U.S. House of Representatives in [1995].[195]

The parents of two Massachusetts high school students sued their school committee, school officials, the school physician, and a safer-sex educator over their children's exposure to ninety minutes of explicit language about avoiding AIDS.[196] Although the parents lost on appeal to the Supreme Court in 1996,[197] most courts are inclined to favor parental or political authority over teachers' rights of expression or students' freedom to learn, particularly when the specters of school disruption,[198] subversion,[199] or sexually offensive speech[200] can be evoked.

Yet, the language of the lower courts, which the Supreme Court let stand in the above AIDS education decision, is a major triumph for progressives: "Although the program may offend the religious sensibilities of the plaintiffs, mere exposure at public schools to offensive programs does not amount to a violation of free exercise. . . . Parents have no right to tailor public school programs to meet their individual religious or moral preferences."[201] This was a case where principled school people prevailed over disgruntled parents. Nevertheless, the decision does not address the right of classroom teachers to oppose censorious school authorities.

Even where antidiscrimination policies exist, they cannot be construed easily to call for curriculum. Protecting homosexual youth from assault or suicide and offering them counseling are seen as separate from textbook contents and library holdings. The first three might be approved as care giving, a generally approved function of schools for some time; the last two are condemned as proselytizing—teaching kids to *be* homosexual. After the Des Moines school board voted for information about gays and lesbians to be "thoughtfully infused" into the curriculum,[202] the superintendent clearly had this distinction in mind when he dissolved the committee that recommended it, denied that he had backed away, and vowed that he still supported nondiscrimination.[203]

Another public representative had no objection to classroom lessons, so long as they were the right ones. The attorney for the New York school board that rejected Children of the Rainbow said in a radio debate that he approved of teaching about homosexuality, provided it was presented alongside drug addiction, alcoholism, and so forth.[204]

There are profound reasons for this opposition. A conscientious examination of identity in a number of curricular areas could free many students from the tyranny of oppressive categories. However these distinctions are not generated and maintained by accident. Privileged people
gain from their imposition and enforcement. Schools have traditionally
carried out the wishes of the powerful to conserve and transmit these social constructions. (See Chapter 2.) Sex education, in particular, has aided
the sexual and social control of women and homosexuals by heterosexual
males.[205] James Sears describes what happens when teachers conscientiously broach this explosive topic:

> Integrating sexuality into the curriculum and acknowledging same-sex feel-
> ings and behaviors as an integral part of the human psyche poses a pro-
> found challenge to the social order and, not surprisingly, threatens many
> persons who benefit most from that existing order or who have been social-
> ized into its norms and beliefs. Schools that encourage the exploration of
> sexuality among their students and faculty have, indeed, unleashed a polit-
> ical whirlwind in which issues of power and dominance, dialectical materi-
> alism and biological determinism, childhood sexual scripts and adult expec-
> tations, become the basis for critical discourse on sexuality.[206]

Therefore, attempts to reform sexuality curricula usually incur resistance
from religious and cultural conservatives, many of them heterosexual
males.

Although the courts have upheld the right of a school to require sex
education for graduation, they have also maintained the right of states to
forbid it.[207] The standard of most courts is embodied in *Zykan v. Warsaw*
(1980), which held that books may be removed from school libraries and
curricula based on the social, political, and moral views of school board
members.[208] Furthermore, in *Fisher v. Fairbanks* (1985), a court found that
a teacher could be fired for using an unapproved novel in a unit on gay
rights. The standard was not the suitability of the book; it was the authority of the administrator to ban its use.[209]

First Amendment protections seem to apply only in the area of staff development. The West Covina teachers who were not permitted to attend
a conference went to court, claiming a right to receive information. The
judge ruled in favor of an optional workshop on the grounds that its content would be beneficial. The school board, however, remained opposed.[210]

Intimidation and monitoring of faculty persists: In Utah's Granite
School District, for example, officials nixed the distribution through
teachers' mailboxes of pamphlets and videos about gay youth but invited
those wanting the materials to get them from front offices.[211]

Elected officials and educational administrators appear to have an *a priori* gatekeeping right to monitor and censor what students read or are otherwise exposed to in schools.[212] Elmira, New York, officials agreed with parents that they should have been informed that a Hindu woman adopted by white parents would mention to a middle and high school diversity assembly that she is a lesbian.[213] The mere fact that an Indian could be homosexual was an impermissible communication, notwithstanding Supreme Court Justice Rehnquist's assertion in *Island Trees v. Pico* (1982) that only particular books may be banned, not the thoughts in them.[214] More promisingly, a lower court judge declared unconstitutional the removal of a gay-positive novel, *Annie on My Mind*,[215] from school libraries in a Kansas town on the grounds that local school boards cannot eliminate books just because they disagree with their ideas.[216] But in a startling reversal of a lower court decision, a Fourth Circuit court agreed with conservative parents that a North Carolina drama teacher had no right to choose a "controversial" play for her students to perform.[217]

*Opt-Out Provisions.* Some have tried to diminish parental opposition by giving them the option of keeping their children out of class when homosexuality is discussed. There is some evidence that this strategy causes minimal disruption in some communities. In Fairfax County, Virginia, for example, the board of education allows opt-out from curricular units in Family Life Education. The result: 2 percent opt out of general sex education lessons; 4 percent opt out of lessons on homosexuality. Wisely, the board rejected an opt-in proposal that would have demanded explicit parental permission for student attendance.[218] (That is the obstacle at Louisville (Ky.) Central High School Council, for example, where gay-themed books are permitted on classroom shelves with the stipulation that students obtain parental permission to read them.[219]) The limited impact of the Fairfax opt-out policy may have something to do with its being an affluent, educated, suburban community near Washington, D.C. A similar provision in a conservative community could decimate sex education classes.

Although a Chapel Hill, North Carolina, high school junior was not allowed to transfer from her American Literature class, she was still excused from reading gay and lesbian selections in a multicultural curriculum. Subsequently all the gay materials were suspended because a resource reading list included titles of books with explicitly sexual passages.[220]

Although opt-out clauses might be employed as a last resort, school authorities should consider where they might lead. Would creationists excuse their children from biology classes? Would historical revisionists be allowed to pull their children out of any school forum in which the

Holocaust would be discussed? Would white supremacists' children be let out of classes that portrayed negritude as good or even morally neutral? What begins as parental rights could transform classrooms into shifting masses of ideological pawns.

*A Nationwide Barrage.*   Suppression was given a political boost when the Speaker of the U.S. House of Representatives denounced gay and lesbian curricula as "serious evidence that things are being taught that are clearly propaganda and clearly recruitment."[221] Conservative columnist George Will joined the chorus. In an imaginary middle-class diatribe against the government, he described public schools: "Their children have come home from school, using the condoms they got there as bookmarks in the books they got there (*Heather Has Two Mommies* and *Daddy's Roommate*)."[222]

Fairfax County, a model of liberal educational practice, developed a Family Life curriculum that included three lessons on homosexuality for grades 9 and 10, featuring a video "What If I'm Gay" in the first year. When the lessons were challenged in 1995, the school board, backed by the League of Women Voters, the PTA, and others, voted to retain them. They agreed, however, to drop a compilation of background readings for teachers and to append state laws against adultery, sodomy, and prostitution. They also added the following disclaimer to the curriculum: "Homosexual behavior is highly controversial in our society with some people viewing it as normal and others viewing it as contrary to normal."[223]

Penny Culliton, a five-year veteran heterosexual English teacher in New Ipswich, New Hampshire, was fired for using E. M. Forster's *Maurice*, Bette Greene's *The Drowning of Stephan Jones*, and May Sarton's *The Education of Harriet Hatfield* with her junior and senior classes. Her principal had forbidden her to do so. In finding her insubordinate, the school board declared she had "demonstrated a clear lack of the judgment requisite for a competent teacher in the district." It did not matter to them that the books had been approved previously or that Culliton had been making references to homosexuality in literature for years. After nine months, Culliton was reinstated by an arbitrator without back pay for the previous school year. The board appealed the ruling, was rejected, and finally reinstated Culliton under protest. As an ironic side note, the board approved the books by a narrow vote for optional reading in an upper-level elective.[224]

Gift copies of *Becoming Visible,* an anthology of gay and lesbian history, sent to eighty-three high school libraries in St. Louis and St. Louis County, were not shelved for student use.[225] The superintendent explained it was not part of his schools' curriculum.[226] Employing a similar strategy to GLSEN's, the International Healing Foundation of Maryland offered free copies of *Alfie's Home* to the nation's schools.[227] The children's picture book is about a troubled boy, sexually abused by an uncle and neglected by his father, who "transitions" from homosexual attractions into healthy heterosexuality.[228]

Books may even perish by association. When someone broke into a Virginia elementary school storeroom and discovered gay titles in a pile of possibly controversial books that had been plucked by a committee from a larger lot, panicked officials destroyed the rest of the 30,000 volumes donated to the schools by a national charity.[229]

An Alameda, California, fifth-grade teacher asked her class if anything exciting had happened to them. Students responded that they had watched the "Ellen Show" coming out episode. When one student said she was "proud" of Ellen for being "brave," the teacher wrote those two words on the board and led a discussion about differences and self-esteem. Parents who had, unbeknownst to the teacher, requested in writing that their children not participate in discussions of homosexuality asked the state to revoke her teaching license, but the state panel ruled in her favor.[230] A Kansas City, Missouri, teacher did lose her job on charges of "sexual misconduct," when her substitute teacher allowed students to enter a previously off-limits book cabinet and remove the volume *Looking at Gay and Lesbian Life*,[231] the teacher's personal reference book.[232]

Responding to homophobic comments from her second-grade class, a San Diego teacher invited her gay son to speak to them. After a session that she described as "a supreme educational moment," the teacher was reprimanded and refused a recommendation because she had not notified parents in advance and would not apologize to them.[233]

The principal of a Solon, Iowa, high school canceled a panel for students on sexual orientation and harassment after receiving calls from the American Family Association and threats of disruption. The panel was to have been introduced to tenth-graders by a family life educator as part of a health awareness week.[234]

A group of sophomores in an honors English class in Massachusetts asked their nontenured teacher if it was possible that Holden Caulfield in *Catcher in the Rye* could be gay. When she asked them for their evidence, several boys objected and later complained to a male teacher. The vice-principal ordered the English teacher to have no further discussion, insisting that is not what *Catcher in the Rye* is about.[235]

A district official in Dallas pulled the plug on a student-produced television show after it featured an interview with a gay man in a black dress and blonde wig. The student, whose parents and teacher had approved the program, insisted the show was educational.[236] A few months later, a Maryland school board overruled its superintendent to allow a high school television production class to air its taped debate on same-gender marriage.[237]

Class visitors might be particularly vulnerable to exaggerated accusations. Although they contested the facts, two San Francisco middle school teachers were suspended for ten days and almost lost their state credentials for purportedly allowing classroom guest speakers on hate crimes to mention sexual acts.[238] Parents of third-, fourth-, and fifth-graders in Hanover, New Hampshire, demanded an apology from their principal and school board because they allowed a performance by a gay singing group, during which singers identified as gay or lesbian and asked students if any of them had two mothers or two fathers.[239]

Mickey Mouse himself cannot escape suspicion. School officials in Bunnell, Florida, rescheduled a trip to Disney World for eighth-graders after parents objected to their children being there on the same day as an annual gay and lesbian event.[240]

School censorship reported by People for the American Way include the following stark incidents:[241]

- Florida objectors used their challenge to Mary Renault's *The Last of the Wine* as an opportunity to screen the right-wing viciously antigay video, "The Gay Agenda," at a school board meeting and to accuse a former Teacher of the Year of being a sexual "predator."
- A Madison, Wisconsin, parent objected to the biography of writer James Baldwin in a middle school library because it was written to "lure" and "attract children at an early age to the gay and lesbian lifestyle."
- The Hattiesburg, Mississippi, superintendent canceled a high school production of the musical Falsettoland after parents alleged that the play's gay theme violated a state criminal obscenity law.
- Texas critics attempted to remove *I Know Why the Caged Bird Sings* from classrooms, citing profanity and the "encouraging" of premarital sex and homosexuality.

And in one last credulity-straining occurrence:

- A California parent claimed the use of Sesame Street in a kindergarten class could promote homosexuality because the characters Bert and Ernie lived together.

In 1998, House Republicans introduced a Parental Freedom Of Information Act, requiring all states and localities to give parents review authority over all curricular materials.[242] Even Miss America became involved that year in the national tug-of-war over censorship, complaining that state and local restrictions against using words like "heterosexual" and "homosexual" were crippling her AIDS awareness campaign, literally banned from in North Carolina schools.[243]

These are just some of the flash points in a widespread offensive against gay and lesbian content in curriculum. Scores of other censorship battles have also been documented. Opponents, fearful of a world in flux, want to keep children from critically examining conventional values and the world their parents have created. At the heart of these skirmishes is profound disagreement over "the scope of free expression, the place of religion in public life, and the extent to which our culture ought to foster—or at least acknowledge—diversity."[244]

*Resisting Censorship.* Progressive parents, educators, and politicians must not abandon the field, yet neither should they fear a free market of ideas in classrooms. They ought to set an example of tolerance for opposing views, not try to win over young people by denigrating those with seemingly strange opinions or odd principles. Adult behavior should be governed by two of the highest virtues of a democracy: pluralism is not weakness and a commitment to diversity can actually bring people together.

The following verbatim excerpts, taken from student evaluations in a high school sociology course, offer proof of these assertions:[245]

- This curriculum made me understand more the kind of problems gay people have had to deal with. I don't necessarily feel that homosexuality is "good," but I am no longer so quick to judge. (African American female)
- It is good that people organize a group to help teach kids to understand the values and feelings of gays and lesbians, so they might understand them and know that they too are humans. (Hispanic male)
- I have always thought what people do is their business, but it has taught me that society and its rules for "norms" can do a job on a group of people. (white female)
- After discussing it with the class I started thinking about it as a prejudice, which is all it is. (white male)
- We need to accept everyone's differences because we want to be accepted ourselves. This course was too short. (Asian American female)
- I realized that I have to let people have the room to change their opinion. . . . When [student's name] sat down to give his presentation on homosexuality . . . I remembered him being against ho-

mosexuals. When he started talking about changing his mind, I was so impressed. I learnt so much just from witnessing that change in him. (white female)

- I was raised not with gays and the only things I heard about gays were remarks and jokes about them. So my view towards them was bad. But listening and studying about them made me get a whole different point of view. . . . Listening of how they march and protest to get equal rights made me think because I am doing the same thing trying to get respect and not to be laughed at or hurt because of my color. (African American female)
- I started to realize that it's okay for people to be gays and lesbians, as long as they don't interfere with me. . . . Being gays or lesbians does not mean that they are totally different persons. . . . I now believe that they should also have rights to do whatever they feel comfortable, as long as they don't change the heterosexuals into homosexual. (Indian Muslim female)
- I've always known that even in the most "liberal" area (ex., Cambridge) where people are supposedly very "p.c." homophobia and ignorance exists. . . . After one of our class discussions I immediately signed up in the Project 10 room to go on the Gay Pride March . . . because I was so outraged. (white female)
- I knew the subject and its effects on our society before I studied gay issues further in this class. But I did not really form my own moral opinion about homosexuality or their rights until our unit. . . . These many facets of a not too long ago "forbidden" subject have made me completely change my previous views toward the gay issue. (Jewish white male)
- Even though I was taught to be homophobic, I am not. [One guest speaker's] willingness to come forward and try to make the topic more clear to others was my final affirmation that homophobia has no basis. (Hispanic male)

These comments are strikingly similar to two San Francisco students' reflections on their tenth-grade reading and discussion of an essay written by a gay Catholic American:[246]

- Before I thought in the Bible it says when two people of the same sex come together it's earthquakes and the world's coming to an end. I was against it. But then I read "Dear Anita" and they have rights, too. . . . I was confused at first. Are they good people or bad people? But then I came to realize they're just people, too.
- At first I was always calling gay people queers and stuff but then we kept talking about it and then like my homophobia just

started to go away because whenever we talked about gay people
it was just throwing stereotypes around, right?

If these responses are typical of what happens when teachers introduce
homosexuality into their curricula, it is no wonder that social conservatives are alarmed. Of course, it is too early to conduct broad research on
the effects of such materials because so few educators are permitted to
use them. Yet smaller-scale studies in enlightened communities could
motivate teachers to forge ahead with units of study.

They should first spend some time cajoling the administration and lobbying school boards. Some may prefer just to begin on their own and quietly do the right thing behind classroom doors as they often have done,
assuming no one will notice. But if they follow that familiar course on a
topic so incendiary, they risk a disastrous exposure that could set back
the cause. Albeit individual courage and initiative are essential to this reform, an incremental team approach is preferable for the long run. Progressive educators who undertake this work need allies to avoid isolation, exhaustion, and defeat. There is just too much resistance to these
curricula to go it alone.

*Engaging the Opposition*

The Freedom Forum First Amendment Center recommends constructive
dialogue to resolve the conflict between parents' rights and education for
democratic living: "Children and schools benefit greatly when parents
and educators work closely together to shape school policies and practices and to ensure that public education supports the societal values of
their community without undermining family values and convictions."[247]

Theirs is a reasonable-sounding formula but not an unambiguous one.
Who constitute "the community?" How are "societal values" arrived at?
And how can schools teach even constitutional principles to children
whose parents cannot agree on its provisions any more than the Supreme
Court can?

The Freedom Forum offers no neat formula, pleading instead for civil
debate. On homosexuality, one of its scholars-in-residence advises teachers to "teach the controversy," but cautions: "Until our society resolves
some of the legal and social disputes surrounding homosexuality, we
should not ask schools to take sides."[248] Would he have offered the same
advice to Alabama teachers in 1960 about lessons on racial equality? Perhaps equivocation is all one can expect from an organization whose
members include the Christian Coalition, the National Education Associ-

ation, the Union of American Hebrew Congregations, and the People for the American Way.

The responsibility in curricular decisionmaking is to be sensitive to all views and still teach for the growth and autonomy of all students. One must be careful to seek out genuine community feelings and not only entertain political posturing. When opposition to curriculum is heartfelt, progressive teachers can only put their faith in continuing respectful dialogue.[249] Because nearly nine out of ten people endorse teaching about cultural pluralism in schools,[250] teachers who favor homosexual inclusion must try to convince a culturally diverse opposition that their causes are one in the same. To be taken seriously, gay and lesbian advocates must be allies to other minorities for curricular equity.

Reformers must indeed meet with parents and other community people for constructive dialogue to limit the influence of the radical Right on public education policy. And in that conversation moderates should learn that some of the loudest opponents of antihomophobia education are not as concerned about homosexuality per se as they appear to be; rather they use antigay hysteria to raise money and amass political power.

Liberals must also demonstrate that learning about gay and lesbian life does not cause young people to become homosexual, although it might encourage those who are struggling with their identities to feel better about themselves. Opponents should know about the harm that comes to both gay and lesbian people and their loved ones from repression and hiding. And they must be shown that gay-positive curricula, far from endangering heterosexual students, help them become more understanding and better adjusted.

The following excerpt was taken from an exam in a class that had studied a gay history unit. It was written by a student who had admitted previously to gay-bashing, a common pastime in his neighborhood:

> One thing that changed me the most, and made [me] become a better person, and made me understand better, was the topic on homosexuals been discriminated against. People now adays, alot of people that I know, don't take this serious. They think it's a big joke to laugh about but in my opinion it is something we all women and men should work on to make people understand the effects of life, so we all could live hopefully forevermore. I must admit myself. I used to hate even hearing the word homosexual. I used to think that they were not regular people, so they should all get eliminated from our society but now I have a different perspective. And because of the class and studying about this topic in particular changed a great deal. People should not be discriminated against no matter what.[251]

Such evidence cannot be easily dismissed.

*Fashioning an Effective Response.* In the spirit of civil discourse, what then are the best responses to the belligerence of such groups as the American Family Association, Concerned Women for America, the Eagle Forum, the Family Research Council, Focus on the Family, the Traditional Values Coalition, and the National Association of Christian Educators/Citizens for Excellence in Education? First, progressives should analyze the specific threat that homosexuality poses to those whose fears and misapprehensions are genuine. Then, with an eye toward moral suasion, gays, lesbians, and their allies must speak the truth to ignorance and bigotry. The most effective gay-affirmative argument is one that appeals to the highest ethical reasoning an opponent can understand. (See Chapter 11.)

Whenever possible, one ought to cite the same American values that conservatives employ. Concerned Women for America has argued, for instance, that students should be free to express their religious beliefs and that schools must encourage open inquiry in all subjects, including world religions.[252] Bravo to the expression of genuine thoughts and feelings and to unrestricted classroom inquiry into the nature of things. Liberals should advance the same goals by calling for such human characteristics as race, ethnicity, spirituality, gender, and sexuality to be openly expressed, rationally examined, and regularly celebrated.

Of course the nonlibertarians on the Right champion only those principles that support their social conservatism. William Bennett's *Book of Virtues*[253] notwithstanding, they inveigh against values education as left-wing propaganda. They are particularly distressed when the embracing of diversity leads to multiculturalism—let alone feminism and tolerance for homosexuality.

Moreover, although the colorful protests of extremists are more likely to be featured in the media, one should not assume that opposition to gay-positive education is their exclusive domain. To many others, homosexuality can be acceptable in the abstract, yet horrifying in its concrete and proximate form. For example, a parent at an exclusive New York private girls' school exclaimed to an antihomophobia trainer, "Are you saying that I'm supposed to be *neutral* [emphasis added] about this? I'm supposed to say to my daughter, 'I don't want you to drink Coke, but it's OK to be a lesbian?'"[254] Numbers of independent schools, especially single-gender ones, demonstrate an institutional version of this mother's annoyance. They believe a reputation for attracting gay and lesbian students riles trustees and wrecks havoc with admissions.[255]

*Model Responses.* Assuming, however, that one encounters opponents with whom one can have a thoughtful exchange, the following are recurring objections to antiheterosexism education, each followed by a suggested reasonable response:

1. The proportion of homosexuals in the population is much less than 10 percent.

     The exact number of gays and lesbians is irrelevant. The rights or respect due to a minority group is not proportionate to their numbers. No one would argue that anti-Semitism is less wrong in countries with few Jews.

2. Homosexuals are not a true minority group like religious and racial minorities.

     As individuals, homosexual people may have nothing other than some part of their sexual orientation in common; they hold a broad range of political, philosophical, and religious beliefs. Their cohesion, to the extent that they are united, is the result of two factors: first, an at least 100-year history as a despised, marginalized, and victimized minority; and second, a vibrant, often heroic, culture of survival, marked by hiding and celebration, humor, tragedy, and persevering love. In other words, homosexual people are linked by elements of history and culture similar to those that bind ethnic, racial, and religious minorities all over the world.

3. Homosexuality is a choice.

     There is some evidence that all sexual orientations are both genetically and environmentally determined, but even if homosexual desire were entirely voluntary, would that make homosexuals any less deserving of autonomy and respect? Significant choices are already protected in our constitution, such as the choice of faith or the choice to be left alone.

4. Homosexuality is a behavior.

     All sexuality is a combination of orientation, identification, and behavior. Like heterosexuality, homosexuality may involve desire/attraction, self-definition, and activities intended to fulfill desire and identity.

5. Homosexuality is a violation of God's law and hence should be off-limits for schools.

     Biblical interpretations vary, nor is any doctrinal reading of the Bible germane to public school policy or curriculum.

6. Gay/lesbian-positive education influences students to become homosexual.

     There is no evidence that any sexual orientation can be caused or changed through education. Education and counseling may help students understand and accept their sexualities.

7. Gay/lesbian-positive education promotes homosexual behavior.

     Factors such as puberty, peer pressure, media images, and adult example may influence young people to become sexually active. Sexuality education in home, school, and community might help them to behave responsibly and safely. Whether it encourages behavior of any kind depends on its content. Lessons that affirm gay and lesbian people must also affirm their sexual expression, but that can be done without encouraging young people to become sexually active before they want to or are ready to be.

8. Gay/lesbian-positive education spreads HIV/AIDS.

Antihomophobia education does not promote sexual activity. Furthermore, because it lessens the stigma that may lead to self-destructive behaviors, it may decrease the incidence of HIV transmission.

9. Gay/lesbian-positive education is antifamily.

Helping families to accept their gay and lesbian members and creating a model for alternative family paradigms increases the number of loving and nurturing environments for young people, older people, and those who raise them and care for them.

10. Gay-positive education is an attack on the innocence and purity of children.

Children's allegedly blissful ignorance is challenged from the moment they become conscious of their environment. Now, as in the past, the world presents information to disillusion a growing child, but there is nothing inherent in homosexuality to sully the purity of children. On the contrary, teaching children to value religious, racial, ethnic, gender, and sexual diversity preserves the innocence of their unbiased hearts.

11. Homosexuality is an inappropriate topic for young children.

Lessons about different kinds of love and respect for different kinds of relationships should begin in the early grades. Too often homophobic name-calling is rampant by middle school years.

12. Sexuality education detracts from "real learning."

Sexuality is a major component of human identity, plays an important role in human relations, and has figured prominently in history, literature, and the fine arts. To prevent the study of sexuality diminishes the scope of legitimate inquiry and the truthfulness of teaching.

13. Sexuality education is political activism.

Most school subjects, even science, have political dimensions or ramifications. Deciding what will be studied and how it will be presented nearly always involves political considerations.

14. Values education should be left to parents and churches.

School curricula are permeated with values, yet most adults still support public education. The values of all Americans are contested daily by means of unprecedented channels of communication. Finding common civic values and learning to live by them is a challenge that students must begin to undertake in school.

15. The values taught in particular schools should be determined by their
    individual communities.

    It is understandable that groups of parents want the schools to re-
    inforce their values. However, a community's values are usually
    more diverse than most people care to admit. An individual's val-
    ues are not determined by majority vote; nor do these values al-
    ways remain static. The principal values that the people of the
    United States embrace by virtue of their citizenship are contra-
    dicted when minorities are singled out for discrimination on the
    basis of the personal or religious beliefs of their oppressors. The
    values of equality and liberty must be promoted in our schools.
16. Schools ought to teach that homosexuality is wrong, but that people
    should not disrespect homosexuals.

    Even adults may fail to understand the distinction. Public schools
    should teach that all sexualities and all sexual identities are worthy
    of understanding and respect and that people should conduct
    themselves accordingly.

American pluralism's great challenge is to balance what separates and
unites individuals of many colors, faiths, cultures, incomes, gender expressions, degrees of physical capacity, sexualities, and political views.
But if this nation's youth learn to probe differences respectfully, to find
commonalities where they exist, and above all, to be comfortable with
both heterogeneity and ambiguity, they will have developed a capacity to
live and work together that preserves the United States and sets an example for the world.[256]

# 14

## Curriculum

*We as teachers have a responsibility to bring the world our students will have to confront—are already confronting—into our classrooms. Anything less than that is professionally and morally irresponsible.*
—Marvin Hoffman, "Teaching Torch Song: Gay Literature in the Classroom"

For gay and lesbian activists, the Rainbow controversy (see Chapter 13) was a singular opportunity to engage nationally with social conservatives on the issue of inclusive education. Instead gay military service became the focal point in the gay rights struggle, and the hoopla over lifting the ban diverted national attention from the schools to the barracks. Gay and lesbian leaders seemed to forget the connection between government policies and the K–12 schooling of the people who make them.

The Rainbow defeat intimidated reformers even in places where significant advances were already being made. In Massachusetts, the governor excised the library and curriculum recommendations of his Commission on Gay and Lesbian Youth (see Chapter 12) and the Brookline High School principal, an ostensible friend, said: "I think we'd be asking for trouble if we introduced something like the Rainbow Curriculum that specifically deals with gay developmental issues, social history, and so forth. I think subtlety is important."[1] Later, in Oregon, a state that had defeated antigay initiatives, Portland Superintendent Jack Bierworth eloquently defended optional sensitivity workshops, yet he stipulated that they not introduce curriculum into the classrooms.[2]

Although such setbacks may represent only a temporary diminution of confidence, evidence mounts that the anti-Rainbow mind-set persists. Many schools still bend over backward to distinguish between acceptable antidiscrimination policies and forbidden classroom lessons. For instance, despite unanimously voted protections for homosexual students in one Maryland county, officials would not permit displays of gay-related books or talks by homosexual speakers in classes. "That would be proselytizing," declared the superintendent.[3]

California's 1997 gay student protection bill AB101 was lambasted by conservative school board members who warned the public that safety issues would degenerate into "lifestyle education" and "be in your reading and language arts curriculum, you can be sure of it." Parents invoked the New York Rainbow curriculum in fear for their rights. The bill's sponsor called the accusations red herrings and weakly denied curricular implications: "The bill doesn't mandate curriculum."[4] Only San Francisco continued to consider the addition of sexual orientation to its multicultural curriculum mandate.[5]

## Why Curriculum?

### Preparation for Life

Teaching about homosexuality is justifiable on pragmatic grounds. To prepare for democracy, students must learn about gays and lesbians as part of the American patchwork.[6] They will, if they have not already done so, eventually study, work, worship, or live beside openly gay and lesbian people. For those who go on to higher education, the meeting may be sooner, as it has been historically for many college students whose prior encounters with diversity were limited. In 1995, there were nearly 1,200 homosexual student organizations inviting notice and dialogue on U.S. college and university campuses.[7]

### Teaching to Student Interests

Another practical reason for an inclusive curriculum is that American adolescents are demonstrably inquisitive on the subject and schools do well to teach to student interests. One factor that prevents the schools from responding is that most adults are embarrassed to admit their own curiosity, fearing it makes them immoral and eccentric. Although they would rather see explicit sex than violence on screen, they assume their neighbors would prefer the opposite. Researchers who have studied this shamefulness believe people's notions of public morality have been skewed by the outspokenness of religious conservatives.[8]

Contrary to the common right-wing assertion, classrooms and class lessons are highly sexualized and antihomosexualized.[9] The oppressive nature of this environment is ripe for student analysis and discussion. A recent national study of comprehensive health education found that 82 percent of adolescents rated human sexuality and sexual relationships of equal or more importance than other subjects taught in school. Although

87 percent of administrators and 79 percent of parents concurred,[10] adults differ on what sex education should look like.

One may argue that the mass media contribute to both an exaggeration and a distortion of human sexuality. Sex acts or allusions to them were found in over half of prime-time shows on the four major networks, according to one study in 1996; another discovered them every four minutes.[11] Children who are exposed to the media may come to think that heterosexual sex is always appropriate and good.[12]

Yet even without the commodification of sex through MTV, teen magazines, film, and advertising, the protracted adolescent period that has developed in our culture has sexual musings, anxieties, and experimentation at its core. Today's students are thinking, talking, and doing sexuality, sometimes beginning a very young age.[13] A 1990 Centers for Disease Control survey found that 40 percent of ninth-graders reported having had sexual intercourse. The number increased to 72 percent by twelfth grade.[14] Although frequency of intercourse may have diminished since then, perhaps in part because of AIDS, the age of first engagement appears to have been slowly getting lower over many years.[15] Peer pressure and media images have much to do with that. Moreover, intercourse represents just a fraction of sexual activity, and sexual ideation in turn dwarfs behavior.

Natural or not, exploited or not, sexual interests are an important part of our youths' universe. Schools should accept the challenge of meeting them where they are. Young people must marvel or laugh at teachers who step gingerly around sexuality, even when the text or students' remarks cry out for frank discussion. Even younger children, who may not be ready for detailed or lengthy explanations, would benefit from the teachable moments that our sexualized mass culture regularly provides.[16]

Furthermore, for all their experience and would-be sophistication on sexual issues, most students' understanding is superficial and warped by commercial interests. To deepen and clarify their knowledge so as to change their attitudes and behaviors, school curricula must explore the meanings and importance of human sexuality both historically and in contemporary life. An honest and profound curriculum not only illuminates the mechanics of sexuality; it also puts it into perspective.

Gay and lesbian sexualities are suitable topics, especially for junior and senior high school students, because they are of compelling concern to them.[17] As adolescents become aware of their own sexual interests, they focus quite naturally on conforming to peer group norms. Is it any wonder then, that sexuality differences, particularly those perceived as extreme, are riveting to them? The social abhorrence with which homosexuality is viewed itself renders it fascinating for teens.

Although many young people feel obliged to react publicly to the subject with dismissive derision or horror, others increasingly do not. Their willingness to discuss homosexuality may indicate a lessening of homophobia or merely the decreasing shock value of a familiar media theme. Some yearn to know it better because it is their own experience; others may want to be reassured of their heterosexuality.

Whatever the cause of their interest, students have become more open to the discourse. The scope and seriousness of their curiosity can be remarkable. The following sections are composed of verbatim excerpts from a one-day sampling of anonymous student questions and comments at one Massachusetts high school in 1994.[18]

### Homophobia and Violence.

- Why the hell would you like guys? p.s.: That's nasty.
- Fags! Why would you love a guy? You can't! They should be shot.
- In my opinion "faggot" is about on the same level of the word "nigger." Both of these are horrible names, but why is faggot so commonly used?
- How do I deal with a family who is completely against homosexuality? I myself am not gay but I have gay friends and it hurts when my family openly says horrible things.
- I have witnessed a great deal of hatred toward gays not only in school but in other places as well. . . . How do you react to hearing hateful and ignorant remarks toward gays?
- Have you ever been the victims of physical violence because of your sexual preference?
- Is there a lot of discrimination against homosexuals? If so, then in what communities do you see it the most?
- Many people are homophobic—do you think society does this to them?
- Do you think it will be harder for you to find a job as a high school history teacher?
- Have you ever lost a job or apartment because of your sexuality?
- How could someone like their own sex? I wouldn't be able to live thinking I might be gay.
- If I was gay I would kill myself.

### Health.

- Do you practice safe sex? Do you worry about getting the HIV virus?

### Politics.

- If gays and lesbians want to be equal why are they so public about their sexuality? Straight people don't go around saying, "We're straight, let's have a parade, or let's spend 4 hours talking about it at high schools."
- Do you think telling people you are gay is important?
- How do you feel about the St. Patrick's Day Parade being canceled because of you [wanting to march]?

### Science.

- If the entire human race became homosexual, it would take no longer than a century for all humans to become extinct.
- Is homosexuality a choice/preference/lifestyle or is it more often biological?
- Are humans the only species with the gay gene?
- Do certain population groups have a higher percent of homosexuality?
- Is homosexuality a brain disorder?
- If you're bisexual, are you still considered gay?
- At what age do most people become or decide they are gay?
- If a gay man sees a beautiful woman naked, do you get excited or aroused (even partially)?

### Human Relations.

- Do you often times find people who aren't homosexual attractive?
- Have you ever dated a man or woman in a heterosexual relationship?
- Do your parents feel like its their fault?
- Have people ever been kicked out of their family because they were a homosexual?
- Do your friends accept you?
- If being gay were a choice, would you have chosen to be gay or straight?
- What would you say to someone who is gay but doesn't ever plan to tell anyone about it?
- If you are interested in someone, how do you go about asking if they're gay?
- How can you tell if someone is gay without them telling you?
- Is it harder to stay in a relationship?

- Are the majority of gay relationships based on love or sexual attraction?
- Do you think gays should be able to marry?
- How do gay couples decide who is going to be the aggressor in sexual situations?
- Are either of you thinking of adopting or do you already have a child?

### *Religion.*

- Do you know anything about the standpoint of the major religions on homosexuality?
- Is it actually in the Bible that being homosexual is wrong? If so, how do you get strong churchgoers to accept homosexuality?

The easy generation of such a list should convince any good teacher that this realm represents a remarkable curricular opportunity in many disciplines.

### *Honest and Complete Curricula*

In addition to these pragmatic considerations—the requirements for democratic living and the genuine interests of students—educators should be spurred by their professional duty to impart accurate and complete information in their classes and counseling sessions. Expurgation is dishonesty. One academic asserts that one cannot omit sex from history any more than one can overlook the importance of religion in it.[19] A teacher must help students see sexuality objectively in all its forms, with their distinctions and congruencies. A superlative pedagogical standard comes from, of all people, a very young film actor who was asked if he minded playing the role of gay poet Arthur Rimbaud. He replied, "My feelings don't matter. What matters is showing the truth of this great poet's life."[20]

Practicality is enhanced, not compromised, by truthfulness, because an intellectually honest curriculum is more vibrant and convincing than a sanitized one. Young people are turned off by made-up lessons that do not reflect the real world.[21] In the words of a pioneer in tolerance education:

When the chasm between the curriculum of the classroom and the daily lives of our students is so wide, students exercise their options. They stop trusting their teachers; the curriculum seems irrelevant. Some continue to play the "game of education," attending class and telling teachers what they want to hear. Others become cynical, indifferent, and apathetic. Still others, alienated and angry, drop out.[22]

This is what can happen when curricula do not encompass the particular shapes of students' lives. Conversely, when they judge that school lessons are about their world, they are more likely to participate. Then they have a chance to think critically about their own experience and that of others around them.

As for homosexuality, educators must not rest with a feint of inclusion. A gesture will not suffice, when teachers might facilitate the discovery of the centuries-long span of same-gender sociality and love. Further, they are in a position to dare older students to interrogate sexuality's socially constructed meanings and their implications for their own identities.

### Help for Gay and Lesbian Youth

The litany of stresses and self-inflicted harms suffered by youth who are struggling with homosexual identities are familiar: alienation, depression, substance abuse, and suicide. (See Chapter 8.) Since many do not receive affirming information from family, friends, or school, they may be more attentive to media representations of sexuality than their heterosexual peers.

It is hard to understand how any homosexual young person who has grown up listening to the American TV talk-show cavalcade could still think that she or he is the only one. The candor and variety of television discussions of sexuality should help relieve isolation and ignorance, but most shows are worrisome. Programming appears to favor sensationalism and ratings over accuracy. Deliberately provocative images and acrimony could confuse or frighten average youth. Secondly, the inclusion of opposing views, a governing principle of TV talk on homosexuality, is problematic because it usually features a rabid homophobic "expert."

News and public affairs programming can also send destructive messages to youth. Congressional hearings on gays in the military and on gay marriage, for example, elicited a stream of negative demeaning testimony. There was very little shown to counter depictions of gays and lesbians as predatory, infected, promiscuous, loveless, and damned. Some coverage of the HIV epidemic furthers this impression.

Dramatic series and movies have historically featured these same characterizations. Comedy, in turn, has traded on fops and amazons. Yet, particularly in the 1990s, rational discussion and good-humored, even flattering portrayals have occurred. The 1995 TV movie about Margaretha Cammemeyer's fight to remain in the military was one of those. It was in fact unique because it did not erase her intimate life. Beyond rendering her competence and courage, it paid homage to her lesbian love relationship.[23]

Others who are gay or lesbian supporting characters in comedic and dramatic series have also begun to break down stereotypes, for example, the gay African American mayor's assistant on *Spin City* or the gay roommate on *Will and Grace*.[24] Walt Whitman, no less, was afforded a sympathetic coming out on a popular series.[25] If these breakthrough programs are profitable, they may signal the beginning of a new era in media.[26] That prospect has in fact drawn suggestions for "gay content" warnings from conservatives[27]and protests from offended youths.[28]

Some of these new characters, adult or adolescent, are merely "ratings week" window dressing. Even the more established ones lack the emotional depth (such as it exists) and the explicit sexuality of their heterosexual counterparts.[29] Of course the 1997 coming out episodes of Ellen Degeneres's sitcom *Ellen* were a boon, albeit short-lived.[30] Although not a teen, she was young, and her vignettes with family, friends, and employer reflected universal concerns.

Granted that doing justice to homosexual adults likely inspires younger people, entertainment television, which plays a central role in setting cultural norms,[31] is still for the most part devoid of adolescent homosexual content. Until *Dawson's Creek* in 1999,[32] no prime-time commercial network featured a homosexual teenager as a continuous character.[33] (The first positive exception, public television's youth-oriented series *My So-Called Life*, was eventually canceled.[34]) Previous incidental representations depicted desperate characters in sexuality confusion and crisis or humorous teens, whose sexuality provoked jest or ridicule.

An African American professor of psychiatry observes that the absence of black heroes in curricula and media leads to psychological disadvantage for many blacks.[35] The same can easily be said of gays and lesbians. The mass media, including the music industry, have often conflated homosexuality with controversy and suffering. Many gay and lesbian youth cannot resist these harmful images.[36] Hampered by geographic or psychic isolation from an affirming subculture, they develop a dismal view of their prospects, perhaps experiencing their homosexuality the way others did fifty years ago.

Even balanced and positive presentations, however, can lead to discouraging outcomes by inciting homophobic comments from others. How many family members offered good-natured or supportive commentary as they sat in their living rooms watching *Ellen*? How many teachers who picked up the student buzz were prepared or willing to conduct impromptu class discussions? And how many expressed a tolerant view? The self-esteem of young gays and lesbians is vitally linked to parent and teacher approval.[37]

Bringing the discussion of homosexuality into the school can enhance these students' development. At the very least, they will not suffer the enforced ignorance that distressed Essex Hemphill, when as a sixth-grader, he sneaked into the adult section of the library to learn about his developing sexuality: "When I finished my month-long reading marathon, I put away the last book, knowing only that I had homosexual tendencies and desires, but beyond that awareness I didn't recognize my-self in any of the material I had so exhaustively read."[38]

Homosexuality does not have to be glamorized to serve as an antidote to lies and stigmatization. Homosexual students will learn through objective study that their lives, like those of some other minorities, are fraught with risk. But they will also learn that there is more to celebrate than to fear. This vital information will also comfort those who discover their homosexual feelings some time after graduating from high school.

Needless to say, homosexual youth would also benefit from increased tolerance. The advent of AIDS and the vitriol in the political debate over gay rights have led to more homophobic assaults. (See Chapter 1.) Schools, a frequent site for such rage and violence, are an opportune place to intervene: "Someone is teaching our kids to hate. But we can teach them how to avoid violence, practice empathy, and see the world through the lens of the other."[39]

*Help for Heterosexual Youth*

Implicit in most campaigns for antihomophobia education is the notion that homosexual young people will be its only beneficiaries. A well-de-vised curriculum offers more than security, self-esteem, and role models for gay and lesbian students. It can have benefits for other youth as well.

First, any learning that lessens the fears and hatred of bigotry helps not only its targets but also the bigots themselves. Prejudice is a debilitating burden. Letting it go allows a stunted mind to grow. Among the aims of multicultural education should be both to protect the oppressed and to "help free students from their own cultural boundaries."[40]

This latter effect on white students was ignored in *Brown v. Board of Education*, which focused on the consequences of discrimination to blacks. Chief Justice Warren may have rightly concluded that black children's segregation "generates a feeling of inferiority as to their status in the community that may affect their hearts and minds in a way unlikely ever to be undone."[41] Yet separation hurt white children too. It crippled their understanding of the human experience by limiting their educational contact with their black neighbors. Integration should stimulate dialogue that enriches all children.

Recognizing the presence of gay and lesbian students, faculty, and families, talking with them, and studying homosexuality enhances their humanity and makes both homosexuals and heterosexuals wiser. This outcome appears underappreciated, even by the Association for Supervision and Curriculum Development, whose 1990 resolution urging the development of "policies, curriculum materials, and teaching strategies that do not discriminate on the basis of sexual orientation," seems directed more at gay and lesbian students "at risk" than to their heterosexual peers disadvantaged by ignorance.[42]

A second benefit for nongay students concerns their own sexual development. One of the penalties of socialization is that many heterosexuals lose their spontaneous relational voice as they reach adolescence. Young boys are taught to banish emotion and empathy and to deny pain in their quest for masculinity. Girls are forced to abandon authentic same-gender relations. They must cut off ties with female confidantes and vie with them in the pursuit of men who may even abuse them for speaking their true feelings.[43]

Sexism and heterosexism are used to enforce these regulations. Young men's sexuality becomes suspect if they express their true feelings to other men, communicate feelingly with women, or listen to the uncensored voices of their female partners. Many males become obsessed with ridding themselves of any emotions or behaviors that appear feminine.[44] They are a source of shame that one psychologist has called "the primary or ultimate cause of all violence, whether toward others or toward the self."[45] Likewise, young women's sexuality is questioned if they are strong in self-expression and true in their assessment of sexist injustice. Young men and women should not be forced by cultural oppression to abandon same-gender closeness and honest relationality.

Teachers and counselors must recognize how a "male-biased curriculum that celebrates ideals of masculinity" contributes to this problem.[46] Although many educators understand the importance of stopping gay and lesbian suicide and bashing, few see how antihomophobia education might lessen other kinds of self-destruction and violence. Studying the range of human sexual feeling and gender expression can help relieve straight-identified students from the pressures of a narrow, inflexible heterosexuality. Some might also come to see the arbitrariness of sexuality labels.

A young man in a conflict resolution project described what happens when one signifier of masculinity, the ownership of a woman, is challenged: "Say a guy is walking down the street with his female, and someone else looks at her. He'll probably turn around and go, 'What you lookin at?' and that right there can escalate into something else." Then he added: "I'd rather be thought a wimp than jeopardize my life."[47] This attitude shift will be advanced when "wimp" and "sissy" have lost their sting.

One heterosexual student expressed just such an altered view after studying a unit on gay and lesbian U.S. history:

> The more we talk about homosexuality in class, the more comfortable I am with the idea, with gay people, with my own sexuality, and with my own male identity. Is/Was this curriculum and these discussions important? About as important as the desegregation of schools in the 50s and the abolition of slavery in the 1800s. We are in the *middle* of a *huge* societal movement, a tremendous change, one more step to a better society.[48]

Presenting homosexuality without embarrassment or condemnation signals a teacher's acceptance of sexuality in general and that may facilitate better communication with all students. Some young people have approached openly gay and lesbian teachers to discuss sexual and relationship issues that they would not broach with anyone else. The students explained that they confided in them because the out teachers seemed to be more open and accepting of people's different experiences than others.[49]

## Curriculum as Change Agent

Media misrepresentation and curricular invisibility do more than hurt a minority's self-image. They also influence the views of the majority, leading to

- feelings of superiority to a minority group that seems to have no culture or past;
- assumptions of no shared beliefs and experiences with the minority;
- false impressions which make the minority seem strange and ends in rejection;
- psychological distance from the minority, which makes aggression easier.[50]

Lies and omissions can be countered in schools with books, fact sheets, and lectures. Without genuine dialogue, however, people's attitudes are less likely to change. (See Chapter 11.) Factual information by itself often leads to disappointing outcomes. One study has demonstrated that anti-Semitism did not decrease when facts about Jews were taught;[51] another found that white prejudice actually increased when information about blacks was presented.[52] Only when new knowledge was combined with discussion, especially unfettered after-class conversations, did attitudes change. A third study found academic instruction had little effect on eighth-graders' prejudice, whereas participation in role plays brought about significant change.[53] There appears to be a need for active participation. Passive listening or viewing is thought to have no impact.[54]

There is nevertheless one important caveat to these conclusions. Although most studies show no immediate change in attitudes brought on by fact presentation alone, it is possible that new information incubates slowly. Curriculum, even without discussion, may thus serve as a gradual inoculation against bigotry.[55]

As to pedagogical format, when a sensitive topic is introduced in a large group, some students shy away from saying what is really on their minds. General discussions can stimulate their thinking, but the direct engagement needed for growth may be better fostered in one-on-one conversations with a peer or an adult.[56] It is wise, therefore, for teachers to ensure that pair-exercises are a part of class activities and also to make themselves available for private conferences.

The possibility that inclusive curriculum by itself is an unproven agent for reducing prejudice does not diminish its positive influence on minorities or the intellectual desirability of complete and accurate instruction.[57] In the final analysis, though, if curriculum is more broadly construed to entail cooperative experiences and guided discourse in a variety of settings, it is almost certain to have a positive effect on how students understand and relate to people who are different from them.

## Minimum Changes to Increase Sensitivity

Teaching about sexuality may be more discouragingly problematic than exploring other kinds of difference (see Chapter 11), but teachers should not underestimate the importance of simply naming sexual orientation when they talk about cultural diversity. For young people just to hear the words periodically in an unembarrassed and accepting tone disrupts their habitual thinking. Beyond this categorical inclusion, teachers must consistently challenge homophobic name-calling and other harassment and urge tolerance. They should also seriously consider the following:

- putting up a "Safe-Zone" sticker;
- spending a few minutes countering a handful of misconceptions;
- putting up a poster of famous gays and lesbians;
- having a special sensitivity session about homophobia;
- inviting guest speakers from the gay/lesbian community;

- celebrating gay pride or National Coming Out Day with posters, panels, and pink triangles.

Just having visible minority group members in a school can promote experiences and dialogue that lead to greater understanding. However, since openly homosexual students and teachers are rare, even where religious and political barriers are absent, opportunities are limited. Most who commit to inclusion under the rubric of general multiculturalism must depend on guest speakers, autobiography, documentary film, or third-person accounts and observations.

An explicit rule against homophobic name-calling can lead to a minimal curriculum when conscientious enforcement begins a lesson in tolerance. Students (or faculty) should not merely be punished for using words like "faggot" or "lezzie" but also told who is being hurt by such language and why it is wrong to defame homosexual people.[58]

*Answering the Inevitable Question.* Often, when teachers include or defend gays and lesbians they are assumed to be homosexual themselves, particularly when they are not known to be married. Students might ask outright, and however one eventually responds, critical questions for them to hear are, "Why do you think I might be?" and "Would my being gay or lesbian influence how you feel about me or about homosexuality?" There are three lessons here. First, not everyone who objects to gay-bashing is homosexual—a needed inducement to heterosexual allies. Second, temporary uncertainty about the teacher's orientation can help students see that sexuality is not always discernible by means of stereotypical markers. Third, they would have to consider what it would mean for them if a teacher they respected and liked was homosexual.

Straight teachers should postpone answering for a short time to investigate students' preconceptions and expectations. Then, lest they be suspected of shameful evasion, they should respond in good ally fashion that being gay or lesbian is no disgrace, as in: "No, I don't happen to be homosexual, though people I love and admire are gay and lesbian. I didn't answer right away because I wanted you to have a chance to think hard about this issue." Homosexual teachers, on the other hand, must have support in the school to undertake what could be a controversial disclosure. (See Chapter 9.)

*Grouping Heterosexism with Other Oppressions.* Schools that undertake homophobia sensitization are often more comfortable including sexual orientation with other tolerance issues than discussing it separately. They may attempt to lessen political repercussions by limiting their actions to incidental mention of homosexuality and use of general antiprejudice exercises. One simulation that has proven successful is the teacher-led stigmatization of an arbitrary group, such as blue-eyed people, for a period of time. This ordeal appears to increase empathy for minorities of different types.[59]

Although it may seem safer to mention gays and lesbians in a larger cluster of groups, that approach is not foolproof in neutralizing hostile responses. Classroom reference to homosexuals is rare enough that students will be naturally inquisitive about their inclusion. Some, particularly members of other minority groups, may not understand or may even resent the apparent equating of homosexual orientation with other minority statuses. Glib superficial answers only make matters worse.

Teachers, of course, have to concede to conformity-minded young people that heterosexuality is the norm and that heterosexism is not the same as all other oppressions. (See Chapter 11.) But they must take care not to get too defensive or to convey disapproval of or discomfort with homosexuality. They also should guard against tokenism and a patronizing attitude, such as sometimes prevails when a minority is given its moment of attention.

General tolerance curricula that cover sexual orientation explicitly are rare and commendable. These include such programs as "The Shadow of Hate," "A Place at the Table," and other materials produced by the Teaching Tolerance Project[60] and curricula from the Equity Institute[61] and Diversity Works.[62] Lessons from the Facing History and Ourselves Project also make reference to homosexuality.[63]

### Beyond Sensitivity

The impact of one-shot curriculum strategies is often evanescent. A well-intended forty-minute show and tell may be no more efficacious than a "zapping" Queer Nation schoolyard distribution of leaflets and condoms—dramatic perhaps, but not a sustained conversation.[64] Even a good comic strip on the tribulations of gay adolescence has to last a dozen episodes.[65]

Gay and lesbian curricula must not become trendy sideshows, conducted apart from the serious daily business of classroom inquiry. To do so is to engage in "fragmentation/isolation,"[66] which separates learning about minorities from the central academic goals of the school. Students sense that such add-on lessons about "the other" are detours from real schooling. The relegation of such lessons to extracurricular purgatory mirrors the segregation of multicultural issues in teacher and administrator training.[67] And that marginalization itself reflects the social reality that schools exist to transmit dominant cultural values and mores rather than to stimulate disruptive inquiry.[68]

Progressive educators have an obligation to do more than broach homosexuality or any other important human difference as an aside.[69]

What is needed in antihomophobia education is sustained and serious discourse within the disciplines of the school. Students must begin to

- understand the nature of sexual identity and same-gender attraction, and how they have been expressed in various times and cultures;
- know about past and current etiologic research;
- analyze how the homosexuality of a historical figure, author, or artist might have influenced his or her life and work;
- know something about the history of the gay/lesbian community in the United States and current issues in gay life;
- appreciate the diversity of gays and lesbians in this country and around the world.[70]

For many years in their zeal to transmit a common culture, schools have given scant attention to the lives and contributions of many minorities. Homosexuality has been completely ignored. To be sure, many gays and lesbians figure in history texts and literature, but their sexuality and its implications are not broached. If the educational mission is to cultivate interest in the truth and to give students the skills to begin searching for it, this kind of purposeful naiveté is counterproductive. Never mind that the whole and absolute truth can never be discovered because it does not exist—students' and teachers' rehearsing variations on a truth is what counts.[71]

Some years ago when scholarship on homosexuality was spotty, good materials were scarce. Today though, the growing academic and independent pursuit of gay studies provides volumes of respected research and provocative theory. The goal should be to make some of this new learning accessible in units for integration into existing K–12 curricula. Independent courses are not inconceivable; yet, if one is to reach those most in need of information—homophobic students and those agonizing over their homosexual identities—one must employ an integrated approach. Haters and closeted adolescents would just not enroll in independent courses.[72] A case in point: A teacher at Newton North High School (Mass.) suspected that not one student chose an optional gay-related assignment for a final project in her literature and film course because no student dared be associated with it.[73] Such was the level of aversion and fear at an otherwise liberal school.

### Beyond Compensation

Teaching about homosexuality is more than informing students about a particular kind of person. It can also challenge them to think about how same-gender attraction became a marker of a type of person in the first

place. They can investigate other characteristics that "make" identity labels and ponder how these tags influence their own understanding of the
past and the present. (See Chapter 2.) In short, teachers and students
could employ new concepts of identity in many curriculum areas and
link sexuality to a variety of equity issues.[74] This transformative paradigm gives the lie to gay/lesbian units as curriculum add-ons, where
"the basic assumptions, perspectives, paradigms, and values of the dominant curriculum remain unchallenged and substantially unchanged, despite the addition of ethnic content or content about women."[75] To the
contrary, homosexual identity theory destabilizes the verities, inverts the
viewpoints, undermines the models, and tests the values. It can be quite
appealing to young people, for whom society's dictates are a locus both
of self-reference and potential rebellion.

Discussions of culturally imposed categories of sexual identity can
lead to poignant conversations among groups of diverse high school students, asking, "Who does this culture say I am and you are? On what
basis does it make those assessments and why should I believe it?" As a
direct consequence of studying homosexuality, students at Cambridge
Rindge and Latin High School have puzzled over what it means to be
Jewish or black in America and what is essential to a woman's identity.
One biracial student spoke about her inability to choose between black
and white, wanting to be both and neither. She did not seem a pathetic
soul, stumped by a fruitless pursuit of racial identity. On the contrary, she
was strong, self-respecting, and impatient with society's bipolar categories and perhaps with any identity based on pigmentation.[76] Her desire to be accepted just as herself was not surprising in a teenager, but her
capacity to inspire others to contest universally accepted racial dichotomies was extraordinary.

As a child of mixed parentage, she had doubtless given much thought
to the question. Nevertheless, it was the discussion of social constructionism, prompted by the issue of homosexuality that gave her the incentive to speak out. Through her example, all students were roused to
examine the power of similar labels to determine their life courses. Gay
and lesbian youth, too, for all the comfort to be found in the safe harbor
of a homosexual identity, might be relieved to find corroboration for its
limited capacity to describe who they are.

## The Disciplines

*Health, Sex Education, and Family Life*

The subject of homosexuality, if it arises at all in schools, is most often referred to in health and HIV curricula, perhaps in some of the thirty-six

states with recommended or mandatory sex education.[77] However, only 46 percent of health teachers in one random sample indicated they formally taught about homosexuality.[78] Of those, 48 percent spent less than a class period on it and 43 percent spent 1 to 2 periods.

Although it is perfectly suitable to discuss some aspects of homosexuality in these venues, health/HIV educators must be wary of medicalization, that is, having students think that homosexuality is inevitably linked with deviance and pathology. Some people actually prefer that students relate heterosexuality to life and health and associate homosexuality with death and sickness.[79] A 1996 bill introduced in the Missouri senate would have prevented teachers and curricula from advocating homosexuality as an acceptable lifestyle but would have allowed negative reference to homosexuality in connection with health and AIDS;[80] and a Marysville, Washington, policy did the same.[81]

Teachers may be likely to make that association themselves: fully one-third of health teachers in the above study deemed gay and lesbian rights "a threat to the American family and its values."[82]

Even when the educator is gay-friendly and the curriculum is accurate, placing the subject under the heading of "health" or "disease prevention" carries its own implications. Indeed some attempts to balance negative associations between AIDS and homosexuality have been targeted by opponents. In California, Republican lawmakers proposed that parents give written permission prior to lessons on AIDS because "schools were contracting with homosexual groups to come in and supposedly teach about AIDS, but they often stepped over their boundaries and were actively promoting the gay culture."[83]

Medicalizing homosexuality in disease prevention education also dehumanizes gays and lesbians. Instruction that deals only with the physiological dimensions of homosexuality reinforces the common misconception that gayness is just about sex. Would we confine the study of *heterosexuality* to health classes—reducing it to plumbing and other technicalities? Heterosexuality, of course, is well depicted in history, literature, and elsewhere, balancing physiological reductionism with other aspects of male-female relationships.

The limited effectiveness of this narrow approach is keenly illustrated at San Ramon Valley (Calif.) High School, where students have been required to take sex education courses inclusive of homosexuality for some time. Homophobia is still a persistent problem: AIDS quilts were defaced with antigay graffiti; gay pride displays were spat upon and students have worn "Straight Pride" t-shirts and protested with Confederate flags.[84]

As for sex education itself, students do not give it credence if it pretends sex is all rational and technical.[85] A purely physiological approach to sex eviscerates its pleasure and spirituality; it also fails to address power in sexual relations. These three axes of analysis—pleasure, spirituality, and power—are as compelling and vital as biology. An honest and complete inquiry into sexuality must delve into these matters.[86] Few schools are able to meet these criteria for heterosexuals; fewer still dare incorporate gay sexuality into their programs.[87]

All students need explicit AIDS education that leads to less risk-taking. However, for the sake of homosexual youth, especially those without connections to the gay community, teachers must avoid portraying gays as a grieving, doomed lot. To be effective, adult HIV prevention affirms gay sexuality and relationships. School-based lessons must do the same.

Family life education should be a more comfortable place for the integration of gay/lesbian content.[88] Family life curricula could offer a comprehensive view of homosexuality that moves "beyond victimization."[89] Seattle's Family Life and Sexual Health (FLASH), for example, is a good beginning: eleventh- and twelfth-graders learn about the Kinsey scale, the difference between homosexual acts and gay identity, the history of antigay prejudice and discrimination, and theories of causation.[90]

Yet, one could go further. Studying the ways that gays and lesbians create alternative families would encompass same-gender domestic arrangements, spousal relationships, child-rearing, extended biological and adopted family, work sharing, and financial planning. Students could gain insight into "the sophisticated level of interpersonal structure and relationship management that lesbians and gay men must achieve."[91]

There is also a valuable discovery in the evidence that core issues like sharing, commitment, communication, and conflict resolution are similar for all couples, and that the differences between men and women are greater than those separating homosexual and heterosexual couples.[92]

The study of homosexual partnerships and parenting would assure homosexual youth of their own potentialities. Moreover, studying how gays and lesbians make families could also help those heterosexual students who are disadvantaged by normative definitions of family. Young women particularly might benefit from seeing that there are other ways to thrive beyond traditional marriage.

Of course some heterosexuals too can provide healthy models of unconventional family life. Still, instructive exceptions to conservative notions of gender role are often found in same-gender relationships.[93] Thus, when a high school student, commonly male, asks a partnered gay male presenter, "Which of you is the husband?" the lesson may truly begin.

Some critics, noting that sex education in the United States privileges white middle-class understandings of sexuality, suggest bringing focus groups of diverse parents into the curriculum design process.[94] That diversity ought to extend to homosexual parents and to supportive parents of gays, lesbians, and bisexuals.

## Social Studies

The social studies—history, political science, sociology, anthropology, and psychology—are fertile ground for gay and lesbian curricula. The topics of primary interest might include the following:

- cross-cultural and trans-historical understandings and representations of same-gender sexuality;
- the importance of certain homosexual people in various eras;
- the evolution of the modern gay identity;
- current gay issues, including legal rights, medicine, activism, and politics.

An 8–10 day curriculum, "The Stonewall Riots and the History of Gays and Lesbians in the U.S.," is one example of a such social studies unit.[95] Used successfully in U.S. history and sociology classes in the Cambridge (Mass.) public high school, the unit begins with contemporary journalistic accounts of the 1969 riots at the Stonewall Inn.[96] These raucous events pull students into a vivid conflict. They are then asked to consider such queries as,

- Who were these rioters?
- Why were they at the Stonewall Inn?
- Had there always been gay people in New York?
- What is the significance of this event historically? Was it a turning point in our national awareness?
- How does it compare with the other homosexual protests?

The curriculum then recapitulates the history of same-gender sexuality from the colonial period through the present, with special attention to urbanization, the impact of the World Wars, the ascendancy of science, and the characteristics of a liberation movement.

The following are selected comments from final examinations:

- I came in thinking I knew at least something about the gay movement, because I know many people who are gay. Yet I knew barely anything about the Stonewall incident. (White female)
- I didn't really care about gays and lesbians before I entered sociology but I learned so much about them. . . . My view of gays

and lesbians when I came into this class changed completely. (Asian female)

- It is very similar to the Black Civil Rights Movement. That helps me understand the movement more. The lesson also helped me to be open-minded to homosexuals. (African-American female)
- I was aware that the gay rights movement is still going on. . . . In this class I learned the history of homosexual identity. (White male)

Another example, *Struggle for Equality: The Lesbian and Gay Community*, published by People About Changing Education (PACE),[97] employs stories and case studies with some New York focus to relate modern gay/lesbian history to the quests for equality of women and people of color. PACE has also published *Transforming the Nation: Lesbian, Gay, Bisexual, and Transgendered U.S. Histories, 1945–1995*, weaving together issues of race and sexuality by decade.[98] A fourth social studies resource is *Becoming Visible*, edited by GLSEN Executive Director Kevin Jennings, the first gay/lesbian history anthology for high school students. It explores a number of cultures over 2,000 years and offers suggested questions and activities.[99] GLSEN has also helped produce *Out of the Past*, a film outlining the lives of several historical figures along with Kelli Peterson's contemporary struggle to found a Gay/Straight Alliance in Salt Lake City.

Although posters of prominent gay and lesbian historical figures are a fine teaser, they are most effective when the images come to life. Most students would not recognize Alan Turing's name, yet they would be fascinated to learn how this gay mathematician helped break the Nazi war codes and start the computer industry.[100] His arrest for homosexual activity, his forced hormone therapy, and his tragic suicide add a significant human rights dimension to his story. Students may also read or see a video of the play *Breaking the Code*, based on his life.[101]

Similar projects can be constructed around the lives of such notables as T. E. Lawrence, Dag Hammerskjöld, Bayard Rustin, Margaret Fuller, Susan B. Anthony, Katharine Lee Bates (lyricist of "America the Beautiful"), and Sweden's Queen Christina. However, teachers must be careful with lists of famous gays and lesbians, since the sexuality of historical figures can be dubious.

That minorities take pride in great forebears is understandable: Jews rejoice in the accomplishments of brethren like Einstein, Fanny Brice, and Lilian Wald; African Americans memorialize heroes like Phyllis Wheatley, W.E.B. DuBois, and Jackie Robinson. Yet complications do arise, for example, when Jews claim Columbus, blacks want Beethoven on their list, and gays point to American presidents. Evidence varies on all of these personages. As for homosexuals in the White House, there are more creditable objections to the surmise that because he shared a bed with another man for three years, Abraham Lincoln was gay[102] than to a similar hypothesis about James Buchanan.[103] In the end, though, both men may be better embodiments of nineteenth-century emotional possibilities than they are of homosexual eroticism. Yet the improbability of the latter should not deter one from honest exploration of the former. Some, like Eleanor Roosevelt, illustrate the limited usefulness of sexuality labels. But at the same time, although one can never know all the details of her female relationships (some with lesbians), students might recognize these ties as a significant factor in her life.[104]

Another area for study is the experience of gays and lesbians in the Holocaust. Several good books provide harrowing accounts,[105] and recent historiography has commemorated their suffering in the U.S. Holocaust Museum in Washington, D.C.[106] Moreover, students could learn that the victimization of Jews, Gypsies, and homosexuals under the Nazis points to important universal features of bigotry.[107] This discovery could open a window on prejudice and dehumanization in the world today. Finally, students could compare anti-Semites who deny that the Holocaust ever happened to those who allege that homosexuals were the perpetrators of it rather than its victims.[108] These are some of the topics that arise from the Facing History and Ourselves materials, including a passage from *One Teenager in Ten* on identities today,[109] Weimar criminal statutes, book burnings, treatment in the camps, and reparations.[110] These should be supplemented with such topics as Magnus Hirschfeld's own homosexuality, testimony of homosexual survivors, and other materials that give greater depth to the subject.

### Language Arts/Literature

Students may surely come to comprehend gay and lesbian lives by reading first- or third-person accounts of them, both fiction and biography, both prose and poetry. They may begin to ask some broad critical questions: Does Gertrude Stein[111] have something in common with Dorothy Allison or Henry James with Truman Capote? Why and how do gays and lesbians make art of their lives? Is there a gay male aesthetic—perhaps an amalgam of irony and outrageousness or exquisite observation and pathos? What common themes emerge from lesbian writing?

They should definitely investigate how some gay and lesbian writers' sexualities might have influenced their views of the world. Or put more abstractly, whether a book by a homosexual author is still a gay book even if it has no discernible gay or lesbian content? These are worthwhile inquiries for English, foreign language, and world literature classes.[112]

Sexuality is not a peripheral matter in understanding any writer and his or her work. Yet when teachers want to explore homosexual inflections, they might find that the faculty consensus on standards of relevance and acceptability have suddenly changed. That is what one teacher discovered when she was criticized for finding homosexual meanings in her literature syllabus:

> A few colleagues have reacted dismissively to what they call "fishing for extraneous debris" in literature. My response: what the narrow eye views as "debris" is in fact central to many human lives. I challenge these colleagues to broaden their vision to include others beside themselves, beside the common Everyman which exclusively dominated literary vision and practice for far too long. . . . We, as readers and teachers, can know that the fear of displacement comes from the fallacy of one center.[113]

Those writers who invite this analysis include both the pantheon of homosexual authors who are already part of the school canon, such as Auden, Albee, Anderson, Baldwin, Hansberry, Forster, Williams, Woolf, Cather, Whitman, Wilde, Proust, Gide, and Verlaine, and those perhaps lesser known, who could be taught: Radcliffe Hall, Amy Lowell, Hart Crane, Isherwood, Renée Vivien, Rita Mae Brown, Nancy Garden, Horatio Alger Jr., David Leavitt, Mishima, Mary Renault, and others.[114]

Writers whose sexualities are open to debate may already be included in existing courses: Dickinson,[115] Tennyson,[116] G. M. Hopkins,[117] Langston Hughes,[118] Melville,[119] Thoreau,[120] Twain,[121] Goethe,[122] Kerouac[123]and others. The crucial point in studying them from a gay or lesbian perspective is not to prove them homosexual, though better cases can be made for some than others. Rather, as one should do with other historical figures, one raises the homosexual possibility to gain insight through hypothesis. If it can be shown that certain authors experienced same-gender attraction, the facts that modern gay labels did not exist 110 years ago or that no evidence can be found of their erotic practice and group affiliation ought not frustrate the enterprise. The valuable academic questions in each case are, Did these feelings have any significance for the author, and was there a *possible* influence on the work?

For example, analysis of Thoreau's poem "Sympathy" ("Lately, alas, I knew a gentle boy") is enriched by considering its homoromanticism. Further, Thoreau's possible homosexuality creates an interesting new criterion for probing the mind-set of *Walden*.[124] This exercise would be intellectually satisfying, even if one could not find reference to gay self-awareness either in *Walden* or in the journals.[125] As Eve Kosofsky Sedgwick has written: "No one *can* know in *advance* where the limits of a gay-centered inquiry are to be drawn, or where a gay theorizing of and through even the hegemonic high culture of the Euro-American tradition may need or be able to lead."[126]

Langston Hughes's poem "Café: 3 A.M." is about undercover police officers arresting "fairies" around 1950.[127] In eleven lines it sketches the cruelty of homophobia, the causes of homosexuality, and archly, not being able to differentiate a lesbian from a policewoman. Besides the provocative issue of Hughes's sexuality,[128] students can think about how being black and writing in Harlem might have shaped his empathetic view of homosexuals. The poem can also serve as an introduction to other Harlem Renaissance figures who were openly gay and lesbian, like Bessie Smith, Gladys Bentley, Ma Rainey, Countee Cullen, and Wallace Thurman.[129]

Some teachers have actually taught Willa Cather's "Paul's Case"[130] without reference to the homosexuality of either the title character or the author. Although it may not be critical to know details about Cather's women companions, "Paul's Case" comes alive with a gay lens. Discovery of Cather's early condemnation of Oscar Wilde and her own masquerade as a man lends even greater nuance to this short story.[131]

A similar argument can be made for studying *Billy Budd* as a tale of repressed homoerotic desire.[132] Alternative readings of *Moby Dick* and "Bartleby the Scrivener" might come from learning about Melville's views of sexuality in the South Sea islands and the passionate relationship between him and Hawthorne.[133] The routine unsensationalized inclusion of homosexual possibilities in the classical high school literature curriculum would have a profoundly positive effect.

Collections of stories by modern gay and lesbian authors offer opportunities as well.[134] When using less-established writers, one must be ready to defend one's selections on grounds of student needs and abilities and the quality of the literature. Teachers have already begun documenting their classroom experiences with newer gay and lesbian texts to guide and encourage their peers.[135]

In the arena of young adult fiction, a number of bibliographies, some well-annotated, have been prepared for teachers and librarians wishing to add gay/lesbian titles to their syllabi and collections.[136] Some of these books lack style or substance; others ignore or slight female and minority homosexuals. Of the approximately sixty books published between 1969 and 1992, only a few have gay or lesbian main characters, and the ones that do mostly portray unhappy or tragic figures.[137] Newer inclusive and positive ones, like Jacqueline Woodson's *From the Notebooks of Melanin Sun*, Paula Boock's *Dare, Truth, or Promise,* and Nancy Garden's *Annie on My Mind*, deserve a place in comprehensive multicultural middle and junior high school collections.[138]

Lastly, language arts teachers should consider gay and lesbian topics for student writing, such as opinion pieces about civil rights questions, research on historical figures, fiction with gay and lesbian characters, and first-person exercises in the voice of a homosexual person.

For gay and lesbian students, personal writing is an outlet for self-expression that is at once tantalizing, daunting, and crucial: "Narrative writing, telling our own stories and telling the truth about our own experience, is essential to the attainment of literacy."[139] Ambivalent and closeted students might not risk the disclosure that genuine, even passionate, writing demands.[140] Nevertheless, teachers could break down this reticence by communicating receptivity, creating respectful and discrete writing groups, or guaranteeing that they will be the only readers of designated pieces. Sometimes, despite such assurances, the voice of the gay or lesbian student remains indirect and the sexuality implied, such as when one young lesbian wrote fantastically about "a matriarchal, female only, cat kingdom."[141]

## The Arts

Teachers should not slight the importance of sexuality in the fine and performing arts. Painting, sculpture, photography, and film are related to sexual imagination and desire as well as to other human qualities. Students in art history and appreciation will find that the homosexuality of certain artists is reflected in their creations.[142] Renaissance art is ripe with homoeroticism in, for example, Michelangelo and Caravaggio.[143] More modern figures include Beardsley, Kahlo, Johns, Rauschenberg, Warhol, and Hockney.

This perspective extends into the fields of music and dance: Tchaikovsky's sexual unhappiness, Benjamin Britten's "Billy Budd," Chopin, Ravel, Copeland, Bernstein, Virgil Thompson, Stephen Sondheim, and the popular music of composers and performers like Billy Strayhorn, Gladys Bentley, Bessie Smith, Elton John, Boy George, KD Lang, and Melissa Etheridge.[144] Finally, students can study the choreography and performance of Diaghilev, Nijinsky, Michael Bennet, and Alvin Ailey.

Correspondingly, young people might need to express views and feelings about sexuality in their own artwork. A Massachusetts high school photography teacher has developed a curriculum in which students document something about which they care deeply. One of the models she uses to inspire them is Duane Michals's photo sequences, demonstrating an unusual approach and technique, an interest in sexuality, and finally, a gay sensibility and content.[145] Self-critiques of technique and content are required. The teacher has found that photography gives gay and lesbian students another language to articulate their identities with varying degrees of directness. One student's work over the course of several years explored her place in her family and eventually her coming out.[146] One effective resource depicting gay and lesbian adolescent lives in photos and text is "The Shared Heart," a traveling exhibition created by Adam Mastoon.[147]

Drama classes can bring the subject to life with performance and role-playing. In her segment of the video "Gay Youth," Gina Gutierrez reads the part of an Orthodox Jewish girl spurned by her family for breaking tradition. Gina then analogizes to gays and lesbians. Young people could perform scenes from full-length plays and screenplays like "The Children's Hour,"[148] "The Sign in Sidney Brustein's Window,"[149] "Torchsong Trilogy,"[150] "As Is,"[151] "The Normal Heart,"[152] "The Color Purple,"[153] "Consenting Adult,"[154] "Falsettos,"[155] "Fifth of July,"[156] and others.[157] Original student work or improvisational pieces evoke an even more personal voice, such as are expressed in the projects "West Los Angeles Fringe Benefits: Queer Youth Theater" and Boston's "True Colors Out Youth Theater," both community-based efforts.[158]

In addition, the arts can be used to persuade and create change. To reduce homophobia in their schools and communities, for example, students might perform skits about gay and lesbian life or design words and images for posters and other displays.

## The Sciences

Although sciences like math, physics, and chemistry have no apparent connection to social issues, they should not be written off.[159] Occasional biographic details of important scientific figures are common curriculum components, especially in the early grades and general science courses. Every student knows about Marie Curie, George Washington Carver, and Charles Darwin. Could they not learn as well that DaVinci, Francis Bacon, Florence Nightingale, John Maynard Keynes, Margaret Mead, and perhaps Washington Carver himself were gay, lesbian, or bisexual? Moreover, particularly in mathematics, hypothetical problems involving domestic situations could be set in homosexual households: "Martha and Jane are buying champagne for their commitment ceremony . . . "

Substantive study is warranted in biology, biochemistry, and psychobiology, where the connections among body, mind, and behavior have been probed. (See Chapter 3.) Science teachers could devise a short unit, like the 3–5 day "The History and Nature of Homosexuality and Its 'Causes,'" which lays out the changing scientific understandings of same-gender desire from ancient Greece to contemporary findings.[160] One of its themes is the influence of culture and politics on scientific inquiry, a crucial topic in the history of science. Students could easily spend a semester weighing the purportedly objective responses of science to such social phenomena as poverty, crime, feminism, and homosexuality. Valuable lessons could be found, for example, in analyzing parallels in past and current diagnoses of the Irish, Jews, blacks, women, homosexuals, and others.

## Physical Education and Sports

There is no branch of curriculum that speaks more directly to gender roles than physical education and sports. On most gym floors and playing fields children encounter the rigid enforcement of gender expectations.[161] The usual modalities include the following:

- segregation by gender;
- encouragement of aggressivity and competitiveness in boys;
- discouragement of aggressivity and competitiveness in girls;
- use of homophobic intimidation and invective to enforce both masculine and feminine behavior.

Heterosexism is common currency in athletics and physical education. Coaches and players are known to motivate male performance with insults. To forge solidarity, build morale, and maximize aggression in male team sports, the same methods are used as are employed in the military. (See Chapter 4.) Fear of being labeled effeminate drives hypermasculinity, and athletes crudely distance themselves from homosexuality through ridicule. Boys frequently assail opposing teams with sexist and homophobic taunts. It is no accident that gay and lesbian students often report harassment by "the jocks."

Gay male professional athletes could help counter these outrages, if they were not generally invisible. Open perhaps with teammates, they are nevertheless rarely public about their sexuality. Some, like Jim Bouton and Greg Louganis, who have come out after their professional careers, may have some influence, but active sports figures would likely have greater positive effect.[162]

By a reverse standard, female athletes are accused of lesbianism in proportion to their skill and dedication to sport. Off the field, girls must go out of their way to be feminine if they want to escape suspicion. Lesbian athletes may shrink from top performance or even from participation. Pat Griffin observes that lesbianism in women's sports is like "a large lavender elephant in the middle of the locker room, ignored by all."[163]

For all the good will generated by a Navratilova, a forbidding homophobia still lingers, for example, in women's golf and tennis. Some feel lesbian golfers threaten the sport by confirming existing prejudice toward female competitors. Others fear tennis would be devastated by numbers of mature lesbians traveling the circuit with younger players.

In any event, teachers and coaches cannot wait for professional athletes to end the bigotry that poisons physical education and sport. They must intervene early to break down sexist assumptions and practices and confront homophobia. This strategy has to include:

- ending gender segregation in physical education;
- exploring motivations for physical fitness, performance, and competition;
- stressing the importance of teamwork;
- understanding the meaning of winning;
- introducing and valuing cooperative games;
- discussing and challenging the social dictates of masculinity and femininity;
- interrupting gender, sexuality-based, and other insults;
- clarifying the differences among and relative acceptability of competitiveness, aggression, and violence on and off the field;
- punishing athletes seriously for sexist and homophobic remarks or actions.

## Libraries

Libraries should be well equipped and accessible to students and teachers seeking comprehensive information on homosexuality and gay and lesbian lives.[164] Especially in schools that forbid instruction on these subjects, the library can be a last resort for desperate, or simply curious, young people. On the grounds that in expanding collections they are not proselytizing, school librarians may have greater discretion in ordering materials than teachers or counselors do.

Money may be an issue. If it did not compromise professional neutrality, the librarian could probably find eager book donors in the community. The Sexual Minority Advisory Council of the Seattle schools, for example, composed a list of titles and secured a grant from the local Pride Foundation to purchase library books. The award raised a flap in the community, but acceptance was left to the discretion of individual librarians.[165] In another instance, a book for gay teens and their friends was allowed to remain on the shelves with the proviso that parents could notify the librarian if they did not want their children to take the volume out.[166] Opposition might be answered by making space as well for books that are critical of homosexuality,[167] although such materials could harm students who give them credence and have no countervailing guidance.

Getting the volumes on the shelves is only the first hurdle, however. Access and privacy concerns must also be addressed. For holdings to reach the most students, they must be discretely obtainable. Many interested young people are understandably worried about expressing their needs to a librarian. Nor do they want to be browsing special sections, reading in open spaces, checking books out, and creating records of their borrowing. All of these qualms are compounded in the presence of peer library assistants.

Librarians ought to minimize the risks. Beyond offering private alcoves, they might scatter gay and lesbian titles throughout the collection, lend materials on an honor system, or put some resources in other parts of the school such as a guidance library or student resource center with open borrowing.[168] A Kansas City, Missouri, public librarian recommends a range of fiction and nonfiction and warns against leaving a title on a phone message or sending notices on postcards.[169] Finally, vandalized or stolen materials should be quickly replaced.

## *Elementary School Curriculum*

The best place to introduce gays and lesbians in preschool and the lower grades is in connection with teasing and name-calling based on gender-role or sexuality.[170] Children can be taught at incremental levels of intellectual and moral sophistication why it is wrong to discriminate against those who are different in ways that should not be condemned. (See Chapter 11.)

After first doing an inventory of classroom images (posters, book illustrations, visitors, and so forth) that contribute to various forms of stereotyping, teachers should set about changing those depictions.[171] The earlier children's contact with difference is initiated, the more certain the inhibition of prejudice.[172] Alvin Poussaint has noted: "There has been a significant movement by educators to address the issues of diversity training, appreciating differences early in the process. There is a movement to get this education into the first, second, and third grade."[173]

**Family Constellations.** In preschools and elementary grades, teachers often start by introducing various kinds of families and relationships in terms that children can understand.[174] This is the approach taken by the Teaching Tolerance Project in their "Starting Small" guide.[175] Sometimes the students themselves are able to provide examples of same-gender family arrangements among people they know. In the pre-K to first-grade classroom, children from various backgrounds are able to engage with each other to piece together an understanding of "love, marriage, divorce, and relationships."[176]

The curriculum should illustrate the daily life of gay families. The outcries over the bedroom scene in *Daddy's Roommate*,[177] which once topped the American Library Association's banned book list[178] were undeserved. A child is able to construe any bedroom as the place where parents sleep.

*Age-Appropriateness.* The gay/lesbian curriculum should keep pace with children's growing comprehension of sexuality.[179] However, a classroom does represent a range of sexual knowledge and maturity that cannot be predicted by grade. In a sexually explicit television age, neither do reading levels necessarily correlate with sexual understanding. How are teachers then to fashion an age-appropriate curriculum?

One education professor warns that raising homosexuality with elementary school children is ill advised, even if some ask about it. He fears such discussion

> may embarrass many of the other children, expose them to things they are not developmentally ready for, undermine their modesty.... At a time when society greatly overstimulates children sexually, schools should not become part of the problem. Rather, they should do everything possible to aid the healthy "quieting" of sexual interest that occurs during elementary-school years.[180]

This view is regrettable. Most children, even the youngest ones, are exposed through the media, if not directly, to a number of disquieting and often sensationalized aspects of life, like greed, anger, violence, death, drug abuse, and drunkenness. One role of parents and teachers is to help young children understand these things. Would anyone suggest that youngsters could not to any degree understand death? Does it help children for teachers to pretend such things do not exist?

Besides, human sexuality is itself not shameful, though its commercial uses and misrepresentations often are. When teachers "quiet" students' sexual interests, even those elicited by exploitative media, they merely aggravate the ignorance instead of teaching responsibly to children's curiosity. Reactionaries seem to believe that sexual interests are equivalent to sexual activity. They are not. Neither, despite legislative intent, do young people cease to be sexual when their natural inquisitiveness is stifled. The corrective for societal overstimulation is thoughtful contextualization, not a blindfold.

Jonathan Silin's work with elementary school students has shown that adults may underestimate children's ability to notice and understand the sexual world around them.[181] Most adults begin by wrongly assuming that a child's sexual imagination and experience begin at puberty. Few people, honestly recalling their own childhood years, would deny that sexual interest and pleasure, however uninformed, began before the age of twelve. Children are also aware to some degree of older people's sexualities and have questions about them. A South Dakota twenty-nine-year veteran teacher was fired and then rehired for his "poor judgment" in responding to fourth-, fifth-, and sixth-grade boys' questions about homosexual intercourse. Although the community faulted his explicitness, they might better have targeted his leading introduction to the topic: "It's something that is very much frowned on; most people do not believe in it; you're going to think it's gross."[182]

Let teachers be guided by student inquiries about sexuality and relationships. Allow peers to respond in their own words with what they know. Such exchanges are common and rarely accurate, but having them in schools permits teacher embellishment and correction. For instance, when one teacher approached a crying first-grader, he asked her, "How do I know if I'm gay?" He had just given a welcome-back kiss to a male friend who had been absent, prompting a girl to remark that he must be gay. The boy also wondered if his father must also be gay because his dad kissed him and told him that he loved him every day.[183] In another instance, a kindergarten teacher came on two girls arguing in the "Housekeeping Corner" over which of them ought to be the "mommy." She suggested that a family could have two mommies, resolving the dispute and beginning a spontaneous lesson.[184]

Children may also be introduced to gay and lesbian families through peer show and tell, picture collages of family groupings, stories from books, teacher storytelling, videos, and class visitors—all vehicles for portraying homosexual people as familiar and nonthreatening, working, playing, and loving human beings. They should be presented alongside, and as part of, other multicultural groups and nontraditional family constellations. One teacher has used a nurturing father bunny in a story to introduce the concept of families without mothers.[185] These first steps in de-stigmatization help all children, those who already suffer from gender stereotyping and homophobia and those who may some day discover their own or a loved one's homosexuality.

In the lower grades, adult explanations are best kept simple for students of limited attentiveness and understanding, although children might know more than the teacher thinks. They could be aware of homosexuality and be familiar with some of the vocabulary used to denote it. Children with homosexual parents, other relatives, or family friends are apt to have more information than others do. Such students are valuable discussants. If other class members voice discomfort with the topic or disapproval, teachers might comfort them with assurances that they understand how they feel, while urging them to respect other students and homosexual people.

In the middle grades, when children can begin more a complex analysis of social justice, they should be able to understand more about diversity within the homosexual community, to recognize heterosexism, and to appreciate the contributions of famous gay and lesbian people to our culture. For example, several classes at an independent K–8 school observed Gay and Lesbian History Month by performing at an all-school assembly. Sixth-graders narrated and acted out the Stonewall riots and the first Gay Pride march; another skit, complete with Native American dancing, explained the berdache tradition; a third presented reports on the origin of the pink triangle and on Colorado's antigay rights Amendment 2; a fourth presented a scene from a young-adult novel about a teenage lesbian; and a fifth performed a short play about homophobic name-calling.[186]

At another assembly, this one in a public middle school, students performed original skits on racial, sexual, and homophobic harassment. In one, a boy excused his failure to catch a ball by claiming the thrower was a "fag" and threw "like a girl." The thrower was then shunned. Another featured a high school student confiding to her best female friend that she was a lesbian. The friend quickly made an excuse to exit, leaving the lesbian to "drop her head in her hands and gently shake in despair."[187] The performances and subsequent question and answer session were a hit.

A teacher at New York's Harvey Milk School has created a web page with "The Story of Harvey Milk" and "Stonewall" for both elementary and middle school viewing.[188] Filmmakers Debra Chasnoff and Helen Cohen have produced a series of videos for use with young students, *Respect for All: Preventing Homophobia Among School-Age Children*.[189] Among its parts: "My Family Is Special" (K–3) is a documentary of nontraditional families; "Don't Call Me That" (grades 3–6) addresses name-calling and teasing; "Shattering Stereotypes" (grades 4–8) portrays gay and lesbian historical figures and professionals.

A 1995 traveling photo exhibit, "Love Makes a Family: Living in Lesbian and Gay Families" captures thirty families with homosexual members in group portraiture with accompanying texts.[190] It is available in two editions, one for grades K–6 and one for older students and adults. An unspoken point of the pictures is that without the explanatory labels, one cannot tell these families from any others.

***Opposition to Curriculum for Younger Students.*** In Amherst, Massachusetts, a town with a sizable homosexual population, parents went to court to bar "Love Makes a Family" from several elementary schools on the grounds that the photographs would create "an intimidating, hostile, humiliating, and sexually offensive education environment."[191] The judge refused to block it.[192] A similar outcry was heard in Madison, Wisconsin,[193] where parents at one school finally decided to have it, as long as dissenters could exempt their children from the viewing.[194]

Some adults are apprehensive about what such images might suggest to young students, particularly whether they might have an impact on their developing sexualities. It is perfectly natural for children and adolescents to fret over what their own same-gender emotions and activities mean. They need to understand that many people have such feelings and experiences and that some of them develop into gays and lesbians, others into heterosexuals, and some into bisexuals. Some others grow tired of limiting labels and reject them altogether. Of course, when teachers do not signal that the heterosexual outcome is better than the others, some parents become distraught, thinking their children are not being properly informed or intimidated.

The governor of Colorado, no less, has found himself discussing homosexuality with fifth- and sixth-graders. Responding to queries about his interests, he said that he had just read a book about a gay Italian soldier in World War II. The Jefferson County schools superintendent opined, "The great thing about the governor, what makes him a wonderful teacher, is that he doesn't talk down to kids. They asked him what he reads and he told them a story that was important to him."[195] Unfortunately, the governor later apologized in response to criticism.

***Exercising Good Judgment.*** Teachers must be ready to stand by their pedagogy when people object, as some invariably do. They must take care, nevertheless, not to set themselves up in an untenable position. An example of each:

- Two North Dakota nurses were guest speakers in an AIDS awareness class for seventh- and eighth-graders. They were accused of "mental rape," even though explicit language and queries came directly from students and some fourteen-year-olds in the district were "on their third sexual partner."[196]
- Invited to a middle school health fair, a New Hampshire community AIDS agency displayed prevention pamphlets with graphic "Safe Sex Guidelines for Gay Men." Parents and administrators were irate.[197]

The nurses in the first incident were responding properly in a controlled setting to specific student concerns. The second incident, though, is problematical because it was too loose. The fair, to which students had been brought, was not a planned response to their questions. Further, there was no mechanism for teachers to shape the environment or even to participate in the students' learning on the spot. Schools have to assume responsibility for teaching and learning when they allow sexually explicit information to reach younger students.

The goal of all the above curricular suggestions is to devote substantial class attention to homosexuality within various disciplines and at many grade levels. However, not every mention of homosexuality needs to become a lesson nor should teachers always anticipate classroom discussion or debate. On the contrary, the issue can be de-sensationalized through frequent appropriate referencing when it is not the main focus. For instance, openly gay or lesbian class speakers might come to talk about their professions or expertise and make only incidental reference to their sexuality. It is desirable that students come to appreciate that sexual orientation, though important, is just one aspect of a person's life.

## Sanitizing

### A Double Standard

Some fearful educators might attempt to tidy up the content. Most would rather teach about orientation and identity than behavior. Yet representations of heterosexual romance, love, and even lust abound in existing curricula. Even the Bible, one of the earliest books of instruction, has its share of sexual tales. None would hesitate to put *Romeo and Juliet*, *Othello*, and *The Return of the Native* on their syllabi. Reaching for diversity, some classes read *I Know Why the Caged Bird Sings*, and *The Autobiography of Malcolm X*. No good teacher could lead discussions of these books without addressing sexual behavior and relationships. Some may even discuss Thomas Jefferson and Sally Hemmings or Jack Kennedy's peccadilloes.

For all that, when it comes to homosexual characters and historical figures, their mere orientation appears to be more than enough to tackle. Their loves and sexual behavior are either unimaginable, and therefore nonexistent, or unspeakable, and therefore an expendable embarrassment. Even so, students know that gays and lesbians have sexual relationships. Some, in fact, assume homosexuality is only about sex. A well-conceived and competently taught curriculum ought to correct that misapprehension by putting the sex into homosexuality without exaggeration or distortion.

If curricula do not extend beyond orientation by speaking to gay and lesbian sexuality then it will appear to have been censored because it is dirty. A teacher's hesitancy, embarrassment, or enforced silence only furthers that supposition. Finally, if a humanities teacher responds to students' sincere questions by referring them to the sex education specialist, homosexuality is needlessly torn from its historical and literary context.

## Making Reasonable Choices

Teachers may have to compromise with majority sensibilities in their choice of texts however. Many excellent homosexual novels, short stories, poems, and plays employ sexual vocabulary and imagery that might discredit the entire enterprise. Just a sentence in an otherwise nonobjectionable story could incite hysterical community reaction. Such has been the history of many fine books touching on controversial matters, Salinger's *Catcher in the Rye* and Malamud's *The Assistant*, for example. Practical judgment dictates matching the level of explicitness to that of acceptable heterosexual writing. Even then, many communities will try to impose a different standard.

Teachers, therefore, must choose carefully and prepare to defend their choices on scholarly and pedagogical grounds. There is little wisdom, for instance, in selecting a reading for ninth-graders that reports on vaginal cigarette smoking in Jazz Age Harlem, no matter how stellar the source.[198] Discretion favors excerpting portions of such a chapter.

## Student Responses

To allay her fears and "cross the boundaries that seemed to be set in unspoken stone," one boarding school teacher planned an elaborate rationale for teaching *The Normal Heart* along with *Romeo and Juliet* and *Master Harold and the Boys* in her ninth-grade drama class: "I recount this thematic and structural analysis of the plays to point out how fully prepared I was to defend my book selection based on literary elements and dramatic theory."[199] In the end her choice was not challenged. *The Normal Heart* prompted stories about gay relatives and friends with AIDS and inspired this student comment: "I didn't realize before reading this book that there are many relationships in which there is a real bond of love between two men. . . . I had no idea that there were gay men who loved other men as much as two heterosexuals do."[200]

Even in the resistance of another student to the play, one senses a potential for growth:

> I found it very unenjoyable to read about the intimate descriptions of relationships between homosexuals. Some would say because I admit that I'm homophobic, but that raises another issue. I may be homophobic, but by

that I mean I'm not comfortable reading, seeing, or hearing about homosexual behavior. I do not have a hate for all homosexuals.[201]

The tension in this ninth-grader between being comfortable and being fair is a promise of her overcoming an aversion to the unfamiliar.

Homosexuality sparks distinct reactions in different populations. Despite the just cited example, gender is often one predictable determinant. (See Chapter 4.) The colorful sexuality in the gay play *Torch Song Trilogy* educed contrasting responses from two seniors in a two-thirds minority magnet high school.[202] The female view was represented by Maria:

When I read this book I felt like I was doing something wrong because of the sex that was mentioned. I feel uncomfortable reading or seeing movies with this kind of activity. But I don't think there is anything wrong with studying this book in school . . . because instead of getting all the dirty stuff of the reading we are allowed to examine how it is written. It even makes us think of homosexuality—that these two people actually love each other.

And a male view from Michael:

The only thing that bugged me was the very sexual, graphic nature of the piece. It just didn't sit too well when I thought about this being done for a class. Our society is very sexual and shouldn't have to hide that fact, but there is a contingent that might really be offended. I guess I would have picked another book, that's all, but it was good.

A profitable class session would explore whether Maria's sensitivity extends to all sexual portrayals, whether Michael's characterization of others' sensibilities includes his own, what he thinks about homosexual relationships, and how these two students might inform or change each other's arguments.

### Including the Negatives

Erotics are not the only target of sanitizers. Curriculum writers are surely tempted to present only the positive features of a minority community, assuming other information to be defamatory. Teachers are not cheerleaders, however. As much as they might want to give hope to homosexual students and correct heterosexist assumptions, they have to fashion a credible curriculum. Mature students see through propaganda and faculty are demeaned by teaching it.

Those for instance who believe that the media's fixation on drag queens and sadomasochists necessitates banishing them from view are overreacting. Consider one archetypal letter to Ann Landers from a thirty-four-year-old closeted gay man: "[I am tired of] the effeminate, limp-wristed, nasal-voiced queens who jump in front of the cameras and make a spectacle of themselves . . . [and] deny all of us the opportunity to be accepted as decent, constructive members of the community."203

An honest curriculum demands that the whole truth be told. It would not shy away from such spectacle nor miss analyzing it, as well as the responses it elicits in the straight and gay communities. Furthermore, it would invite students to compare this man's dismay to insider critiques of "embarrassing" behavior in other minority groups such as Jews, blacks, Irish, and Hispanics. A vivid lesson on what it means to internalize the voice of oppression would be a great gift.

The wording of the Massachusetts Department of Education's student rights regulations regarding curricular diversity may have it right:

> What you learn in courses must fairly present the culture, history, activities, and contributions of all people and groups. Overall, the books and other educational materials your school buys must include examples and situations which show men, women, and members of minority groups in positive roles.204

The key word is "fairly." Although one need not balance every ennobling chapter with a vicious one, curricular truth telling does require the delicate inclusion of flawed characters and ignominious episodes.

History and literature lessons should recognize not only homosexual icons like social reformer Jane Addams and politician Harvey Milk, and authors Walt Whitman and Virginia Wolf; they should also extend to the nefarious, Ernst Roehm and Roy Cohn, for example. The dubious, like Jean Genet, should also be mentioned and others who merely push the boundaries of propriety, like Pat Califa and Leslie Feinberg. In other words, the same spirit that embraces homosexuality as a rightful part of the curriculum also recognizes the varieties of gay and lesbian experience. Not only is homosexuality broader than white, Western, and male; it is also neither uniformly liberal, eternally beneficent, nor totally undisturbing.

By presenting a truthful portrait, one also guards against critics who accuse gay-positive educators of having their own agenda of misrepresentation and their own interest "in image and self-promotion, in panegyric and hagiography, in past grievances and scores to settle."205

Simultaneously, one must be cautious about texts that confirm negative stereotypes, including the unavoidable dire end of homosexual characters. Poor reading choices and poorly guided discussion can reinforce negative attitudes rather than challenging them.206 The treacherous perversity of Claggart in "Billy Budd," for example, or the suicide in "Paul's Case," demands commentary. Students must learn to distinguish between individual and group traits and between those that are innate and those that are induced. Although we cannot blame heterosexism for every gay imperfection, both its societal and internalized forms can lead to misery and wretched behavior. Teachers ought to balance a pathetic, sad, or evil portrait with a more representative affirming view. The latter are afforded generally by modern depictions.

Good curriculum gives gay, lesbian, bisexual, and transgendered students the deep satisfaction of seeing something of themselves in the lessons of the school. It gives them a sense of rootedness in the culture and a glimpse of people whose lives inspire or warn. Heterosexual students, for their part, have their universe stretched. They see how much they have in common with homosexual people and what they do not share. Both discoveries are instructive and personally enriching.[207]

## Publishers

Publishers' profit-driven aversion to risk holds curricula back from greater inclusiveness. Reformers who demand more diversity are sometimes accused of being politically correct and of wanting to dilute a curriculum's impact and diminish its rigor. Moves to depict the lives of minorities and women are attacked as balkanizing, distorting, and even unpatriotic. In the political center, Arthur Schlesinger Jr. decries multiculturalism as an agent of national disunity.[208] On the left, Tod Gitlin worries over the role of identity politics in breaking up the progressive alliance.[209] And the Right have an apoplexy when sexuality is added to a multicultural perspective they already despise.[210]

Gays and lesbians would probably consider it an achievement to follow the path of women into textbooks, though women themselves still have a way to go:

> For two decades, educators and women's history specialists have pressured textbook publishers to integrate women's history material into the body of each chapter of text. And the result? Women's history has been upgraded all right—from little boxes squeezed in the page margins, to half-page and full-page boxes, all the way to separate sections and chapters. . . . Many experts maintain . . . that presenting women's history in isolation encourages teachers and students to skip over the new and unfamiliar material.[211]

Most textbook publishers are guided by the wishes of their largest markets, states with centralized curriculum-setting authority like California and Texas. Adult and student lobbyists did persuade California's curriculum committee to mandate inclusion of homosexuality in health texts, but that was the limit of its largesse. In Texas, on the other hand, Holt, Rinehart and Winston held to its principles by pulling out of competition when the state board of education ordered 300 changes in its health textbook. Among the unacceptable passages were references to teenage homosexuality and illustrations of self-examination for breast and testicular cancers.[212]

Facing such responses to health texts, where omission of homosexuality is unconscionable, is it any wonder that publishers are loath to include gays and lesbians in history and literature? Even in college history textbooks, reference to homosexuals is superficial at best.[213] One recent review of more than fifteen U.S. history texts found that "none mentioned lesbians, some mentioned gay men via the AIDS epidemic and the Names Quilt, and only one mentioned their March on Washington in 1987."[214] The gay and lesbian civil rights movement is entirely ignored in high school history texts, although AIDS sometimes appears, often inaccurately.[215]

Voyager Company and the American Social History Project[216] put several gay and lesbian vignettes in their CD-ROM "Who Built America?" In the mid-1990s it won the American Historical Association's biennial prize for "the most outstanding contribution to the teaching and learning of history." After distributing 12,000 copies of the disc free with new computer shipments to public schools, Apple Computer stopped providing it in response to public objections and Voyager's refusal to remove references to turn-of-the-century homosexuality, to birth control, and to abortion. Taken from historical documents and oral histories, these segments amounted to the equivalent of 40 pages and 15 minutes of sound out of the 5,000 pages and over 4 hours of sound.[217]

On the other hand, Chelsea House Publishers has launched two book series for the general and adolescent audience: Lives of Notable Gay Men and Lesbians (over forty titles); and Issues in Lesbian and Gay Life (over thirty titles).[218]

## National Curriculum Projects

A few prominent organizations want to make gay and lesbian curricula a part of the nation's schoolwork. The Sex Information and Education Council of the U.S. (SIECUS) has developed "Guidelines for Comprehensive Sexuality Education" (1991). A K–12 document that includes "Sexual Identity and Orientation," it covers key concepts on the subject of homosexuality at four levels of difficulty.

Project 21, an offshoot of the Gay and Lesbian Alliance Against Defamation, is a consortium of organizations and individuals that has been lobbying curriculum-setting authorities at the state and local levels since 1990 to change policy and has provided resources to classrooms and libraries. They have also written capsule biographies of prominent literary and historical figures and other units for elementary through high school.[219]

The Gay, Lesbian, and Straight Education Network's Gay and Lesbian History Month Project assists teachers in bringing displays and lectures to their districts.[220] GLSEN's first gay/lesbian history conference featured ten workshops and three plenaries with prominent historians and writers, and experienced teachers.[221] It has also sponsored student essay contests and book distributions. Some local chapters have begun comprehensive curriculum projects.[222]

The Harvard Gay and Lesbian School Issues Project has developed a number of curricular units in history, literature, and science for incorporation into existing high school courses. A staff development manual, bibliographies, and other aids for teachers are also available.[223]

The Secondary Schools Curriculum Development Project of the American Council of Learned Societies has published a series of pamphlets and curricular suggestions.[224] The Center for Research on Women at Wellesley College offers guidelines for inclusive teaching.[225] And Amnesty International publishes a gay/lesbian teacher's resource guide and curriculum outline.[226]

## Faculty Training

More than falsehood and misrepresentation, "a sexual silence dominates schools of education."[227] Therefore most teachers are not ready for the task demanded of them in this chapter: In one survey 67 percent of administrators rated their teachers "not adequately prepared" to teach human sexuality and sexual relationships.[228] That younger health teachers in one study were not as comfortable teaching about homosexuality as their more experienced colleagues is a further indictment of university preparation.[229]

Curricular incorporation of homosexuality is particularly dependent on staff development, from the standpoints both of content and methodology. Regardless of the commitment from central offices, the project will rise or fall on teacher knowledge, skill, and comfort level. Faculty must be primed even to introduce the subject in the classroom. They have to work out their own feelings about homosexuality, be trained to handle extreme student or parent responses, and be ready for the "are you one of them" query.

Teachers can indeed learn to deal with this subject as they have accommodated to other controversial issues. Nevertheless, a degree of will-

ingness to use these curricula is a prerequisite. It would be a mistake at
the outset to force all faculty to teach about homosexuality, especially
without proper training. A reluctant, unhappy teacher is worse than none
at all. Many students are good insincerity and sarcasm detectors. It
would set the effort back for teachers to give the impression they were
being forced to undertake a curriculum about which they were queasy or
which they opposed.

Some training is not optional. Every teacher must be sensitized to heterosexist behaviors, taught how to interrupt them, and required to do so.
If some were still uncomfortable with curriculum, it would be better to
begin with those who are willing. Curricular change can not flourish as a
top-down mandate. Once a critical mass of support has been established
among cooperative faculty at the grass roots, further persuasion may be
attempted, lesson plans shared, and so on.

Two effective videos have been made for elementary school staff development. The first, Chasnoff and Cohen's 75-minute *It's Elementary:
Talking About Gay Issues in School* uses classroom footage from seven public and independent schools to motivate faculty to raise name-calling,
family diversity, and gay/lesbian stereotypes with students. The second,
*Both of My Moms' Names Are Judy* was produced by the Lesbian and Gay
Parents Association as part of their workshop "Overcoming Homophobia in the Elementary Classroom."[230] In just 10 minutes it presents a be-
guiling lineup of racially diverse children, ages 7–10, talking about their
love for their homosexual family members, how they feel about homophobic harassment, and the school changes they would like to see.

However teacher comfort and good intentions are still not enough.[231]
Some mastery of the content is also essential, and it is widely lacking.
Only recently have a small number of colleges offered gay studies elec-
tives; a handful may integrate some material into broader courses. One
can have little assurance that either incoming or veteran educators have
had any academic exposure. In a study of secondary health teachers, although 37 percent felt comfortable teaching about homosexuality, only 20
percent believed themselves competent to do so. In addition, 66 percent
identified the mass media as their chief source of information on the subject.[232]

To begin curricular infusion without proper training is to court failure.
The least homophobic teacher may be incapable of giving accurate basic
information. It is arguably better not to bring up homosexuality at all
than to repeat even well-intended stereotypes or disproved theories.
They do not have to be omniscient; they and their students can always
find answers together. Nonetheless, sexuality, like race, is an area in
which a modicum of ignorance can be harmful. For example, one high
school English teacher, using a short story about an African American

lesbian in a tenth-grade class, answered the causation question by explaining how domineering mothers are thought to make their sons gay.[233] At another school a health teacher was asked, "How do you know if you're gay?" She responded, "Well, you just know."[234] She might have been uncomfortable going any deeper, or more likely, the panel discussion, which constituted the school's only formal training, was insufficient preparation for any teacher.

One woman has observed that before she felt ready to teach competently about gays and lesbians, she had to do a bit of real intellectual work. For her, reading a half dozen books was indispensable. Her intent was not to become an expert but to be informed enough to teach students to examine definitions and see them in historical context.[235]

In the 1970s, not many teachers or curriculum specialists were prepared to tackle African, Asian, Hispanic American, or women's studies materials. Most required compensatory education, and today many have brought themselves up to speed on certain facets of multiculturalism. For homosexuality to be added to the mix there must be comprehensive staff development, including both introductory sensitization and such substantive topics as etiology, homophobia/heterosexism, and gay history.

### A Last Word

The suggestions in this chapter for refashioning curriculum and instruction cannot be implemented without hard work over a long haul, but what valuable reform would ever be achieved without that? There is of course the cheering thought that new materials are being produced on this topic at an unprecedented pace.

In fact the intensity of new developments over the last five years on the topic of homosexuality has been such that is has been a challenge to keep some of the chapters of this book relevant and manageable. New research on gay, lesbian, bisexual, and transgender youth, teachers, and families, an evolving politics and culture, and new books for young readers are every day making it harder to keep up—yet also offering educators such a richness of resources that ultimately our work will be less difficult.

My greatest hope is that some parts of this volume—particularly the sections on homophobia, heterosexism, violence, and self-destruction—will one day be read as curious historical artifacts of an unenlightened age.

# Notes

## Introduction

1. See, for example, John D'Emilio, *Sexual Politics, Sexual Communities: The Making of a Homosexual Minority in the United States, 1940–1970* (Chicago: Univ. of Chicago Press, 1983); and H. Abelove, M. Barale, and D. Halperin, eds., *The Lesbian and Gay Studies Reader* (New York: Routledge, 1993).

2. See Eric Rofes, "Queers, Education Schools, and Sex Panic," paper presented at the annual meeting of the American Educational Research Association, San Francisco, 21 Apr. 1995; and Eric Rofes, "Gay Issues, Schools, and the Right-Wing Backlash," *Rethinking Schools* 11, 3 (Spring 1997): 4–6.

3. See Sarah Rengel Phillips, "The Hegemony of Heterosexuality: A Study of Introductory Texts," *Teaching Sociology* 19 (October 1991): 454–463.

4. Karen L. Butler, "Prospective Teachers' Knowledge, Attitudes, and Behavior Regarding Gay Men and Lesbians," ERIC Microfiche: ED379251; and James T. Sears, "Personal Feelings and Professional Attitudes of Prospective Teachers Toward Homosexuality and Homosexual Students: Research Findings and Curriculum Recommendations," revision of a paper presented at annual meeting of American Educational Research Association, San Francisco, 27–31 Mar. 1989, ERIC Microfiche: ED312222.

5. See Dennis Carlson, "Gayness, Multicultural Education, and Community," *Educational Foundations* 8, 4 (Fall 1994): 5–25.

## Chapter 1

1. Nathan Glazer, *We Are All Multiculturalists Now* (Cambridge: Harvard Univ. Press, 1997).

2. On the analogous persistence of racism and heterosexism in America, see Michael Bronski, *The Pleasure Principle: Sex, Backlash, and the Struggle for Gay Freedom* (New York: St. Martin's Press, 1998).

3. People for the American Way, "Hostile Climate" (Washington, D.C., 1997).

4. "Breaking the Silence," report (London: Amnesty International, 1997).

5. See Liz Galst, "Reel Hate," Supplement to the *Boston Phoenix*, October 1993, 10–11.

6. Chris Black, "Pollsters Say Some Voters Lie," *Boston Globe*, 10 November 1989.

7. Gallup poll, March 15–17, 1996, reported in *Los Angeles Times Syndicate*, 4 April 96; 55 percent agreed that homosexuality is always wrong in a *Wall Street Journal* poll, 5 March 1998.

8. National Gay and Lesbian Task Force report, "From Wrongs to Rights," Washington, D.C., May 1998.

9. "Juror Outlook Survey," *National Law Journal*, 1 November 1998. Cited in Nat Hentoff, "The War Against Gays and Lesbians," *Village Voice*, 17–23 November 1998.

10. *New York Times* and CBS News poll of 1,048 teens, as reported in Laurie Goodstein and Marjorie Connelly, "American Teenagers Are Both Worldly and Devoid of Cynicism," *New York Times*, 30 April 1998.

11. Gallup Youth Survey, January–March 1998. Reported in "Gallop Poll Results, *Erie (Pa.) Morning News*, 6 May 1998.

12. Alan Wolfe, *One Nation, After All* (New York: Viking, 1998).

13. "The Moderate Majority," (Alan Wolfe interview) *Boston Globe*, 8 March 1998.

14. Oregon Ballot Measure #9, 1992.

15. People for the American Way, *People for the American Way News* 1, 2 (Winter 1995): 8.

16. National Gay and Lesbian Task Force Policy Institute et al., *Beyond the Beltway: State of the States, 1995* (Washington, D.C.: NGLTF, July 1995).

17. National Gay and Lesbian Task Force, reported in Karyn Hunt, "Thousands Gather for Gay Pride," *Associated Press*, San Francisco, 30 June 1996.

18. The states are California, Connecticut, Hawaii, Massachusetts, Minnesota, New Hampshire, New Jersey, Rhode Island, Vermont, and Wisconsin. Lambda Legal Defense and Education Fund, March 1998. Cited in *Associated Press*, 6 March 1998.

19. Matt Green, unpublished paper on Newton North High School (Mass.), Harvard Graduate School of Education, 12 December 1995.

20. See for example, announcement for "Joint International Conference on Developing Religious, Racial, and Ethnic Tolerance," Orlando, Fla., 20–22 March 1997, sponsored by over 30 prominent school, government, community, civil rights, and religious organizations, *Youth Today* (November–December 1996): 47.

21. In 1992, 7 out of 8, according to the National Center for Juvenile Justice, *Juvenile Offenders and Victims: A Focus on Violence* (Pittsburgh, 1995), although the rate of arrest for these crimes increased faster for girls between 1986 and 1995; see Lynn Phillips, *The Girls Report* (Washington, D.C.: National Council for Research on Women, 1998).

22. L. Berkowitz and J. A. Green, "The Stimulus Qualities of the Scapegoat," *Journal of Abnormal Social Psychology* 64 (1962): 293–301.

23. M. J. Monteith, P. G. Devine, and J. R. Zuwerink, "Self-Directed Versus Other-Directed Affect as a Consequence of Prejudice-Related Discrepancies," *Journal of Personality and Social Psychology* 64 (1993): 198–210.

24. Richard D. Ashmore and Frances K. DelBoca, "Psychological Approaches to Understanding Intergroup Conflict," in *Towards the Elimination of Racism*, ed. Phyllis Katz (New York: Pergamon, 1976), 80.

25. Peter Finn and Taylor McNeil, *The Response of the Criminal Justice System to Bias Crime: An Exploratory Review,* submitted to the National Institute of Justice, U.S. Department of Justice (Cambridge, Mass.: Abt Associates, 1987).

26. Southern Poverty Law Center, "1994 Hate Crime Recap: A Year of Close Calls," *Klanwatch Intelligence Report* 77 (March 1995): 4.

27. National Coalition of Anti-Violence Programs, cited in "Nationline Report: Fewer, More Violent Gay Hate Crimes in '95," *USA Today,* 13 March 1996.

28. Report of the National Coalition of Anti-Violence Programs (New York: New York City Anti-Violence Project, 1997).

29. Report of the National Coalition of Anti-Violence Programs (New York: New York City Anti-Violence Project, 1998).

30. Report of the National Coalition of Anti-Violence Programs, cited in Ula Ilnytzky, "Crimes Against Gays More Hateful and Aggressive in 1998," *Associated Press,* 6 April 1999.

31. N.Y.P.D. Bias Unit figures reported in Michael Cooper, "Killing Shakes Complacency of Gay Rights Movement," *New York Times,* 21 October 1998, 1.

32. B. Miller and L. Humphreys, "Lifestyles and Violence: Homosexual Victims of Assault and Murder," *Qualitative Sociology* 3, 3 (1980): 169–185.

33. 1994 Report of New York City Gay and Lesbian Anti-Violence Project, cited in Christopher Muther, "Study: Anti-Gay Killings More Brutal Than Most," *Bay Windows* (Boston), 22 December 1994, 3–4; and in "Murders of Gay Men and Lesbians More Brutal, Police Less Effective," *In Newsweekly,* 1 January 1995, 2.

34. *Anti-Gay/Lesbian Violence, Victimization, and Defamation in* 1993 (report) (Washington, D.C.: National Gay and Lesbian Task Force Policy Institute, 1994.)

35. Ibid.

36. Jack Levin and Jack McDevitt, *Hate Crimes: The Rising Tide of Bigotry and Bloodshed* (New York: Plenum, 1993).

37. 1994 Report of New York City Gay and Lesbian Anti-Violence Project, cited in Christopher Muther, "Study: Anti-Gay Killings More Brutal Than Most," *Bay Windows* (Boston), 22 December 1994, 3–4.

38. G. Herek, "Hate Crimes Against Lesbians and Gay Men: Issues for Research and Policy," *American Psychologist* 44, 6 (1989): 25–43; K. T. Berrill, "Antigay Violence in the United States: An Overview," in *Hate Crimes: Confronting Violence Against Lesbians and Gay Men,* ed. G. M. Herek and K. T. Berrill (Newbury Park, Calif.: Sage, 1992), 19–45.

39. Karen Franklin has found thrill-seeking and peer dynamics are key elements among male perpetrators of antigay hate crimes in "Psychosocial Motivations of Hate Crimes Perpetrators: Implications for Educational Interventions," paper presented at the 106th annual convention of the American Psychological Association, San Francisco, 16 August 1998.

40. "Eight Teenagers Arrested in Weekend Assault on Gay Man," *Los Angeles Times,* 16 April 1996, B4.

41. Howard Chua-Eoan, "Crime: That's Not a Scarecrow," *Time,* 19 October 1998.

42. Daniel Doyle, quoted in Donna Minkowitz, "It's Still Open Season on Gays," *Nation,* 23 March 1992, 368.

43. Eric Pooley, "With Extreme Prejudice: A Murder in Queens Exposes the Frightening Rise of Gay-Bashing," *New York* (Magazine), 8 April 1991.

44. H. G. Bissinger, "The Killing Trail," *Vanity Fair*, February 1995, 80–88, 142–145.

45. Charles Burress, "Confessed Stockton Slayer Tells Motive," *San Francisco Chronicle*, 22 August 1996.

46. Dennis O'Brien and TaNoah Morgan, "Suspect Sought in Wounding of Cross-Dresser," *Baltimore Sun*, 8 November 1998.

47. "Hate Crimes Against Gay Men in Palm Springs," MSNBC, 12 November 1988.

48. The greatest number of monthly incidents occur in June, which is Gay Pride Month nationally, according to the National Coalition of Anti-Violence Programs, cited in David Tuller, "Gay Hate Crimes Down Slightly," *San Francisco Chronicle*, 12 March 1997.

49. Nationline, *USA Today*, 5 January 1996, 3A.

50. Anna Quindlen, "Silence Fosters Gay-Bashing," *New York Times*, 31 October 1992.

51. Alison Mitchell, "Armey Supports Lott's Views of Homosexuals," *New York Times*, 17 June 1998.

52. Thomas B. Edsall, "Forecasting Havoc for Orlando," *Washington Post*, 10 June 1998.

53. National Gay and Lesbian Task Force, *Anti-Gay and Lesbian Victimization: A Study by the National Gay and Lesbian Task Force in Cooperation with Gay and Lesbian Organizations in Eight U.S. Cities* (New York: NGLTF, 1984).

54. American Association of University Women, *Hostile Hallways: The AAUW Survey on Sexual Harassment in America's Schools* (Washington, D.C.: AAUW Educational Foundation, 1993), 23.

55. See Deborah Locke, "Youth's Intolerance of 'Different' Can Destroy Lives," *St. Paul Pioneer Press*, 2 January 1997.

56. Scott A. Giordano, "Newspaper Reports That Student Who Shot Classmates Was Target of Harassment," *Bay Windows* (Boston), 22 October 1998.

57. Jordana Hart, "Northampton Confronts a Crime, Cruelty," *Boston Globe*, 8 June 1998.

58. Poll of 3,123 "A" or "B" average high school students, published in *Who's Who Among American High School Students*, 1998 edition, quoted in Carol Ness, "Prejudice Among Teens on the Rise," *San Francisco Examiner*, 12 November 1998.

59. Joyce Hunter, "Violence Against Lesbian and Gay Male Youths," *Journal of Interpersonal Violence* 5, 3 (September 1990): 295–300.

60. Confidential report to the author, July 1997.

61. Bert Tenhave, on Christopher Lydon's "The Connection," National Public Radio (WBUR-Boston), 17 August 1995.

62. Study conducted by Children Now and the Kaiser Family Foundation, released December 1996, reported in Nancy Hass, "Sex and Today's Single-Minded Situations," *New York Times*, 26 January 1997.

63. See Michael Putzel, "White House Forces Elders to Resign over Remarks," *Boston Globe*, 10 December 1994.

64. Pat Robertson, in a fund-raising letter for the Christian Coalition, Chesapeake, Va., 1994, 3. For a series of publications on right-wing exploitation of homophobia, contact Political Research Associates, 678 Massachusetts Ave., Suite 702, Cambridge, Mass., 02139, (617) 661-9313.

65. A. C. Kinsey, W. B. Pomeroy and C. E. Martin, *Sexual Behavior in the Human Male* (Philadelphia: W. B. Saunders, 1948); A. C. Kinsey, W. B. Pomeroy, C. E. Martin, and P. H. Gebhart, *Sexual Behavior in the Human Female* (Philadelphia: W. B. Saunders, 1953).

66. A 1993 sex survey by Batelle Human Affairs Research Center, Seattle; a 1994 male survey by the University of Chicago; and a 1989 national phone survey by the *San Francisco Examiner;* all cited in Carol Ness, "3.2 Percent of U.S. Voters Are Gay, Survey Reports," *San Francisco Examiner,* 25 April 1996, 1.

67. R. E. Fay, C. F. Turner, A. D. Klassen, and J. H. Gagnon, "Prevalence and Patterns of Same-Gender Contact Among Men," *Science* 243 (1989): 338–348.

68. Robert T. Michael, Edward Laumann, John Gagnon, and Gina Kolata, *Sex in America: A Definitive Survey* (Boston: Little, Brown, 1994).

69. "The Gay Agenda," The Report, No Special Rights Committee PAC, 1992; "The Gay Agenda in Public Education," A Ty and Jeanette Beeson Production, The Report, Springs of Life Church, Los Angeles, 1993.

70. John Carlson, "The Selling of Homophobia," *In Newsweekly* (Boston), 19 February 1995.

71. See Elisabeth Young-Bruehl, *The Anatomy of Prejudices* (Cambridge: Harvard Univ. Press, 1966).

72. See Chapter 3.

73. William Shakespeare, *Twelfth Night or What You Will*, Act II, Scene 5, line 69.

74. National Gay and Lesbian Task Force Policy Institute et al., *Beyond the Beltway.*

75. Phi Delta Kappa/Gallup Poll, May 1996, reported in Deb Riechmann, "Private School Taxes Unpopular," *Associated Press,* 27 August 1996.

76. "Teaching That Gays and Lesbians Don't Exist" (graph), *Advocate,* 6 February 1996, 16.

77. Jeff Mapes, "OCA Files Anti-Gay Rights Initiative Targeting Schools," *Oregonian,* 25 August 1998.

78. Television advertisement for the Barry Goldwater for President Campaign.

79. Chip Berlet, "The Right Rides High," *Progressive,* October 1994, 22–29.

80. Published by Oregon's "No Special Rights Committee," 1992.

81. E. L. Pattullo, "Straight Talk About Gays," *Commentary,* December 1992, 21–24. Reprinted with Permission

82. Ibid., 23.

83. Ibid., 23–24.

84. See William J. Bennett, "Gay Marriage? A Man and a Woman Needed for the 'Honorable Estate,'" *St. Louis Post Dispatch,* 23 May 1996.

85. George Will, "Rainbow Curriculum," *Boston Sunday Globe,* 6 December 1992, A39.

86. Ambrose Evans-Pritchard, "On This Campus, Straight Is Queer—Some 'Hets' Go Along to Get Along," *Washington Times,* 27 March 1996, A2.

87. See Urvashi Vaid, Randy Shilts, Sarah Schulman, Simon Levay et al., "Ideals and Strategies: We Can Get There From Here," *Nation,* 5 July 1993, 26–31.

88. "Right Answers: Dee Mosbacher Interviews John Schlafly," *10 Percent* (Spring 1993): 66.

89. See, for example, James Bennet, "Clinton Is Greeted Warmly as He Speaks to Gay Group," *New York Times,* 9 November 1997; and Katharine Q. Seelye, "Citing 'Primitive Hatreds,' Clinton Asks Congress to Expand Hate-Crime Law," *New York Times,* 7 April 1999, A18.

90. From the White House transcript of "Meet the Press," 8 December 1997.

91. Kevin Galvin, "Clinton Asks Hate-Law Expansion," *Associated Press,* 6 April 1999. The curriculum will be a public-private partnership involving the federal Departments of Education and Justice with AT&T, the Anti-Defamation League, and others.

92. From the White House transcript of "Meet the Press," 8 December 1997.

93. "Clinton Agrees with Gore on Ellen," *UPI,* 20 October 1997.

94. *Newsweek* poll, 22–23 May 1996, reported in David A. Kaplan and Daniel Klaidman, "A Battle, Not the War," *Newsweek,* 3 June 1996.

95. Gary B. MacDonald, Raymond O'Brien, Karen J. Pittman, and Mary Kimball, "Adolescents and HIV: Defining the Problem and Its Prevention," Commissioned Paper #12 (Washington, D.C.: Center for Youth Development and Policy Research, Academy for Educational Development, February 1994).

96. For example, William Bennett, cited in "Under Surveillance" column, *Advocate,* 6 February 1996, 14.

97. S. 1513.

98. Chris Bull, "Back to the Future," *Advocate,* 15 November 1994.

99. After being called a fag by a colleague, Representative Barney Frank (D.-Mass.) observed that those congresspeople who assured him it was OK with them if he was gay would lose their "funding" if they were teachers saying the same thing to a public school student; see *Bay Windows,* 2 February 1995, 4.

100. Jill Smolowe, "The Unmarrying Kind," *Time,* 29 April 1996, 68.

101. Michael Matza, "Challenge to a School Policy on Gays Polarizes a N.H. Town," *Philadelphia Inquirer,* 25 March 1996.

102. David W. Dunlap, "Congress Debates School Curriculums on Sexual Values," *New York Times,* 10 December 1995.

103. Available from GLSEN, 121 West 27th St., Suite 804, New York, NY 10001, (212) 727-0135

## Chapter 2

1. Michael G. Shively and John P. Dececco, "Components of Sexual Identity," in *Psychological Perspectives on Lesbian and Gay Male Experiences, ed.* L. D. Garnets and D. C. Kimmel list the first four. I add the fifth.

2. Societal intolerance for gender ambiguity leads doctors and parents to such surgeries. See Natalie Angier, "New Debate Over Surgery on Genitals," *New York Times,* 13 May 1997.

3. J. Money and P. Tucker, *Sexual Signatures: On Being a Man or a Woman* (Boston: Little, Brown, 1975); R. Green, *Sexual Identity Conflict in Children and*

*Adults* (New York: Basic Books, 1974); E. E. Macoby and C. N. Jacklin, *Psychology of Sex Differences* (Stanford: Stanford Univ. Press, 1974); J. Money and A. A. Ehrhart, *Man and Woman, Boy and Girl: The Differentiation and Dimorphism of Gender Identity from Conception to Maturity* (Baltimore: Johns Hopkins Univ. Press, 1972); R. Sears, "Development of a Gender Role," in *Sex and Behavior, ed.* F. A. Beach (New York: Wiley, 1965), 133–163.

4. J. Kagan, "The Concept of Identification," *Psychological Review* 65 (1958): 296–305.

5. A. Kinsey, W. Pomeroy, and C. Martin, *Sexual Behavior in the Human Male* (Philadelphia: W. B. Saunders, 1948).

6. M. G. Shively and J. P. DiCecco, "Components of Sexual Identity," *Journal of Homosexuality* 3 (1977): 41–48.

7. F. Klein, "The Need to View Sexual Orientation as a Multi-Variable Dynamic Process: A Theoretical Perspective," in *Homosexuality/Heterosexuality: Concepts of Sexual Orientation*, ed. D. S. McWhirter, S. A. Sanders, and J. M. Reinisch (New York: Oxford Univ. Press, 1990).

8. J. Money, *Gay, Straight, and In Between: The Sexology of Erotic Orientation* (New York: Oxford Univ. Press, 1988).

9. John Boswell, *Christianity, Social Tolerance, and Homosexuality* (Chicago: Univ. of Chicago Press, 1980); Jonathan Ned Katz, *Gay and Lesbian Almanac* (New York: Harper & Row, 1983); John D'Emilio, *Sexual Politics, Sexual Communities: The Making of a Homosexual Minority in the United States, 1940–1970* (Chicago: Univ. of Chicago Press, 1983).

10. Boswell, *Christianity, Social Tolerance, and Homosexuality*. In his *Before the Closet: Same-Sex Love from Beowulf to Angels in America* (Chicago: University of Chicago Press, 1998), Allen J. Frantzen claims Boswell missed extensive evidence of universal church condemnation.

11. J. Boswell, *Same Sex Unions in Premodern Europe* (New York: Villard, 1994).

12. J. Boswell, "Categories, Experience, and Sexuality," in *Forms of Desire: Sexual Orientation and the Social Constructionist Controversy*, ed. Edward Stein (New York: Routledge, 1992), 133–174.

13. Boswell, *Christianity, Social Tolerance, and Homosexuality*.

14. "L'Ombre de Deschauffours," cited in Claude Courouve, *Vocabulaire de l'homosexualité masculine* (Paris: Payot, 1985), 64.

15. Plutarch's discussion on his "Dialogue on Love", in Boswell, "Categories, Experience, and Sexuality," 169, note 60.

16. Bernadette Brooten, *Love Between Women: Early Christian Responses to Female Homoeroticism* (Chicago: Univ. of Chicago Press, 1997). See also Bernadette Brooten, "Of Love Spells and Lesbians in Ancient Rome" (interview with Edouard Fontenot), *Harvard Gay and Lesbian Review* 1, 2 (Spring 1994): 11–14.

17. Brooten, *Love Between Women*, 105.

18. "The Homosexual Role," *Social Problems* 16, (Fall 1968): 182–192.

19. Robert Padgug, "Sexual Matters: On Conceptualizing Sexuality in History," in *Forms of Desire: Sexual Orientation and the Social Constructionist Controversy*, ed. Edward Stein (New York: Routledge, 1992), 53.

20. Alan H. Goodman, "Problematics of 'Race' in Contemporary Biological Anthropology," in *Biological Anthropology: The State of the Science*, ed. Noel T. Boaz

and Linda D. Wolfe (Bend: International Institute for Human Evolutionary Research, 1997), 221–243.

21. C. Guillaumin, "Race et native: Système des marques, idée de groupe naturel et rapport sociaux," *Plureil* 11 (1977). See also Noel Ignatiev, *How the Irish Became White* (New York: Routledge, 1995).

22. Renee Graham, "How Black Is Black?" *Boston Globe*, 19 January 1993, 51.

23. David M. Halperin, *One Hundred Years of Homosexuality* (New York: Routledge, 1990), 8; Boswell, *Christianity, Social Tolerance, and Homosexuality*.

24. Sigmund Freud, *Three Essays on the Theory of Sexuality*, trans. James Strachey (New York: Basic Books, 1964), 33.

25. Halperin, *One Hundred Years*, 160.

26. Ibid., 47. In a later essay, Halperin further elucidates the differences between the older partner's *eros* (passionate sexual desire) and *philia* (nonerotic love)—the only kind of reciprocal feeling permitted the boy without shameful life-long consequences. The exchange was highly regulated: a puerile erection was fine, but for the boy to enjoy penetration or want to penetrate his elder brought dishonor. Halperin also cautions against seeing the much older universal Cretan rite of passage (i.e., a boy's sexual abduction by a man) as a direct precursor of Athenian practice. See David M. Halperin, "Questions of Evidence: Commentary on Koehl, DeVries, and Williams," in *Queer Representations: Reading Lives, Reading Cultures*, ed. Martin Duberman (New York: New York Univ. Press, 1997), 39–54.

27. Ibid., 70.

28. Ibid., 2–3.

29. E. Bethe, "Die dorishe Knabenlieve: Ihre Ethik und ihre Idee," *Rheinisches Museum fur Philologie* 62 (1907): 438–475; Harald Patzer, "Die Griechische Knabenliebe," sitzungsberichte der Wissenschaftlichen Gesellschaft an der Hohann Wolfgang Goethe-Universitat Frankfurt am Main, 19.1, Weisbaden (1982).

30. K. J. Dover, *Greek Homosexuality* (Cambridge: Harvard Univ. Press, 1975).

31. See Michael Rocke, *Forbidden Friendships: Homosexuality and Male Culture in Renaissance Florence* (New York: Oxford Univ. Press, 1996).

32. M. Duberman, M. Vicinus, and G. Chauncy Jr., eds., *Hidden from History: Reclaiming the Gay and Lesbian Past* (New York: Meridian, 1990), 484, note 6.

33. Mary McIntosh, "The Homosexual Role," in *Forms of Desire: Sexual Orientation and the Social Constructionist Controversy*, ed. Edward Stein (New York: Routledge, 1992), 34.

34. Randolph Trumbach, "London's Sodomites: Homosexual Behavior and Western Culture in the Eighteenth Century," *Journal of Social History* 11 (1977/1978).

35. Jeffrey Weeks, "'Sins and Diseases': Some Notes on Homosexuality in the Nineteenth Century," *History Workshop* 1 (1976): 211–219; Jeffrey Weeks, *Coming Out: Homosexual Politics in Britain from the Nineteenth Century to the Present* (London: Quartet Books, 1977).

36. H. Hossli, "Eros, Die Mannerliebe der Griechen, ihre Beziehungen zur Geschichte, Leteratur and Gesetzgebung aller Zeitung, oder Forschungen uber platonische Liebe, ihre Wurdigung und Entwordigung fur Sitten-, Natur- and Volkerkunde (Munster, Switzerland, 1836); on Ulrichs see James D. Steakley, *The Homosexual Emancipation Movement in Germany* (New York: Arno Press, 1975); J.

A. Symonds, "A Problem in Greek Ethics, being an inquiry into the phenomenon of sexual inversion, addressed especially to medical psychologists and jurists," (London, 1901).

37. Halperin, *One Hundred Years*, 155, note 2.

38. Havelock Ellis, *Sexual Inversion = Studies in the Psychology of Sex*, vol. 2., 3rd ed. (Philadelphia: Davis, 1921).

39. Halperin, *One Hundred Years*, 159, note 17.

40. See Jonathan Ned Katz, *The Invention of Heterosexuality* (New York: Dutton, 1995).

41. Lee Edelman, *Homographesis: Essays in Gay Literary and Cultural Theory* (New York: Routledge, 1994) 39.

42. Eve Kosofsky Sedgwick, *Tendencies* (Durham: Duke Univ. Press, 1993), 66.

43. Padgug, "Sexual Matters," 43–68.

44. Thomas Szasz, *The Manufacture of Madness* (New York: Delta Books, 1970).

45. Carroll Smith-Rosenberg, "Discourses of Sexuality and Subjectivity: The New Woman, 1870–1936," in *Hidden from History: Reclaiming the Gay and Lesbian Past*, ed. M. Duberman, M. Vicinus and G. Chauncy Jr. (New York: Meridian, 1990), 267.

46. Justice Bradley decision upholding the right of a state to prohibit women from practicing law, *Bradwell v Illinois*, 83 US 130 (1872).

47. Smith-Rosenberg, "Discourses of Sexuality," 270.

48. Ibid., 269.

49. Esther Newton, "The Mythic Mannish Lesbian," in *The Lesbian Issue: Essays from Signs*, ed. Estelle Freedman et al. (Chicago: Univ. of Chicago Press, 1985), 7–25.

50. Smith-Rosenberg, "Discourses of Sexuality," 270–271. See also Sheila Jeffries, *The Spinster and Her Enemies* (London: Pandora, 1987); Celia Kitzinger, *The Social Construction of Lesbianism* (London: Sage, 1987); Celia Kitzinger, "Liberal Humanism as an Ideology of Social Control," in *Texts of Identity*, ed. K. Gergen and J. Shotter (London: Sage, 1989), 82–98.

51. Michel Foucault, *The History of Sexuality*, vol. 1 (New York: Random House, 1978). Halperin, *One Hundred Years*, 42.

52. Halperin, *One Hundred Years*, 49.

53. For example, see ibid., 159, note 21, for Bullough as one.

54. Ibid., 161, note 32.

55. Ibid., 46. On New Guinea, see G. H. Herdt, *Guardians of the Flutes: Idioms of Masculinity* (New York: McGraw-Hill, 1981).

56. Boswell, "Categories, Experience, and Sexuality."

57. Ibid., 146.

58. Kitzinger, *Social Construction*, 147; for a critique of socially constructed gender, see Phyllis Burke, *Gender Shock: Exploding the Myths of Male and Female* (New York: Anchor, 1996.)

59. Katz, *Gay and Lesbian Almanac*, 62.

60. Egyptologist Greg Reeder, in John McCoy, "Evidence of 'Same-Sex Desire' Exists as Early as 2400 B.C.," *Dallas Morning News*, 20 July 1998.

61. Steven Epstein, "Gay Politics, Ethnic Identity: The Limits of Social Constructionism," *Socialist Review* 93/94 (May–August 1987): 24.

62. See Halperin, *One Hundred Years*, 32, footnote.

63. Katz, *Gay and Lesbian Almanac*, 62.

64. Marc Stein, "British Gay Left" (interview with Jeffrey Weeks), in *Gay Community News*, 30 October–5 November 1988.

65. Halperin, *One Hundred Years*, title chapter, part 2.

66. Ibid., 225 (addendum).

67. Boswell, *Christianity, Social Tolerance, and Homosexuality*, 44.

68. Boswell, "Categories, Experience and Sexuality," 137, note 8.

69. Epstein, "Gay Politics, Ethnic Identity," 24.

70. Kitzinger, *Social Construction*, 144.

71. Epstein, "Gay Politics, Ethnic Identity," 43–48.

72. Dennis Altman, *Homosexual Oppression and Liberation* (New York: Avon, 1971), esp. ch. 3, "Liberation: Toward the Polymorphous Whole."

73. Epstein, "Gay Politics, Ethnic Identity," 38.

74. In 1997 the gay neighborhood in Chicago was afforded the same designation status (signs and banners, etc.) as Greektown, Chinatown, and other ethnic neighborhoods. See Dirk Johnson, "Chicago Recognizes District as Symbol of Gay Life," *New York Times*, 27 August 1997.

75. Epstein, "Gay Politics, Ethnic Identity," 45.

76. James T. Sears, "Responding to the Sexual Diversity of Faculty and Students: Sexual Praxis and the Critically Reflective Administration," in *Educational Administration in a Pluralistic Society*, ed. Colleen A. Capper (Albany: State Univ. of New York Press, 1993), 147.

77. James T. Sears, "Researching the Other/Searching for Self: Qualitative Research on (Homo)Sexuality in Education," *Theory into Practice* 31, 2 (Spring 1992): 149–156.

78. Jacquelyn N. Zita, "Gay and Lesbian Studies: Yet Another Unhappy Marriage," in *Tilting the Tower: Lesbians Teaching Queer Subjects*, ed. Linda Garber (New York: Routledge, 1994).

79. Ibid., 270.

80. Kitzinger, *Social Construction*, 154.

81. Ibid., 153.

82. Halperin, *One Hundred Years*, 42.

83. Kitzinger, *Social Construction*, 156.

84. Halperin, *One Hundred Years*, 53.

85. Jean Piaget, *The Psychology of Intelligence* (Totowa, N.J.: Littlefield, Adams, 1981); Jean Piaget, *Judgment and Reasoning in the Child* (Totowa, N.J.: Littlefield, Adams, 1976).

86. Lawrence Kohlberg, *Essays on Moral Development*, vol. 2, *The Psychology of Moral Development* (San Francisco: Harper & Row, 1984).

87. Epstein, "Gay Politics, Ethnic Identity," 34

88. Gilbert Herdt and Andrew Boxer, *Children of Horizons: How Gay and Lesbian Teens Are Leading a New Way Out of the Closet* (Boston: Beacon Press, 1993), 179.

89. L. D. Garnets and D. C. Kimmel, "Origins of Sexual Orientation," in *Psychological Perspectives on Lesbian and Gay Male Experiences*, ed. L. D. Garnets and D. C. Kimmel (New York: Columbia University Press, 1993), 112.

90. An excellent resource for students is Jan Clausen, *Beyond Gay or Straight: Understanding Sexual Orientation* (Philadelphia: Chelsea House, 1997).

91. Audre Lorde, *Zami: A New Spelling of My Name* (Watertown, Mass: Persephone Press, 1982).

92. William G. Tierney, "On Method and Hope," in *Power and Method: Political Activism and Educational Research*, ed. Andrew Gitlin (New York: Routledge, 1994).

93. Halperin, *One Hundred Years*, 70.

94. Sears, "Researching the Other," 149–156.

95. See Anne Fausto-Sterling, "The Five Sexes: Why Male and Female Are Not Enough," *Sciences* 33, 2 (March–April 1993): 20–26.

96. Anne Fausto-Sterling, in William O. Beeman, "What Are You: Male, Merm, Herm, Ferm, or Female?" *Baltimore Sun*, 17 March 1996, 1F.

97. See Natalie Angier, "New Debate over Surgery on Genitals," *New York Times*, 13 May 1997. One pediatric endocrinologist opines that surgery after the age of 18 months is too psychologically risky (Melvin Grumbach in Delia M. Rios, "Doc's Quick Look at Baby Determines Path Through Life," *Chicago Tribune*, 23 February 1997).

98. NBC, *Saturday Night Live*, mid-1990s.

99. See Leslie Feinberg, *Transgender Warriors: Making History from Joan of Arc to Dennis Rodman* (Boston: Beacon Press, 1996).

100. Dean Labate, Executive Director of the Callen-Lorde Community Health Center in a letter to *Time*, 24 August 1998.

101. William G. Tierney, "On Method and Hope," in *Power and Method: Political Activism and Educational Research*, ed. Andrew Gitlin (New York: Routledge, 1994).

102. Lisa Duggan, "Making It Perfectly Queer," *Socialist Review* 22, 1 (January–March 1992): 11–21.

103. Michelle Quinn, "High-Profile Peninsula Therapist, Author Insists Having a Boyfriend Doesn't Mean She Isn't Gay," *San Jose Mercury News*, 23 October 1997. Jan Clausen, in her *Apples and Oranges: My Journey Through Sexual Identity* (Boston: Houghton Mifflin, 1999), avoids that trap by calling herself a "hasbian" and a "floating woman." The latter, of course, speaks to liquidity. (See Chapter 6.)

104. F. L. Whitam and R. M. Mathy, *Male Homosexuality in Four Societies: Brazil, Guatemala, the Philippines, and the United States* (New York: Praeger, 1986).

105. Halperin, *One Hundred Years*, 61.

106. W. Davenport, "Sexual Patterns and Their Regulation in a Society of the Southwest Pacific," in *Sex and Behavior*, ed. F. A. Beach (New York: John Wiley & Sons, 1965), 164–207; G. H. Herdt, ed., *Ritualized Homosexuality in Melanesia* (Berkeley: Univ. of California Press, 1984);J. Money and A. A. Ehrhardt, "Gender-Dimorphic Behavior and Fetal Sex Hormones," in *Recent Progress in Hormone Research*, ed. E. B. Astwood (New York: Academic Press, 1972), 735–754.

107. G. H. Herdt, *Guardians of the Flutes: Idioms of Masculinity*, rev. ed. (Chicago: Univ. of Chicago Press, 1994); John Money, "Sin, Sickness, or Status? Homosexual Gender Identity and Psychoneuroendocrinology," in *Psychological Perspectives on Lesbian and Gay Male Experiences*, ed. L. Garnets and D. Kimmel (New York: Columbia Univ. Press, 1993).

108. Thomas Almaguer, "Chicano Men: A Cartography of Homosexual Identity and Behavior," in *The Lesbian and Gay Studies Reader*, ed. H. Abelove, M. Barale, and D. Halperin (New York: Routledge, 1993).

109. See Esther Newton, "Of Yams, Grinders, and Gays: The Anthropology of Homosexuality," paper delivered at the Gays, Lesbians, and Society lecture series, New York City, 17 October 1987, published in *Out/Look* (Spring 1988): 28–37

110. Martin Duberman, "A Matter of Difference," *Nation*, 5 July 1993.

111. Pat Caplan, ed., *The Cultural Construction of Sexuality* (London: Tavistock, 1987), 24.

## Chapter 3

1. For example, see *U.S. News and World Report*, 13 November 1995; *Time*, 9 September 1991; *Newsweek*, 24 February 1992; and *CBS This Morning*, ABC's *Good Morning, America*, *NBC Nightly News*, NBC's *Nightline* all in July 1993.

2. L. D. Garnets and D. C. Kimmel, *Psychological Perspectives on Lesbian and Gay Male Experiences* (New York: Columbia Univ. Press, 1993), 110.

3. John Bancroft, in Martha Irvine, "Study Says Gender Identity May Be Malleable After All," *Associated Press*, 6 July 1998.

4. Quoted in Ernst Jones, *The Life and Work of Sigmund Freud*, vol. 3, *The Last Phase: 1919–1939* (New York: Basic Books, 1957), 195–196.

5. For Freud's analysis of a rebellious but healthy lesbian, see Sigmund Freud, "The Psychogenesis of a Case of Homosexuality in a Woman," in *Standard Edition of the Complete Psychological Works of Sigmund Freud*, ed. James Strachey (London: Hogarth Press, 1953–1974), 18: 145–172.

6. Sigmund Freud, *Three Essays on the Theory of Sexuality, 1905* (New York: Avon, 1962), 25.

7. See T. F. Murphy, "Freud Reconsidered: Bisexuality, Homosexuality, and Moral Judgment," *Journal of Homosexuality* 9 (1984): 65–78.

8. From a letter to an American mother of a homosexual, cited in Henry Abelove, "Freud, Male Homosexuality, and the Americans," *Dissent* (Winter 1996). Freud added, "Many highly respectable individuals of ancient and modern times have been homosexuals."

9. Ronald Bayer, *Homosexuality and American Psychiatry: The Politics of Diagnosis* (Princeton: Princeton Univ. Press, 1981), 21–40.

10. Irving Bieber et al., *Homosexuality: A Psychoanalytic Study of Male Homosexuals* (New York: Basic Books, 1962), 310–314.

11. Sandor Rado, *Psychoanalysis of Behavior II* (New York: Grune & Stratton, 1962).

12. Bieber et al., *Homosexuality*, 310–314.

13. See David W. Dunlap, "Gay Rights Split Analyst Father and His Gay Son," *New York Times*, 24 December 1995.

14. Bayer, *Homosexuality and American Psychiatry*, 34–38.

15. Evelyn Hooker, "Male Homosexuals and Their 'Worlds,'" in *Sexual Inversion*, ed. Judd Marmor (New York: Basic Books, 1965), 92.

16. Richard A. Isay, *Being Homosexual: Gay Men and Their Development* (New York: Farrar, Straus & Giroux, 1989); A. P. Bell, M. S. Weinberg, and S. K. Hammersmith, *Sexual Preference: Its Development in Men and Women* (Bloomington: Indiana Univ. Press, 1981).

17. Nancy J. Chodorow, *Femininities, Masculinities, Sexualities: Freud and Beyond* (Lexington: University Press of Kentucky, 1994), 68.

18. Ibid., 61–62.

19. Ibid., 63.

20. J. Michael Bailey, "Biological Perspectives on Sexual Orientation," in *Lesbian, Gay, and Bisexual Identities over the Lifespan: Psychological Perspectives*, ed. A. R. D'Augelli and C. Patterson (New York: Oxford Univ. Press, 1995), 119.

21. A. P. Bell and M. S. Weinberg, *Homosexualities: A Study of Diversity Among Men and Women* (New York: Simon & Schuster, 1978).

22. See Judith Hopper, "A New Germ Theory," *Atlantic Monthly*, February 1999.

23. Jim Weinrich, *Sexual Landscapes* (New York: Charles Scribner's Sons, 1987).

24. Bailey, "Biological Perspectives," 125.

25. For a summary of genetic research on homosexuality, see Chandler Burr, *A Separate Creation: The Search for Biological Origins of Sexual Orientation* (New York: Hyperion, 1996).

26. J. M. Bailey and R. C. Pillard, "A Genetic Study of Male Sexual Orientation," *Archives of General Psychiatry* 48 (1991): 1089–1096; J. M. Bailey, R. C. Pillard, M. C. Neale, and Y. Agyei, "Heritable Factors Influence Female Sexual Orientation," *Archives of General Psychiatry* 50 (1993): 217–223.

27. Bailey and Pillard, "A Genetic Study of Male Sexual Orientation."

28. Edward Stein, "Evidence for Queer Genes: An Interview with Richard Pillard," *GLQ: A Journal of Lesbian and Gay Studies* 1, 1 (1993): 93–110.

29. Dean H. Hamer, Stella Hu, Victoria A. Magnuson, Nan Hu, and Anglea M. L. Pattatucci, "A Linkage Between DNA Markers on the X-Chromosome and Male Sexual Orientation," *Science* 261, 5119 (July 16, 1993): 321–328. Also Dean Hamer and Peter Copeland, *The Science of Desire: The Search for the Gay Gene and the Biology of Behavior* (New York: Simon and Schuster, 1994).

30. See J. Michael Bailey, Richard C. Pillard, and Robert Knight, "Is Sexual Orientation Biologically Determined?" *CQ Researcher* 3, 9 (5 March 1993): 209.

31. Howard Altman, "The Hand of Fate," in *One in Ten*, supplement to the *Boston Phoenix*, June 1995, 8.

32. Heino Meyer-Bahlburg, "Psychoendocrine Research on Sexual Orientation: Current Status and Future Options," *Progress in Brain Research* 61, ed. G. J. DeVries, J.P.C. DeBruin, H.M.B. Uylings, and M. A. Corner (Amsterdam: Elsevier, 1984): 375–398.

33. Melvin Konner, "She and He," *Science* 3, 7 (September 1982): 54–61; C. Burr, "Homosexuality and Biology," *Atlantic Monthly*, March 1993, 45–65.

34. See Simon LeVay, *The Sexual Brain* (Cambridge: MIT Press, 1993).

35. John Money, "Sin, Sickness, or Status? Homosexual Gender Identity and Psychoneuroendocrinology," in *Psychological Perspectives on Lesbian and Gay Male Experiences*, ed. L. D. Garnets and D. C. Kimmel (New York: Columbia Univ. Press, 1993).

36. "'Bisexual' Fish Found in Japan," *San Francisco Examiner* (AP), 14 November 1995.

37. Results reported by John Money, "Prenatal and Postnatal Factors in Gender Identity," in *Animal Models in Human Psychobiology*, ed. George Serban and Arthur Kling (New York: Plenum Press, 1976), and reconsidered by Milton Diamond and H. Keith Sigmundson, "Sex Reassignment at Birth: Long-Term Review and Clin-

ical Implications," *Archives of Pediatric and Adolescent Medicine* 151, 3 (March 1997): 298–304.

38. Susan J. Bradley, Gillian D. Oliver, Avinoam B. Chernick, and Kenneth J. Zucker, "Experiment of Nature: Ablatio Penis at 2 Months, Sex Reassignment at 7 Months, and a Psycho-Sexual Follow-Up in Young Adulthood," *Pediatrics* 102, 1 (July 1998): e9.

39. Money, "Sin Sickness or Status," 130–167.

40. Bailey, "Biological Perspectives on Sexual Orientation," 112–113.

41. Heino F. L. Meyer-Bahlburg et al., "Prenatal Estrogens and the Development of Homosexual Orientation," *Developmental Psychology* 31, 1 (1995): 12–21.

42. See Diana Baumrind, "Commentary on Sexual Orientation: Research and Social Policy Implications," *Developmental Psychology* 31, 1 (1995): 131.

43. Sheri A. Berenbaum and Elizabeth Snyder, "Early Hormonal Influences on Childhood Sex-Typed Activity and Playmate Preferences: Implications for the Development of Sexual Orientation," *Developmental Psychology* 31, 1 (1995): 31–42.

44. Burr, "Homosexuality and Biology."

45. D. F. Swaab and M. A. Hofman, "An Enlarged Suprachiasmatic Nucleus in Homosexual Men," *Brain Research* 537 (1990): 141–148.

46. Simon LeVay, "A Difference in Hypothalamic Structure Between Heterosexual and Homosexual Men," *Science* 253 (1991): 1034–1037.

47. Laura Allen and Roger Gorski, "Sexual Orientation and the Size of the Anterior Commisure in the Human Brain," *Proceedings of the National Academy of Sciences* 89 (1992): 7199–7202.

48. Bailey, "Biological Perspectives on Sexual Orientation," 114–116.

49. Anne Fausto-Sterling, "Society Writes Biology/Biology Constructs Gender," *Daedalus* 116, 4 (1987): 61–75; W. Byne and B. Parsons, "Human Sexual Orientation: The Biologic Theories Reappraised," *Archives of General Psychiatry* 50 (1993): 228–239; L. Gooren, "Biomedical Theories of Sexual Orientation: A Critical Examination," in *Homosexuality/Heterosexuality: Concepts of Sexual Orientation*, ed. D. P. McWhirter, S. A. Sanders, and J. M. Reinish (New York: Oxford Univ. Press, 1990): 71–87.

50. Garnets and Kimmel, *Psychological Perspectives*, 5; Meyer-Bahlburg, "Psychoendocrine Research on Sexual Orientation," 375–398.

51. Garnets and Kimmel, *Psychological Perspectives*, 110; David M. Halperin, *One Hundred Years of Homosexuality* (New York: Routledge, 1990), 51

52. Ray Blanchard, Kenneth J. Zucker, Susan J. Bradley, and Caitlin S. Hume, "Birth Order and Sibling Sex Ratio in Homosexual Male Adolescents and Probably Prehomosexual Feminine Boys," *Developmental Psychology* 31, 1 (1995): 22–30.

53. Ray Blanchard and Anthony F. Bogaert, "Homosexuality in Men and Number of Older Brothers," *American Journal of Psychiatry* 153, 1 (January 1996): 27–32.

54. Burr, "Homosexuality and Biology," 60; Bailey, "Biological Perspectives on Sexual Orientation," 125; Jiang-Ning Zhou, Michel A. Hofman, Louis J. G. Gooren, Dick F. Swaab, "A Sex Difference in the Human Brain and Its Relation to Transexuality," *Nature* 378, 6552 (2 November 1995): 68–71.

55. Money, "Sin, Sickness, or Status?" 163.

56. S. Marc Breedlove, "Sex on the Brain," *Nature*, 389, 6653 (October 1997): 801.

57. Nicholas Wade, "Mating Game of Fruit Fly Is Traced to Single Gene," *New York Times*, 12 December 1996.

58. For a critique of simplistic genetic causation arguments, see Philip Kitcher, *The Lives to Come: The Genetic Revolution and Human Possibilities* (New York: Simon & Schuster, 1997).

59. Dean Hamer, "Sexual Orientation: Biology and Society," talk given at conference, Harvard University, 19–20 April 1997.

60. "Scientists Find New Evidence of Homosexuality Gene," *Associated Press*, 6 August 1996.

61. Dean Hamer, in Anastasia Toufexis, "New Evidence of a 'Gay' Gene," *Time*, 13 November 1995.

62. Burr, "Homosexuality and Biology," 64–65.

63. Simon LeVay, *Queer Science: The Use and Abuse of Research into Homosexuality* (Cambridge: MIT Press, 1996); Carla Golden, "Do Women Choose Their Sexual Identity?" (essay), *Harvard Gay and Lesbian Review* 4, 1 (Winter 1997): 18–20.

64. Dean Hamer and Peter Copeland, *Living with Our Genes: Why They Matter More Than You Think* (New York: Doubleday, 1998).

65. Dennis McFadden and Edward G. Pasanen, "Comparison of the Auditory Systems of Heterosexuals and Homosexuals," *Proceedings of the National Academy of Sciences*, 95, 5 (3 March 1998): 2707–2713.

66. N. G. Waller, B. A. Kojetin, T. J. Bouchard, D. T. Lykken, and A. Tellegen, "Genetic and Environmental Influences on Religious Interests, Attitudes, and Values: A Study of Twins Reared Apart and Together," *Psychological Science* 1 (1990): 138–142.

67. See LeVay, *Queer Science*.

68. Cited in William Byne and Edward Stein, "Varieties of Biological Explanation," (essay), *Harvard Gay and Lesbian Review* 4, 1 (Winter 1997): 13–15.

69. John DeCecco, *Sex, Cells, and Same-Sex Desire*(in press); Rev. Lou Sheldon, in Traci Watson and Joseph P. Shapiro, "Is There a 'Gay Gene'?" *U.S. News and World Report*, 13 November 1995.

70. See Garland Allen, *Thomas Hunt Morgan: The Man and His Science* (Princeton: Princeton Univ. Press, 1978).

71. Aaron Greenberg, in Carol Ness, "Lawyer Suggests Abortion If a Test Could Prove Fetus Has 'Gay Gene,'" *San Francisco Examiner*, 26 August 1998.

72. Remarks to *London Daily Telegraph*, 16 February 1997, quoted in Lisa Keen, "DNA Discoverer Backs Aborting Gay Fetuses," *Washington Blade*, 28 February 1997.

73. Chandler Burr, "Why Conservatives Should Embrace the Gay Gene," *Weekly Standard*, 9 December 1996.

74. For example, a *U.S. News* and Bozell poll revealed that 69 percent of those who think homosexuality is completely or mostly hereditary/genetic favored gay rights, compared to 45 percent of the entire sample. U.S. News/Bozell Worldwide Nature-Nurture Survey, 6–9 February 1997, reported in Wray Herbert, "Politics of Biology," *U.S. News and World Report*, 21 April 1997.

75. See Byne and Stein, "Varieties of Biological Explanation," 13–15; and Jan Clausen, *Beyond Gay or Straight: Understanding Sexual Orientation* (Philadelphia: Chelsea House, 1997), 73.

76. Lee Siegel, "Same Sex Seagulls," *Salt Lake (Utah) Tribune*, 8 May 1997.

77. A. Chaudhuri and A. K. Sinha, "Odd Couples: A Male-Male Pairing in the Tropical Tasar Silkmoth, Antheraea mylitta (Saturniidae)," *News of the Lepidopterists' Society* 39, 3 (Summer 1997).

78. Ross Clark, "After the Black Sheep . . . the Pink Sheep," *Sunday Telegraph* (London), 9 March 1997.

79. That fact does not seem to have influenced the estimated 3,000 gay visitors to a Dutch safari park, whose special theme of homosexual acts among animals required guides to point out same-gender acts when observable among the displayed species. Reported in Lewis Dorlinsky, "Birds Do It, Bees Do It," *San Francisco Chronicle*, 5 September 1997. The tour de force of this kind of scholarship must be Bruce Bagemihl's *Biological Exhuberance: Animal Homosexuality and Natural Diversity* (New York: St. Martin's Press, 1998), which, at 751 pages, documents many instances of homosexuality, bisexuality, and transgenderism in the wild.

80. See for example Mona Charren, "Even If It Is Genetic, Homosexuality Is Wrong," *Columbus (Ohio) Ledger-Enquirer*, 11 December 1996; also religious positions cited in Burr, "Why Conservatives Should Embrace the Gay Gene."

81. See Lisa Milligan, "Church: Religious Groups Doubt 'Gay Gene' Theory," *Modesto (Calif.) Bee*, 28 June 1998.

82. See chapter 10 in Burr, *A Separate Creation*.

83. See for example, Carl Campbell Brigham, *A Study of American Intelligence* (Princeton: Princeton Univ. Press, 1923; reissued by Millwood N.Y.: Kraus Reprint Co., 1975). And R. J. Herrnstein, *IQ in the Meritocracy* (Boston: Little, Brown, 1973).

84. Richard J. Herrnstein and Charles Murray, *The Bell Curve: Intelligence and Class Structure in American Life* (New York: Free Press, 1994).

85. Garnets and Kimmel, *Psychological Perspectives,* 114.

86. Barbara Beckwith, "How Magazines Cover Sex Difference Research: Journalism Abdicates Its Watchdog Role," *Science for the People* (July-August 1984): 18–22.

87. Jacquelyn B. James, "His and Hers," *Boston Globe*, 25 May 1995.

88. Karen Messing, "The Scientific Mystique: Can a White Lab Coat Guarantee Purity in the Search for Knowledge About the Nature of Women?" in *Woman's Nature: Rationalizations of Inequality,* ed. Marian Lowe and Ruth Hubbard (New York: Pergamon Press, 1983), 75–88.

89. Bayer, *Homosexuality and American Psychiatry,* 65.

90. See comments of Charles Socarides in Jay Rayner, "Shrink Resistant," *Guardian*, 25 April 1995.

91. Halperin, *One Hundred Years of Homosexuality*, 50.

## Chapter 4

1. Richard D. Ashmore and Frances K. DelBoca, "Psychological Approaches to Understanding Intergroup Conflicts," in *Towards the Elimination of Racism,* ed. Phillis A. Katz (New York: Pergamon, 1976), 100.

2. A. P. MacDonald Jr., "Homophobia: Its Roots and Meanings," *Homosexual Counseling Journal* 3, 1 (1976): 23–33; G. Weinberg, *Society and the Healthy Homosexual* (New York: St. Martin's Press, 1972).

3. See Gregory K. Lehne, "Homophobia Among Men," in *The Forty-Nine Percent Majority: Reading on the Male Role,* ed. D. David and R. Brannon (Reading, Mass.: Addison Wesley, 1975). For measurement of homophobia on a fear and aversion scale, see Barry Sepekiff, "The Development of an Instrument to Measure Homophobia Among Heterosexual Males," diss., New York University, 1985, *Dissertation Abstracts* 4, 1 (July 1986): 93-A.

4. G. M. Herek, "Assessing Heterosexuals' Attitudes Toward Lesbians and Gay Men: A Review of Empirical Research with the ATLG Scale," in *Lesbian and Gay Psychology: Theory, Research, and Clinical Applications,* vol. 1, ed. Beverly Greene and Gregory M. Herek (Thousand Oaks, Calif.: Sage, 1994), 224.

5. N. M. Henley and F. Pinkus, "Interrelationship of Sexist, Racist, and Antihomosexual Attitudes," *Psychological Reports* 42 (1978): 83–90; M. E. Kite, "Psychometric Properties of the Homosexuality Attitude Scale," *Representative Research in Social Psychology* 19, 2 (1992): 3–18; L. A. Kurdek, "Correlates of Negative Attitudes Toward Homosexuals in Heterosexual College Students," *Sex Roles* 18 (1988): 727–738.

6. M. E. Kite, "When Perceptions Meet Reality: Individual Differences in Reactions to Lesbians and Gay Men," in *Lesbian and Gay Psychology: Theory, Research, and Clinical Applications,* vol. 1, ed. Beverly Greene and Gregory M. Herek (Thousand Oaks, Calif.: Sage, 1994), 28.

7. J. F. Dovidio and S. L. Gaertner, eds., *Prejudice, Discrimination, and Racism: Theory and Research* (Orlando, Fla.: Academic Press, 1986); H. Sigall and R. Page, "Current Stereotypes: A Little Fading, A Little Faking," *Journal of Personality and Social Psychology* 18 (1971): 247–255; Virginia Slims, *The 1990 Virginia Slims Opinion Poll: A 20-Year Perspective of Women's Issues,* Chicago, 1990.

8. M. E. Kite, "Psychometric Properties of the Homosexuality Attitude Scale," *Representative Research in Social Psychology* 19, 2 (1992): 3–18; M. E. Kite, B. E. Whitley Jr., and S. T. Michael, "Are Attributions About AIDS Victims Affected by the Social Desirability of the Source of Infection?" paper presented at the meeting of the Midwestern Psychological Association, Chicago, 1992.

9. Gallup poll reported in B. Turque, "Gays Under Fire," *Newsweek,* 14 September 1992, 35–40. Also Gallup poll, March 15–17, 1996, reported in *Los Angeles Times Syndicate,* 4 April 1996.

10. G. M. Herek, "Stigma, Prejudice, and Violence Against Lesbians and Gay Men," in *Homosexuality: Research Implications for Public Policy,* ed. J. C. Gonsiorek and J. D. Weinrich (Newbury Park, Calif.: Sage, 1991), 66–80.

11. Governor's Task Force on Bias-Related Violence, *Final Report,* 1988. (Available from Division of Human Rights, 55 W. 125th St., New York, N.Y., 10027).

12. Kite, "When Perceptions Meet Reality," 33.

13. For example, see M. J. Monteith, P. G. Devine, and J. R. Zuwerink, "Self-Directed Versus Other-Directed Affect as a Consequence of Prejudice-Related Discrepancies," *Journal of Personality and Social Psychology* 64, 2 (1993): 201.

14. E. Aronson and J. M. Carlsmith, "Experimentation in Social Psychology," in *Handbook of Social Psychology,* vol. 2, 2nd ed., ed. G. Lindzey and E. Aronson

(Reading, Mass.: Addison-Wesley, 1968), 1–79; M. E. Kite, "Psychometric Properties of the Homosexuality Attitude Scale," *Representative Research in Social Psychology* 19, 2 (1992): 3–18. Note similar observation made of race attitude studies in Yehuda Amir, "The Role of Intergroup Contact in Change of Prejudice and Ethnic Relations," in *Towards the Elimination of Racism*, ed. Phillis A. Katz (New York: Pergamon, 1976), 290–291.

15. Kite, "When Perceptions Meet Reality," 33.

16. A. H. Eagly, *Sex Differences in Social Behavior: A Social Role Interpretation* (Hillsdale, N.J.: Lawrence Erlbaum, 1987).

17. Kite, "When Perceptions Meet Reality."

18. See discussion of "categorization tendencies" in Richard D. Ashmore and Frances K. DelBoca, "Psychological Approaches to Understanding Intergroup Conflicts," *Towards the Elimination of Racism*, ed. Phillis A. Katz (New York: Pergamon, 1976), 88.

19. See G. M. Herek, "Beyond 'Homophobia': A Social Psychological Perspective on Attitudes Toward Lesbians and Gay Men," *Journal of Homosexuality* 10, 1–2 (1984): 1–21; Herek, "Assessing Heterosexuals' Attitudes."

20. G. M. Herek, "On Heterosexual Masculinity: Some Physical Consequences of the Social Construction of Gender and Sexuality," *American Behavioral Scientist* 29, 5 (1986): 563–577.

21. See Brice Wachterhauser, "Prejudice and Reason," in *Bigotry, Prejudice, and Hatred: Definitions, Causes, and Solutions*, ed. Robert M. Baird and Stuart E. Rosenbaum (Buffalo, N.Y.: Prometheus Books, 1992), 139–144.

22. Kite, "When Perceptions Meet Reality," 32.

23. Florence H. Davidson, in "Studies of Prejudice Prompt Researcher to Call for Character Education," *Brown University Child and Adolescent Behavior Letter* 11, 5 (May 1995): 1, 7.

24. Elisabeth Young-Bruehl, *The Anatomy of Prejudices* (Cambridge: Harvard Univ. Press, 1996).

25. Lawrence Kohlberg, *Essays on Moral Development*, vol. 2, *The Psychology of Moral Development* (San Francisco: Harper & Row, 1984).

26. See, for example, Mary Jeanne Larrabee, ed., *An Ethic of Care: Feminist and Interdisciplinary Perspectives* (New York: Routledge, 1993).

27. Ashmore and DelBoca, "Psychological Approaches," 96.

28. R. D. Ashmore, "Solving the Problem of Prejudice," in *Social Psychology*, ed. B. E. Collins (Reading, Mass.: Addison-Wesley, 1970).

29. Ashmore and DelBoca, "Psychological Approaches," 93.

30. See Theodore R. Warm, M.D., on teasing in "Children Go Through Stages of Teasing," *Brown University Child and Adolescent Behavior Letter* 11, 5 (May 1995): 1–2.

31. Karen Franklin, "Psychosocial Motivations of Hate Crimes Perpetrators: Implications for Educational Interventions," paper presented at the 106th annual convention of the American Psychological Association, San Francisco, 16 August 1998, 7.

32. Personal communication to author, July 1997.

33. Florence H. Davidson, in "Studies of Prejudice Prompt Researcher to Call for Character Education," *Brown University Child and Adolescent Behavior Letter*, 11, 5 (May 1995): 1, 7.

34. Elsa C. Arnett, "Gays Find Some Social Changes Harder to Win," *Detroit Free Press*, 16 April 1998.

35. Ashmore and DelBoca, "Psychological Approaches," 96.

36. Ibid., 106.

37. John Wayne Plasek and Janicemarie Allard, "Misconceptions of Homophobia," *Journal of Homosexuality* 10 (1984): 23–37.

38. ABC Evening News, 16 October 1998.

39. James T. Sears, "Responding to the Sexual Diversity of Faculty and Students: Sexual Praxis and the Critically Reflective Administrator," in *Educational Administration in a Pluralistic Society*, ed. Colleen A. Capper, (Albany: State Univ. of New York Press, 1993), 148.

40. Tyrone Beason, "Boys Skirt the Rules—'No Dress Code' Sparks Protest by Students," *Seattle Times*, 6 April 1996.

41. U.S. Department of Health and Human Services Report, 1993, cited in "Three Horrific Abuse Cases Leave Officials Grasping for Answers," *Boston Globe*, 4 December 1995, 12.

42. Richard D. Mohr, "Gay Basics: Some Questions, Facts, and Values," in *Bigotry, Prejudice, and Hatred: Definitions, Causes, and Solutions*, ed. Robert M. Baird and Stuart E. Rosenbaum (Buffalo, N.Y.: Prometheus Books, 1992), 167–182.

43. See, for example, George Mosse, *The Image of Man: The Creation of Modern Masculinity* (New York: Oxford Univ. Press, 1996). On the historical similarities between anti-Semitism and homophobia, see Warren J. Blumenfeld, "History/Hysteria: Parallel Representations of Jews and Gays, Lesbians, and Bisexuals," in *Queer Studies: A Lesbian, Gay, Bisexual, and Transgender Anthology*, ed. Brett Beemyn and Mickey Eliason (New York: State Univ. of New York Press, 1996), 146–162.

44. G. M. Herek, "Religion and Prejudice: A Comparison of Racial and Sexual Attitudes," *Personality and Social Psychology Bulletin* 13, 1 (1987): 56–65; G. M. Herek, "Heterosexuals' Attitudes Toward Lesbians and Gay Men: Correlates and Gender Differences," *Journal of Sex Research* 25 (1988): 451–477; G. M. Herek and E. K. Glunt, "Interpersonal Contact and Heterosexuals' Attitudes Toward Gay Men: Results from a National Survey," *Journal of Sex Research* 30 (1993): 239–244.

45. See Pierre L. Van Den Berghe, "The Biology of Nepotism," in , *Prejudice, and Hatred: Definitions, Causes, and Solutions*, ed. Robert M. Baird and Stuart E. Rosenbaum (Buffalo, N.Y.: Prometheus Books, 1992), 125–138.

46. Plasek and Allard, "Misconceptions of Homophobia," 29.

47. Herek, "Stigma, Prejudice, and Violence." Also, for example, national polls show that 84 percent support equal rights in job opportunities (Princeton Survey Research Associates, cited in Elsa C. Arnett, "Gays Find Some Social Changes Harder to Win," *Detroit Free Press*, 16 April 1998).

48. Kite, "When Perceptions Meet Reality," 37.

49. Immanuel Kant, *Fundamental Principles of the Metaphysics of Morals* (New York: Liberal Arts Press, 1949); John Rawls, *A Theory of Justice* (Cambridge: Belknap Press of Harvard Univ. Press, 1971).

50. The recalcitrant psychiatrist Charles Socarides uses this argument in a letter to *Commentary* (March 1993): "[Homosexuality] drives the sexes in opposite directions [so it] cannot make a society or keep one going for very long."

51. Ron Simmons, "Some Thoughts on the Challenges Facing Black Gay Intellectuals," in *Brother to Brother: New Writings by Black Gay Men*, ed. Essex Hemphill (Boston: Alyson Publications, 1991), 211.

52. See Dorothy Riddle, J. A. Hower, M. Bankins, and S. Crahen, "The Scale of Homophobia," *ACPA/NASPA Celebration*, Chicago 1987.

53. See Diana L. Eck, *On Common Ground: World Religions in America* (New York: Columbia Univ. Press, 1997).

54. James W. Fowler, *Stages of Faith: The Psychology of Human Development and the Quest for Human Meaning* (San Francisco: Harper & Row, 1981).

55. Herek, "Religion and Prejudice," 56–65; Herek, "Heterosexuals' Attitudes Toward Lesbians and Gay Men"; Herek and Glunt, "Interpersonal Contact and Heterosexuals' Attitudes," 239–244.

56. G. W. Allport and J. M. Ross, "Personal Religious Orientation and Prejudice," *Journal of Personality and Social Psychology* 5 (1967): 432–443.

57. Ibid.

58. Herek, "Assessing Heterosexuals' Attitudes," 219.

59. See the critique of Christian justifications of African American slavery in Peter Gomes, *The Good Book: Reading the Bible with Mind and Heart* (New York: William Morrow, 1996).

60. The references are respectively to Representative Robert Barr, Republican from Georgia, during the 1996–1997 session and to Michael Bowers, Georgia Attorney General and title figure in *Bowers v. Hardwick*, 106 S.Ct. 2841 (1986).

61. Paul Galloway, "NU Professor's Bible Lesson: There Are No Gospel Truths," *Chicago Tribune*, 6 March 1998.

62. Herek, "Stigma, Prejudice, and Violence."

63. Suzanne Pharr, *Homophobia: A Weapon of Sexism* (Little Rock, Ark.: Chardon Press, 1988).

64. Richard A. Isay, *Being Homosexual: Gay Men and Their Development* (New York: Avon, 1989), 81, 128; also R. J. Stoller, *Presentations of Gender* (New Haven: Yale Univ. Press, 1985).

65. M. E. Kite, "Individual Differences in Males' Reactions to Gay Males and Lesbians," *Journal of Applied Social Psychology* 22 (1992): 1222–1239; M. . Kite and K. Deaux, "Attitudes Toward Homosexuality: Assessment and Behavioral Consequences," *Basic and Applied Social Psychology* 7 (1986): 137–162.

66. Kite, "When Perceptions Meet Reality," 34.

67. K. Preston and K. Stanley, "'What's the Worst Thing . . . ?' Gender-Directed Insults," *Sex Roles* 17 (1987): 209–219.

68. D. Altman, *Homosexual Oppression and Liberation* (New York: Outerbridge and Dienstfrey, 1971), 69–70.

69. A. I. Henderson, "Homosexuality in the College Years: Developmental Differences Between Men and Women," *Journal of American College Health* 32 (1984): 216–219; R. Lewis, "Emotional Intimacy Among Men," *Journal of Social Issues* 31, 1 (1978): 108–121.

70. Jean Baker Miller, *Toward a New Psychology of Women* (Boston: Beacon Press, 1976), 112.

71. Adrienne Rich, "Compulsory Heterosexuality and Lesbian Existence," in *Lesbian and Gay Studies Reader*, ed. H. Abelove, M. Barale, and D. Halperin (New York: Routledge, 1993), 230.

72. Sheela Raja and Joseph P. Stokes, "Assessing Attitudes Toward Lesbians and Gay Men: The Modern Homophobia Scale," *Journal of Gay, Lesbian, and Bisexual Identity* 3, 2 (1998): 113–134.

73. M. E. Kite and K. Deaux, "Gender Belief Systems: Homosexuality and the Implicit Inversion Theory," *Psychology of Women Quarterly* 11 (1987): 83–96.

74. M. D. Storms, M. L. Stivers, S. M. Lambers, and C. A. Hill, "Sexual Scripts for Women," *Sex Roles* 7 (1981): 699–707.

75. K. Deaux and L. L. Lewis, "Structure of Gender Stereotypes: Interrelationships Among Components and Gender Label," *Journal of Personality and Social Psychology* 46 (1984): 991–1004.

76. Deaux and Lewis, "Structure of Gender Stereotypes"; G. M. Herek, "Attitudes Toward Lesbians and Gay Men: A Factor-Analytic Study," *Journal of Homosexuality* 10, 1–2 (1984): 39–52; Storms et al., "Sexual Scripts."

77. E. Levitt and A. Klassen, "Public Attitudes Toward Homosexuality: Part of the 1970 National Survey by the Institute for Sex Research," *Journal of Homosexuality* 1 (1974): 29–43.

78. J. E. Krulewitz and J. E. Nash, "Effects of Sex Role Attitudes and Similarity on Men's Rejection of Male Homosexuals," *Journal of Personality and Social Psychology* 38 (1980): 67–74; M. R. Laner and C. R. Laner, "Personal Style or Sexual Preference: Why Gay Men Are Disliked," *International Review of Modern Sociology* 9 (1979): 215–228; M. R. Laner and C. R. Laner, "Sexual Preference or Personal Style? Why Lesbians Are Disliked," *Journal of Homosexuality* 5 (1980): 339–356.

79. A. P. MacDonald Jr., J. Huggins, S. Young, and R. A. Swanson, "Attitudes Toward Homosexuality: Preservation of Sex Morality or the Double Standard?" *Journal of Consulting and Clinical Psychology* 40 (1973): 161; B. S. Newman, "The Relative Importance of Gender Role Attitudes to Male and Female Attitudes Toward Lesbians," *Sex Roles* 21 (1989): 451–465; B. E. Whitley Jr., "The Relationship of Sex-Role Orientation to Heterosexuals' Attitudes Toward Homosexuals," *Sex Roles* 17 (1987): 103–113.

80. Herek, "Religion and Prejudice"; Herek, "Heterosexuals' Attitudes Toward Lesbians and Gay Men"; Herek and Glunt, "Interpersonal Contact and Heterosexuals' Attitudes."

81. Kite, "Individual Differences in Males' Reactions"; M. E. Kite, "Sex Differences in Attitudes Toward Homosexuals: A Meta-Analytic Review," *Journal of Homosexuality* 10, 1–2 (1984): 69–81; Herek, "Heterosexuals' Attitudes Toward Lesbians and Gay Men"; R. Braungart and M. Braungart, "From Yippies to Yuppies: Twenty Years of Freshman Attitudes," *Public Opinion* 11, 3 (1988): 53–57; R. Coles and G. Stokes, *Sex and the American Teenager* (New York: Harper and Row, 1985); B. Glassner and C. Owen, "Variations in Attitudes Toward Homosexuality," *Cornell Journal of Social Relations* 11 (1979): 161–176; S. Hong, "Sex, Religion, and Factor Analytically Derives Attitudes Towards Homosexuality," *Australian Journal of Sex, Marriage, and Family* 4, 3 (1983): 142–150; K. Larsen, M. Reed, and S. Hoffman, "Attitudes of Heterosexuals Toward Homosexuality: A Likert-Type Scale and Construct Validity," *Journal of Sex Research* 16, 3 (1980): 245–257; A. MacDonald and R. Games, "Some Characteristics of Those Who Hold Positive and Negative Attitudes Toward Homosexuals," *Journal of Homosexuality* 1, 1 (1974): 9–27; F. Minnigerode, "Attitudes Toward Homosexuality: Feminist Attitudes and Sexual Conservatism," *Sex Roles: A Journal of Research* 2, 4 (1976): 347–352; K. Nyberg and

J. Alston, "Homosexual Labeling by University Youths," *Adolescence* 12, 48 (1977): 541–546; M. Young and J. Wertvine, "Attitudes of Heterosexual Students Toward Homosexual Behavior," *Psychological Reports* 51, 2 (1982): 673–674.

82. Herek, "On Heterosexual Masculinity"; S. F. Morin and E. M. Garfinkle, "Male Homophobia," *Journal of Social Issues* 34 (1978): 29–47.

83. C. S. Gentry, "Social Distance Regarding Male and Female Homosexuals," *Journal of Social Psychology* 127 (1987): 199–208; Herek, "Heterosexuals' Attitudes Toward Lesbians and Gay Men,"; Kite, "Sex Differences in Attitudes Toward Homosexuals"; B. E. Whitley Jr., "Sex Differences in Heterosexuals' Attitudes Toward Homosexuals: It Depends upon What You Ask," *Journal of Sex Research* 24 (1988): 287–291; Sheela Raja and Joseph P. Stokes, "Assessing Attitudes Toward Lesbians and Gay Men: The Modern Homophobia Scale," *Journal of Gay, Lesbian, and Bisexual Identity* 3, 2 (1998): 113–134.

84. G. M. Herek and E. K. Glunt, "An Epidemic of Stigma: Public Reactions to AIDS," *American Psychologist* 48, 5 (1993): 886–891.

85. 1995 *Times Mirror* poll.

86. Sue Kiefer Hammersmith, Interview on Homophobia, *Advocate*, 30 April 1985.

87. Victor J. Seidler, "Reason, Desire, and Male Sexuality," in *The Cultural Construction of Sexuality*, ed. Pat Caplan (New York: Tavistock, 1987), 99.

88. Kite, "When Perceptions Meet Reality," 42.

89. Ibid., 47.

90. Hammersmith, Interview.

91. Herek, "Religion and Prejudice," 56–65; G. M. Herek, "Can Functions Be Measured? A New Perspective on the Functional Approach to Attitudes," *Social Psychology Quarterly* 50 (1987): 285–303; Herek, "Heterosexuals' Attitudes Toward Lesbians and Gay Men."

92. R. Christopher Qualls et al., "Racial Attitudes on Campus: Are There Gender Differences?" *Journal of College Student Development* 6, 6 (1992): 524–530.

93. M. Forstein, "Homophobia: An Overview," *Psychiatric Annals* 18 (1988): 33–36; J. C. Gonsiorek, "Mental Health Issues of Gay and Lesbian Adolescents," *Journal of Adolescent Health Care* 9 (1988): 114–122; J. Loulan, *Lesbian Sex* (San Francisco: Spinsters, 1984); A. K. Malyon, "Psychotherapeutic Implications of Internalized Homophobia in Gay Men," *Journal of Homosexuality* 7 (1982): 59–70; Pharr, *Homophobia: A Weapon of Sexism*; J. Sophie, "Internalized Homophobia and Lesbian Identity," *Journal of Homosexuality* 14 (1988): 53–66.

94. Jack Thomas, "David Brudnoy's Secret Struggle," interview with David Brudnoy, *Boston Globe*, 7 November 1994.

95. A. Shidlo, "Internalized Homophobia: Conceptual and Empirical Issues in Measurement" in *Lesbian and Gay Psychology: Theory, Research, and Clinical Applications*, vol. 1, ed. Beverly Greene and Gregory M. Herek (Thousand Oaks, Calif.: Sage, 1994), 180.

96. R. A. Alexander, "The Relationship Between Internalized Homophobia and Depression and Low Self-Esteem in Gay Men," diss., Univ. of California at Santa Barbara, 1986; Malyon, "Psychotherapeutic Implications of Internalized Homophobia in Gay Men,"; W. D. Nicholson and B. C. Long, "Self-Esteem, Social Support, Internalized Homophobia, and Coping Strategies of HIV+ Gay Men," *Journal of Consulting and Clinical Psychology* 58 (1990): 873–876.

97. Alexander, "The Relationship Between Internalized Homophobia"; Malyon, "Psychotherapeutic Implications of Internalized Homophobia in Gay Men"; A. J. Sbordone, "Gay Men Choosing Fatherhood," diss., City Univ. of New York, 1993.

98. Malyon, "Psychotherapeutic Implications of Internalized Homophobia in Gay Men"; D. G. Finnegan and D. Cook, "Special Issues Affecting the Treatment of Male and Lesbian Alcoholics," *Alcoholism Treatment Quarterly* 1 (1984): 85–98; R. C. Friedman, "Couple Therapy with Gay Couples," *Psychiatric Annals* 21 (1991): 485–490; K. D. George and A. E. Behrent, "Therapy for Male Couples Experiencing Relationship and Sexual Problems," *Journal of Homosexuality* 14 (1988): 77–88; G. Lehne, "Homophobia Among Men," in *The Forty-Nine Percent Majority: The Male Sex Role,* ed. D. David and R. Brannon (Reading, Mass.: Addison Wesley, 1976), 66–88; L. Margolies, M. Becker, and K. Jackson-Brewer, "Internalized Homophobia: Identifying and Treating the Oppressor Within," in *Lesbian Psychologies: Explorations and Challenges,* ed. Boston Lesbian Psychologies Collective (Urbana: Univ. of Illinois Press, 1987), 229–241.

99. American Psychiatric Association, *Diagnostic and Statistical Manual of Mental Disorders,* 3rd ed. (Washington, D.C.: APA, 1980); J. C. Gonsiorek, "The Use of Diagnostic Concepts in Working with Gay and Lesbian Populations," *Journal of Homosexuality* 7 (1982): 9–20; Malyon, "Psychotherapeutic Implications of Internalized Homophobia in Gay Men"; A. Martin, "Some Issues in the Treatment of Gay and Lesbian Patients," *Psychotherapy: Theory, Research, and Practice* 19 (1982): 341–348; Sophie, "Internalized Homophobia," 53–66.

100. J. C. Gonsiorek, "Gay Male Identities: Concepts and Issues," in *Lesbian, Gay, and Bisexual Identities over the Lifespan,* ed. A. R. D'Augelli and C. J. Patterson (New York: Oxford Univ. Press, 1995), 33.

101. Shidlo, "Internalized Homophobia," 181.

102. J. Crocker and B. Major, "Social Stigma and Self-Esteem: The Self-Protective Properties of Stigma," *Psychological Review* 96 (1989): 608–630.

103. G. W. Allport, *The Nature of Prejudice* (Cambridge, Mass.: Addison-Wesley, 1954).

104. Ibid.

105. Sophie, "Internalized Homophobia."

106. J. C. Gonsiorek, "Mental Health Issues of Gay and Lesbian Adolescents," *Journal of Adolescent Health Care* 9 (1988): 114–122; Gonsiorek, "Gay Male Identities," 33.

107. Sophie, "Internalized Homophobia."

108. L. G. Nungesser, *Homosexual Acts, Actors, and Identities* (New York: Praeger, 1983); S. Folkman, R. S. Lazarus, C. Dunkel-Schetter, A. DeLongis, and F. J. Gruen, "Dynamics of a Stressful Encounter: Cognitive Appraisal, Coping, and Encounter Outcomes," *Journal of Personality and Social Psychology* 50 (1986): 992–1003; A. P. MacDonald, "The Importance of Sex-Role to Gay Liberation," *Homosexual Counseling Journal* 1, 4 (1974): 169–180; W. D. Nicholson and B. C. Long, "Self-Esteem, Social Support"; Sbordone, "Gay Men Choosing Fatherhood"; Shidlo, "Internalized Homophobia."

109. Henry Adams, Leston W. Wright, and Bethany Lohr, "Is Homophobia Associated with Homosexual Arousal?" *Journal of Abnormal Psychology* 105, 3 (1996): 440–445.

110. Seidler "Reason, Desire, and Male Sexuality," 99. On the correspondence between self-discrepancy along masculine traits and homophobia, see Peter S. Theodore and Susan A. Basow, "Heterosexual Masculinity and Homophobia: A Reaction to the Self," paper presented at the 106th annual convention of the American Psychological Association, San Francisco, 16 August 1998.

111. "Toll in Condom Plan Prison Riots Rises to Six," *Los Angeles Times* (from wire services), 23 August 1997.

112. Allport, *The Nature of Prejudice.* Also L. Kohlberg and D. Candee, "The Relation of Judgment to Action," in *Moral Development and Moral Behavior,* ed. W. Kurtines and I. Gewirtz (New York: Wiley, 1984).

113. M. Fishbein and I. Ajzen, "Attitudes Toward Objects as Predictors of Single and Multiple Behavioral Criteria," *Psychological Review* 81 (1974): 59–74; I. Ajzen, "The Attitude Behavior Relation: On Behaving in Accordance with One's Attitudes," in *Consistency in Social Behavior: The Ontario Symposium,* vol. 2, ed. M. P. Zanna, E. T. Higgina, and C. P. Herman (Hillsdale, N.J.: Lawrence Erlbaum, 1982), 3–15; S. Epstein, "The Stability of Behavior: II. Implications for Psychological Research," *American Psychologist* 35 (1980): 790–806; S. Epstein, "Aggregation and Beyond: Some Basic Issues on the Prediction of Behavior," *Journal of Personality* 51 (1983): 360–392.

114. W. Mischel, "The Interaction of Person and Situation," in *Personality at the Crossroads: Current Issues in Interactional Psychology,* ed. D. Magnusson and N. S. Endler (Hillsdale, N.J.: Lawrence Erlbaum, 1977), 333–352; T. C. Monson, J. W. Hesley, and L. Chernick, "Specifying When Personality Traits Can and Cannot Predict Behavior: An Alternative to Abandoning the Attempt to Predict Single-Act Criterias," *Journal of Personality and Social Psychology* 43 (1982): 385–399.

115. R. P. Abelson, "Three Modes of Attitude-Behavior Consistency," in *Consistency in Social Behavior: The Ontario Symposium,* vol. 2, ed. M. P. Zanna, E. T. Higgins, and C. P. Herman (Hillsdale, N.J.: Lawrence Erlbaum, 1982).

116. D. D. Stein, "The Influence of Belief Systems on Interpersonal Preference: A Validation Study of Rokeach's Theory of Prejudice," *Psychological Monographs: General and Applied* 616 (1966).

117. Kite, "When Perceptions Meet Reality," 45.

118. P. G. Devine, M. Monteith, J. R. Zuwerink, and A. J. Elliot, "Prejudice with and Without Compunction," *Journal of Personality and Social Psychology* 60 (1991): 817–830; Monteith et al., "Self-Directed Versus Other-Directed Affect."

119. Kite, "Individual Differences."

120. C. Gray, P. Russell, and S. Blockley, "The Effects upon Helping Behavior of Wearing Pro-Gay Identification," *British Journal of Social Psychology* 30 (1991): 171–178.

121. T. A. Fish and B. J. Rye, "Attitudes Toward a Homosexual or Heterosexual Person with AIDS," *Journal of Applied Social Psychology* 21 (1991): 651–667; M. R. Stevenson, "Social Distance from Persons with AIDS," *Journal of Psychology and Human Sexuality* 4 (1991): 13–20.

122. A. E. Gross, S. K. Green, J. T. Storck, and J. M. Vanyur, "Disclosure of Sexual Orientation and Impressions of Male and Female Homosexuals," *Personality and Social Psychology Bulletin* 6 (1980): 307–314 ; S. B. Gurwitz and M. Marcus, "Effects of Anticipated Interaction, Sex, and Homosexual Stereotypes on First

Impressions," *Journal of Applied Social Psychology* 8 (1978): 47–56; J. E. Krulewitz and J. E. Nash, "Effects of Sex Role Attitudes and Similarity on Men's Rejection of Male Homosexuals," *Journal of Personality and Social Psychology* 38 (1980): 67–74.

123. Kite and Deaux, "Attitudes Toward Homosexuality."

124. Kite, "When Perceptions Meet Reality," 46.

125. National Gay and Lesbian Task Force, *Anti-Gay Violence and Victimization and Defamation in 1986* (Washington, D.C.: NGLTF, 1987). Available from NGLTF, 1517 U Street NW, Washington, D.C. 20009.

126. E. Weissman, "Kids Who Attack Gays," *Christopher Street*, August 1978, 9–13.

127. A. V. Horowitz and H. R. White, "Gender Role Orientations and Styles of Pathology Among Adolescents," *Journal of Health and Social Behavior* 28 (1987): 158–170.

128. G. M. Herek, "Hate Crimes Against Lesbians and Gay Men: Issues for Research and Policy," *American Psychologist* 44, 6 (1989): 953.

129. U.S. Army Regulation 635-200, chap. 15, sec. 15-2(A), "Policy": "Homosexuality Is Incompatible with Military Service."

130. Committee on the Armed Services 93-32, "Hearing to Receive Testimony from Current and Former Members of the Military Services of Gay Men and Lesbians in the Armed Forces," 11 May 1993.

131. Matthew Brelis, "Lewd Hazing on Cutter Detailed," *Boston Globe*, 8 April 1998.

132. Major Kathleen G. Bergeron, in Committee on the Armed Services, 93–32, "Hearing to Receive Testimony."

133. Note that under "don't ask, don't tell" not only public homosexual acts are forbidden, but also private off-duty and off-base behavior with the observation that such requirements apply to both homosexuals and heterosexuals (Official Guidelines on homosexual conduct in the armed forces, *Congressional Quarterly*, 24 July 1993). Heterosexuals are not being held to that standard and they never have; officers have been driven to visit with prostitutes while their military chauffeur waited outside (Donald M. Murray, "Combatting Hypocrisy, Homophobia," *Boston Globe*, 2 February 1993).

134. Craig Donegan, "For Military's Men, Change Comes Slowly, with Great Resistance," *Congressional Quarterly*, reprinted in *Bay Windows* (Boston), 16 May 1996.

135. See, for example, Whidbey Island Naval Air Station in Randy Shilt's *Conduct Unbecoming: Gays and Lesbians in the U.S. Military* (New York: St. Martin's Press, 1993), 720.

136. See "Army Faces Obstacle: A Less-Macho Image," *Wall Street Journal*, 15 July 1997.

137. L. A. Kauffman, "Praise the Lord, and Mammon," *Nation*, 26 September 1994, 3–8.

138. See Harvey Cox in Peter S. Conellos, "A Promise or a Threat?" *Boston Globe*, 19 July 1997; and Joe Conason, Alfred Ross, and Lee Cokorinos, "The Promise Keepers Are Coming," *Nation* 263, 10 (7 October 1996): 11–19.

139. The Scouts have barred homosexuals since their founding in 1910.

140. "Alabama Exhibitionist Inmates to Get a Sort of Scarlet Letter," *Boston Globe* (AP), 19 May 1995, 16.

141. "Renaming Street to Pansy Circle Could Deter Gangs, Police Say," *Associated Press*, 8 April 1998.


## Chapter 5

1. See Vicki L. Eaklor, "Of Politics and History: Gay Americans in and out of Textbooks," *AHA Perspectives*, October 1991.

2. See, for example, James Burnham, "Early References to Homosexual Communities in American Medical Writings," *Medical Aspects of Human Sexuality* 7 (1973): 40–49.

3. Evelyn A. Hooker, "The Adjustment of the Male Overt Homosexual," *Journal of Projective Techniques* 21 (1957): 17–31; see also Ronald Bayer, *Homosexuality and American Psychiatry: The Politics of Diagnosis* (Princeton: Princeton Univ. Press, 1981).

4. George Chauncey, *Gay New York: Gender, Urban Culture, and the Making of the Male Gay World, 1890–1940* (New York: Basic Books, 1994), 9.

5. See Martin Duberman, "A Matter of Difference," *Nation*, 5 July 1993, 22–24.

6. Epistle to the Romans (1:26)

7. Jonathan Ned Katz, *Gay and Lesbian Almanac* (New York: Harper & Row, 1983), 59.

8. Ibid., 31.

9. Ibid., 29.

10. Ibid., 32.

11. John D'Emilio, "Gay Politics and Community in San Francisco Since World War II," in *Psychological Perspectives on Lesbian and Gay Male Experiences*, ed. L. D. Garnets and D. C. Kimmel (New York: Columbia Univ. Press, 1993), 59–79.

12. Chauncey, *Gay New York*, 10.

13. Katz, *Gay and Lesbian Almanac*, 165, 259.

14. Chauncey, *Gay New York*.

15. Ibid., 4; and George Chauncey, "The Way We Were," *Village Voice* 31, 26 (1 July 1986): 29.

16. Chauncey, *Gay New York*, 7.

17. See Johnathan Ned Katz, "1892–1915: The Homosexual Underworld in American Cities," chap. 1 in *Gay American History: Lesbians and Gay Men in the U.S.A.: A Documentary* (New York: Crowell, 1976), 61–90.

18. Katz, *Gay American History*, 62.

19. Ibid., 65.

20. Ibid., 65–66.

21. Ibid., 66–67.

22. Ibid., 75.

23. Chauncey, *Gay New York*, 6.

24. Katz, *Gay American History*, 71–72.

25. Ibid., 73.

26. Ibid., 76–80.

27. Ibid., 80–82.

28. Lilian Faderman, *Odd Girls and Twilight Lovers: A History of Lesbian Life in Twentieth-Century America* (New York: Penguin Books, 1991), 73–75.

29. John D'Emilio, *Sexual Politics, Sexual Communities: The Making of a Homosexual Minority in the United States, 1940–1970* (Chicago: Univ. of Chicago Press, 1983), 98.

30. Faderman, *Odd Girls*, 14.

31. Ibid., 130.

32. Martin Duberman, "A Matter of Difference," *Nation*, 5 July 1993, 22–24.

33. Faderman, *Odd Girls*, 30.

34. Neil Miller, *Out of the Past: Gay and Lesbian History from 1869 to the Present* (New York: Vintage Books, 1995), 58.

35. Carol Smith-Rosenberg, "Discourses of Sexuality and Subjectivity: The New Woman, 1870–1936," in *Hidden from History: Reclaiming the Gay and Lesbian Past*, ed. Martin Duberman, Martha Vicinus, and George Chauncey Jr. (New York: Penguin Books, 1989), 271.

36. Faderman, *Odd Girls*, 25.

37. See Estelle Freedman, *Maternal Justice: Miriam Van Waters and the Female Reform Tradition* (Chicago: Univ. of Chicago Press, 1996).

38. Richard von Krafft-Ebbing, *Psychopathia Sexualis* (Stuttgart: F. Enke, 1888).

39. Faderman, *Odd Girls*, 54.

40. See Katz, *Gay American History*, esp. ch. 2, "Treatment: 1884–1974."

41. Miller, *Out of the Past*, 233.

42. Timothy F. Murphy, "Redirecting Sexual Orientation: Techniques and Justifications," *Journal of Sex Research* 29, 4 (1992): 501–523; Katz, *Gay American History*, ch. 2; A. P. Bell and M. S. Weinberg, *Homosexuality: An Annotated Bibliography*, ed. Martin S. Weinberg and Alan P. Bell (New York: Harper and Row, 1972); James Harrison, "Changing Our Minds," documentary film, 1992.

43. See British Broadcasting Company documentary film "Dark Secret," 1996, for the stories of some even killed by aversion therapies in Britain in the 1960s and 1970s.

44. From Lord Alfred Douglas's 1894 poem "Two Loves."

45. Edouard Bourdet, *La Prisonnière*, trans. Arthur Hornblow Jr. (New York: Brentano's, 1926).

46. Katz, *Gay and Lesbian Almanac*, 428.

47. Ibid., 463.

48. D'Emilio, *Sexual Politics*, 132.

49. New York paper *Brevities*, in Katz, *Gay and Lesbian Almanac*, 486–487.

50. Sukie de la Croix (pseud.), "Gay Activist Henry Gerber," *Chicago Tribune*, 31 July 1998.

51. Miller, *Out of the Past*, 333–334.

52. Allan Bérubé, "Marching to a Different Drummer: Lesbian and Gay GIs in World War II," in *Hidden from History: Reclaiming the Gay and Lesbian Past*, ed. Martin Duberman, Martha Vicinus, and George Chauncey Jr. (New York: Penguin Books, 1989), 384.

53. Bérubé, "Marching," 389.

54. Ibid., 385.

55. Ibid., 386.

56. Ibid., 385.

57. Ibid., 392.

58. D'Emilio, *Sexual Politics*, 46.

59. Alfred C. Kinsey, W. B. Pomeroy, and C. E. Martin, *Sexual Behavior in the Human Male* (Philadelphia: W. B. Saunders, 1948); Alfred C. Kinsey, W. B. Pomeroy, C. E. Martin, and P. H. Gebhard, *Sexual Behavior in the Human Female* (Philadelphia: W. B. Saunders, 1953).

60. Bayer, *Homosexuality and American Psychiatry*, 43.

61. Ibid., 45.

62. Ibid., 43–44.

63. D'Emilio, *Sexual Politics*, 41.

64. Katz, *Gay American History*, 150–151.

65. Ibid., 141.

66. Ibid., 144.

67. Ibid., 153.

68. On Hoover, see Anthony Summers, *Official and Confidential: The Secret Life of J. Edgar Hoover* (London: Victor Gollancz, 1993); on Cohn, see Miller, *Out of the Past*, 266–267.

69. Katz, *Gay American History*, 155.

70. From *The New York Post*, in Katz, *Gay American History*, 146.

71. D'Emilio, *Sexual Politics*, 42–43.

72. Katz, *Gay American History*, 154.

73. D'Emilio, *Sexual Politics*, 44.

74. Ibid., 44–45.

75. Ibid., 45.

76. Ibid., 44.

77. Karen M. Harbeck, "Gay and Lesbian Educators: Past History/Future Prospects," in *Coming Out of the Classroom Closet: Gay and Lesbian Students, Teachers, and Curricula*, ed. Karen M. Harbeck (New York: Haworth Press, 1992), 125.

78. D'Emilio, *Sexual Politics*, 46–49.

79. Katz, *Gay American History*, 167–181.

80. D'Emilio, *Sexual Politics*, 49–51.

81. Katz, *Gay American History*, 616.

82. Ibid., 627.

83. In the tension between the National Gay and Lesbian Task Force and the Human Rights Campaign, for example.

84. Katz, *Gay American History*, 626.

85. Ibid., 162–163.

86. Ibid., 649.

87. D'Emilio, *Sexual Politics*, 101.

88. Katz, *Gay American History*, 634–635.

89. Ibid., 646.

90. Ibid., 648.

91. D'Emilio, *Sexual Politics*, 106.

92. Katz, *Gay American History*, 640.

93. Ibid., 644.

94. D'Emilio, *Sexual Politics*, 209.

95. Katz, *Gay American History,* 306–315.

96. Franklin Kameny, from a letter to *ONE* (magazine), 27 August 1960, cited in D'Emilio, *Sexual Politics,* 151.

97. D'Emilio, *Sexual Politics,* 153.

98. Her debate with Kameny was published in *The Ladder.* See Katz, *Gay American History,* 642.

99. Donald Webster Cory (pseud.), *The Homosexual in America: A Subjective Approach* (New York: Greenberg, 1951).

100. D'Emilio, *Sexual Politics,* 167.

101. Katz, *Gay American History,* 644–645.

102. Martin Duberman, *Stonewall* (New York: Dutton, 1993), 286–287, note 3; and D'Emilio, *Sexual Politics,* 168.

103. Masha Gessen, "Twenty-Five Gay and Lesbian Years," *Advocate* 613, 6 October 1992.

104. D'Emilio, *Sexual Politics,* 165.

105. Ibid., 231.

106. Quoted in Donn Teal, *The Gay Militants* (New York: Stein & Day, 1971), 17–18.

107. "Gay Power Comes to Sheridan Square" and "Full Moon Over Stonewall: View from Inside," *Village Voice,* 3 July 1969, both from Teal, *The Gay Militants,* 19.

108. Teal, *The Gay Militants,* 20.

109. Ibid., 21.

110. Leo Skir, cited in Teal, *The Gay Militants,* 24.

111. Ibid.

112. Owen Keehnan, "Interview with Edmund White," *Men's Style* (magazine), March-April 1995, 23.

113. Teal, *The Gay Militants,* 41–42.

114. Toby Marotta, *The Politics of Homosexuality* (Boston: Houghton Mifflin, 1981), 71–72.

115. Marotta, *The Politics of Homosexuality,* 74–76.

116. See for example Anne Moody, *Coming of Age in Mississippi* (New York: Dial Press, 1968).

117. Martin Duberman, *Cures: A Gay Man's Odyssey* (New York: Dutton, 1991), 161.

118. Katz, *Gay American History,* 642.

119. Teal, *The Gay Militants,* 35.

120. Gessen, "Twenty-Five Gay and Lesbian Years."

121. On the emulation of African American models of protest, see Marotta, *The Politics of Homosexuality,* 96–97.

122. Ibid., 93; and Miller, *Out of the Past,* 373.

123. See Simon Karlinsky, "Russia's Gay Literature and Culture: The Impact of the October Revolution," in *Hidden from History: Reclaiming the Gay and Lesbian Past,* ed. Martin Duberman, Martha Vicinus, and George Chauncey Jr. (New York: Penguin Books, 1989), 347–364; Lourdes Arguelles and B. Ruby Rich, "Homosexuality, Homophobia, and Revolution" in *Hidden from History: Reclaiming the Gay and Lesbian Past,* ed. Martin Duberman, Martha Vicinus, and George Chauncey Jr. (New York: Penguin Books, 1989), 48; John Lauritsen and David Thorstad, *The*

*Early Homosexual Rights . Movement, 1864–1935* (New York: Times Change Press, 1974), 62–70; and Marotta , *The Politics of Homosexuality,* 130–131.

124. Steven Epstein, "G ay Politics, Ethnic Identity: The Limits of Social Constructionism," *Socialist Rev iew* 93/94 (May–August 1987): 45.

125. D'Emilio, *Sexual Pol. itics,* 228.

126. On Friedan's and N( )W's hostility, see Miller, *Out of the Past,* 374–376.

127. Faderman, *Odd Girls,* 212.

128. National Institute of 1 Mental Health, *Final Report of the Task Force on Homosexuality* (Washington, D.C.: 1 NIMH, 1969), 32.

129. Bayer, *Homosexuality a nd American Psychiatry,* 51–52; for a list of Hooker's often reprinted articles, see D' Emilio, *Sexual Politics,* 112, note 12.

130. Bayer, *Homosexuality an d American Psychiatry,* 118.

131. Ibid., 60–64.

132. Henry Abelove, "Freud , Male Homosexuality, and the Americans," *Dissent* (Winter 1996): 67–68.

133. Bayer, *Homosexuality and American Psychiatry,* 64.

134. Ibid., 60.

135. Ibid., 167.

136. Ibid., 217.

137. *Bowers v. Hardwick,* 478 US ' 186 (1986).

138. Gessen, "Twenty-Five Gay and Lesbian Years."

139. "Sodomy Law Furthers '1 Moral Welfare' Says Georgia Court," *ACLU Newswire,* 12 March 1996.

140. G. M. Herek, "Illness, Stigma ι, and AIDS," in *Psychological Aspects of Serious Illness,* ed. G. R. Vanden Bos and P. T. Costa (Washington, D.C.: American Psychological Association, 1990).

141. Julie Irwin, "Law Denying Ga y Protection Stands," *Cincinnati Enquirer,* 14 October 1998.

## Chapter 6

1. Anonymous, letter to Arthur Lipk in, teacher, Cambridge Rindge and Latin School, 12 January 1987.

2. See, for example, Erik Erikson, *Iden tity, Youth, and Crisis* (New York: Norton, 1968).

3. J. Schippers, "Gay Affirmative Coun: sel ing and Psychotherapy in the Netherlands," paper presented at meeting of th ie American Psychological Association, Boston, August 1990.

4. B. Ponse, *Identities in the Lesbian World: The Social Construction of Self* (Westport, Conn.: Greenwood Press, 1978); B. Ponse, "Lesbians and Their Worlds," in *Homosexual Behavior: A Modern Reappraisal,* ed. J. 1 Marmor (New York: Basic Books, 1980), 157–175; D. G. Wolfe, *The Lesbian Communi ty* (Berkeley: Univ. of California Press, 1979); D. M. Cronin, "Coming Out among L esbians," in *Sexual Deviance and Sexual Deviants,* ed. E. Goode and R. R. Troiden (New York: William Morrow, 1974), 268–277; J. M. Gagnon and W. Simon, "Hom osexuality: The Formulation of a Sociological Perspective," in *Approaches to Devi iance: Theories, Concepts, and Research Findings,* ed. M. Lefton, J. K. Skipper Jr., and ( .. H. McGaghy (New York: Appleton-

Century-Crofts, 1968), 349–361; J. M. Gagnon and W. Simon, *Sexual Conduct: The Social Sources of Human Sexuality* (Chicago: Aldine, 1973); D. W. Cory and J. P. LeRoy, *The Homosexual and His Society: A View from Within* (New York: Citadel Press, 1963).

5. Gagnon and Simon, "Homosexuality: The Formulation"; Gagnon and Simon, *Sexual Conduct;* M. T. Saghir and E. Robbins, *Male and Female Homosexuality: A Comprehensive Investigation* (Baltimore: Williams & Wilkins, 1973); E. Hooker, "Male Homosexuals and Their 'Worlds,'" in *Sexual Inversion: The Multiple Roots of Homosexuality,* ed. J. Marmor (New York: Basic Books, 1965), 83–107.

6. Ponse, *Identities in the Lesbian World;* Ponse, "Lesbians and Their Worlds"; Wolf, *The Lesbian Community;* Hooker, "Male Homosexuals."

7. Eli Coleman, "Developmental Stages of the Coming Out Process," in *Homosexuality: Social, Psychological, and Biological Issues,* ed. W. Paul, J. D. Weinrich, J. C. Gonsiorek, and M. E. Hotvedt (Thousand Oaks, Calif.: Sage, 1982).

8. V. C. Cass, "Homosexual Identity Formation: Testing a Theoretical Model," *Journal of Sex Research* 20 (1984): 143–167.

9. Richard R. Troiden, "The Formation of Homosexual Identities," in *Gay and Lesbian Youth,* ed. Gilbert Herdt (New York: Harrington Park Press, 1989.)

10. A. M. Boxer and B. J. Cohler, "The Life Course of Gay and Lesbian Youth: An Immodest Proposal," *Journal of Homosexuality* 17, 3–4 (1989): 315–355.

11. Celia Kitzinger and S. Wilkinson, "Transitions from Heterosexuality to Lesbianism: The Discursive Production of Lesbian Identities," *Developmental Psychology* 31, 1 (1995): 95–104.

12. H. L. Minton and G. J. McDonald, "Homosexual Identity Formation as a Developmental Process," *Journal of Homosexuality* 9 (1984): 91–104.

13. Richard R. Troiden, "The Formation of Homosexual Identities," in *Gay and Lesbian Youth,* ed. G. Herdt (Binghamton, N.Y.: Harrington Park Press, 1989), 47.

14. Kristine L. Falco, *Psychotherapy with Lesbian Clients: Theory into Practice* (New York: Brunner/Mazel, 1991), 90.

15. J. Gramick, "Developing a Lesbian Identity," in *Women-Identified Women,* ed. T. Darty and S. Potter (Palo Alto, Calif.: Mayfield, 1984), 31–44; F. Suppe, "In Defense of a Multidimensional Approach to Sexual Identity," *Journal of Homosexuality* 10 (1984): 7–14.

16. Falco, *Psychotherapy with Lesbian Clients,* 91.

17. Ponse, *Identities in the Lesbian World.*

18. D. P. McWhirter and A. M. Mattison, *The Male Couple: How Relationships Develop* (Englewood Cliffs, N.J.: Prentice-Hall, 1984).

19. Troiden, "The Formation of Homosexual Identities," 47–48.

20. J. C. Gonsiorek, "Mental Health Issues of Gay and Lesbian Adolescents," *Journal of Adolescent Health Care* 9 (1988): 114–122.

21. G. Herdt and A. Boxer, *Children of Horizons* (Boston: Beacon Press, 1993), 20.

22. L. D. Garnets and D. C. Kimmel, "Introduction: Lesbian and Gay Male Dimensions in the Psychological Study of Human Diversity," in *Psychological Perspectives on Lesbian and Gay Male Experiences,* ed. L. D. Garnets and D. C. Kimmel (New York: Columbia Univ. Press, 1993), 14, note 2.

23. See L. Kohlberg and D. Candee, "The Relation of Judgment to Action," in *Moral Development and Moral Behavior,* ed. W. Kurtines and I. Gewirtz (New York: Wiley, 1984).

24. J. Henken, "Conceptualizations of Homosexual Behavior Which Preclude Homosexual Self-Labeling," *Journal of Homosexuality* 9, 4 (1984): 53–63.

25. R. R. Troiden, *Gay and Lesbian Identity: A Sociological Analysis* (New York: General Hall, 1988); C. de Monteflores and S. Schultz, "Coming Out: Similarities and Differences for Lesbians and Gay Men," *Journal of Social Issues* 34, 3 (1978): 59–72; Henken, "Conceptualizations."

26. E. Hetrick and D. Martin, "Developmental Issues and Their Resolution for Gay and Lesbian Adolescents," *Journal of Homosexuality* 14, 1–2 (1987): 25–43; Joyce Hunter and Robert Schaecher, "Lesbian and Gay Youth," in *Planning to Live: Evaluating and Treating Suicidal Youths in Community Settings*, ed. M. Rotheram-Borus, J. Bridle, and N. Obolensky (Tulsa: Univ. of Oklahoma Press, 1990).

27. "Massachusetts Youth Risk Behavior Survey 1997," report (Malden: Massachusetts Department of Education, August 1998). The figure was 31.6 percent versus 11.8 percent in 1995. (See Chapter 8.)

28. John Reid, *The Best Little Boy in the World* (New York: G. P. Putnam, 1973), 31.

29. J. C. Gonsiorek, "Mental Health Issues of Gay and Lesbian Adolescents," *Journal of Adolescent Health Care* 9 (1988): 118.

30. Reid, *The Best Little Boy*, 32.

31. Gonsiorek, "Mental Health Issues," 118.

32. J. T. Sears, *Growing Up Gay in the South* (New York: Harrington Park Press, 1991), 202–231.

33. Sears, *Growing Up Gay*, 211.

34. Saghir and Robbins, *Male and Female Homosexuality*, 1973.

35. M. Hunt, *Sexual Behavior in the 1970s* (New York: Dell, 1974).

36. B. Miller, "Gay Fathers and Their Children," *The Family Coordinator* 28 (1979): 544–552; S. Schafer, "Sexual and Societal Problems of Lesbians," *Journal of Sex Research* 12, 1 (1976): 50–79; J. Fast and H. Wells, *Bisexual Living* (New York: Pocket Books, 1975).

37. F. Klein, *The Bisexual Option: A Concept of One Hundred Percent Intimacy* (New York: Arbor House, 1978); F. Klein, *The Bisexual Option*, 2nd ed. (New York: Harrington Park Press, 1993); Beverly Greene, "Lesbian and Gay Sexual Orientation: Implications for Clinical Training, Practice, and Research," in *Lesbian and Gay Psychology: Theory, Research, and Clinical Applications*, ed. B. Greene and G. M. Herek (Thousand Oaks, Calif.: Sage, 1994): 1–24; J. Money, *Gay, Straight, and In Between: The Sexology of Erotic Orientation* (New York: Oxford Univ. Press, 1988); L. Garnets and D. Kimmel, "Lesbian and Gay Male Dimensions in the Psychological Study of Human Diversity," in *Psychological Perspectives on Human Diversity in America: Master Lectures*, ed. J. Goodchilds (Washington, D.C.: American Psychological Association, 1991): 143–192.

38. Heather Wishik and Carol Pierce, *Sexual Orientation and Identity: Heterosexual, Lesbian, Gay, and Bisexual Journeys* (Laconia, N.H.: New Dynamics Publications, 1995), 202.

39. L. D. Garnets and D. C. Kimmel, "Origins of Sexual Orientation," in *Psychological Perspectives on Lesbian and Gay Male Experiences*, ed. L. D. Garnets and D. C. Kimmel (New York: Columbia University Press, 1993), 111.

40. P. W. Blumstein and P. Schwartz, "Bisexuality: Some Social Psychological Issues," in *Psychological Perspectives on Lesbian and Gay Male Experiences,* ed. L. D. Garnets and D. C. Kimmel (New York: Columbia Univ. Press, 1993).

41. A. P. Bell, M. S. Weinberg, and S. K. Hammersmith, *Sexual Preference: Its Development in Men and Women* (Bloomington: Indiana University Press, 1981).

42. Ruth Westheimer, "Ask Doctor Ruth," King Features Syndicate, 29 June 1996.

43. Martin S. Weinberg, in Shankar Vedantam, no title, *Knight-Ridder/Tribune Business News,* 1 August 1996.

44. P. W. Blumstein and P. Schwartz, "Bisexuality: Some Social Psychological Issues," in *Psychological Perspectives on Lesbian and Gay Male Experiences,* ed. L. D. Garnets and D. C. Kimmel (New York: Columbia Univ. Press, 1993).

45. Beverly Greene, "Lesbian and Gay Sexual Orientation: Implications for Clinical Training, Practice, and Research," in *Lesbian and Gay Psychology: Theory, Research, and Clinical Applications,* ed. Beverly Greene and Gregory Herek (Thousand Oaks, Calif.: Sage, 1994), 4–5.

46. Herdt and Boxer, *Children of Horizons,* 166–172.

47. Garnets and Kimmel, "Introduction: Lesbian and Gay Male Dimensions," 14.

48. J. C. Gonsiorek, "Gay Male Identities: Concepts and Issues," in *Lesbian, Gay, and Bisexual Identities over the Lifespan,* ed. A. R. D'Augelli and C. J. Patterson (New York: Oxford University Press, 1995), 37–38.

49. Carmen de Montefores, "Notes on the Management of Difference," in *Psychological Perspectives on Lesbian and Gay Male Experiences,* ed. L. D. Garnets and D. C. Kimmel (New York: Columbia Univ. Press, 1993), 218–247.

50. Hetrick and Martin, "Developmental Issues," 39.

51. See Roy Cain, "Stigma Management and Gay Identity Development," *Social Work* 36, 1 (1991): 67–73.

52. Troiden, "The Formation of Homosexual Identities," 53–54.

53. Ibid., 69.

54. Saghir and Robbins, *Male and Female Homosexuality.*

55. Troiden, *Gay and Lesbian Identity;* A. P. Bell and M. S. Weinberg, *Homosexualities: A Study of Diversity Among Men and Women* (New York: Simon & Schuster, 1978); A. P. Bell, M. S. Weinberg, and S. K. Hammersmith, *Sexual Preference: Its Development in Men and Women* (Bloomington: Indiana Univ. Press, 1981).

56. Herdt and Boxer, *Children of Horizons,* 181.

57. Gramick, "Developing a Lesbian Identity," 31–44; S. Schaefer, "Sexual and Social Problems of Lesbians," *Journal of Sex Research* 12 (1976): 50–69.

58. C. de Montefores and S. J. Schultz, "Coming Out: Similarities and Differences for Lesbians and Gay Men," *Journal of Social Issues* 34, 3 (1978): 59–72.

59. Troiden, "The Formation of Homosexual Identities," 59.

60. Margaret Schneider, "Sappho Was a Right-On Adolescent: Growing Up Lesbian," in *Gay and Lesbian Youth,* ed. G. Herdt (Binghamton, N.Y.: Harrington Park Press, 1989), 111–130.

61. Herdt and Boxer, *Children of Horizons,* 181.

62. Mary B. Harris and Gail K. Bliss, "Coming Out in a School Setting: Former Students' Experiences and Opinions About Disclosure," in *School Experiences of Gay and Lesbian Youth,* ed. Mary Harris (Binghamton, N.Y.: Haworth Press, 1998).

63. B. Zuger, "The Role of Familial Factors in Persistent Effeminate Behavior in Boys," *American Journal of Psychiatry* 126 (1970): 1167–1170; R. Green, "One Hundred Ten Feminine and Masculine Boys: Behavioral Contrast and Demographic Similarities," *Archives of Sexual Behavior* 5 (1976): 425–446; R. Green, "Gender Identity in Childhood and Later Sexual Orientation: Follow-Up on 78 Males," *American Journal of Psychiatry* 142 (1985): 339–341; G. Zuger, "Effeminate Behavior Present in Boys from Childhood: Ten Additional Years of Follow-Up," *Comprehensive Psychiatry* 19 (1978): 363–369.

64. Richard Green, *The "Sissy Boy Syndrome" and the Development of Homosexuality* (New Haven: Yale Univ. Press, 1986).

65. J. Michael Bailey and Kenneth J. Zucker, "Childhood Sex-Typed Behavior and Sexual Orientation: A Conceptual Analysis and Quantitative Review," *Developmental Psychology* 31, 1 (1995): 43–55.

66. J. C. Fracher and M. S. Kimmel, "Hard Issues and Soft Spots: Counseling Men About Sexuality," in *Handbook of Counseling and Psychotherapy with Men,* ed. M. Scher, M. Stevens, G. Good, and G. A. Eichenfield (Newbury Park, Calif.: Sage, 1987); Gagnon and Simon, *Sexual Conduct.*

67. G. Herdt, "Gay and Lesbian Youth, Emergent Identities, and Cultural Scenes at Home and Abroad," *Journal of Homosexuality* 17, 1–4 (1989): 1–42; P. Paroski, "Healthcare Delivery and the Concerns of Gay and Lesbian Adolescents," *Journal of Adolescent Health Care* 8 (1987): 188–192; P. C. Larsen, "Gay Male Relationships," in *Homosexuality: Social, Psychological, and Biological Issues,* ed. W. Paul, J. D. Weinrich, J. C. Gonsiorek, and M. E. Hotvedt (Thousand Oaks, Calif.: Sage, 1982), 219–232; T. S. Weinberg, "On 'Doing' and 'Being' Gay: Sexual Behavior and Homosexual Male Self-Identity," *Journal of Homosexuality* 4, 2 (1978): 143–156.

68. J. Hencken, "Conceptualizations of Homosexual Behavior Which Preclude Homosexual Self-Labeling," *Journal of Homosexuality* 18, 1–2 (1984): 53–63.

69. P. Blumstein and P. Schwartz, "Intimate Relationships and the Creation of Sexuality," in *Gender in Intimate Relationships: A Microstructural Approach,* ed. B. Risman and P. Schwartz (Belmont, Calif.: Wadsworth, 1989), 120–129; G. D. Wilson, "Male-Female Differences in Sexual Activity, Enjoyment, and the Fantasies," *Personality and Individual Differences* 8 (1987): 125–127.

70. Troiden, "The Formation of Homosexual Identities"; Schippers, "Gay Affirmative Counseling."

71. Gramick, "Developing a Lesbian Identity."

72. V. A. Vetere, "The Role of Friendship in the Development and Maintenance of Lesbian Love Relationships," *Journal of Homosexuality* 8, 2 (1983): 51–65; S. Schaefer, "Sociosexual Behavior in Male and Female Homosexuals," *Archives of Sexual Behavior* 6 (1977): 355–364.

73. J. Harry, "Gay Male and Lesbian Relationships," in *Contemporary Families and Alternative Lifestyles: Handbook on Research and Theory,* ed. E. Macklin and R. Rubin (Beverly Hills, Calif.: Sage, 1983): 216–234.

74. Blumstein and Schwartz, "Intimate Relationships"; Vetere, "The Role of Friendship."

75. Sara Lucia Hoagland, *Lesbian Ethics: Toward New Value* (Palo Alto, Calif.: Institute of Lesbian Studies, 1988); Marilyn Frye, *The Politics of Reality: Essays in*

*Feminist Theory* (Freedom, Calif.: Crossing Press, 1983). See C. Kitzinger, S. Wilkinson, and R. Perkins, "Heterosexuality," *Feminism and Psychology* 2, 3 (1992): 293–509, for intentional lesbianism as a political tool to replace essentialism.

76. Adrienne Rich, "Compulsory Heterosexuality and Lesbian Existence," in *The Gay and Lesbian Studies Reader*, ed. H. Abelove, M. A. Barale, and D. M. Halperin (New York: Routledge, 1993).

77. J. T. Sears, *Growing Up Gay in the South*, 224.

78. A. R. D'Augelli, "Lesbian and Gay Male Development: Steps Toward an Analysis of Lesbians' and Gay Men's Lives," in *Lesbian and Gay Psychology: Theory, Research, and Clinical Applications*, ed. B. Greene and G. M. Herek (Thousand Oaks, Calif.: Sage, 1994), 127.

79. Blumstein and Schwartz, "Bisexuality," 168–184.

80. J. C. Gonsiorek, "Gay Male Identities," 31.

81. Blumstein and Schwartz, "Bisexuality," 177.

82. Troiden, "The Formation of Homosexual Identities," 43–74; J. T. Sears, "The Impact of Gender and Race on Growing Up Lesbian and Gay in the South," *National Women's Studies Association Journal* 1 (1989): 42–57; A. P. Bell and M. S. Weinberg, *Homosexualities: A Study of Diversity*; M. S. Weinberg and C. Williams, *Male Homosexuals: Their Problems and Adaptations* (New York: Oxford Univ. Press, 1974).

83. P. A. Sergio and J. Cody, "Physical Attractiveness and Social Assertiveness Skills in Male Homosexual Dating Behavior and Partner Selection," *Journal of Social Psychology* 125 (1985): 505–514; P. Blumstein and P. Schwartz, *American Couples: Money, Work, Sex* (New York: Morrow, 1983).

84. G. D. Wilson, "Male-Female Differences in Sexuality, Enjoyment and Fantasies," *Personality and Individual Differences* 8 (1987): 125–127; V. Green, "Experimental Factors in Childhood and Adolescent Sexual Behavior: Family Interactions and Previous Sexual Experiences," *Journal of Sex Research* 21 (1985): 157–182; D. E. Phyllis and M. H. Gramko, "Sex Differences in Sexual Activity: Reality or Illusion," *Journal of Sex Research* 21 (1985): 437–448; M. Hunt, *Sexual Behavior in the 1970s* (Chicago: Playboy, 1974).

85. L. A. Lewis, "The Coming Out Process for Lesbians: Integrating a Stable Identity," *Social Work* (September-October 1984): 464–469.

86. Catherine Roberts, Harvard University, personal communication, 1998.

87. Troiden, "The Formation of Sexual Identities," 70.

88. D. Palladino and Y. Stevenson, "Perceptions of the Sexual Self: Their Impact on Relationships Between Heterosexual Women," *Women and Therapy* 9 (1990): 231–253; E. Blackwood, "Breaking the Mirror: The Construction of Lesbianism and the Anthropological Discourse on Homosexuality," *Journal of Homosexuality* 11, 3–4 (1985): 1–17; A. Faraday, "Liberating Lesbian Research," in *The Making of the Modern Homosexual*, ed. K. Plummer (London: Hutchinson, 1981), 112–129.

89. Suzanna Rose, "Sexual Pride and Shame in Lesbians," in *Lesbian and Gay Psychology: Theory, Research, and Clinical Applications*, ed. B. Greene and G. M. Herek (Thousand Oaks, Calif.: Sage, 1994), 71–83.

90. Bell and Weinberg, *Homosexualities: A Study of Diversity*, 138.

91. Lewis, "The Coming Out Process for Lesbians," 468.

92. B. K. Vance and V. Green, "Lesbian Identities: An Examination of Sexual Behavior and Sex Role Attribution as Related to Age of Initial Same-Sex Sexual Encounter," *Psychology of Women Quarterly* 8, 3 (1984): 293–307.

93. Laura S. Brown, "Lesbian Identities: Concepts and Issues," *Lesbian, Gay, and Bisexual Identities over the Lifespan: Psychological Perspectives,* ed. Anthony R. D'Augelli and Charlotte J. Patterson (New York: Oxford University Press, 1995), 3–23.

94. Ibid., 20.

95. Rich, "Compulsory Heterosexuality."

96. N. Chodorow, *The Reproduction of Mothering* (Berkeley, Univ. of California Press, 1978).

97. C. Golden, "Our Politics and Choices: The Feminist Movement and Sexual Orientation," in *Lesbian and Gay Psychology: Theory, Research, and Clinical Applications,* ed. B. Greene and G. M. Herek (Thousand Oaks, Calif.: Sage, 1994), 54–70.

98. C. Kitzinger and S. Wilkinson, "Transitions from Heterosexuality to Lesbianism: The Discursive Production of Lesbian Identities," *Developmental Psychology* 31, 1 (1995): 95–104.

99. Ponse, *Identities in the Lesbian World.*

100. "On a Straight Tip, Intimacy Between Females Is 'In,'" *Philadelphia Inquirer,* 29 August 1996.

101. G. Remafedi, "Homosexual Youth: A Challenge to Contemporary Society," *JAMA* 258, 2 (1987): 233; J. Gonsiorek and J. Weinrich, eds., *Homosexuality: Research Implications for Public Policy* (Newbury Park, Calif.: Sage, 1991), 8; C. Kitzinger and S. Wilkinson, "The Precariousness of Heterosexual Feminist Identities," in *Making Connections: Women's Studies, Women's Movements,* ed. M. Kennedy, C. Walsh, and V. Walsh (London: Taylor and Francis, 1993), 24–36.

102. Garnets and Kimmel, "Introduction: Lesbian and Gay Male Dimensions," 11.

103. P. C. Rust, "'Coming Out' in the Age of Social Constructionism: Sexual Identity Formation Among Lesbian and Bisexual Women," *Gender and Society* 7, 1 (1993): 50–77; D'Augelli, "Lesbian and Gay Male Development," 118–132.

104. R. C. Fox, "Coming Out Bisexual: Identity, Behavior, and Sexual Orientation Self-disclosure," unpublished doctoral diss., California Institute of Integral Studies, San Francisco, 1993; P. C. Rust, "The Politics of Sexual Identity: Sexual Attraction and Behavior Among Lesbian and Bisexual Women," *Social Problems* 39, 4 (1992): 366–386; P. C. Rust, "'Coming Out' in the Age of Social Constructionism," 50–77; C. Golden, "Diversity and Variability in Women's Sexual Identities," in *Lesbian Psychologies: Explorations and Challenges,* ed. Boston Lesbian Psychologies Collective (Urbana: Univ. of Illinois Press, 1987), 18–34.

105. Diane Richardson, "Recent Challenges to Traditional Assumptions About Homosexuality: Some Implications for Practice," in *Psychological Perspectives on Lesbian and Gay Male Experiences,* ed. L. D. Garnets and D. C. Kimmel (New York: Columbia Univ. Press, 1993), 117–129.

106. Robert T. Michael, Edward Laumann, John Gagnon, and Gina Kolata, *Sex in America: A Definitive Survey* (Boston: Little Brown, 1994).

107. Michael Szymanski, "Movies Reflect the Undefined Sexuality of Youth," *Real People* (Bimonthly, New York, N.Y.), June 1997.

108. Blumstein and Schwartz, "Bisexuality: Some Social Psychological Issues"; E. R. Weise, ed., *Closer to Home: Bisexuality and Feminism* (Seattle: Seal Press, 1992); D. Haldeman, "Sexual Orientation Conversion Therapy for Gay Men and Lesbians: A Scientific Examination," in J. Gonsiorek and J. Weinrich, eds., *Homosexuality: Research Implications for Public Policy* (Newbury Park, Calif.: Sage, 1991); C. Golden, "Diversity and Variability in Women's Sexual Identities"; and Ponse, *Identities in the Lesbian World.*

109. Brown, "Lesbian Identities: Concepts and Issues," 14.

## Chapter 7

1. See Gilbert Herdt, "Introduction: Gay and Lesbian Youth, Emergent Identities, and Cultural Scenes at Home and Abroad," in *Gay and Lesbian Youth*, ed. Gilbert Herdt (Binghamton, N.Y.: Harrington Park Press, 1989), 16–20.

2. Lee Song-sun, "In My View (Readers' Forum): 'Coming Out of the Closet,'" *(Seoul) Korea Herald*, 21 November 1998.

3. See Gilbert Herdt and Andrew Boxer, *Children of Horizons: How Gay and Lesbian Teens Are Leading a New Way Out of the Closet* (Boston: Beacon Press, 1993), 241.

4. Taiwan, for example, as illustrated in the following headlines: "Taiwan Government to Air Radio Show for Gays," *Reuters*, 27 June 1996; and "Taiwan to See Its First Gay Wedding," *Reuters*, 14 July 1996.

5. One 1998 poll, for example, showed some differences on two variables: 57 percent of blacks said homosexuality was "morally wrong," compared to 50 percent of whites; 69 percent of blacks opposed gay marriage, compared with 63 percent of whites. Roper Center poll, cited in Lekan Oguntoyinbo, "Black Gays a Social Force," *Detroit Free Press*, 30 March 1999.

6. See George Chauncey, *Gay New York: Gender, Urban Culture, and the Making of the Gay Male World, 1890–1940* (New York: Basic Books, 1994); John D'Emilio, *Sexual Politics, Sexual Communities: The Making of a Homosexual Minority in the United States, 1940–1970* (Chicago: Univ. of Chicago Press, 1983); Lilian Faderman, *Odd Girls and Twilight Lovers: A History of Lesbian Life in Twentieth-Century America* (New York: Columbia Univ. Press, 1991); and Jonathan Ned Katz, *Gay/Lesbian Almanac: A New Documentary* (New York: Harper and Row, 1983).

7. Faderman, *Odd Girls and Twilight Lovers*, 167–174.

8. Herdt, "Introduction," 8; Bob Tremble, Margaret Schneider, and Carol Appathurai, "Growing Up Gay or Lesbian in a Multicultural Context," in *Gay and Lesbian Youth*, ed. G. Herdt (Binghamton, N.Y.: Harrington Park Press, 1989), 261; and Emery S. Hetrick and A. Damien Martin, "Developmental Issues and Their Resolution for Gay and Lesbian Adolescents," *Journal of Homosexuality*, 14, 1–2 (1987): 39.

9. Hetrick and Martin, "Developmental Issues," 39–40; for working-class Latinos, see Tomas Almaguer, "Chicano Men: A Cartography of Homosexual Identity and Behavior," in *The Lesbian and Gay Studies Reader*, ed. H. Abelove, M. Barale, and D. Halperin (New York: Routledge, 1993), 264–265.

10. Governor's Commission on Gay and Lesbian Youth, "Prevention of Health Problems Among Gay and Lesbian Youth: Making Health and Human Services Accessible and Effective for Gay and Lesbian Youth" (Boston: Governor's Commission on Gay and Lesbian Youth, August 1994), 37.

11. Bernie Sue Newman, "The Effects of Traditional Family Values on the Coming Out Process of Gay Male Adolescents," *Adolescence* 28, 109 (Spring 1993): 213–226.

12. Beverly Greene, "Ethnic-Minority Lesbians and Gay Men: Mental Health and Treatment Issues," in *Journal of Consulting and Clinical Psychology* 62, 2 (1994): 243–251.

13. "Cornel West on Heterosexism and Transformation: An Interview," special issue of the *Harvard Educational Review*, 66, 2 (1996): 356–367.

14. Essex Hemphill, introduction to *Brother to Brother: New Writings by Black Gay Men*, ed. Essex Hemphill (Boston: Alyson, 1991), xv.

15. Cheryl Clarke, "The Failure to Transform: Homophobia in the Black Community," in *Home Girls: A Black Feminist Anthology*, ed. Barbara Smith (New York: Kitchen Table, Women of Color Press, 1983), 200; L. Dyne, "Is D.C. Becoming the Gay Capital of America?" *Washingtonian*, September 1980, 96.

16. Clarke, "The Failure to Transform," 198.

17. Hemphill, introduction to *Brother to Brother*, xvi.

18. J. R. Porter, *Dating Habits of Young Black Americans* (New York: Kendall & Hunt, 1979). See also *Harvard Crimson* 6 (November 1991), for reporter Eliot Morgan's interview with Afro-centrist university professor Leonard Jeffries.

19. Alycee Lane, "Pride at Home," *BLK*, July 1990, 13. Reprinted with permission.

20. See Eldridge Cleaver, "Notes on a Native Son," in *Soul on Ice* (New York: Dell, 1968), 97–111.

21. See discussion of Kunjufu Hare et al. in Ron Simmons, "Some Thoughts on the Challenges Facing Black Gay Intellectuals," in *Brother to Brother: New Writings by Black Gay Men*, ed. Essex Hemphill (Boston: Alyson, 1991), 212–215.

22. Angus Shaw, "Demonstrators Force Gay Activists to Abandon Exhibit," *Associated Press*, 2 August 1996. See also Angus Shaw, "Zimbabwe's Mugabe, at Book Fair, Assails Homosexuals as 'Perverts,'" *Boston Globe*, 2 August 1995; "Zimbabwe's Mugabe Attacks Homosexuals Again," *Reuters*, 28 February 1996; and "Zimbabwe Government Bans Gays from Book Fair Again," *Reuters*, 24 July 1996.

23. Namibian President Sam Nujoma, in *(Windhoek, Namibia) Namibian*, 30 January 1997. See also Cris Chinaka, "Castrate Gays, Zimbabwe Campaigner Says," *Reuters*, 5 March 1997.

24. David Tuller, "Lesbians, Gays Seek Asylum from Persecution Abroad," *San Francisco Chronicle*, 13 January 1997.

25. Rosalind Bentley, "Gays to Share Tales of 'Cures' at 'Shelter from Hate' Conference," *(Minneapolis) Star Tribune*, 11 October 1997.

26. "The Myth of Homosexuality in Kenya Society," *(Nairobi, Kenya) Daily Nation*, Wednesday Magazine: Special Report, 24 June 1998.

27. Robert Staples, *Black Masculinity: The Black Man's Role in American Society* (San Francisco: Black Scholar Press, 1982) 88.

28. In "Agenda," *Advocate*, 17 November 1995.

29. Ice Cube, as quoted in Earl Ofari Hutchinson, Ph.D., "My Gay Problem, Your Black Problem," *Chicago Defender* (newspaper), 14 June 1997.

30. Marlon Riggs, "Black Macho Revisited: Reflections of a SNAP! Queen," in *Brother to Brother: New Writings by Black Gay Men*, ed. Essex Hemphill (Boston: Alyson, 1991), 254.

31. Riggs, "Black Macho Revisited," 254.

32. See, for example, John Blake, "Resistance Strong in Black Pews," *Atlanta Journal Constitution*, 31 May 1998; and Donette Dunbar, "Black Churches and Gays," *Omaha World-Herald*, 18 April 1998.

33. "Malcom," in James T. Sears, *Growing Up Gay in the South* (Binghamton, N.Y.: Harrington Park Press, 1991), 58.

34. See the film *All God's Children*, Dee Mosbacher and Frances Reid, directors; Dee Mosbacher, Frances Reid, and Sylvia Rhue, producers, 1996.

35. Christopher Clark, "Farrakhan Targets Gay Men During KC Rally," *(Boston) Bay Windows*, 14, 49, November 29–December 4, 1996, 14. For analysis of Farrakhan, Ben-Jochanan, and others, see Simmons, "Some Thoughts on the Challenges Facing Black Gay Intellectuals," 222–224; and Irene Monroe, "Louis Farrakhan's Ministry of Misogyny and Homophobia," in *The Farrakhan Factor*, ed. Amy Alexander (New York: Grove Press, 1998), 275–298. Also Steven Gray, "Farrakhan Speaks Out at Dorchester Mosque," *Boston Globe*, 8 August 1997.

36. See Clarke, "The Failure to Transform," 199; Hemphill, introduction to *Brother to Brother*, xxviii; and Greene, "Ethnic-Minority Lesbians and Gay Men," 246; and A. Poussaint, "An Honest Look at Black Gays and Lesbians, *Ebony*, September 1990, 124, 126, 130–131.

37. See Clarke, "The Failure to Transform," 206; and Tania Abdulahad, Gwendolyn Rogers, Barbara Smith, and Jameelah Waheed, "Black Lesbian/Feminist Organizing: A Conversation," in *Home Girls: A Black Feminist Anthology*, ed. Barbara Smith (New York: Kitchen Table, Women of Color Press, 1983), 313.

38. Opinion of Robert Penn, assistant director of education for prevention services, Gay Men's Health Crisis, in Liz Galst, "Silent Scream: AIDS Is Quietly Devastating the Black Gay Arts Community," *Boston Phoenix*, 19 February 1993. See also Philip Brian Harper, "Eloquence and Epitaph: Black Nationalism and the Homophobic Impulse in Responses to the Death of Max Robinson," in *The Lesbian and Gay Studies Reader*, ed. Henry Abelove, Michele Aina Barale, and David Halperin (New York: Routledge, 1993), 159–175.

39. bell hooks, "Homophobia in Black Communities," *Zeta Magazine* 1, 3 (1988): 36.

40. Hemphill, introduction to *Brother to Brother*, xxviii.

41. Heather Wishik and Carol Pierce, *Sexual Orientation and Identity: Heterosexual, Lesbian, Gay, and Bisexual Journeys* (Laconia, N.H.: New Dynamics, 1991), 81.

42. See Taylor Branch, *Parting the Waters: America in the King Years, 1954–1963* (New York: Simon & Schuster, 1988), 196–197, 861–862.

43. Reference in Earl Ofari Hutchinson, "My Gay Problem, Your Black Problem," *Chicago Defender*, 14 June 1997.

44. See account of a 1993 speech by Khalid Abdul Muhammad, national spokesman for the Nation of Islam in *BLK* 5, 3 (March 1994): 22–23.

45. Steven Corbin, in Galst, "Silent Scream."

46. See hooks, "Homophobia in Black Communities," 36–37.

47. Greene, "Ethnic-Minority Lesbians and Gay Men," 243–251.

48. See hooks, "Homophobia in Black Communities," 36; and Larry Icard, "Black Gay Men and Conflicting Social Identities: Sexual Orientation Versus Racial Identity," *Journal of Social Work and Human Sexuality* 4 (1986): 87.

49. Audre Lorde, *ZAMI: A New Spelling of My Name* (Watertown, Mass.: Crossing Press, 1982), 224.

50. Tania Abdulahad et al., "Black Lesbian/Feminist Organizing," 301.

51. Clarke, "The Failure to Transform," 197.

52. For example, E. Lynn Harris, *Invisible Life: A Novel* (New York: Anchor, 1994).

53. Co-star Damon Wayans continued to gay-bash "faggots" in his club act. See Richard Johnson, "Rough Humor," *New York Post*, 18 May 1998.

54. Earl Ofari Hutchinson, "A Diminished View of Manhood," *Salon* (online magazine), 6 April 1998.

55. Alice Walker, *The Color Purple* (New York: Harcourt, Brace, Jovanovich, 1992).

56. See Alice Walker, *The Same River Twice: Honoring the Difficult: A Meditation on Life, Spirit, Art, and the Making of the Film* The Color Purple, *Ten Years Later* (New York: Scribner, 1996).

57. Gloria Naylor, *Women of Brewster Place* (New York: Viking Press, 1982).

58. Whitney Houston, for example, who has repeatedly denied a lesbian relationship with her manager.

59. Joseph Beam, "Brother to Brother: Words from the Heart," in *In the Life: A Black Gay Anthology*, ed. Joseph Beam (Boston: Alyson, 1986), 231.

60. Informal congressional hearing during the March on Washington for Lesbian and Gay Civil Rights, April 1993.

61. T. Beame, "Young, Gifted, Black, and Gay: Dr. Julius Johnson," *Advocate*, 8 July 1982, 25.

62. See, for example, Revon Kyle Banneker (pseud.), "Marlon Riggs Untied," *OUT/LOOK* 10 (Fall 1990): 18; and Shawn Hinds, "Mayor Ken Reeves, Cambridge, Massachusetts," *BLK* 5, 1 (January 1994): 8.

63. Hemphill, introduction to *Brother to Brother*, xxii.

64. hooks, "Homophobia in Black Communities," 38.

65. *Tongues Untied*, Marlon Riggs, director, 1989.

66. Audre Lorde, "There Is No Hierarchy of Oppressions," *Interracial Books for Children Bulletin* 14, 3–4 (1983): 9.

67. Barbara Smith, introduction to *Home Girls: A Black Feminist Anthology*, ed. Barbara Smith (New York: Kitchen Table, Women of Color Press, 1983), xxxii.

68. Greene, "Ethnic-Minority Lesbians and Gay Men," 246.

69. Marlon Riggs, "Tongues Untied," in *Brother to Brother: New Writings by Black Gay Men*, ed. Essex Hemphill (Boston: Alyson, 1991), 203.

70. For an analysis, see Isaac Julien and Kobena Mercer, "True Confessions: A Discourse on Images of Black Male Sexuality," in *Brother to Brother: New Writings by Black Gay Men*, ed. Essex Hemphill (Boston: Alyson, 1991), 169–170.

71. Charles Silverstein, *Man to Man: Gay Couples in America* (New York: Morrow, 1981), 164–165.

72. Lane, "Pride at Home," 14. Reprinted with permission.

73. Hemphill, introduction to *Brother to Brother*, xx.

74. Banneker (pseud.), "Marlon Riggs Untied," 18.

75. Huey P. Newton, "A Letter from Huey to the Revolutionary Brothers and Sisters About the Women's Liberation and Gay Liberation Movements," *Gay Flames, Pamphlet No. 7*, 1970, quoted in Hemphill, introduction to *Brother to Brother*, xxiv.

76. Deb Price, "Gays Owe Black Caucus Deep Thanks," *San Jose (Calif.) Mercury News*, 21 December 1995.

77. *Congressional Record*, 104th Congress, 11 July 1996.

78. Senate debate on Defense of Marriage Act, 10 September 1996. *Congressional Record*, S 10105.

79. Terry Wilson, "King's Widow Stands Up for Gay Rights," *Chicago Tribune*, 1 April 1998.

80. Bob Drogin, "South Africa: Gays Chalk Up New Rights to Nation's Cruel History," *Los Angeles Times*, 31 December 1996.

81. Donald G. McNeil Jr., "In a New South Africa, Homosexuals Find Resistance to Change," *New York Times*, 18 November 1997.

82. Jonathan Petre, "Outcry As Leading Bishop Backs Gay Clergy," *Telegraph* (London), 22 June 1997, 16.

83. 1436 U St. NW, Suite 200, Washington, D.C. 20009. Tel: (202) 483-6786. Email: nbgllf@aol.com

84. *All God's Children*, Dee Mosbacher and Frances Reid, directors; Dee Mosbacher, Frances Reid, and Sylvia Rhue, producers. Women Vision, 3145 Geary Blvd., Box 421, San Francisco, CA 94118.

85. Carla Trujillo, ed., *Chicana Lesbians: The Girls Our Mothers Warned Us About* (Berkeley: Third Woman Press, 1991).

86. See Marta A. Navarro, "Interview with Ana Castillo," in *Chicana Lesbians: The Girls Our Mothers Warned Us About*, ed. Carla Trujillo (Berkeley: Third Woman Press, 1991), 122–123; and Emma Pérez, "Sexuality and Discourse: Notes from a Chicana Survivor," in *Chicana Lesbians: The Girls Our Mothers Warned Us About*, ed. Carla Trujillo (Berkeley: Third Woman Press, 1991), 174–179.

87. Pérez, "Sexuality and Discourse," 174–175.

88. Carla Trujillo, "Chicana Lesbians: Fear and Loathing in the Chicano Community," in *Chicana Lesbians: The Girls Our Mothers Warned Us About*, ed. Carla Trujillo (Berkeley: Third Woman Press, 1991), 189; and Oliva M. Espín, "Issues of Identity in the Psychology of Latina Lesbians," in *Psychological Perspectives on Lesbian and Gay Male Experience*, ed. Linda D. Garnets and Douglas C. Kimmel (New York: Columbia Univ. Press, 1993), 353.

89. Trujillo, "Chicana Lesbians: Fear and Loathing," 190.

90. A. Carballo-Dieguez, "Hispanic Culture, Gay Male Culture, and AIDS: Counseling Implications," *Journal of Counseling and Development*, 68 (1989): 26–30.

91. Cherríe Moraga, *Loving in the War Years* (Boston: South End Press, 1983), 111.

92. Octavio Paz, *The Labyrinth of Solitude: Life and Thought in Mexico* (New York: Viking Penguin, 1985, c1961).

93. Raimundo Pereira, in Laurie Goering, "Violence Against Gay Brazilians Comes Out in Open," *Chicago Tribune*, 4 April 1997.

94. Almaguer, "Chicano Men," 261.

95. Marvin Goldwert, "Mexican Machismo: The Flight from Femininity," *Psychoanalytic Review* 72, 1 (1985): 161–169.

96. See, for example, Huseyin Tapinc, "Masculinity, Femininity, and Turkish Male Homosexuality," in *Modern Homosexualities: Fragments of Lesbian and Gay Experience*, ed. Ken Plummer (London: Routledge, 1992), 39–49; and Neil Miller, "Egypt: In the Realm of the Polymorphous Perverse," in *Out in the World: Gay and Lesbian Life from Buenos Aires to Bangkok* (New York: Random House, 1992), 67–92.

97. Almaguer, "Chicano Men," 262–263.

98. H. Hidalgo, "The Puerto Rican Lesbian in the United States," in *Women-Identified Women*, ed. T. Darty and S. Potter (Palo Alto: Mayfield, 1984), 105–150; E. Morales, "Latino Gays and Latina Lesbians," in *Counseling Gay Men and Lesbians: Journey to the End of the Rainbow*, ed. S. Dworkin and F. Gutierrez (Alexandria, Va.: American Association for Counseling and Development, 1992), 125–139; and Goering, "Violence Against Gay Brazilians."

99. Jarrett Barrios, in Alisa Valdis, "Coming Out in Spanish," *Boston Globe*, 23 July 1998.

100. Joseph Hanania, "Facing Their Fears," *Los Angeles Times*, 20 May 1997.

101. Florangela Davila, "Persecuted for Being Gay, Venezuelan Starts Over in the United States," *Seattle Times*, 11 June 1996.

102. Goering, "Violence Against Gay Brazilians"; and elected Deputy Fernando Gabeira, in "Rio's Gays March for Tolerance and Right to Marry," *Reuters*, 29 June 1997.

103. "Asylum for Gays Is a Policy That Needs Protecting," *Philadelphia Daily News*, 14 June 1997.

104. See Annick Prieur, *Mema's House, Mexico City: On Transvestites, Queens, and Machos* (Chicago: Univ. of Chicago Press, 1998).

105. Phil Gunson, "Cuba's Gay Cabaret Defies the Party," *Scripps-Howard News Service*, 15 February 1998.

106. Anthony Faiola, "In Dramatic Change, Gays Are Winning Acceptance in Argentina," *Washington Post*, 28 September 1997.

107. Robert W. Gardner, Bryant Robey, and Peter C. Smith, *Asian Americans: Growth, Change, and Diversity* (Washington, D.C.: Population Reference Bureau, 1989), 8.

108. *Trikone Magazine*, P.O. Box 21354, San Jose, CA 95151.

109. C. S. Chan, "Issues of Identity Development Among Asian American Lesbians and Gay Men," *Journal of Counseling and Development* 68 (1989): 18.

110. Trinity A. Ordona, "The Challenges Facing Asian and Pacific Islander Lesbian and Bisexual Women in the U.S.: Coming Out, Coming Together, Moving Forward," in *The Very Inside: An Anthology of Writing by Asian and Pacific Islander Lesbian and Bisexual Women*, ed. Sharon Lim-Hing (Toronto: Sister Vision, 1994), 389.

111. J. Kehaulani and Ju Hui "Judy" Han, "'Asian Pacific Islander': Issues of Representation and Responsibility," in *The Very Inside: An Anthology of Writing by Asian and Pacific Islander Lesbian and Bisexual Women*, ed. Sharon Lim-Hing (Toronto: Sister Vision, 1994), 377–378.

112. Chan, "Issues of Identity Development," (1989) 19; Linda Wong, "Mini Liu, Long-Time Activist," in *The Very Inside: An Anthology of Writing by Asian and Pacific Islander Lesbian and Bisexual Women*, ed. Sharon Lim-Hing (Toronto: Sister

Vision, 1994), 351; Nayan Shah, "Sexuality, Identity, and the Uses of History," in *A Lotus of Another Color: An Unfolding of the South Asian Gay and Lesbian Experience,* ed. Rakesh Ratti (Boston: Alyson, 1993), 119; and Tremble, Schneider, and Appathurai, "Growing Up Gay or Lesbian in a Multicultural Context," 260.

113. Chan, "Issues of Identity Development," (1989) 19.

114. Shah, "Sexuality, Identity, and the Uses of History," 117.

115. C. K. Bradshaw, "A Japanese View of Dependency: What Can Amae Psychology Contribute to Feminist Theory and Therapy?" in *Women and Therapy* 9, 1–2 (1990): 67–86; H. Pamela, "Asian American lesbians: An Emerging Voice in the Asian American Community," in *Making Waves: An Anthology of Writings By and About Asian American Women,* ed. Asian American Women United of California (Boston: Beacon Press, 1989), 282–290; C. S. Chan, "Asian Lesbians: Psychological Issues in the Coming-Out Process," *Asian American Psychological Association Journal* 12, 1 (1987): 16–18; T. Gock, "Issues in Gay Affirmative Psychotherapy with Ethnically/Culturally Diverse Populations," paper presented at the 94th annual convention of the American Psychological Association, Washington, D.C., August 1986; W. S. Wooden, H. Kawasaki, and R. Mayeda, "Lifestyles and Identity Maintenance Among Gay Japanese-American Males," *Alternative Lifestyles* 5 (1983): 236–243; S. P. Shon and D. Y. Ja, "Asian Families," in *Ethnicity and Family Therapy,* ed. M. McGoldrick, J. K. Pearce, and J. Giordano (New York: Guilford Press, 1982), 208–229; and Connie S. Chan, "Issues of Sexual Identity in an Ethnic Minority: The Case of Chinese American Lesbians, Gay Men, and Bisexual People," in *Lesbian, Gay, and Bisexual Identities over the Lifespan: Psychological Perspectives,* ed. Anthony D'Augelli and Charlotte Patterson (New York: Oxford Univ. Press, 1995), 95.

116. Chan, "Issues of Identity Development," (1989) 19.

117. Ibid.

118. Susan Y. F. Chen, "Slowly but Surely, My Search for Family Acceptance and Community Continues," in *The Very Inside: An Anthology of Writing by Asian and Pacific Islander Lesbian and Bisexual Women,* ed. Sharon Lim-Hing (Toronto: Sister Vision, 1994), 81.

119. Kitty Tsui, "A Chinese Banquet: For the One Who Was Not Invited," in *The Very Inside: An Anthology of Writing by Asian and Pacific Islander Lesbian and Bisexual Women,* ed. Sharon Lim-Hing (Toronto: Sister Vision, 1994), 155.

120. R. S., "South African, Indian, and Gay," letter, *Trikone* 2, 4 November 1987, 2.

121. Alice Y. Hom, "Stories from the Homefront: Perspectives of Asian American Parents with Lesbian Daughters and Gay Sons," *Amerasia Journal* 20, 1 (1994): 19–32.

122. Chan, "Issues of Sexual Identity," (1995) 96.

123. See Neil Miller, "The Emperor's New Clothes," in *Out in the World: Gay and Lesbian Life from Buenos Aires to Bangkok* (New York: Random House, 1992), 144–181; and Steven O. Murray, "The Discreet Charm of Gay Life in Japan in the Early 1980s," in *Oceanic Homosexualities* (New York: Garland Publishing, 1992), 371–373.

124. Recent survey by a "leading daily," cited in Hiromi Sasamoto, "Gays Want Equality with Heterosexual Couples," *Daily Yomiuri* (Tokyo), 24 December 1998.

125. Russel Skelton and Andrew Donaldson, "Japan's Lesbians Step Out," *The Age* (Melbourne, Australia), 11 October 1997. For a sketch of attitudes and conditions in Japan, see Neil Miller, *Out in the World: Gay and Lesbian Life from Buenos Aires to Bangkok* (New York: Random House, 1992).

126. "Tokyo Court Bans Book Containing Letters by Gay Author," *Associated Press*, 30 March 1998.

127. Chan, "Issues of Identity Development," (1989) 17.

128. Interview, in Hom, "Stories from the Homefront," 28.

129. C. Chan, "Cultural Considerations in Counseling Asian American Lesbians and Gay Men," and E. Morales, "Latino Gays and Latina Lesbians," both in *Counseling Gay Men and Lesbians: Journey to the End of the Rainbow*, ed. S. Dworkin and F. Gutierrez (Alexandria, Va.: American Association for Counseling and Development, 1992); Pamela, "Asian American Lesbians," 282–290.

130. Interview in Hom, "Stories from the Homefront," 27.

131. Ibid.

132. S. Murray, "The Underdevelopment' of Modern/Gay Homosexuality in Mesoamerica," in *Modern Homosexualities: Fragments of Lesbian and Gay Experience*, ed. K. Plummer (New York: Routledge, 1992), 29–38.

133. "Rage in Thailand over Ban on Gay Teachers," *San Francisco Examiner*, 24 January 1997.

134. Ken McLaughlin, "Vietnamese Views on Gays Changing with the Times," *San Jose Mercury News*, 29 April 1997.

135. See, for example, Seth Faison, "Tolerance Grows for Homosexuals in China," *New York Times*, 2 September 1997.

136. Philip Gambone, "Cultural Revolution," *Boston Phoenix*, 12 March 1997.

137. Julie Chao, "Chinese Still Reluctant to Accept Homosexuality," *San Francisco Examiner*, 11 January 1997.

138. Kaushalya Bannerji, "No Apologies," in *A Lotus of Another Color: An Unfolding of the South Asian Gay and Lesbian Experience*, ed. Rakesh Ratti (Boston: Alyson, 1993), 59.

139. Anu, "Who Am I ?" in *The Very Inside: An Anthology of Writing by Asian and Pacific Islander Lesbian and Bisexual Women*, ed. Sharon Lim-Hing (Toronto: Sister Vision, 1994), 20. Reprinted with permission.

140. Ordona, "The Challenges Facing Asian and Pacific Islander Lesbian and Bisexual Women in the U.S.," 19–21.

141. Bannerji, "No Apologies," 60.

142. See also Alice Y. Hom, "In the Mind of An/Other," in *The Very Inside: An Anthology of Writing by Asian and Pacific Islander Lesbian and Bisexual Women*, ed. Sharon Lim-Hing (Toronto: Sister Vision, 1994), 274.

143. See Min-Yeung, "Sleeping with the Enemy? Talking About Men, Race, and Relationships," interview, *OUT/LOOK* 15 (Winter 1992): 30–38.

144. Ibid., 32–33.

145. Anu, "Who Am I ?" 19. Reprinted with permission.

146. Hom, "In the Mind of An/Other," 272–273.

147. Vivien W. Ng, "Homosexuality and the State in Late Imperial China," in *Hidden from History: Reclaiming the Gay and Lesbian Past*, ed. Martin Duberman, Martha Vicinus, and George Chauncey Jr. (New York: Meridian, 1989), 76–78. See

also Bret Hinsch, *Passions of the Cut Sleeve: The Male Homosexual Tradition in China* (Berkeley: Univ. of California Press, 1990).

148. Shah, "Sexuality, Identity, and the Uses of History," 121.

149. See Serena Nanda, *Neither Man nor Woman: The Hijras of India* (Belmont, Calif.: Wadsworth, 1990).

150. See Arvind Kumar, "Hijras: Challenging Gender Dichotomies," in *A Lotus of Another Color: An Unfolding of the South Asian Gay and Lesbian Experience*, ed. Rakesh Ratti (Boston: Alyson, 1993), 90–91.

151. Greene, "Ethnic-Minority Lesbians and Gay Men, " 246–247.

152. See, for example, Walter Williams, *The Spirit and the Flesh* (Boston: Beacon Press, 1986); and Paula Gunn Allen, "Lesbians in American Indian Cultures," in *Hidden from History: Reclaiming the Gay and Lesbian Past*, ed. M. Duberman, M. Vicinus, and G. Chauncey Jr. (New York: Meridian, 1989), 106–117.

153. See, for example, Harriet Whitehead, "The Bow and the Burden Strap: A New Look at Institutionalized Homosexuality in Native North America," in *The Gay and Lesbian Studies Reader*, ed. H. Abelove, M. Barale, and D. Halperin (New York: Routledge, 1993), 498–527.

154. Ibid., 512.

155. Evelyn Blackwood, "Sexuality and Gender in Certain Native American Tribes: The Case of Cross-Gender Females," *Signs: Journal of Women in Culture and Society* 10, 1 (1984): 27–42.

156. Whitehead, "The Bow and the Burden Strap," 506.

157. Ibid., 508.

158. Blackwood, "Sexuality and Gender in Certain Native American Tribes," 27–42.

159. Ibid.

160. Whitehead, "The Bow and the Burden Strap," 511.

161. Ibid., 510.

162. Ibid., 506, 510; and W. W. Hill, "Note on the Pima Berdache," *American Anthropologist*, 40 (1938): 273–279.

163. Will Roscoe, "The Zuni Man-Woman," *OUT/LOOK* (Summer 1988): 56–69.

164. See Ramón Gutiérrez, "Must We Deracinate Indians to Find Gay Roots?" *OUT/LOOK* (Winter 1989): 61–67.

165. Whitehead, "The Bow and the Burden Strap," 516.

166. Jonathan Katz, *Gay American History: Lesbians and Gay Men in the U.S.A.* (New York: Crowell, 1976), 278.

167. See D'Emilio, *Sexual Politics;* and Chauncey, *Gay New York.*

168. Will Roscoe, "Living the Tradition: Gay American Indians," in *Gay Spirit: Myth and Meaning,* ed. Mark Thompson (New York: St. Martin's Press, 1987), 69–77.

169. Bannerji, "No Apologies," 63.

170. Shah, "Sexuality, Identity, and the Uses of History," 116.

171. "Asylum for Gays Is Policy That Needs Protecting," *Philadelphia Daily News,* 14 January 1997.

172. David Beresford, "Army Gave Gays Shock Treatment," *Manchester Guardian,* 17 June 1997.

173. Adrian Bridge, "Gay Call to Boycott Wine from Romania," *Independent* (London), 22 January 1997.

174. Kathy Evans, "Kuwait Sacks Professor Who Dared to Speak of Gays," *Manchester Guardian*, 29 March 1997.

175. Vera Haller, "Intolerance of Homosexuals in Italy Underscored by Tragedy," *Washington Post*, 15 February 1998.

176. Tremble, Schneider, and Appathurai, "Growing Up Gay or Lesbian in a Multicultural Context," 261.

177. Ibid., 257.

178. For example, see "Egypt: In the Realm of the Polymorphous Perverse," chapter 2 in Miller, *Out in the World*.

179. Tremble, Schneider, and Appathurai, "Growing Up Gay or Lesbian in a Multicultural Context," 261.

180. For a counterargument to proscriptive Torah readings, see Hershel Goodman, "'Myth' of Torah Opposition to Homosexuality," *Forward Magazine*, letter to the editor, 24 April 1998. See also Chapter 11, note 136.

181. American National Conference of Catholic Bishops, "Always Our Children," 30 September 1997.

182. In Bill Reel, "A 'Cure' for Gays? Maybe Yes, Maybe No," *Newsday* (New York), 19 July 1998.

183. See, for example, "Pope Takes Aim at Same-Sex Marriage," *Agence France-Presse*, 19 February 1998; "Pope Praises Family Life," *Associated Press*, 6 June 1998.

184. An orthodox gay synagogue, opening in the Jerusalem Open House, Israel, was to be the first of its kind in the world. See Robby Berman, "Double Identity," *Jerusalem Post Magazine*, 17 July 1998. Also see *Trembling Before God*, a film by Sandi Dubowski (email: simcha2000@aol.com) on the lives of orthodox and Hassidic gay and lesbian Jews.

185. Shah, "Sexuality, Identity, and the Uses of History," 117.

186. See Adrienne Rich, "Compulsory Heterosexuality and Lesbian Existence," in *The Gay and Lesbian Studies Reader*, ed. H. Abelove, M. Barale, and D. Halperin (New York: Routledge, 1993), 227–254.

187. See, for example, *Black Is . . . Black Ain't*, Marlon Riggs, director, 1995.

188. Chan, "Issues of Sexual Identity," (1995) 99. Also see Herdt, "Introduction," 18

189. Peou Lakhana, "Tha Phi Neah Yeung The . . . ? (Only the Two of Us?)," in *The Very Inside: An Anthology of Writing by Asian and Pacific Islander Lesbian and Bisexual Women*, ed. Sharon Lim-Hing (Toronto: Sister Vision, 1994), 161.

190. Jan Clausen, *Beyond Gay or Straight: Understanding Sexual Orientation* (Philadelphia: Chelsea House, 1997), 50, implies (wrongly, I believe) that Western cultural sexism renders such a judgment of non-Western heterosexism inadmissible.

## Chapter 8

1. Ilan H. Meyer, "Minority Stress and Mental Health in Gay Men," *Journal of Health and Social Behavior* 36 (March 1995): 38–56.

2. Scott L. Hershberger and Anthony R. D'Augelli, "The Impact of Victimization on the Mental Health and Suicidality of Lesbian, Gay, and Bisexual Youth," *Developmental Psychology* 31, 1 (1995): 65–74; A. M. Boxer and B. J. Cohler, "The Life

Course of Gay and Lesbian Youth: An Immodest Proposal for the Study of Lives," *Journal of Homosexuality* 17 (1989): 315–355; Caitlin C. Ryan and Donna Futterman, *Lesbian and Gay Youth: Care and Counseling* (New York: Columbia Univ. Press, 1997); K. Cwayna, G. Remafedi, and L. Treadway, "Caring for Gay and Lesbian Youth," *Medical Aspects of Human Sexuality* 25 (1991): 50–57; J. C. Gonsiorek, "Mental Health Issues of Gay and Lesbian Adolescents," *Journal of Adolescent Health Care* 9 (1988): 114–122; R. Kournay, "Suicide Among Homosexual Adolescents," *Journal of Homosexuality* 13, 4 (1987): 111–117; G. Remafedi, "Adolescent Homosexuality: Psychosocial and Medical Implications," *Pediatrics* 79 (1987): 331–337; G. Remafedi, "Homosexual Youth: A Challenge to Contemporary Society," *Journal of the American Medical Assn.* 258 (1987): 222–225; G. Remafedi, "Male Homosexuality: The Adolescent's Perspective," *Pediatrics* 79 (1987): 326–330; L. Garnets, G. M. Herek, and B. Levy, "Violence and Victimization of Lesbians and Gay Men: Mental Health Consequences," *Journal of Interpersonal Violence* 5 (1990): 366–383.

3. Tom Moroney, "Coming Unhinged over Hand-Holding Ban," *Boston Globe*, 21 January 1995.

4. Esther D. Rothblum, "'I Only Read About Myself on Bathroom Walls': The Need for Research on the Mental Health of Lesbians and Gay Men," *Journal of Consulting and Clinical Psychology* 62, 2 (1994): 213–220; Charlotte Patterson, "Sexual Orientation and Human Development: An Overview," *Developmental Psychology* 31, 1 (1995): 3–11; see also Working Groups, Workshop on Suicide and Sexual Orientation, "Recommendations for a Research Agenda in Suicide and Sexual Orientation," *Suicide and Life-Threatening Behavior* 25, Supplement (1995): 82–87.

5. See Ritch Savin-Williams, "Verbal and Physical Abuse as Stressors in the Lives of Lesbian, Gay Male, and Bisexual Youths: Associations with School Problems, Running Away, Substance Abuse, Prostitution, and Suicide," *Journal of Consulting and Clinical Psychology* 62, 2 (1994): 262.

6. Anthony R. D'Augelli and Scott L. Hershberger, "Lesbian, Gay, and Bisexual Youth in Community Settings: Personal Challenges and Mental Health Problems," *American Journal of Community Psychology* 21, 4 (1995): 421–448.

7. G. Remafedi, J. A. Farrow, R. W. Deisher, "Risk Factors for Attempted Suicide in Gay and Bisexual Youth," *Pediatrics* 87, 6 (1991): 869–875.

8. Hershberger and D'Augelli, "The Impact of Victimization," 65–74.

9. Cliff O'Neill, "Top CDC Official Says Gay Teens Need Help," *Bay Windows*, 23 January 1991; Shira Maguen, "Teen Suicide: The Government's Cover-Up and America's Lost Children," *Advocate*, 24 September 1991, 40–47.

10. Thirty-three states conduct CDC Youth Risk Behavior Surveys. Only Massachusetts, Vermont, and Maine allow questions on homosexual behavior. Maine has not analyzed this data.

11. James T. Sears, "Alston and Everetta: Too Risky for School?" in *At-Risk Students: Portraits, Policies, Programs, and Practices*, ed. Robert Donmoyer and Raylene Kos (Albany: State Univ. of New York Press, 1993), 154.

12. Office of National AIDS Policy, "Youth and HIV/AIDS: An American Agenda," Executive Summary (Washington, D.C.: Office of National AIDS Policy, March 1996). Also see, for example, D. L. Sondheimer et al., "Legal, Ethical, and Social Complexities in Conducting HIV-Related Research Involving Adolescents," paper presented at First International Conference on AIDS, San Francisco,

1985. The conference was sponsored by the World Health Organization, Geneva, Switzerland.

13. Seattle, Washington, schools have also used this instrument. For updates, contact Safe Schools Coalition of Washington: (206) 233-9136.

14. Commonwealth of Massachusetts, Dept. of Education, *Youth Risk Behavior Survey Results, 1993, 1995, 1997*. In 1995, 59 schools participated in the survey and 4,159 students responded (77 percent rate). This is an overall response rate of 72 percent with accuracy to plus or minus 3 percent. Results were statistically weighted by the CDC. In 1997: 58 schools, 3,982 student respondents (79 percent rate), accuracy to plus or minus 3 percent).

15. R. H. DuRant, D. P. Krowchuk, and S. H. Sinal, "Victimization, Use of Violence, Drug Use at School Among Male Adolescents Who Engage in Same-Sex Sexual Behavior," *Journal of Pediatrics* 133, 1 (1988): 113–118.

16. Safe Schools Coalition of Washington, *Safe Schools Anti-Violence Documentation Project Third Annual Report* (Seattle: Safe Schools Coalition, 1996).

17. G. Remafedi, M. Resnick, R. Blum, and L. Harris, "Demography of Sexual Orientation in Adolescents," *Pediatrics* 89 (1992): 714–721.

18. Robert Garofalo, R. Cameron Wolf, Shari Kessel, Judith Palfrey, and Robert H. DuRant, "The Association Between Health Risk Behaviors and Sexual Orientation Among a School-Based Sample of Adolescents," *Pediatrics* 101, 5 (1998): 900–901.

19. J. Gonsiorek, "The Use of Diagnostic Concepts in Working with Gay and Lesbian Populations," in *Homosexuality and Psychotherapy: A Practitioner's Handbook of Affirmative Models*, ed. J. Gonsiorek (Beverly Hills, Calif.: Sage, 1982), 9–20.

20. Gordon Allport, *The Nature of Prejudice* (Reading, Mass.: Addison Wesley, 1954).

21. G. M. Herek, "Stigma, Prejudice, and Violence Against Lesbians and Gay Men," in *Homosexuality: Research Implications for Public Policy*, ed. J. Gonsiorek and J. Weinrich (Newbury Park, Calif.: Sage, 1991).

22. J. C. Gonsiorek and J. R. Rudolph, "Homosexual Identity: Coming Out and Other Developmental Events," in *Homosexuality: Research Implications for Public Policy*, ed. J. C. Gonsiorek and J. D. Weinrich (Newbury Park, Calif.: Sage, 1991), 1–12; Eva D. Olson and Cheryl A. King, "Gay and Lesbian Self-Identification: A Response to Rotheram-Borus and Fernandez," *Suicide and Life-Threatening Behavior* 25, Supplement (1995): 35–39.

23. John C. Gonsiorek, "Gay Male Identities: Concepts and Issues," in *Lesbian, Gay, and Bisexual Identities over the Lifespan: Psychological Perspectives*, ed. A. R. D'Augelli and C. J. Patterson (New York: Oxford Univ. Press, 1995), 28–29.

24. Anthony R. D'Augelli, "Lesbian and Gay Male Development: Steps Toward an Analysis of Lesbians' and Gay Men's Lives," in *Lesbian and Gay Psychology: Theory, Research, and Clinical Applications*, ed. Beverly Greene and Gregory M. Herek (Thousand Oaks, Calif.: Sage, 1994), 120.

25. Mary Jane Rotheram-Borus, Helen Reid, Margaret Rosario, Ronan Van Rossem, and Roy Gillis, "Prevalence, Course, and Predictors of Multiple Problem Behaviors Among Gay and Bisexual Male Adolescents," *Developmental Psychology* 31, 1 (1995): 83. Sarah Fitzharding, doctoral candidate at Cambridge University (U.K.) in 1998, is investigating resilience by interviewing successful adults.

26. The data are preliminary as of March 1999 and cannot be published.

27. Karen J. Pittman and Michele Cahill, "A New Vision: Promoting Youth Development," testimony before the House Select Committee on Children, Youth, and Families, Commissioned Paper no. 3 (Washington, D.C.: Academy for Educational Development, September 1991).

28. E. Hooker, "The Adjustment of the Male Overt Homosexual," *Journal of Projective Techniques* 21 (1957): 18–31; E. S. Hetrick and A. D. Martin, "Developmental Issues and Their Resolution for Gay and Lesbian Adolescents," *Journal of Homosexuality* 14, 1–2 (1987): 25–43; E. S. Hetrick and A. D. Martin, "The Stigmatization of the Gay and Lesbian Adolescent," *Journal of Homosexuality* 15 (1988): 165.

29. S. Dworkin and F. Gutierrez, "Opening the Closet Door," in *Counseling Gay Men and Lesbians: Journey to the End of the Rainbow,* ed. S. Dworkin and F. Gutierrez (Alexandria, Va.: American Assoc. of Counseling and Development, 1992), xvii–xxvii; L. Garnets and D. Kimmel, "Lesbian and Gay Male Dimensions in the Psychological Study of Human Diversity," in *Psychological Perspectives on Human Diversity in America: Master Lectures,* ed. J. Goodchilds (Washington, D.C.: American Psychological Assoc., 1991), 143–192; L. Garnets et al., "Issues in Psychotherapy with Lesbians and Gay Men: A Survey of Psychologists," *American Psychologist* 46 (1991): 964–972; J. Gonsiorek and J. Weinrich, "The Definition and Scope of Sexual Orientation," in *Homosexuality: Research Implications for Public Policy,* ed. J. Gonsiorek and J. Weinrich (Newbury Park, Calif.: Sage, 1991); L. M. Markowitz, "Homosexuality: Are We Still in the Dark?" *Family Therapy Networker* (Vienna, Va.: Family Therapy Network, 1991), 26–29, 31–35.

30. See Savin-Williams, "Verbal and Physical Abuse," 261–269. In addition to the Massachusetts Youth Risk Behavior Survey results from 1993 and 1995, see R. H. DuRant et al., "Victimization, Use of Violence," 113–118, for an analysis of Vermont's YRBS.

31. Safe Schools Coalition of Washington, *Safe Schools Anti-Violence Documentation Project.*

32. Bill Bartleman, "Gay Implication Spurred Teasing: Carneal," *Paducah (Ky.) Sun,* 26 June 1998.

33. "Boy Charged in Attack on Gay," *Colorado Springs Gazette Telegraph* (AP), 5 April 1996.

34. Document of the Maine Department of the Attorney General, 4 October 1996.

35. Dennis Roberts, "Gay Bashing or Not, Crime Is Heinous," *Modesto Bee,* 2 March 1999.

36. Pamela J. Podger, "Assaulted Novato Gay Teen Gets Support," *San Francisco Chronicle,* 17 February 1999.

37. Unpublished incident report to the Massachusetts Dept. of Education, personal communication, 1994.

38. Shira Maguen, "Teen Suicide: The Government's Cover-Up and America's Lost Children," *Advocate,* 24 September 1991, 40–47.

39. G. Remafedi, "Male Homosexuality," 326–330.

40. Mason-Dixon Political/Media Research, 25–27 August 1997, reported in Lisa Keen, "Survey Finds Most Parents Would Support a Gay Child," *Washington Blade,* 5 September 1997.

41. L. Gross, S. K. Aurand, and R. Addessa, *Violence and Discrimination Against Lesbian and Gay People in Philadelphia and the Commonwealth of Pennsylvania* (Philadelphia: Philadelphia Lesbian and Gay Task Force, 1988). Available from the Philadelphia Lesbian and Gay Task Force, 1501 Cherry St., Philadelphia, PA 19102.

42. R. M. O'Brien, *Crime and Victimization Data* (Beverly Hills, Calif.: Sage, 1985).

43. Chris Muther, in Governor's Commission on Gay and Lesbian Youth, *Making Schools Safe for Gay and Lesbian Youth: Breaking the Silence in Schools and in Families*, Education Report, 25 February 1993, 8.

44. Concerned Students of Des Moines, "Homophobia in Schools Project," reported in Kellye Carter,"Group Monitors Pervasiveness of Comments," *Des Moines Register*, 7 March 1997.

45. Governor's Commission on Gay and Lesbian Youth, *Making Schools Safe for Gay and Lesbian Youth*, 9–11.

46. Paul Gibson, "Gay Male and Lesbian Youth Suicide," in *Report of the Secretary's Task Force on Youth Suicide*, vol. 3, ed. M. R. Feinleib, DHHS Publication No. ADM-89-1623 (Washington, D.C.: U.S. Dept. of Health and Human Services, 1989), 110–142; Governor's Commission on Gay and Lesbian Youth, *Making Schools Safe for Gay and Lesbian Youth*, 10.

47. Safe Schools Coalition of Washington, *Safe Schools Anti-Violence Documentation Project*.

48. Erin Van Bronkhorst, "Study: Gay Kids Being Raped in Schools," *Bay Windows*, 7 September 1995.

49. Joyce Hunter and Robert Schaecher, "Gay and Lesbian Adolescents," in *Encyclopedia of Social Work*, 19th ed., ed. Richard L. Edwards et al. (New York: National Assn. of Social Workers, 1995), 1055, 1058.

50. National Gay and Lesbian Task Force Policy Institute, *Anti-Gay/Lesbian Violence, Victimization, and Defamation in 1993* (Washington, D.C.: NGLTF, 1993).

51. Ibid.

52. G. Remafedi, "Adolescent Homosexuality: Psychosocial and Medical Implication," *Pediatrics* 79 (1987): 331–337.

53. Remafedi, "Male Homosexuality," 326–330.

54. National Gay and Lesbian Task Force, *Anti-Gay/Lesbian Violence;* and Remafedi, "Male Homosexuality," 326–330; R. C. Savin-Williams, "Theoretical Perspectives Accounting for Adolescent Homosexuality," *Journal of Adolescent Health Care* 9, 2 (1988): 95–104.

55. Hetrick and Martin, "Developmental Issues," 25–43.

56. National Network of Runaway and Youth Services, *To Whom DO They Belong? Runaway, Homeless, and Other Youth in High-Risk Situations in the '90s* (Washington, D.C., 1990).

57. Hetrick and Martin, "The Stigmatization," 165.

58. Lee Fearnside, in Governor's Commission on Gay and Lesbian Youth, *Making Schools Safe for Gay and Lesbian Youth: Breaking the Silence in Schools and in Families*, Education Report, 25 February 1993, 13.

59. Jack Foley, "Gilroy High Runs Ad for Gay Center: Parents, Pastor Critical," *San Jose Mercury News*, 16 May 1996.

60. A. R. D'Augelli, "The Development of a Helping Community for Lesbians and Gay Men: A Case Study in Community Psychology," *Journal of Community Psychology* 17 (1989): 18–29; R. R. Troiden and E. Goode, "Variables Related to the Acquisition of a Gay Identity," *Journal of Homosexuality* 5, 4 (1980): 383–392.

61. J. P. Hollander, "Restructuring Gay and Lesbian Social Networks: Evaluation of an Intervention," *Journal of Gay and Lesbian Psychotherapy* 1 (1989): 63–71; A. R. D'Augelli, C. Collins, and M. Hart, "Social Support Patterns of Lesbian Women in a Rural Helping Network," *Journal of Rural Community Psychology* 8 (1987): 12–22; F. R. Lynch, "Non-ghetto Gays: A Sociological Study of Suburban Homosexuals," *Journal of Homosexuality* 13, 4 (1987): 13–42; A. E. Moses and J. A. Buckner, "The Special Problems of Rural Gay Clients," in *Counseling Lesbian Women and Men: A Life Issues Approach,* ed. A. E. Moses and R. O. Hawkins Jr. (St. Louis: C. V. Moby, 1980), 173–180; M. S. Weinberg and C. Williams, *Male Homosexuals: Their Problems and Adaptations* (New York: Oxford Univ. Press, 1974).

62. Jennifer Weiner, "Prom Night: Some of Them Felt Closed Out of the Big Dance in High School, So Dozens of Gay Teenagers and Young Adults Attended the Alternative Prom Saturday at the Warwick," *Philadelphia Inquirer,* 4 June 1996; Tara Shioya, "Gay Prom Makes Proud Return," *San Francisco Chronicle,* 14 June 1996; "Pride Prom Offered as Alternative for Gay Students," *Lincoln (Neb.) Journal,* 8 March 1996; Aline McKenzie, "Good Times Mark First Prom for Gay Teens," *Dallas Morning News,* 31 May 1998.

63. Aaron Fricke, *Reflections of a Rock Lobster* (Boston: Alyson Press, 1981).

64. "Teen Can Wear Gown to Prom," *Associated Press,* 24 March 1999.

65. Two examples of opposite experiences: "Gay Teen-Ager and His Male Date Spark Controversy at Senior Prom," *Louisville Courier-Journal,* 4 May 1997; Heather Stone, "A Night to Remember: Two Gays Find the Prom Can Be a Dream—Not the Nightmare It Was in 1980," *Detroit News,* 6 June 1997.

66. For example, Ellen Bass and Kate Kaufman, *Free Your Mind: The Book for Gay, Lesbian, and Bisexual Youth and Their Allies* (New York: HarperCollins, 1996).

67. For example, the IYG Youth Hotline, (800) 347-TEEN, described in Donovan R. Walling and Christopher T. Gonzalez, "How the IYG Helps Gay Teens at Risk," in *Open Lives: Safe Schools,* ed. Donovan R. Walling (Bloomington, Ind.: Phi Delta Kappa Educational Foundation, 1996), 245–250.

68. For example, *Gay '90s,* a radio show in St. Louis with a 17-year-old cohost, profiled in Amy Adams Strongheart, "Message of Hope for Sexual Minority," *St. Louis Post Dispatch,* 2 February 1996.

69. For example, *Gay and Lesbian Community Forum* on America On Line, *Pride* on Compuserve, and *PlanetOut* on Microsoft Network (www.gayhelp.com).

70. Examples: lyric.talkline.info@tlg.net (Lavender Youth Recreation and Information Center); info@outproud.org and www.outproud.org; www.oasismag.com (Oasis Magazine); http://www.youth.org/loco/PERSONProject/ (The P.E.R.S.O.N. Project).

71. See, for example, Bruce Mirken, "Message in a Cyberbottle: A Lifeline for Gay Teens," *Pacifica News Service,* 13 December 1997.

72. Gay and Lesbian Alliance Against Defamation (GLAAD) has begun a research project on the effects of these filters on access by gay/lesbian youth.

73. Michelle Slatalla, "Software Filters Prove an Imperfect Solution," *Philadelphia Inquirer,* 27 March 1997. Also, *Access Denied,* Gay and Lesbian Alliance Against Defamation Report, December 1997 (available at 1-800-GAY-MEDIA).

74. Deana F. Morrow, "Social Work with Gay and Lesbian Adolescents," *Social Work* 38, 6 (1993): 655–660.

75. See Michael Thomas Ford, *Outspoken: Role Models from the Lesbian and Gay Community* (New York: William Morrow, 1998).

76. See Diana Baumrind, "Commentary on Sexual Orientation: Research and Social Policy Implications," *Developmental Psychology* 31, 1 (1995): 132.

77. Jane Meridith Adams, "For Many Gay Teens Torment Leads to Suicide Tries," *Boston Globe,* 3 January 1989.

78. K. E. Gillow and L. L. Davis, "Lesbian Stress and Coping Methods," *Journal of Psychosocial Nursing* 25, 9 (1987): 28–32.

79. Weinberg and Williams, *Male Homosexuals: Their Problems and Adaptations.*

80. L. A. Kurdek, "Perceived Social Support in Gays and Lesbians in Cohabiting Relationships," *Journal of Personality and Social Psychology* 54 (1988): 504–509.

81. J. Harry, *Gay Couples* (New York: Praeger, 1984).

82. Donald B. Reed, "High School Gay Youth: Invisible Diversity," paper presented at the annual meeting of the American Educational Research Association, Atlanta, April 12–16, 1993.

83. Hetrick and Martin, "The Stigmatization," 172.

84. Marshall Forstein, M.D., Lecture on gay, lesbian, and bisexual adolescent health issues, Lesley College, 20 May 1994.

85. J. Jacobs, *Adolescent Suicide* (New York: Wiley, 1971).

86. Teresa DeCrescenzo of Los Angeles's Gay and Lesbian Adolescent Social Services, in S. Maguen, "Teen Suicide: The Government's Cover-Up and America's Lost Children," *Advocate,* 24 September 1991, 40–47.

87. Alan L. Berman, "The Adolescent: The Individual and Cultural Perspective," *Suicide and Life-Threatening Behavior* 27, 1 (1997): 12.

88. *Let's Talk Facts About Teen Suicide,* pamphlet (Washington, D.C.: American Psychological Association, June 1998).

89. P. Gibson, "Gay and Lesbian Youth Suicide," paper presented at U.S. Dept. of Health and Human Services and the National Institute of Mental Health. Washington, D.C., 11 June 1986.

90. See especially, David Shaffer, Prudence Fisher, R. H. Hicks, Michael Parides, and Madelyn Gould, "Sexual Orientation in Adolescents Who Commit Suicide," *Suicide and Life-Threatening Behavior* 25, Supplement (1995): 64–71.

91. See especially, P. J. Meehan, J. A. Lamb, L. E. Saltzman, and P. W. O'Carroll, "Attempted Suicide Among Young Adults: Progress Toward a Meaningful Estimate of Prevalence," *American Journal of Psychiatry* 149 (1992): 41–44.

92. John C. Gonsiorek, Randall L. Sell, and James D. Weinrich, "Definition and Measurement of Sexual Orientation," *Suicide and Life-Threatening Behavior* 25, Supplement (1995): 40–51.

93. Virginia Uribe and Karen Harbeck, "Addressing the Needs of Lesbian, Gay, and Bisexual Youth: The Origins of PROJECT 10 and School-Based Intervention," in *Coming Out of the Classroom Closet: Gay and Lesbian Students, Teachers, and Curricula,* ed. K. Harbeck (Binghamton, N.Y.: Harrington Park Press, 1992).

94. Commonwealth of Massachusetts, Dept. of Education, *Youth Risk Behavior Survey Results, 1995, 1997.*

95. Safe Schools Coalition of Washington, *Safe Schools Anti-Violence Documentation Project.*

96. G. Remafredi, J. A. Farrow, and R. W. Deisher, "Risk Factors for Attempted Suicide in Gay and Bisexual Youth," *Pediatrics* 87, 6 (1991): 869–875.

97. Hershberger and D'Augelli, "The Impact of Victimization," 65–74.

98. Remafredi, "Adolescent Homosexuality," 331–337.

99. Remafredi, Farrow, and Deisher, "Risk Factors for Attempted Suicide," 869–875.

100. Mary J. Rotheram-Borus et al., "Suicidal Behavior and Gay-Related Stress Among Gay and Bisexual Male Adolescents," *Journal of Adolescent Research* 9, 4 (1994): 498–508.

101. Christopher Bagley and Pierre Tremblay, "Suicidality Problems of Gay and Bisexual Males: Evidence from a Random Community Survey of 750 Men Aged 18 to 27," in *Suicidal Behaviors in Adolescents and Adults: Taxonomy, Understanding, and Prevention,* ed. C. Bagley and R. Ramsay (Brookfield, Vt.: Avebury, 1997). See also Pierre J. Tremblay, "The Homosexuality Factor in the Youth Suicide Problem," paper presented at the sixth annual conference of the Canadian Association for Suicide Prevention, Banff, Alberta, 11–14 October 1995.

102. A. R. D'Augelli, and Scott L. Hershberger, "Lesbian, Gay, and Bisexual Youth in Community Settings: Personal Challenges and Mental Health Problems," *American Journal of Community Psychology* 21, 4 (1995): 421–448.

103. Steven Obuchowsky, in Governor's Commission on Gay and Lesbian Youth, *Making Schools Safe for Gay and Lesbian Youth: Breaking the Silence in Schools and in Families,* Education Report, 25 February 1993, 8.

104. J. Hunter, "Violence Against Lesbian and Gay Male Youths," *Journal of Interpersonal Violence* 5, 3 (1990): 295–300.

105. Safe Schools Coalition of Washington, *Safe Schools Anti-Violence Documentation Project.*

106. Hershberger and D'Augelli, "The Impact of Victimization," 65–74.

107. Kim Westheimer, presentation, Healthy Boston Coalition, 47 West St., Boston, 17 April 1996.

108. Doreen Cudnik, "Why Did Robbie Kirkland Have to Die?" *Gay People's Chronicle* (Cleveland), 21 February 1997.

109. Hershberger and D'Augelli, "The Impact of Victimization," 65–74.

110. Remafedi, Farrow, and Deisher, "Risk Factors for Attempted Suicide," 869–875.

111. "Q and A with John Gonsiorek," presentation at "Children from the Shadows VI," conference, University of Hartford, 19 March 1999.

112. Bradford N. Bartholow, Lynda S. Doll et al., "Emotional, Behavioral, and HIV Risks Associated with Sexual Abuse Among Adult Homosexual and Bisexual Men," *Child Abuse and Neglect: The International Journal* 18, 9 (1994): 747–761. Researchers in the Massachusetts Department of Education led by Carol Goodenow have begun to assess the "involuntary sex" factor as a risk determinant.

113. Gary Remafedi, Simone French, Mary Story, Michael Resnick, and Robert Blum, "The Relationship Between Suicide Risk and Sexual Orientation: Results of a Population-Based Study," *American Journal of Public Health* 88, 1 (1998): 57–60. A new study using 1995 Massachusetts YRBS data links homosexuality directly with boys' suicide attempts; lesbian girls' suicidality appears to be mediated by drug use and violence/victimization behaviors. *See* R. Garofalo, R.C. Wolf, L.S. Wissow, E.R. Woods, E. Goodman, "Sexual Orientation and Risk of Suicide Attempts Among a Representative Sample of Youth," *Archives of Pediatric Adolescent Medicine* 153, 5 (1999): 487–493.

114. Carol Goodenow, personal communication relating to an unpublished analysis of the Massachusetts YRBS, November 1998.

115. Ronald F. C. Kourany, "Suicide Among Homosexual Adolescents, *Journal of Homosexuality* 13 (1987): 111–117.

116. The 24-hour Trevor Helpline is devoted exclusively to gay or questioning youth: (800) 850–8078.

117. Devin Beringer, in Governor's Commission on Gay and Lesbian Youth, *Making Schools Safe for Gay and Lesbian Youth: Breaking the Silence in Schools and in Families*, Education Report, 25 February 1993, 15.

118. Renee Graham, "Amid Higher Suicide Rate, Schools Help Gay Youths Cope," *Boston Globe*, 19 April 1991.

119. Maguen, "Teen Suicide," 44.

120. B. Jaye Miller, "From Silence to Suicide: Measuring a Mother's Loss," in *Homophobia: How We All Pay the Price*, ed. Warren J. Blumenfeld (Boston: Beacon Press, 1992), 89.

121. See Leroy Aarons, *Prayers for Bobby: A Mother's Coming to Terms with the Suicide of Her Gay Son* (New York: HarperCollins: 1995); on another family's suffering, see Molly Fumia, *Honor Thy Children: One Family's Journey to Wholeness* (Berkeley: Conari, 1997).

122. L. Brown, "Lesbians, Weight, and Eating: New Analyses and Perspectives," in *Lesbian Psychologies: Exploration and Challenges*, ed. Boston Lesbian Psychologies Collective (Urbana: Univ. of Illinois Press, 1987), 294–309; Michael Siever, "Sexual Orientation, Gender, and Socioculturally Acquired Vulnerability to Eating Disorders," *Dissertation Abstracts International* 50 (1989): 11B.

123. J. T. Sears, "Responding to the Sexual Diversity of Faculty and Students: Sexual Praxis and the Critically Reflective Administrator," in *Educational Administration in a Pluralistic Society*, ed. C. Capper (New York: State Univ. of New York Press, 1993), 139.

124. M. Siever, "Sexual Orientation and Gender as Factors in Socioculturally Acquired Vulnerability to Body Dissatisfaction and Eating Disorders," *Journal of Consulting and Clinical Psychology* 62, 2 (1994): 252–260; Daniel J. Carlat, "Eating Disorders in Males: A Report on 105 Patients," *American Journal of Psychiatry* 10 (1982): 52–65.

125. Massachusetts YRBS 1997.

126. Donald B. Reed, "High School Gay Youth: Invisible Diversity," paper presented at the annual meeting of the American Educational Research Association, Atlanta, 12–16 April 1993.

127. Gilbert Herdt and Andrew Boxer, *Children of Horizons: How Gay and Lesbian Teens Are Leading a New Way Out of the Closet* (Boston: Beacon Press, 1993), 20.

128. Gonsiorek, "Mental Health Issues," 114–122; A. D. Martin, "Learning to Hide: The Socialization of the Gay Adolescent," *Adolescent Psychiatry* 10 (1982): 52–65.

129. Eli Coleman, "The Development of Male Prostitution Activity Among Gay and Bisexual Adolescents," in *Gay and Lesbian Youth*, ed. Gilbert Herdt (Binghamton, N.Y.: Harrington Park Press, 1989), 131–149; Debra Boyer, "Male Prostitution and Homosexual Identity," in *Gay and Lesbian Youth*, ed. Gilbert Herdt, 151–184; Victoria A. Brownworth, "America's Worst Kept Secret: AIDS Is Devastating the Nation's Teenagers, and Gay Kids Are Dying by the Thousands," *Advocate*, 24 March 1992, 41.

130. Research by Wilder Research Center, cited in Maja Beckstrom, "Project's Goal: House Homeless Gay Youth," *St. Paul Pioneer Press*, 29 June 1997.

131. R. C. Savin-Williams, "Theoretical Perspectives Accounting for Adolescent Homosexuality," 95–104.

132. Victims Services/Travelers Aid, *Streetwork Project Study* (New York: Victim Services, 1987–1990).

133. Lynette Holloway, "For Group of Young People, Village Piers Mean Home," *New York Times*, 18 July 1998.

134. D. Allen, "Young Male Prostitute: A Psychosocial Study," *Archives of Sexual Behavior* 9 (1980): 399–426; J. Cates, "Adolescent Sexuality," *Child Welfare* 66, 4 (1987): 353–364; *Male and Female Adolescent Prostitution: Huckleberry House Sexual Minority Youth Services Project* (Washington, D.C.: Dept. of Health and Human Services, 1981); F. Matthews, *Familiar Strangers: A Study of Adolescent Prostitution* (Toronto: Central Toronto Youth Services, 1987); D. Weisberg, *Children of the Night: A Study of Adolescent Prostitution* (Lexington, Mass.: Lexington Books, 1985).

135. *Report of the Secretary's Task Force on Youth Suicide* (Washington, D.C.: U.S. Dept. of Health and Human Services, 1989); Governor's Commission on Gay and Lesbian Youth, "Prevention of Health Problems Among Gay and Lesbian Youth," August 1994, 48; N. Hammond, "Chemical Abuse in Lesbian and Gay Adolescents," paper presented at the Symposium on Gay and Lesbian Adolescents, Minneapolis, May 1986; Francine Shiflin and Mirtha Solis, "Chemical Dependency in Gay and Lesbian Youth," *Journal of Chemical Dependency Treatment* 5, 1 (1992): 67–76.

136. M. J. Rotheram-Borus, G. C. Luna, T. Marotta, and H. Kelly, "Going Nowhere Fast: Methamphetamine and HIV Infection," in *The Context of HIV Risk Among Drug Users and Their Sexual Partners*, ed. R. J. Battjes, Z. Sloboda, and W. C. Grace, NIH Publication no. 94-3750 (Washington, D.C.: U.S. Government Printing Office, 1994), 155–182.

137. M. Rosario, M. J. Rotheram-Borus, and H. Reid, "Gay-Related Stress and Its Correlates Among Gay and Bisexual Male Adolescents of Predominantly Black and Hispanic Backgrounds," *Journal of Community Psychology* 24, 2 (1996): 136–159.

138. M. Rosario, J. Hunter, and M. J. Rotheram-Borus, unpublished data on lesbian and gay adolescents, HIV Center for Clinical and Behavioral Studies, New York State Psychiatric Institute, 1992.

139. Safe Schools Coalition of Washington, *Safe Schools Anti-Violence Documentation Project*.

140. Rotheram-Borus, Reid, Rosario, Van Rossem, and Gillis, "Prevalence, Course, and Predictors," 83.

141. Garofalo, Wolf, Kessel, Palfrey, and DuRant, "The Association Between Health Risk Behaviors and Sexual Orientation," 900–901.

142. Erik Erikson, *Identity, Youth, and Crisis* (New York: Norton, 1968).

143. W. Massiglo, "Attitudes Toward Homosexual Activity and Gays as Friends: A National Survey of Heterosexual 15–19-Year-Old Males," *Journal of Sex Research* 30 (1993): 12–17.

144. T. Roesler and R. Deisher, "Youthful Male Homosexuality," *Journal of the American Medical Assn.* 219 (1972): 1018–1023.

145. R. H. DuRant et al., "Victimization, Use of Violence," 113–118.

146. G. Remafedi, "Fundamental Issues in the Care of Homosexual Youth," *Medical Clinics of North America* 74 (5 September 1990): 1173.

147. Hetrick and Martin, "The Stigmatization," 171.

148. "Peter," in Shane Town, "Is It Safe to Come Out Yet?: The Impact of Secondary Schooling on the Positive Identity Development of Ten Young Gay Men, or 'That's a Queer Way to Behave,'" paper presented at the annual meeting of the American Psychological Association, New York, April 1996.

149. National Academy of Sciences, reported in Warren E. Leary, "U.S. Rate of Sexual Diseases Highest in Developed World," *New York Times*, 20 November 1996.

150. Remafedi, "Adolescent Homosexuality," 331–337.

151. J. Zenilman, "Sexually Transmitted Diseases in Homosexual Adolescents," *Journal of Adolescent Health Care* 9 (1988): 139–143; U.S. Centers for Disease Control, *HIV/AIDS Surveillance* (U.S. CDC: Atlanta, Georgia, June 1990–1992); AIDS Committee of Massachusetts, *A Survey of AIDS-Related Knowledge, Attitudes and Behaviors Among Gay and Bisexual Men in Greater Boston* (Boston: AIDS Committee of Massachusetts, June 1991); AIDS Office, Bureau of Epidemiology and Disease Control, San Francisco City Clinic Special Programs for Youth and San Francisco Dept. of Welfare, *The Young Men's Survey: Principal Findings and Results* (San Francisco: June 1991).

152. Study of the San Francisco AIDS Office, reported in Sabin Russell, "AIDS Rate Drops for Young Gays," *San Francisco Chronicle*, 23 January 1997.

153. Researchers found the same prevalance of unsafe sex and drug use among both groups, so the reason for the discrepancy is unclear.

154. Jonathan Bor, "Young Gays: Fear Recedes, Risks Rise," *Baltimore Sun*, 15 August 1997 (article concerning ongoing U.S. Centers for Disease Control and Prevention's Young Men's Survey).

155. U.S. Centers for Disease Control, *HIV/AIDS Surveillance Report* 6, 2 (U.S. CDC: Atlanta, Georgia, 1994).

156. Daniel Q. Haney, "Study: AIDS Still Spreading Fast Amongst Young Gay, Bisexual Men Having Unsafe Sex," *Bay Windows* (AP), 15 February 1996.

157. M. Rosario, J. Hunter, M.J. Rotheram-Borus, unpublished data on lesbian and gay adolescents, HIV Center for Clinical and Behavioral Studies, New York State Psychiatric Institute, 1992.

158. Craig Waldo, of the University of California at San Francisco, on research presented at World AIDS Congress, Geneva, 1998, in Thomas H. Maugh II,

"High-Risk Behavior by Gay Males More Common with Low Self-Esteem," *Los Angeles Times*, 2 July 1998.

159. AIDS Prevention Studies (CAPS), University of California at San Francisco, reported in David Tuller, "Study of Gays Reveals Deadly Guessing Game," *San Francisco Chronicle*, 18 March 1997.

160. Fenway Community Health Center report, in *In Newsweekly*, 25 December 1994.

161. A survey of almost 22,000 men by the San Francisco Department of Public Health, cited in Mike Cooper, "U.S. Sees Increase in Risky Behavior by Gay Men," *Reuters*, 28 January 1999.

162. J. Hunter and Robert Schaecher, "Lesbian and Gay Youth Suicide," in *Planning to Live: Evaluating and Treating Suicidal Teens in Community Settings*, ed. M. J. Rotheram-Borus, J. Bradley, N. Obolensky (Tulsa: Univ. of Oklahoma Press, 1990).

163. M. J. Rotheram-Borus, M. Rosario, H.F.L. Meyer-Bahlburg, C. Koopman, S. C. Dopkins, and M. Davies, "Sexual and Substance-Use Behaviors Among Homosexual and Bisexual Male Adolescents in New York City, *Journal of Sex Research* 31, 1 (1994): 47–58.

164. Lena Einhorn and Michael Polgar, "HIV-Risk Behavior Among Lesbians and Bisexual Women," *AIDS Education and Prevention* 6, 6 (1994): 519–523.

165. Sexually Active Men Study: Chicago, Denver, San Francisco, reported in *Bay Windows*, 26 January 1995.

166. Lisa M. Krieger, "Many No Longer See Unsafe Sex as Taboo," *San Francisco Examiner*, 5 January 1998.

167. See, for example, Robert B. Hays et al., "Why Are Young Gay Men Engaging in High Rates of Unsafe Sex?" paper delivered at the International Conference on AIDS, San Francisco, 1985.

168. Richard Saltus, "With AIDS Treatment, New Hints of Risky Sex," *Boston Globe*, 14 August 1997.

169. Sexually Active Men Study, reported in *Bay Windows*, 26 January 1995.

170. Bor, "Young Gays: Fear Recedes, Risks Rise."

171. Dr. Barbara Warren, director of mental health and social service program at Lesbian Gay Community Services Center, New York, in David W. Dunlap, "In Age of AIDS, Love and Hope Can Lead to Risk," *New York Times*, 27 July 1996, 7.

172. Gamalier de Jesus, counselor at New York Blood Center's Project Achieve, in David W. Dunlap, "In Age of AIDS, Love and Hope Can Lead to Risk," *New York Times*, 27 July 1996, 7.

173. Ian Young, an excerpt from the book *The AIDS Cult: Essays on the Gay Health Crisis*, ed. John Lauritsen and Ian Young (Provincetown, Mass.: Askleopios, 1997) in *Art and Understanding* 31 (May 1997): 46–48.

174. For example, "Human Sexuality Seminar," Alexandria City Public Schools (Va.), 1991–1992.

175. Hetrick and Martin, "Developmental Issues," 14.

176. Maguen, "Teen Suicide," 45.

177. Hetrick and Martin, "Developmental Issues," 38.

178. H. Voth, *The Castrated Family* (Kansas City, Mo.: Sheed, Andrews & McMeel, 1977); M. Decter, "The Boys on the Beach," *Commentary* 70, 3 (1980): 34–48.

179. E. Rofes, "I Thought People Like That Killed Themselves": Lesbians, Gay Men, and Suicide (San Francisco: Grey Fox, 1993).

180. Susan L. Morrow, "Career Development of Lesbian and Gay Youth: Effects of Sexual Orientation, Coming Out, and Homophobia," in School Experiences of Gay and Lesbian Youth, ed. Mary Harris (Binghamton, N.Y.: Haworth Press, 1998).

181. Gonsiorek, "Mental Health Issues," 114–122.

182. See WGBH film When a Kid Is Gay, 1995. To obtain a copy of this video, send a blank VHS Tape and SASE to: Community Programming, WGBH, 125 Western Ave., Boston, MA 02134.

183. Report of the Secretary's Task Force on Youth Suicide.

184. E. Erikson, Childhood and Society, 2nd ed. (New York: Norton, 1963).

185. Sasha Lewis, Sunday's Woman: A Report on Lesbian Life Today (Boston: Beacon, 1979).

186. Hetrick and Martin, "The Stigmatization," 173–174.

187. American Academy of Pediatrics Committee on Adolescents, "Homosexuality and Adolescence," Pediatrics 72 (1983): 249–250.

188. R. A. Buhrke, "Female Student Perspectives on Training in Lesbian and Gay Issues," Counseling Psychologist 17 (1989): 629–636.; D. Graham et al., "Therapist's Needs for Training in Counseling Lesbians and Gay Men," Professional Psychology 15 (1984): 482–496; B. Greene, "Lesbian and Gay Sexual Orientations: Implications for Clinical Training, Practice, and Research," in Lesbian and Gay Psychology: Theory, Research, and Clinical Applications, ed. B. Greene, and G. M. Herek (Thousand Oaks, Calif.: Sage, 1994), 17–18. There are some exceptions, for example, Counseling and Psychotherapy with Gay, Lesbian, and Bisexual Clients, a semester seminar at Memphis State University, given in 1993 by Dr. Burl Gilliland and Bob Hughes.

189. Stacey Harris, in the Governor's Commission on Gay and Lesbian Youth, Prevention of Health Problems Among Gay and Lesbian Youth, August 1994, 20.

190. Greene, "Lesbian and Gay Sexual Orientations."

191. Christopher Bellonci, in the Governor's Commission on Gay and Lesbian Youth, Prevention of Health Problems Among Gay and Lesbian Youth, August 1994, 41–42.

192. K. Cwayna, G. Remafedi, and L. Treadway, "Caring for Gay and Lesbian Youth," Medical Aspects of Human Sexuality (July 1991): 50–57.

193. L. M. Markowitz, "Homosexuality: Are We Still in the Dark," Family Therapy Networker (January-February 1991): 26–29, 31–35; Garnets et al., "Issues in Psychotherapy with Lesbians and Gay Men," 964–972; Committee on Lesbian and Gay Concerns, Final Report of the Task Force on Bias in Psychotherapy in with Lesbians and Gay Men (Washington, D.C.: American Psychological Assoc., 1990).

194. See, for example, Ann Landers, "A High School Student, Certain He's Homosexual, Is Contemplating Suicide," Philadelphia Inquirer, 25 May 1997.

195. Garnets et al., "Issues in Psychotherapy," 964–972; N. Youngstrom, "Lesbians and Gay Men Still Find Bias in Therapy," APA Monitor (July 1991): 24–25.

196. Shannon Minter, "Project to Stop the Abusive Confinement and Treatment of Lesbian, Gay, Bisexual, and Transgender Adolescents," unpublished monograph, National Center for Lesbian Rights, 870 Market St., Suite 570, San Francisco, CA 94102, 1993; "Misguided Treatment for Gay and Lesbian Adolescents,"

*Brown Univ. Child and Adolescent Development Letter* 10, 7 (1994): 5. Also, "It's Who I Am," *Seventeen*, November 1996; Barbara Walters report, *ABC 20/20*, 27 September 1996.

197. In response to Parents Friends and Families of Lesbians and Gays (P-FLAG), Transformation Christian Ministries (Washington, D.C.) has founded Parents and Friends of Ex-Gays (P-FOX) to urge and support the "healing of homosexuals." Organizers claimed 23 chapters nationwide in 1998 and projected 30 more within a year (*PR Newswire*, 5 March 1998).

198. See Phyllis Burke, *Gender Shock: Exploding the Myths of Male and Female* (New York: Anchor, 1996).

199. Sexual orientation "deprogramming" is still the goal of some programs operated in religious and in pseudopsychiatric contexts. The National Center for Lesbian Rights reported in 1992 that it assisted an adolescent lesbian from California who had escaped from a so-called sexual orientation treatment center in Utah. The young woman had been sent there pursuant to an individual educational plan (IEP) developed by her school and mother in response to the girl's lesbianism. Her tuition was paid by the school district (Liz Hendrickson, "Dear Friend of NCLR," National Ctr. for Lesbian Rights, San Francisco, December 1992). A protestant minister reported in 1992 that his denomination offered him access to a "Christian counseling program" designed to change his sexual orientation from gay to straight (H. Wishik and C. Pierce, *Sexual Orientation and Identity: Heterosexual, Lesbian, Gay, and Bisexual Journeys* [Laconia, N.H.: New Dynamics, 1995], 237).

200. See, for example, "Gender Identity Disorder," *Child Therapy News* 3, 4 (1996), published by the Center for Applied Psychology, Inc., P.O. Box 61587, King of Prussia, PA 19406.

201. Eli Coleman and Gary Remafedi, "Gay, Lesbian, and Bisexual Adolescents: A Critical Challenge to Counselors," *Journal of Counseling and Development* 68 (September-October 1989): 36–40.

202. Gary Remafedi, in Maguen, "Teen Suicide," 45.

203. J. H. Price and S. K. Telljohan, "School Counselors' Perceptions of Adolescent Homosexuals," *Journal of School Health* 89 (1991): 714–721.

204. A. Glenn and R. Russel, "Homosexual Bias Among Counselor Trainees," *Counselor Education and Supervision* 25, 3 (1986): 222–229; M. Schneider and B. Tremble, "Training Service Providers to Work with Gay or Lesbian Adolescents: A Workshop," *Journal of Counseling and Development* 65, 2 (1986): 98–99; M. Thompson and W. Fishburn, "Attitudes Toward Homosexuality Among Graduate Counseling Students," *Counselor Education and Supervision* 17, 2 (1977): 121–130.

205. Sears, "Responding to the Sexual Diversity," 129.

206. J. T. Sears, "Attitudes, Experiences, and Feelings of Guidance Counselors About Working with Homosexual Students," paper presented at the American Educational Research Association, New Orleans, 1988. ERIC Document no. 296 210.

207. Sara Lonberg Lew, in Jane O'Connor, "A Study of the Brookline High School Gay/Straight Alliance," unpublished paper, Harvard University Graduate School of Education, 12 December 1995, 13–14.

208. Beth Zemsky, "Coming Out Against All Odds: Resistance in the Life of a Young Lesbian," in *Women, Girls, and Psychotherapy: Reframing Resistance,* ed. Carol Gilligan, Annie G. Rogers, and Deborah L. Tolman (New York: Harrington Park Press, 1991), 198.

209. Kristine L. Falco, *Psychotherapy with Lesbian Clients: Theory into Practice* (New York: Brunner/Mazel, 1991), 103.

210. D. McDermott, L. Tyndall, and J. W. Lichtenberg, "Factors Related to Counselor Preference Among Gays and Lesbians," *Journal of Counseling and Development* 68 (September-October 1989): 31–35.

211. Sara Lonberg Lew, in Jane O'Connor, "A Study of the Brookline High School Gay/Straight Alliance," unpublished paper, Harvard University Graduate School of Education, 12 December 1995, 4.

212. Schneider and Tremble, "Training Service Providers," 98–99.

213. Coleman and Remafedi, "Gay, Lesbian, and Bisexual Adolescents"; Schneider and Tremble, "Training Service Providers"; Wendell Ricketts, "Homosexuality in Adolescence: The Reification of Sexual Personalities," *Journal of Social Work and Human Sexuality* 5, 1 (1986): 35–49; J. C. Gonsiorek, "Mental Health Issues of Gay and Lesbian Adolescents," *Journal of Adolescent Health Care* 9 (1988): 120; Lewis, *Sunday's Woman.*

214. Hetrick and Martin, "Developmental Issues," 38.

215. M. Glasser, "Homosexuality in Adolescence," *British Journal of Medical Psychology* 50 (1977): 217–225; R. C. Sorenson, *Adolescent Sexuality in Contemporary America* (New York: Work Publishing, 1973).

216. Gonsiorek, "Mental Health Issues," 120.

217. William J. Bennett, "Gay Marriage? A Man and a Woman Needed for the 'Honorable Estate,'" *St. Louis Post Dispatch,* 23 May 1996.

218. Lewis, *Sunday's Woman.*

219. Ricketts, "Homosexuality in Adolescence."

220. K. Plummer, "Going Gay: Identities, Life Cycles, and Life Styles in the Male Gay World," in *The Theory and Practices of Homosexuality,* ed. J. Hart and D. Richardson (London: Routledge and Kegan Paul, 1981), 108.

221. James T. Sears, "Researching the Other/Searching for Self: Qualitative Research on [Homo]Sexuality in Education," *Theory into Practice* 31, 2 (1992): 155.

222. Paul H. Cottell Jr., "A Queer Youth," in special issue of the *Harvard Educational Review* 66, 2 (1996): 186.

223. "Everetta," as quoted in J. T. Sears, "Alston and Everetta: Too Risky for School?" in *At-Risk Students: Portraits, Policies, Programs, and Practices,* ed. R. Donmoyer and Raylene Kos (Albany: State Univ. of New York Press, 1993), 158–159.

224. "Andy," in Shane Town, "Is It Safe to Come Out Yet?"

225. C. Silverstein, "Behavior Modification and the Gay Community," paper presented at the annual convention of the Association for Advancement of Behavior Therapy, New York, October 1972.

226. See, for example, Jeffrey Beane, "'I'd Rather Be Dead Than Gay': Counseling Gay Men Who Are Coming Out," *Personnel and Guidance Journal* (December 1981): 222–226.

227. C. Socarides, *The Homosexualities and the Therapeutic Process* (Madison, Conn.: International Universities Press, 1991); and J. Nicolosi, *Reparative Therapy of Male Homosexuals* (Northvale, N.J.: Jason Aronson, 1991).

228. "Misguided Treatment for Gay and Lesbian Adolescents," *Brown Univ. Child and Adolescent Behavior Letter* 10, 7 (July 1994): 5.

229. British Medical Association, *Homosexuality and Prostitution* (London: British Medical Association, 1955); T. F. Murphy, "The Ethics of Conversion Therapy," *Bioethics* 5 (1991): 123–138; E. M. Pattison and M. L. Pattison, "'Ex-Gays': Religiously Mediated Change in Homosexuals," *American Journal of Psychiatry*, 137 (1980): 1553–1562; W. . Masters and V. E. Johnson, *Homosexuality in Perspective* (Boston: Little, Brown, 1979); R. E. Hemphill et al., "A Factual Study of Male Homosexuality," *British Medical Journal* 1 (1958): 1317–1322; M. T. Saghir and E. Robbins, *Male and Female Homosexuality* (Baltimore: Williams and Williams, 1973); C. A. Tripp, *The Homosexual Matrix* (New York: McGraw-Hill, 1975).

230. J. Money, "Sin, Sickness, or Status? Homosexual Gender Identity and Psychoneuroendocrinology," *American Psychologist* 42 (1987): 384–399; J. Money, *Gay, Straight, and In-Between: The Sexology of Erotic Orientation* (New York: Oxford Univ. Press, 1988); B. Zuger, "Is Early Effeminate Behavior in Boys Early Homosexuality?" *Comprehensive Psychiatry* 29 (1988): 509–519; A. D. Martin, "The Emperor's New Clothes: Modern Attempts to Change Sexual Orientation," in *Innovations in Psychotherapy with Homosexuals*, ed. Emery S. Hetwick and Terry S. Stein (Washington, D.C.: American Psychiatric Press, 1984); and Judd Marmor, "Clinical Aspects of Homosexuality," in *Homosexual Behavior: A Modern Reappraisal*, ed. Judd Marmor (New York: Basic Books, 1980). Also W. C. Menninger, *Psychiatry in a Troubled World* (New York: Macmillan, 1948); D. C. Haldeman, "Sexual Orientation Conversion Therapy for Gay Men and Lesbians: A Scientific Examination," in *Homosexuality: Research Implications for Public Policy*, ed. J. C. Gonsiorek and J. Weinrich (Newbury Park, Calif.: Sage, 1991), 149–160.

231. R. Bayer, *Homosexuality and American Psychiatry: The Politics of Diagnosis* (New York: Basic, 1991), 33–34, 37–38.

232. See, for example, Elizabeth Gilbert, "Queer and Loathing," *Spin Magazine,* June 1996; Ward Harkavy, "Slay It with a Smile: Paul Cameron's Mission to Stop Homosexuality Is Hard to Swallow," *Westword Magazine* (Denver), 3 October 1996.

233. Rick Weiss, "Psychologists' Society Adopts Resolution Seeking to Limit Gay 'Conversion' Therapy," *Washington Post*, 15 August 1997.

234. Robert Weller, "Psychiatrists Converting Gays," *Associated Press*, 11 December 1998.

235. E. Coleman, "Changing Approaches to the Treatment of Homosexuality: A Review," in *Homosexuality: Social, Psychological, and Biological Issues*, ed. J. D. Weinrich, J. C. Gonsiorek, and M. E. Hotvedt (Beverly Hills, Calif.: Sage, 1982), 81–88; K. Freund, "Should Homosexuality Arouse Therapeutic Concern?" *Journal of Homosexuality* 2 (1977): 235–240; Douglas C. Haldeman, "The Practice and Ethics of Sexual Orientation Conversion Therapy," *Journal of Consulting and Clinical Psychology* 62, 2 (1994): 221–227.

236. E. Coleman, "Toward a New Model of Treatment of Homosexuality: A Review," *Journal of Homosexuality* 3 (1978): 345–359; Gonsiorek, "Mental Health Issues"; E. S. Hetrick and A. D. Martin, "More on Ex-Gays: A Response to Pattison and Pattison," *American Journal on Psychiatry* 138 (1981): 1510–1511; A. C. Kinsey, W. B. Pomeroy, C. E. Martin, *Sexual Behavior in the Human Male* (Philadelphia: W. B. Saunders, 1948); Richard A. Isay, *Being Homosexual: Gay Men and Their Develop-*

*ment* (New York: Farrar Straus & Giroux, 1989). The arguments for and against the possibility of cure are garnered respectively by the National Association for Research and Treatment of Homosexuality (by Dr. Charles Socarides et al.) and the National Lesbian and Gay Health Association (by Drs. Ariel Shidlo, Michael Schroder et al.) A website for former ex-gays has been established by Doug Upchurch through http://member.aol.com/exexgay (email through exexgay@ aol.com).

237. Susana Aikin and Carlos Aparicio, directors, *POV: The Transformation*, produced by American Documentary, Inc., 1996.

238. Gonsiorek, "Gay Male Identities," 29.

239. See Timothy F. Murphy, "Redirecting Sexual Orientation: Techniques and Justifications," *Journal of Sex Research* 29, 4 (1992): 520.

240. For counseling resources, see the *Bisexual Resource Guide* (Cambridge, Mass.: Bisexual Resource Center, 1999).

241. Ruth Westheimer, *Ask Doctor Ruth*, King Features Syndicate, 29 June 1996.

242. M. E. Reilly and J. M. Lynch, "Power Sharing in Lesbian Relationships," *Journal of Homosexuality* 19 (1990): 1–30; P. Blumstein and P. Schwartz, *American Couples: Money, Work, Sex* (New York: Wm. Morrow, 1983); J. Harry and W. B. DeVall, *The Social Organization of Gay Males* (New York: Praeger, 1978).

243. Blumstein and Schwartz, *American Couples*.

244. D. P. McWirter and A. M. Matthison, *The Male Couple: How Relationships Develop* (Englewood Cliffs, N.J.: Prentice-Hall, 1984).

245. Lawrence A. Kurdek, "Developmental Changes in Relationship Quality in Gay and Lesbian Cohabiting Couples," *Developmental Psychology* 31, 1 (1995): 86–94.

246. See, for example, Kath Weston, *Families We Choose: Lesbians, Gays, Kinship* (New York: Columbia Univ. Press, 1991).

247. AIDS Prevention Studies (CAPS), University of California at San Francisco, reported in David Tuller, "Peer Pressure for Safer Sex," *San Francisco Chronicle*, 14 August 1996.

248. See James T. Sears, "Dilemmas and Possibilities of Sexuality Education, Reproducing the Body Politic," in *Sexuality and the Curriculum: The Politics and Practices of Sexuality Education*, ed. James T. Sears (New York: Teachers College Press, 1992), 7–33.

249. See Jonathan Silin, "School-Based HIV/AIDS Education: Is There Safety in Safer Sex," in *Sexuality and the Curriculum: The Politics and Practices of Sexuality Education*, ed. James T. Sears (New York: Teachers College Press, 1992), 267–283.

250. For example: The Safe Homes Project (Massachusetts Prevention Center, Worcester, Mass.); Gay and Lesbian Adolescent Social Services (Boston); and Gay and Lesbian Adolescent Social Services (West Hollywood, California).

251. Marshall Forstein, M.D., lecture on gay, lesbian, and bisexual adolescent health issues, Lesley College, 20 May 1994.

252. "Sasha," in Shane Town, "Is It Safe to Come Out Yet?"

253. A. P. Bell and M. S. Weinberg, *Homosexualities: A Study of Diversity Among Men and Women* (New York: Simon & Schuster, 1978); J. Bradford and C. Ryan, *National Lesbian Health Care Survey: Mental Health Implications* (Washington, D.C.: National Lesbian and Gay Health Foundation, 1987); S. K. Hammersmith and M.

S. Weinberg, "Homosexual Identity: Commitment, Adjustments, and Significant Others," *Sociometry* 36, 1 (1973): 56–78; J. Miranda and M. Storms, "Psychological Adjustment of Lesbians and Gay Men," *Journal of Counseling and Development* 68 (1989): 41–45.

254. C. Rand, D. L. Graham, and E. Rawlings, "Psychological Health and Factors the Court Seeks to Control in Lesbian Mother Custody Trials," *Journal of Homosexuality* 8, 1 (1982): 27–39.

255. B. Murphy, "Lesbian Couples and Their Parents: The Effect of Perceived Parental Attitudes on the Couple," *Journal of Counseling and Development* 68 (1989): 46–51.

256. D. W. Cramer and A. S. Roach, "Coming Out to Mom and Dad: A Study of Gay Males and Their Relationships with Their Parents," *Journal of Homosexuality* 15, 3–4 (1988): 79–91; J. W. Wells and W. B. Kline, "Self-Disclosure of Homosexual Orientation," *Journal of Social Psychology* 127 (1987): 191–197.

257. Sara Lonberg Lew, in Jane O'Connor, unpublished paper, Harvard University Graduate School of Education, 12 December 1995, 4.

258. C. Hetherington, "Life Planning and Career Counseling with Gay and Lesbian Students," in *Beyond Tolerance: Gays, Lesbians, and Bisexuals on Campus,* ed. N. J. Evans and V. A. Wall (Alexandria, Va.: American College Personnel Association, 1991), 131–145; B. Campbell and S. L. Morrow, "Influences Affecting Career Development of Lesbians, Gays, and Bisexuals," poster presentation, annual convention of the American Psychological Association, New York, N.Y., August 1995.

259. Esther D. Rothblum, "Lesbians and Physical Appearance: Which Model Applies?" in *Lesbian and Gay Psychology: Theory, Research, and Clinical Applications,* ed. Beverly Greene and Gregory Herek (Thousand Oaks, Calif.: Sage, 1994).

260. A senior at Lutheran High School, Denver, was not allowed to graduate because he would not obey a dress code that disallowed his gay self-expression, including at various times "leather pants," "platform tennis shoes," and a "necklace" (Mike McPhee, "Dress Code Drives Away Gay Student," *Denver Post,* 3 February 1998).

261. Rotheram-Borus, Reid, Rosario, Van Rossem, and Gillis, "Prevalence, Course, and Predictors," 84.

262. J. Hunter and R. Schaecher, "AIDS Prevention for Lesbian, Gay, and Bisexual Adolescents," *Families in Society* 75, 6 (1994): 346–354.

263. Michael Matza, "Challenge to a School Policy on Gays Polarizes a N.H. Town," *Philadelphia Inquirer,* 25 March 1996.

264. Nanette K. Gartrell, "Boundaries in Lesbian Therapist-Client Relationships," in *Lesbian and Gay Psychology: Theory, Research, and Clinical Applications,* ed. Beverly Greene and Gregory Herek (Thousand Oaks, Calif.: Sage, 1994).

265. Beverly Greene, "Ethnic-Minority Lesbians and Gay Men: Mental Health and Treatment Issues," *Journal of Consulting and Clinical Psychology* 62, 2 (1994), 243–251.

266. Bettina Boxall, "Gay Youth Agency's Woes Show Work's Risk," *Los Angeles Times,* 25 March 1996.

267. Troix Bettencourt, in *Prevention of Health Problems Among Gay and Lesbian Youth,* Governor's Commission on Gay and Lesbian Youth, August 1994, 50.

268. Rotheram-Borus et al., "Sexual and Substance Use Behaviors," 47–58.

269. Bettencourt, in *Prevention of Health Problems* , 19.

270. Carol Gilligan, "Women's Psychological Development: Implications for Psychotherapy," in *Women, Girls, and Psychotherapy: Reframing Resistance,* ed. Carol Gilligan, Annie G. Rogers, and Deborah L. Tolman (New York: Harrington Park Press, 1991), 27.

271. Cramer and Roach, "Coming Out to Mom and Dad," 79–92.

272. State laws are far from uniform on this matter. See David Buckel, "A Legal Sketch of the Issues of Parental Consent and Related Tort Liability in the Context of Youth Service Providers Working with Lesbian, Gay, Bisexual, and Transgendered Youth," Lambda Legal Defense and Education Fund, New York, 14 September 1995.

273. Gary P. Mallon, "Gay and No Place to Go: Assessing the Needs of Gay and Lesbian Adolescents in Out-of-Home Care Settings," *Child Welfare* 71, 6 (1992): 547–556.

274. Cramer and Roach, "Coming Out to Mom and Dad," 79–92.

275. L. Brown, "Lesbians, Gay Men, and Their Families: Common Clinical Issues," *Journal of Gay and Lesbian Psychotherapy* 1, 1 (1989): 65–77.

276. David Masello, *New York Times Magazine,* 2 January 1994, 13. Copyright © 1994 by *The New York Times.* Reprinted by permission.

277. April Leavech et al., "Sexual Orientation Disclosure to Parents: Problem Solving and Social Support," paper presented at the annual convention of the American Psychological Association, Washington, D.C., 14–18 August 1992.

278. See, for example, Cramer and Roach, "Coming Out to Mom and Dad," 79–92.

279. J. L. DeVine, "A Systemic Inspection of Affectional Preference Orientation and the Family of Origin," *Journal of Social Work and Human Sexuality* 2 (1984): 9–17

280. Herdt and Boxer, *Children of Horizons,* 216.

281. Cramer and Roach, "Coming Out to Mom and Dad," 79–92.

282. Erik Strommen, "Hidden Branches and Growing Pains: Homosexuality and the Family Tree," in *Homosexuality and Family Relations,* ed. F. Bozett and M. B. Sussman (Binghamton, N.Y.: Haworth Press, 1990), 9–34.

283. B. E. Robinson, L. H. Walters, and P. Skeen, "Response of Parents to Learning That Their Child Is Homosexual and Concern over AIDS: A National Study," *Journal of Homosexuality* 18, 1–3 (1989): 59–80; C. Griffin, M. Wirth, and A. Wirth, *Beyond Acceptance: Parents of Lesbians and Gays Talk About Their Experiences* (Englewood Cliffs, N.J.: Prentice-Hall, 1986).

284. Ann Muller, *Parents Matter* (New York: Naiad Press, 1987).

285. DeVine, "A Systemic Inspection of Affectional Preference Orientation," 9–17; L. Collins and N. Zimmerman, "Homosexual and Bisexual Issues," in *Sexual Issues in Family Therapy,* ed. J. C. Hansen, J. D. Woody, and R. H. Woody (Rockville, Md.: Aspen Publications, 1983).

286. T. Sauerman, "Read This Before Coming Out to Your Parents," publication of P-FLAG, P.O. Box 24565, Los Angeles, CA 90024.

287. Interview in Alice Y. Hom, "Stories from the Homefront: Perspectives of Asian American Parents with Lesbian Daughters and Gay Sons," *Amerasia Journal* 20, 1 (1994): 25.

288. E. F. Strommen, "'You're a What?': Family Members' Reactions to the Disclosure of Homosexuality," *Journal of Homosexuality* 18, 1–2 (1989): 37–58; DeVine, "Systemic Inspection of Affectional Preference Orientation," 9–17.

289. Sauerman, "Read This Before Coming Out."

290. Interview in Alice Y. Hom, "Stories from the Homefront," 25.

291. *Developmental Stage Model for Family and Friends of Gays, Lesbians, Bisexuals, and Transgendered People* (Boston: P-FLAG, 1996).

292. DeVine, "A Systemic Inspection," 9–17.

293. See Marlene Fanta Shyer and Christopher Shyer, *Not Like Other Boys* (Boston: Houghton Mifflin, 1996).

294. Agnes G. Herman, "The Answer Most Feared," *Hadassah Magazine,* May 1988, 34–35.

295. Robinson, Walters, and Skeen, "Response of Parents," 59–80; C. Griffin, M. Wirth, and A. Wirth, *Beyond Acceptance*; L. Kleinberg, *Coming Home to Self, Going Home to Parents: Lesbian Identity Disclosure*, Stone Center Work in Progress Series, no. 24 (Wellesley, Mass.: Wellesley College, 1986); L. Collins and N. Zimmerman, "Homosexual and Bisexual Issues," in *Sexual Issues in Family Therapy*, ed. J. C. Hansen, J. D. Woody, and R. H. Woody (Rockville, Md.: Aspen, 1983), 82–100.

296. Robert A. Bernstein, "Paving Good Intentions: One Father Responds," *Bay Windows*, 19 May 1988.

297. See Strommen, "Hidden Branches and Growing Pains," 19.

298. C. Jones, *Understanding Gay Relatives and Friends* (New York: Seabury Press, 1978).

299. Edward S. Morales, "Ethnic Minority Families and Minority Gays and Lesbians," in *Homosexuality and Family Relations*, ed. F. Bozett and M. B. Sussman (Binghamton, N.Y.: (Haworth Press, 1990).

300. D. Atkinson, G. Morten, and D. Sue, *Counseling American Minorities* (Dubuque Ia.: William C. Brown, 1979); Greene, "Ethnic-Minority Lesbians and Gay Men," 243–251.

301. R. C. Savin-Williams and R. G. Rodriguez, "A Developmental, Clinical Perspective on Lesbian, Gay Male, and Bisexual Youths," in *Adolescent Sexuality: Advances in Adolescent Development*, ed. T. P. Gullotta, G. R. Adams, and R. Montemayor (Newbury Park, Calif.: Sage, 1993).

302. Bell and Weinberg, *Homosexualities: A Study of Diversity*; M. J. Rotherham-Borus, J. Hunter, and M. Rosario, "Suicidal Behavior and Gay-Related Stress Among Gay and Bisexual Male Adolescents," *Journal of Adolescent Research* 9, 4 (1994): 498–508; Remafedi, Farrow, and Deisher, "Risk Factors for Attempted Suicide," 869–876.

303. Alycee J. Lane, "Pride at Home," *BLK*, July 1990. Reprinted with permission.

304. Susan Ferriss, "Young Gay Latinos Are Finding and Founding Support Groups in the City That Embrace Both Cultures," *San Francisco Examiner,* 1 June 1997.

305. Website: www.blk.com/blk/blk magazine

306. E. Acosta, "Affinity for Black Heritage: Seeking Lifestyle Within a Community," *Washington Blade,* 11 October 1979; V. Mays, S. Corchran, and S. Rhue, "The Impact of Perceived Discrimination on the Intimate Relationships of Black Lesbians," *Journal of Homosexuality* 25, 4 (1993): 1–15.

307. C. Chan, "Asian Lesbians: Psychological Issues in the 'Coming Out' Process," *Asian American Psychological Association Journal* 12 (1987): 16–18; C. Chan, "Issues of Identity Development Among Asian American Lesbians and Gay Men," *Journal of Counseling and Development* 68 (1989): 16–20.

308. Greene, "Ethnic-Minority Lesbians and Gay Men," 243–251.

309. Olivia M. Espín, "Cultural and Historical Influences on Sexuality in Hispanic/Latin Women: Implications for Psychotherapy," in *Pleasure and Danger: Exploring Female Sexuality*, ed. Carole Vance (London: Routledge and Kegan Paul, 1984), 149–163.

310. Mark Pope, "The 'Salad Bowl' Is Big Enough for Us All: An Argument for the Inclusion of Lesbians and Gay Men in Any Definition of Multi-Culturalism," *Journal of Counseling and Development*, 73, 3 (1995): 301–304.

311. See, for example, Kathryn Snider, "Race and Sexual Orientation: The (Im)possibility of These Intersections in Educational Policy," special issue of the *Harvard Educational Review*, 66, 2 (1996): 294–302.

312. Eduardo Aparicio, in Enrique Fernandez, "Something's Queer in 'Macho' Society," *Fort Lauderdale Sun Sentinal*, 2 February 1998.

313. Leopoldo Negron Cruz, in the Governor's Commission on Gay and Lesbian Youth, *Prevention of Health Problems Among Gay and Lesbian Youth*, 35.

314. On changes in the Catholic Church, see, for example: Gary Heinlein and Lama Bakri, "Bishop Assails Gay Policy," *Detroit News*, 16 February 1997; Mark I. Pinsky, "Catholics Launch Ministry for Gays," *Orlando (Fla.) Sentinel*, 6 February 1997; "Rochester Mass Held for Gays," *Associated Press*, 2 March 1997; Ann Rodgers-Melnick, "Catholic Gay and Lesbian Meeting Set," *Pittsburgh Post-Gazette*, 28 February 1997.

315. PFLAG offers two publications for parents of transgender youth: Mary Boenke, *Our Trans Children*, pamphlet (Washington, D.C.: PFLAG, 1999); and Mary Boenke, *Trans Forming Families* (Imperial Beach, Calif.: Walter Trook, 1999).

316. Linda Wong, "Mini Liu, Longtime Activist," in *The Very Inside: An Anthology of Writing by Asian and Pacific Islander Lesbian and Bisexual Women*, ed. Sharon Lim-Hing (Ontario, Canada: Sister Vision Press, 1994), 351.

317. B. Aoki, "Gay Asian Americans: Adapting Within the Family Context," paper presented at the 91st annual convention of the American Psychological Association, Anaheim, California, August 1983.

318. Susan Y. F. Chen, "Slowly but Surely, My Search for Family Acceptance and Community Continues," in *The Very Inside: An Anthology of Writing by Asian and Pacific Islander Lesbian and Bisexual Women*, ed. Sharon Lim-Hing (Ontario, Canada: Sister Vision Press, 1994), 82.

319. Marta Navarro, "Interview with Ana Castillo," in *Chicana Lesbians: The Girls Our Mothers Warned Us About*, ed. Carla Trujillo (Berkeley: Third Woman Press, 1991), 123.

320. Greene, "Ethnic-Minority Lesbians and Gay Men," 243–251; Morales, "Ethnic Minority Families"; Alisa Valdis, "Coming Out in Spanish," *Boston Globe*, 23 July 1998.

321. Olivia M. Espín, "Issues of Identity in the Psychology of Latina Lesbians," in *Lesbian Psychologies: Explorations and Challenges*, ed. Boston Lesbian Psychologies Collective (Urbana: Univ. of Illinois Press, 1987), 35–51.

322. One such group for Catholic Parents is the Catholic Parents Network, St. Francis Chapel and City Ministry Center, 58 Weybosset St., Providence, RI 02903, (401) 331–6510, ext. 137.

323. Chen, "Slowly but Surely," 79–84.

324. Kaushalya Bannerji, "No Apologies," in *A Lotus of Another Color: An Unfolding of the South Asian Gay and Lesbian Experience*, ed. Rakesh Ratti (Boston: Alyson, 1993), 62.

325. See, for example, C. Chan, "Cultural Considerations in Counseling Asian American Lesbians and Gay Men," and E. Morales, "Latino Gays and Latina Lesbians," both in *Counseling Gay Men and Lesbians: Journey to the End of the Rainbow*, ed. S. Dworkin and F. Gutierrez (Alexandria, Va.: American Association for Counseling and Development, 1992); L. Garnets and D. Kimmel, "Lesbian and Gay Male Dimensions in the Psychological Study of Human Diversity," in *Psychological Perspectives on Human Diversity in America*, ed. J. Goodchilds (Washington, D.C.: American Psychological Association, 1991); B. Greene, "African American Lesbians: Triple Jeopardy," in *The Psychology of African American Women*, ed. A. Brown-Collins (New York: Guilford Press, in press).

326. Alice Y. Hom, "Stories from the Homefront."

327. Tomas Almaguer, "Chicano Men: A Cartography of Homosexual Identity and Behavior," in *The Lesbian and Gay Studies Reader*, ed. H. Abelove, M. Barale, and D. Halperin (New York: Routledge, 1993).

328. Edward S. Morales, "Third World Gays and Lesbians: A Process of Multiple Identities," paper presented at the 91st annual convention of the American Psychological Association, Anaheim, California, August 1983.

329. Greene, "Ethnic-Minority Lesbians and Gay Men," 243–251; Morales, "Ethnic Minority Families."

330. Marlon Riggs, director, *Tongues Untied*, 1989.

## Chapter 9

1. Anonymous, 1992.

2. Name withheld, 1991.

3. "Rockport Comfort Barometer," in cooperation with Roper Starch, cited in "Survey Shows About Half of All Americans Support Gay Teachers," PRNewswire report, *(San Francisco) Bay Area Reporter*, 26 September 1997. In a 1998 poll 55 percent of Americans approved the hiring of homosexuals as elementary teachers (double the support of 1977), according to the National Gay and Lesbian Task Force's report, *From Rights to Wrongs*, May 1998. The sticking point may be the issue of openness.

4. "Across the USA: News from Every State," *USA Today*, 6 April 1998.

5. *The Gay Agenda in Public Education*, A Ty and Jeanette Beeson Production, The Report, Springs of Life Church, Los Angeles, 1993.

6. See, for example, Paul Cameron, William L. Playfair, and Stephen Wellum, "The Longevity of Homosexuals: Before and After the AIDS Epidemic," *Omega–Journal of Death and Dying* 29, 3 (1994): 249–272. Cameron was dropped from the APA in 1983 for "unprofessional conduct, willfully misrepresent[ing] his professional qualifications and affiliations and purposes." He was also repri-

manded by the ASA in 1985: "The American Sociological Association officially and publicly states that Paul Cameron is not a sociologist and condemns his consistent misrepresentation of sociological research." *Ground Zero News* (Colorado Springs), 10 September 1996.

7. Michael R. Wickline, "Walton Claims Moscow Teacher Is Openly Gay," *Lewiston (Idaho) Tribune,* 21 May 1996.

8. Karen M. Harbeck, "Gay and Lesbian Educators: Past History/Future Prospects," in *Coming Out of the Classroom Closet: Gay and Lesbian Students, Teachers, and Curricula,* ed. Karen M. Harbeck (New York: Harrington Park Press, 1992), 129.

9. Ibid., 122.

10. For example, in the legislative debate on the Massachusetts gay and lesbian civil rights bill in the 1980s.

11. Harbeck, "Gay and Lesbian Educators," 125–126, 128–129.

12. Willard Waller, *The Sociology of Teaching* (New York: Russell & Russell, 1961), 147–148.

13. "Jack Kemp and the Issues" (reprinted statements of 1987 "television and newspaper interviews"), *New York Times,* 11 August 1996, 26.

14. Jackie M. Blount, "Manly Men and Womanly Women: Deviance, Gender Role Polarization, and the Shift in Women's School Employment," special issue of *Harvard Educational Review* 66, 2 (1996): 318–338.

15. Ibid., 320.

16. Waller, *The Sociology of Teaching,* 143.

17. Blount, "Manly Men and Womanly Women," 328.

18. *Digest of Educational Statistics* (Washington, D.C.: National Center for Education Statistics, 1995), Tables 68 and 66.

19. Dan Woog, *School's Out: The Impact of Gay and Lesbian Issues on America's Schools* (Boston: Alyson, 1995), 293.

20. T. R. Fischer, "A Study of Educators' Attitudes Toward Homosexuality," doctoral diss., Univ. of Virginia, *Dissertation Abstracts International* 43 (1982): 3294A; M. Olson, "A Study of Gay and Lesbian Teachers," *Journal of Homosexuality* 13, 4 (1987): 73–81; S. S. Nickeson, "A Comparison of Gay and Heterosexual Teachers on Professional and Personal Dimensions," *Dissertation Abstracts International* 41 (1980): 3956A, Univ. Microfilms no. DA 8015601; A. A. Sciullo, "Tolls at Closet Doors: A Gay History for Teachers," *Dissertation Abstracts International* 45 (1984): 497A, Univ. Microfilms no. DA 8412076; D. Smith, "An Ethnographic Interview Study of Homosexual Teachers' Perspectives," *Dissertation Abstracts International* 46 (1985): 66A, Univ. Microfilms no. DA 8506864; K. Jennings, ed., *One Teacher in Ten: Gay and Lesbian Educators Tell Their Stories* (Boston: Alyson, 1994); Pat Griffin, "Identity Management Strategies Among Lesbian and Gay Educators," *Qualitative Studies in Education* 4, 3 (1991): 189–202; E. Rofes, *Socrates, Plato, and Guys Like Me: Confessions of a Gay Schoolteacher* (Boston: Alyson, 1985); E. Fogarty, "Passing as Straight: A Phenomenological Analysis of the Experience of the Lesbian Who Is Professionally Employed," *Dissertation Abstracts International* 41, 6 (1980): 2384B. See "Horror Stories," Part 3 in Rita M. Kissen, *The Last Closet: The Real Lives of Lesbian and Gay Teachers* (Portsmouth, N.H.: Heineman, 1996), 71–117.

21. Matt Green, unpublished paper on Newton North High School (Mass.), Harvard Graduate School of Education, 12 December 1995, 11.

22. Green, unpublished paper, 11.

23. Kissen, *The Last Closet*, 68–69.

24. Griffin, "Identity Management Strategies," 193.

25. Blount, "Manly Men and Womanly Women," 330.

26. B. Michael Hunter, "I Have Come Here to Die," in *One Teacher in Ten: Gay and Lesbian Educators Tell Their Stories*, ed. Kevin Jennings (Boston: Alyson, 1994), 73–74.

27. Refuted in, for example, R. S. Kempe and C. H. Kempe, *The Common Secret: Sexual Abuse of Children and Adolescents* (New York: W. H. Freeman, 1984); and in Carole Jenny, "Quality Assurance: A Response to the 'Backlash' Against Child Sexual Abuse Diagnosis and Treatment," *Journal of Child Sexual Abuse* 2, 3 (1993): 89–98.

28. National Gay and Lesbian Task Force web site, December 1998. www.NGLTF.org.

29. R. A. Dyer, "Two Men Charged Under State's Sodomy Law," *Houston Chronicle*, 5 November 1998.

30. *Gaylord v. Tacoma School District No. 10*, 85 Wash. 2d 348, 88 Wash. 2d 286, 559 P. 2d 1340 (1977), Cert. denied (1977).

31. *Marc Morrison v. State Board of Education*, 74 Cal. Rptr. 116; 1 Cal. 3d 214; 461 P. 2d 365; 82 Cal. Rptr. 175, (1969); *Burton v. Cascade School District Union High School No. 5*, 353 F. Supp. 254 (1973), 512 F. 2d 850 (1975), Cert. denied, 423 U.S. 859 (1975); *Board of Education of Long Beach v. Jack M.*, 139 Cal. Rptr. 700, 566 P. 2d 602, 603 (Cal. 1977).

32. *Rowland v. Mad River Local School District*, 730 F. 2d 444 (6th Cir. 1984), Cert. denied, 470 U.S. 1099 (1985).

33. Harbeck, "Gay and Lesbian Educators," 127. Contact NEA Human and Civil Rights Division (202) 822–7700 or email: mbailey@nea.org for resources, including an NEA pamphlet, "Strengthening the Learning Environment, an Employee's Guide to Lesbian and Gay Issues."

34. For example, see Kissen, *The Last Closet*, 74.

35. Their finding in *Bowers v. Hardwick*, 478 U.S. 186 (1986) that states may outlaw homosexual behavior was not overruled in *Romer v. Evans*, 116 S. Ct. 1620 (1996), which found that gay rights legislation may not itself be outlawed by states. It is being argued whether their denial of certiorari in a Cincinnati case (no. 97-1795, October 13, 1998) limits the Romer decision to statewide actions or has no bearing on Romer.

36. Human Rights Campaign, 1101 14th St. NW, Washington, D.C. 20005.

37. John Ashcroft (R-Mo.), Proceedings of the U.S. Senate, 10 September 1996.

38. Orrin Hatch (R-Utah), in Lee Davidson, "Demos' Anti-Bias Measure Could Lead to Hiring Quotas for Gays, Hatch Says," *Deseret News*, 7 September 1996.

39. Update to Kenneth D. Wald, James W. Button, Barbara A. Rienzo, *All Politics Is Local: Analyzing Local Gay Rights Legislation* (Washington, D.C.: National Gay and Lesbian Task Force, 1997), 6 April 1999, personal communication. Nevada became the eleventh state in May 1999.

40. In addition to Oklahoma and California, the states of North Carolina, Nevada, Texas, and Arkansas considered similar legislation. See Harbeck, "Gay and Lesbian Educators," 138, note 34.

41. Kellye Carter, "'Students' vs. 'Parents': Petitions Reflect Divisions on Policy," *Des Moines Register*, 18 April 1996; Kellye Carter, "Petitioners Support Gay

Issue, Thousands Urge Board to Keep Language in School Policy," *Des Moines Register*, 24 April 1996; and Kathy A. Bolten, "School Board Hears Opinions, Defines 'Sexual Orientation,'" *Des Moines Register*, 10 July 1996.

42. Laura Kurtzman, "Board Decision Under Fire, Benefits for Unmarried Couples Spark S.J. Protest," *San Jose Mercury News*, 8 March 1996.

43. "Court Orders Gay Teacher Reinstated," *United Press International*, 19 May 1998.

44. "Experts: Tenure Is Crane's Best Defense," *Grand Rapids Press*, 17 December 1995; "Don't Take Away Our Teacher," *Between the Lines*, Michigan's Community News for Lesbians, Gays, Bisexuals, and Friends, January 1996; "School Suspends Officials over Anti-Gay Mailing," *Detroit News*, 13 March 1996; Jill Smolowe, "The Unmarrying Kind," *Time*, 29 April 1996; *USA Today*, 30 July 1996; "Gay Teacher Tells Why He Quit," *Chicago Tribune*, 31 July 1996; Melanie Eversley, "Embattled Gay Teacher Resigns Byron Center," *Detroit Free Press*, 30 July 1996; "Gay Teacher Forced Out of Conservative High School Dies at Thirty-Two" (obituary), *Detroit News*, 4 January 1997.

45. Jeffrey P. Haney, "Weaver Lawsuit Whittled Down," *Deseret News*, 17 March 1999.

46. Mary L. Bonauto, "A Legal Overview of the Rights of Gay, Lesbian, and Bisexual Teachers," in *One Teacher in Ten: Gay and Lesbian Educators Tell Their Stories*, ed. K. Jennings (Boston: Alyson, 1994), 257–276.

47. Marjorie Cortez, "Disclosure May Attract High Price," *Deseret News* (Salt Lake City), 27 February 1996.

48. Again, see *Rowland v. Mad River School District*.

49. Mike Carter, "Lesbian Coach Sues School District," *Associated Press*, 21 October 1997; Sheila R. McCann, "Teacher Sues over School's Gag Order," *Salt Lake Tribune*, 22 October 1997; Gwen Florio, "She's Out; Now Parents Want Her Ousted," *Philadelphia Inquirer*, 14 November 1997; Jeff Call, "Charged Crowd Speaks Out on Weaver," *Deseret News*, 20 November 1997; Edward L. Carter, "Lawsuit Says Coach Encouraged Lesbianism," *Deseret News*, 23 December 1997; Joe Costanzo, "Nebo District Breaks Silence," *Deseret News*, 27 December 1997; Ryan Van Benthuysen, "Girls Claim Weaver Lawsuit Unfounded," *Daily Herald* (Provo, Utah), 30 December 1997; Jeffrey P. Haney, "Weaver Opposing Lawyer in Eye of Storm," and Jeff Call, "Life Has Been a Roller Coaster for Teacher, Partner," *Deseret News*, 25 January 1998.

50. Hilary Groutage, "Lesbian Teacher Wins Suit Against Nebo Schools," *Salt Lake Tribune*, 26 November 1998. $1500 was the amount of her lost coaching salary.

51. Haney, "Weaver Lawsuit Whittled Down."

52. Richard Mohr, *Gays/Justice: A Study of Ethics, Society, and Law* (New York: Columbia Univ. Press, 1988); Richard Mohr, *A More Perfect Union: Why Straight America Must Stand Up for Gay Rights* (Boston: Beacon Press, 1994).

53. *Romer v. Evans* dissent by Justice Scalia, joined by Chief Justice Rehnquist and Justice Thomas, S. Ct. 730 F. 2d at 449 (1996).

54. S. 1740.

55. Harbeck, "Gay and Lesbian Educators," 127.

56. G. Hechinger and F. Hechinger, "Should Homosexuals Be Allowed to Teach?" *McCall's* (March 1978): 100, 160–163.

57. Harbeck, "Gay and Lesbian Educators," 131.

58. Faye Penn, "Out of the Classroom Closet," *QW* (New York City periodical), 11 October 1992, 12.

59. Joyce Hunter and Robert Schaecher, "Stresses on Lesbian and Gay Adolescents in Schools," *Social Work in Education* (Spring 1987): 187.

60. J. T. Sears, *Growing Up Gay in the South* (Binghamton, N.Y.: Harrington Park Press, 1991), 399–400.

61. David Buckel, in Martha Irvine, "More Gay Teachers Coming Out, But Not Without Controversy," *Associated Press*, 6 April 1998.

62. Kissen, *The Last Closet*, 89–91.

63. Dale Martin, "Offering Students Sexual Identity Haven," *Daily Review* (Alameda, Calif.), 25 March 1996, 13.

64. Gretchen Schuldt, "Lawsuit Filed over Alleged Slurs, Threat to Gay Teacher," *Milwaukee Journal Sentinel*, 2 January 1999.

65. Tony Prince, "One Teacher in Ten Thousand: Out in Kentucky," in *One Teacher in Ten: Gay and Lesbian Educators Tell Their Stories*, ed. Kevin Jennings (Boston: Alyson, 1994), 137–138.

66. Dave Rasdal, "Teacher Feels Vindicated by Firing Ruling," *Cedar Rapids (Ia.) Gazette*, 30 December 1995. For additional examples, see Kissen, *The Last Closet*, ch. 8, "He Handed Me a Letter . . . ," 97–109.

67. For example, see Kissen, *The Last Closet*, 81.

68. Elaine Herscher, "Coming Out at School," *San Francisco Chronicle*, 11 March 1998.

69. Pat Griffin, "From Hiding Out to Coming Out: Empowering Lesbian and Gay Educators," in *Coming Out of the Classroom Closet: Gay and Lesbian Students, Teachers, and Curricula*, ed. K. Harbeck (New York: Harrington Park Press, 1992), 167–196; Kate Adams and Kim Emery, "Classroom Coming Out Stories: Practical Strategies for Productive Self-Disclosure," in *Tilting the Tower: Lesbians Teaching Queer Subjects*, ed. Linda Garber (New York: Routledge, 1994), 32.

70. Among a few noteworthy exceptions is Dave Ellison, an assistant principal at Barnard-White Middle School in Union City, California (former Teacher of the Year) and Larry Alegre, a San Francisco elementary school assistant principal.

71. Survey conducted by Anthony Costa, Fairfield University. Garrett Stack is a principal at a Stratford elementary school. Both cited in Dan Woog, *School's Out*, 293 and 44.

72. D. Smith, "An Ethnographic Study of Homosexual Teachers," *Dissertation Abstracts International* 46, 1 (1985): 66-A.

73. Suzanne Sutley, in *QW*, 11 October 1992, 12.

74. Bettina Boxall, "A Painful Lesson for a Gay Teacher," *Los Angeles Times*, 18 June 1994, A31.

75. Rodney Wilson, "Telling Our Stories, Winning Our Freedom," in *One Teacher in Ten: Gay and Lesbian Educators Tell Their Stories*, ed. K. Jennings (Boston: Alyson, 1994): 200–207. Also David Ruenzel, "Coming Out," *Education Week*, 21 September 1994, 22–26.

76. Joan Little and Phyllis Brasch Librach, "Homosexual Teacher Here Is 'Out,' But Scores Stay Closeted," *St. Louis Post-Dispatch*, 16 August 1994, 1a.

77. Joan Little, "Gay Teacher Wins His Tenure," *St. Louis Post-Dispatch*, 19 April 1995, 1b.

78. Boxall, "A Painful Lesson," A31.

79. On signaling vulnerability, see Kissen, *The Last Closet*, 99.

80. Griffin, "Identity Management Strategies," 194–199. (Cf., Monteflores and Troiden stigma management strategies in Chapter 6.).

81. Hope E. Burwell, "Skeleton Key," in *One Teacher in 10: Gay and Lesbian Educators Tell Their Stories*, ed. Kevin Jennings (Boston: Alyson, 1994), 30.

82. Ibid., 37.

83. Kissen, *The Last Closet*, 47

84. Ruth Irwin, "You Can't Tell Him I'm Not," in *One Teacher in Ten: Gay and Lesbian Educators Tell Their Stories*, ed. Kevin Jennings (Boston: Alyson, 1994), 100–105.

85. M. Olson, "A Study of Gay and Lesbian Teachers," *Journal of Homosexuality* 13, 4 (1987): 73–81.

86. Gary Campbell, "Coming Out of the Cloakroom," in *One Teacher in Ten: Gay and Lesbian Educators Tell Their Stories*, ed. Kevin Jennings (Boston: Alyson, 1994), 131–136.

87. Al Ferreira, personal communication, 1987; K. Jennings, "I Remember," in *One Teacher in Ten: Gay and Lesbian Educators Tell Their Stories*, ed. Kevin Jennings (Boston: Alyson, 1994), 24.

88. Sandy Dorfman and Cindy Bingham, Framingham, Massachusetts Public Schools, personal communication, 1996.

89. Thomas Patrick Juul, "A Survey to Examine the Relationship of the Openness of Self-Identified Lesbian, Gay Male, and Bisexual Public School Teachers to Job Stress and Job Satisfaction," paper presented at the annual meeting of the American Educational Research Association, Atlanta, 12–16 April 1993. ERIC Microfiche no. ED378079.

90. For examples, see Kissen, ch. 4, "Being Invisible," in *The Last Closet*, 41–56.

91. See, for example, Rita M. Kissen, "Voices from the Glass Closet: Lesbian and Gay Teachers Talk About Their Lives," paper presented at the annual meeting of the American Educational Research Association, Atlanta, 12–16 April 1993, ERIC Microfiche no. ED363556; Karen Amy Snelbecker, "Speaking Out: A Survey of Lesbian, Gay, and Bisexual Teachers of ESOL in the U.S.," Master's Thesis, School for International Training, 1994. ERIC Microfiche no. ED375680.

92. James T. Sears, "Responding to the Sexual Diversity of Faculty and Students: Sexual Praxis and the Critically Reflective Administrator," in *Educational Administration in a Pluralistic Society*, ed. Colleen A. Capper (Albany: State Univ. of New York Press, 1993), 121.

93. Kissen, *The Last Closet*, 54.

94. See also Thomas Patrick Juul, "Tenure, Civil Rights Laws, Inclusive Contracts, and Fear: Legal Protection and the Lives of Self-Identified Lesbian, Gay Male, and Bisexual Public School Teachers," paper presented at the annual meeting of the American Educational Research Association, New York, 26–28 October 1994. ERIC Microfiche no. ED377565.

95. Terri Gruenwald, "Ms. G. Is a Lesbian," in *One Teacher in Ten: Gay and Lesbian Educators Tell Their Stories*, ed. Kevin Jennings (Boston: Alyson, 1994), 147–155.

96. Ibid., 155.

97. See Kissen, *The Last Closet*, 58.

98. Ibid., 102–103.

99. Griffin, "From Hiding Out to Coming Out," 195.

100. Barbara Blinick, "Out in the Curriculum, Out in the Classroom: Teaching History and Organizing for Change," in *Tilting the Tower: Lesbians Teaching Queer Subjects*, ed. Linda Garber (New York: Routledge, 1994), 142.

101. Kissen, *The Last Closet*, 41

102. See Adams and Emery, "Classroom Coming Out Stories," 31–32.

103. Anonymous teacher, personal conversation.

104. See, for example, Jim Bridgman, "Yes I Am," in *One Teacher in Ten: Gay and Lesbian Educators Tell Their Stories*, ed. Kevin Jennings (Boston: Alyson, 1994), 123–130.

105. Al Ferreira, Cambridge Rindge and Latin High School, Reggie Sellars, Noble and Greenough School, Kathy Henderson, Phillips Academy (Andover), and Patricia Smith, The Pike School, in "The Contributions of Gay and Lesbian Teachers," panel discussion at the Third Annual Gay, Lesbian, Straight Teachers Network Conference, Milton Academy, Milton, Mass., 1 March 1993.

106. Lee Romney, "Teen's Attack Investigated," *Los Angeles Times*, 13 June 1996.

107. Reggie Sellars, "Working My Way Back Home," in *One Teacher in Ten: Gay and Lesbian Educators Tell Their Stories*, ed. Kevin Jennings (Boston: Alyson, 1994), 244–253.

108. "Cornel West on Heterosexism and Transformation: An Interview," special issue of *Harvard Educational Review* 66, 2 (1996): 356–367.

109. See Kissen, *The Last Closet*, 64–65, for example.

110. See Michele Barale, "The Romance of Class and Queers: Academic Erotic Zones," in *Tilting the Tower: Lesbians Teaching Queer Subjects*, ed. Linda Garber (New York: Routledge, 1994), 21.

111. For an example, see Kissen, *The Last Closet*, 48.

112. Nancy Boutilier, "Reading, Writing, and Rubyfruit Jungle: High School Students Respond to Gay and Lesbian Literature," *OUT/LOOK* 15 (Winter 1992): 76.

113. "Family Sues over Teacher-Student Pants-Pulling Incident," *Associated Press*, 28 May 1996.

114. Susan Dodge and Brenda Warner Rotzoll, "A Dramatic Test of Tolerance," *Chicago Sun-Times*, 10 July 1998; Rosalind Bentley, "Second Transgender Teacher to Come Out in Blaine," *Minneapolis Star Tribune*, 7 November 1998.

115. Rosalind Bentley, "Transgendered Teacher Says She Was Driven Out," *Minneapolis Star Tribune*, 4 March 1999.

## Chapter 10

1. A. Bell and M. Weinberg, *Homosexualities* (New York: Simon & Schuster, 1978); K. Jay and A. Young, *The Gay Report* (New York: Summit, 1979).

2. Charlotte J. Patterson, "Lesbian Mothers, Gay Fathers, and Their Children," in *Lesbian, Gay, and Bisexual Identities over the Lifespan: Psychological Perspectives*, ed. A. R. D'Augelli and Charlotte J. Patterson (New York: Oxford Univ. Press, 1995), 262.

3. Elena Marie DiLapi, "Lesbian Mothers and the Motherhood Hierarchy," *Journal of Homosexuality* 18, 1–2 (1989): 101–122; P. Falk, "Lesbian Mothers," *American Psychologist* 44, 6 (1989): 941–947; E. Gibbs, "Psychosocial Development of

Children Raised by Lesbian Mothers: A Review of Research," *Women and Therapy* 8, 5 (1988): 65–75; C. Patterson, "Children of Lesbian and Gay Parents," *Child Development* 63 (1992): 1025–1042; P. Turner, L. Scadden, and M. Harris, "Parenting in Gay and Lesbian Families," *Journal of Gay and Lesbian Psychotherapy* 1, 3 (1990): 55–65.

4. Patterson, "Lesbian Mothers, Gay Fathers and Their Children," 262.

5. V. Casper, S. Shultz, and E. Wickens, "Breaking the Silences: Lesbian and Gay Parents and the Schools," *Teachers College Record* 94 (1992): 109–137.

6. David A. Baptiste Jr., "Psychotherapy with Gay/Lesbian Couples and Their Children in Stepfamilies: A Challenge for Marriage and Family Therapists," *Journal of Homosexuality* 14, 1–2 (1987): 223–238.

7. Casper, Schultz, and Wickens, "Breaking the Silences"; N. Polikoff, "This Child Does Have Two Mothers: Redefining Parenthood to Meet the Needs of Children in Lesbian Mother and Other Nontraditional Families," *Georgetown Law Review* 78 (1990): 459–575; S. Pollack and J. Vaughn, *Politics of the Heart: A Lesbian Parenting Anthology* (Ithaca: Firebrand Books, 1987).

8. Editors of the Harvard Law Review, *Sexual Orientation and the Law* (Cambridge: Harvard Univ. Press, 1990); Patricia J. Falk, "Lesbian Mothers: Psychosocial Assumptions in Family Law," *American Psychologist* 44, 6 (1989): 941–943.

9. "Killer Defends Child Custody," *Boston Globe* (AP), 3 February 1996. Jackie Hallifax, "Court Rules Against Lesbian Mother in Custody Fight with Killer Dad," *Associated Press*, 30 August 1996.

10. Jackie Hallifax, "Lesbian Who Lost Custody of Daughter to Killer Dad Dies," *Associated Press*, 22 January 1997.

11. W. Ricketts, *Lesbians and Gay Men as Foster Parents* (Portland: National Child Welfare Resource Center, Univ. of Southern Maine, 1991); W. Ricketts and R. Achtenberg, "Adoption and Foster Parenting for Lesbians and Gay Men: Creating New Traditions in the Family," in *Homosexuality and Family Relations*, ed. F. W. Bozett and M. B. Sussman (New York: Harrington Park Press, 1990). Also, see for example, Donna Leinwand, "Gay Adoption Ban Upheld," *Miami Herald,* 29 July 1997.

12. Judith Stacey, "The Father Fixation," *Utne Reader,* September–October 1996.

13. Carol Ness, "State Eyes Gay Adoption," *San Francisco Examiner,* 2 September 1996.

14. "Custody Case Centers on N.C. Validity of Lesbian Adoption," *Charlotte Observer* (AP), 12 July 1997.

15. L. Stuart Ditzen, "Court Allows Lesbian to Seek Custody," *Philadelphia Inquirer,* 21 September 1996.

16. Diane Raymond, "In the Best Interests of the Child: Thoughts on Homophobia and Parenting," in *Homophobia: How We All Pay the Price,* ed. Warren Blumenfeld (Boston: Beacon Press, 1992), 116.

17. "Gay Mom Can See Her Son; Lover Cannot," *Associated Press,* 22 August 1996.

18. "VA Court Reverses Ruling in Case of Lesbian Mother," *Washington Post,* 30 July 1997.

19. Zinie Chen, "Lesbian Can't See Son with Lover," *Associated Press,* 4 March 1998.

20. Elizabeth Bartholet, in *USA Today,* 14 November 1995, 3A.

21. *Adoption of Galen,* 425 Mass. 201 (1997); *In re MMD and BHM,* 662 A. 2d 837 (1995); *In re petition of F.M. and D.M. to adopt Olivia M.,* 274 Ill. App. 3d 989 (1995); *Adoption of Evan,* 583 NYS 2d 997 (1992); "Court Says Lesbian Adoption Can Be Considered," *Associated Press,* 2 August 1997.

22. *Holtzman v. Knott,* 116 S.Ct. 475 (1995).

23. Court of Appeals of Georgia, *In the Interest of R.E.W.,* No. A95A1989 (1996).

24. Terry Wilson, "Appeals Court Lets Lesbian Mom Keep Kids," *Chicago Tribune,* 18 December 1996; and "Bisexual Woman Gets Custody of Her 2 Kids," *Chicago Sun-Times* (AP), 18 December 1996.

25. "Gay Father Now Legally Allowed to Show Affection," *Associated Press,* 26 December 1996.

26. Estes Thompson, "N.C. Court Nixes Gay Dad's Custody," *Associated Press,* 30 July 1998.

27. "Lesbian Loses Custody of Child," *Montgomery (Ala.) Advertiser* (AP), 26 June 1998.

28. Bruce Dunford, "Trial Begins Tuesday in Hawaii's Same-Sex Marriage Case," *Associated Press,* 8 September 1996.

29. Carey Goldberg, "A Victory for Same-Sex Parenting, at Least," *New York Times,* 5 December 1996.

30. See Judith Stacey, *In the Name of Family: Rethinking Family Values in a Postmodern Age* (Boston: Beacon Press, 1996).

31. B. Miller, "Gay Fathers and Their Children," *Family Coordinator* 28, 4 (1979): 544–552.

32. Arthur Leonard, personal communication.

33. J. J. Bigner and F. W. Bozett, "Parenting by Gay Fathers," in *Homosexuality and Family Relations,* ed. F. W. Bozett and M. B. Sussman (New York: Harrington Park Press, 1990), 155–176; M. Crosbie-Burnett and L. Helmbrecht, "A Descriptive Empirical Study of Gay Male Stepfamilies," *Family Relations* 42 (1993): 256–262.

34. Charlotte Patterson, in Paul Recer, "Lesbians' Kids Emotionally Sound," *Associated Press,* 4 April 1997.

35. J. T. Sears, "Challenges for Educators: Lesbian, Gay, and Bisexual Families," *High School Journal* 77, 1–2 (1993–1994), 139. Patterson, "Lesbian Mothers, Gay Fathers, and Their Children," 281–283; J. Gottman, "Children of Gay and Lesbian parents,' in *Homosexuality and Family Relations,* ed. F. Bozett and M. Sussman (New York: Haworth Press, 1990), 177–196; Diana Baumrind, "Commentary on Sexual Orientation: Research and Social Policy Implications," *Developmental Psychology* 31, 1 (1995): 130–136. For a summary of the shortcomings in 8,000 research articles on lesbian and gay families, see Katherine R. Allen, "The Families of Lesbians and Gay Men: A New Frontier in Family Research," *Journal of Marriage and the Family* 57, 1 (1995): 111–127.

36. Patterson, "Lesbian Mothers, Gay Fathers, and Their Children," 281–283.

37. Sears, "Challenges for Educators," 145; Patterson, "Lesbian Mothers, Gay Fathers, and Their Children," 283–285.

38. F. Bozett, "Gay fathers: How and Why Gay Fathers Disclose Their Homosexuality to Their Children," *Family Relations* 29 (1980): 173–179, B. Miller, "Unpromised Paternity: The Lifestyles of Gay Fathers," in *Gay Men: The Sociology of Male Homosexuality,* ed. M. Levin (New York: Harper & Row, 1979), 239–252.

39. M. Hotvedt and J. Mandel, "Children of Lesbian Mothers," in *Homosexuality: Social, Psychological, and Biological Issues,* ed. W. Paul, J. Weinrich, J. Gonsiorek, and M. Hotvedt (Beverly Hills, Calif.: Sage, 1982), 275–285; Miller, "Gay Fathers and Their Children," 544–552.

40. N. Polikoff, "This Child Does Have Two Mothers," in *Families We Choose: Lesbians, Gays, Kinship,* ed. K. Weston (New York: Columbia Univ. Press, 1991).

41. R. Green, J. Mandel, M. Hotvedt, J. Gray, and L. Smith, "Lesbian Mothers and Their Children: A Comparison with Solo Parent Heterosexual Mothers and Their Children," *Archives of Sexual Behavior* 15, 2 (1986): 167–184; C. Rand, D. Graham, and E. Rawlings, "Psychological Health and Factors the Court Seeks to Control in Lesbian Mother Custody Trials," *Journal of Homosexuality* 8, 1 (1982): 27–39; N. Thompson, B. McCandless, and B. Strickland, "Personal Adjustment of Male and Female Homosexuals and Heterosexuals," *Journal of Abnormal Psychology* 78 (1971): 237–240; E. DiLapi, "Lesbian Mothers and the Motherhood Hierarchy"; A. Bell and M. Weinberg, *A Study of Diversity Among Men and Women* (New York: Simon & Schuster, 1978); B. S. Harris, "Lesbian Mother Child Custody: Legal and Psychiatric Aspects," *Bulletin of the American Academy of Psychiatry and the Law* 5 (1977): 75–89; M. Riley, "The Avowed Lesbian Mother and Her Right to Child Custody: A Constitutional Challenge That Can No Longer Be Denied," *San Diego Law Review* 12 (1975): 799–864; S. Golombok, A. Spencer, and M. Rutter, "Children in Lesbian and Single-Parent Households: Psychosexual and Psychiatric Appraisal," *Journal of Child Psychology and Psychiatry and Allied Disciplines* 24, 4 (1983): 551–572.

42. Golombok, Spencer, and Rutter, "Children in Lesbian and Single-Parent Households."

43. K. Ehrlichman, "Lesbian Mothers: Ethical Issues in Social Work Practice," *Women and Therapy* 8, 5 (1988): 207–223; M. Kirkpatrick, "Clinical Implications of Lesbian Mother Studies," *Journal of Homosexuality* 14, 5 (1987): 201–211.

44. J. Miller, R. B. Jacobsen, and J. Bigner, "The Child's Home Environment for Lesbian vs. Heterosexual Mothers: A Neglected Area of Research," *Journal of Homosexuality* 7, 1 (1981): 49–56.

45. J. Loulan, "Psychotherapy with Lesbian Mothers," in *Contemporary Perspectives on Psychotherapy with Lesbians and Gay Men,* ed. T. Stein and C. Cohen (New York: Plenum, 1986), 181–208.

46. Scott Stradler, "Non-Custodial Gay Fathers: Considering the Issues," paper presented at the annual convention of the American Psychological Association, Toronto, 20–24 August 1993.

47. F. W. Bozett, "Children of Gay Fathers," in *Gay and Lesbian Parents,* ed. F. W. Bozett (New York: Praeger, 1987), 39–57.

48. B. Hoeffer, "Children's Acquisition of Sex-Role Behavior in Lesbian-Mother Families," *American Journal of Orthopsychiatry* 51, 3 (1981): 536–544; Turner, Scadden, and Harris, "Parenting in Gay and Lesbian Families," 55–65. B. M. Mucklow and G. K. Phelan, "Lesbian and Traditional Mothers' Responses to Adult Response to Child Behavior and Self-Concept," *Psychological Reports* 44 (1979): 880–882; M. Kirkpatrick, C. Smith, and R. Roy, "Lesbian Mothers and Their Children: A Comparative Survey," *American Journal of Orthopsychiatry* 51, 3 (1981): 545–551; A. E. Moses and R. O. Hawkins Jr., *Counseling Lesbian Women and Gay Men: A Life-Issues Approach* (St. Louis: C. V. Mosby, 1982).

49. F. Bozett, "Gay Men as Fathers," in *Dimensions of Fatherhood*, ed. S. Hanson and F. Bozett (Beverly Hills, Calif.: Sage, 1985), 327–352; Golombok, Spencer, and Rutter, "Children in Lesbian and Single-Parent Households," 551–572; Hoeffer, "Children's Acquisition of Sex Role Behavior in Lesbian-Mother Families," 536–544; B. E. Robinson and P. Skeen, "Sex-Role Orientation of Gay Fathers Versus Gay Nonfathers," *Perceptual and Motor Skills* 55 (1982): 1055–1059.

50. B. McCandlish, "Against All Odds: Lesbian Mother Family Dynamics," in *Gay and Lesbian Parents*, ed. F. Bozett (New York: Praeger, 1987), 23–38.

51. Charlotte Patterson, "Families of the Lesbian Baby Boom: Parents' Division of Labor and Children's Adjustment," *Developmental Psychology* 31, 1 (1995): 115–123.

52. Fiona Tasker and Susan Golombok, "The Well-Being of Children Raised in Two-Parent Lesbian Mother Families," paper presented at national meeting of the Society for Research on Child Development, Washington, D.C., 3 April 1997. For a summary of Tasker's research on lesbian parents, see Fiona L. Tasker and Susan Golombok, *Growing Up in a Lesbian Family: Effects on Child Development* (New York: Guilford Press, 1997).

53. R. Rivera, "Legal Issues in Gay and Lesbian Parenting," in *Gay and Lesbian Parents*, ed. F. Bozett (New York: Praeger, 1987), 199–227. M. Riley, "The Avowed Lesbian Mother and Her Right to Child Custody"; M. Hall, "Lesbian Families: Cultural and Clinical Issues," *Social Work* 23 (1978): 380–385; M. Hotvedt and J. Mandel, "Children of Lesbian Mothers," in *Homosexuality: Social, Psychological, and Biological Issues*, ed. W. Paul, J. Weinrich, J. Gonsiorek, and M. Hotvedt (Beverly Hills, Calif.: Sage, 1982), 275–285; Miller, "Gay Fathers and Their Children," 544–552.

54. M. Harris and P. Turner, "Gay and Lesbian Parents," *Journal of Homosexuality* 12, 2 (1985–1986): 101–113: K. Lewis, "Children of Lesbians: Their Points of View," *Social Work* 25, 3 (1980): 198–203; D. Matteson, "The Heterosexually Married Gay and Lesbian Parent," in *Gay and Lesbian Parents*, ed. F. Bozett (Westport, Conn.: Praeger, 1987), 138–161.

55. Miller, "Gay Fathers and Their Children."

56. Charlotte J. Patterson, "Children of Lesbian and Gay Parents," *Advances in Clinical Psychology* 19 (1977): 235–282.

57. A recent study (Abigail J. Stewart et al., *Separating Together: How Divorce Transforms Families* [New York: Guilford, 1997]) places more emphasis on the discord than on the divorce itself.

58. Golombok, Spencer, and Rutter, "Children in Lesbian and Single-Parent Households"; Kirkpatrick, Smith, and Roy, "Lesbian Mothers and Their Children," 545–551; Lewis, "Children of Lesbians," 198–203; C. Patterson, "Children of the Lesbian Baby Boom: Behavior Adjustment, Self-Concepts, and Sex-Role Identity," in *Psychological Perspectives on Lesbian and Gay Issues*, vol. 1, *Lesbian and Gay Psychology: Theory, Research, and Clinical Applications*, ed. B. Greene and G. Herek (Thousand Oaks, Calif.: Sage, 1994), 156–175; S. Huggins, "A Comparative Study of Self-Esteem of Adolescent Children of Divorced Lesbian Mothers and Divorced Heterosexual Mothers," *Journal of Homosexuality* 18, 5 (1989): 123–137; D. Puryear, "A Comparison Between the Children of Lesbian Mothers and the Children of Heterosexual Mothers," unpublished doctoral diss., California School of Professional Psychology, Berkeley, 1983. S. Huggins, "A Comparative

Study of Self-Esteem of Adolescent Children of Divorced Lesbian Mothers and Divorced Heterosexual Mothers," in *Homosexuality and the Family*, ed. F. Bozett (New York: Haworth Press, 1989), 123–135; M. Hotvedt and J. Mandel, "Children of Lesbian Mothers"; S. Golombok and F. Tasker, "Adults Raised as Children in Lesbian Families," *American Journal of Orthopsychiatry* 65, 2 (1995): 203–215.

59. Golombok and Tasker, "Adults Raised as Children in Lesbian Families," 203–215.

60. David K. Flaks, Ilda Ficher, Frank Masterpasqua, and Gregory Joseph, "Lesbians Choosing Motherhood: A Comparative Study of Lesbian and Heterosexual Parents and Their Children," *Developmental Psychology* 31, 1 (1995): 105–115. Also Raymond W. Chan, , Barbara Raboy, Charlotte J. Patterson, "Psychosocial Adjustment Among Children Conceived via Donor Insemination by Lesbian and Heterosexual Mothers," paper presented at national meeting of the Society for Research on Child Development, Washington, D.C., 3 April 1997.

61. Huggins, "A Comparative Study of Self-Esteem of Adolescent Children," 123–135.

62. Patterson, "Families of the Lesbian Baby Boom," 115–123.

63. Unpublished research by Gill Dunne of Cambridge University, England, cited in Louise Jury, "Lesbians 'Are Better Parents,'" *The Independent* (London), 15 February 1999.

64. Huggins, "A Comparative Study of Self-Esteem of Adolescent Children"; Lewis, "Children of Lesbians"; Green et al., "Lesbian Mothers and Their Children."

65. Golombok, Spencer, and Rutter, "Children in Lesbian and Single-Parent Households," 551–572; Hoeffer, "Children's Acquisition of Sex-Role Behavior in Lesbian-Mother Families," 536–544; Kirkpatrick, Smith, and Roy, "Lesbian Mothers and Their Children," 545–551. J. S. Gottman, "Children of Gay and Lesbian Parents," *Marriage and Family Review* 14, 3–4 (1990): 177–196; A. Steckel, "Psychosocial Development of Children of Lesbian Mothers," in *Gay and Lesbian Parents*, ed. F. Bozett (New York: Praeger, 1987), 75–85; Patterson, "Children of the Lesbian Baby Boom," 156–175; F. Bozett, "Gay Fathers: Evolution of the Gay Father Identity," *American Journal of Orthopsychiatry* 51 (1981): 552–559; F. Bozett, "Gay Fathers; Identity Conflict Resolution Through Integrative Sanctions," *Alternative Lifestyles* 4 (1981): 90–107; R. Green, "Sexual Identity of 37 Children Raised by Homosexual or Transsexual Parents," *American Journal of Psychiatry* 135, 6 (1978): 692–697; Miller, "Gay Fathers and Their Children"; J. Paul, "Growing Up with a Gay, Lesbian, or Bisexual Parent: An Exploratory Study of Experiences and Perceptions," unpublished doctoral diss., Univ. of California, Berkeley. *Dissertation Abstracts International* 47, 7 (1986): 2756A; Susan Golombok and Fiona Tasker, "Do Parents Influence the Sexual Orientation of Their Children? Findings from a Longitudinal Study of Lesbian Families," *Developmental Psychology*, 32, 1 (1996): 3–11. Also, Patterson, "Children of Lesbian and Gay Parents," 235–282.

66. Hoeffer, "Children's Acquisition of Sex-Role Behavior."

67. Kirkpatrick, Smith, and Roy, "Lesbian Mothers and Their Children." Also J. Hare, J. and L. Richards, "Children Raised By Lesbian Couples: Does the Context of Birth Affect Father and Partner Involvement?" *Family Relations*, 42 (1993): 249–255.

68. D. Riddle, "Relating to Children: Gays as Role Models," *Journal of Social Issues* 34, 3 (1978): 38–58.

69. S. I. Hand, "The Lesbian Parenting Couple," unpublished doctoral dissertation, Professional School of Psychology, San Francisco, 1991; D. McPherson, "Gay Parenting Couples: Parenting Arrangements, Arrangement Satisfaction, and Relationship Satisfaction," unpublished doctoral dissertation, Pacific Graduate School of Psychology, Palo Alto, California, 1993.

70. Green et al., "Lesbian Mothers and Their Children," 175–181.

71. Ibid.

72. E. DiLapi, "Lesbian Mothers and the Motherhood Hierarchy."

73. Steckel, "Psychological Development of Children of Lesbian Mothers," 75–85.

74. Golombok and Tasker, "Do Parents Influence the Sexual Orientation of Their Children?" 3–11.

75. J. Michael Bailey, David Bobrow, Marilyn Wolfe, and Sarah Mikach, "Sexual Orientation of Adult Sons of Gay Fathers," *Developmental Psychology* 31, 1 (1995): 124–129.

76. See, for example, David Kirby, "The Second Generation," *New York Times*, 7 June 1998.

77. See for example, Laura Benkov, *Reinventing the Family: The Emerging Story of Lesbian and Gay Parents* (New York: Crown, 1994).

78. Sears, "Challenges for Educators," 143; also, Benkov, *Reinventing the Family*, esp. ch. 8, "What the Children Must Learn: Facing Homophobia."

79. Harris and Turner, "Gay and Lesbian Parents," 101–113; Matteson," The Heterosexually Married Gay and Lesbian Parent"; B. Miller, "Counseling Gay Husbands and Fathers," in *Gay and Lesbian Parents*, ed. F. Bozett (Westport, Conn.: Praeger, 1987), 175–187.

80. Sears, "Challenges for Educators," 143.

81. P. Turner, L. Scadden, and M. Harris, "Parenting in Gay and Lesbian Families," paper presented at the first annual Future of Parenting Symposium, Chicago, March 1985; N. Wyers, *Lesbian and Gay Spouses and Parents: Homosexuality in the Family* (Portland, Oregon: School of Social Work, Portland State University, 1984).

82. J. P. Paul, "Growing Up with a Gay, Lesbian, or Bisexual Parent: An Exploratory Study of Experiences and Perceptions," unpublished doctoral dissertation, University of California at Berkeley, 1986.

83. Bigner and Bozett, "Parenting by Gay Fathers," 155–175; Bozett, "Children of Gay Fathers"; Lewis, "Children of Lesbians: Their Points of View"; Paul, "Growing Up with a Gay, Lesbian, or Bisexual Parent"; N. Wyers, "Homosexuality in the Family: Lesbian and Gay Spouses," *Social Work* 32, 2 (1987): 143–148; A. Steinhorn, "Lesbian Mothers, the Invisible Minority: Role of the Mental Health Worker," *Women and Therapy* 1, 4 (1982): 35–48; Turner et al., "Parenting in Gay and Lesbian Families."

84. Sears, "Challenges for Educators," 151.

85. S. B. Pennington, "Children of Lesbian Mothers," in *Gay and Lesbian Parents*, ed. F. Bozett (New York: Praeger, 1987), 58–74; Lewis, "Children of Lesbians."

86. Pennington, "Children of Lesbian Mothers"; Lewis, "Children of Lesbians."

87. Miller, "Gay Fathers and Their Children."

88. Sears, "Challenges for Educators," 142.

89. Rachel Gold, "Needs Differ for Children of Gays," *Focuspoint* (Minneapolis), 25 June–1 July 1997.

90. Pamela Hill, "Persecution of Innocence," *Northwest Arkansas Times*, 7 December 1996.

91. J. T. Sears, "Responding to the Sexual Diversity of Faculty and Students: Sexual Praxis and the Critically Reflective Administrator," in *Educational Administration in a Pluralistic Society*, ed. Colleen A. Capper (Albany: State Univ. of New York Press, 1993), 120.

92. Bozett, "Children of Gay Fathers."

93. "Bill," in Lynn Minton Reports: Fresh Voices, "When a Parent Is Homosexual," *Parade Magazine*, 11 September 1994, 14. Reprinted with permission.

94. Sears, "Challenges for Educators," 146.

95. "Shaundra," in Lynn Minton Reports: Fresh Voices, "When a Parent Is Homosexual," *Parade Magazine*, 11 September 1994, 14. Reprinted with permission.

96. Patterson, "Lesbian Mothers, Gay Fathers, and Their Children."

97. Gibbs, "Psychological Development of Children Raised by Lesbian Mothers," 65–75.

98. From Elaine Wickens, "Penny's Question: 'I Will Have a Child in My Class with Two Moms—What Do You Know About This?'" *Young Children*, March 1993, 27.

99. Bozett, "Children of Gay Fathers."

100. Summarized from Beverly Fletcher, unpublished paper, Harvard Graduate School of Education, 15 December 1995.

101. See also Margie Carter, "Supporting the Growing Identity and Self-Esteem of Children in Gay and Lesbian Families," paper presented at the annual conference of the National Association for the Education of Young Children, Anaheim, California, 10–14 November 1994.

102. See, for example, "Happy Families Are Not Alike," *People Magazine*, 10 June 1996, 50–57.

103. GLPCI P.O. Box 50360, Washington, D.C. 20091; and COLAGE 2300 Market St. #165, San Francisco, CA 94114. Ph: (202) 583-8029; email: kidsofgays@aol.com

104. See a collection of short fictional treatments of the subject in Cindy Rizzo, Jo Schneiderman, Lisa Schweig, Jan Shafer, and Judith Stein, eds., *All the Ways Home: Parenting and Children in the Lesbian and Gay Communities* (Norwich, Vt.: New Victoria Publishers, 1995).

## Chapter 11

1. John D. Anderson, "School Climate for Gay and Lesbian Students and Staff Members," *Phi Delta Kappan* 76 (October 1994): 151–154.

2. Heterosexual pedophiles outnumber gay pedophiles 11 to 1, according to Kurt Freund and Robin J. Watson, "The Proportions of Heterosexual and Homosexual Pedophiles Among Sex Offenders Against Children: An Exploratory Study," *Journal of Sex and Marital Therapy* 18, 1 (1992): 34–43.

3. Del Stover, "The At-Risk Kids Schools Ignore," *Executive Educator* 14 (March 1992): 28–31.

4. Milbrey Wallin McLaughlin and David D. Marsh, "Staff Development and School Change," *Teachers College Record* 80 (September 1978): 69–94.

5. See Wendy Schwartz, "Improving the School Experience for Gay, Lesbian, and Bisexual Students," *ERIC Digest* 101 (October 1994).

6. K. Deaux and M. E. Kite, "Thinking About Gender," in *Analyzing Gender: A Handbook of Social Science Research*, ed. B. B. Hess and M. M. Ferree (Newbury Park, Calif.: Sage, 1987), 92–117.

7. Sue Kiefer Hammersmith, interview, *Advocate*, 30 April 1985.

8. For employing moral argument against homophobia, see Chai Feldblum, "Sexual Orientation, Morality, and the Law: Devlin Revisited," *University of Pittsburgh Law Review* 57 (Winter 1996): 237.

9. Elliot Aronson, "Stateways Can Change Folkways," in *Bigotry, Prejudice, and Hatred: Definitions, Causes, and Solutions*, ed. Robert M. Baird and Stuart E. Rosenbaum (Buffalo, N.Y.: Prometheus, 1992), 186.

10. Marshall Kirk and Hunter Madsen, *After the Ball: How America Will Conquer Its Fear and Hatred of Gays in the '90s* (New York: Doubleday, 1989); Bruce Bawer, *A Place at the Table: The Gay Individual in American Society* (New York: Poseidon Press, 1993).

11. J. Martin Stafford, "In Defense of Gay Lessons," *Journal of Moral Education* 17 (1988): 16.

12. Kirk and Madsen, *After the Ball*, 136–137.

13. See "Cornel West on Heterosexism and Transformation: An Interview," special issue of *Harvard Educational Review* 66 (Summer 1996): 356–367.

14. See Florence H. Davidson and Miriam M. Davidson, *Changing Childhood Prejudice: The Caring Work of the Schools* (Westport, Conn.: Bergin and Garvey/Greenwood Press, 1995). Although they ignore homophobia, their Kohlbergian approach is instructive.

15. M. Rokeach, *The Nature of Human Values* (New York: Free Press, 1973). See also Glenn S. Pate, "Research on Reducing Prejudice," *Social Education* (April-May 1988): 287–289. For concurrence of higher stage moral reasoning with tolerance, see also Ann Breslin, "Tolerance and Moral Reasoning Among Adolescents in Ireland," *Journal of Moral Education* 11 (January 1982): 112–127.

16. See L. Kohlberg and D. Candee, "The Relation of Judgment to Action," in *Moral Development and Moral Behavior*, ed. W. Kurtines and I. Gewirtz (New York: Wiley, 1984).

17. For an argument against mere integration, see Alfie Kohn, *No Contest: The Case Against Competition* (Boston: Houghton Mifflin, 1986), 150–151.

18. See Charles Y. Glock et al., *Adolescent Prejudice* (New York: Harper and Row, 1975).

19. Alvin Poussaint, interview, *Klanwatch Intelligence Report*, October 1995, 14.

20. Samuel L. Gaertner and John F. Dovidio, "Toward the Elimination of Racism: The Study of Intergroup Behavior," in *Bigotry, Prejudice, and Hatred: Definitions, Causes, and Solutions*, ed. Robert M. Baird and Stuart E. Rosenbaum (Buffalo, N.Y.: Prometheus Books, 1992), 205.

21. Yehuda Amir, "The Role of Intergroup Contact in Change of Prejudice and Ethnic Relations," in *Towards the Elimination of Racism*, ed. Phyllis A. Katz (New York: Pergamon Press, 1976), 272.

22. Gregory M. Herek, "Assessing Heterosexuals' Attitudes Toward Lesbians and Gay Men: A Review of Empirical Research with the ATLG Scale," in *Lesbian*

*and Gay Psychology: Theory, Research, and Clinical Applications,* ed. Beverly Greene and G. M. Herek (Thousand Oaks, Calif.: Sage, 1994), 219.

23. Ibid., 219.

24. Gregory M. Herek, "Stigma, Prejudice, and Violence Against Lesbians and Gay Men," in *Homosexuality: Research Findings for Public Policy,* ed. J. C. Gonsiorek and J. D. Weinrich (Newbury Park, Calif.: Sage, 1991), 60–80.

25. *Newsweek* poll of 779 adults, in "Gay in America," *San Francisco Examiner,* 25 June 1996.

26. Gallup poll, 15–17 March 1996, in *Los Angeles Times Syndicate,* 4 April 1996.

27. Andrew Hodges and David Hutter, *With Downcast Gays: Aspects of Homosexual Self-Oppression* (Toronto: Pink Triangle Press, 1974); and National Coming Out Day, a project of the Human Rights Campaign, Washington, D.C.

28. Amir, "The Role of Intergroup Contact," 272.

29. Gary B. Melton, "Public Policy and Private Practice: Psychology and Law on Gay Rights," *American Psychologist* 44 (June 1989): 939.

30. Alvin Poussaint, in Alison Bass, "New Studies on Prejudice Point to Possible Remedies," *Boston Globe,* 17 April 1993, 27.

31. Phyllis A. Katz, "Attitude Change in Children: Can the Twig be Straightened?" in *Towards the Elimination of Racism,* ed. Phyllis A. Katz (New York: Pergamon Press, 1976), 224. See also Amir, "The Role of Intergroup Contact," 246.

32. S. W. Cook, "The Systemic Analysis of Socially Significant Events: A Strategy for Social Research," *Journal of Social Issues* 18 (1962): 76.

33. G. W. Allport, *The Nature of Prejudice* (Reading, Mass.: Addison-Wesley, 1954).

34. Amir, "The Role of Intergroup Contact," 252.

35. Ibid., 288.

36. Ibid., 277–278.

37. Ibid., 270.

38. Aronson, "Stateways Can Change Folkways," 188–190.

39. Amir, "The Role of Intergroup Contact," 289.

40. Ibid., 279–280.

41. Ibid., 268.

42. Audre Lorde, "There Is No Hierarchy of Oppressions," *Interracial Books for Children Bulletin* 14, 3–4 (1983).

43. Teaching and Curriculum Summer Component, Harvard Graduate School of Education, August 1996.

44. See, for instance, an account of a heterosexual female African American teacher's failure to reach the black boys on the subject of homophobia, in Rita M. Kissen, *The Last Closet: The Real Lives of Lesbian and Gay Teachers* (Portsmouth, N.H.: Heineman, 1996), 35.

45. Higher Education Research Institute, Univ. of California at Los Angeles, cited in Paul Varnell, "College Freshmen: A Class Act," *Bay Windows* (Boston), 19 February 1998.

46. American Council on Education Fall Survey of 240,000 entering freshmen, *Associated Press,* 1 August 1986.

47. G. M. Herek and E. K. Glunt, "Public Reactions to AIDS in the United States," in *The Social Psychology of HIV Infection,* ed. J. B. Pryor and G. D. Reeder (Hillsdale, N.J.: Erlbaum, 1993), 229–261; P. Irwin and N. L. Thompson, "Accep-

tance of the Rights of Homosexuals: A Social Profile." *Journal of Homosexuality* 3 (1977): 107–121; K. L. Nyberg and J. P. Alston, "Analysis of Public Attitudes Toward Homosexual Behavior," *Journal of Homosexuality* 2 (1976): 99–107.

48. G. M. Herek and E. K. Glunt, "AIDS-Related Attitudes in the United States: A Preliminary Conceptualization," *Journal of Sex Research* 28 (1991): 99–123; Herek and Glunt, "Public Reactions to AIDS in the United States"; G. M. Herek and E. K. Glunt, "Interpersonal Contact and the Heterosexuals' Attitudes Toward Gay Men: Results from a National Survey," *Journal of Sex Research* 30 (1993): 239–244.

49. Lisa Keen, "Harris Poll Turns Up Surprising Results," *Washington (D.C.) Blade,* 28 August 1998.

50. For example, see H. Proshansky, "The Development of Intergroup Attitudes," in *Review of Child Development Research,* vol. 2, ed. I. W. Hoffman and M. L. Hoffman (New York: Russel Sage Foundation, 1966).

51. Katz, "Attitude Change in Children," 221.

52. Amir, "The Role of Intergroup Contact," 265.

53. Barbara Blinnick, "Out in the Curriculum, Out in the Classroom: Teaching History and Organizing for Change," in *Tilting the Tower: Lesbians Teaching Queer Subjects,* ed. Linda Garber (New York: Routledge, 1994), 145.

54. Since Bridge's departure, an effective faculty workshop was held and a student group formed. Virginia Uribe and Kathy Gill, Directors, Gay and Lesbian Education Commission, personal interview, 4 December 1995.

55. Aronson, "Stateways Can Change Folkways," 187.

56. Ibid., 186.

57. Heather Wishik and Carol Pierce, *Sexual Orientation and Identity: Heterosexual, Lesbian, Gay, and Bisexual Journeys* (Laconia, N.H.: New Dynamics, 1995), 18–19.

58. Lynn Minton, "Fresh Voices," *Parade Magazine,* 26 August 1996.

59. For an inspiring example of Latina girls challenging Latino boys on homophobia, see Kissen, *The Last Closet,* 37.

60. Amir, "The Role of Intergroup Contact," 281.

61. See Brenda Dorn Conrad, "Cooperative Learning and Prejudice Reduction," *Social Education* (April-May 1988): 283–286.

62. Elizabeth Anne Grady, "After Cluster School: A Study of the Impact in Adulthood of a Moral Development Intervention Project," doctoral dissertation, Harvard Graduate School of Education, 1994, esp. 82–85 and 142–144.

63. See C. Higgins Power and L. Kohlberg, *Lawrence Kohlberg's Approach to Moral Education: A Study of Three Democratic High Schools* (New York: Columbia Univ. Press, 1989).

64. Robert Slavin, in Alison Bass, "New Studies on Prejudice Point to Possible Remedies," *Boston Globe,* 17 May 1993, 27.

65. Aronson, "Stateways Can Change Folkways," 192–199.

66. Gaertner and Dovidio, "Toward the Elimination of Racism," 207.

67. See Eric Rofes, "Making Our Schools Safe for Sissies," in *The Gay Teen,* ed. Gerald Unks (New York: Routledge, 1995), 79–84.

68. In Cambridge and Andover, for example.

69. Scott Miller, letter, *South County Journal,* St. Louis, Missouri, 23 November 1995. Reprinted with permission. An article about Miller's letter appeared in *The*

*Cougar's Tale,* the Affton High School newspaper: Sabrina Bido, "Former Students Speak Out About Being Gay at Affton Senior High," 17 January 1996.

70. Bido, "Former Students Speak Out."

71. Beatrice B. Gordon, in Dan Beyers, "No Gay Bias, No 'Proselytizing,' No End to Montgomery Debate," *Washington Post,* 1 April 1996.

72. See John Martin Rich, "Discipline and Moral Development," in *High School Journal* 76 (December–January 1993): 139–144.

73. Burke Stinson, AT&T spokesman, in Kara Swisher, "Diversity Training: Learning from Past Mistakes," *Washington Post,* National Weekly Edition, 13–19 February 1995, 20.

74. Thomas Petzinger, "AT&T Class Teaches an Open Workplace Is Profitably Correct," *Wall Street Journal,* 11 October 1995, B1.

75. A teacher at the Cambridge (Mass.) Friends' School asks, "As a school, are we saying the kids have to support this? What if a child's background teaches that homosexuality is not right?" in the video *It's Elementary: Talking About Gay Issues in School,* directed by Debra Chasnoff and Helen Cohen, Women's Educational Media, 1996.

76. Lou Chibbaro Jr. and Clint Steib, "Chantilly Students Divided by Kissing Incident," *Washington (D.C.) Blade,* 11 April 1997.

77. See, for example, "Homosexual Activists Win One in Columbus, Now Target Ohio . . . ," *Mission America* (P.O. Box 21838, Columbus, OH 43221), Summer 1998.

78. Colleen A. Capper, "Administrator Practice and Preparation for Social Reconstructionist Schooling," in *Educational Administration in a Pluralistic Society,* ed. Colleen A. Capper (Albany: State Univ. of New York Press, 1993), 298.

79. "Clubs Law Keeps Sinking," editorial, *Salt Lake Tribune,* 14 May 1996.

80. Michael Calsetta, in Beyers, "No Gay Bias."

81. See Petullo argument in Chapter 1.

82. Dan Coulter, Boston Latin School GSA Advisor, personal interview, June 1996.

83. See Ellsworth's, "Why Doesn't This Feel Empowering?" 43–70.

84. Jessica Saunders, "Man Acquitted in Alabama School Arson," *Boston Globe,* 21 October 1995, 3.

85. Pontifical Commission for the Family, "Human Sexuality: Truth and Significance," *Boston Globe,* 21 December 1995.

86. Larry Parnass, "Display Criticized as Anti-Gay," *Daily Hampshire Gazette* (Northampton, Mass.), 15 October 1998.

87. "Teacher's Comments Spur Suit," *Associated Press,* 5 August 1996.

88. Rachel Layne, "Parents Seek Compensation for Child's 'Pain' over Gay Teacher," *Boston Globe,* 11 March 1996.

89. Christine Bedell, "Gay Teacher Files Complaint After Five Pupils Transferred," *Bakersfield Californian,* 22 November 1998.

90. Christine Bedell, "School Board Rules Against Gay Teacher," *Bakersfield Californian,* 11 January 1999.

91. Christine Bedell, "State: School Violated Anti-Discrimination Laws," *Bakersfield Californian,* 9 March 1999. A very similar case involving a student transferred from a lesbian teacher's class in Hemet, California, was still pending be-

fore the board in February. Don C. Smith, "Gay Teacher Awaiting Action," *Hemet News,* 14 February 1999.

92. Bob Egelko, "Teacher Says He's Unlikely to Return to Class Despite Victory," *Associated Press,* 11 March 1999.

93. John M. Glionna, "District, Gay Teacher Settle: Policy Revised," *Los Angeles Times,* 19 March 1999.

94. Ibid.

95. Kara Swisher, "Diversity Training: Learning from Past Mistakes," *Washington Post,* National Weekly Edition, 13–19 February 1995, 20.

96. Paloma McGregor, "Portland Schools: Promoting Sensitivity to Gays?" *Newhouse News Service,* 3 January 1996.

97. Haley Barbour, *Meet the Press,* 22 January 1995, as reported in the *Advocate,* 4 July 1995, 12.

98. This technique has been used in Cambridge, Newton, and Arlington, Massachusetts.

99. "Students Gauge Their Tolerance for . . . Intolerance," *Boston Globe,* 16 June 1996, 67.

100. Michael Handler, personal correspondence, 7 June 1995.

101. "High School Paper Pulled," *St. Paul (Minn.) Pioneer Press,* 3 April 1996.

102. Personal interview, Massachusetts Dept. of Education Workshop, Andover, 5 March 1996.

103. "New PTA Chapter Aims to Help Gay Students and Their Parents," *Knight-Ridder News Wire,* 5 March 1998.

104. Kris Henry, "School Emphasizing Tolerance Opens," *Dallas Morning News,* 3 September 1997; Liz Stevens, "School Aims to Give Gay, Lesbian Teens a Sense of Self-Worth," *Minneapolis Star Tribune,* 9 November 1998. Contact: c/o Becky Thompson, 4038 Cedar Springs, Box 104, Dallas, TX 75219.

105. For remarks on such a program in the Toronto, Canada, public schools, see Kathryn Snider, "Race and Sexual Orientation: The (Im)possibility of These Intersections in Educational Policy," special issue of *Harvard Educational Review* 66, 2 (1996): 294–302.

106. See Preface.

107. Capper, "Administrator Practice and Preparation," 288–313.

108. Ibid., 310.

109. C. E. Sleeter, ed., *Empowerment Through Multicultural Education* (Albany: State Univ. of New York Press, 1991).

110. Capper, "Administrator Practice and Preparation," 290.

111. D. Willower, "Educational Administration: Philosophy, Praxis, Professing," National Council of Professors of Educational Administration, Madison, Wisconsin, 1992.

112. Colleen A. Capper, "Educational Administration in a Pluralistic Society: A Multiparadigm Approach," in *Educational Administration in a Pluralistic Society,* ed. Colleen A. Capper (Albany: State Univ. of New York Press, 1993), 12–15.

113. See L. Kohlberg and R. Mayer, "Development as the Aim of Education," *Harvard Educational Review* 42 (1972): 449–496.

114. Nicholas C. Burbules and Suzanne Rice, "Dialogue Across Differences: Continuing the Conversation," in *Teaching for Change: Addressing Issues of Differ-*

*ence in the College Classroom,* ed. Kathryn Geismar and Guitele Nicoleau (Cambridge: *Harvard Education Review,* Reprint Series 25, 1993), 14.

115. A good argument that seeks refuge from despair through coalition-building is Elizabeth Ellsworth's, "Why Doesn't This Feel Empowering? Working through the Repressive Myths of Critical Pedagogy," 43–70.

116. James T. Sears, "Responding to the Sexual Diversity of Faculty and Students: Sexual Praxis and the Critically Reflective Administrator" in *Educational Administration in a Pluralistic Society,* ed. Colleen A. Capper (Albany: State Univ. of New York Press, 1993), 151.

117. Carol Shakeshaft, "Commentary: Administrators as Barriers to Change?" in *Sexuality and the Curriculum: The Politics and Practices of Sexuality Education,* ed. James T. Sears (New York: Teachers College Press, 1992), 328–336.

118. See, for example, GLSEN report on southeastern Michigan schools, available from GLSEN Detroit-Birmingham, Tel: (810) 646-8784.

119. Jeff Perotti, Massachusetts Department of Education presentation, Suffolk University, 10 February 1995.

120. Massachusetts Department of Education conference at Lesley College, Cambridge, Spring 1995.

121. Gay and Lesbian Advocates and Defenders, *The Legal Rights of Public School Students and Teachers* (294 Washington St., Suite 740, Boston, MA 02108), October 1997.

122. "Suit Says Schools Failed to Protect Gay Student," *New York Times,* 29 March 1996; Mark Walsh, "Gay Students Press Abuse Claims Against Districts," *Education Week,* 24 April 1996, 5.

123. Similar advice had given to a high school student, the victim of an infamous Arkansas beating. See Pamela A. Hill, "Hate Crime," *Northwest Arkansas Times,* 6 December 1996.

124. Terry Wilson, "School District Can Be Sued on Gay Harassment," *Chicago Tribune,* 8 January 1996.

125. Karl Karlson, "After Lawsuit, Nabozny Ready to Get On with Life," *Saint Paul Pioneer Press,* 1 December 1996.

126. "Civil Rights Complaint Filed Against Teen-Ager for Harassment," *Associated Press,* 2 May 1997.

127. Florangela Davila, "Boy Bullied as Gay Sues Kent Schools," *Seattle Times,* 24 July 1997; "Taunted Gay Teen Takes a Stand," *Garden Island* (Lihue, Kauai, Hawaii), 10 September 1997.

128. "Settlement Reached in Lawsuit Filed by Gay Student," *Associated Press,* 7 November 1998.

129. Elaine Herscher, "Lawsuit over Anti-Gay Harassment," *San Francisco Chronicle,* 23 April 1998; and Stacy Finz, "Judge Allows Gay Harass Suit," *San Franciso Chronicle,* 8 November 1998.

130. "Former Student Sues Educators," *Associated Press,* 12 November 1997.

131. Carol Ness, "Schools Face Suit over Slur," *San Francisco Examiner,* 20 July 1997; "Settlement Possible in Pacifica, CA Schools Harassment Case," *Bay City News Service,* 3 July 1998; and "Settlement Reached in Pacifica School Harassment Case," *Pacifica Tribune,* 5 August 1998.

132. Carlos Illescas, "Cheerleader Complains of Harassment," *Denver Post*, 3 March 1998.

133. M. Walsch, "Gay Students Press Abuse Claims Against Districts," *Education Week*, 24 April 1996, 5.

134. "Homophobia Cited in Lawsuit," *Philadelphia Gay News*, 2 August 1996, 10.

135. Kim Wessel and Thomas Nord, "Spencer Girl Harassed at School Awarded $220,000," *Louisville Courier-Journal*, 5 September 1998.

136. Mark Stodghill, "Duluth School District Sued by Former Student," *Duluth News–Tribune*, 13 March 1999.

137. Peter Freiberg, "School District Agrees to Deter Harassment," *Washington (D.C.) Blade*, 29 June 1998.

138. Larry Bleiberg, "Gays, Lesbians Included in DISD Policy," *Dallas Morning News*, 28 March 1996, 33A.

139. Notice from David S. Buckel, Staff Attorney, Lambda Legal Defense and Education Fund, New York, 8 April 1997.

140. Art Coleman, in Carol Ness, "Feds Push to End Gay Youth Bashing," *San Francisco Examiner*, 31 October 1998. The Supreme Court ruled in mid-1999 *(Davis v. Monroe County Board of Education)* that districts receiving federal money are liable for deliberate indifference to sexual harassment that is "so severe, pervasive and objectively offensive that it denies its victims the equal access to education that Title IX is designed to protect." *See* "The Supreme Court," *New York Times*, 25 May 1999, A25.

141. U.S. Department of Education Office for Civil Rights and the National Association of Attorneys General, *Protecting Students from Harassment and Hate Crimes, A Guide for Schools* (Washington, D.C.: U.S. Department of Education, 1999).

142. Pew Research Center, "The Diminishing Divide ... American Churches, American Politics," as reported in Gustav Neibur, "Americans Say Religion and Politics Can Mix, Survey Finds," *New York Times*, 25 June 1996.

143. See, for example, Pat Burson, "New Group of Catholics Forms to Fight Homophobia in Church," *St. Paul (Minn.) Pioneer Press*, 17 April 1996.

144. See especially David Reich, "Giving Comfort in Despair: Unitarian Universalist Youth and Gay-Straight Alliances," *The World: The Journal of the Unitarian Universalist Association* 10, 3 (1996): 18–20; Tineke Boddé, *Is Homosexuality a Sin?* (Washington, D.C.: P-FLAG, 1992). (Publication available from P-FLAG, 1101 14th St. NW, Suite 1030, Washington, D.C., 20005, tel: (202) 638-4200.) Also, Andrew Sullivan, *Virtually Normal: An Argument About Homosexuality* (New York: Alfred A. Knopf, 1995); and Peter Gomes, *The Good Book: Reading the Bible with Mind and Heart* (New York: Wm. Morrow, 1996); "Homosexuality: Not a Sin, Not a Sickness," Universal Fellowship of Metropolitan Community Churches, 1990 (5300 Santa Monica Blvd., Suite 304, Los Angeles, CA 90029); John McNeill, *The Church and the Homosexual* (Boston: Beacon Press, 1988); and 1996 position of Reform Judaism and Union of American Hebrew Congregations.

145. Tanya Schevitz, "Students Learn Tolerance for Gays, Lesbians," *San Francisco Chronicle*, 13 November 1998.

146. Ronald F. Thiemann, *Religion in Public Life: A Dilemma for Democracy* (Washington, D.C.: Georgetown Univ. Press, 1996).

147. Allport, *The Nature of Prejudice*, 296.


# Chapter 12

1. James T. Sears, "Responding to the Sexual Diversity of Faculty and Students: Sexual Praxis and the Critically Reflective Administrator," in *Educational Administration in a Pluralistic Society*, ed. Colleen A. Capper (Albany: State Univ. of New York Press, 1993), 126.

2. The following two reports were issued subsequently by the State of Massachusetts: "Making Colleges and Universities Safe for Gay and Lesbian Students," Report and Recommendations of The Governor's Commission on Gay and Lesbian Youth, July 1993; "Prevention of Health Problems Among Gay and Lesbian Youth: Making Health and Human Services Accessible and Effective for Gay and Lesbian Youth," The Health and Human Services Report of the Governor's Commission on Gay and Lesbian Youth, August 1994.

3. This budget is divided between the Department of Education and Department of Public Health.

4. Contact: Heidi Holland, GLYS Project Director, Health Care of Southeastern Massachusetts, 942 West Chestnut St., Brockton, MA 02401, tel: (800) 530-2770.

5. Chapter 76, Section 5 of the Massachusetts General Laws, State Publication no. 17659-16-5000-1/95-DOE.

6. "Competencies for Certified Educators," 1995 Massachusetts Dept. of Education Certification Regulations, 7.11.

7. Charles McCarthy, class presentation, Harvard University Extension School, 11 January 1996.

8. Tom Rose, "Town GOP Head: Schools Promote Homosexuality," *Arlington Advocate*, 19 October 1995, 1.

9. Kathryn Cremens-Basbas, Arlington High School GSA advisor, personal interview, December 1995.

10. J. edward Pawlick, *An Intelligent Discussion About Homosexuality* (Wellesley, Mass.: Massachusetts News, 1998).

11. Andy Dabilis, "Gays Say Sherborn Lawyer Sent 'Hate Mail,'" *Boston Globe*, 22 January 1999.

12. Pat Griffin, Univ. of Massachusetts–Amherst, "Seventeen Reasons to Address Homophobia in Schools," "Assessment and Action Objectives," "A Strategic Plan for Changing Schools," and "A School Climate Assessment Instrument."

13. Woburn high school principal, retold by Jeff Perrotti, personal communication, March 1999.

14. Jeff Perotti, Safe Schools administrator, Massachusetts Dept. of Education, personal interview, 1995.

15. See, for example, Robert Peterkin, "Anti-Harassment Guidelines," *Superintendents Circular* 22, 11 June 1987, referred to in Sears, "Responding to the Sexual Diversity of Faculty and Students," 126.

16. David S. Buckel, Staff Attorney, Lambda Legal Defense and Education Fund, "Stopping Anti-Gay Abuse of Students in Public High Schools: A Legal Perspective," 1996.

17. One student has claimed as part of a suit that his counselor violated his confidentiality by telling his father he was gay. "Homophobia Cited in Lawsuit," *Philadelphia Gay News,* 2 August 1996, 10.

18. Arthur Lipkin, *A Staff Development Program for Antihomophobia Education in the Secondary Schools,* dissertation, Univ. of Massachusetts, 1990 (Ann Arbor, Mich.: University Microfilms International Dissertation Information Service, 1990). Gay identified participants were not included in the study.

19. A similar award is given at South High School in Minneapolis.

20. Pam Brown, Peggy Gillespie, and Gigi Kaeser, *Love Makes a Family: Living in Lesbian and Gay Families, A Photograph-Text Exhibit,* Amherst, Massachusetts, 1995.

21. Contact: Emmy Howe, Welcoming Schools, CRLS-R302, 459 Broadway, Cambridge, MA 02138, tel: (617) 349-6727.

22. See Lisa Bennett, "Break the Silence," *Teaching Tolerance* 6, 2 (1997): 24–29.

23. Arlington and Belmont.

24. Lexington High School GSA advisor, at a Governor's Commission meeting with GSA advisors, 12 November 1998.

25. Robert Powell, "Project 10 East at Cambridge Rindge and Latin School: Striving for 'Permanent Institutional Change,'" unpublished paper, Harvard Graduate School of Education, 18 December 1994.

26. E. S. Hetrick and A. D. Martin, "Developmental Issues and Their Resolution for Gay and Lesbian Adolescents," *Journal of Homosexuality* 14 (1987): 41.

27. Cameron Wolf, Arthur Lipkin, and Rob Garofolo, "Analysis of Risk Behavior Survey," Cambridge public schools, unpublished study, 1995.

28. Safe Schools Coalition of Washington State, *Safe Schools Anti-Violence Documentation Project,* Annual Report, 1996.

29. For information on the DOE study, contact Kim Westheimer (781) 388-3300, and for the University of Massachusetts, e-mail Pat Griffin: griffin@educ.umass.edu

30. Anonymous writing by GSA member, Concord-Carlyle High School, 1996.

31. Gavin Daly, "Students Rally for Gay/Straight March," *Boston Globe,* 21 May 1995, 34.

32. Jordana Hart, "Youths Uplifted at Gay/Straight Pride Celebration," *Boston Globe,* 17 May 1998.

33. See Chapter 13.

34. *Boston Herald,* 20 May 1993, 1.

35. See, for example, "Homosexual Lifestyle Promoted by Education Report," *Pilgrim Family Citizen* 5 (June 1993). *Pilgrim Family Citizen* is a monthly publication of the Pilgrim Family Institute, Danvers, Massachusetts.

36. Jonathan Yenkin, "Weld Says 'One Size Fits All' Sex Ed a Mistake," *In Newsweekly,* 26 February 1995.

37. General Laws Chapter 71, Section 32A. See also Doris Sue Wong, "Sex Ed Notification Bill Sails Through Senate," *Boston Globe,* 4 April 1995; Allison Bass and Doris Sue Wong, "New Mass. Law Allows Patients to Check Up on Doctors' Records," *Boston Globe,* 8 October 1996, B5. Success in this law's passage led to the filing of another bill mandating that none of these topics could be broached without explicit parent permission, an "opt-in" provision.

38. Fred Kuhr, "Governor's Youth Commission Proposes Addressing Anti-Gay Feelings Beginning in Grade School," *Bay Windows*, 5 September 1996, 1, 4.

39. Trinity Communications, Inc., "The Commonwealth of Massachusetts Dept. of Education's Safe Schools Program for Gay and Lesbian Students: A Quantitative Evaluation," August 1994.

40. "Community in a Flutter over Gay Rights Flag at Orange," *Associated Press*, 19 June 1996.

41. Jordana Hart, "Northampton Confronts a Crime, Cruelty," *Boston Globe*, 8 June 1998.

42. Phyllis Labanowski, in Laurie Loisel, "A Teen's Death in Northampton," *Daily Hampshire (Mass.) Gazette*, 20 June 1998.

43. Justine Underhill, personal interview with a Grover Cleveland Middle School teacher, in "'Benign Neglect': Implementation of Anti-Homophobia Curriculum in an Urban Public School System," unpublished paper, Harvard Graduate School of Education, 15 December 1994.

44. The suggestion was made by the author.

45. Jordana Hart, "As Gays Gather, Lawrence Parents to March Kids Out," *Boston Globe*, 11 June 1998.

46. Christopher Muther, "Hope for Gay Kids," *Bay Windows*, 15–21 September 1994, 11.

47. E. W. Creedon, Office of the Superintendent, Quincy, Mass., personal interview, 9 January 1995.

48. Joseph Nicolosi, "Some Thoughts on Pro-Gay Counseling Programs," *Student Assistance Journal*, November-December 1994, 14–16.

49. Robert Roy, parent, in Phoebe Mitchell, "Westhampton School Panels Put on Hold," *Daily Hampshire Gazette*, 4 May 1994.

50. James Lower, in John Madden, "Parents Say Homophobia Workshop Was 'Degrading,'" *Beverly Times*, 6 June 1994.

51. Michael Lerner, "'The Best Thing We've Ever Done': Newton North, the Gay/Straight Alliance, and 'The Shared Heart,'" unpublished paper, Harvard Graduate School of Education, 1997.

52. Jim Ko, "The Wellesley H.S. Gay-Straight Alliance," unpublished paper, Harvard Graduate School of Education, 10 January 1997.

53. The Governor's Commission on Gay and Lesbian Youth held three public hearings between 12 December 1994 and 3 June 1995 at three locations across the state.

54. Lucy Grinnell, junior at Duxbury High School, in unpublished transcript of public hearings conducted by the Governor's Commission on Gay and Lesbian Youth, 12 December 1994 to 3 June 1995, 1.

55. Debbie Birch, teacher at Andover High School, in unpublished transcript of public hearings conducted by the Governor's Commission on Gay and Lesbian Youth, 12 December 1994 to 3 June 1995, 2.

56. Lindsay Moore, senior at Concord-Carlisle Regional High School, in unpublished transcript of public hearings conducted by the Governor's Commission on Gay and Lesbian Youth, 12 December 1994 to 3 June 1995, 3.

57. John Pollock, student at Belmont High School, in unpublished transcript of public hearings conducted by the Governor's Commission on Gay and Lesbian Youth, 12 December 1994 to 3 June 1995, 4.

58. Eric Dupree, student at North Bedford High School, in unpublished transcript of public hearings conducted by the Governor's Commission on Gay and Lesbian Youth, 12 December 1994 to 3 June 1995, 5.

59. Trinity Communications, Inc., "The Comm. of Mass. Dept. of Education's Safe Schools Program for Gay and Lesbian Students: A Quantitative Evaluation," August 1994, for example 10, 17, and 29.

60. Less than 20 percent compliance according to "The Comm. of Mass. Dept. of Education's Safe Schools Program for Gay and Lesbian Students: A Quantitative Evaluation," 13.

61. No research has been conducted yet, but observation and personal discussion with advisors confirm this.

62. Trinity Communications, Inc., "The Comm. of Mass. Dept. of Education's Safe Schools Program for Gay and Lesbian Students: A Quantitative Evaluation," 16.

63. Edgar A. Kelley and Elizabeth A. Dillon, "Staff Development: It Can Work for You," *NAASP Bulletin* 62 (April 1978): 1–8.

64. Milbrey Wallin McLaughlin and David D. Marsh, "Staff Development and School Change," *Teachers College Record* 80 (September 1978): 69–94.

65. Kristina Brenneman and Sean Gardiner, "Schools to Shelve Controversial Sex Ed Survey," *Middlesex (Mass.) News,* 3 January 1996. The same questionnaire nearly got a teacher fired at Algonquin Regional High School in Massachusetts: Elaine Thompson, "Sexuality Stirs Up a Fuss in Northboro," *Worcester Telegram and Gazette,* 19 February 1996.

66. "School to Drop Controversial Sex Ed Material," *Associated Press,* 1 March 1996.

67. Paula Kluth, "'There Was One Particularly Involved Student Here Last Year' . . . (And the Ninety-Nine Other Excuses of Belmont High School)," unpublished paper, Harvard Graduate School of Education, 16 December 1994. In the three years since these events, the Belmont GSA has revived with significant teacher support. In 1997, an all-school assembly and classroom discussions signaled further progress.

68. André Joseph, at a Governor's Commission meeting with GSA advisors, 12 November 1998.

69. Acton-Boxborough has a similarly constituted Safe Schools Team.

70. Project 10 East was temporarily hobbled by Al Ferreira's illness.

71. Kathleen Glennon, cochair of the Massachusetts Teachers Association Lesbian/Gay Employment and Civil Rights Committee, at a Governor's Commission meeting with GSA advisors, 12 November 1998.

72. Susan Ryan-Vollmar, "With Silber at Helm, Will Gay Youth Programs Be Safe in State Schools?" *Bay Windows,* 9 November 1995, 14.

73. Kenneth Olson, "BU's Silber Lining," *Boston Network,* weekly newspaper at Boston University, 28 April 1988; "Interview with John Silber," *Boston University Daily Free Press,* 3 May 1989.

## Chapter 13

1. Lambda Legal Defense and Education Fund, *Improving School Policies and State Laws: A Landmark Compendium of Model Policies and Laws* (New York: LLDEF,

October 1997). (Lambda Legal Defense and Education Fund is located at 120 Wall St., Suite 1500, New York, NY 10005).

2. See Dan Woog, *School's Out: The Impact of Gay and Lesbian Issues on America's Schools* (Boston: Alyson, 1995) for overview.

3. David Buckel, *Stopping Anti-Gay Abuse of Students in Public High Schools: A Legal Perspective* (New York: Lambda Legal Defense and Education Fund, 1996); also, as of 1 July 1997, Section 10-15c of the Connecticut general statutes (Public Act no. 97-247).

4. Rhode Island Board of Regents Policy Statement on Discrimination Based on Sexual Orientation, 30 May 1997.

5. Maria Miro Johnson, "Students: Teachers Do Little to Curb Harassment of Gays," *Providence Journal-Bulletin,* 13 January 1998.

6. Kauanoe Bombard, "Island Voices: Gay Youth Still at Risk," *Honolulu Advertiser,* 4 June 1998.

7. "Gay, Lesbian Youths Call for Laws Barring Discrimination," *Dallas Morning News* (AP), 21 March 1999.

8. Dionne Searcey, "Legislators Told About Harassment of Gays in Schools," *Seattle Times,* 11 March 1999.

9. Robert B. Gunnison, "Assembly Rejects Ban on Gay Bias in Schools," *San Francisco Chronicle,* 5 June 1997; Laura Aurella, "Opening Eyes to High School Hate Crimes," *Contra Costa Times* (Walnut Creek, Calif.), 5 July 1998.

10. Kathie A. Smith, "Rally for Gay Youth," *Modesto Bee,* 22 March 1999; Lynda Gledhill, "Assembly Panel OKs Bill Protecting Gay, Lesbian Students," *San Francisco Chronicle,* 8 April 1999.

11. Several other gay or lesbian school board presidents have served in California and one in Cambridge, Mass.

12. David Tuller, "San Francisco Holds Its First Hearing for Gay Youths Today," *San Francisco Chronicle,* 26 September 1996.

13. Director, Pam Walton. Available from Wolfe Video, P.O. Box 64, New Almaden, CA 95042 (40 min.).

14. "San Francisco Moves to Protect Gay Youth," *New York Times,* 19 May 1996.

15. "San Francisco Moves to Protect Gay Youth."

16. Carol Ness, "Out at an Early Age," *San Francisco Examiner,* 30 June 1996.

17. See Steven Z. Athanases, "A Gay-Themed Lesson in an Ethnic Literature Curriculum: Tenth Graders' Responses to 'Dear Anita,'" special issue of *Harvard Educational Review* 66, 2 (1996): 231–256.

18. Vanise Wagner, "Students Combat Anti-gay Stigmas," *San Francisco Examiner,* 23 March 1997.

19. Ness, "Out at an Early Age."

20. Cynthia Laird, "San Francisco Unified School District Staff Diversity Training," *Bay Area Reporter,* 26 February 1998.

21. On the ambivalence of the Provincetown community to school antihomophobia programs, see Jason Pring, "Antibias Push Defended in Provincetown," *Boston Globe,* 22 August 1997; and K. C. Myers, "Parents Want Input on Use of Bias Language," *Cape Cod Times,* 26 November 1997.

22. "Official Business; Five-Year Member Elected as L.A. School Board President for the Record," *Daily News of Los Angeles,* 2 July 1996, B4.

23. Virginia Uribe, "The Implementation of District-wide Counseling Program for Lesbian and Gay Youth: Los Angeles Unified School District-Secondary Division," dissertation, Sierra Univ., 1988.

24. Los Angeles Unified School District, Office of Instruction, Memorandum no. 36, 29 May 1992.

25. Patricia Nell Warren, "L.A. Board of Education Terminates Gay and Lesbian Education Commission," *News You Didn't See on TV* (on-line publication from wildcatprs@aol.com), 26 March 1998.

26. Sandy Kleffman, "But They Get No Special Policy," *San Jose Mercury News*, 11 January 1997.

27. Elaine Herscher, "Parents in Uproar over Gay Education in Fremont," *San Francisco Chronicle*, 28 October 1997.

28. David Goll, "Livermore Teen-agers Protest Anti-gay Attitudes," *Contra Costa Times* (Walnut Creek, Calif.), 27 February 1998.

29. "Science Teacher's Coming Out Prompts Complaints," *Associated Press*, 29 December 1997; Claudette Langley, "Board Upholds Teacher Complaint," *San Leandro (Calif.) Times*, 14 May 1998.

30. Elaine Herscher, "Teacher Sues over Ban on Controversial Subjects," *San Francisco Chronicle*, 18 February 1999.

31. Steve Ryfle, "Consent Issue Fuels Debate over School Gay Groups," *Los Angeles Times*, 8 April 1996.

32. "Gay Students Convince Board to Drop Plan," *Pasadena (Calif.) Star News*, 9 May 1996.

33. Rich Kane, "Halls of Revolution," *OC (Orange County, Calif.) Weekly*, 21 November 1997.

34. "Gay in America—School Life," *San Francisco Examiner*, 25 June 1996.

35. Ness, "Out at an Early Age."

36. "Gay in America—School Life."

37. Ness, "Out at an Early Age."

38. *San Marino (Calif.) Tribune*, 16 January 1997, as reported in *GLAAD Alert* (Gay and Lesbian Alliance Against Defamation, Los Angeles, internet bulletin), 14 February 1997.

39. Ness, "Out at an Early Age."

40. John Myers, personal interview, 8 August 1996.

41. North Colonie Central Schools Assistant Superintendent Gregory Carey, in Carolyn Shapiro, "Airing Out School Closets," *The Record* (Troy, N.Y), Sunday edition, 2 November 1997.

42. The Address of CSS-NYS is P.O. Box 2345, Malta, NY 12020.

43. Sara Neufeld, "Schools Urged to Fight Gay Bias," *Newsday* (New York City), 19 October 1998.

44. Jesse Green, "This School Is Out," *New York Times Magazine*, 13 October 91.

45. Stan Karp, "Trouble over the Rainbow," *Rethinking Schools* 7 (Spring 1993): 8–10.

46. As part of its effort to drive a wedge between African Americans and gays, the Traditional Values Coalition (Anaheim, Calif.) sponsored a video, "Gay Rights/Special Rights," Jeremiah Films, shown nationally to PTAs and other groups.

47. Elise Harris, "School Daze," *OUT*, August-September 1993, 118.

48. See Ntanya Lee, Don Murphy, and Lisa North, "Sexuality, Multicultural Education, and the New York City Public Schools," *Radical Teacher* 45 (1994): 12–16.

49. Harris, "School Daze," 119.

50. Midge Decter, "Homosexuality and the Schools," *Commentary*, March 1993, 19–25.

51. Leslea Newman, *Heather Has Two Mommies* (Boston: Alyson, 1989); Leslea Newman, *Gloria Goes to Gay Pride* (Boston: Alyson, 1991).

52. Harris, "School Daze," 119.

53. "Board of Education Approves Curriculum," *In Newsweekly* (Boston), 26 February 1995.

54. *Struggle for Equality: Lesbian and Gay Community*, prepared as part of the Multicultural Education Curriculum by the New York City Mayor's Office for the Gay and Lesbian Community, October 1989.

55. Margaret Cerullo, GLSEN Conference, Milton Academy, Milton, Massachusetts, 1994.

56. See Lee, Murphy, and North, "Sexuality, Multicultural Education, and the New York City Public Schools," 12–16.

57. Pennsylvania Board of Education, Title 22, Chapter 5, General Policies at Section 5(4)(c).

58. Rita Addessa, "Multiracial-Multicultural-Gender Education Equity at Risk Outcomes, Philadelphia and Pennsylvania," Philadelphia Lesbian and Gay Task Force Report, Executive Summary, 1995.

59. Report of the Governor's Task Force on Gay and Lesbian Minnesotans, 22 March 1991.

60. Peg Cullen, "Programs for Gay Teens: Religious Rights in Peril," *St. Paul Pioneer Press*, 25 February 1997 (guest column by the president of the Catholic Defense League, St. Paul).

61. Thomas J. Collins, "St. Paul Taxpayers to Fund Controversial Out for Equity School Program," *St. Paul Pioneer Press*, 11 December 1996.

62. Rosalind Bentley, "Programs Teach Elementary Students Tolerance for Gays," *Star Tribune* (Minneapolis), 26 June 1998.

63. "St. Paulite Assails School Guide on Homosexuality," *St. Paul Pioneer Press* (AP), 12 July 1997.

64. "Report: Students Feel Safer in School," *Star Tribune* (Minneapolis), 11 March 1998.

65. Inara Verzemnieks, "Handling Teens' Homosexuality: School Systems Seek a Proper Approach," *Washington Post*, 30 September 1996.

66. Ibid.

67. "A Matter of Justice and Compassion: Meeting the Needs of Lesbian, Bisexual, and Transgendered Youth," 2nd Annual Diversity Conference, sponsored by Parents, Families, and Friends of Lesbians and Gays (P-FLAG), Wichita, Kansas, 1995.

68. Laura Meade Kirk, "How Bad Is It for Homosexual Teens?" *Providence Journal*, 6 December 1995.

69. Jennifer Juarez Robles, "Gay Students Struggle to Cope with Attitudes," *Detroit Free Press*, 25 February 1997; Tracy Van Moorlehem, "Schools Tackle Job of Protection for Gays," *Detroit Free Press*, 6 November 1998.

70. Leigh Bardugo, "They're Here, They're Queer," *Hartford Advocate*, 20 October 1998.

71. Children from the Shadows is organized and sponsored by True Colors, Inc.: Sexual Minority Youth and Family Services of Connecticut, P.O. Box 1855, Manchester, CT 06045-1855, (860) 649-7386, Robin Passariello McHaelen, Executive Director.

72. Juanita Poe, "Tension in Classrooms Brings Gay Issues to the Fore," Grant Pick, "In with the Out Crowd," *Chicago Tribune*, 19 October 1998; *Chicago Reader*, 11 December 1998.

73. Deneen Smith, "Gay Teen Group Raises Some Hackles," *Waukegan News-Sun*, 22 February 1999.

74. Tracy Phariss, personal interview, GLSEN/Colorado, 1 September 1996.

75. Carlos Illescas, "DPS Eyes Gay-Rights Measure," *Denver Post*, 7 January 1999.

76. Equality Colorado, P.O. Box 300476, Denver, CO 80203, (303) 839-5540, personal communication, 8 April 1999.

77. Erin Emery, "Young Lesbian Finds Comfort in Support Group," *Colorado Springs Gazette Telegraph*, 3 September 1996.

78. Ian Ith, "Gay Teens Find Support Through Sharing of Troubles and Triumphs," *Seattle Times*, 29 October 1998.

79. Eugene J. Patron "Project Y.E.S. Gives Gay Youth Support During Adolescence," *Miami Herald*, 30 March 1997.

80. Lydia Martin, "GED Program Offered for Gay Dropouts," *Miami Herald*, 9 January 1997.

81. Lynn Porter, "School Board Moves to Help Gay, Lesbian Students," *Tampa Tribune*, 24 March 1999.

82. Kellie Patrick, "School Board Backs Off Special Protection for Gay Students," *South Florica Sun-Sentinel*, 18 March 1999.

83. Regional Research Institute for Human Services, Portland State Univ., P.O. Box 751, Portland, OR 97207.

84. Seattle Commission on Children and Youth, "Report on Gay and Lesbian Youth in Seattle," November 1988.

85. Woog, *School's Out*, 95–100.

86. Brian Weber, "School Program Fights Biases," *Rocky Mountain News*, 26 November 1995.

87. "Gay High School Students Need Support Groups," *Arizona Republic* (Phoenix), 9 January 1997.

88. Kelly Pearce,, "School's Gay Club a First," *Arizona Republic*, 25 February 1999.

89. Rosalind Rossi, "Gay Student Elected Nonvoting School Board Member," *Chicago Sun-Times*, 1 August 1997.

90. Colleen Carroll, "School Board Bars Discrimination Against Gay and Lesbian Students, *St. Louis Post-Dispatch*, 14 January 1998.

91. Emily Graham, "Board Broadens Harassment Policy," *Iowa State Daily*, 31 March 1999.

92. Deb Price, "Novi Teen Exemplifies Next Generation of Gay Activism," *Detroit News*, 8 May 1998.

93. NASSP Director of Urban Services Gwendolyn Cooke, cited in Grant Pick, "In with the Out Crowd," *Chicago Reader*, 11 December 1998. Cooke did not investigate nonurban schools.

94. Robin L. Reale, "Lunch Bunch Digests Views," *Herald-Sun* (Durham, N.C, 31 March 1997; Laura Brown, "Gay Students Win Groups in Cobb, Decatur High Schools," *Southern Voice* (Atlanta), 12 November 1997.

95. Chip Wilson, "Father Harassed for Urging Gay Tolerance," *Charlotte (N.C.) Observer*, 9 January 1998.

96. Mike Lowry, personal letter to superintendents, 14 January 1997.

97. Karen Hucks, "Activist Seeks Help for Gays in Schools," *Morning News Tribune* (Tacoma, Wash.), 19 March 1997.

98. "Dean Asks High School Students for Tolerance," *Associated Press*, 8 May 1998.

99. Donna Harrington-Lueker, "Teaching Tolerance," *Executive Educator*, May 1993, 14–19.

100. Micah Sifry, response to a letter from Abraham Foxman, *Nation*, 19 April 1993, 2.

101. Letter from Leonard Zakin, ADL New England Regional Director, to *Concord (Mass.) Journal*, 26 June 1997.

102. See, for example, program for 1997 Summer Institute, 21–25 July 1997, Brandeis University.

103. Presented to Dylan Larke, Marshfield (Mass.) High School, 29 May 1997.

104. Mary Johnson and Margot Stern Strom, *Facing History and Ourselves: Holocaust and Human Behavior* (Brookline, Mass.: Facing History and Ourselves, 1989).

105. Alan L. Stoskopf and Margot Stern Strom, *Choosing to Participate: A Critical Examination of Citizenship in American History* (Brookline, Mass.: Facing History and Ourselves Foundation, 1990).

106. *Facing History and Ourselves: Holocaust and Human Behavior* (Brookline, Mass.: Facing History and Ourselves Foundation, 1994).

107. Doug Cumming, "Georgia Commission Deletes Homosexual References in Guide," *Atlanta Journal-Constitution*, 7 January 1999.

108. *A Guide to Enhancing the Cultural Competence of Runaway and Homeless Youth Programs*, Family and Youth Services Bureau, U.S. Department of Health and Human Services, January 1994.

109. Karen A. McLaughlin and Kelly J. Brilliant, *Healing the Hate* (Newton, Mass.: Education Development Center, 1997). (Funded and distributed by U.S. Dept. of Justice, Office of Juvenile Justice and Delinquency Prevention, P.O. Box 6000, Rockville, MD 20849-6000.) (Funded and distributed by U.S. Dept. of Justice, Office of Juvenile Justice and Delinquency Prevention, P.O. Box 6000, Rockville, MD 20849-6000.)

110. NYAC, 1711 Connecticut Ave. NW, Suite 206, Washington, D.C. 20009. Tel: (202) 319-7596; e-mail: NYouthAC@aol.com

111. *Back to School Campaign Report* (New York: Gay, Lesbian, Straight Education Network, 1998) The report was endorsed by the National Education Association, the American Federation of Teachers, and the National Association of School Psychologists.

112. For a comprehensive list of GLSEN programs and services, see its web site: http://www.glsen.org.

113. Resolution C-26, National Education Association, 1990, in "Teaching and Counseling Gay and Lesbian Students," NEA Human and Civil Rights Action Sheet, undated, 1.

114. "Teaching and Counseling Gay and Lesbian Students," 2.

115. Ibid.

116. Resolution B-9, National Education Association, July 1994.

117. By 1997 the History Month Project was cosponsored by the Gay and Lesbian Alliance Against Defamation (GLAAD) and a host of other national gay/lesbian organizations. Web site: www.glaad.org/glaad/history-month/index.html

118. Nina George Hacker, "NEA Resolution B–9: Anything but Benign," *Family Voice*, January 1996.

119. "Celebrating Gay and Lesbian History Month in Public Schools Is Not Just a Bad Idea—It's a Resolution of the National Education Association," paid advertisement, *Cleveland Plain Dealer* and other newspapers, 13 October 1995. Nina George Hacker in the January 1996 edition of Concerned Women for America's *Family Voice* explains that the 49 percent figure was based on "research" by Dr. Judith Reisman using 166 gay male biographical references in the 1994–1995 *Alyson Almanac*. Reisman arrived at her figure by counting the frequency of "mentions of pedophilia in positive terms."

120. Jessea Greenman, "Teachers' Group Chalks One Up to Homophobia," *GLAAD Images* (Newsletter of the Gay and Lesbian Alliance Against Discrimination), May-June 1996, 9.

121. Erin Anderson, "Gay History Not Part of Curriculum," *Rapid City Journal*, 14 October 1995.

122. Rodney Wilson, personal correspondence, 25 September 1995.

123. Jim Merkel, "No Plans to Observe Gay Month Officials Say," *Oakville-Mehlville Journal*, 1 November 1995.

124. Rodney Wilson, personal correspondence, 1995.

125. Lisa Kim Bach, "East Allen Denounces Homosexual Behavior," *Fort Wayne (Ind.) News-Sentinel*, 20 December 1995.

126. Gary Harmon, President of the Knox County Education Association, in "No Gay History Month, TEA Says," *Commercial Appeal* (Memphis, Tennessee), 21 September 1995.

127. Bob Anez, "NEA Resolution on Gay and Lesbian History Month Still Riling Conservatives," *Bay Windows* (AP), 12 October 1995.

128. Anderson, "Gay History Not Part of Curriculum."

129. Alan Edwards, "Views of National Group Spurring Utahans to Drop Out," *Deseret News*, 7 May 1996.

130. Kathleen Lyons, in Christina Connor, "Anti-Homosexual Ad Is Misleading, Say Educators," *Commercial Appeal* (Memphis, Tenn.), 16 November 1995.

131. Charles Ericksen, in Jo Mannies, "Anti-Gay Ad Draws Criticism," *St. Louis Post-Dispatch*, 18 November 1995.

132. Hacker, "NEA Resolution B-9."

133. Keith Geiger, NEA President, letter, October 1995; "NEA Head Defends Gay History Month Resolution," *In Newsweekly* (Boston), 5 November 1995.

134. Greenman, "Teachers' Group Chalks One Up to Homophobia," 22.

135. Nancy Cassad, NEA/GLC Pacific Region Coordinator, letter, *Caucus Connection* 9 (a publication of the Gay and Lesbian Caucus of the NEA), 3 March 1997.

136. NEA/Gay Lesbian Caucus, press release, 9 October 1998.

137. Brian Weber, "School Board Debates Gay Poster Plan," *Rocky Mountain News*, 3 November 1995.

138. "Panel OKs Gay Listings for Teen Handbook," *Fairfax (Va.) Journal* (AP), 10 April 1997.

139. Paulene Poparad, "Poster Appeal Won't Be Filed," *News-Dispatch* (Michigan City, Ind.), 9 January 1998.

140. Joseph Spector, "Safe or Out?" *Danbury (Conn.) News-Times*, 16 March 1997.

141. Joseph Spector, "Group Rallies to Help Retired Teacher," *Danbury News-Times*, 25 March 1997.

142. Bardugo, "They're Here, They're Queer."

143. "Story on Gay Students Pulled, *In Newsweekly*, 21 May 1995.

144. Gwen Florio, "In Colorado City, Conservatives Target Gay, Sex Issues in Schools," *Philadelphia Inquirer*, 17 January 1996.

145. Todd Bensman, "Censorship or Caution?" *Dallas Morning News*, 8 June 1998.

146. Nancy Roberts Trott, "Anti-Gay Policy Has Students Feeling Cheated, Teachers Fearing for Jobs," *Associated Press*, 3 March 1996; "Merrimack School Board Repeals Homosexual Policy," *Associated Press*, 4 June 1996.

147. Pontifical Commission for the Family, "Human Sexuality: Truth and Significance," *Boston Globe*, 21 December 1995.

148. Molly Guthrie, "Catholics Sue for Data on Gay Students' Program," *St. Paul Pioneer Press*, 25 November 1995.

149. Press release, Lambda Legal Defense and Education Fund, Washington, D.C., 7 July 1997.

150. Bryan Sierra, "Lawmaker Questions Kinsey Study," *United Press International*, 7 December 1995.

151. David W. Dunlap, "Opponents of Gay Topics Press Crusade, *New York Times*, 11 October 1995, B7.

152. "Hostile Climate," Report of People for the American Way, Washington, D.C., 1998.

153. Jeffrey S. Ghannam, "Policy Leaves Out Sexual Orientation," *Detroit Free Press*, 11 June 1996.

154. Craig Garrett, "District Drops Gay Policy," *Detroit News*, 20 August 1997.

155. Kerry McCray, "Schools Face Test on Gay Spending," *Modesto (Calif.) Bee*, 4 May 1997.

156. "School District Opts to Skip Gay Seminar," *Los Angeles Times*, 26 October 1995.

157. "WSU Cancels Gay Conference over Fears for Safety," *Oregonian* (Portland), 4 June 1998.

158. "Students Protest Elizabethtown Pro-Family Resolution," *Associated Press*, 8 October 1996.

159. Chip Berlet, Political Research Associates, 120 Beacon St., Somerville, MA 02144, personal interview, 1993. On the use of gay issues as wedge issues, see Eric Rofes, "Gay Issues, Schools, and the Right-Wing Backlash," *Rethinking Schools* 11, 3 (1997): 1.

160. "In Tennessee, a Move for Genesis," *Boston Globe* (AP), 5 March 1996.

161. *Board of Education of the West Side Community Schools v. Mergens*, 496 U.S. 226 (1990).

162. Jennifer Skordas, "High School Students May Start Gay Club," *Salt Lake Tribune*, 22 December 1995; Jerry Spangler, "Leavitt Joins Growing Chorus Against a Gay Club at East," *Deseret News*, 10 February 1996.

163. Jerry Spangler and Nicole Bonham, "Gay Club Issue May Mean End of School Clubs," *Deseret News*, 1 February 1996.

164. Hillary Groutage, "West, Highland Seek OK for Gay Clubs," *Salt Lake Tribune*, 6 February 1996.

165. Marjorie Cortez, "Board Votes to Ban All Non-Curricular Clubs," *Deseret News*, 21 February 1996.

166. "S.L. Students Walk Out, March in Protest," *Deseret News*, 23 February 1996.

167. Dion M. Harris, "Protesters Say Club Ban Is a Human Rights Issue," *Deseret News*, 3 March 1996.

168. James Brooke, "Will Banning of Clubs to Block Gay Groups Spread Across the Country?" *New York Times*, 28 February 1996.

169. Jerry Spangler, "Utah Senate OKs Restrictions on Schoolteachers' Activities," *Deseret News*, 23 February 1996; Marjorie Cortez, "Plurality Objects to Banning All Clubs," *Deseret News*, 17 March 1996.

170. Joe Costanzo, "Is It Really All or Nothing on School Clubs?" *Deseret News*, 23 February 1996; "Utah School Boards Association Seeks District Willing to Fight in Court over Gay Club Ban," *Bay Windows* (AP), 29 February 1996; Loren Webb, "Schools Could Ban Just Gay Clubs," *Salt Lake Tribune*, 10 March 1996.

171. Brooke, "Will Banning of Clubs to Block Gay Groups Spread Across the Country?"

172. Dan Harrie and Tony Semerad, "Legislature Passes Ban on Gay Clubs" *Salt Lake Tribune*, 18 April 1996.

173. Ibid.

174. Samuel A. Autman, "Senator Offers 'Proof' Gay Clubs Are Bad," *Salt Lake Tribune*, 18 April 1996.

175. Marjorie Cortez, "Legislator Wants to Amend Law That Restricts Student Clubs," *Deseret News*, 5 July 1996.

176. Marjorie Cortez, "Salt Lake District Reviews Loophole on Clubs," *Deseret News*, 31 July 1996.

177. Dan Harrie, "Gay Club Ban: What Will It Cost You?" *Salt Lake Tribune*, 20 April 1996.

178. Katherine Kapos, "Granite OKs Strict Club Policy," *Salt Lake Tribune*, 23 July 1997.

179. Marjorie Cortez and Lucinda Dillon, "Student Clubs Get Some Pointers," *Deseret News*, 18 January 1997.

180. Ben Fulton, "It's a Bash," *Salt Lake Weekly*, 16 November 1997; Robert Bryson, "Clubs, Schools Seek Mediation to End Dispute," *Salt Lake Tribune*, 9 June 1998; Hillary Groutage, "Mediation Does Not Resolve Gay/Straight Alliance Lawsuit," *Salt Lake Tribune*, 17 July 1998.

181. Hilary Groutage, "Gay Club Denied Request for Official Status," *Salt Lake Tribune*, 26 November 1998.

182. Joe Costanzo, "School Board's Motives Off-Limits," *Deseret News*, 9 January 1999.

183. "Meridan Would Consider Similar Ban," *Idaho Statesman* (Boise), 22 February 1996.

184. Rosemary Shinohara, "School Board Compromises on Student Clubs," *Anchorage Daily News*, 2 February 1997.

185. Shirin Parsavand, "Gay Group Suffers a Setback," *Daily Gazette* (Schenectady, N.Y.), 25 February 1997.

186. David Olinger "School Gay-Rights Group Sues," *Denver Post*, 23 January 1998; Brian Weber, "Students Start Club for Gays at East High," *Rocky Mountain News*, 30 September 1998.

187. Cara DeGette, "Students Lose Bid for School Gay Club," *Denver Post*, 5 February 1999.

188. Randy Furst, "Gay Straight Alliance to Have Limited Status in Orono Schools," *Star Tribune* (Minneapolis), 14 August 1998.

189. Shannon Marshall, "Students Try to Form WASP—A Support Group for Gay and Lesbian Teens," *Sun-Sentinel* (Fort Lauderdale, Fla.), 28 February 1996.

190. Terry Wilson, "Club for Gay Teens Shows Its Pride," *Chicago Tribune*, 27 June 1996.

191. "1994–1995 Report: Attacks on the Freedom to Learn," People for the American Way, 2000 M Street NW, Suite 400, Washington, D.C. 20036.

192. Ibid.

193. Ibid.

194. Mark Leccese, "What Parents Want to Know," *Cambridge TAB*, 7 March 1995.

195. "Attacks on the Freedom to Learn."

196. Judy Rakowsky, "Students, Parents Lose Sex-Ed Lawsuit," *Boston Globe*, 25 October 1995.

197. Kate Zernike, "High Court Refuses to Hear Parents' Sex-Education Lawsuit," *Boston Globe*, 5 March 1996.

198. *Solmitz v. Maine Administrative School District No. 59*, 495 A. 2d 812, 817–18 (1985).

199. *Hazelwood School District v. Kuhlmeier*, 484 U.S. 260, 108 S.Ct. 562 (1988).

200. *Bethel School District No. 403 v. Fraser*, 478 U.S. 675, 106 S.Ct. 3159 (1986).

201. Karen Avenoso, "Falmouth Group Loses Appeal on Condoms in School," *Boston Globe,* 9 January 1996.

202. "School Board Supports Gay Curriculum," *In Newsweekly,* 8 January 1995.

203. "Effort to Teach Tolerance Toward Gays Is Dropped by Des Moines Schools," *Bay Windows,* 26 January 1995.

204. John D. Hartigan, Legal Counsel for School Board 24, Queens, N.Y., on *Talk of the Nation,* National Public Radio, 22 December 1992.

205. J. T. Sears, "Dilemmas and Possibilities," in *Sexuality and the Curriculum: The Politics and Practices of Sexuality Education,* ed. James T. Sears (New York: Teachers College Press, 1992), 7.

206. J. T. Sears, "Responding to the Sexual Diversity of Faculty and Students: Sexual Praxis and the Critically Reflective Administrator," in *Educational Administration in a Pluralistic Society,* ed. Colleen A. Capper (Albany: State Univ. of New York Press, 1993), 149.

207. J. A. Whitson, "Sexuality and Censorship in the Curriculum: Beyond Formalistic Legal Analysis," in *Sexuality and the Curriculum: The Politics and Practices of Sexuality Education,* ed. James T. Sears (New York: Teachers College Press, 1992), 61.

208. *Zykan v. Warsaw,* 631 F. 2nd 1300, 7th Cir. (1980).

209. *Fisher v. Fairbanks North Star Borough School District,* 704 P. 2nd 213, Alaska (1985).

210. Guy DeRosa, "California Court Finally Rules in Favor of Gay Issues Workshop," *Caucus Connection* (Publication of the Gay and Lesbian Caucus of the NEA), March 1996, 6.

211. Jennifer Toomer, "Granite Won't Distribute Video on Gay Teens," *Deseret News* (AP), 22 April 1996.

212. Whitson, "Sexuality and Censorship," 65–67.

213. "Proceed with Caution: Warn About Topics" (Editorial), *Star-Gazette* (Elmira, N.Y.), 4 March 1996.

214. *Island Trees . . . School District v. Pico,* 457 U.S. 853 (1982).

215. Nancy Garden, *Annie on My Mind* (Toronto: Collins, 1982).

216. Loren King, "Kansas Judge Rules School's Removal of Gay Book Is Unconstitutional," *Bay Windows,* 7 December 1995.

217. Michael D. Simpson, "Defeat for Academic Freedom," *NEA Today* (a publication of the National Teachers Association), May 1998.

218. Stephanie Burns, Fairfax County, Virginia, Lesbian and Gay Citizens Association, Annandale, Va., speaking at the 8th Annual NGLTF Creating Change Conference, Detroit, Michigan, 1995.

219. Veda Morgan, "Central High Council Votes to Keep Explicit Novels," *Louisville (Ky.) Courier-Journal,* 13 January 1998.

220. "High School Student Excused from Reading Books by Gay Authors," *Bay Windows,* 30 September 1993; "Sexual Orientation Reading Unit Suspended at N.C. High School," *Bay Windows,* 21 October 1993.

221. Newt Gingrich, at Kennesaw, Georgia, town meeting, 14 January 1995, reported in Chris Bull, "Family Matters," *Advocate,* 7 April 1995, 12.

222. George F. Will, "10 Easy Points," *Boston Globe,* 27 January 1995.

223. Sheila Walsh, "Fairfax Approves Sex Ed Plan," *Washington Blade,* 17 April 1995.

224. Jane Eklund, "NH Teacher Fired for Using Gay-Themed Books," *Bay Windows*, 28 September 1995; "Ruling Favors Rehiring Teacher," *Boston Globe* (AP), 9 April 1996; Penny Culliton, personal communication, 28 May 1996; Holly Ramer, "Family Supports Return of Fired Teacher," *Associated Press*, 28 August 1996.

225. Kevin Jennings, ed., *Becoming Visible: A Reader in Gay and Lesbian History for High School Students* (Boston: Alyson, 1994).

226. Joan Little, "New Book on History of Gays Left Unshelved at Most Schools," *St. Louis Post-Dispatch*, 23 November 1995, 2B.

227. Richard Cohen, *Alfie's Home* (Sioux Falls, S.D.: South Dakota Family Policy Council, 1993).

228. *South Dakota Citizen*, published by the South Dakota Family Policy Council, Sioux Falls, S.D., November 1995.

229. Anne Saita, "Hertford School Destroys 30,000 Donated Books with Gay Titles Mixed In," *Norfolk-Virginian Pilot*, 4 March 1997.

230. Lori Olszewski, "Talk of 'Ellen' Fuels Move to Fire Teacher," *San Francisco Chronicle*, 15 July 1997; Elaine Herscher, "'Ellen' Discussion Takes Its Toll on Alameda Teacher," *San Francisco Chronicle*, 3 November 1997; Elaine Herscher, "State Licensing Panel Clears Teacher in 'Ellen' Incident," *San Francisco Chronicle*, 16 December 1997.

231. Warren J. Blumenfeld and Diane Raymond, *Looking at Gay and Lesbian Life* (New York: Philosophical Library, 1988).

232. Kansas City School District correspondence, with regard to Ginny Harris, 1994–1995.

233. Tony Perry, "Attempt to Teach Tolerance Backfires," *Los Angeles Times*, 29 June 1994, A3.

234. Becky Stover and Cindy Hadish, "Solon School Drops Planned Session on Gays," *Gazette* (Cedar Rapids, Ia.), 15 November 1995.

235. Anonymous student in "Gay and Lesbian Issues in Education," Harvard Extension School, Fall 1995.

236. "Dallas School Censors Broadcast," *Associated Press*, 23 January 1997.

237. Dan Beyers, "Montgomery to Air Controversial Tape," *Washington Post*, 24 April 1997.

238. Nanette Asimov, "Teacher Defends Sex Talk to Class," *San Francisco Chronicle*, 26 February 1997.

239. "Parents Irate over Message of Gay Singing Group," *In Newsweekly*, 26 February 1995.

240. "Parents Goofy over Gays," *Bay Windows*, 10 June 1993.

241. "Attacks on Freedom to Learn."

242. Lawrence J. Goodrich, "Giving Parents a Peek at School Lesson Plans," *Christian Science Monitor*, 15 June 1998.

243. Eun-Kyung Kim, "Miss America Chides Sex Ed Programs," *Associated Press*, 16 April 1998.

244. "Attacks on Freedom to Learn."

245. Cambridge Rindge and Latin School students of Carol Siriani, June 1992 and June 1993.

246. For a detailed report on teacher praxis and student responses to Brian MacNaught, "Dear Anita: Late Night Thoughts of an Irish Catholic Homosex-

ual," in *On Being Gay: Thoughts of Family, Faith, and Love* (New York: St. Martin's Press, 1988); Steven Z. Athanases, "A Gay-Themed Lesson in an Ethnic Literature Curriculum: Tenth Graders' Responses to 'Dear Anita,'" in special issue of the *Harvard Educational Review* 66, 2 (1996): 231–256.

247. "Religious Liberty, Public Education, and the Future of American Democracy: A Statement of Principles," Freedom Forum First Amendment Center, Vanderbilt University, 1207 18th Ave. South, Nashville, TN 37212.

248. Charles Haynes, "Tolerance and Civility Should Be Taught in Schools," *Saratogian* (Saratoga Springs, N.Y.), 17 May 1997.

249. See discussion of this dilemma in Janie Victoria Ward and Jill McLean Taylor, "Sexuality Education for Immigrant and Minority Students: Developing a Culturally Appropriate Curriculum," in *Sexuality and the Curriculum: The Politics and Practices of Sexuality Education*, ed. James T. Sears (New York: Teachers College Press, 1992), 183–201.

250. The National Conference in Southern Poverty Law Center Report, July 1994, 5.

251. Male student at Cambridge Rindge and Latin School, 1992.

252. Janet Parshall, "Let Us Pray? . . . Religion in the Schools," Harvard Education Forum, panel discussion, Cambridge, Massachusetts, 21 March 1995.

253. William Bennett, *The Book of Virtue: A Treasury of Great Moral Stories* (New York: Simon & Schuster, 1993).

254. Elisabeth Bumiller, "Elite All-Girls School Faces the Gay Issue," *New York Times*, 13 June 1997.

255. Ibid.

256. See James Sears, *Conversations for an Enlarging Public Square: Religion and Public Education* (New York: Teachers College Press, 1996).

## Chapter 14

1. Robert Weintraub, in Michael Sadowski, "Breaking the Silence: An Assessment of Gay Issues Programming at Brookline High School," unpublished paper, Harvard Graduate School of Education, 20 December 1994, 8.

2. Paloma McGregor, "Portland Schools: Promoting Sensitivity to Gays?" *Newhouse News Service*, 1 March 1996.

3. Paul L. Vance, in Dan Beyers, "No Gay Bias, No 'Proselytizing,' No End to Montgomery Debate," *Washington Post*, 1 April 1996.

4. Laine McKern, Conejo Valley Unified School District Trustee, in Kate Folmar, "Trustees Aim to Fight Bill Protecting Gay Students," *Los Angeles Times*, 17 March 1997.

5. Julian Guthrie, "Call to Add Gay Titles to School Book List," *San Francisco Examiner*, 11 March 1998.

6. J. A. Banks and C. A. McGee Banks, eds., *Multicultural Education: Issues and Perspectives* (Boston: Allyn and Bacon, 1993).

7. National Gay and Lesbian Task Force Campus Project, 1995, as cited in C. F. Shepard, F. Yeskel, and C. Outcalt, *Lesbian, Gay, Bisexual, and Transgender Campus Organizing: A Comprehensive Manual* (Washington, D.C.: NGLTF Policy Institute, 1995).

8. E. Donnerstein and D. Linz et al., "Estimating Community Standards: The Use of Social Science Evidence in an Obscenity Prosecution," *Public Opinion Quarterly* 55, 1 (1991): 80–112.

9. Donald B. Reed, "The Sexualized Context of American Public High Schools," paper presented at the annual meeting of the American Educational Research Assoc., New Orleans, 4–8 April 1994.

10. "Values and Opinions of Comprehensive School Health Education in U.S. Public Schools: Adolescents, Parents, and School District Administrators," American Cancer Society and the Gallup Organization (May 1994), 10, 23, and 33.

11. *U.S. News and World Report* Study and Robert and Linda Lichter, reported in Linda Chavez, "Hollywood Execs Are Out of Touch," *USA Today*, 18 April 1996.

12. Kyle Weeks, "Family Planning Perspectives," *Boston Globe*, 16 February 1995.

13. C. S. Haignere, "Planned Parenthood–Harris Poll Findings: Teens' Sexuality, Knowledge, and Beliefs," paper presented at the Annual Children's' Defense Fund National Conference, Washington, D.C., 1987; M. Zelnik and F. K. Shah, "First Intercourse Among Young Americans," *Family Planning Perspectives* 15 (1983): 64–70.

14. CDC, reported in *Boston Globe*, 5 January 1992.

15. Robert T. Michael, John H. Gagnon, Edward O. Laumann, and Gina Kolata, *Sex in America: A Definitive Survey* (Boston: Little, Brown, 1995).

16. Debra Haffner of the Sexuality Information and Education Council of the U.S. (SIECUS), in Felicia R. Lee, "Is the Dreaded 'Big Talk' Passé?" *New York Times*, 2 May 1996.

17. See Steven Z. Athanases, "A Gay-Themed Lesson in an Ethnic Literature Curriculum: Tenth-Graders' Responses to 'Dear Anita,'" in special issue of the *Harvard Educational Review* 66, 2 (1996): 231–256.

18. Workshops presented by Arthur Lipkin and Theresa Urist, Swampscott High School, Swampscott, Massachusetts, Spring 1994.

19. James Anthony Whitson, "Sexuality and Censorship in the Curriculum: Beyond Formal Legalistic Analysis," in *Sexuality and the Curriculum: The Politics and Practices of Sexuality Education*, ed. James T. Sears (New York: Teachers College Press, 1992), 69, 71.

20. Leonardo DiCaprio, interviewed by Bryant Gumbel, *NBC Today Show*, 2 November 1995.

21. Whitson, "Sexuality and Censorship in the Curriculum," 73–74.

22. Margot Stern Strom, "Fighting Hate's Hidden Curriculum," *Boston Globe*, 27 December 1992.

23. Jeff Bleckner, director, *Serving in Silence*, 1995, starring Glenn Close and Judy Davis.

24. As of April 1999, there were 25 lesbian, gay, bisexual, or transgender characters on prime time, according to the Gay and Lesbian Alliance Against Defamation's TV Scoreboard (http://www.glaad.org/glaad/scoreboard/index.html).

25. *Dr. Quinn, Medicine Woman*, CBS, April 1997.

26. In 1997, there were 22 recurring homosexual characters on prime time, according to the Gay and Lesbian Alliance Against Defamation (GLAAD).

27. Lisa de Moraes, "Call for Gay TV Rating Derided," *Boston Globe*, 4 March 1999.

28. "Teenagers Protest Homosexual Theme in Television Show," *Associated Press*, 12 March 1999.

29. Lisa de Moraes, "The Outer Limits: Gay TV Characters Break New Ground, Old Taboos," *Washington Post*, 3 March 1999.

30. Bruce Handy, "Ellen Degeneres: Yes, I'm Gay," *Time* (cover story), 14 April 1997.

31. K. C. Montgomery, *Target Prime Time: Advocacy Groups and the Struggle over Entertainment Television* (New York: Oxford Univ. Press, 1989).

32. Gary Levin, "TV's New Flirtation: Young Gay Characters," *USA Today*, 23 February 1999.

33. Alfred P. Kielwasser and Michelle A. Wolf, "Mainstream Television, Adolescent Homosexuality, and Significant Silence," *Critical Studies in Mass Communication* 9 (119): 350–373.

34. Many PBS stations have carried good gay programming, although constant right-wing attacks on government funding put their long-term commitment in doubt. Of course, most adolescents are watching major network programming anyway.

35. Alvin Poussaint, in Effrain Hernandez Jr., "Pouissant Urges Team Concept in Fighting Racism," *Boston Globe*, 31 January 1990.

36. See Kielwasser and Wolf, "Mainstream Television," 364.

37. R. C. Savin-Williams, *Gay and Lesbian Youth: Expressions of Identity* (New York: Hemisphere, 1990); T. S. Weinberg, *Gay Men, Gay Selves: The Social Construction of Homosexual Identities* (New York: Irvington, 1983).

38. Essex Hemphill, ed. *Brother to Brother: New Writings by Black Gay Men* (Boston: Alyson, 1991), xvi.

39. Strom, "Fighting Hate's Hidden Curriculum."

40. J. A. Banks, "Multi-Cultural Education: For Freedom's Sake," *Educational Leadership* 49, 4 (1991–1992): 32.

41. *Brown v. Board of Education*, 347 U.S. 483 (1954).

42. ASCD, Resolutions 1990, Alexandria, Va.

43. Carol Gilligan, *In a Different Voice: Psychological Theory and Women's Development* (Cambridge: Harvard Univ. Press, 1982).

44. See M. Mac An Ghaill, *The Making of Men: Masculinities, Sexualities, and Schooling* (Buckingham: Open Univ. Press, 1994).

45. James Gilligan, *Violence: Our Deadly Epidemic and Its Causes* (New York: Putnam, 1996).

46. Shane Town, "Is It Safe to Come Out Yet?: The Impact of Secondary Schooling on the Positive Identity Development of Ten Young Gay Men, or 'That's a Queer Way to Behave,'" paper presented at the annual meeting of the American Psychological Association, New York, April 1996.

47. Joshua Rodriguez, in "Lynn Minton Reports: Fresh Voices, Tough Teens Talk About a Program That Works," *Parade Magazine*, 8 January 1995.

48. White male public high school senior, personal interview, 1992.

49. A. Fererria et al., "Celebration: The Contributions of Lesbian and Gay Teachers," a presentation at the GLSTN Conference, Milton Academy, Milton, Mass., 1 March 1993.

50. R. D. Ashmore and F. K. Del Boca, "Psychological Approaches to Understanding Intergroup Conflicts," in *Towards the Elimination of Racism*, ed. Phyllis A. Katz (New York: Pergamon Press, 1976), 98.

51. H. E. Kagan, *Changing the Attitude of Christian Toward Jew: A Psychological Approach Through Religion* (New York: Columbia Univ. Press, 1952).

52. J. D. McNeill, "Changes in Ethnic Reaction Tendencies During High School," *Journal of Educational Research* 53 (1960): 199–200.

53. M. L. Hayes and M. E. Conklin, "Intergroup Attitudes and Experimental Change," *Journal of Experimental Education* 22 (1953): 19–36.

54. S. Kraus, "Modifying Prejudice: Attitude Change as a Function of the Race of the Communicator," *Audiovisual Communication Review* 10 (1960): 12–22; W. Elrod, "The Effect of Persuasive Communication on Interracial Attitudes," *Contemporary Education* 39 (1968): 148–151.

55. Phyllis A. Katz, "Attitude Change in Children: Can the Twig Be Straightened," in *Towards the Elimination of Racism,* ed. Phyllis A. Katz (New York: Pergamon Press, 1976), 223.

56. See Dean R. Smith, "The Responses of Gay and Straight Readers to Young Adult Novels about Homosexuality," paper presented at the annual meeting of the National Council of Teachers of English, Orlando, Fla., 16–21 November 1994.

57. Katz, "Attitude Change in Children," 223.

58. See, for example, Leonore Gordon, "What Do We Say When We Hear 'Faggot'?" and "Countering Homophobia: A Lesson Plan," *Bulletin on the Council for Interracial Books for Children* 14, 3–4 (1983): 25–27 and 28–29.

59. M. J. Weiner and F. E. Wright," Effects of Undergoing Arbitrary Discrimination upon Subsequent Attitudes Toward a Minority Group," *Journal of Applied Social Psychology* 3 (1973): 94–102.

60. Southern Poverty Law Center, 400 Washington Ave., P.O. Box 548, Montgomery, AL 36101-0548.

61. See, for example, the film *Sticks, Stones, and Stereotypes,* Equity Institute, 48 N. Pleasant St., Amherst, MA 01002.

62. Diversity Works, 201 North Valley Rd., Pelham, MA 01002. Tel. (413) 256-1868.

63. Facing History and Ourselves, 16 Hurd Rd., Brookline, MA 02146.

64. "New Kids in School," *Advocate,* 24 September 1991.

65. Lynn Johnston, *For Better or Worse,* Universal Press Syndicate, 1993. For a reprint of the series, see "Coming Out in the Comics: A Look at Lynn Johnston's 'For Better or For Worse,'" in *Open Lives/Safe Schools,* ed. Donovan R. Walling (Bloomington, Ind.: Phi Delta Kappa Educational Foundation, 1996), 145–157.

66. Colleen A. Capper, "Administrator Practice and Preparation for Social Reconstructionist Schooling," in *Educational Administration in a Pluralistic Society,* ed. Colleen A. Capper (Albany: State Univ. of New York Press, 1993), 297.

67. Ibid.

68. For a critique both of such marginalization and of the mission of schools, see Kathryn Snider, "Race and Sexual Orientation: The (Im)possibility of These Intersections in Educational Policy," in special issue of the *Harvard Educational Review* 66, 2 (1996): 294–302.

69. See Nina Hersch Gebelco, "Prejudice Reduction in Secondary Schools," *Social Education* (April-May 1988): 276–279.

70. See, for example, Lutz van Dijk, *Coming Out: Gays and Lesbians from Around the World* (Lelystad, Netherlands: Stichting IVIO, 1998).

71. See Glorianne M. Leck, "Queer Relations with Education Research," in *Power and Method: Political Activism and Educational Research,* ed. Andrew Gitlin (New York: Routledge, 1994).

72. See Ian Barnard, "Bibliography for an Anti-Homophobic Pedagogy: A Resource for Students, Teachers, Administrators, and Activists," *Feminist Teacher* 7, 3 (1993): 50–52.

73. Matt Green, unpublished report, 12 December 1995.

74. See James T. Sears, "Dilemmas and Possibilities of Sexuality Education: Reproducing the Body Politic," in *Sexuality and the Curriculum: The Politics and Practices of Sexuality Education,* ed. James T. Sears (New York: Teachers College Press, 1992), 19; James T. Sears, "Researching the Other/Searching for Self: Qualitative Research on [Homo]Sexuality in Education," *Theory into Practice* 31, 2 (1992): 149–156.

75. J. A. Banks, "A Curriculum for Empowerment, Action, and Change," in *Empowerment Through Multicultural Education,* ed. C. E. Sleeter (Albany: State Univ. of New York Press, 1991), 130.

76. Her attitude is beginning to be expressed among a new generation of multiracial Americans. See "Rally Held for Multiracial Category on 2000 Census," *Boston Globe* (AP), 21 July 1996, A21.

77. Debra Haffner of the Sex Information and Education Council of the United States, in Kim Painter, "The AIDS Epidemic's Legacy of Change," *USA Today,* 5 June 1996.

78. Susan K. Telljohan and James H. Price, "Teaching About Sexual Orientation by Secondary Health Teachers," *Journal of School Health* 65, 1 (1995): 20.

79. See Sue Ellen Case, "Tracking the Vampire," in *Differences: A Journal of Feminist Cultural Studies* 3, 2 (1991): 1–20.

80. Senate Bill No. 600, 88th General Assembly, Missouri State Legislature.

81. Nancy Montgomery, "Controversial Marysville Sex-Ed Policy Irks Teachers," *Seattle Times,* 16 December 1997.

82. Telljohan and Price, "Teaching About Sexual Orientation by Secondary Health Teachers," 19.

83. Brad Hayward, "GOP Urges Parental Consent for AIDS Ed," *Scripps-McClatchy News Service,* 17 May 1996.

84. Emelyn Cruz Lat and Eric Brazil, "Gay Pride Display Stirs Up Danville School," *San Francisco Examiner,* 7 June 1998.

85. Sears, "Dilemmas and Possibilities," 14.

86. For information on the political dimension of sex education, see Lynn Phillips and Michelle Fine, "What's 'Left' in Sexuality Education?" in *Sexuality and the Curriculum: The Politics and Practices of Sexuality Education,* ed. James T. Sears (New York: Teachers College Press, 1992), 242–249.

87. See Gary B. MacDonald, Raymond O'Brien, Karen J. Pittman, and Mary Kimball, "Adolescents and HIV: Defining the Problem and Its Prevention," Commissioned Paper no. 12 (Washington, D.C.: Center for Youth Development and Policy Research, Academy for Educational Development, February 1994).

88. See Kim DeAndrade, "Teaching About Gay Men and Lesbians in the FLE Classroom," *FLEducator* (Winter 1992–1993): 8–11; "Human Sexuality Seminar," Alexandria City Public Schools (Virginia), 1991–1992.

89. See M. Greene, "The Passions of Pluralism: Multiculturalism and the Expanding Community," *Educational Researcher* 22, 1 (1993): 13–18.

90. Elise Harris, "School Daze," *OUT*, August-September 1993, 118.

91. Anthony R. D'Augelli, "Teaching Lesbian/Gay Development: From Oppression to Exceptionality," in *Coming Out of the Classroom Closet: Gay and Lesbian Students, Teachers, and Curricula*, ed. Karen M. Harbeck (Binghamton, N.Y.: Harrington Park Press, 1992), 217.

92. Lawrence A. Kurdek, "The Nature and Correlates of Relationship Quality in Gay, Lesbian, and Heterosexual Cohabiting Couples: A Test of the Individual Difference, Interdependence, and Discrepancy Models," in *Lesbian and Gay Psychology: Theory, Research, and Clinical Applications*, ed. Beverly Greene and Gregory M. Herek (Thousand Oaks, Calif.: Sage, 1994).

93. See Paul M. Puccio, "Teaching the Literature of Lesbian and Gay Experience: An Assimilationist View," paper presented at the annual meeting of the National Council of Teachers of English, Baltimore, Md., 17–22 November 1989, 9–10. ERIC Microfiche no. 320164.

94. Janie Victoria Ward and Jill McLean Taylor, "Sexuality Education for Immigrant and Minority Students: Developing a Culturally Appropriate Curriculum," in *Sexuality and the Curriculum: The Politics and Practices of Sexuality Education*, ed. James T. Sears (New York: Teachers College Press, 1992).

95. Harvard Gay and Lesbian School Issues Project, 1991.

96. For an interesting sociological analysis of the news coverage of homosexuals from World War II to the present, see Edward Alwood, *Straight News: Gays, Lesbians, and the News Media* (New York: Columbia Univ. Press, 1996).

97. 115 West 28th St., #3-R., New York, NY, 10001. Tel. (212) 643-7867.

98. Ntanya Lee and Alex Robertson Textor, *Transforming the Nation: Lesbian, Gay, Bisexual, and Transgendered U.S. Histories, 1945–1995* (New York: School Voices Press, 1998).

99. Kevin Jennings, *Becoming Visible: A Reader in Gay and Lesbian History for High School and College Students* (Boston: Alyson, 1994).

100. See Andrew Hodges, *Alan Turing: The Enigma* (New York: Simon and Schuster, 1983).

101. Hugh Whitemore, *Breaking the Code* (New York: Samuel French, 1987–1988).

102. W. Scott Thompson, "Was Abraham Lincoln Gay? A Divided Man to Heal a Divided Age," unpublished paper, Tufts University, Fletcher School of Law and Diplomacy, October 1995.

103. Jonathan Ned Katz, *Gay American History* (New York: Meridian, 1976), 647.

104. Blanche Wiesen-Cook, "Eleanor—Loves of a First Lady," *Nation*, 5 July 1993. See also Rodger Streitmatter, *Empty Without You*, in press.

105. See Richard Plant, *The Pink Triangle* (New York: Henry Holt, 1986); Heinz Heger, *The Men with the Pink Triangle* (Boston: Alyson, 1980); and the recently published novel based on a memoir for middle school to high school students, Lutz van Dijk's *Damned Strong Love: The True Story of Willi G. and Stephan K.*, translated from the German by Elizabeth D. Crawford (New York: Holt, 1995); also a web site: http://www.cs.cmu.edu/afs/cs/user/scotts/ftp/bulgarians/pink.html.

106. Dan Levy, "Emerging from Holocaust's Shadow," *San Francisco Chronicle*, 31 March 1996.

107. See Daniel Goldhagen, "There Is No Hierarchy Among Victims," opinion, *New York Times*, 18 January 1997.

108. Adam Dickter, "Anti-Gay Group Targets Museum," *Jewish Week*, 12 April 1996.

109. Ann Heron, ed., *One Teenager in Ten: Writings by Gay and Lesbian Youth* (Boston: Alyson, 1983).

110. See *Facing History and Ourselves: Holocaust and Human Behavior, Resource Book* (Brookline, Mass.: Facing History and Ourselves National Foundation, 1994).

111. An interesting documentary film on Gertrude Stein and her coterie of Left Bank lesbians (including Colette, Janet Flanner, and Sylvia Beach) is Greta Schiller's *Paris Was a Woman*, directed by Greta Schiller, produced by Greta Schiller, Andrea Weiss, and Frances Berrigan (1995 U.S./1996 Great Britain).

112. See, for example, R. F. Hammett, "A Rationale and Unit Plan for Introducing Gay and Lesbian Literature into the Grade Twelve Curriculum," in *Becoming Political: Readings and Writings in the Politics of Literacy Education*, ed. P. Shannon (Portsmouth, N.H.: Heinemann, 1992).

113. Vicky Greenbaum, "Literature Out of the Closet: Bringing Gay and Lesbian Texts and Subtexts Out in High School English," *English Journal* 83, 5 (1994): 71–74.

114. See Robert F. Williams, "Gay and Lesbian Teenagers: A Reading Ladder for Students, Media Specialists, and Parents," *ALAN Review* 20, 3 (1993): 12–17.

115. See, for example, Adrienne Rich, "Vesuvius at Home: The Power of Emily Dickinson," in *On Lies, Secrets, and Silence: Selected Prose 1966–1978* (New York: W. W. Norton, 1979).

116. See short biographic essay by Donald Hall, in Claude J. Summers, ed., *The Gay and Lesbian Literary Heritage* (New York: Henry Holt, 1995), 696–699.

117. See Robert Bernard Martin, *Gerard Manley Hopkins: A Very Private Life* (New York: G. P. Putnam, 1991).

118. See Arnold Rampersad, *The Life of Langston Hughes*, vol. 1, *1902–1941, I, Too, Sing America* (New York: Oxford Univ. Press, 1986).

119. See Robert K. Martin, *Hero, Stranger, and Captain: Male Friendship, Social Critique, and Literary Form in the Sea Novels of Herman Melville* (Chapel Hill: Univ. of North Carolina Press, 1986).

120. See Walter Harding, *The Days of Henry Thoreau: A Biography* (Princeton: Princeton Univ. Press, 1982).

121. See Andrew Jay Hoffman, *Inventing Mark Twain: The Lives of Samuel Langhorn Clemens* (New York: Wm. Morrow, 1997).

122. Karl Hugo Pruys, *Die Liebkosungen des Tigers: Eine Erotische Goethe-Biographie* (The tender caress of the tiger: An erotic Goethe biography) (Berlin: Edition Q, 1997).

123. Ellis Amburn, *Subterranean: The Hidden Life of Jack Kerouac* (New York: St. Martin's Press, 1998).

124. Henry Abelove, "From Thoreau to Queer Politics," *Yale Journal of Criticism* 6, 2 (1993): 17–27.

125. Walter Harding, "Thoreau's Sexuality," *Journal of Homosexuality* 21, 3 (1991): 23–45.

126. Eve Kosofsky Sedgwick, *Epistomology of the Closet* (Berkeley: Univ. of California Press, 1990), 53. Sedgwick's emphasis.

127. Langston Hughes, "Cafe 3 A.M.," from *Montage of a Dream Deferred* (New York: Henry Holt, 1951).

128. Five members of the California Librarians Black Caucus objected anonymously to the use of a Langston Hughes poem on a poster for Lesbian and Gay History Month at the Los Angeles Public Library. New posters were printed. Mark Haile, "Librarians Protest Use of Langston Hughes Poetry," *BLK*, July 1991, 23.

129. Eric Garber, "A Spectacle in Color: The Lesbian and Gay Subculture of Jazz Age Harlem," in *Hidden from History: Reclaiming the Gay and Lesbian Past*, ed. M. Duberman, M. Vicinus, and G. Chauncy Jr. (New York: Meridian, 1990).

130. Willa Cather, "Paul's Case," *Five Stories* (New York: Vintage, 1956).

131. Claude J. Summers, "A Losing Game in the End: Aestheticism and Homosexuality in Cather's 'Paul's Case,'" *Modern Fiction Studies* 36 (Spring 1990): 103–119; Eve Kosofsky Sedgwick, "Across Gender, Across Sexuality: Willa Cather and Others," *South Atlantic Quarterly* 88, 1 (1989): 63.

132. See Kathy J. Phillips, "'Billy Budd' as Anti-Homophobic Text," *College English*, 56, 8 (1994): 896–910.

133. A. L. Rowse, *Homosexuals in History: A Study of Ambivalence in Society, Literature, and the Arts* (New York: Macmillan, 1977), 296.

134. See, for example, Bennett L. Singer, ed., *Growing Up Gay/Growing Up Lesbian: A Literary Anthology* (New York: New Press, 1993); David Leavitt and Mark Mitchell, eds., *The Penguin Book of Gay Short Stories* (New York: Viking, 1994).

135. See, for example, Nancy Boutilier, "Reading, Writing, and Rubyfruit Jungle: High School Students Respond to Gay and Lesbian Literature," *OUT/LOOK* 15 (Winter 1992); Marvin Hoffman, "Teaching Torch Song: Gay Literature in the Classroom," *Rethinking Schools* 8, 4 (1994): 17; Vicky Greenbaum, "Literature Out of the Closet: Bringing Gay and Lesbian Texts and Subtexts Out in High School English," *English Journal* 83, 5 (1994): 71–74. Also Penny Culliton, "Inclusive English Curricula," 1997, a self-published guide, Mascenic High School, Mascenic, N.H.

136. See, for example, Christine Jenkins, "Heartthrobs and Heartbreaks: A Guide to Young Adult Books with Gay Themes," *OUT/LOOK* 1, 3 (1988): 82–92; Dennis Sumara, "Gay and Lesbian Voices in Literature: Making Room on the Shelf," *English Quarterly* 25, 1 (1993): 30–34; Christine Jenkins, "Young Adult Novels with Gay/Lesbian Characters and Themes, 1969–1992: A Historical Reading of the Content, Gender, and Narrative Distance," *Journal of Youth Services in Libraries* 7, 1 (1993): 43–55; "Books on Lesbian and Gay Issues," (bibliography adapted from one by Sarah-Hope Parmeter, University of California at Santa Cruz) *Rethinking Schools* 8, 4 (1994): 19; Michael Allyn Jackson, "20 Novels for Gay and Lesbian Youth," (bibliography) (New York: American Council of Learned Societies, Secondary Schools Curriculum Development Project, 1995); David E. Wilson, "The Open Library: YA Books for Gay Teens," *English Journal* (November 1984): 60–63; Sandra Chapman, *The Power of Children's Literature: A Review of Books with Gay and Lesbian Themes* (New York: Bank Street College of Education, 1996).

137. Michael Thomas Ford, "Gay Books for Young Readers: When Caution Calls the Shots," *Publishers Weekly*, 21 February 1994, 24–27.

138. Jacqueline Woodson, *From the Notebooks of Melanin Sun* (New York: Blue Sky Press 1995); Nancy Garden, *Annie on My Mind* (Toronto: Collins, 1982); Paula

Boock, *Dare, Truth, or Promise* (Dunedin, New Zealand: Longacre Press, 1997). Also: Marion Dane Bauer, ed., *Am I Blue? Coming Out from the Silence: A Collection of Short Stories by Notable Young Adult Gay/Lesbian Fiction Writers* (New York: Harper Trophy: 1994); and Tony Grima, ed., *Not the Only One: Lesbian and Gay Fiction for Teens* (Boston: Alyson, 1994); Liza Ketchum, *Blue Coyote* (New York: Simon and Schuster, 1997); Francesca Lia Block, *Weetzie Bat* (New York: HarperCollins, 1989); Francesca Lia Block *Baby Be-Bop* (New York: HarperCollins, 1995); M. E. Kerr, *Deliver Us from Evie* (New York: HarperCollins, 1994); M. E. Kerr, *"Hello, I Lied"* (New York: HarperCollins, 1997); Nancy Garden, *Good Moon Rising* (New York: Farrar Straus Giroux 1996); and three books by E. Lynn Harris, *Invisible Life* (New York: Anchor Books, 1994), *Just As I Am* (New York: Doubleday, 1994), and *This Too Shall Pass* (New York: Doubleday, 1996).

139. Ellen Louise Hart, "Literacy and the Empowerment of Lesbian and Gay Students," paper presented at the annual meeting of the Conference on College Composition and Communication, Seattle, 16–18 March 1989, 2.

140. See Hart, "Literacy and the Empowerment of Lesbian and Gay Students," 5.

141. Leslie Smith, "Writers Who Are Gay and Lesbian Adolescents: The Impact of Social Context," paper presented at the annual meeting of the Conference on College Composition and Communication, Seattle, 16–18 March 1989.

142. On the resistance to such interpretations, see Martin Duberman, "Is There Room for Privacy on the Canvas?" *New York Times*, 7 September 1997.

143. James M. Saslow, *Ganymede in the Renaissance: Homosexuality in Art and Society* (New Haven: Yale Univ. Press, 1986).

144. See Philip Kennicott, "Music's New Genre: Sexual Preference," *Saint Louis Post Dispatch*, 16 June 1996; Meryle Secrest, *Stephen Sondheim: A Life* (New York: Alfred A. Knopf, 1998); and, for example, Anthony Holden, *Tchaikovsky: A Biography* (New York: Random House, 1996); and David Hajdu, *Lush Life: A Biography of Billy Strayhorn* (New York: Farrar Straus and Giroux, 1996).

145. A wonderful tribute by one gay artist to another is Duane Michals's more recent *Salute, Walt Whitman* (Santa Fe, N.M.: Twin Palms, 1996).

146. Cynthia Katz, teacher at Concord Academy, personal interview, Concord, Mass., June 1994.

147. The Shared Heart, P.O. Box 562, Brookline, MA 02146, Tel: (617) 536-7050, nos. 1, 27.

148. Lillian Hellman, *The Children's Hour* (New York: Alfred A. Knopf, 1934).

149. Lorraine Hansberry, *The Sign in Sidney Brustein's Window* (New York: New American Library, 1966).

150. Harvey Fierstein, *Torch Song Trilogy* (New York: Samuel French, 1979).

151. William M. Hoffman, *As Is* (New York: Random House, 1985).

152. Larry Kramer, *The Normal Heart* (London: Methuen in assoc. with the Royal Court Theater, 1986).

153. See V. A. Lankewish, "Breaking the Silence: Addressing Homophobia with *The Color Purple*," in *Social Issues in the Classroom*, ed. C. M. Hurlburt and S. Totten (Urbana, Ill.: National Council of Teachers of English, 1992), 219–230.

154. Gilbert Cates, director, *Consenting Adult*, based on the 1975 novel by Laura Z. Hobson.

155. William Finn, *Falsettos* (New York: Samuel French, 1995).

156. Lanford Wilson, *Fifth of July* (New York: Hill and Wang, 1979.)

157. Collections include Don Shewey, ed., *Out Front: Contemporary Gay and Lesbian Plays* (New York: Grove Press, 1988); William M. Hoffman, ed., *Gay Plays: The First Collection* (New York: Avon, 1979). Also see Sam Able, "Gay and Lesbian Studies and the Theater Curriculum," *Theater Topics* 4, 1 (1994): 31–44.

158. See Enrique Lavin, "Spoken by Heart," *Los Angeles Times,* 7 January 1998; and Christopher Muther, "Theater of Self-Exploration," *Boston Globe,* 24 May 1998.

159. For a rare discussion of including matters of sexual orientation, see "Dialogue Corner" in *Journal of Science Teacher Education* 6, 4 (1995): 204–206.

160. "The History and Nature of Homosexuality and Its Causes," Harvard Graduate School of Education Gay and Lesbian School Issues Project, Arthur Lipkin, Longfellow Hall 210, Cambridge, MA 02138.

161. Michael A. Messner and Donald F. Sabo, *Sex, Violence, and Power in Sports: Rethinking Masculinity* (Freedom, Calif.: Crossing Press, 1994); Susan K. Cahn, *Coming On Strong: Gender and Sexuality in Twentieth-Century Women's Sport* (New York: Free Press, 1994); Myriam Miedzian, *Boys Will Be Boys: How We Encourage Violence in Our Sons and What We Can Do to Stop It* (New York: Doubleday, 1991).

162. See Dan Woog, *Jocks: True Stories of America's Gay Male Athletes* (Los Angeles: Alyson, 1998).

163. Pat Griffin, "Changing the Game: Homophobia and Sexism in Women's Sport," *Quest* 44, 2 (1992): 251–265; see also Pat Griffin, *Strong Women, Deep Closets: Lesbians, Sports, and Homophobia* (Champaign, Ill.: Human Kinetics, 1998).

164. See Carolyn Caywood, "Reaching Out to Gay Teens," *School Library Journal* 39, 4 (1993): 50.

165. Jolayne Houtz, "District Official Regrets Gay-Books Confusion," *Seattle Times,* 22 May 1997; "School Books on Gay Families Stir Seattle," *New York Times,* 2 November 1997.

166. Lee Elby, "Book for Gay Teens Will Stay on Library Shelves," *Pittsburg Tribune-Review,* 5 August 1997.

167. See Herbert Foerstel, "Conflict and Compromise over Homosexual Literature," *Emergency Librarian* 22, 2 (1994): 28–30.

168. See, for example, Gary Klein, "Helping Students Find Sensitive Material: A Guide to Literature on Homosexuality for Librarians and Faculty," unpublished paper, 1993, ERIC Microfiche #ED359990.

169. Helma Hawkins, in Rasheeda Crayton, "Librarians Discuss Serving Gay Youths," *Kansas City (Mo.) Star,* 12 March 1998.

170. See Susan Corbett, "A Complicated Bias," *Young Children* 3 (March 1993): 29–31.

171. See, for example, "Images Checklist for Anti-Bias Environments" (pamphlet, adapted by Ellen Wolpert, Jamaica Plain, Mass., (617) 522-8778, from *Anti-Bias Curriculum Tools for Empowering Young Children,* Council on Interracial Books for Children.)

172. Yehuda Amir, "The Role of Intergroup Contact in Change of Prejudice and Ethnic Relations," in *Towards the Elimination of Racism,* ed. Phyllis A. Katz (New York: Pergamon Press, 1976), 259–260.

173. Interview in *Klanwatch Intelligence Report,* October 1995, 14, a publication of the Southern Poverty Law Center, 400 Washington Ave., P.O. Box 548, Montgomery, AL 36101-0548.

174. See Virginia Wolf, "The Gay Family in Literature for Young People," *Children's Literature in Education* 20, 1 (1989): 51–58; and "Reading Resources: Support Services for Gay, Lesbian, and Bisexual Youth," available from San Francisco United School District, School Health Programs Dept., 1512 Golden Gate Avenue, San Francisco, CA 94115, tel: (415) 749-3400.

175. *Starting Small: Teaching Tolerance in Preschool and the Early Grades*, a publication of the Southern Poverty Law Center, 400 Washington Ave., P.O. Box 548, Montgomery, AL 36101-0548.

176. Virginia Casper, Harriet K. Cuffaro, Steven Schultz, Jonathan G. Silin, and Elaine Wickens, "Toward a Most Thorough Understanding of the World: Sexual Orientation and Early Childhood Education," special issue of *Harvard Educational Review* 66, 2 (1996): 271–293; Betsy J. Cahill and Rachel Theilheimer, "'Can Tommy and Sam Get Married?' Questions About Gender, Sexuality, and Young Children," *Young Children* (January 1999): 27–31.

177. Michael Willhoite, *Daddy's Roommate* (Boston: Alyson, 1990).

178. "Queer Books for Kids Top Ban List," *In Newsweekly*, 19 February 1995.

179. See, for example, lesson plans for grades K–5, available from the Buena Vista Lesbian and Gay Parents Group, 1541 Alabama St., San Francisco, CA 94110.

180. Thomas Lickona, in *National Guidelines for Sexuality and Character Education*, Medical Institute for Sexual Health (P.O. Box 4919, Austin, TX 78765), 1996.

181. Jonathan Silin, *Sex, Death, and the Education of Children: Our Passion for Ignorance in the Age of AIDS* (New York: Teachers College Press, 1995).

182. *Collins v. Faith School District*, #46-2, #19959, Supreme Court of South Dakota, 1998 SD17; 574 N.W. 2d889. Opinion filed 25 February 1998.

183. Beverly Fletcher, unpublished paper, Harvard Extension School, 15 December 1995.

184. Teacher, Cambridge, Mass., personal correspondence, 1995.

185. See Elaine Wickens, "Penny's Question: 'I Will Have a Child in My Class with Two Moms—What Do You Know About This?'" *Young Children*, March 1993, 27–28.

186. The Fayerweather Street School, Cambridge, Mass., as described in Liza Featherstone, "Stonewall for Sixth-Graders," in *One in 10*, supplement to *Boston Phoenix*, 8 March 1996, 8.

187. Ottoson Middle School Assembly, Arlington, Mass., Spring 1996.

188. Address: http://member.aol.com/Matthew Bam/HMilk.htm

189. Women's Educational Media, 2180 Bryant St. #203, San Francisco, CA 94110. Tel. (415) 641-4616, e-mail WEMDHC@aol.com.

190. Pam Brown and Peggie Gillespie, P.O. Box 1216, Amherst, MA 01004-1216. See also *Love Makes a Family: Portraits of Lesbian, Gay, Bisexual, and Transgender Parents and Their Families*, photographs by Gigi Kaeser, ed. Peggy Gillespie (Amherst, Ma: Univ. of Massachusetts Press, 1999).

191. Nick Grabbe and Phyllis Lehrer, "Exhibit Foes Get Hearing," *Amherst Bulletin*, 10 May 1996, 1.

192. Laurie Loisel, "Judge Refuses to Halt Exhibit," *Daily Hampshire Gazette* (Northampton, Mass.), 16 May 1996.

193. "Gay Photo Show Debated," *St. Paul Pioneer Press*, 28 April 1996, B3.

194. Scott Russell, "Gay Photo Exhibit OK'd," *Capital Times*, 3 May 1996.

195. Bill Scanlon, "Romer Discusses Gays at Elementary School," *Rocky Mountain News*, 16 May 1996.

196. Tim Mayer, "Parents Protest Class on AIDS," *Rapid City (S.D.) Journal*, 23 January 1996.

197. "Irate Parents Complain About Gay Safer Sex Pamphlet Handed Out to Middle School Kids," *Bay Windows* (AP), 13 June 1996.

198. Eric Garber, "A Spectacle in Color: The Lesbian and Gay Subculture of Jazz Age Harlem," in *Hidden from History: Reclaiming the Gay and Lesbian Past*, ed. Martin Duberman, Martha Vicinus, and George Chauncy (New York: Penguin Books, 1989), 318–331. A teacher at Algonquin Regional High School (Mass.) almost lost his job over this choice.

199. Boutilier, "Reading, Writing, and Rubyfruit Jungle," 72.

200. Ibid., 73.

201. Ibid., 75.

202. Hoffman, "Teaching Torch Song," 17.

203. "Gay Man Is Tired of Misrepresentation," *Boston Globe*, 12 October 1992.

204. Chap 76, Sec.5, State Publication no. 17659-16-5000-1/95-DOE.

205. Gilbert T. Sewall, "California: The Story Continues," *Social Studies Review: A Bulletin of the American Textbook Council* 6 (1990): 12.

206. J. Baker, "An Ethnographic Study of Cultural Influences on the Responses of College Freshmen to Contemporary Appalachian Short Stories, unpublished Ed.D. dissertation, Virginia Polytechnic Institute and State University, 1990. ERIC Document no. ED321264.

207. See Paul M. Puccio, "Teaching the Literature of Lesbian and Gay Experience: An Assimilationist View," paper presented at the annual meeting of the National Council of Teachers of English, Baltimore, Md., 17–22 November 1989. ERIC Microfiche no. 320164.

208. Arthur Schlesinger Jr., *The Disuniting of America: Reflections on a Multicultural Society* (New York: Norton, 1991).

209. Todd Gitlin, *The Twilight of Common Dreams* (New York: Metropolitan Books, 1995).

210. See, for example, Dinesh D'Souza, *Illiberal Education: The Politics of Race and Sex on Campus* (New York: Free Press, 1991); and Russell Jacoby, *Dogmatic Wisdom: How the Culture Wars Divert Education and Distract America* (New York: Doubleday, 1994).

211. Judith E. Harper, "There's History, and Then There's Her Story," *Boston Globe*, 30 March 1997, E3.

212. "Publisher Gives Up on Texas," *Rethinking Schools* 8, 4 (1994).

213. Vicki L. Eaklor, "Of Politics and History: Gay Americans In and Out of Textbooks," *Perspectives* (American Historical Association newsletter) 29, 1 (1991): 17–19.

214. Barbara Blinick, "Out in the Curriculum, Out in the Classroom: Teaching History and Organizing for Change," in *Tilting the Tower: Lesbians Teaching Queer Subjects*, ed. Linda Garber (New York: Routledge, 1994), 147.

215. See, for example, Glencoe/Macmillan/McGraw-Hill's *American Odyssey* (Mission Hills, Calif., 1991); and Holt, Rinehart and Winston's *The Story of America*.

216. At the City University of New York.

217. *New York Daily News,* 8 February 1995; and American Social History Project, personal communication, 12 February 1995.

218. Chelsea House Publishers, Dept. GL-2 Box 914, 1974 Sproul Rd., Broomall, PA 19008-0914, tel. (800) 848-BOOK.

219. Project 21, c/o GLAAD/SFBA for Project 21, 514 Castro St., Suite B, San Francisco, CA 94114.

220. Originally founded by Rodney Wilson. See Pat Wingert and Steven Waldman, "Did Washington Hate Gays?" *Newsweek,* 16 October 1996.

221. First Annual Lesbian and Gay History Month Celebration, Cambridge, Mass., 29 October 1994.

222. Contact GLSEN at 121 West 27th St., Suite 804, New York, NY 10001. e-mail: GLSEN@glsen.org

223. "A Staff Development Manual for Anti-Homophobia Education in the Secondary Schools"; "Strategies for the Teacher Using Gay/Lesbian Related Materials in the High School Classroom"; "The Stonewall Riots and the History of Gays and Lesbians in the United States"; "The History and Nature of Homosexuality (and Its 'Causes')"; "Looking at Gay and Lesbian Literature"; "Reading List: Some Works of Noted Authors with Gay/Lesbian Content"; "Reading List: Books About Homosexuality and Coming Out for Young People"; "The Case for Gay and Lesbian Curriculum"; "Bibliography," the Harvard Graduate School of Education Gay and Lesbian School Issues Project, Arthur Lipkin, Longfellow Hall 210, Cambridge, MA 02138.

224. See Michael Jackson, "Things for Teachers of Gays and Lesbians to Tell Their Students," "What Not to Teach About Gays and Lesbians in the Classroom," 1983, American Council of Learned Societies, 850 S. Genessee Ave., Los Angeles, CA 90036-4617.

225. *Integrating the Curriculum: Teaching About Lesbians and Homophobia,* available from Publications Dept., Center for Research on Women, 106 Central St., Wellesley, MA 02181-8259.

226. *Breaking the Classroom Silence,* available from Amnesty International, 53 West Jackson, Rm. 1162, Chicago, IL 60604.

227. Sears, "Dilemmas and Possibilities," 28.

228. "Values and Opinions of Comprehensive School Health Education in U.S. Public Schools: Adolescents, Parents, and School District Administrators," American Cancer Society and the Gallup Organization, May 1994, 40.

229. Telljohan and Price, "Teaching About Sexual Orientation by Secondary Health Teachers," 21.

230. Lesbian and Gay Parents Association, Box 43206, Montclair, NJ 07043.

231. See, for example, Greta Gaard, "Opening Up the Canon: The Importance of Teaching Lesbian and Gay Literatures," *Feminist Teacher* 6, 2 (1992): 30–33.

232. Telljohan and Price, "Teaching About Sexual Orientation by Secondary Health Teachers," 20.

233. Anonymous, Cambridge Rindge and Latin School, 1992.

234. Paula Katze, unpublished paper, Harvard Graduate School of Education, 8 December 1995.

235. Ann Louise Keating, "Heterosexual Teacher, Lesbian/Gay/Bisexual Text: Teaching the Sexual Other(s)," in *Tilting the Tower: Lesbians Teaching Queer Subjects,* ed. Linda Garber (New York: Routledge, 1994), 96–107.

# Index